FROM DUSK 'TIL DAWN

An Insider's View of the Growth of the Animal Liberation Movement

The Story Our Government Does Not Want Told

Keith Mann

Puppy Pincher Press

First published in Great Britain in 2007 by Puppy Pincher Press
BM2636
London
WC1N 3XX

ISBN 978-0-9555850-0-5

Reprinted October 2007

Printed on FSC certified paper using vegetable based ink and bound with adhesive containing no animal products

Disclaimer:
Nothing in these pages is intended to incite, encourage or promote duplication or repetition of any event, activity or action. I document the violence inflicted on animal advocates and animals not to incite more of the same but because it happens and seldom gets reported. I explore the actions of animal advocates because they too are significant events in a growing social movement seeking change. The reaction to them is also significant. Each of these issues affects us all. I hope by exploring them in this way we can begin to bring them to an end

www.fromdusktildawn.org.uk

Contents

Endorsements

As an animal protectionist, even I feel humbled and useless when I read of Keith Mann's life and risks. No matter who says what, it is such as Keith who are the real heroes of modern society. There can be nothing brave about going to Iraq to kill Iraqi civilians—stay here, in England, and face the slaughterhouses of the Death Industry, and their factory farms and their torture laboratories of dread. *The Daily Mail* terms pro-vivisectionists as 'boffins' and denounces anti-torture activists as 'extremists'—thankfully some of us aren't so dim.

How vicious life would be without visionaries such as Keith, and the bravery and unified vision of the ALF. One way or another books such as Keith's make us more aware of ourselves because they tell us what we are—or aren't—doing to help other beings. That so many corporations and power-maniacs openly and eagerly despise animal rights activists is evidence of the guilt of those corporations. What else could it be?

MORRISSEY

Keith Mann's *From Dusk 'til Dawn* takes the reader on a roller coaster ride through the history of the animal rights movement, focusing in the main on an area in which the author could be said to be something of a specialist. At times uplifting, at times uproariously funny, at times desperately bleak, the book is part autobiographical and part historical document. Mann attempts to do what no other writer in the field has attempted so far: to bring together the many strands of thought from which the early animal rights direct action movement drew its inspiration, and to provide a very personal perspective on the chronology of events.

Mann's humanity speaks to us, urges us to look at the world through the eyes of the meek and defenceless, who have no voice to speak for them except those who are prepared to stand out on a limb, to risk their lives and their liberty in alerting the world to the cruelty our species visits upon billions of animals every year. Galvanised by the author's indestructible optimism, we cannot fail to be convinced that each single deed or action we undertake in the name of animal rights takes us one tiny step further on the journey towards finding a compassionate way of co-existing with all life on earth.

From Dusk 'til Dawn is a very personal account written by someone who has dedicated most of his life in the pursuit of his truth. Uncompromising he may be—subversive he is not. His is only one expressed view and one voice among a growing number that seek to change a global injustice that remains unmatched in the history of the human species. It is in making so public his own personal views that he challenges us to find our own way of fighting to make this world a more harmonious place to live, without either being passive or submitting to compromise.

John Feldmann
(Lead singer and guitarist with the band Goldfinger)

This is a heartfelt account from an ALF insider and deserves the attention of anyone who wants to know how a failure to implement change through legal channels has created a disenchanted liberation force to reckon with. It is a huge work, often raw, but reading only a part of it should wake people up to the filth and horror of treating animals as 'things'.

Ingrid Newkirk
(PETA: People For The Ethical Treatment Of Animals)

Acknowledgements

With thanks to Rolanda Ware, Louise, Ingrid Newkirk, Alice Barton, Brendan, Paul, Kate, Moira, Hannah, Al Green, Noel Molland and Steve Poole for help with the production of, or for contributing to, this book.

For Mike Hill, Jill Phipps, Barry Horne, Davy Barr, Valerie Mohammed, Deborah Bourke, Vicky Moore, Caralyn Hudson and Gari Allen—dear friends and dedicated campaigners whose absence is humanity's loss. For Tom Worby, who never had a chance; for those vets who have helped when no others would, and for the unsung heroes who take risks for others. For the animals we rescued who were recovered by the police and sent back; for my Mum—my Special Mum; and of course for those who give their everything to help others—you are my heroes and make life here worth fighting for. For the animals.

Only after the last tree has been cut down. Only after the last river has been poisoned. Only after the last fish has been caught. Only then will you find that money cannot be eaten.

Cree Indian prophecy

Foreword

Keith Mann's name is in many minds synonymous with the ALF. I first came across him when I was dedicating a lot of time to supporting prisoners and the animal rights movement. He was brought to my attention because he was both a prisoner and an animal rights activist. Having never met him, and armed with only a photo of him, I joined his supporters in regular letter writing and the lobbying of MPs on his behalf.

Having served time in prison as an ALF activist, Mann is something of a cause célèbre in the global animal rights movement for his uncompromising stance on the issue of animal exploitation. Eminently personable, he never attempts to paint himself as anything other than what he is–a cheeky and affable Mancunian lad, with an overriding desire to see an end to the suffering of animals. I first met him on a demonstration and I thought it was going to be one of those mystical experiences, like you get when you meet Nelson Mandela, but all I got from him was a piece of vegan cake and a leaflet about another demo. It is this passion that has motivated him to break unjust laws. It informs his actions and his life choices, and it is this passion that speaks to us when we read *From Dusk 'til Dawn*, his first book.

Those who know the author personally will recognise the often chatty, anecdotal style in his writing, which is conversational and not restricted by the 'house style' of a publisher worried about the bottom line. It allows you to read this book from cover to cover or dip into it at leisure, though its subject matter and sheer scale do not make it easy bedtime reading.

Mann is a natural storyteller, with a hell of a story to tell. It does not end happily ever after, nor does it offer glib solutions to the tyranny of oppression. What it does offer is hope, and that is its feel-good factor. As the book's title suggests, it provides a background to the dawning of a new consciousness, though it also gives a knowing wink to the reader who recognises that the hours before dawn are the hours when most direct actions take place.

The history of what we would consider the modern animal rights movement is barely 100 years old; it is a movement still in its infancy. This book is a part of that unfolding history. In my humble opinion there have been times when the animal rights movement has lost its way, when sections of it have got bogged down in what are almost academic arguments about language or image, or even personalities. At times like these we tend to forget about what the struggle is really about and begin to sound like bureaucratic hippies. This book reminds us why we are here. Sometimes being able to look back helps in seeing the way forward. Knowing your roots can promote your growth. Agree with Mann or not, you cannot fail to be moved by his moral arguments and his appeal to the humanity that potentially resides in us all to work towards rebuilding a world on the principles of true equality with life itself being the yardstick.

Benjamin Zephaniah

Prologue

Beginnings

> All truth passes through three stages. First, it is ridiculed. Second, it is violently opposed. Third, it is accepted as being self-evident...
>
> *Arthur Schopenhauer (1788-1860) German philosopher*

I was brought up in the northern mill town of Rochdale in the 1970s with my younger brother. My dad was a caretaker for many years in a not unpleasant tower block. My mum did everything else. I have no awful memories of my childhood, I just mourn its passing. Rochdale nestles at the foot of the tree-bare Pennines, which cut off Lancashire from Yorkshire, but is only ten miles from the sprawl of Manchester.

Aside from collecting birds' eggs—for which I am eternally remorseful—I was little exposed to the country way of life until I left school in 1982 and went out with some local hunt saboteurs who had been distributing leaflets on an information stall in the high street. Meeting people like that selflessly trying to help others—particularly animals who have no voice—was inspirational. Meeting true country folk was too, but for very different reasons. If they were so readily predisposed to violence against a group of kids out waving placards against the killing foxes, then what chance was there for the foxes and animals in their sights? Rather than scare me away with their violence, they rooted my resistance. Very independent and more keen on actively living life and not especially keen on the educational system, I made it through my exams and got out of there lickety-split. As a kid, I had always wanted to be a footballer and 'play for England' until the moment I found out what we as a society were doing to other animals.

My first rescue was a domestic rabbit. I used to walk past her on the way to school, and saw her sitting there, day, after day, after day in a box in a yard. I snuck out and took her home in a holdall after pleading for weeks anonymously with the homeowner to do something to make life better for the rabbit. It was a happy ending for that rabbit and my views on 'theft' changed forever. Soon after, as a proud ALF activist, I lifted a large tub of goldfish from behind the counter on a fairground stall and ran off home while my mate distracted the stall attendant. We didn't have a bath for weeks as it was occupied by fifty-three goldfish whom we later placed in good ponds around Rochdale.

Their newfound freedom was another step on the ladder, leading to even more 'heinous crimes', few of which I am able to confess. I have spent at lot of time standing in the street talking to people and trying to make them think about respecting animals. I've hidden for hours in hedges and sneaked around places that haunt me for the cruelty that I witnessed. Needless to say, this is not for some kind of perverted kick or to prove to myself that it happens, but in order to confirm its existence to others and to try and do something about it. There is something thrilling about this, of course—the rush of adrenalin that comes from facing the unknown—alarms, a chase, live animals, dead animals, prison, none or all of it.

I've probably been at my lifelong happiest and saddest in this environment and very scared too. I can't think what I would rather have been doing were it not this, despite the invited trauma and ever present risk of serious physical harm. I've fallen from a building and through a roof, jumped through a first floor window and swum a river in a pair of wellies and then had to get on a bus, dripping wet and beg a free ride! I've been shot at while trying to rescue animals; I've put my own car window through with a ball bearing that bounced back off someone else's property; I've been spat on, punched and driven at, covered in a bucket of elephant piss by an angry clown, chased through woodland by men with spades and arrested, charged and convicted for things I haven't done. I've felt utter despair and been driven to distraction—and action—by the endless procrastinating and indifference of officialdom and I've been locked in prison and made to go without food because of my objections to the abuse of animals.

All this aside from the indescribable suffering and cruelty I've witnessed first hand. But it's precisely that, and being able to do something about some of it, that has made it all worthwhile. These close calls are nothing; the lucky breaks and the confrontations recharge my batteries rather than drain me, as, of course, do the victories in every life saved or opinion altered. The angrier I see the people I oppose and listen to their reasons for what they do, the more I empathise with the animals they are messing with and feel compelled to act. My only regret is getting caught. It has given me a voice but taken away the anonymity that allowed me to take those risks. I have a lot to say, but I preach that words are cheap and actions are everything. Allow me this lengthy contradiction.

From the moment my eyes were opened to the terrible cruelty we inflict on other animals, I have avoided being sucked into a career, and being tied to a mortgage. I prefer to rescue other Earth creatures and will go to my grave counting those I saved and be content I did my best. Anything else would make my life seem futile. Spare cash is merely a distant memory of a time when I was fixing vacuum cleaners for a living. The path I have chosen is one I view as my destiny and the peak of my football 'career' is as a centre forward in a Top Security prison team. My World Cup was beating the screws' best team three years on the trot!

Being unable or unwilling to ignore the reality of animal suffering has got me into no end of trouble and strife but I think has played a part in alleviating and preventing some of it. I can't imagine that winning ten World Cup competitions would give me anything like the same satisfaction I feel after convincing someone to stop encouraging slaughterhouses and factory farms or by placing a neglected animal in a safe loving home for the rest of its life on Earth. I have never hurt anyone for being cruel but have defended myself when under attack and have done a lot of things to help desperate animals to which I can't confess, not out of any sense of shame but because I'd be arrested and sent to prison. That this happens to people like me in a nation of animal lovers never ceases to amaze me as does the fact this nation treats other animals so appallingly. I write this book to document not so much my journey but that of a movement of people just like me who want to make the world a better place for all.

About The Book

> It's a strange sort of terrorist campaign to say the least that is waged for 20 years without killing anybody.
>
> *The Observer, July 1992*

They'd try and tell me the best way is education, which is ultimately the goal, but how do you draw attention to something so corrupt and secretive that it has its own laws and is violently defended by those same forces who use the law and the police to resist all attempts to effect change, if not by using extra-political methods? Write a book? But who will read it? No, there shouldn't be violent confrontations over little animals, ladies batoned and CS sprayed, kids cut by razor wire, there shouldn't be rocks thrown at riot police and through windows, but there shouldn't be tortured animals dying in cages either and it's no good complaining. Whatever the legal detail of the efforts people make to save these animals, it's hardly surprising they do. Watch *The Animals Film*, *Behind The Mask* or *Earthlings* and tell me you aren't moved to at least agree with the sentiments expressed by those so readily dubbed extremists. I suggest society would be better, not worse, for more of these people and less of what they fight. Prove me wrong! To make criminal activity right or glamorous is not the purpose of this book. I merely document the progress of an advancing movement that utilises direct action. I obviously don't necessarily agree with every thought or deed of all who are labelled animal lovers or extremists, in much the same way as you wouldn't expect or assume all meat eaters side with the actions of their kith and kin. I would, I have to say, be far more ashamed of this stance were I in the latter camp! I comment on this because of the ludicrous assumption that the actions of an animal liberator are the responsibility of a global movement of many diverse individuals.

It was while I was in prison in February 1992 that I decided to try to put together a book telling the story of the ALF. Having the time on my hands at last to do so, my original plan was to create a simple-to-reference guide—a chronology of dates and events, if you like—in a single publication. The only place this had been done thus far was in ALF newsletters, which generally tend to be read by a few and then discarded by most or stored away. For such a monumental human initiative as the emancipation of animals, it seemed to me inappropriate that a more detailed overview was not available. There are many books looking at the issues surrounding specific areas of animal abuse, as well as campaigner's handbooks and novels, but none have detailed the actions of the activists on the front line, and the state's response to this phenomenon in thinking.

I had intended to complete the book by 1993, when I was expecting to reach trial and move on to the next stage of my life, whether that ended up being in or out of prison. While in custody, I managed to acquire early animals rights archives as a reference guide, and I scribbled away trying to formulate something more than simply a diary of actions. Unfortunately, what the ALF and others do is much the same today as it always was. Most of the actions are similar in many respects, and there's only so much you can say about rescuing chickens and blowing hunting horns. That said, as I found, there is a big story here, as you will find!

Story or not, however, I did have other things on my mind at the time I started writing the first draft of the book. Namely: escaping from custody! I had always promised myself that, should I get sent to prison, I would do my utmost to make a quick exit, and I managed that after much effort before the book had been completed. As it is, that was just as well, because that was 1993 and a great deal has happened since that would otherwise have been omitted from these pages.

It was one morning in June 1993; Manchester detectives escorted me out of Walton Prison in Liverpool. I left behind my belongings in my cell, expecting to return that night. However, providence brought me an opportunity to make good my ambition to become an escapee, and I never returned there. It is fully expected that the property of a prisoner who escapes or is moved will go missing, and I was certain that was precisely what would happen to my files and ramblings. As it was, the only things that weren't returned to me by the prison authorities were items of value like my Walkman, radio, stamps, dictionary and so on. To my amazement, the paperwork—along with my clothes and legal documents—were later handed out to my mum. Some time after that, the manuscript joined me in Sussex where I was holed up and where I intended to complete it. Ill disciplined as I am for spending hours in front of a computer writing, after a couple of months I had only slightly advanced the project when Sussex police caught up with me and confiscated it along with a variety of other items. It had progressed little in a year and the omens weren't good.

Listed as 'Miscellaneous Papers' on the police search sheets, it would have been easy for them to disappear into the official black hole. But miraculously, they re-emerged and some months later, I managed to get them snook into Full Sutton prison under some other guise, where I slowly transferred my scribbles to type in the computer class. At a rate of two hours a day, three days a week (barring removal from the class for cell searches, prison lock-downs, staff meetings, strikes and the flooding of the department) it made for slow progress. Oh, and added to which, the small matter of me being on the course to learn computer skills, not write a book, as I was reminded when rumbled. I knew my time at Full Sutton would be limited, and that I would need to complete the manuscript as best I could before being moved on somewhere where I would be less free to pursue my own agenda.

Best part done months later, I smuggled the work out on disk for it to be further worked on and passed on to a publisher. The first willing editor had to pass the project over soon after, following an unconnected arrest on incitement charges over other material he had allegedly written. The next willing recipient left it under his bed for a year, much to my dismay. He was apologetic, but that didn't help me draw a line under my little project. Then there was a third offer from an ALF activist in Canada. A little off the beaten track perhaps, but he had seen a draft and was keen to help. Indeed, it appeared that they would be able to do all the work out there and pay for publishing it if need be. If they were as efficient as they were keen, what did I have to lose? Somehow, despite the apparent enthusiasm of all those concerned, progress was negligible. This had a lot to do with police raids and everyone being so busy with other things.

Never did I imagine when I recovered the disk three years later, that I would find it, not a publication-ready manuscript with all the necessary alterations and updates I'd expected, but in much the same state as it had been when I'd smuggled it out so long ago. Clearly it hadn't helped matters that the Royal Canadian Mounted Police had in the interim period raided the home of their favourite animal liberator and taken the manuscript into custody along with most of his valued possessions.

Lesson learnt by a slightly circuitous route, I decided that if you want something done, you have to do it yourself. While I was getting nowhere fast with the book, the political situation back home had changed and there was a clampdown on the prison system, which made book-writing difficult, not least for me because my hidden back-up disk copy had slipped into a wall void on B Wing and become forever lost. The atmosphere in the Education department, as elsewhere, had deteriorated as screws imposed Michael Howard's call for a more austere prison regime. I'd meanwhile been offered a job as a gym orderly, and I didn't need asking twice to spend all day in the gym. There was no way I could find to get the updated (not) disk back in to me, so I tried to get it back in its printed form via the mail to work on. I could then update and alter in my cell and pass it backs out to try again. Easy. But for prison rules. One of Howard's many new rules (encouraged by the aggressive, self-interested Prison Officers Association) was that family and friends couldn't send in books any longer. Instead, any you wanted had to be ordered through the library and paid for out of private allowance. Sadly, this wasn't a book yet—just A4 photocopied pages, which I hoped would be a book one day, so no problem, right? Ha!

The day the papers arrived in the mail, someone with more than a safely recommended level of power for a Jobsworth decided that I couldn't have it because it hadn't been ordered via the library.

'New rules.'

Trying to explain to him the futility of trying to order a book from myself that hadn't yet been published was hopelessly frustrating. He wasn't going to be made to look a fool or back down from his interpretation, instead maintaining: 'If we allow you to have it, they will all get round it that way.'

'And the problem with prisoners using their initiative and a lot of photocopy paper to get themselves a book sent in for less than the cost of the real version?' I queried.

'You're not having it!'

The manuscript and I were banned from seeing each other and it stayed like that until my release three years later, by which time it needed a great deal of reworking. Still, having recovered my life and being in the middle of a campaign to close the Shamrock monkey farm, it progressed slowly. Even then, it went off with the police once more, along with computers and so on, as they raided the homes of animal activists. With the passing of Shamrock a year later and making time to write, I passed my idea on for advice and I got it. It turned out the whole thing needed 'A big fat edit.' It was only three years, two campaigns, two house moves and two new computers later that I found the time, resources and inspiration I needed to completely redo the whole thing and put it all together near enough in its present form.

The story of the Animal Liberation Movement is a story shared—one that documents the struggles of many who make up this rich, diverse movement, driven by tens of thousands of people around the world of whom I'm just one. I had intended to make the book a historical document, not a personal journey, but others felt differently about the tone I had adopted in the earlier drafts. They convinced me I should make it more personal and tell my story, and so it has become something of a personal overview of the movement, with autobiographical overtones. In restructuring the book, I had to make a decision whether or not to include prison stories, since prison too, is fascinating in its own way, but I decided the material would be best left to another volume. Whether you ever get to read more than the glimpse that follows in these pages of that stage in my life is another matter, bearing in mind that I started writing notes for this project in Liverpool Prison in 1992 when the first salvo in the long-running hunting with hounds saga was fired, and its now 2007. (I finally passed the transcript on for final proofing on 18 February 2005—the day of the hunting ban.)

One final point: before I finished the manuscript, the Labour Government went to Parliament with their latest round of laws to further criminalise dissenting voices, notably those opposing vivisection. They also gained the power to stop anyone 'glorifying terrorism.' Now, it seems to me that by banging on about how great our troops in Iraq are behaving and how great it is that we are there at all is doing precisely that—glorifying terrorism. So why haven't those responsible been arrested? If not for war crimes then surely there's enough evidence he is breaking these new laws? Some people say that rescuing animals is terrorism, usually the people who have had animals stolen, I don't agree. Nor do I believe that this law was passed to stop people supporting the rescue of animals in danger of suffering serious physical and emotional harm, or to put it another way terrorism. That said I seek not to glorify any of it, as you will see there are few rewards for such behaviour in our society. Indeed you may be killed or arrested and imprisoned if you do, even if you simply protest, but protest you must! This book is a document of fact, it tells a story of a historical struggle of which our society should be immensely proud. It puts into perspective the reality of what people do to protect the animal kingdom and highlight the plight of the same. It is nothing to fear. At the time of writing it isn't yet an offence punishable with seven years in prison to agree with liberating animals from torture—just for glorifying terrorism—but who knows what tomorrow will bring as the State Sledgehammer seeks to smash the Animal Rights Nuts?!

Despite all the false starts and obstacles, the book is now complete. It is not a definitive version of the history of the movement, but the story as I see it. It is a story that will continue to be re-written and be added to by many others over the coming years until animal liberation is finally achieved. It is dedicated to the countless animal victims who have suffered and died, and continue to suffer and die at the hands of our species and our obsession with power and wealth; it is dedicated to the many brave and wonderful people who have contributed to the struggle. The book has been a labour of love. What you see in these pages are the fruits of that labour. I hope you find it enlightening.

Starting with a brief but not exhaustive summary of the early history of the movement, this book is primarily a personal perspective on the growth of the Animal Liberation Movement, which began to burgeon in the 1960s. The book takes you on tour with the ALF as activists carry out raids and advance the cause. Or perhaps set it back years? You decide. It's a story as yet untold.

You will hopefully gain a better understanding of the thinking and motivation of some of the people who risk prison and worse by challenging laws and traditions, who go undercover or switch sides. The views expressed are mine, though there are many players in this game with many opinions, but I lay before you my view of things in a collection of stories that make up this phenomenon we call the Animal Liberation Movement. I've put together interviews with activists past and present, archival material and personal experience. I don't agree with everything people do in the name of animal rights or encourage repetition by referring to it. To set out my stall, let me make clear I object so greatly to the use of violence that I joined the ALF. I separate violence against the individual from damage done to inanimate objects. The latter moves me not a jot, the other always will.

This work is one view from the front line of a sea of change in the way we treat other beings. The actions of animal activists are often described as extremist and it's a word I will repeat. While it may be a fair description in the eyes of some, be under no illusions about my views. In a sentence: there is nothing animal liberation activists have done in four decades of campaigning that comes even close to being as extreme as the violence inflicted on any one of the countless million animals exploited every single day. For me, the deciding factor in this war in this Age Of Grotesque Cruelty is the body count: on the one hand colossal, and on the other zero. I ask that you make up your own minds and be swayed by no one to accept that violence is the only way.

This movement has always had a life of its own, with no-one at the controls dictating the rules or the best course of action, just a few suggesting guidelines or a direction for the individual to interpret as they see fit or to discard altogether; the rules are unwritten but the central edict is: don't use violence or incite others to do so. That's all. That's a good rule, no? The best Commandment. As an animal sympathiser faced with the horrific truths about animal abuse, it's a hard path to follow, and one often wonders: why follow it? To make animal abusers feel safe in what they do? For animal abuse industries to flourish? These are questions for the individual's conscience, but ironically, it seems that holding that viewpoint and acting on it in a society based on violence, may very well lead one to be branded inhuman, violent, terrorist or extremist and locked in prison! Albert Einstein once said: 'The world is a dangerous place, not because of those who do evil but because of them that look on and let them do it.' We break the rules to end the bloodshed, not to pursue it.

There's a lot more to 'animal extremism' than two words and some screaming editorials, as you will see. We are deliberately being sold a distorted story. Books on 'A Thousand Recipes Without Animal Products', '1001 Confrontations in the Hunting Field' and 'A Protester's Guide To Police Stations' would help paint the picture. There are many individual struggles forming this movement, many stories worth telling from many brave souls less well known than I am. I hope this inspires someone or everyone reading it to tune in, switch on and speak up for the animals. What matters is not what others are doing but what *we* are doing to make a difference. If we do nothing we lose our right to condemn those who do something.

Due to the nature of the ALF's activities, I couldn't hope to document everything experienced by those involved, but a pretty good picture follows. Images too. Keen to portray the movement photographically I've sought to compile a comprehensive dossier, however some key events aren't recorded, images have become lost, have been taken in police raids or are simply being stored in boxes under beds. My experiences are intermingled and other details have been gleaned from archives, ex-activists and colleagues with long memories, and proud 'criminal' histories. I hope it's all accurate; it's not for want of trying. If nothing else, I hope it serves to entertain and inform you and puts things into some sort of perspective. I've looked long and hard at all aspects of animal exploitation and questioned many in the struggle as to their motives for their dedication to the cause. I've been an ALF activist and vegan for many years. I am therefore what some might describe as an animal extremist. If so then I'm proud to be thus labelled if it means I object to every aspect of animal abuse and will compromise on none, but one thing I must make clear: for me, premeditated physical violence must end today. With that the ALF would go away.

Hopefully, after reading this, you will get a fuller understanding of the movement. I hope it will raise questions about the use of animals, the treatment of protesters, and the way-out stories the media tell. There is no financial reward and no glory. It's a selfless occupation, which increasingly carries a risk of arrest, imprisonment, violence and even death. But the rewards are huge and for some outweigh the risks. It's about animals and a whole lot more.

The Chicken Run

You have no enemies you say.
Alas my friend, the boast is poor.
He who has mingled in the fray
Of duty that the brave endure,
Must have made foes. If you have none,
Small is the work that you have done.
You've hit no traitor on the hip,
You've dashed no cup from perjured lip,
You've never turned a wrong to right,
You've been a coward in the fight.

Man Without Enemies by Charles Mackay (1814—1889)

Somewhere in the Hampshire countryside…

It is cold, very, very dark and eerily silent except for the sound of wild animals scurrying about in the undergrowth. There are rats everywhere, but nothing compared to the numbers inside the buildings. They aren't really the focus of anyone's attention, though it's hard to ignore them as they run over some of the humans squatting on their territory. This is less than a fun night out for any of this team, but for two or three silent sufferers in the undergrowth waiting for word to move in, this is a living nightmare. Not bad out of sixteen people! How many friends can you persuade to hide up in a dark, spooky remote woodland late at night with rats scuttling around, and with worse yet to come? Bet you wouldn't find many takers! And it isn't just that you have to trust wild rats—you have to trust your work mates, and be certain that they don't mind running the risk of spending some time in prison as a reward, and not dropping you in it.

This is southern England, Good Friday, circa 2003. Within this isolated woodland are hidden volunteers from the Animal Liberation Front. Also hidden from the outside world are three huge warehouses and a stench like no other. Inside the stinking warehouses, there are so many female chickens in cages stacked in rows you would be literally overcome by the stench before you could count them. All are incarcerated in egg units laying Farm Fresh Eggs to fill supermarket shelves with cheap chickens' periods. No one cares enough to do anything about what goes on here except for the small group on site and others of a like-mind who not only boycott the product, but also break these birds out to take them to a better life.

That we allow this form of mass cruelty to take place is a gross indictment of our claim to being a sophisticated society of animal lovers and this farm is far from an isolated case. Such units can contain tens of thousand juvenile red hens, descendants of the red jungle fowl of Southeast Asia. Its modern incarcerated cousin is exploited to the absolute extreme. Back in the 1970s these 'chicken sheds', as these monstrous places are so called, could hide endless double-decker buses so vast was their size and this mass exploitation has been expanding ever since.

One of the earliest rescue raids on just such a chicken shed not a million miles from here was carried out by six friends who met at an animal welfare meeting in the south of England in 1975; seen as rather eccentric then, in today's society they would be described by animal farmers, the mainstream media and politicians as 'extremists.' Overnight, they became 'activists', endlessly on the lookout for the animal abuse about which they were so outraged. One Sunday afternoon, they simply parked their cars on a grass verge, climbed over a gate, walked across a field to the rear of a farm in Hampshire—'the county of cruelty' as one called it—and unbolted the first shed door they came to. The scene was exactly the same then as it is now, 30 years later. Same county, different farm. Countless birds crammed in cages sounding decidedly unhappy. Fearful of being shot or caught by an angry farmer, and with only a few homes secured, the group were out of there with a bird each in less than 15 minutes. It took that long because the wretched cages wouldn't open. It's a lesson many budding rescuers have had to learn on the job through experience: all the cage doors are different! They all agreed afterwards that they could have rescued more had they been calmer at the time but it was a start—the start of something bigger: animal rights 'extremism'! It was a simple but effective thing to do, and it was to be done again and again, with activists taking more and more time to rescue more and more birds. Battery hens: plentiful, uncomplicated and exploited mercilessly have inspired generations of activists to overstep the boundaries of legitimate protest.

The Good Friday raiders have to wait until the last of the workers have gone home for the night before moving in, but it's essential to act quickly the moment it's safe. There's a lot of work to do. Bizarrely, it is still possible to simply open the doors to some of these units and walk in. Such is the sprawl of filth and the death; it appears it simply isn't worth locking the doors. One would surely want to hide this grotesque example of how to do something bad badly, but stuck out in the middle of nowhere with only fields and a clump of trees around the stinking, infested shit storage units, who's going to look? No one in his or her right mind would voluntarily go inside. As long as eggs keep coming out, nothing else matters. Only a small number of activists are prepared to wade through the waste pits below the cages. Occasionally the farmer will drive a tractor in to scoop out the mountain of droppings, dead birds and broken eggs and scatter them on his fields, but aside from that, this is a hidden world.

As soon as the last of the workers have driven down the track and out of the woodland, balaclavas are adjusted and people emerge from their hiding places. Until two hours earlier, most didn't even know what they would be doing; they just knew they would be needed. It's never a pleasant experience confronting cruelty, but as difficult as it is for some to deal with, the pain of trying is easier than doing nothing. Opening the rotten wooden door at the base of the first unit exposes a fresh nightmare for those with a phobia for rats. Those who'd previously been to recce the site had warned them about this, but for all that, their description failed to impart the true picture.

There's almost no describing the full horror of the scenes inside these units. The smell is the first thing that hits you and it does quite literally hit you. Imagine the accumulated festering waste of thousands of chickens piled high. There's waste below the cages for as far as torchlight can see, the peaks are like the Alps rising toward the sky. Above them are the pale feet of baby birds, their toes on wire above the mess and a thick mass of grey, ancient cobwebs around the cages and girders and walls, forming like a second skin on the structure of the building, hanging in the dank air. Underneath and on top of the compacted waste are thousands of rats; the floor seems to move with them—they *are* the floor. They stop and stare and scurry, looking for food, fallen crumbs, eggs, dead chickens. They run into your legs and over your feet. They run over piles of feathers scattered among the waste.

One rat stands on top of a pile and looks down at the intruders. The pile of feathers is a live bird fallen from a cage, but she's been down there some time and has no life left in her to complain. She might be stuck or starving or injured—who cares? Her head stays firmly buried in her chest. The rat thought her a good vantage point so she's good for something. The birds resign themselves to their fate. There's not a lot they can do about it; there's nowhere to run, nowhere to hide and no way out. You fall down there, you die down there. Unless you are one of the lucky ones that gets to meet an 'extremist'.

The team first split into working groups to comb each of the pits for the fallen birds who have slipped the net during loading, round up or escaped from broken cages. Only the farmhands know how they get there and they don't give a damn. It's hard to tell at first glance whether a bundle of feathers in the dirt is alive or dead. Many get huge weights of congealed waste stuck to their legs rendering them unable to move, so they just sit there until they die. There are birds at every level of life, death and decomposition in these pits. Some are just able to blink in the torchlight—that close to death—either weighted to the spot or caught in a deep pool of sodden waste formed under a dripping water pipe. Slowly rotting to death. It's no reward for the huge obligation demanded from them at a few weeks of age.

It's enough to direct someone with faultless enthusiasm to elicit the rescue of these birds, but it isn't that easy according to Leah, a 17-year-old trainee dental nurse on her first raid. Her older sister who does this kind of thing routinely has asked her along. Leah writes later:

> It took us so long going through our unit, the third one, because of the amount of water in there. We thought it must have been the same in them all but I realised later we got the short straw! It was like wading through quicksand. The four of us got stuck up to our knees more than once and we had to keep rescuing each other and our boots! The worst of it was spending ages struggling through to a bird in the distance only to find it was dead. One I waded through to was ninety percent sunk with only her blinking eye to attract me, but she died in my arms. She was tiny and weighed nothing. I guess her dream came true and someone came to take her to the sunny farmyard she'd heard was pictured on the side of the egg boxes, but it was too much for her little body to cope with. It was the saddest thing I think has ever happened to me.
>
> It made me feel so proud to be with all those other people, really different people, all working really hard to save some chickens. I was brought up to think about all life. My old school friends mostly eat meat and just don't care; they just wouldn't understand why anyone would bother stopping eating chicken, never mind doing this! But when you see it for real, you can't turn

> away. Gina (not her real name) had tried to keep me away from this side of being an 'animal lover' to protect me, but I needed to experience something like this to make me realise what I need to do with my life. Fixing people's teeth isn't going to be it! You can smell the meat inside people, you know!

There are dozens of living birds in each of the pits and many more dead ones. There are little colonies of black beetles in and under the corpses, the floor beneath them alive as they recoil en masse from the torchlight back into the shit. The surviving birds are the first to be loaded into bread crates and piled in the back of one of the vehicles backed up to the entrance doors. It's cramped and will be like that for a few hours, but its five-star accommodation compared to what they have had to endure so far in their short lives.

By the time the Unit 3 team gets back to Unit 1, someone has cut a big hole in the caging above the pits near the doors where the waste isn't so deep. Birds are being passed down and transferred into big bright coloured plastic laundry bags, four or five in each one. The only colour in this dreadful place. There is a human conveyor belt of bags and birds moving gradually from cages to crates to who knows where. Do they know these humans have good intentions, or is this it: that terrible, final journey to the slaughterhouse?

There is a lookout posted in the woods by the gate, but no one is expected to return to the farm until early in the morning. Everyone has a lot to lose should they be caught red-handed in the middle of a 'conspiracy'—not least the owners of the horseboxes on site loaned on a promise they will be returned safely—but the work is being done at a careful, steady, relaxed pace. Rushing things is a waste of valuable energy and besides, these birds are fragile. According to reports and observations, many birds suffer at least one broken bone during the round up for slaughter and whilst they are unloaded at the other end. No one along that route cares, that's for sure.

Upstairs among the cages, the miserable individual stories are far outnumbering those down below. 'How many can we take?' is Leah's first hopeful query, after she has been helped up to the aisles to do a shift. There's no way you can take them all without far more hands or far more time. There are just too many and they're stacked up high, huddled five to a cage. Perhaps less if cage mates have died, leaving space to stretch a little, perhaps something soft to stand on for a while. But which ones do you take? The first you come to seems to be the best method, that way you don't beat yourself up choosing who gets to spend the next ten years pottering around pecking and chasing moths and who gets shipped to the slaughterhouse physically worn out and traumatised to be brutally killed. It's a cruel world, but whose fault is that? Surely not the fault of vegan 'extremists' breaking from the ranks of the norm?

There are so many aisles it would be easy to lose everyone else. There are so many birds, probably 100,000, each one so programmed to resume the routine of eating that they begin as the torch brings light to the darkness. That's what they do for eighteen hours of artificial daylight: eat. Indeed all chickens behave this way—they see a light and they eat! And dust bathe. And lay eggs. And therein lies the problem: they can lay daily and are forced to do so with the flick of a switch. They all look broken and resigned. What are their other options? They fight, hence the debeaking process that slices off the tip of their beak and limits the amount of damage they can do to each other. Some sound really disturbed. Periodically there will be a pained scream in a distant aisle—that of a bird finally broken, driven insane, dying? Who knows? You'd never find her. It sounds like it'd be too late anyway.

There are some birds lying on the floor outside the cages, not quite dead. Others are dead. They've been pulled out as failures, no longer profitable. As the weeks turn to months, the overcrowding is resolved as naturally as can be in this environment and by the end of the cycle, by the end of the year, there may be just one bird left. No one cares much as long as they've lived long enough to leave a sufficient profit in their wake—but pump them with as many antibiotics as you like, you can't make them stay alive, laying eggs forever. They are very fragile.

The sad thing is, they do stay alive and continue laying those precious eggs long after the year they're incarcerated in a cage if you just leave them alone. Instead of which, they're forced to the extreme for a few more eggs. Compared to the vast numbers exploited, ALF's rescue statistics are pitiful. Nevertheless, since 1975 many thousands of individuals have been whisked out of this kind of living hell and onto the Animal Liberation Underground Railroad where they have been able to live out their lives in peace.

Three hours later, one horsebox full of birds trundles slowly out of the woods as a second one pulls in, lights dimmed, and reverses to the doors. For the hard working raiders this is a pleasure after all.

It's hard for anyone to say how they're all doing because the birds were spread far and wide, but over six hours that night this small group bagged up, boxed up and sent on their way over a thousand chickens to good homes. The 'girls' were driven first to prearranged safe houses from where they were later distributed to people keen to live alongside them in mutual harmony in back gardens, allotments, farms and smallholdings, long after fertility.

Bizarrely, this compassionate way of life is viewed as 'criminal behaviour' in the eyes of the law. If the police track down the birds they'll be put back in cages. They are someone's property after all and it matters little if they suffer, you're not allowed to rescue them. So what can you do? Let's see.

Weeks after the Animal Liberation Front raid on the Wallops Wood Farm, the Royal Society for the Prevention of Cruelty to Animals (RSPCA) were informed of the conditions and encouraged to investigate. The RSPCA is supposed to help animals: 'RSPCA Action For Animals'—it says so on the promos. Staggeringly, the RSPCA Inspector didn't even bother to check out the farm's conditions, and said he didn't even need to see the video footage because a poultry expert—a vet he knew—had been shown the footage and assured him that there was nothing illegal in the way the birds were slowly wasting away in the pits or dying on the floor outside the cages. The Inspector was happy to agree while the Expert shrugged his shoulders and said such cruelty is a trade-off if we want cheap eggs. The RSPCA clearly does not prioritise animal welfare above profit.

Oddly enough, Trading Standards at the local council and its special Animal Welfare Department are the people to contact, if you are keen on wasting your time. They'd been to Wallops Wood before and animal welfare charities and campaign groups all agree that Trading Standards inspection teams turn up without warning and they were certainly pretty quick off the mark here. However, the inspectors rapidly cooled down and the charities and the volunteer groups all concur that in reality prosecutions rarely happen. A year earlier, Trading Standards were called to the same place and coincidentally turned up at the farm the day after the units had been 'depopulated' and the spent society of little ladies within decamped to the slaughterhouse for conversion into chicken stock or something like. Apparently they aren't much good for anything else! The inspectors weren't directed to look under the units, only in the cages and as the cages were empty the place was given a clean bill of health. Tipped off a second time, they made another visit to the farm and were directed specifically to the waste pits below the cages. They were equipped with video footage taken by the raiders, depicting the suffering of fallen stock, footage of rats in cages with laying hens, the filth, and hens crammed in cages. They'd seen it all before and weren't minded to do anything about it.

They told the farmer off and said they advised him to fish out the birds below the units but only one month later there were dozens of live hens still there. What the farmer had done as a priority was replace the old wooden walls with huge solid steel ones bolted from the inside to keep out prying eyes, effectively sealing in from rescuers the birds that fall and making the situation worse. Anyone care? Trading Standards in Hampshire were themselves more concerned that people had entered this site without protective clothing and may have transferred disease, and wanted names! The question of the appalling conditions in which the birds were forced to live did not even enter their radar! Only the extremists have since been into those stinking cellars and the aisles above to rescue other birds. By way of contrast, a 42-year-old man who was found guilty in 2004 of causing unnecessary suffering to 2,000 birds that were found dead, dying, diseased and living in utter squalor at his farm was given a conditional discharge and ordered to pay £75 costs. Two men arrested for rescuing some birds from the cages had their homes raided, spent months on bail and were fined £1,000 each.

The Early Years

From The Dawn Of Time

> Blind obedience to authority is the enemy of truth.
>
> *Albert Einstein*

It is hard, if not impossible, to say when exactly the Animal Liberation Movement started. The much referred to 'Movement' we have today has evolved over many thousands of years, each generation working on and expanding the ideas of those who went before. This is an example of human evolution at its best and most constructive. As early as the sixth century BC, Pythagoras was advocating vegetarianism; he believed that once the body was dead, the souls of humans transmigrated to animals. Pythagoras reportedly told a man abusing a puppy: 'Do not kick him. In his body is the soul of a friend of mine. I recognised his voice when he called out.' Of course he may also have been on drugs!

Moving on through the decades, it is said Plutarch (46-120 AD) was one of, if not the first, animal liberation writer. He was also one of the most influential. Plutarch's writings strongly advocated abstinence from meat, and as the centuries unfolded, other ideas started to emerge. Thomas More's *Utopia*, published in 1516, described hunting as: 'the lowest, the vilest and most abject part of butchery.' Perhaps one of the most outspoken yet little acknowledged 'animal extremists' of the time was Leonardo da Vinci (1452—1519) Italian painter, architect, sculpture and engineer. The talented da Vinci was a committed vegetarian, perhaps even vegan, pondering how the taking of milk from the cows amounted to stealing and describing humans as 'burial places' for animals. He would often buy caged birds from vendors in order to set them free and his distaste for the cruelty of meat consumption is recorded by some biographers and other writers, but in his own words:

> King of the animals—as thou hast described him—I should rather say king of the beasts, thou being the greatest—because thou doest only help them, in order that they give thee their children for the benefit of the gullet, of which thou hast attempted to make a sepulchre for all animals; and I would say still more, if I were allowed to speak the truth.

By the early 1700s, the concept of animal liberation was starting to find a footing in the writings of the day. In 1711, the Earl of Shaftesbury published *Characteristic,* which was a doctrine of benevolence using similar arguments to those of Plutarch. Meanwhile, other essayists such as Alexander Pope openly challenged the animal abusers. Pope was heavily influenced in his writings by the work of Plutarch and eagerly admitted to such, arguing strongly against vivisection and other forms of animal cruelty.

Throughout the 18th century, more and more people took up the idea of benevolence towards animals. In 1738, the Methodist preacher John Wesley openly condemned blood sports. Poets also pressed the cause of animal liberation, with the likes of Burns and Blake declaring kinship with animals. Blake's poetry was strong and powerful and written in a form, which everyone could understand. His famous poem *Auguries Of Innocence* neatly summed up his message:

A robin redbreast in a cage
Puts all heaven in a rage.
A dove-house filled with doves and pigeons
Shudders Hell through all religions.
A dog starved in his master's gate
Predicts the ruin of the state.
A horse misused on the road
Calls to heaven for human blood
Each outcry of the hunted hare
A fibre of the brain does tear.
A skylark wounded on the wing
A Cherubim does cease to sing.
The game cock clipped and armed for fight
Does the rising sun affright.

William Blake

The 18th century was very important in the advancement of the animal liberation philosophy and movement. A flood of progressive ideas and theories expanded and built on the foundations laid by earlier thinkers. In 1790, one American sect prohibited the wearing of clothing derived from animals and forbade the eating of their flesh. In 1789, writer Jeremy Bentham published *Introduction to the Principles of Morals and Legislation.* It was in this book that he penned the oft-quoted line, which is as relevant today as it was then: 'The question is not, can they reason? Nor, can they talk? But, can they suffer?' With these famous words, he encapsulated the guiding principle of today's liberation movement: opposition to suffering whatever its perceived justification.

Eighteenth-century writings called for compassion and kindness towards animals and strongly advocated vegetarianism. However, one book published at that time took the animal liberation argument one step further, making a ground-breaking connection between human and animal rights, examining as it did the similarities between the arguments advocating both. In 1792, the liberal feminist Mary Wollstonecraft published *A Vindication of the Rights of Women*. This book was and is heralded as a landmark in the liberal feminist movement, though of course not everyone greeted the book with a warm welcome. That same year, in a rather pathetic attempt to ridicule the work, Thomas Taylor published a book entitled *A Vindication of the Rights of Brutes*. Taylor showed that the same arguments being used to advance the rights of women could be used to advance the rights of animals, and that idea was even more ludicrous in his view. Taylor had no real intention of wanting to advance the Animal Liberation Movement and his book was written more as an attack on the arguments used in Wollstonecraft's book. However, little did this chauvinist realise that the arguments he penned in mockery were to be taken up by future generations to further the very cause against which he was fighting, i.e. the emancipation of others.

One ancient Chinese verse says:

> For hundreds of thousands of years, the stew in the pot has brewed hatred and resentment that is difficult to stop. If you wish to know why there are disasters of armies and weapons in the world, listen to the piteous cries from the slaughterhouse at midnight.

It neatly sums up the sort of bigotry that Taylor expounded in his attempt to belittle two worthy causes. Where open-mindedness towards, and compassion for the 'other' are absent, there too, cruelty is given free reign. Yet it seemed that only the radical thinkers could connect the dots.

The Victorian Era

> We can easily forgive a child who is afraid of the dark; the real tragedy is when men are afraid of the light.
>
> *Plato*

By the start of the 19th century, the Animal Liberation Movement was finding itself well supplied with new ideas on the way to rights of animals, and books were regularly written throughout the era. *An Essay on Abstinence From Animal Food, As A Moral Du*ty was written by Joseph Ritson and published in 1802.

Joseph Ritson was born in Stockton in 1752. He died in London in 1803, the year after his book was published. Like many 18th and 19th century writers of this description, he was heavily influenced by the writings of Plutarch. However, unlike Plutarch, Ritson was an atheist. As the book's title suggests, Joseph Ritson was 100% against the consumption of meat, denouncing it for its cruelty to non-human animals, and advocating it for the positive health aspects of abstention. He suffered much ridicule for his views, and as one who abstains myself, this isn't hard to imagine, given the level of ridicule and ignorance still prevalent 200 years later!

He went even further in his analysis of the moral duty of avoiding meat and rounded an all-encompassing attack on the whole meat-eating culture and the oppression of other species. He argued that there were links between meat eating and mental illness (long before BSE) and between meat eating and violence, an observation that has more recently been recognised as fact. He also suggested that all cruelty and injustice was rooted in human arrogance, which fostered a myopic refusal to recognise the similarities between Homo sapiens and other animals. Others, arguing that humans were different (and therefore superior) to other animals, reinforced the notion, which encouraged human slavery, permitting the perceived superior being to exploit those deemed different and thus inferior. Joseph Ritson's powerful and persuasive arguments influenced many other animal liberation writers, including the great poet Shelley, who said that the vegetarian diet 'strikes at the very root of evil.'

As the wealth of thinking and material continued to grow, it is unsurprising that people started to form groups and societies in order to further their ideas. (What is surprising is that the fight for progress in alleviating the suffering of other animals is regarded in the 21st century as the preserve of thinkers who are often deemed criminal and even terrorists...)

Britain's first animal protection society was formed in 1808 during a Royal anniversary celebration meal in Liverpool, when a group of like-minded people came together. Sharing stories they had experienced of animal cruelty, they decided to form an animal protection group—The Society for Preventing Wanton Cruelty to Brute Animals.

The aims of the society members were very clear. They hoped to operate by exercising coercion. They boycotted products manufactured by dint of wanton cruelty, published details of animal cruelty in the newspapers and awarded prizes to essayists who promoted animal welfare ideas. One of the first people to receive the praise of the SPWCBA was the author of an article printed in a London magazine in 1762, which showed how honey could be obtained from bees without having to kill them. (Yet over 200 years later, how many people today are aware of the fact that Queen bees have their wings clipped to keep the hives in the same place and are artificially inseminated by decapitated males? Their honey, naturally stored to get them through the winter months, is replaced with a nutrient-deficient glucose or corn syrup, synthetic pesticides and antibiotics).

Sadly, this well-meaning collection of radically minded individuals was unable to sustain the society for long and it folded. On a happier note, Lewis Gompertz founded the Animal Friend Society, a group of highly enlightened campaigners. He was born into a Jewish family in 1779, was a committed follower of his faith and a champion for the rights of women, blacks, the poor and all oppressed beings. He was also a dedicated vegan, despite the fact he believed this would eventually kill him, and refused to ride in a horse-drawn carriage. In 1824, he published his first book for animal liberation entitled *Moral Inquiries On The Situation Of Man And Of Brute* in which he set out an argument that is still drawn on for information by animal liberationists nearly 200 years on. It is a highly comprehensive work and looks at all forms of animal cruelty including issues such as wool production, which are serious but side issues for the embattled Animal Liberation Movement.

The earliest animal welfare law was Richard Martin's Act of 1822, which banned the cruel treatment of cattle. It has failed terribly. In 1835, the Act was extended to outlaw bull and bear baiting, cock fighting and dog fighting. Modern day suggestions that this was a class thing are reinforced by the fact there was little interest in calling for a ban on hunting as Martin himself participated on his Irish estate and needed the sympathy of the landed classes to pass any legislation.

June 1824 saw the formation of what is thought to be the world's second animal protection organisation. Meeting in London, a group of people comprising social reformers, MPs and members of the Church joined together to form the Society for the Prevention of Cruelty to Animals. This was only more successful in that it has lasted to this day. Sadly its history of achievement beyond that is at best slight. A few years after its foundation in 1840, the Society was awarded a Royal prefix by Queen Victoria and became known as the Royal Society for the Prevention of Cruelty to Animals (RSPCA). Lewis Gompertz was one of the founding members of the original Society alongside the Evangelical William Wilberforce. The first secretary was the Reverend Arthur Broome. However, under his management and within two years of its formation, it fell into serious financial difficulties. Because the Society couldn't pay its debts, Broome was imprisoned. Whilst he was away, Gompertz, who had been his right-hand man, took charge.

He was a hard-working and energetic member of the SPCA and as secretary he managed to steer it through its financial difficulties and set it back on a firm footing. But six years later, conflict broke out. Gompertz discovered that one of the members was involved in behaviour 'inimical to the institution.' Others were clearly pro-hunting, but before he was able to have the miscreant thrown out, a smear campaign against Gompertz accused him of promoting Pythagorean ideas in his writings. Such a charge should really be a positive thing, but the SPCA was already being steered in the direction, in which its successor wallows to this day, where, ironically, the boardroom scorns such radical ideas as that of animal liberation.

In an act of overt religious intolerance and despite all that Gompertz had done for the society, the SPCA decided that only Christians could save animals. So it was that in 1832, Gompertz resigned as secretary and went on to establish the aforementioned Animal Friend Society. Not surprisingly, this more radical society was soon outstripping the work of the welfarists. Sadly, then, as today, the journal of the AFS—*The Animals Friend/Progress of Humanity*—was used as a vehicle to expose the failings of other activists and specifically those of the SPCA. One of the people whom it exposed was Lord Suffield, a so-called animal welfarist who had his own pack of staghounds! One incident records that whilst he was out supposedly conserving wild animals, his pack chased a deer for twenty-three miles. It died on the run. The pace of the chase is reported to have been 'almost unparalleled for its severity.'

As well as exposing the hypocrisy of people like Suffield, the journal looked at many forms of animal abuse and educated people in an unprecedented fashion. However, in 1846 Gompertz was forced to retire due to ill health, and without his hard work and visionary thinking, the AFS fell into decline and eventually ceased to exist. He died in 1861 but, before he did, he left one final legacy in the form of *Fragments In Defence Of Animals*, published in 1852.

Most exciting of all the groups to emerge during the Victorian era was the Band of Mercy and its radical action approach to helping animals. In 1845 the RSPCA undertook an educational campaign in schools. One of the leading lights of this campaign was the human rights activist Catherine Smithies who was a dedicated anti-slavery campaigner.

To understand what happened next it is important to appreciate that during this time a number of youth groups had emerged calling themselves the Bands of Hope. These were members of the Temperance movement and all pledged never to drink alcohol. (Indeed, similarly, there are many animal activists and vegans today who are 'Straight Edgers': those abstaining from drink and drugs and so on. Although this life style is ancient but at the same time advanced, it still only has a minority following).

Looking at the Bands of Hope, Catherine Smithies believed that if people were willing to form groups to abstain from alcohol, then they might also be encouraged to abstain from animal cruelty. And so it was that in the 1870s she set to work forming the Bands of Mercy.

These early BoM groups are steeped in legend for the Animal Liberation Movement. On the surface they were like any Victorian youth group—listening to lectures and readings and singing songs and reciting poems like *Don't Rob the Birds of Their Eggs, Boys*. They also took part in tableaux and parades during which each member carried a letter that spelt out 'A Band of Mercy.' They spread legends about faithful animals to redress the imbalance of suggested indifference. One such classic—and possibly the most famous—tale of animal fidelity was that of Greyfriars Bobby.

The story goes that in 1858, a labourer called Grey died and was buried in the Greyfriars churchyard in Edinburgh. During his life, Grey had been the devoted companion of a small dog named Bobby. After the man's death, Bobby would spend every day on his dead friend's grave, and no matter how many times he was dislodged, he would always return. A restaurant keeper would feed Bobby and in due course, the little dog became a much-loved member of the Greyfriars community. Then one day someone decided that Bobby had to fall into line and needed to have a dog licence.

Horrified that their little canine friend might be executed because he had no owner and thus no licence, the whole community, although poor, rallied round and raised the money needed to buy one. So touched was he by the action of the community, that the Lord Provost exempted Bobby from the dog tax and gave him a collar inscribed 'Greyfriars Bobby', which he presented to the dog in 1867.

Bobby died in 1872 by the grave of his much-loved human companion, and in his memory, the Baroness Burdett-Coutts raised a fountain in Bobby's honour. Other animals since then have earned recognition for their voluntary service to humanity yet few have received even the most basic level of compassion, let alone the honour of being recognised for their contribution, at times of war, for example.

On the surface, the Bands of Mercy were just youth animal welfare groups. Yet beneath this sanitary image lay a radical attitude towards direct action for animal liberation. Although the direct action in which they engaged pales by comparison to that of today's radical animal liberation groups, they were their latter-day equivalent.

Their best-known action, immortalised in a Victorian play, was to sabotage hunting rifles—a simple, effective tactic that rendered the rifles useless and thus saved lives. Although in reality there was no killing in the field, the theatrical script centred around a narrative in which a hunter died when his rifle exploded in his face after young activists had damaged it by pouring liquid down the barrel and soaking the cartridges in warm water.

While awareness and direct action was on the increase, thinkers of the time continued to write groundbreaking texts on the subject of animals. During the latter part of the 19th century, one of the most important works to be published was Henry Salt's book of 1892: *Animal Rights Considered In Relation To Social Progress*. Outlining the principles of 'animal rights' and arguing against almost every form of cruelty, from the treatment of domestic animals to vivisection, this book is widely regarded as a major landmark in the development of our thinking towards animal liberation.

In the early 1900's, London witnessed serious public disorder (known as the Brown Dog riots) over a monument erected to commemorate a mongrel, whose suffering in repeated experiments was made public by two female Scandinavian students studying physiology at various medical colleges in the City. The two Swedes—anti-vivisectionists Lizzy Lind Af Hageby and Leisa K. Schartau—were the earliest undercover investigators in the field and their book *The Shambles of Science*, published in 1903, was one of the first really important documents to come out of the growing anti-vivisection movement. Reading the graphic accounts today is heartbreaking, yet despite the furore at the time, the horrors of vivisection have continued unabated. The extract below gives a brief insight into what the two Swedes saw on a regular basis in the lecture theatres: animals (with their abdominal cavities open, rib cages and organs removed) were subjected to hours' long experiments, regularly without anaesthetic, and displayed obvious signs of extreme suffering. If they survived this ordeal, they were used in further experiments.

> A large dog, stretched on its back on an operation board, is carried into the lecture-room by the demonstrator and the laboratory attendant. Its legs are fixed to the board, its head is firmly held in the usual manner, and it is tightly muzzled. There is a large incision in the side of the neck, exposing the gland. The animal exhibits all signs of intense suffering; in his struggles, he again and again lifts his body from the board, and makes powerful attempts to get free. The lecturer, attired in the blood-stained surplice of the priest of vivisection, has tucked up his sleeves and is now comfortably smoking a pipe, whilst with hands coloured crimson he arranges the electrical circuit for the stimulation that will follow. Now and then he makes a funny remark, which is fully appreciated by those around him.
>
> The lecturer has gone out of the room. When the lecturer re-enters, the dog's struggles are changed into convulsive tremors of the whole body. This is nothing unusual; the animals seem to realise the presence of their tormentors long before they touch them. Dogs whose heads are covered so that they cannot see will nevertheless show signs of the utmost terror when their vivisectors approach them.
>
> The lecturer describes certain experiments on dogs amid the laughter of the audience. The oesophagus had been cut and a fistula established, so that the food taken fell down on the floor instead of passing into the stomach. The dogs ate and ate and

ate—they were frightfully hungry—and were much surprised to see the food fall out; they tried again with the same result. They could go on like that for hours.

Of the brown dog who became immortalised in the Brown Dog debacle, we know this: the brown terrier, with scars from previous operations, was stretched on its back on an operation board, its legs fixed to the board, its head clamped in a special holder and its mouth tightly muzzled to keep it quiet before the audience in the lecture theatre. The dog was cut open and then stimulated electrically as it struggled throughout the half-hour ordeal.

In 1903, the National Anti-vivisection Society (NAVS) drew public attention to the brown dog's suffering and fired up a huge debate about vivisection. The NAVS, founded in 1875 as the Victoria Street Society, was largely responsible for lobbying for the Cruelty to Animals Act, which stayed in force for more than 100 years. Stephen Coleridge, a barrister committed to the anti-vivisection cause and honorary secretary of the NAVS, was quoted wildly observing: 'the deep and abiding humanity of the British race would be offended beyond measure by what was happening in such dens of infamy. They would in their irresistible thousands set free the victims in their cages, smash to atoms the horrible instruments of torture and leave every laboratory in the kingdom in heaps of ruins.' The affair had roused the public to the anti-vivisection cause like nothing before and there was a definite public mood that this vile practice should be outlawed. Sadly Coleridge's chosen path was to be one of gradual change through legislation, as with other influential anti-vivisectionists of the time, and it would be a further three score and ten before another public outcry to match that of 1903 would awaken the British public to go set free the victims, of which there were nearly 20,000 recorded in 1903. 100 years later, there are some three million sacrificed annually in this country alone and at time of writing, the numbers are once again on the increase.

In 1906 a seven-foot memorial drinking fountain with a sculptured bronze dog on the top was erected in a park in Battersea, South London, in the memory of the brown dog and other victims of vivisection. Such was the consternation amongst vivisecting medical students that it was necessary to patrol and alarm the monument to protect it from them. Some still tried to trash it and were arrested. Others ran amok and fought with police, hundreds of them calling for the monument to be removed, waving stuffed toy dogs on sticks as they did, angry at the message the memorial was putting out. Four and a half years later less than sympathetic local councillors under police guard removed the monument in the dead of night. But thousands of locals and anti-vivisectionists kept the issue alive. They demonstrated their anger and marched to Trafalgar Square, giving hope to the cause, but the onset of the First World War would change everything and dampen the campaign against vivisection and it was to be quite some time before animals were taken into consideration again. A new monument was erected in its place in Battersea Park in December 1985.

The Emergence Of Direct Action

> Compassion for animals is intimately connected with goodness of character; and it may be confidently asserted that he who is cruel to animals cannot be a good man.
>
> *Arthur Schopenhauer (1788-1860) German philosopher*

The Victorian era and beyond saw the setting up of many different animal liberation and welfare groups and societies, some of them opposed to vivisection, others pro-vegetarian. By the start of the twentieth century, anti-blood sports groups had emerged. By the mid 20th century, there was even a society for vegans, more confident of longevity than their predecessors! In the main, their campaigning strategies avoided taking any direct action and tended instead towards focusing their energies on education and legislation. Time has shown that this is generally a woefully slow process, which has effected little change in over a hundred years of campaigning.

Despite the fact that Pythagoras had advocated vegetarianism in the 6th century BC, by the end of the Second World War there were only an estimated 100,000 vegetarians in the UK. And despite over a hundred years of parliamentary campaigns for animal protection, every abuse has continued to increase and new forms of exploitation have emerged.

Even when animal protection legislation was proposed, those with an interest in animal exploitation often corrupted it, a situation we continue to live with. Sir George Greenwood introduced the Animal Protection Bill of 1911, which is regarded as the anchor of animal welfare regulation. Helping Greenwood secure the Bill's passage through parliament was the blood sport enthusiast the Reverend Bowen. In exchange for Bowen's help, Greenwood made no mention of hunting in his Bill other than to make clear it would not be affected by the Act. Because Greenwood bowed to the whims of blood sports enthusiasts, the Animal Protection Act afforded no protection to any wild animal, unless the animal was temporarily restrained in some way. The Act also introduced the counterproductive concept of 'unnecessary suffering', which to this day effectively means that animals will suffer if it's deemed necessary by the abuser. By way of protection for animals, the Act offers little but a token gesture. Not surprisingly therefore, by the time post-war British society had stabilised, the thinking of radical-minded 'animal lovers' in the late 1950s was that something more effective was needed in the quest for the liberation of the long suffering animal kingdom.

And so it began. In August 1958, the Devon and Somerset Staghounds became the focus of a high-profile attempt by the once nearly radical League Against Cruel Sports (LACS) to lay false scents with a 'secret chemical.' *The Daily Telegraph* reported incredulously: 'opponents of stag hunting who have so far failed to stop the sport, are resorting to sabotage.'

This small act brought LACS some very welcome publicity, and the campaign was kept going intermittently for at least the next two seasons. The League's new chairman, Raymond Rowley, carried this pioneering approach forward in the early 60s. As the focus of League actions shifted to the South East and Midlands, membership increased dramatically and Rowley's dream of a 'revitalised' LACS began to look possible. In the Midlands for instance, the LACS gained 400 new members during November 1962 after false trails were laid against the North Warwickshire FH and the Albrighton Woodland. 'Anything the League does will have a sting to it', Rowley told the press, announcing that he was about to launch 'new' harassing tactics.

League militants, like pensioner Gwen Barter, had been grabbing headlines during 1962 with actions of their own. In March, she brought the Norwich Staghounds to a halt by climbing onto the front of the deer-cart; and in February she prevented the East Kent FH from digging out when she sat in a foxhole. 'There was nothing we could do', confessed the huntsman, 'we just stopped digging out the fox and went away.'

Since its foundation in 1927, the League had been anything but dynamic. It had achieved no legislative success in over 30 years, and had only recently hit upon the idea of creating wildlife sanctuaries in the South West. The membership was largely inactive and elderly and media attention was negligible before Rowley took over. As a pressure group, the LACS were a dismal reflection of the public activism of CND offshoots like the Committee of 100. Not only did the Committee win massive publicity for CND, but also it appealed strongly to a more youthful audience. Former Tory MP, Howard Johnson, voiced the hopes of many when he told the League's 1963 AGM: 'I have a vision in the coming stag and foxhunting season of whole numbers of you sitting in the roadway at meets of the hunt doing exactly what the anti-nuclear demonstrators do.' That month, Spies For Peace broke with the Committee of 100, published the influential *Beyond Counting Arses* and launched a more militant campaign of anti-war sabotage.

It has been suggested that the Hunt Saboteurs Association (HSA) was the inevitable result of the League's progress along these lines being held back by its more traditionalist members. It is tempting to suppose that Rowley hoped to appease both camps by assisting in the setting up of a direct action unit to run separately but in tandem with LACS. He now denies this. He certainly did not attempt to withdraw League support for sabotage until well after the HSA had decided upon an independent existence and its active membership was rising. Rowley engaged a solicitor and helped actively with the HSA's first major court case following the Culmstock Otterhound incident in May 1964, when, according to the HSA's first news bulletin:

> The incident took place during the lunch break of the Culmstock Otterhounds' meet at Colyford, Devon. 20 Saboteurs had been with the hunt for two hours when the assault took place. One of our cars was sandwiched between a Land Rover and another car. About 20 followers attacked our members with brass-tipped otter poles and whips. They bashed and dented the car roof and bonnet, let down the tyres and even tried to turn over and set it on fire whilst our members were still inside. The car driver, Leo Lewis, café proprietor of Paignton, was dragged from the car. He was struck with poles and punched heavily in the face. Three of our girls in the car were slashed with whips and punched. They were terrified, as the attackers seemed to go berserk. One of the assailants shouted: 'That will teach you a lesson to interfere with our sport'.

The car driver had his jaw broken. Another Devon hunt later brought out 100 farm workers to deal with a handful of sabs.

As late as 1966 Rowley was expressing his 'regret' at the HSA's 'independent' development from the League. Following the peace movement's example, he took 100 activists on a 'dawn attack' with 'secret chemicals' against the Old Berkeley's Boxing Day meet at Amersham in 1963. The first chairman of HSA, and its founder, was John Prestige, a 21-year-old freelance journalist from Brixham in Devon. According to *The Guardian*, he 'picked the first of his supporters' on 15 December 1963. 'He is the founder of the Hunt Saboteurs Association', declared the paper, 'which has the support of the LACS, whose chairman, Raymond Rowley, says is willing to make available all the latest know-how on how to sabotage a hunt.' Prestige, it was announced, was to travel to London 'for instructions... that trained action groups could be set up all over the country.' According to both Rowley and Prestige however, no formal meeting between the League and the HSA ever took place. Prestige adheres to the traditional view that HSA came about because 'the League didn't seem to be doing anything.'

He told *The Daily Herald* of his intentions: 'We aim to make it impossible for people to hunt, by confusing the hounds. The movement is being financed by a small legacy of mine and the 2/6d membership fee.' There were also two early donations of £500 each. One hundred members were enrolled in the first week and Prestige remembers receiving 1000 letters in the first ten days. An office was set up at Fore St, Brixham and staffed by the HSA's first secretary, an ex-Palladium dancer called Joyce Greenaway. Prestige led his small group into action for the first time on Boxing Day 1963, as the South Devon FH met at Torquay. 'We did so well that day that they cancelled the hunt', Prestige claimed. 'The local butcher gave us 50 pounds of meat and we fed it to the hounds. We used hunting horns. Nothing like that had ever really happened before and it caused absolute chaos! We did a lot of research on horn blowing and did the job very, very well. The police were completely bemused.' So would today's anti-hunt activists, who are for the most part vegan and would balk at the contradiction of feeding dead animals to the hounds to save foxes. During the following weeks, considerable effort was put, into developing new chemical formulas for confusing hounds. 'The main trouble', commented one early member, 'is finding something effective against them, but at the same time harmless.' It was not until April 1964 that 'Chemical X', the HSA's first scent-dulling compound, was used (against the Culmstock).

On 10 January 1964, the second HSA strike was carried out against the South Devon FH. Tactics at this time were described by a reporter after a strike against the Dart Vale and Holden Harriers: horns were blown, roads blockaded, aniseed sprayed and 'highly flavoured meat' was tipped in front of the hounds from the back of a landrover. The hunt killed twice. Within a month, the movement suffered a setback when Norman Redman, leader of the Littlehampton group, became the HSA's first casualty to arbitrary policing. Arrested for feeding the Chiddingfold's hounds on 15 February, Redman was fined £15 for 'insulting behaviour' and bound over for two years. Although saboteurs now regard such treatment as an occupational hazard, the fledgling movement took the judgement very seriously and Prestige was moved to write to Redman in May, forbidding him to break the terms of his sentence. 'We CANNOT allow you to take any active part in sabotage', he stressed in the letter, which caused Redman some annoyance and contributed to his later alienation from the movement.

Within the first four months, HSA groups had sprung up at Portsmouth, Street (Somerset) Weybridge, and Littlehampton. The Street group, run by Joyce Cebo, boasted 40 members by December 1964 and was harassing the Mendip Farmers and the Sparkford Vale on a regular basis. A group at Bournemouth was being formed; another in London, and Derek Lawrence was trying to turn Midlands LACS over to the HSA. Ian Pedler joined the moribund Bristol branch of LACS, revitalised it and then set up an HSA group from its ashes. Prestige felt able to claim, perhaps fancifully, that Boxing Day '64 would see 700 saboteurs in action from Sussex to Nottinghamshire. There were certainly large joint strikes on the Whaddon Chase and the Surrey Union where smoke bombs and rook scarers were added to the usual armoury for dramatic affect. A capable self-publicist with good media contacts, Prestige began spreading rumours around Fleet Street that HSA would raid an unspecified fox farm early in 1965 and that a helicopter would shortly be brought into action against various foxhunts. Twelve months after founding the HSA, he estimated there had been 120 strikes altogether, mostly in the West Country.

The next serious instances of anti-saboteur violence occurred during 1965. In February, three members of the Bournemouth group were attacked with an axe and a starting handle by thugs from the Sparkford Vale. Although a hunt supporter was fined £15 for breaking a saboteur's guitar with the axe (!) eight sabs were fined £10 each for 'threatening behaviour' (throwing flour bombs). But worse, much, much worse was to come.

Following the Culmstock Otterhunt incident at Colyford when sabs were viciously attacked, 70 saboteurs turned out against the same hunt a week later and sent them home in disarray, but the damage inflicted by the subsequent court hearing was far reaching. The hunt thugs were successfully convicted but seven saboteurs were bound over for a year to keep the peace. It was not the last time the courts would use this tactic and it took the aggrieved seven (who included Lewis and Prestige) so much by surprise that none of them took any further part in hunt sabotage. Prestige had in any case become disillusioned by the politicisation of HSA as a result of 'left wingers' joining the movement.

The legal offensive against the Brixham group threw the national organisation into a state of chaos. Communication between groups in an age where telephones and cars were not necessarily available, had never been that easy, but now complaints that HQ were not replying to letters became common. Pedler, Cebo and Dave Wetton wrote regularly to one another—Have we got any money...? Is Prestige still chairman...? If not, who is...? And so on. Eventually the job went to Pedler. Then in April 1965 came the Norman Redman fiasco. Redman was irritated by the HSA's insistence that he should take no part in any sabotage until his bind-over expired. Feeling 'disowned' by the movement, and in Jean Pyke's view, 'keen to get back at his old friends', Redman suddenly accepted an invitation to ride with the Crawley and Horsham FH. The national press, for whom the HSA was still good copy, rushed to the meet with pens and cameras poised to hear Redman hold forth about 'infantile' hunt saboteurs. The London and Littlehampton groups quickly organised a strike against the hunt and had the satisfaction of seeing Redman tumble headlong from his horse into a thorn bush! Still, this was an episode the HSA could well have done without. Eager to capitalise on this rare example of beneficial publicity, the British Field Sports Society (BFSS) tried for a short while to use Redman as pro-hunting speaker in debates but he soon lost interest and faded from the picture.

By the end of 1965, the HSA's honeymoon period was definitely over. Some groups were buckling under the continuous assaults of courts and heavies. 'I seem to have done nothing recently but get kicked and knocked about', considered Joyce Cebo feelingly, 'I think it is best to do things undercover now.' The Street group switched to sabotage by stealth before the meet rather than confrontation during it. But the group did not survive beyond the summer of 1966.

The burden of organisation began to fall more and more upon Wetton's London group. They were certainly the most active by 1967 although fresh groups with new energy were developing steadily. These emerged in Warwickshire and Hampshire in 1965, and in the following year, Cambridge, Northampton, Brighton, Hertfordshire, Yeovil, and Essex University all went active. October 1966 saw the first strike notched up in the North when David Hansen and Stuart Sutcliffe took a group from Keighley out against the Airedale Beagles at Silsden. A publicity conscious pop singer called Lady Lee announced she was forming an 'army' of saboteurs (including Billy Fury, Wayne Fontana and Peter Noone from Herman's Hermits!) but, perhaps fortunately, the venture came to nothing.

In the 1964/5 season, Wetton's group tackled 20 Foxhunts, four cub hunts, two hare hunts and seven otterhunts. An impressive tally for a group of people with less access to reliable transport and communications than their modern descendants. In January 1966 this group became the first to experiment with high frequency sound as a sabotage method.

He and Pedler effectively kept the HSA together as funds were divided between the pair, and they motivated and cajoled anti-hunt activists around the country. It was touch and go but the HSA had come a long way. Pedler drafted an HSA 'Manifesto' in 1965. In it, he made a prediction that is hereby partially fulfilled: 'There have been many incidents, too many to name here. But some day, when we have won, someone will write a book telling of all that has happened.'

Prestige's direct approach, once put into practice, was to have far-reaching implications, and was to provide a blueprint that would arguably prove far more effective than anything achieved by the League and other armchair opponents of animal abuse.

The HSA was set up to tackle hunting in the killing fields and proved to be highly effective. It was a glorious step-forward for those who believed more had to be done for the animals and, almost overnight, direct action came to be viewed as a significant strategy to effect change.

According to hunt supporter Nicholas Kester, however, the motivation was far from altruistic: 'Frequently protesters are recruited with the promise of a day's anarchy, a packed lunch and a bounty of some £20. One must ask: if these funds were to be withdrawn, how many supporters would show? The antis are predominantly urban students for whom a bit of beer money is quite tempting.' If indeed such was the case, since they were exposing themselves to the extreme violence of hunt supporters, the recruiting fees were woefully inadequate! Others have implied similar values drive saboteurs to act demonstrating a poor understanding of their adversaries.

It's one thing taking a beating in order to spare the hunted animal (and for many sabs it's been almost acceptable) but it's too much when the animal is killed as well. This violence coupled with the indifference and even complicity from the police, led first to the resurgence of the Band of Mercy and later to the formation of the ALF. It has also resulted in people being killed.

The Band Of Mercy

> Animals are our younger brothers and sisters, also on the ladder of evolution but a few rungs lower. It is an important part of our responsibilities to help them in their ascent, and not to retard their development by cruel exploitation of their helplessness.
>
> *Air-Chief Marshal Lord Dowding*

It was the violence and obscenity of cub hunting (now referred to as Autumn Hunting so it doesn't sound so bad) a ritual designed to teach young hounds how to hunt by using the season's fox cubs, that inspired the more radical activists of the Band of Mercy to begin a campaign of economic sabotage against the vehicles of hunts in the south of England. Half a dozen activists first hit the Whaddon Chase, the Vale of Aylesbury, and the Puckeridge and Thurlow foxhunts immobilising their vehicles the night before hunting. Others followed. It was 1973.

The initial result was financial and physical hassle for the hunts in question; the bonus was that it also prevented hunt members from getting to meets on time or sometimes at all. Still, not many sabs at that time were sold on the notion of covert sabotage raids as acceptable campaign tactics, but, as time went by, others couldn't fail to see the effect and were drawn to join the ranks.

These were annoying tactics and those on the receiving end weren't impressed. That just inspired the raiders more! Within months, the BoM extended the scope of their target groups to include other forms of animal abuse. No one really noticed at the time but the nice level playing field was being dug up. It was to start filling with potholes for many, from fur farmers in Sweden to vivisectors in Brazil, leading to comments such as: 'The people responsible for this are not animal lovers—there's something wrong in their heads' (made by a once comfortable animal abuser the morning after a visit from activists).

Early in November 1973, a fire broke out at a new laboratory complex under construction for the Hoechst pharmaceutical company at Milton Keynes in Buckinghamshire. It was clearly a deliberate fire but was not immediately attributed to 'animal lovers.' At the time, no group claimed responsibility, principally because it appeared to those who lit the flames that the fire hadn't taken hold and they felt it would have drawn attention to it, thus making a return visit difficult. Ronnie Lee was able to go back to the site and Cliff Goodman accompanied him. Both were hunt saboteurs, vegans and visionaries in a hostile environment. They were confident of a future for this growing evolution of human thinking and reasoned that women were climbing the ladder, the slaves had been freed, so why not the animals? Why not! It was surely logical for this nation—if any—to go out of its way to free the animals from slavery and the deliberate infliction of harm.

Possessed of a good knowledge of the tactics of other revolutionary groups and with a clear—if highly ambitious—vision of a world future without animal exploitation, the two men began to lay the foundations for change. Profoundly moved by the horrors of vivisection—the deliberate infliction of lasting harm on sentient animals—they took several gallons of petrol and poured it around the annex of the Hoechst building. They went up to the top floor and set several fires, then went down each floor and did the same, making good their escape as the place lit up the night sky behind them. The attack caused £46,000 worth of damage and crucially the BoM communiqué made the news:

> The building was set fire to in an attempt to prevent the torture and murder of our animal brothers and sisters by evil experiments. We are a non-violent guerrilla organisation dedicated to the liberation of animals from all forms of cruelty and persecution at the hands of mankind. Our actions will continue until our aims are achieved.

Fighting talk indeed. Between then and the following summer, the BoM's activities focused on hunt kennels in Hertfordshire and Buckinghamshire and on two boats moored in the Wash in Lincolnshire, which were licensed by the Home Office for use in seal culling. Fire extensively damaged one and the other was wrecked: neither would be used again in the killing of any more seals, but most importantly, no other boat owners were prepared to risk the same fate and the seal culling stopped. For good. It was a simple but significant victory for a noble cause finding its feet.

Covert fact finding investigations around known vivisection labs had uncovered a list of laboratory animal supply companies, confirming countless targets for the new band of empowered activists and soon a coordinated campaign was launched. In one raid, two vehicles (used to transport animals to laboratories) belonging to the Carworth animal-breeding centre at Huntingdon were burnt out and another immobilised.

There were similar attacks on suppliers in Wales, Hertfordshire, the

West Country, Buckinghamshire, Lincolnshire and Cambridgeshire. These and other actions received extensive news coverage and for the first time drew attention to the wide-scale animal abuse taking place in the laboratories. It soon became obvious that the animal abusers were taking the BoM and its threats seriously, and the Laboratory Animal Breeders Association issued a memo warning all its members of the BoM and its damaging attacks.

Even in the stagnant animal protection movement of the time, there was unease about this new level of protest. Some worried that law breaking would alienate the public from the cause. As one activist noted: 'There was no one talking about these issues until we arrived on the scene.' This is perhaps confirmed by the reaction of Sidney Hicks from the British Union for the Abolition of Vivisection (BUAV) who told *The Guardian* following one sabotage raid that: 'An act like this is worse than vivisection.' This was an extraordinary statement coming from an organisation campaigning against vivisection, but it was not to be the last word on the subject from the BUAV, who over the coming years would seem to voice as many objections to the work of animal liberators as they did to vivisection. Even the HSA of the time objected to this 'heavy handed' escalation in tactics, fearing it was damaging their image. They even offered a reward of £250 for information on the Band of Mercy ruffians, who would not, they said, be handed over to the police but instead 'dealt with' internally.

The BoM, however, were unrepentant and focused instead on the task in hand, mostly concentrating on economic sabotage in order to make animal abuse unprofitable. The only known BoM liberation raid in which animals were rescued caused the farm to close down through fear of a return visit. Just six guinea pigs were rescued in this raid—the first of many thousands of animals to come out in the years ahead.

During this period of activity, three members of the group were arrested as they prepared to set fires at the premises of the Oxford Laboratory Animal Colonies (OLAC) near Bicester for a second time. After spotting the activists, a security guard called the police who cornered the men in the farmyard. 23-year-old solicitor's clerk, Ronnie Lee, 31-year-old engineer Cliff Goodman and 20-year-old computer programmer Robin Howard suddenly found themselves out of work and locked in prison, charged variously with fourteen counts including causing £57,000 worth of damage to various premises. The publicity generated by the arrests and trial of the Bicester Three attracted a great deal of public sympathy and positive publicity helped by support from

Lee's MP, the Free Church Minister Ivor Clemiston. These were significant arrests but, in the long term, the show trial backfired on the authorities as these things often do. Lee and Goodman were each given a three-year prison sentence after admitting the charges and released in the spring of 1976 having served 12 months. Howard was given a 12 month suspended sentence and £500 fine. Significantly, the judge accepted they were men of sincerity and integrity and not common criminals.

In prison, the highly motivated Lee continued to generate publicity by going on hunger strike to protest at the lack of provision for vegans. Prison authorities soon accepted his request to be fed a non-animal diet but kept it basic! Anyone who has experience of the modern prison diet will appreciate just how basic it would have been back then but for Lee it was progress. It was vegan, which meant no animal had suffered.

Following these arrests, illegal actions virtually ground to a halt; the only one of note took place in 1975 at Alderley Edge in Cheshire, the vast base of Imperial Chemical Industries (ICI). On his first visit to the premises, Michael Huskisson, a 21-year old zoologist, broke into one of the complex of dog units and rescued two beagles of the infamous tobacco-smoking variety, which had been recently highlighted in the national press. Soon bonding with the two very individual rescued dogs and rapidly drawn into the notion of animal liberation, he returned for more but was spotted, arrested and charged with burglary. John Bryant, a 33-year-old LACS sanctuary manager was charged with handling 'stolen property': the rescued beagle dogs. For the fledgling BoM things had taken a turn for the worst.

Appropriately, the case went nowhere and they were both acquitted because ICI dropped the allegations. The company had suffered an enormous amount of bad publicity following the exposure of their smoking beagle experiments, which they had been conducting to 'prove' that there was no link between smoking and cancer. They wished at all costs to avoid further hostile publicity, but that was already brewing. 'The Beagle Burglars'—as they were described by *The Daily Mirror*—said they weren't connected to any group but were 'simply people who care' and would have taken more dogs had they been able to find homes. They were unrepentant. Two of the dogs taken by Huskisson—Major and Noddy—were never recovered, but a third called Snap was returned to ICI and her awful fate. In what can be seen with hindsight as a refreshing show of benevolence, the prosecutor in the case noted in summing up:

> We accept that whatever the defendants did in connection with this case, was done out of genuine motive. It is clear they believed the dogs were being treated cruelly and each of the defendants was justified in his action. The prosecution hold no view on whether the experiments were cruel or not, but it is right to say that a Government investigation had agreed that although there were better ways of carrying out such experiments, they should continue to their conclusion.

Enter The Animal Liberation Front

> The moment we make connections between what we know and how we live, evil collapses.
>
> *Maneke Ghandi. Minister for animal welfare in India*

Labs raided, locks glued, products spiked, depots ransacked, windows smashed, construction halted, mink set free, fences torn down, cabs burnt out, offices in flames, car tyres slashed, cages emptied, phone lines severed, slogans daubed, muck spread, damage done, electrics cut, site flooded, hunt dogs stolen, fur coats slashed, buildings destroyed, foxes freed, kennels attacked, businesses burgled, uproar, anger, outrage, balaclava clad thugs. It's an ALF thing!

By design, the Animal Liberation Front has caused much controversy since its earliest days. The ALF is an organisation of sorts, loosely made up of people who see a need to break criminal laws for the furtherance of what is often referred to by those involved as a higher moral law. They do so in order to alleviate the suffering of animals that have been deliberately denied the protection of animal welfare legislation and are legally exploited for sport, profit and pleasure.

The motives behind the actions of 'bunny-huggers' have been deliberately distorted over the years by the media, government agencies and animal abuse industries, who operate at the heart of this nation of so-called animal lovers. Those who stand for these sections of society know only too well that an honest representation of ALF activists and animal abuse would garner widespread public sympathy for the cause. Even without the blessing of the news media, the ALF has earned itself a broad support base. People who do care enough to act against animal abuse have seen that for all their fine words, those in power don't care and never will, as long as there are profits to be made from animal exploitation.

The Animal Liberation Front in reality isn't so much an organisation, more a banner—a title, an umbrella name, or a state of mind if you like—under which individuals and groups of people claim responsibility for illegal actions, which are designed to either directly or indirectly help the cause of animals. Anyone can be an ALF activist: there is no membership form to fill in—all that is required is that activists are vegan or at least vegetarian. It isn't a dismissal or kneecapping offence or anything like that—it just kind of goes without saying, and someone failing to recognise this obvious contradiction is missing the whole point. A primary undertaking is that all actions should cause no physical harm to other humans or animals. There is no hidden agenda.

The policy of the ALF is very straightforward: to rescue animals from suffering and to cause financial hardship to those who profit from their exploitation, in order to make that exploitation unprofitable, unpleasant and unappealing. ALF actions are often undertaken as retribution against someone who has committed an act of cruelty. Animals are rescued from cruel and neglectful pet owners, experimental laboratories and their suppliers, from zoos, fur farms, pet shops, factory farms, lobster pots and anywhere else they don't belong. The targets are therefore not surprising: laboratories, fur shops and farms, hunt kennels, intensive farms, butchers' shops, windows, vehicles, buildings, cages, snares and traps—anything connected with animal abuse, the people responsible for it, and their profits. The fundamental principles of the ALF's philosophy are neatly summarised in a statement published in The Animal Liberation Front Supporters Group newsletter in 1995. A Declaration Against Speciesism:

> Inasmuch as we believe that there is ample evidence that many other species are capable of feeling, we condemn totally the infliction of suffering upon our brother and sister animals, and the curtailment of their enjoyment, unless it be necessary for their own benefit. We do not accept that a difference in species alone (any more than a difference in race) can justify wanton exploitation or oppression in the name of science or sport, or for food, commercial profit or other human gain. We believe in the evolutionary and moral kinship of all animals and we declare our belief that all sentient creatures have rights to life, liberty and the quest for happiness. We call for the protection of these rights.
>
> *Animal Liberation Front Support Group*

ALF activists aren't necessarily animal lovers or people haters, but a quite average sample of society motivated by their sense of outrage at animal abuse. They risk their own lives and liberty rather than await the will of politicians who tend to work to protect those with vested interests. In this, the Government are ably assisted by the media, whose inflammatory newspaper headlines distort the truth—in short, activists are 'Animal Lib Loonies', 'Animal Mobs', 'Terror Groups', 'Animal Fanatics', 'Animal Rights Terrorists', Thugs, 'Animal Crackers' and

'Extremists.'

Headlines with a pejorative slant, which scream: 'Terror Mob Release Dogs', 'Lib Gang Smash Lab' or 'Libbers Release Rats' are designed to misinform readers. They suggest a false picture of a gang of crazed loonies at large, rampaging across the country, smashing their way into laboratories and releasing rabid animals into the wild, tormenting kindly business folk as they go. The truth is rather different: these are generally well thought out rescue raids, the object of which is to ensure that neglected and abused animals are taken away to safe, lifelong homes with the minimum of disturbance and stress. Some might think this is a barmy thing to be doing with your life, but the rewards reaped from every life saved are unsurpassable in my experience. Real job satisfaction and surely the way ahead for the human animal.

In view of the relative immaturity of the ALF, it has achieved a considerable amount in our society. Bad press, yes, but no other organisation has directly saved more lives: none have even come close. The ALF has been extremely successful in its aims. Their raids contribute not only to crippling established businesses like the trade in animal furs, but also draws attention to cruelty without resorting to the use of physical violence. Every animal freed from its torment and every bit of publicity that opens up debate is a small victory in this monumental war on terror and is seen as a job well done. Taking a neglected dog from its existence in a back garden shed is as important to that dog as is a major clearout raid on a high security vivisection laboratory liberating hundreds of animals, and it's usually the same people responsible.

There is no particular way in which people get involved with the ALF: there are no recruiting sergeants outside school gates or a call to arms outside the health food store. Like-minded people meet and try to stop animal abuse legitimately and later agree their preference for nocturnal activities: these are the 'cells.' One active cell alongside which I've spent time was formed one evening at a football tournament in Manchester. The two men, both in their early twenties, hadn't met since school but immediately recognised each other while playing in opposing teams. They knew each other from classes but hadn't been particularly close at school. That soon changed after close of play and the friendship grew as they found out that both of them were not only vegan, but also similarly minded as to the radical approach they wanted to adopt to address animal rights issues. Since then, they have been involved in many 'raiding parties' on the property of animal abusers, sometimes out together and at other times working with like-minded individuals. You couldn't pick them out from the rest of the players on the pitch.

Few ALF activists start out on the path of animal liberation thinking about breaking the law, but are soon convinced of the effectiveness of such an approach compared to the other options available. The animals can only benefit in the long term from their plight being constantly highlighted or by the increased pressure on those who abuse them or in the short term by being given their life back. Animal abuse thrives in secrecy and keeping animals behind closed doors is essential to maintaining that secrecy, so all publicity, which exposes or challenges this necessarily, contributes to its downfall. Most grass-roots campaigners will state, with some sadness, this is most often achieved outside the confines of the law.

Some activists carry out small-scale acts on a regular basis, some routinely firebomb targets, others do both every now and then, while some just can't help themselves and try to do everything at once. They will go to prison before their time. I've hung out with specialists in animal rescue who don't actually like animals that much, not even handling them. In the end, its about personal preferences and priorities. It can take months to organise a liberation raid and cost a great deal: surveillance and fund-raising are essential and animals have to be moved around and homed. The firebombing of a fleet of lorries, on the other hand, can be organised in a moment and cost next to nothing. I know because I've done it. Cutting the funding of the so-called extremists would have a knock-on affect on the rescue of animals, while encouraging those who don't need much funding for a can of paint stripper or half a house brick. Incendiary devices cost nothing to construct.

However individuals choose to hit a target, an immense amount of care is taken to ensure no life is put at risk. While few would mourn the passing of a vivisector or slaughter man, fewer still think it's right to start killing them. It wouldn't be good press and would be arguably less productive than attacking their profits. While fire is seen as the best option for inflicting maximum damage, many attacks have been aborted where a potential risk of it spreading was identified. Fire-fighters know the dangers involved in fighting fires and are instructed not to risk themselves unnecessarily for the protection of property. How can an inanimate object like a truck or a wooden shed be compared to a life? The crux of the ALF fire raisers argument! Of course it can't; it doesn't even come into the equation for anyone with their priorities in order. But those who profit from the suffering and exploitation of others don't list their priorities in this order, and a similarly muddled respect for property is often reflected in the law courts. Activists who find themselves before the courts labelled 'animal rights extremists' for an ALF rescue raid can expect a more severe sentence than the average thug on the street shoving a broken glass into someone's face. If proof were needed that the ALF is forcing political attention, then the law courts are that proof.

ALF 'extremists' are often accused by animal abusers (a general term I use to refer to all who participate in some way in the physical or psychological torment of animals and birds for their use) of having a reckless disregard for human life and an inhuman desire to injure or kill people. Nothing could be further from the truth. Apart from maintaining a policy of non-violence—however bankrupt that policy might appear in light of the continued torments inflicted on animals and the lack of political action to stop it—since its formation the ALF has never targeted human beings. If the intention was to harm the animal abusers whose property is the focus, those targeted could surely be picked off at will. But there is a conscious effort made to avoid physical violence. A great deal of work goes into opening the doors to these places and tracking down the people responsible for the cruelty within. It would probably be as easy a job to organise the assassination of one, as it would be to break into their garage to sabotage their car. It's a deliberate and sinister misrepresentation of the truth to suggest that animal activists are trying, hoping or intending to cause injury or death, however the facts speak for themselves.

Critics of ALF campaigns often voice 'concerns' that such criminal behaviour is counterproductive and that the due process of the law is the only way to proceed, but history tells a different story, as does the reality of modern protest. The suffragettes broke all the rules and used fire and violence to good effect to highlight the discrimination of women and help secure equal representation, or the vote at least. Asking politely of their oppressors failed laughably. Fighters of the Resistance used explosives and guns, and killed innocent people, as well as the guilty, when trying to overcome Nazi rule in Europe. The ANC saw the need to take up arms to fight the system of apartheid in South Africa, which was responsible for endless violence, torture and death and not readily open to reasoned argument. Slaves of racism in the West Indies felt they had no choice but to resort to violence to liberate themselves, as has just about everyone throughout history apart from Gandhi who was blessed by great timing and an enormous following.

Were they all wrong? Can it reasonably be argued they would have been able to achieve their aims by legally defined methods alone? Not reasonably it can't. Few of us put our neck on the line lightly but some will do whatever they see is necessary to change things if there is resistance from those in power. This is a natural process.

It was June 1976 when the Animal Liberation Front rose out of the remnants of the BoM. A couple of dozen new activists were drawn in by the publicity surrounding the trial of the Bicester Three, the ICI exposé, and the desire to create inroads where other organisations had so obviously failed. The Band of Mercy wasn't considered to be a sufficiently forceful name to represent the vanguard of the revolution that was envisaged, so it was ditched and the now (in) famous title—the Animal Liberation Front—was adopted in its place.

It was by now becoming more generally accepted that animals were being cruelly exploited on a vast scale for fun, out of habit and for financial gain, and a few thinkers saw that there was potential to draw attention to and maybe even put an end to some of it. More young people than ever before were now able and prepared to get involved in direct action for animals, and, in the twelve months since the ALF's inception, property was sabotaged to the tune of half a million pounds.

The first of the ALF liberation raids took place at the laboratory of the drug company Pfizer at Sandwich in Kent. Three pregnant beagles—which later gave birth to thirteen puppies—were rescued in a well-planned raid by a group of friends who employed the use of a stolen boat to cross a strategic river and avoid security guards. Unlike the quite astounding security that not surprisingly surrounds today's animal research laboratories (including Pfizer) in the early years of active opposition, security wasn't such a big problem. Over the years, liberationists have had to adapt their methods to the pace of change to keep up with security improvements, and technologies, which have been the inevitable knock-on effect of paranoia among those in the animal abuse industries, caused by damaging raids.

In November that year, thirteen beagles were rescued from OLAC (Western) Ltd. at Chapel Issac in mid Wales, a massive beagle factory then described by activists as the 'biggest dog breeding station in Europe, encased in a ten foot wall and high wire fencing.' The offices of the public face of vivisection, the Research Defence Society (RDS) in

London were also raided in the dead of night and a great deal of intelligence was recovered, including the home addresses of animal researchers. In a call to the RDS following the raid, the caller explained: 'This is the ALF. We have your files. We think you are pretty sick people.'

At that time, unlike thirty years later, there was little appetite for actions which specifically targeted people's homes as opposed to the centres of abuse. In stark contrast to today's environment, vivisectors were left largely unmolested at home.

Even for those exposed to the very real horrors of vivisection, the nice, gentle, polite English attitude prevailed. In their labs, however, they were less comfortable and not quite sure what might happen next as the activists toured them and made some noise. This polite approach would last only another three years before patience started to run out and the work of the vivisectors increasingly began to follow them home where the focus for the activists' attention would eventually outweigh even the reviled centres of abuse.

Although in the main it was hunting types and those who experiment on animals who were targeted in the early days, factory farmers and other animal abusers were soon brought into the limelight. Over £90,000 was reportedly lost when 1,500 arctic blue foxes were released from the Dalchonzie fur farm in Scotland in October 1976. Still active many years later, one of the team I tracked down told me:

> I was nay totally sure at the time it was the right thing tay do, but my pal said they needed my help so I agreed. The silence in the car on the way there made me even more uncomfortable. We'd never done anything like this before and knew we could get into trouble. We hardly spoke for the whole journey. I thought it was me rubbing off on the others. It was only once we got into the farm and started opening the cages and watched the foxes run away, some stopping to look back as if to thank us for returning their freedom, that I realised my life had changed. This was totally the right thing tay do! We were buoyant on the way back, singing and joking. We'd all been nervous to start with and not one hundred percent sure but we were now, and into something really exciting. It was like being liberated at the same time as the foxes.

The ALF was by now well established in the UK. In 1977 alone, a handful of activists rescued over two hundred animals from laboratory supply companies. As a result, the need for non-active participation in raids soon became as important to the ALF as the raiders themselves; an efficient network of potential homes for rescued animals was gradually being established and put to use. Over the coming years, many thousands of animals were to be rescued from factory farms and laboratories across the world, and all would be in need of good homes, thus making such a network invaluable to the cause.

One of the first raids of 1977 turned sour when the rescued animals were re-captured and returned to the lab, and Ronnie Lee (a pattern developing here) was arrested and later imprisoned for their theft. Frank Evans, the owner of Evans Laboratory Animal Breeding Centre at Carlshalton in Surrey spoke to the police after the raid:

> The function of the laboratory is to breed mice for medical research. I sell mice to hospitals and research laboratories. At any one given time I would estimate that there are approximately ten thousand mice at my laboratory. On Thursday 17 February 1977 at about 4.30pm I locked up my premises as usual and everything was secure.
>
> Then the following day, Friday the 18th at about 8.00am, I arrived at the laboratory to start work. On arriving I found my premises had been broken into and damage caused. First of all I saw that slogans had been sprayed on the walls of the laboratory.
>
> These slogans were to the effect of STOP ANIMAL EXPERIMENTS and STOP ANIMAL CRUELTY. Then I noticed a large window to my office had been smashed. Then on going through the laboratory, I found that the petty cash from my tea club was missing. I then noticed my telephone wires had been cut. On checking the laboratory itself, I found that three trays of mice had been taken. Two of these trays contained 50 mice each and the third contained 25. The value of the trays is at least £25. That makes a total of £55. I have also noticed that a book is missing which I cannot place a value on. This book is a record of various things that I have built up over the years and the loss of the book causes inconvenience.

Not quite blowing up trains or flying passenger planes into

buildings, but in today's political landscape, this kind of behaviour would rank alongside something they call terrorism, a term which is so overused it has become meaningless other than to say the authorities don't like you.

Ronnie Lee, whom one reporter described as, 'The most gentle person I ever met'—and few could reasonably disagree—was becoming known to the police as a business-like individual at odds with his oft reported and far less fearsome, slight bespectacled appearance. He was playing a key role in building the ALF strategy. Unaware the police knew his new address, he took the mice back there. Later that same day, his home was raided once again and all the mice were recovered and returned to the breeding centre for execution. Eight months later, he was found guilty of burglary and sent back to prison for a year. He said after sentencing: 'The prosecuting council said that the law exists so that the weak shall not be oppressed. It seems that the opposite is the case. It seems that the law exists so that the weak shall be oppressed. It allows animals to be exploited.'

The first ALF success involving the tactic of economic sabotage came after a small team broke into the Consultox lab in North London and caused £80,000 damage. This was a substantial financial loss and consequently the lab went out of business shortly afterwards. Countless others (and I have tried to count them) from butchers to laboratories, factory farms to department stores have since succumbed to the ALF's none too subtle, but nonetheless not unreasonable demands for fair treatment of animals. Victories such as the closure of a fur farm or pet shop or laboratory were and are often only achieved because of the complementary work done by legal campaign groups and vice versa. In effect, they publicise the horrors uncovered by the ALF, and apply legal pressure through protests and boycotts; in other words, while the 'fluffies', as they are referred to, are occupying the front door, the ALF go in the back. For some targeted individuals, however, the mere discovery of a broken back door and the implied threat of more to come are sufficient inducement for them to call it a day.

Outside the UK, there was also a mood for change fermenting. In early 1977, a group calling itself the Undersea Railroad carried out an audacious plan to rescue two bottlenose dolphins from a laboratory in Hawaii University, where they were being used in experiments on their communication ability. The test subjects, named Puka and Kea, had been abducted from the Gulf of Mexico six years earlier. The Undersea Railroad's founders, two students who were also surfers and were part of the project, had become disillusioned with the remorseless experiments. The dolphins were being denied further stimulation in their individual barren tanks through deprivation of playthings as a way to try to encourage better cooperation with the scientists.

Steve Sipman and Kenny Le Vasseur were probably the only real friends these dolphins had, and it was easy for them to work on conditioning them for their release. Working late into the night and at weekends, the two covertly taught the dolphins as best they could how to fish for themselves. Having spent six years in small, five foot round concrete enclosures being hand fed frozen fish it could have been a slow process but they were keen to learn—and play—and perhaps even sensed that they were heading for a better life. And they were.

The two men enlisted the help of sympathisers and on 29 May, the team went to work on the plan the moment their co-workers at the lab had left for their long weekend away. The execution of the plan turned out to be remarkably simple. It does of course help to have someone on the inside when trying to pull off something like this but even then, there are plenty of potential pitfalls. Lifting the animals using a winch was one. It broke under the weight. In the end, a combination of pure determination, foam for comfort and safety, ropes to lift, wet sheets, treats and a VW van made it work. Lifting the dolphins was easy and when they were safely loaded they were driven to the shore. Dressed for surfing, our two heroes carefully transferred their friends to the sea, then—loaded up with treats—they paddled out on surfboards in the hope of coaxing Puka and Kea into the open water.

Puka was always the feistier of the two and she headed for the ocean quicker than you could say: 'Watch out dolphin friendly tuna.' Kea, however, hung around the shore for a few days to the delight of locals and surfers and managed to avoid attempts to recapture her. Back at the lab the following morning, in place of the missing animals were two blow-up plastic dolphins and a confession written for all to see:

GONE SURFING—Puka, Kea, Kenny and Steve.

The two men handed themselves in after holding a press conference the next day and were later convicted of felony theft, but they gained the approbation of—among others—The American Society for Animal Rights, who said: 'Animals have waited a long time for this.' While their names have faded into relative obscurity, the international media interest they attracted played no small part in drawing attention to captive dolphins. This simple act was the first such successful liberation, and others have followed in the years since, along with the rehabilitation of dolphins held hostage to human entertainment around the world: so much so, that in the UK they had all gone within twenty years.

Early in 1978 in the UK, the ALF was struck a telling blow when five of its more active members were imprisoned following two trials. Gary Treadwell, aged 21, David Hough, a 48-year-old company director and Michael Huskisson, 24 (who had last been seen rooting around ICI's labs) were sent down after being convicted of damaging the grave of huntsman John Peel, the infamous fox hunter's hero. After a lifetime of hunting down and digging up live foxes, he was himself disturbed in his 20-year old resting place at Saint Kentigern's Church at Caldbeck in the Lake District—a shrine to today's bloodsport fanatics. The idea for the stunt was fuelled by years of seeing hunters digging out live foxes to chase and kill them, a barbaric tradition, which some thought warranted something noteworthy. The headstone was overturned and left in the partly dug grave were a stuffed fox head, pinched from a hunting pub, and a note with the words: 'Go blow your horn till your face turns blue.'

Just £70-worth of damage was caused, but that wasn't really the point. It wasn't the cost of repairs that caused the storm: the general consensus was that you shouldn't go around damaging graves and threatening to dig up dead people. The offenders were expecting to be fined for their stunt, but the judge wasn't impressed by their motives and sent them to prison for nine months each. Gary Treadwell said later, 'I considered the publicity over the action was a little over-dramatic and I couldn't understand the fuss being made—it was little different from those who went into Egyptian tombs and dug up the remains inside and were congratulated.' Indeed, but this was nothing compared to the reaction a similar stunt would have in years to come.

That same year, Judge Suzanne Norwood, presiding over a case of burglary and criminal damage at the offices of the pro-hunt lobby group the British Field Sports Society (BFSS) in London, told the defendants in a blast of refreshing enlightenment: 'I can understand you breaking into a vivisection laboratory and letting out the animals, but typewriters and calculator machines had not caused any harm to animals.' Gary Treadwell was sent to prison for another nine months but wasn't that put out as he was already there; twenty-year-old Aubrey Thomas was sent down for six months, and Christopher

Morrisey was remanded in custody for three weeks but later acquitted.

The same month, three women and two men in their early twenties, including Aubrey Thomas, were put on trial for rescuing 12 hens worth £18 from a 40,000-bird factory farm at Sayers Common in Sussex. They were later acquitted after arguing that they had been taking the birds to the Ministry of Agriculture for examination and so weren't intending to permanently deprive the owner. At the time of the arrest, only Robin Howard spoke to police with a request: 'If I admit the break-in on my own, could you let the others go?' The answer was no, the police wanted to prosecute.

These arrests, trials and jailings, and the associated aggro had a marked effect on the activity of the infant ALF. Consequently, although things never came to a complete standstill, it wasn't until well into 1979 that a resurgence took place. For example, in the summer, around 100 feather-bare battery hens were rescued during a raid on a factory farm at Middle Wallop in Wiltshire. Newspapers reported ALF warnings of more raids to come and gave more good publicity to the cause. In August the Shangri-La battery farm at Stevenage, Hertfordshire was also raided and another 70 hens rescued. The owner denied to journalists that there were any cruel goings-on at the farm, claiming ALF criticisms were unfounded because his birds got fed regularly on a balanced diet! Seemingly happy with this, he posed for photographs in one of his sheds in front of the now familiar sight of endless rows of hens tightly packed into cages.

At the time, since such scenes were alien to the public, activists viewed this publicity with optimism, for then, as now, there was a prevailing hope that on seeing evidence of these atrocities, others would be galvanised into action. Sadly, this was—and is—rarely the case. The small minority affected are vastly outnumbered by those who either forget what they've seen, those who abnegate from taking any responsibility because 'someone else' will do something about it, or those who simply don't care. Expectations from the publication of such images are overly optimistic—it seldom, if ever, has the desired effect: rather than do something to stop cruel practices, the government and industry tend to work out ways of preventing further exposés.

During the same month, several greens belonging to the exclusive Coombe Hill Golf Club in Kingston, Surrey, were damaged in protest against the use of the club's facilities by the Association of Fur Traders. It was a shift in tactics, which widened the definition of culpability for areas of animal cruelty. On 1 August, *The Daily Telegraph* suggested that to date, the ALF had successfully accomplished £1 million worth of damage, a figure the damage-doers considered to be more than a conservative estimate.

As the number of activists prepared to risk their liberty increased, so did the amount being spent on security. In the longer term, the knock-on effect was that future vivisection laboratories would be built concealed on top of multi storey buildings or underground. Those still on ground level, especially the bigger commercial labs and universities, were increasingly protected by expensive security systems. Of course, that hasn't always been enough to keep people out. As the saying goes: Where there's a will, there's no wall (or something like that!).

Elsewhere, reports of actions began to trickle into the UK ALF HQ from, amongst other places, Canada, France, Holland and the USA. The Dutch ALF emerged in 1977, starting with a raid on a battery farm at Windhaven. Over a brief period, they also rescued twelve beagles from a laboratory in Zeist, released over 200 mink and three foxes from factory fur farms and 400 pheasants reared for shooting. They also rescued sheep and ponies which were being ill-treated by a Dutch politician, took dozens of hens from factory farms and 21 cats from a laboratory supplier and in one night, sprayed hundreds of silver foxes on three farms with dye that spoiled their fur.

In France, extensive publicity was generated when 57 dogs destined for laboratory experiments were snatched. In Canada, many newspapers covered the story of a raid in which 14 guinea pigs, five rabbits and a cat were rescued from a hospital for sick children in Toronto; amazingly, among the photographs published was that of a mutilated cat with no ears—known simply as Cat 452—at the laboratory. The ALF told the press: 'It was like walking into Frankenstein's room—there were dogs that had been de-vocalised, a pig covered in burns and 18 cats with their ears cut off. We picked up the maximum number of animals we could carry and walked past the nurses, We felt sure they wouldn't stop us to ask what we were doing with all these mutilated animals in front of the children and it worked. The authorities will call this theft but we are law-abiding people and prefer to think of this as civil disobedience. What we saw in there made us really feel very sick.' Other animals in the unit included piglets with burns, rabbits in slings with broken legs and an irradiated lamb implanted in its mother.

If France wasn't surprising enough, it was unprecedented in Japan to see direct action being used to save the lives of non-humans, though it should be pointed out that the protagonist here was an American. 36-year-old Dexter Cate was an environmentalist who was put on trial accused of releasing 250 dolphins awaiting slaughter. He was found guilty of obstructing the legitimate business of fishermen, having rowed through the high rolling surf of the Kasumoto Bay late one night to cut fishing nets and free the trapped dolphins on Iki island near Nagasaki. The fishermen viewed the dolphins as 'gangsters of the sea' for eating 'their' fish and called them 'vermin', a label widely used to describe those creatures whom animal abusers don't like in this part of the world. Cate was expected to get three years in jail and be heavily fined for his crime but the judges decided the three months spent on remand and a six-month suspended sentence was punishment enough.

In America, the International Animal Liberation Front (IALF) rescued 60 gerbils and 32 rats from the psychology department of the University of South Florida; the gerbils had suffered in psychology experiments, while the rats had undergone surgery. Meanwhile, back where it all began: A. Tuck & Son Ltd at Battlesbridge in Essex, a laboratory animal breeding station which was visited several times in 1977, was raided again in July 1980 and 500 mice were taken. In Northamptonshire, the Faccenda Chickens depot was paid a visit, painted and had 15 of its lorries 'immobilised.'

One of the more famous raids of this period involved the rescue of beagle dogs from Wickham laboratories in Hampshire and was widely reported in the national press. Among the photographs published was one, which remains one of the most famous images of a masked activist carrying a rescued beagle to safety. The ongoing coverage helped to refute claims made by their abusers that the dogs would have died without the drugs, which they had been pumping into them.

The 1980's

> I am sometimes asked 'Why do you spent so much of your time and money talking about kindness to animals when there is so much cruelty to men?' I answer: 'I am working at the roots.'
>
> *George Angell (1823-1909) Founder of the Massachusetts Society for the Prevention of Cruelty to Animals in 1863*

Wickham—Round One

The Wickham Animal Laboratories are part of a complex, which included a large veterinary practice founded by William Cartmell, a practising Ministry of Agriculture vet and a vivisector. It had been chosen as a possible ALF target after rumours emanated they were testing things on animals there, but a preliminary look at the premises was not encouraging. Wickham is a busy little village and the labs are situated by the main road and were at the time, for the most, part surrounded by cottages owned by Cartmell and his staff. On the remaining side there was a new housing estate.

The first reconnaissance trip struck gold: the street lights in the housing estate were all out, probably due to repair work, and there was a large gap in the fencing surrounding the laboratory. A light was on in the office and a briefcase had been left outside the building; presumably its owner was in the office. Two activists nipped in, took the briefcase and legged it. The haul was to prove invaluable.

There were copies of a business prospectus with coloured photos of various animals undergoing experimentation and details of the work undertaken by the laboratory where inhalation experiments using smoke, dust, gasses and aerosols can be administered to the whole body or head alone. Also confirmed were irritancy tests, skin sensitisation and experimental surgery being carried out by the laboratory on a wide range of animals. There was also a business diary containing many addresses with contact names and a letter detailing business arrangements for the expansion of Wickham labs at Torbay Farm a few miles away. There was a very interesting document relating to the purchase of beagle puppies from Allington Farm at Porton Down, the MoD secret testing laboratories in Wiltshire. These were dogs, which were to weigh no more than three kilograms (i.e. the smaller the better); the puppies were to be injected with a Pfizer cat vaccine and then transported to Beecham laboratories. All really spooky stuff and a real revelation. There was also evidence of similar transactions with Fisons. Three more visits were made to establish exactly where the dogs were housed at Wickham and to ascertain methods of entry and exit, and then it was all systems go.

In early March 1981, the team met near Winchester railway station shortly before midnight and were joined by a local freelance journalist. Arriving at Wickham, they parked their cars close to a padlocked but unused gate near the housing estate at the rear of the labs. The advance party, armed with a sledgehammer for the kennel block door and bolt cutters for the gates and padlocks, went into the laboratory compound through the garden of a bordering house. Once the padlock on the gate had been cut, the rest of the group entered and positioned themselves with four lookouts at strategic points. A pack of beagles make a lot of noise when aroused so speed was essential. The door gave way with little trouble and the cutters made short work of the cage. There were three dogs in each pen and they were lively; as one was taken from the first pen to be opened, the other two bolted from the grounds. This wasn't the plan but at least they had a chance. The other dogs—11 altogether–were picked up safely and carried to the waiting cars, which then left in different directions in order to maximise the chances of some of the animals getting safely away. The puppies were quiet, if a little bewildered, and soon settled down for their journey. They stayed at their initial destination while tests were made to ensure that they were not ill or contagious in any way, and were later sent to their new homes.

Cartmell later described the raiders as, 'Anarchistic burglars who should be shown up for what they are.' He didn't suggest how that might happen. Publicity was extensive and gave rise to a mood of optimism that those in favour of animal rights could do something to make a difference. Others also clamoured for a piece of the press attention, some establishing a niche for themselves as being among those on whom the press could rely to condemn such actions as 'criminal.'

Taking On The Vivisectors

> One person with a belief is equal to a force of 99 who only have interests.
>
> *John Stuart Mill, 19th century philosopher*

By the beginning of the 1980s, the homes of vivisectors had become fair game and on one occasion, some three dozen were hit in a single nationally coordinated action, mostly with paint. The polite approach was being done away with, as it was evident that cruelty wouldn't simply be stopped by focusing on the labs where the abusers could hide and ignore the protests outside. Raids on fur farms were also on the increase, and the industry began to fold. Shop windows were being broken almost nightly in the UK and a mass of publicity was being generated. Never before had so much attention been focused on the plight of animals and the mindset of those seeking their liberation. In the next few years there would be a steady increase in ALF activity and publicity reaching its peak during 1984, a year full of surprises for those thinking they'd seen what they so readily term 'extremism' at its worst.

In Scotland, Australia and West Germany, small-scale covert liberation raids and damage attacks gave way to larger scale operations; there was a definite sense that the movement was a growing global phenomenon indicative of a world wide mood for change. Meanwhile, Animal Liberation Front activists in the UK were trying something different. For the sympathetic observer and potential activist it was great copy; for those behind closed doors it was a nightmare; for the authorities it was time to wake up and get to grips with the potentially revolutionary concept of mass public participations in daylight lab invasions.

It did in fact take just two of these raids to demonstrate that although good for publicity, mass participation was too risky a business. In the first large-scale daytime action, dozens of activists stormed the Safepharm animal testing laboratory near Derby in the West Midlands and rescued animals. That was all good and well, but the media had been invited by organisers and captured some of the raiders on film as they left, compromising a number. Brendan McNally was one who was later arrested and remanded in custody for two months for his involvement and breaching bail on other offences. In protest at this, demonstrations were held outside the prison and outside Leicester University's Psychology labs, which led to a break-in, the destruction of lab torture equipment and the rescue of a number of animals. Several other Safepharm raiders who were identified from press photographs were later given suspended prison sentences for their involvement. Such was the novelty of seeing these heroic day raiders go to prison, that when McNally was released, he was honoured by being given the role of BUAV Vice President.

A week after the Safepharm raid on Valentine's Day, activists acting under the flag of 'Operation Valentine' poured in through the front gates of the Life Science Research laboratories at Stock in Essex. Over the next 40 minutes, rats, beagles and mice were rescued from the notorious vivisection complex, £76,000 damage was caused but over 60 people were arrested. As a consequence of the raid and subsequent lost orders, over 40 lab workers were laid off. The ensuing three trials of 29 defendants cost over £1 million to stage, resulting in the eventual imprisonment of eight activists. On appeal, their sentences were reduced—Steve Boulding's to nine months, Steve Davis' to three months, Peter Sales' to two months and Mark Corsini to 200 hours community service. Linda Harman and Christopher Davis were given conditional discharges and Randy Burroughs got three months in prison but was released prematurely when prison authorities confused his paperwork. Brendan Delaney ended up with 150 hours community service after initially being given four months inside. One key prosecution witness—one of 69 called—was a local who worked at the lab and who took down vehicle registration details, phoned just about everyone he could think of to report the incursion and even found some raiders' stashed tools. The judge for his part commented that he was glad vivisection existed and of course did the defendants no favours. He promptly dismissed one jury member who had wept as one of the defendants described to the court some of the experiments that went on in the labs, and he refused permission for an ex-worker (who had left Life Science out of disgust) to give evidence because he said it would be irrelevant.

Prison sentences weren't excessive by today's standards, but being arrested, charged, restrained by bail conditions and having the threat of prison looming large can seriously impact on individuals' lives, especially those who wouldn't otherwise have ever ended up anywhere near the criminal justice system. At times like this, the accused need all the support they can get, but it was a complaint of many of those going through these trials that there was no coordinated support from sympathisers, with the result that they felt isolated from the huge public support there was for these actions.

The risks involved in organising a mass of people in this way were obvious, though it was considered there was still a lot be gained by such raids which had rocked the foundations of established abuse industries, but as ALF tactics they were abandoned following the Stock raid to allow for more concentration on the covert approach, proven to be as effective but less risky.

The Animal Liberation Leagues

> Boundless compassion for all living things is the surest and most certain guarantee of pure moral conduct. Whoever is filled with it will assuredly injure no one...
>
> *Arthur Schopenhauer (1788-1860) German philosopher*

The Northern Animal Liberation League (NALL), on the other hand positively extolled the virtues of mass participation daylight invasions, and the benefits were there for all to see, not least the wider public who were getting to see inside vivisection labs and factory farms for the first time. Formed in 1980 by activists based in the Northwest of England, and operating under the slogan 'Over The Wall When They Least Expect It', the NALL worked to bring together all concerned in a coordinated drive against animal abuse: the NALL would do the job of both the ALF and the public campaigning groups.

The policy of the NALL was to cause only minimum damage when gaining entry to places in order to focus press attention on the cruelty and not to steal animals but to photograph them and recover information. This was about exposing animal abuse to the general public and involving as many people as possible in direct action and giving them a feel for these places. Having this hands-on experience made returning in the dead of night easier for those moved to act by what they'd seen and ill-content with causing minimal damage and leaving the animals behind and left the NALL with a positive image.

The attention drawn to these mass invasions, coupled with an endless flow of images from places seldom before exposed to public view, would inspire the formation of the Central Animal Liberation League, South Eastern Animal Liberation League, Eastern Animal Liberation League, Southern Animal Liberation League, Western Animal Liberation League, and the Scottish Action Group for Animals who snatched a pack of beagles in a day time raid on Organon labs in Motherwell, Scotland in Dec 1983.

The first and probably most successful NALL action took place one Sunday morning in the summer of 1980 at the notorious government-run Babraham Agricultural Research Centre in Cambridge. This raid set the pace for the rest of the fledgling movement to follow. Dubbed 'Frankenstein Farm' by the media, the former country house now houses animals which are interfered with and altered in a variety of intriguing ways which confuse the average mind but are aimed at increasing the profitability of their exploited bodies for the meat industry. The raiders had hit the big time here. Around 100 activists got into the farm buildings unchallenged and split into groups, one small team seeking evidence from the locked windowless buildings, the other larger group creating a diversion. They recovered from a number of buildings graphic evidence of the worst excesses of human cruelty. Amongst other freakish things, there were pigs with electrical contraptions fixed to their skulls and wired to the brain, cows with glass portholes fixed into their stomachs through which their heartless captors could shove their arms and remove the contents, and goats with udders grafted to their necks. A spokesman at the labs complained after that the incursion, and in particular the use of camera flashes, caused 'severe stress to the experimental animals' and that apparently the poor creatures 'were put out by the whole thing.' Ah, bless.

The raiders, of all shapes, sizes and disguises, photographed the scenes in various labs. Most left before police arrived in sufficient numbers to detain the camera crews, although 18 people were arrested. One man detained had found his way alone into a secluded experimental area and photographed something he said looked like a cross between a goat and a horse. He explained years later what he'd seen: 'I'd read all I could find on the subject (vivisection) after a teacher at school brought it up in Current Affairs and it disturbed me but I still wasn't sure it could be as shocking as described in some literature. Instinctively I felt I didn't trust the idea of vivisection and I went on some demonstrations and talked to people who had their own horror stories but firsthand experience Babraham was something else. It was surreal yet very real; everything I'd imagined in my worst nightmares. There were a lot of distressed and abnormal looking animals to make sense of in such a brief period of time. It was an emotional overload the like of which no other life experience has given me to this day. By the time I'd located the poor horse, whatever, I'd seen it all and it was time to leave. People were shouting that staff were trying to make arrests and the police had arrived.'

Officers from Cambridgeshire Police grabbed him on the way out and took him into custody. On arrival, the primary concern of the police was to secure this particular building and they rapidly had it surrounded to prevent anyone else getting inside. The captured raider was later released without charge, but police in the meantime managed to 'lose' his camera and the film of the strange creature.

Most officers had been patrolling the vivisection-riddled streets of

Cambridge in numbers at the time of the raid, apparently expecting protests there. Arranging this was a cute move by raid organisers but hardly likely to warm police organisers to the cause (not that cooperating has reaped much reward and respect since, as repeated contact with this force over coming years has shown).

The use of stolen pets in vivisection has always aroused strong emotions; hence the industry campaign to promote the use of purpose bred animals as somehow less capable of suffering. Blackie was one of a handful of dogs removed by the NALL from Sheffield University in 1980 and later identified by his owner in the resulting publicity and reunited with her. While admissions have been few and far between, there have always been rumours and suspicions and recently, with the release of once-secret papers, it was revealed the Medical Research Council had been paying cat thieves £1 or £2 to bring in cats from the streets of London. This was during the 1950s, when 6,000 cats were used in experiments, half the number demanded by a growing industry. Two of these thieves, Frederick Oldham, a scrap metal merchant, and Joseph Biscoe, a road sweeper, were arrested in 1952 and convicted of stealing nine cats. Despite the thriving trade in stolen pets for fur and vivisection and the incredible suffering inflicted upon them, the only prosecutions since then have been of people rescuing animals from labs and suppliers. Those ruthless enough to steal people's pets for supply to such places have attracted no political will to prosecute.

The findings of the Babraham investigation were widely publicised and teased ever more people into the world of animal liberation campaigning. It would be difficult to convince most people of the existence of this world without such graphic evidence. A world that would, to all intents and purposes, not exist without those whom political leaders and media commentators so easily dismiss as criminals, thugs and terrorists. There was a positive theme developing here whereby people went for a sneak around some place that rumours suggested was iffy, took some pictures of animals subjected to something or other unpleasant, left and contacted the press, who ran a story. It's what the abusers dread. It's what animals behind closed doors need. Exposure.

Babraham footage and that of many similar raids attracted a mass of local, national and international publicity, which in turn brought in lots of new blood to the Movement and opened many eyes to the dark and seldom exposed world of what they call 'scientific research' and 'animal husbandry.' These spectacular raids were grabbing the imagination of the media, the public and the movement alike, though with distinctly opposing effects and they all wanted to be involved in some way. As commonplace as they are now, video cameras were first adopted and put to good use by the SEALL during this period but were soon on the wish list of anyone serious about exposing and ending animal abuse. Really, all that was spectacular about these raids was the secrets they revealed. Everyone involved, without exception, was anxious; some were scared, few were experienced, none paid and not everyone knew each other. There were no helicopters, abseiling or parachute drops. All there was—and so often is—was a group of loosely connected people and a plan that probably won't work to the letter, as they seldom do. But it is the will to try that makes it special. Do nothing, nothing happens and nothing changes. Wangle a way into a secret building where secret experiments are carried out and wander around taking photographs and documents and bingo! The findings make it spectacular.

The Royal College Of Surgeons

Never despair, but if you do, work on in despair.

Edmund Burke

Another major SEALL coup came with a well-publicised raid on the prestigious Royal College of Surgeons at Buxton Brown Farm, Downe in Kent in August 1984, where hundreds of monkeys and thousands of other animals are used in experiments including long-term dental and diet-related research. The 60-strong raiding party recovered bundles of documents, with the unprecedented result that the BUAV brought a case against the RCS, who were found guilty of wantonly and unreasonably causing unnecessary suffering to a ten-year-old macaque monkey. This notoriety gained them a derisory £250 fine and unwanted media coverage, which shattered the college's reputation.

SEALL claimed that the ventilation system in the lab had broken down and a ten-year old female crab-eating macaque called Mone had severely dehydrated as temperatures soared to 92F. Other animals at the lab had suffered broken limbs and had been found trapped in their cages, which had been in use since 1966. Some were cut free while others died, unable to reach water. Monkey expert and prosecution witness Cyril Rosen of The International Primate Protection League described the conditions at the lab as akin to Victorian slums and criticised the surgeons for keeping experimental and breeding monkeys together, and in three-foot-square aluminium cages. 'You would not expect humans to live like this, so why animals?' he asked, not unreasonably.

Mr John Cooper, the vet employed by the RCS, gave evidence in court for the college. Paradoxically, given that a vivisection laboratory employed him, Cooper was described as a 'dedicated veterinary surgeon.' Clearly, having a vet on the RCS payroll was good for business not just because it helped keep valuable animals alive, but helped to appease the public. Cooper's view was that to provide the dehydrated monkey Mone—the focus of all the media interest—with an extra water bottle would have made his job more difficult as he had to be able to see into the cages and this would have caused an obstruction. His stance on the torture of distressed wild monkeys was: 'My prime objective was to improve the health of the animals. My job is to make them healthy first. If research is to be good—it has to be made good and not half-baked.' (And not involve stressed-out caged animals...) A vet going out of his way to make healthy animals sick might sound like an aberration but there are more than a few who will do this if they are paid well enough as we will see.

Another Defence witness (another vet) former President of the British Veterinary Association and zoo inspector, thought the conditions at the RCS very satisfactory and stated that, in her view, animals are happier in captivity than in the wild and that physical isolation is fine as long as they can see and hear other monkeys. Further, that these types of monkeys don't need exercise to stay healthy!

It is a prerequisite of those who seek to inflict severe physical damage on an animal to have a healthy one to begin with, but the greatest contradiction for a vet whose stated duty is to care for animals and make them well. Another witness for the RCS, their chief Animal Technician, claimed in court that he only worked at the lab because of a love of animals and guessed that was why others did. He stated that keeping monkeys in small aluminium boxes was just as much a way of helping to improve the environment of the animals as it was a way of protecting staff, and that housing them alone made monitoring their health easier.

Just four days before the SEALL raid, a Home Office appointed lab inspector had visited the RCS and had not only given it a clean bill of health, but also praised the high standard of animal care! This is a recurring theme, which has been turned on its head by evidence gathered during every illegal incursion or undercover investigation. Suffice it to say, that all those who visited the RCS uninvited, explicitly disagreed with the Home Office inspector's findings.

Michael Huskisson was 31 now and among those who disagreed (more and more the older he's got, and the more he's learnt) and was about to be punished for his views once again. He was convicted for his part in the raid after agreeing to give voluntary testimony in court to his involvement. He was well away from the scene by the time the police had arrived, but when it became apparent that some of the RCS material might be used to prosecute them, it proved necessary for someone to stand up in court and testify to witnessing the damaging internal 'incident reports' being taken from the labs during the raid. Without such a testimony, the material would have been worthless as evidence.

Deployed on the day to photograph monkeys for SEALL, Huskisson gave evidence in court for the BUAV. He claimed that in the melee, he had been handed the documents and then passed them on himself to those whose job it was to bag all useful material and move it to a safe house for analysis. This admission was tantamount to walking into prison and took exceptional bravery. Having walked away from the scene of the crime, it would have been easy to let the whole thing go and get on with other projects, but here was a golden opportunity to have a very real impact on the workings of the prestigious RCS, and Huskisson knew he was best placed to do it. Their future was potentially in the hands of one person, the one brave enough to invite punishment. It was made clear from the start that prison was inevitable but so was the acquittal of the RCS without this witness. Difficult choice?

Effectively, Mike Huskisson pleaded guilty to involvement in the burglary in order to reveal the secret inner workings of the RCS, but claimed he had acted without dishonesty and didn't intend to permanently deprive the lab of its shocking material, which was the main focus of both prosecution cases. Accepting he hadn't done any damage or stolen anything himself, the jury swallowed the argument that he was guilty of complicity with others and convicted him. Keen to make an example for those others, the judge sent him to prison for 18 months.

Following the highly publicised exposure of the RCS' failings, they were convicted of and fined for cruelty to Mone. The other charges were dismissed, despite the college's admission that 52 animals had suffered unnecessarily, a fact which Home Office inspectors had somehow managed to miss during their inspections. Inspectors had visited the RCS on 18 June 1984, the day a female called Rage died from dehydration. Mone collapsed four days later. To add insult to his injury, the RCS were acquitted on a legal technicality a year later, returning to their Prestigious Institution status in the eyes of the law, despite the fact that the material recovered—which detailed the neglect of, and suffering inflicted upon, monkeys in the RCS labs—can never be altered. The RCS remains somewhere secret—a place you certainly wouldn't want to be if you were an animal.

Meanwhile, established state sponsored businesses were becoming dismayed at the loss of their anonymity and the potential for damage to their property. The pharmaceutical and farming interests were leaning on friends in government (some were in government) and it wasn't long before police resources were committed to unravelling the Liberation League phenomenon before any more damage was done.

Imperial Chemical Industries

Ideas are funny things. They won't work unless you do.

Unknown

Just two NALL activists were imprisoned following the trial for their part in the large-scale invasion of the ICI labs at Alderley Park in Cheshire in April 1984, when 300 activists swamped the site and sought out the usual nasties to the disbelief of staff on the premises. The effect of the state's response to yet another high profile raid was far more devastating. This damaged ICI less than the earlier smoking beagles exposé; though the minimum damage policy of the NALL was circumnavigated during this raid in order to deal with lab security. At least one beagle was also rescued.

The behaviour of the police in dealing with the young, inexperienced activists detained in Cheshire proved a problem; less than half of those arrested remained silent amid fears of violence and of statements being concocted for them. Some made full confessions and even named people they knew were involved but hadn't been arrested.

Dave Callender and Robin Smith, key activists and well-known organisers in regional hunt sab and animal rights groups, were presented as leaders of the raid during the three-month show trial that followed at Knutsford County Court and were sent to prison for nine months, six suspended. Callender was arrested on site and was held for a week in Macclesfield Police station but said nothing. Smith was a high-profile figure in the ongoing ICI campaign and was arrested two weeks after the raid. He also maintained his right to silence. Fifteen others arrested and similarly charged with 'Unlawful Assembly with Intent to Burgle', were threatened with prison from the beginning and adjusted their lives accordingly but were eventually fined and given community service orders. Others had charges dropped as the case proceeded. Not the worst outcome, but the ordeal tested resolve and relationships and slowly killed off a thriving regional movement. The Northwest of England had been an exciting place to be during the early 1980s, but the mood changed following the ICI raid and the knock-on effect on individuals and local groups who had borne the majority of arrests was far more serious than the actual punishment meted out. By the time the trial had concluded a year after the raid, the power had been sucked out of the movement in the Northwest and the ICI campaign had died away.

The NALL had led the way in the North, but SEALL became the unofficial trailblazers of the Animal Liberation Movement in the south of England following the successful mass invasion of Wellcome laboratories in Dartford in Kent in September 1983 when dozens of activists occupied the roof, took photographs and ransacked offices.

Wellcome were exposed on national TV and claimed they had suffered over £250,000-worth of damage. Even though it took the police an hour to arrive, seventy people—some inside the labs—were arrested in all, but the protesters' lack of urgency was equalled by that of the authorities, and no one was punished with anything other than being bound over to keep the peace. It was clear that a lot of these companies would rather avoid attracting further publicity than seek convictions (as shown with ICI's smoking beagles) and that made such forays all the more inviting. The reality was, however, that mass raids had a very limited shelf life as the authorities began to develop a strategy to deal with the problem.

Operating at a time when the press were sympathetic, the SEALL put the video camera to good use and grabbed extensive media coverage. Their well-publicised raids inspired activists everywhere and encouraged the launch of a fresh campaign—guaranteed to draw in widespread support—against Shamrock Farms in Sussex who were importing monkeys for experimentation. Activists also raided and exposed Surrey University labs; here again those arrested (mainly on the roof at the time) were bound over. It was no deterrent, but the warning signs were that without better planning, the arrests could cause major problems if charges followed. As it was, the only person sentenced was a woman who was convicted of theft and assault after driving her car through the security gate with a rescued lab dog on the back seat.

Mass arrests were a wake up call for SEALL organisers, who learnt fast. It was something of a honeymoon period for the movement, and the powers that be were beginning to get stirred by the raids and their negative impact on their regulated animal research programmes. It was only a matter of time before the iron fist of 'commercial concern' would come crashing down and media coverage turn nasty.

Before that happened and those at the top had realised the negative impact of people opening the window onto animal abuse, Channel 4 screened *The Animals Film* at its launch in the early 80's. This was three hours of pure horror, more shocking and real than the best horror film, depicting all aspects of animal abuse in unimaginable, graphic detail. It was the stuff of nightmares. It changed the direction of my life, as I know it changed the lives of many others. I was overwhelmed by the cruelty, and it occurred to me early on that, whatever animal liberators (who were, as some claimed, 'criminals') were accused of doing—they were acting in the interest of the animals and that's all that should matter. These people were risking their own safety to prevent the awful suffering of others. How fantastic—to actually be rebelling against the systems that indoctrinate us into accepting that animal cruelty is a necessary evil; that make us swallow the horrors which, as children, we instinctively know are unacceptable! It was a revelation to many: I, for one, was no longer convinced by the rhetoric. Always for the underdog—or just the dog—I soon took sides and put my broken heart on my sleeve.

Return To Wickham

> Tests on animals have led to around 100 drugs being thought potentially useful for stroke; not one has proved effective in humans. You don't need to be a balaclava-wearing animal rights activist to question the value of animal studies in this area of medical research.
>
> *The First Post. 25 January 2007*

Focusing on exposing the criminal behaviour of animal abusers, and planning meticulously, by October 1984 the SEALL had prepared and conducted three simultaneous raids on laboratory premises in Hampshire. Non purpose-bred dogs in RCS kennels and information recovered from the RCS and Sheffield University raids had exposed a pet-stealing ring operating in the Hampshire area. SEALL activists were convinced stolen pets were being distributed to the likes of the RCS and Wickham laboratories via APT Consultancy—a supply company run by David Walker, another vet, and Cottagepatch Kennels in Southampton.

This was the most ambitious of all the League raids, and the third large scale SEALL action in 60 days, but it was seemingly doomed to failure from the outset thanks to information the police were apparently receiving from an informant operating within SEALL. Inevitably the League idea was becoming a victim to its own success; due to the large numbers of people involved in operations, it was easy for the authorities and corporations to infiltrate. That these raids happened at all was something of an achievement, given the information leak and the ever-enthusiastic Hampshire Police. But all three were executed precisely as planned and Scotland Yard, who had placed key activists under surveillance in anticipation of the raids, were furious at the ineptitude of their Hampshire colleagues who had somehow managed to bungle the job and make only a handful of arrests. It turned out that their informant had passed back to detectives one slightly inaccurate but vitally important detail.

The SEALL raids were planned for the Sunday, and not the Saturday on which police had set up their ambush at the three sites. It was a fruitless stake out and when nothing happened that Saturday, Hampshire detectives went back to base. The next day, dozens of SEALL activists simultaneously invaded the premises of APT and Cottagepatch and Wickham laboratories. Management and staff were still on alert, however, and at APT—the home address of David

Walker—raiders were confronted by the owner, armed with a shotgun. Animal dealer, gunman, Research Director of Wickham's animal testing labs and vet, Walker was hit over the head when a scuffle broke out as trespassers defended themselves against his aggression and disarmed him. Elsewhere, workers attacked other raiders but their injuries were superficial. The police fed the media and used Walker's bruise to portray all activists as mindless thugs intent on violence, and the businessmen who poisoned animals as helpless humanitarians, victimised for being engaged in life-saving research for the sake of humanity. This certainly wasn't what I was seeing around me pouring out of the labs in photographs, on paper and on film, and I recognised that it wasn't a one-off misunderstanding of the facts. It was the beginning of a long-term strategy to defame a movement, which seeks to make radical changes to the status quo.

Coverage was extensive, and footage of the raids was shown on national TV news. In all, nineteen people were arrested, mostly at APT, and charged with a variety of conspiracy offences, leading to another show trial that would mark the end of the SEALL. Charges of conspiracy to burgle, cause criminal damage, to assault and to rob all three sites were laid against the defendants—the 'Wickham 19' as they became known. The Chief Constable of Hampshire did his best to hype up the charges by suggesting to the press that if anyone died as a result of the scuffle then 'murder charges will follow.' He must have known that people don't usually die from abrasions? The police were also talking about ten-year sentences, which had the desired effect of shaking up some of the more susceptible defendants who were initially remanded in custody and coerced into making statements to the police. Even with that, the police were so worried that they didn't have enough evidence; they tried to nobble the jury!

Of the fifty-eight potential jury members, twenty-five admitted the police approached them in a prejudicial manner. Such an incredible revelation would normally be sufficient to have a case dropped, but this one wasn't and instead a whole new jury was sworn in. Still the prosecution had a hard time of things, and watched 12 of the defendants be acquitted of all charges, and just seven found guilty on a single count at the end of a nine-week-long political trial that the police had predicted would be the one that would smash the radical Animal Liberation Movement.

Over a year after the raids, 55 year-old Mike Nunn, a reformed butcher and SEALL organiser was sent down for three years; Gordon

Bryant (24)—12 months; John Quirke (26) and Sally Miller (24)—nine months; John Curtin (21)—six months; Sue Baker (25)—five months and Kevin Williams (24)—three months. The extensive knowledge, which the police had gathered during their investigation of SEALL meant it could no longer effectively operate and, on the day of the sentencing, the South East Animal Liberation League officially disbanded itself.

A bungled police operation, vets torturing animals, stolen pets in labs and jury fixing aside, perhaps the most notable aspect of this case is the fact that four of the defendants gave evidence before the jury and admitted their part in the raids. They argued that they had only acted with good intent because it was believed Wickham were using stolen dogs in experiments and that the average person would agree with their actions. The people on the jury agreed and found them not guilty. This had potentially huge implications for the animal liberation cause. In addition, the high profile defence campaign organised by SEALL drew constant attention to Wickham after the event, kept the impending trial in the headlines and included a series of public meetings, street stalls, phone-blockades and mass leaflet drops. Tracy Young of the Style Council released a pop record about the Wickham 19. It was—all told—an impressive show of solidarity and an example for others to follow.

Unilever

> When you've got terrorism, foreign counterintelligence, kidnapping of babies, bank robberies, and hijackings, breaking into an animal facility just doesn't stack up very high.
>
> *Reluctant but naïve police investigator*

In August 1984, 200 hundred Eastern Liberation League activists invaded the highly fortified Unilever research laboratories in Bedfordshire while staging a public demonstration outside. The high perimeter fence around the complex was made of apparently impregnable tempered steel, which should have kept out prying eyes. However, this uncuttable fence (part of a multi-million-pound computerised security system installed two years earlier) was no match for strong determination and a hired commercial petrol-driven stone cutter. Carrying crowbars and sledgehammers, various teams looking for animals and documents jumped through a hole cut in the fence, ran the eight hundred yards to the complex and broke into labs and office buildings. It looked slick but because of the huge scale of the operation and the relative inexperience of many participants in anything illegal, and lack of knowledge as to what was happening, once files and photographs had been recovered, not everyone made a hasty retreat from the site when it was time to leave. Small groups were still milling around when police began pouring into the area an hour after the invasion began and alarms started squealing. The lack of an escape plan was a fundamental flaw in the audacious raid and effectively put paid to further mass invasions of this nature.

Only three of the 42 that were arrested on the day were still actually in the grounds; others were in surrounding fields, but most were arrested in vans as they left the area. The softly, softly approach of the police extracted far fewer statements than in Cheshire, but, in hindsight, it mattered not. As was the norm, few of those arrested had ever been in trouble before, but they most certainly were now. All were charged with conspiracy to burgle and were assured a place in the greatest show trial to date.

There was very little evidence against the majority of those arrested except that they were around when windows were broken and buildings entered, and that wasn't illegal because some were only there for a demonstration and were indeed on one and it wasn't their fault there was a burglary at the same time. Not until now that is!

Things were changing; the police and courts were getting their act together and such raids were being viewed far more seriously than the breach of the peace many had anticipated. Part of the evidence included a computerised printout of times to the second each door and window of the Unilever complex was breached, and there was CCTV footage. Some of those arrested had glass cuts in their shoes which was all the evidence there was against them but that essentially meant they had walked over broken glass, which may well have been outside buildings but was within the grounds, and that would prove to be enough.

This was devastating news for many. Nancy Phipps was one. Calm, quiet and compassionate, she was soon to be a grandmother. With her to protest the vile experiments conducted at Unilever were her two stunning teenage daughters. To them, like many others there that day all that should have been of concern to anyone was the way animals were being poisoned inside those labs to test new products, not a few broken windows. Arrested and charged, a year in prison was suddenly looming as they nervously awaited the outcome of the case against them, as indeed did the rest of the movement.

During court proceedings, one of her own legal team made something of a joke of 'Grandmother Phipps' clothing on the day of the demo: 'Raiders wearing pretty floral dresses, members of the jury! Come on!' It was no joke, and it wasn't meant to be, but it was funny because it was ludicrous that this caring family and others like them were standing accused in the dock and looking at a prison sentence. Nancy Phipps' emotional account takes us through the sandblast that aged her, and sealed her commitment to fighting all the harder for the rights of animals. The trial shook the foundations of the Animal Liberation Movement.

> We sat there, four human beings ranged along the hard wooden bench of the cell. Debbie, Dee, Jill and myself. Surely the most traumatic day we would ever experience. Eventually the door opened and we were allowed to sit in slightly more pleasant surroundings alongside our barristers. Smoking, disjointed conversation, everyone trying to lighten the atmosphere. Little jokes exchanged, everyone so tense, nerves so taut, you could almost feel the vibrations.
>
> Later the others filtered in, slowly in twos and threes, and we sat there supported by each other. All of us locked together in a ring

of solidarity. Mentally preparing to take whatever the State was deciding for us, in our case through a jury, the people of our land. Were they prepared to listen to our silent plea for humanity and compassion? What is compassion? Not much of that around these days. After six weeks of being on trial and listening throughout to voices which told of animals being subjected to diabolical experiments. In this case not even to further the phoney cause of medical science, but for the dubious pursuit of ever-new brands of toothpaste, shampoo, floor polish etc.

The list is endless as are the mindless experiments. How many pounds of toothpaste can be fed to a rat before it explodes? Not even the mealy-mouthed cant of the vivisectors' usual whine: 'Would you sooner we experimented on a child than on an animal?' can be used in this case. We sit together and wonder. Does the great British public (in this instance, twelve people plucked willy-nilly from the great mass of humanity) really care? Have they the wit or intelligence to listen to our reason for doing what we did? Or are they blinded by the voice of authority, the Establishment in the figure of the judge, in our case a dyed-in-the-wool reactionary and a man well known for his hatred of blacks, gays, CND supporters and females. (Well over half of the population of this green and pleasant land). The summing up was a farce. We'd been pronounced 'Guilty' before the jury even rose. Were there enough human beings amongst the jury to understand, or even realise?

The hours dragged on. The hands of the clock finally pointed to 3.30pm. Zero hour. A whisper was heard at the door. Anxious faces stared, voices tried to speak, but no sound came from the constricted throats. Slowly the room emptied. Three of us left. Red-haired Mike gave me a reassuring hug then one for Jill and the three of us climbed the stairs, holding on to each other tightly, giving each other our strength. In the small room adjoining the court, we joined Debbie and Dee. Then slowly we filed into the courtroom to join the others. Fourteen of us in the last trial of three. 'Members of the jury have you reached your Verdict?' 'We have'. I hold on tightly to Jill's hand. Delia. Guilty. Debbie. Guilty. The toneless voice drones on. Boris, Giles, Mike. We heard a shout from the public gallery. It was cleared by the police before the last

> Guilty was pronounced. One found 'Not Guilty'. One out of the fourteen! No reason. They had to let one go. A glimmer of compassion to show they'd given the matter some thought. And he was the youngest after all. And so the establishment won. It extracted its pound of flesh. Another setback for the frightened, tortured prisoners we call animals. A setback, yes, but we are not defeated. We will languish in our prison cells, but there are many more on the outside with love and support, and their anger. For we cannot be crushed by the State. For we know our cause is just. We fight for the gentle creatures of the earth. And our fight will go on until every animal on this earth is allowed to live out its natural life with respect and dignity.

Nancy Phipps and her youngest daughter Leslie were sent to prison for six months; Jill Phipps was 'let off' with a two-year suspended sentence, in a surprising show of compassion from a man who appeared to have none, because—he said—she was expecting a baby. Luke would not be a prison baby.

At the conclusion of the three major trials at Northampton and Leicester crown courts, 27 people were convicted and, of these, 25 were sent to prison for between six months and 2 ½ years—a total of 41 years! This was a rude awakening for an ambitious but naïve movement and it was time to take stock, to regroup and to look after our gentle friends.

Peter Anderson got two years, Boris Barker six months, David Carre two years, Alan Cooper two years, Nigel Couch two years, Beverley Cowley two years, Carl Egan two years, Giles Eldridge two years suspended, Alistair Fairweather 18 months, Karl Garside 18 months, Keith Griffin two years, Sally Levitt two years, Delia Lowick two years, Eric Marshall 18 months, Mike McKrell 18 months, Sally Miller 12 months, Virginia Scholey 18 months, Debbie Smith two years, Nick Sweet two years, Jim Snook two years, Duncan Thorpe two years, Paul Watkins 30 months, Gari Allen 18 months and Julian Webster 12 months. Greg Avery was acquitted.

The trial process lasted over four months in total and cost the taxpayer in excess of £2 million pounds for £11,000 worth of damage to windows of a multi-national company torturing animals. In his summing up the judge described the defendants as, 'enemies of society.'

Many defendants spoke from the heart of the cruelties they sought to oppose and with remarkably little hatred for the perpetrators. These were young lives in turmoil. That this diverse group of people were heading for prison left sympathetic observers dazed once it actually happened and they were taken downstairs to the cells. Surely this couldn't be for real? For helping animals? What if the police had stopped every van? There might have been 200 locked up! Who would have been left to pick up the pieces then?

This case had dragged on for many months and there had been many hints that prison was the likely conclusion, but there always are; we always hear of the maximum possible sentence when someone is charged, but the outcome is seldom so grim. There were no criminals in the dock that day, none looked like it or acted like it or sought to be considered so. But they all needed food now they were being treated as such and were securely locked up in the cells. Prisons don't do food very well at the best of times and this lot, not surprisingly, were mostly vegans! There were visits to organise, animals to look after, kids to comfort, letters to be written. Who'd pay the mortgage? What about jobs? They'd be lost. Would they cope with prison? Would prison cope with them!

The EALL had achieved more than just rattling the Unilever Empire in its brief history but this significant event was the end of the Eastern Animal Liberation League, which effectively ceased to exist the day of the raid. In contrast to the SEALL trial, which had a strong regional support campaign, a lack of coordination for the Unilever case again left defendants largely to their own devices. With over 80 League activists facing prison by the end of 1984, what was needed more than anything else was a solid support base. Without it, a movement is fragile and easily broken, something that was addressed with the formation of Support Animal Rights Prisoners following the Unilever trials. This distributed far and wide the details of detainees and raised funds to support their welfare and encouraged supporters to look after prisoners. This was a little like locking the door after the horse had been liberated but it was here that the ground was prepared for an invaluable prisoner support network—one that serves its purpose admirably to this day.

Central Animal Liberation League

> We cannot do everything at once but we can do something at once.
>
> *Calvin Coolidge*

By 1985 all but the Central Animal Liberation League operationally had ceased to exist. The idea had run its course — it simply couldn't survive for long using such tactics. The SALL was never broken nor was the WALL, but they never really presented a threat before the League tactics became outdated. The risks were too high, there were too many people involved and the police had learnt to respond quickly to panic calls for help from those on the receiving end, who were for their part shelling out massively on elaborate security measures to keep out prying eyes.

The CALL adopted a more cautious approach in light of the mass arrests sustained elsewhere and as a result proved highly effective in avoiding a similar fate. They gathered some of the most damaging footage of the Bizarre World Of The Animal Technician thus far recovered and in doing so rescued and re-homed over a hundred animals during many bold incursions. Beatrice was a 15 year-old rhesus monkey used in arthritis research and to this day somehow remains the only monkey ever to be rescued by raiders from a British laboratory. Bereft of human contact but for surgery and injections, she was delighted to be taken from her cage during the rescue and would never part with the blanket she was given to keep her warm during the journey away from the lab. Other activists, dressed as window cleaners, rescued guinea pigs in their buckets from hospital burn experiments in Birmingham, an action which generated widespread regional coverage. Evidence obtained included rabbits with their front paws removed at Oxford University's Nuffield Orthopaedic Centre and decapitated monkey heads and remains of bats found in a fridge at Animal Supplies London Ltd from where four van-loads of documents were recovered detailing a shady world of animal trafficking.

Two rhesus monkeys who had been subjected to eye mutilation experiments at Oxford University Park Farm were seen desperately clinging to each other in abject terror as the door of the unit opened and humans appeared in view. This footage proved devastating for the vivisectors and their apologists. So too the filming of experiments on rats, pigs, mice, rabbits, ferrets, polecats, primates, pigeons and sheep at the John Radcliffe Hospital, again owned by Oxford University. The university had always denied point blank carrying out such experiments but was forced into a corner when presented with video and documentary evidence and suddenly had no choice but to confess: 'Yes, we are admitting we use all sorts of animals.' It was a spectacular about-turn forced by CALL raiders, and not the last lie to be uncovered at Oxford University. Not by a long stretch.

What they weren't admitting was that they were using people's pets. No matter how much some folk want vivisection to continue if they think they may benefit somehow, few want their own animals to be used, preferring the victims be special 'purpose bred' versions. Vivisectors hope that specifying an animal has been bred specifically for the purpose of being experimented on makes it OK, and want us to believe its suffering is less than one used to being cuddled, taken for walks and fed treats. To others this is muddled thinking in the extreme, as is that which says mice are like little people and will provide cures for every human ill.

Relying less on quantity and more on quality, the CALL had proven plenty. Entering the premises of Roebuck Farm in Hertfordshire in 1986, which was the haunt of a defunct animal trading company called Animal Supplies Ltd, they exposed the trade between zoos and the vivisectors. Windsor Safari Park supplied the animal dealers with baboons, Ravenstone Zoo supplied rhesus monkeys and baboons, Chessington Zoo provided them with rhesus and African Green monkeys, bonnet and stump-tailed macaques and capuchins. Animal Supplies then sold the creatures to the likes of Huntingdon Life Sciences (HLS), Smith & Nephew and Pfizer for their use and abuse.

Another investigation found that London Zoo had supplied the Wellcome laboratories with owl monkeys during the 1980's so they could set up their own breeding colony; the Isle of Wight Zoo supplied primate dealers Shamrock Farm with macaques and squirrel monkeys, and Ravensden Zoo in Northampton sent macaques, cebus, aotus and squirrel monkeys to their vivisector-induced deaths. London Zoo even has Home Office licensed vivisection labs on site! There, at their Nuffield Laboratory of Comparative Medicine, they have experimented on wallabies to try to find ways to stop their collection from dying, bled goats until they were anaemic and injected bacteria into mice and rabbits, amongst other things. Conservation at its best!

Focusing on rescues, CALL was no less capable of generating results. CALL raids were well planned and well executed, but its raiding parties also had their fair share of good fortune. Back at base in Oxford in the summer of 1985, CALL again hit the headlines with a raid that was to become one of the most publicised animal liberation raids ever. Of the two-dozen brave, but all-the-same nervous, individuals being driven towards Oxford University's Park Farm on the outskirts of the city this July Sunday, there were few who hadn't been before. As a remote breeding station for the various university departments fiddling with animals, Park Farm had become a magnet for protesters and raiders alike. Out beyond the farm manager's accommodation, there were a variety of outbuildings within the fenced compound, housing different species of animals from mice to cats to monkeys. Security was comparatively minimal in parts, especially around the kennels.

Some of the team who had been snooping around the compound noticed that in the kennels, otherwise known as Death Row, there were what appeared to be domestic dogs, not just the typical beagles that are bred to excess and used in research for their placid nature. Here there was an Old English sheepdog, a spaniel with a docked tail, collies and mongrels of all descriptions. And not only did they look like they once lived with someone but they responded readily on command to 'Sit', 'Stay' and 'Gimme your paw.' If these weren't people's pets, they were doing a very good impersonation.

Commandeering the farm's own van to the rear of the kennels, it was then easy enough to access the site by chopping a hole in the fence, forcing a way into the kennels and, with some cajoling, escort out the prisoners. Some were just excited to be taken on a lead for a walk. A few weren't so sure of what had become of their life or who this odd looking bunch were with no faces—just eyes—kidnapping dogs, so they had to be carried out. Few, clearly, were lab-bred animals. One mongrel was even wearing an identity barrel on his collar, but this was found to be empty. It came that close to proving what many suspected about the depth to which some will stoop to satisfy the market for experimental tools. Without a name and address there remained only deep suspicion, circumstantial evidence and a bunch of mangy mutts.

Within hours of the raid, 30 anonymous dogs were suddenly a headline national news story. Footage of the raid and the dogs was plastered over the TV bulletins and lots of questions were posed, but there was a suspicious silence from Park Farm and Oxford University. Neither was able to manage any explanation as to what these animals were doing in vivisection kennels or where they'd come from.

CALL produced a report detailing the findings. It had been

discovered that large numbers of dogs were dying in University labs with as many as 138 'unrelated mongrel dogs' used in just one experiment. University bosses were having trouble explaining how the raiders had managed to find themselves various unidentifiable mongrels—Greyhounds, Labradors, Alsatians, terriers and even an Old English sheepdog—while raiding their kennels at Park Farm. Forced to comment by a story that wouldn't go away because of a public outcry, the University claimed their accredited supplier had 'accidentally' bred a mongrel litter and sold them cheaply. That didn't make it right of course and still didn't explain how there were so many unrelated, domesticated dogs of all ages in their kennels, some far older than would be profitably sold by a lab breeder for whom a quick turnover of puppies is essential. The University Vice Chancellor claimed the dogs were exercised daily at Park Farm and taught to walk to heel, and so on, so CALL produced video evidence showing that, while under surveillance for the preceding two months, not once during the day to day running were the dogs exercised or trained in any way shape or form. All lied out, but not prepared to tell the truth, the University retracted their statement and fell silent again.

A year earlier, a number of activists had been arrested after a raid in which 17 dogs including Greyhounds, Labradors, Collies and mongrels had been rescued from Laundry Farm in Cambridge. In a previous raid, a Rhodesian Ridgeback and a spaniel had been amongst the dogs rescued. During the trial, the defence case rested on the claim that dogs held there were stolen pets. One witness was a member of the public who had recognised her dog from the raiders' publicity photographs taken later. A laboratory technician from the farm admitted that no questions were asked about the source of the animals and was clearly stumped when he was cross examined about the cost effective business of their suppliers' who were supposedly breeding, feeding and then housing dogs in their kennels for up to two or three years (or more as some were older) with the intention of selling them for just £25 each, as was the asking price for dogs at the time. (The point being that there would be a healthy profit to be made in selling a stolen dog but only a loss to be made doing it the way it was claimed).

All of which added weight to the defence case, but, again, there wasn't enough hard proof and at the conclusion of the trial, Hilly Bevan was sentenced to six months in prison suspended for five and her four co-defendants were acquitted of all charges.

Back at Park Farm, and aware of the allegations that the farm was in possession of stolen property, Thames Valley Police were keen to get involved, but not, as you would hope, in pursuit of the truth regarding the dogs' true source. Instead, they wanted the animals back. Their removal from and return to Park Farm was the primary concern of the police so that they could continue on to their intended destination to an Oxfordshire laboratory. (In the public interest, of course).

Intense police investigations led to the arrest of eight people and the recovery of eight dogs from one address, seven of which were delivered straight back to Park Farm, who claimed them as their property. One person was charged. Apart from the obvious distasteful and provocative nature of this action, it is normal practice for stolen property to be kept in the possession of the police pending the outcome of legal proceedings, or at least until the identity of the lawful owner is proven. There was clearly something to be suspicious about here, but the police showed no interest whatsoever in trying to trace the real owner of the dogs or ascertain the dubious source, effectively giving the seal of approval to those who engage in stealing domestic animals for testing things on.

This news stunned observers. How could they do that to those dogs? Not just horrified and angered as many consequently were but utterly single minded, within days SEALL activists were sneaking around at Park Farm. Still not as secure as it might be, the brazen team re-entered the site, accessed the kennels and re-rescued four of the dogs returned by the police, including the Old English sheepdog. These exceptionally lucky dogs never went back to Park Farm again! The animal liberators have though.

Around the country, local groups were springing up everywhere, activists were out on the streets with information stalls; all were full of enthusiasm to spread the word. And the word wasn't just 'animal': people were suffering too because of animal abuse. How especially gross! It was a grim message, but according to some the world was going to have to change! Vivisection, fur shops and slaughterhouses were all in the news. Dangerous drugs, leg hold traps and degenerative diseases, all because of human greed. The enthusiasm was infectious, one person inspiring the next with their efforts. Diverse groups were getting involved in the UK and elsewhere, and direct action for the animals was the new struggle. There were a million battles ahead.

Above left: Class of 1964: Street HSA pose for the press during the Culmstock court case. Above right: Hill Grove Farm defendants outside court. May 1982. Arrested attempting to rescue lab bound cats from an Oxford breeder, they were later fined and given suspended sentences. In today's political climate they are 'terrorists'.

Above: January 1966 Bristol hunt sabs. Ian Pedler left.

Below: Dave Wetton looking singularly unimpressed during the anti-Redman demo. April 1965.
Right: Ronnie Lee, one of the founders of the Animal Liberation Front.

Below: The public invades the secret government warfare research laboratories at Porton Down in 1982. More secure barriers very quickly sprang up around such places to keep out prying eyes.

Above: Anti-hunt activist Gwen Barter obstructing Norwich Staghounds' deer-cart. March 1962.

Above: Circus worker using a hacksaw to try and remove protester from Blocking the entrance to a show. (Alec Smart)

Above: Beagles forced to smoke. ICI, Cheshire 1975 (Sunday People)

Above left: Sending a message that the ALF is still active. Merseyside ALF raid carried out in response to imprisonment of ALF leaders in Feb 1987.
Above right: Resources aplenty: A police helicopter intimidates hunt saboteurs at a Midlands Fox Hunt. 1988. (Edward Hirst)

Tally Ho!

Above left: Nurturing disrespect.
Above right: A sabotaged shooting tower. Germany 1988.

Hunt supporter expresses his views to a bloodsport opponent.

Above: An elephant forced to roller-skate. Below: US campaigners barricade fur sales using concrete filled barrels and bike locks.

Above: Groups of hunt saboteurs gather for the annual grouse shoots on the north Yorkshire moors. 1988.

Above: Hunt saboteur Joe Hashman takes control of beagle pack using horn calls.

The Animal Market

> We have just learned that the brains, offal etc of cattle in the abattoir is being fed to battery hens, whose litter is then fed back to cows.
>
> *Green World, Green Party newsletter, March '96*

From 1980 until a successful conclusion 2 ½ years later, one of the most significant campaigns of the era was waged on the Club Row animal market in London. When approached by campaigners seeking action to curb the cruelty and neglect for which the place was notorious, this Victorian attraction was described by the likes of the RSPCA and MPs to be 'An immovable object of British heritage' which was 'Regularly inspected' and was 'Operating within the law.' The usual drivel. The reality was that the market was a magnet for animal abusers and as close as an animal comes to hell for those on sale—the equivalent of a school playground for paedophiles. Shivering, pathetic, terrified animals would be taken from stinking, rusty cages piled in side streets and shoved into the back of vans belonging to anyone with money; since vivisectors like a steady supply for their pleasure, they were of course regular customers of the market, to the absolute horror of local animal campaigners. Protest marches attracted the largest number of animal-friendly demonstrators gathered together in London since the beginning of the century. There were pickets, acts of civil disobedience causing disruption, lobbying of councillors, MPs and other officials, and various irritating acts of sabotage.

Simple and obvious, the approach of this campaign was to be a blueprint for the future. There was a growing feeling that distant goals were achievable with persistence and determination; campaigners and activists used every opportunity to irritate, expose and annoy those claiming they were maintaining some sort of heritage. The pay off for perseverance was only a matter of time. Many said it couldn't be done, that opponents were few and this was a long established business venture supported by the government and tradition. But gradually attitudes changed and what was obviously right, shone bright. Hearing the same facts about cruelty and suffering angrily repeated over and over again, traders became weary of the endless opposition and eventually Tower Hamlets council was persuaded to stop the trade in live animals on their patch. It had worked; here was something for activists everywhere—persistent people do have power and animal exploitation does not have to go unchallenged just because it's always been so!

The early 1980s provided important experience for the growing direct action movement; the short-lived phenomenon of mass raids proved invaluable for information gathering, and for exposing those in the business of animal exploitation, but it was a risky business. But the end of the Leagues did not mark an end of headaches for those in the animal abuse industries, for whom life was about to appear less and less attractive the more time passed—something that I would view as inevitable as human thinking evolves.

Meanwhile, it was back to Plan A for the raiding parties, who were regrouping. History has shown that in matters of social change around the world, the cell structure approach has persistently proved the most effective. In the case of the animal liberation struggle, it allows small teams to operate independently of each other without any command structure, and to work alongside—not inside—public campaigns. Most significantly, if compared to the Leagues, when things go wrong, as they surely will, the cost isn't so high.

Countless groups have emerged over the years to fight animal abuse. In America, actions have been claimed by the ALF, the Urban Gorillas, the Band of Mercy, the Animal Rights Militia and the Farm Animal Freedom Fighters; Elainten Vapataus Rintama is the Finnish ALF; in Australia, the ALF and Animal Freedom Fighters have been active; in Spain—Frente de Liberación Animal; in France—Le Front Pour La Liberation Des Animaux (FLA) Arch De Noe, the Green Brigades and Operation Four Paws; in Sweden—Djurens Belfrielse Front (DBF) and the Wild Minks; in Holland & Belgium—Dieren Bevrijdings Front; Denmark—Dyrenes Befrielses Front (DBF); Italy—Fronte Liberazione Animale (FLA); in Norway—Dyrenes Frigjørings Front; Switzerland, Germany and Austria—Tier Befreiungs Front; Argentina—Frente de Liberación Animal (FLA) and in the UK—the Poultry Liberation Organisation (PLO) the Animal Rights Militia (ARM) and Hunt Retribution Squad (HRS) the Justice Department (JD) and others. Most are dedicated to animal rescue and economic sabotage, but the ARM, Green Brigades and JD have demonstrated their desire to physically hurt animal abusers, particularly vivisectors. The HRS has threatened to do likewise to hunters, but hasn't. All have succeeded in keeping the animal rights issue in the public domain.

On 30 November 1982, out of the blue, packages described as letter bombs—but with the capacity to ignite rather than explode—were sent to the leaders of the four main political parties in Britain, Margaret Thatcher included. It seems to have been more a symbolic gesture than with intent to do harm and none reached its target, but a claim enclosed with the devices was made on behalf of the Animal Rights Militia (ARM). This was a group never previously heard of, but in whose name others have since gone on to act against more likely targets, such as vivisectors. Not many in the movement, nor the press at the time, were convinced that animal rights activists were responsible and the police were stuck for obvious suspects, thrown no doubt by later claims of responsibility made on behalf of both the Irish National Liberation Army and the Angry Brigade! One theory, supported by the ALF Supporters Group, who were as radical as any and equally as confused and dismissive about the alleged source of these parcels, was that it could be linked to the Canadian Government, who were under pressure from animal rights groups and their own fishermen over the annual Canadian seal massacre. Indeed, some years before, an attempt had been made by persons unknown to blow up a plane carrying anti-seal-hunt campaigners to the Canada ice flows suggesting the lengths some people will go to to protect their lifestyles.

Digging The Duke

> It is not enough that we do our best; sometimes we have to do what is required.
>
> *Winston Churchill*

The Hunt Retribution Squad gained notoriety on Boxing Day 1984, the biggest day in the hunting calendar, when activists dug three feet down into the grave of the ex-master of the Duke of Beaufort foxhunt—the Tenth Duke, Hugh Arthur Fitzroy Somerset, a close friend of the Queen. The graveyard at the Badminton Parish church in Gloucester was daubed and the cross removed. In a written statement to the Press Association, the group claimed: 'The intention was to remove the remains from the grave and to scatter him around Worcester Lodge. We also planned to remove his head and dispatch it to Princess Anne, a fellow blood junkie. It's time the perverted hunters had a taste of their own medicine.' The statement was accompanied by a photograph of three hooded figures around the upended cross from the grave daubed with the word 'Shit.' Second thoughts prevented anything quite so grisly taking place that night, but the press loved the idea all the same. The intention was, of course, to make animal abuse controversial.

The HRS had first emerged in October 1984 when a London-based magazine featured a dramatic picture of a group of hooded activists holding chainsaws, axes, clubs and bats threatening hunters with serious physical retribution for their attacks on saboteurs and wild animals. This was the first time animal activists had advocated violence, but these were threats that never materialised. Thanks partly to the shortage of news between Christmas and the New Year, but probably more due to the ghoulish undertones of the graveyard stunt; it generated a lot of publicity, not much of it favourable. This came as no surprise to anyone involved in the action or anyone who remembered the disturbance of John Peel's grave a few years earlier. Those involved weren't expecting there to be much positive coverage, rather stressing the notion that all publicity is good publicity. This was a long-lasting spectacle in the memory of hunt supporters and the media but the latter eventually got bored with these dramatic, but mostly hollow, threats and saboteurs continued to suffer very real hunt violence.

A number of suspects were rounded up on suspicion of involvement in the stunt and two were later charged. Terry Helsby and John Curtin were subsequently convicted of desecrating the grave and sent to prison for two years. Helsby's mother had recognised him from a publicity photograph and contacted the police. A partly obscured hire car number plate seen on one photograph also helped immortalise them as gravediggers.

Operation Greystoke

> The assumption that animals are without rights, and the illusion that our treatment of them has no moral significance, is a positively outrageous example of Western crudity and barbarity. Universal compassion is the only guarantee of morality...
>
> *Arthur Schopenhauer (1788-1860) German philosopher*

The notion that actions speak louder than words spread fast and within ten years, direct action for animals had taken hold in the most unlikely places. France, a country not best known for its animal friendliness, let alone liberators, saw some spectacular actions in the 1980s. One of the more notable raids was Operation Greystoke, the liberation of a colony of baboons from a lab. Patrick Sacco's gripping personal account of the raid is complemented by that of Christian Huchedé, who runs the sanctuary where nearly all the baboons are still alive and well today:

> When in 1985, detailed inside information became available to us about the location of the primate house at the CNRS laboratories, we had no hesitation about what had to be done. In targeting a national institution like CNRS, we would be making an important symbolic gesture, much in the same way as INSERM was to be several years later. It was the symbol of the battle against a violent institution, a state research centre; it was not merely a question of denouncing an abuse, it was a question of highlighting an abuse that took place with full legal sanction.
>
> The baboons, who were of the papio-papio genus, were at that time being used in photo-sensitive research into epilepsy. The primates were kept locked in cages some one metre square; resin electrode boxes had been fixed to the base of their cranium through which electrodes were connected to certain areas in their brain.
>
> They were subjected to daily ordeals by researchers, who flashed lights directly into their eyes at various frequencies in order to induce epileptic seizures; researchers were also attempting to isolate at which precise moment and at which frequency the seizures were triggered. In their wild habitat in Gambia, epilepsy occurs naturally in the baboon and CNRS researchers (led by

Professor Naquet, the scientist conducting the study) wanted to understand what triggered these epileptic episodes. In attempting to do so, they had been torturing some of the primates for ten years. Many of the animals were too large for their cages and did not even have sufficient room to stand upright.

Since the experiments were being carried out on an open campus, we were able to obtain detailed information about the laboratory from sympathisers of the cause who knew exactly where the baboons were housed. Once the information had been verified, we were confident that the animals could be liberated, so over the next four months, we prepared for the raid. The CNRS was put under surveillance and the building was watched virtually every night; we did test runs opening doors and windows to see how the guard reacted, and we met up two or three times a week to discuss work in progress and see if all had gone according to plan thus far.

But crucially, of course, we had also to think about the 'post-liberation' aspect of the operation; we needed to find somewhere safe for the primates after they had been freed, as well as medicine and veterinary surgeons, who could remove the apparatus from their heads. We discussed the matter with vets who specialised in primate behaviour, believing that we might eventually be able to release the animals back into their natural environment—we even travelled to Holland to meet experts in charge of a primate rehabilitation centre. They strongly advised us against any attempt to release the baboons, stressing that their long years in captivity (some of them were born at CNRS) would have blunted their instinct for survival in the wild. We heeded their advice.

We had further to consider making preliminary contact with the media who would have to film the unfolding operation. The aim of the exercise was to create a media spectacle that would publicly denounce animal experimentation. The most delicate subject to be tackled was the question of finding trustworthy individuals who had the necessary competence, motivation and discretion, and who would be prepared to risk their careers should everything go pear-shaped.

Once all these prerequisites had been met and we felt that, in every other aspect, we were well prepared, we were ready for the operation and at one o'clock on the morning of 1 April, 21 people, including camera crews, were all in position. There were three lookouts with walkie-talkies, and one martial arts expert whose role was to act as a bodyguard in the event of a problem.
The two trucks arrived, and their motors were left to run at low revs in readiness for reversing into position in front of the animal house window. From this moment, a minimum of noise was allowed, and those taking part in the operation were required—should communication be necessary—to use pseudonyms in order to minimise any possibility of their being recognised.

Having removed the protective bars from the window, and then the window itself, ten people entered the animal house along with the camera crew. Since the TV equipment required very bright lighting, the window was completely blacked out as a precautionary measure, so that no light could be seen from the outside.

While someone daubed the walls with the words: 'Science without conscience is the death of the soul', the rest of us detached the cages in which the sick baboons were being kept. In order to calm them down, we took the precaution of covering the cages, which reassured them, although I remember that this time, unlike other occasions when we had gone in to see them, the primates were utterly silent—one would have almost believed that they understood that we were there to save them...

Once we had completed this first stage, we lifted the heavy cages one after the other through the window to carry them to the waiting trucks, in an atmosphere of almost reverential silence. The whole thing was pretty disturbing as the laboratory, which was located on the ground floor, was surrounded by buildings, which no doubt housed researchers, and we couldn't help wondering: would they see us...?

The entire operation lasted between 45 minutes to an hour. After this phase had been completed, everyone moved off to a pre-arranged location. I took the steering wheel of one of the trucks and drove it to a nearby parking lot, then returned to the lab to check that nothing had been forgotten. It was at this moment, having done a head count, that I realised that one of us was missing—one of the look-outs was still at her position and hadn't seen that we had completed the liberation—apparently she had dropped the walkie-talkie that had been around her neck while she lay in hiding behind a bush…

OK. So we had finished the first half of the job. The second half now remained to be completed. We now had to get rid of the cages, which were simply too cumbersome for a 1,000 km journey. We also had to divide the primates into two groups: those with electrode boxes, and those without. We had previously located with some difficulty a spot for this purpose in a long-forgotten clearing in the forest of Rambouillet. Once there we removed the 17 cages and, having anaesthetised the baboons, gently lifted them out.

Of the 17 baboons, eight had no electrode implants, so they were taken straight to the Refuge de l'Arche at Château Gontier, where they arrived at dawn. Meanwhile, the other nine were taken in the opposite direction to the South of France, where a vet awaited to operate on them in his home to remove the implants. For maximum 'camouflage', they travelled in my camper van in potato sacks for the entire duration of the 1,000 km journey, which ended the following night.

We undertook both journeys in a heightened state of anxiety; the raid, and the disappearance of the animals, which had been discovered at dawn, was headline news on the radio, and it was reported that road blocks had been set up to recapture the animals. It looked like we were for the chop…

Making myself available in the event that I might be needed, I stayed with the baboons for 15 days, keeping an eye on their progress and observing their behaviour. We had absolutely no idea whether they would get on with each other, nor did we have a clue whether they would adapt to any food other than the proprietary laboratory food pellets to which they were accustomed.

> There were a number of us at the house: the vet, a militant friend who was also a nurse, and Doctor Kalmar, who has since died, but who was a militant anti-vivisectionist. It was they who removed the electrode implants, and who saw to the aftercare as well as the integrating of the animal. I was completely stunned when I entered the animals' holding cage: I was mindful of maintaining a respectful distance that would feel safe to them, but the baboons completely accepted me…
>
> The integration of the group went extraordinarily well—indeed, far better than we could ever have hoped, and three weeks later, they were reunited with the rest of their group at Château-Gontier.
>
> When they arrived, they weren't taken to an island straight away, as it was important to keep them away from public scrutiny at the Refuge de l'Arche. The affair was in the newspapers for quite some time, and even if Christian Huchedé knew exactly what he was doing, for him there was no question of doing anything less.
>
> The baboons were hidden for several months, at the end of which time they were moved to two islands prepared for them by animal lovers. All the experts had assured us that baboons couldn't swim, and we believed that they would not be able to escape from their islands; as it turned out, several years later, one of the baboons did escape and was found in the garden of a neighbouring property. After that, an electrified fence was put around the perimeter of one island, to stop them going in the water.

Christian Huchedé, who is in charge of the Refuge de l'Arche at Château-Gontier, the sanctuary where the rescued monkeys were homed, recalls how the animals became acclimatised to their newfound 'freedom':

> It's difficult to be absolutely exact about some of the specifics with regard to the Greystoke baboons; they were not identified on arrival, and were joined by a group of 32 others in 1989, and have since formed an important social group. What is certain is that the oldest individuals in the group are among those liberated during

Operation Greystoke. They are therefore over 30 years old today. Among them is a female we call 'La Tondue'—literally the shaved one; she was one of those who had had electrode implants, and to this day, her hair has never grown back on her head.

Interestingly, one recognises those from her group because, for identification, she plucks their hair so that they become bald like her. One must in addition remember that on 1 April 1985, only seven baboons arrived at the sanctuary, and the others arrived later.

When the first Greystoke animals arrived, we already had several baboons from various sources such as circuses, zoos and those previously kept in private collections. As soon as we housed the first arrivals in a structure where they would be in visual contact with the baboons already living at the sanctuary, we were shocked by their complete lack of communication skills. No vocalisation, no complaints, no groans of satisfaction, no grooming, just frightened body language, and real terror. Whenever we approached their home, they would climb the bars and would crouch there motionless for long periods of time waiting for us to leave.

It took about six months for them to begin to trust humans. The young volunteers working there at the time (who were under 15 years of age) spent many hours with them to reassure them, to show them things, to teach them how to peel a banana, for example, or to open a monkey nut. It was clear that the baboons had had no previous experience of fruit—they had never eaten anything other than proprietary laboratory food. Slowly, having grown in confidence around humans and through contact with the other baboons that they could see and hear, they began to communicate by groans and cries and in grooming sessions.

It was at this point that we decided to introduce them to other baboons that were already at the refuge. There was no visible aggression or rivalry because they had watched, heard and touched each other through the bars. The others, arriving individually, were placed in holding cages inside the baboon house and were released into the group after a certain period of time.

When we took in 32 baboons in January in 1989, we released all of them together onto two islands surrounded by water, which we had prepared and which they still inhabit to this day…

As to the two baboons who did not survive for very long, I recall above all a juvenile female who was weak and had only one arm. She only survived a few months, and was undoubtedly killed by the others because of her disability or weakness…in any case, it was not because they fell ill.

(Translation from the French first published in Arkangel 30)

Heists & Hoaxes

> I want to emphasise that animal rights extremist activity is not terrorism.
>
> *The head of the anti-terrorist branch, 1995*

The Green Brigades, on the other hand, were at the sharper end of this revolt. While having a similar desire to end animal experiments, they adopted far more aggressive tactics. They only just came short of achieving unmatched notoriety in the nervous world of laboratory animal breeding when they blew up the premises of an animal dealer at Lewarde in Northern France. By sheer fluke, the owner suffered only minor injuries. A year later, a policeman was injured when a bomb exploded outside the home of another animal dealer. If things didn't all go to plan, it was not for lack of intent. The activists of Operation Four Paws, meanwhile, weren't to be outdone in the race to force the boundaries of the French struggle for animals in laboratories. Disguised activists flagged down a van delivering dogs to a laboratory outside Rennes; the driver was taken out, had his hair cut off and his face daubed with red indelible paint. He was left by the roadside and ten dogs were driven away. Two weeks later, another team of activists raided laboratories at the university of Paris and rescued 50 frogs and 20 pigeons, destroying paperwork and lab equipment before they left. France was full on!

Elsewhere, a Viennese court fined a 37 year-old scientist at the Austrian Academy of Sciences approximately £450 at the end of 1985, after he was found guilty of carrying out five animal liberation raids on laboratories at the Pharmacological Institute of Vienna between March and September 1985. Herr Peter Mueller had worked for five years at the brain research department of the academy and had himself carried out animal experiments. He finally saw the light after injecting 76 rats in order to provoke epileptic fits and then being ordered to dispose of their bodies because the test results conflicted with what was stated in existing medical literature.

Peter Mueller actually carried out six raids but was prosecuted for just five, because the animals he found in one lab were in such a pitiful condition that the authorities decided against raising this issue in court.

As a result of the Mueller case, the public prosecutor launched an inquiry into conditions at the vivisection labs. Herr Mueller had embarked on a series of lone nightly raids in his car, climbing through fanlights and rescuing a total of 31 animals—dogs, rabbits and goats—which he delivered to the homes of animal lovers whom he knew. He was finally caught attempting to liberate a goat but refused in court to disclose where he had taken the animals he had freed.

These were simple acts of compassion, which drew a lot of attention and admiration. Mueller was made unemployed as a result of his new-found liberated lifestyle but had his fine paid by a number of sympathetic actors and entertainers. The magazine *Man Of The Month* and the actor Frank Hoffman founded a prize in Austria for 'The Most Courageous Animal Action Of The Year.' Peter Mueller was the first recipient. (Interestingly, while Austria is not widely seen as a nation of animal lovers, as a nation, it can be proud it has more safe places for vegetarians and vegans to eat than anywhere else and has gone on to become the first country in the world to ban the battery cage and introduce groundbreaking legislation to protect animals in numerous other areas).

In Germany more of the same was produced with several small teams at work.

> In one spacious bus there was still plenty of room. There were just four in, but a couple more were due. Six activists desperate to do something to help the animals and, as long as no one gets hurt, they don't care what it is. Spirits are high because everyone knows that some more animals are due to be rescued from the horrors of the laboratory tonight. They've been together before for the same purpose and it was the most special time, each time the best night out ever.
>
> During the drive, a plan of the site at Mainz University is passed round and scrutinised, and intelligence shared. The night patrols on the premises are made at rather infrequent intervals, so great care will be needed. The message is—no risks—if only for the sake of the animals. They were going into the Goods section of the bus, which contains several cages. These should soon be full; a thought that puts silly grins onto expectant faces and makes hearts beat faster. They are animals, but what will the new passengers actually look like? No one knows what's in there…
>
> It is 7.30pm when the bus arrives at the service station. Thanks to the switch over to wintertime it is already pitch dark. Are the

others already here? Everyone looks about expectantly. Soon someone gives a hearty wave. The others climb into the bus; the doors are shut and greetings whispered. This is it!

The plan of the university is unrolled again, tactics discussed in detail and individual roles fixed. Nerves are fortified with a final flask of tea and then it's time. It's only a short drive before the transporter cruises along the street towards the university area. No going back now. As if! With a sharp look out for any night watchmen, all is called clear. All out! Lookouts then take up their positions, while the others unload the cages and containers. Everyone whispers. These are quickly, quietly passed over the fencing and carried up to the institute building. There's a soft rattling sound then a wait in total silence for two minutes. One of the team has forced a window open—he gives the all-clear sign and two dark shadows disappear easily through the window into the dark rooms of the animal bunker. It's really dark. A filthy smell hits the nostrils. Someone could have easily tripped over that large sheet of corrugated metal left lying on the ground. Whose fault would that be? This place isn't inviting intruders!

Rabbit boxes stand out in the beam of the torch, pink eyes gone red. There are only twelve boxes, each containing one animal. The rabbits look up tensely and seem anxious about what's going to happen to them. They should be, because it isn't usually good. There's no time to worry about that for long, knowing that things will soon be better for the animals. They're immediately loaded into the comfortable transport boxes. This is soon completed. The smell is still appalling.

A look at the second room is a shock. At least four hundred rats crammed together in tiny breeding cages are gazing up with their tiny pink eyes. But there's room in the once huge bus to take less than half that! Fuck! It is terribly painful to realise that some of these intelligent creatures must be left behind, but there's no room for them! After a short discussion about the situation, a decision is made to leave behind the mother rats with their suckling youngsters, so as to spare the very youngest ones the stress of transportation. There's no way of switching the rats from their cages into others, due to the lack of space, so they're taken in the breeding cages directly from the shelves.

Suddenly a warning whistle is heard. Outside, a night watchman is passing slowly on his bicycle. Everyone freezes, not making a sound. Please go away! Nothing more is to be seen of the lookouts because they've hidden in the bushes. The cyclist goes past the building making only a superficial inspection of it. Two minutes later—the all-clear signal allows everyone to breathe again. Such a fine line between success and failure!

Now begins the most difficult part of the operation. Load up. The cages are gently handed through the window and stacked out of view behind the undergrowth. The containers are quite heavy and the shifters are soon out of breath. The transporter, meanwhile, drives slowly and so quietly up to the gateway of the university site. Luckily the gate is not locked and the van reverses in. People move quickly and loading is unhindered. Once the final cage is placed into the transporter, it's time to get away fast with the valuable freight and raiders back to the original meeting place. It's all gone to plan, the van returns safely, and the team splits in two. Three take the cargo to a safe house and the others, wishing them luck on their journey, are then left to ponder what's just happened. Happy with the night's work? No!

It's OK for those in the van, with rescued animals to sort out, but the spirits of the remaining three are rather dampened on account of the mother rats and their offspring they've left behind. There's no comfort knowing that they remain in a place that means certain death with probably worse first. Quite a few rats will fit in their car! Drive back there now and go back in? Good homes will certainly be found for the rats. It doesn't take long to decide, the preparatory access work has already been done and there is not much time left before dawn.

Back on site within a flash, a lookout stays outside while the other two climb into the building once more. It's still dark and it still stinks! And the rats are still waiting for their lives to change for the better. As many boxes are squeezed into the car as it can take. Again, nobody sees what's going on and the sense of achievement has been reached. They've done all they can. During the homeward journey little lumps of cheese are shared among the rats—probably they've never eaten anything so tasty!

They love it. Now there's joy at a good night's work and something good to celebrate! Simple, effective direct action. Or is it unacceptable violence? Spine chilling terrorism? I'll share some facts—you decide.

An article in *The Face* in October 1982 said of the ALF: 'Agree with them or not, they are forcing the pace of change.' And such indeed appeared to be the case. With the foundation of the ALF Supporters Group in the UK in 1982, money had started to find its way to the activists on the ground, and raid reports came back. Those who couldn't get actively involved now had a way of helping those that did. As 'The SG' newsletter became more widely read, it soon became clear just how widespread actions were, and how far the notion of animal liberation had travelled. Reports were sent in anonymously to the SG, then compiled in newsletters and Action Reports and redistributed. Very deliberately the fires were being stoked. From Canada to South Africa, Australia to Ireland and all corners of the UK there were reports of direct action for animals and it was inspiring more of the same. The newsletters also provided a forum for debate, an exchange of tactics and novel ideas, and activity was, in no uncertain terms, incited. The SG, essentially, linked like minds. The personal details of known animal abusers were listed and readers invited to 'adopt an animal abuser' and dedicate their energies to them. And when there was a problem with homing animals, open appeals were made requesting homes. But public appeals for homes for what the authorities see as stolen property—much the same as the distribution of inciting material—wasn't something they could allow to continue unchecked.

Ronnie Lee had by this point become the ALF's official Press Officer. He was a lone voice for all the actions of others in a sea of change, ever prepared to shove his head above the parapet and put animals before human greed. He was something of an extremist in the eyes of officials, but a beacon to those who fought against the injustices of animal abuse. This was a voluntary position that eventually gained him the 'honour' of being the longest serving ALF prisoner. Even more unfortunate is that this dubious honour has since been lost.

Lee was the voice of the activists and a recognisable figure to anyone even slightly interested in the issues. Utterly uncompromising, he was readily available to explain the ALF to wanting journalists, TV crews and anyone that would listen, and wrote regular columns in the SG newsletters. He was publicly causing and heading for trouble but content within himself that this ALF creature was well and truly off the leash and no matter how many arrests were made the ALF was here to stay.

A coordinated four-pronged raid codenamed Operation Bright Eyes had netted the ALF 163 rabbits from factory farms in Scotland, Essex, Suffolk and Gloucester. It was 1984 and acts of economic sabotage had reached an all-time high in the UK and elsewhere. At South Mimms in Hertfordshire, the Imperial Cancer Research Fund's Clare Hall laboratory suffered around £100,000 in fire damage, while in Cambridgeshire, activists caused a massive £1.5 millions worth of damage at the Parke Davis vivisection laboratory. In West Germany, the Hazleton (now Covance) contract-testing lab at Munster suffered a million pounds' worth of damage and the Dutch ALF set fires in a laboratory in Utrecht, which cost the lab £250,000.

Probably the most controversial tactics of all in the expanding campaign of economic sabotage have been the contamination scares. Although most have been simple or elaborate hoaxes, they have proved very successful in attracting publicity, not much of it sympathetic. Activists blinding shoppers now? You'd think so. A few months prior to the mother of all contamination scams in the summer of 1984, bottles of doctored Elida Gibbs Sunsilk shampoo were discovered in Boots stores in Southampton, London and Leeds. A warning had been sent to a national newspaper and Boots were forced to remove every single bottle of the product from their shelves nationwide. A spokesman said: 'It's a mammoth task, but it has to be done.' It was music to the ears of the activists. It was also an expensive operation for the company, and had to be repeated a month later when more dodgy shampoo turned up in Hull, East Yorkshire.

Three people were later arrested there. It transpired that a single bottle of shampoo had been placed in a local supermarket contaminated with weak bleach; the bottle had been put to the back of the shelf with very loud and obvious warnings attached. As one of those involved so decisively put it when I asked about this apparently reckless act: 'Only a friggin' blind shoplifter could have come to use the stuff once we'd finished with it!' Due to the novelty of this action, the police had no case law to follow so the three were eventually charged with causing a Blemish Of The Peace and, having pleaded guilty soon after, were bound over to refrain from causing further indiscretions for two years. The charge was dug out of 17th century law as the only one likely to stick at the time. The laws surrounding the contamination of goods have since been radically rewritten and now carry a far heavier sentence as do many offences excluding sex crimes, the abuse of animals and illegal wars.

There were also contaminated turkey scares in over 30 towns and cities across the UK. These actions, which have proved effective in highlighting certain animal issues, were also instrumental in pinning the extremist, people-hating label to animal activists. They have nevertheless invariably been carried out in line with ALF policy of avoiding causing physical harm to others. It is an honourable oft stated position, which too few humans care enough to really consider applying to their daily actions.

The Sweet Truth

A journey of 1000 miles begins with a single step.

Chairman Mao Tse-Tung

Contaminations rapidly reached a peak in November when dozens of Mars Bars marked with a large X were placed in ten shops in and around Leeds, Manchester, Salisbury and Plymouth. Chocolate bars were delivered to the offices of *The Sunday Mirror* and the BBC. The bars had been laced with a small amount of Alphakil rat poison, which is said to only be harmful to humans when taken in large doses. Bars marked with the infamous X also carried a note explaining that the reason behind the targeting of the product was that the Mars company was funding tooth decay experiments at London's Guy Hospital. Inevitably, the media had a field day: 'We Don't Care If People Die' screamed the headline in one national newspaper, followed by stories of consumers falling ill and being rushed to hospital, poisoned.

The government's vivisection front man of the day was Home Office Under Secretary, David Mellor, whose role appeared to be to disseminate lies, deceit and misinformation. He announced: 'It beggars belief that these people are prepared to sacrifice children on the altar of their own fanaticism.' Extreme rhetoric of this kind was soon to become the norm from government officials, vivisectors and many in the media, and has marched on shamelessly into the new millennium.

Ironic as it is, Mellor was the Minister responsible for the ill being of millions of animals bred for the scientists to fiddle with. That's a fact. The level of suffering is well documented. Poison in chocolate bars was fiction, and the ALF later issued a statement admitting the whole thing had been an elaborate hoax and raised an intriguing question as to why so many people had fallen ill after eating chocolate bars! Further irony lay in the fact that the vivisectors were looking to develop a vaccine to 'cure' rampant tooth decay, mostly suffered by children and caused by sugar-filled confectionery products!

The likelihood of anyone being harmed by unwittingly eating one of the X-contaminated sugar bars was as likely as a blind shoplifter doing themselves a mischief with the dodgy shampoo, yet the media machine, aided by officials in government, used the opportunity to create a state of terror amongst the public. Mars were forced to recall every single bar on sale in the UK, a process that cost the company around £3 million. That was the activists' fault. The experiments being carried out on monkeys, which involved feeding them a sugar rich diet were stopped. That was also the activists' fault. With any stretching of the ripening imagination, this wasn't the sort of action likely to get a positive reaction from the media, but publicity was extensive beyond the wildest dreams of those involved, and that was the point. It got results.

Similar actions have been part of the ALF armoury since then, mainly aimed at the cosmetics industry, with Boots and L'Oreal bearing the brunt. The meat industry, with the Christmas turkey a particular favourite for no particular reason, has also had to deal with its share of tampering.

The Animal Squad

Man is the only animal that blushes—or needs to.

Mark Twain

Another animal rights group? Not quite! The threats of the HRS and others, the Mars Bar affair, and the general scale of animal rights activity were causing concern in the world of animal exploitation and pressure was forcing those in power to do something to stop the menace of enlightenment from spreading any further. By the middle of 1984, the ALF was being credited with causing over 6 million pound's worth of damage a year—and claiming much more—while recording up to six actions a night across the UK. Whatever the fine detail, it was the busiest time for the ALF. The meat trade, fur and hunting fraternities and the pharmaceutical industry were applying so much collective pressure that Scotland Yard formed a special squad whose express role was to deal with the Animal Liberation Front and other animal groups agitating for change.

The nation of 'animal lovers' had brought the Animal Rights National Index (ARNI) into the arena to contain the animal lovers! The squad was to be based at New Scotland Yard where only serious criminals like the Ripper, the Great Train Robbers and so on had previously attracted such attention. Initially known as the ALF Squad and then the National Index of Animal Rights Extremists, its purpose was to collate information on those trying to protect animals, to record actions, monitor phone calls and scrutinise the movers and shakers. It soon became obvious that the reach of the ALF Squad extended beyond ALF activists and sympathisers and would eventually include anyone involved in the animal protection movement. Plain clothed officers were found mingling with demonstrators to see who was talking to whom, to find out who was organising the 'atrocities', and to try to pick up some gossip. Gossiping is what people do so it has potential be a fruitful exercise!

Inevitably, in keeping with the advance of technology, these early exercises have been somewhat supplanted by a greater technological sophistication: today's political police pride themselves on their video cameras so that as well as mingling covertly, they also overtly film perfectly law abiding protesters, sometimes for hours on end. Borring! These Evidence Gatherers operate in pairs: while one officer directs the camera operator, the other captures as many faces as possible on film, for the record and in order to intimidate. The large numbers of police mustered to monitor some of today's protests is quite staggering.

The Eighties Animal Squad (ARNI) put together a regular bulletin to inform and update regional forces, particularly those with an ALF problem. This was of course a confidential internal document but, very early on in its history, copies of the bulletin and other intelligence fell into my hands, I think by accident. I was home watching the clock as I had a couple of detectives coming round. This is normally a good reason to be out of the house but they had made an appointment to return some of the things they'd taken on an earlier visit when they definitely weren't invited. I had been accused of an assault on a hunt and criminal damage to McDonald's windows, but they were obliged to conclude, on the basis that there was no evidence, that I was guilty of neither.

Anyway, months later, in the boot of their car were loads of bags containing my belongings, not a single item of which could have proven my guilt in these allegations, but they figured it necessary—and not for the last time—to deprive me of it all nonetheless. Polite half-hearted greetings over, we unloaded the car boot and carried my belongings back indoors. I didn't realise it at the time, but amongst the haul were two large black bags that weren't mine. It was of course nice to have my things back after so long but best of all was to have theirs! They left.

I checked through the bags and I couldn't believe my eyes when I saw what they'd given me. Angry Cop had asked of Affable Cop, when grabbing the first bag from the boot, if everything in there was mine. Affable Cop answered in the affirmative. I had overheard this, but just to be on the safe side, I was out of the house in a flash once I'd realised they'd given me a large pile of police surveillance photographs and negatives, files, copies of ARNI circulars and details of ALF Squad operations in the Manchester area! At a friend's house we spread out the juicy booty over the kitchen table and feasted! All at once, rumours about extensive surveillance were confirmed beyond any doubt. There had been agents positioned overlooking fur shops, McDonald's outlets, circuses and anywhere else intelligence had revealed that protesters might be gathering. Even the homes of occasional protesters, were targeted—people whom I, for one, thought unworthy of any police interest given that their presence on the front line of the struggle was sporadic at best. The police thought differently. Everyone who was pro animal was a crime suspect. Spies observed 'Ginger' doing the weekly shopping, 'Pig tail' was with her laden with soya milk. In an instant I knew what the police knew about who went to what supermarkets, even when their parents had visited them. But what of the bombers and hoaxers? Where were they when all this shopping was going on?

In many cases, the 'intelligence' for these costly time consuming surveillance operations had come from public meetings or fliers advertising them as leafleting sessions or public protests. There was nothing sinister going on outside any of the protest sites where perhaps half a dozen leaflet givers had gathered, but the political police were deeply involved in something! The ARNI circulars outlined and hyped up ALF tactics and potential targets; there were details of known activists alongside mug shots and vehicle registrations, and advice on action to take and who to inform of incidents involving the 'Extremists.' There was a clear intent to inflate the threat posed. You'd think that 600 snapshots of a couple of vegans bringing home the shopping wouldn't be that useful for anything other than target practice for dairy farmers; the only conclusion was that the police were extremely interested in animal rights protesters. There was little apparent return for the detectives on the evidence they'd gathered around Manchester, but this work made it possible for them to link contacts and create files and profiles on people who objected to the status quo.

Cocksparrow

> If [man] is not to stifle human feelings, he must practice kindness toward animals, for he who is cruel to animals becomes hard also in his dealings with men. We can judge the heart of man by his treatment of animals.
>
> *Immanuel Kant (1724-1804)*

Elsewhere, the police were having more obvious success but with less effort. Cocksparrow Farm in Warwickshire was the sort of place to which animal rights protesters tended to migrate en masse, and with disturbing regularity for the farmer and his family. One of only six remaining fox fur farms, this place was the most unpleasant. It was January 1984 when, following weeks of preparation, the Sheffield ALF hatched a plan to breach the fences at Cocksparrow (over 100 miles south in Warwickshire) and whisk away some of the foxes. Planners had used protests at the farm as an opportunity to suss out the possibilities. While others were throwing themselves at police lines in an attempt to force an entry, distracting attention, a couple of South Yorkshire's thinkers were taking note of the telephone lines, access roads and escape routes. For this once profitable compound of captives in cages, the business plan was steadily being re-written.

Everyone who had seen Cocksparrow wanted to get rid of it. Over the high fence you could watch the ragged sad looking foxes pacing repetitively in their cages utterly frustrated with their lot. It wasn't just the ALF newsletters that had incited direct action but that repetitive pacing, which pains all decent human beings. Foxes really don't like captivity and the time had come to stress the point!

When the night finally arrived for the Yorkshire posse in the winter of 1984/5, the adrenalin was in full flow as they headed towards the Midlands equipped with a few tools and some sacks. There were two aims: the first was to take away foxes for whom homes had already been secured; the second was to damage as much of the farm's equipment as possible. Economic sabotage to some, criminal damage to others.

It's one thing to have the nerve and some initiative but you need luck too. Driving through Tamworth just ten miles from the farm, something happened that would prove costly. WPC Reeves was on patrol. She was drawn to a passing Transit van. Always a draw.

> I am a police constable of the Staffordshire police stationed at Tamworth. At approximately 0240 hours on Thursday 5 January, I was in full police uniform in a marked police vehicle. As I was travelling along Upper Gungate, Tamworth I saw a vehicle approach me. I could see that the front nearside headlight of the vehicle was not illuminating. The registration number of the vehicle was YWY 20X. It was a white Ford transit van and across its rear doors it had the words Beauchief Van Hire and a Sheffield telephone number. I followed the van and at 0243 hours I stopped it on the A51. I approached the driver of the vehicle and said, 'Can you tell me where you are going?' The driver replied, 'I'm from Barnsley. We're going to Cardigan in South Wales.' I said, 'What's your name?' He replied: 'Andrew Horbury.' I looked at the back of the van and saw approximately six persons. They were asleep on what looked like canvas sacking.

So what? They'd done nothing wrong and the van was allowed to go on its way. Further investigation revealed that both headlights were in fact working perfectly well, but that was immaterial too. Still, there followed a heavy debate on whether to go ahead with the plan. Some said yes others no—put it off. In the end the decision was left to the driver, the only person whom the police had identified. He would be the most likely to get nicked later. No one would have blamed him had he opted out, but going back was out of the question. Horbury was known to the police and knew the increased risk he was taking if they went ahead and the police established the obvious link with his van full of people and a break in at the fur farm down the road. But he was unmoved by the situation. 'No way. Not now. We've come this far and the foxes are still there.' Words like pennies from heaven for the animal liberators in the back.

A little over two hours after it was stopped, the van—now heavily disguised—eased its way up the narrow lane leading to the farm as telephone wires were pulled down. The long-awaited Cocksparrow raid was on. The lightly sleeping farmer, Nirbahal Singh Gill, didn't take long to stir.

> My concern is the breeding of foxes for their fur. The foxes are arctic blue foxes. On Thursday 5 January 1984 I was at home asleep when, at about 4.40 am, I was woken by the dogs. At the pens there are five dogs on running wires guarding the perimeter

of the pens. To begin with I ignored the noises. I got out of bed and looked through the bedroom curtains. I saw a van reversing along the concrete path to the back of the pens. The van's lights were on, there were people around the van, and I could see four at this stage. The van was a white Transit. I then went out in my nightclothes to the door. I opened the door and there were several people between the pens and my house. As soon as I went I saw torch lights, these were directed in my face and they said 'Get back inside or we are going to shoot you.' This was repeated two or three times, by more than one in the group. The only thing I could see of them was that they all had masks completely covering their faces. I could not identify any accents.

I then came back inside and tried to telephone the police. I tried the telephone but it wasn't working. I assumed at this stage that the wires had been fetched down. I went outside again to the farmhouse because that also had a telephone, but the group threatened me again, they came face to face with me. I then noticed one of them was a girl by her voice. They repeatedly threatened me, saying they were going to shoot me if I didn't get back inside. I could not see whether they had a weapon or not because they kept flashing torches in my face. The van was still down at the pens.

I then went to the back door and went to the north side of the pens without being seen, I got the dog from there and walked back to the front of the temporary building. I spoke to my wife and she told me the telephone wasn't working there either. I then said to my wife: 'I'll have to go and get my motorbike.' The three did not have any conversation with my wife, but when I went to walk to the building with my bike the three came again to me. The dog was still with me. They said, 'Get back inside or we'll shoot you, we don't want to hurt you but if you cause us trouble, we will.' Just before I got back inside I saw another three or four people over by the barn buildings. I could hear a lot of noise around the two buildings. I came to the back door again and went with my dog across to the Andrews' house some 200 yards away.

There I saw Mrs. Andrews and asked to use her telephone, she said it was out of order, the line's dead. I said: 'Will you please

> put one of your vehicles in the lane to block the way and I will pay for any damage?' She did not have the time to reply because I heard the noise of the van leaving. I then walked to the gate of her house and saw the van was passing me, the registration no. was KAY, I think the suffix was 'Y'. I then came back towards the farm. I could still see some of the torches at the farm so I went onto the road, walking through the fields to avoid being seen. I got to the main road and tried two houses before I woke someone. I used their telephone and called the police. I waited there until the police came then drove down the lane and I ran and informed them that the people had only been gone a few minutes. I made a quick search of the farm and noted that some foxes had been taken and there was a lot of damage. Thirty foxes were taken, total value £6,000. The total value of the damage was £5,787,50.

Within an hour, the group was well on its way back to Sheffield. The foxes were taken to a safe house from where they would be re-homed once they were acclimatised, and every one else dropped off to head home. Jubilation at a job well done had obscured the memory of WPC Reeves, but WPC Reeves was very much in on this and on hearing about the raid, told senior officers about her encounter with the Tranny. Warwickshire detectives contacted colleagues in Sheffield and the net closed in. When Horbury returned with the hired van, he found a reception committee waiting for him. Forget losing your deposit, this is the worst thing that happens back at the car hire place when you and their vehicle have been up to no good! Handing the thing back signs seals and delivers a good night out, but this time it signalled the start of some sleepless ones.

Horbury and passenger Mandy Barratt were arrested on suspicion of burglary. Police discovered nothing about the whereabouts of the foxes or the others involved in the rescue, but both were charged the next day with conspiracy to commit criminal damage and theft, and released on strict conditions. Over a year and a half and a dozen magistrates' hearings later, the trial began at Warwick Crown Court and sympathisers packed the public gallery.

According to some observers, Gill's evidence appeared to have been manipulated with the help of the police, but it couldn't be proven and, given the forensic link between the van and the farm, it mattered little. Mandy Barratt had innocently accompanied Horbury to return the van and had an alibi for the night of the raid that the prosecution couldn't challenge. For Horbury, there was no way out and there were whispers of a six-month prison sentence if convicted, not so much because of the disappearance of the foxes but because of the threats of violence made to Gill, albeit by others.

The day of the verdict the judge, Michael Harrison-Hall, hitherto a doddery senile fool, who had appeared to be best part dead, suddenly sprang into life and turned full of anger and loathing. He had a problem with this type of offender and was about to show it. Performing for court observers, his face reddened as he spat his conclusion at his anxious victim: 'This was a gross violation of a man's property. Your motives do not interest me. On both counts to run concurrently you will go to prison for two years.'

The irony of being accused of committing a gross violation of the man's 'property' when the man was going to first anally electrocute and then strip the property in question of their skin!

Two years was a severe punishment for such an offence and signalled the step up in the ante that the impending Liberation League sentences confirmed very publicly.

The Silver Spring Monkeys

> A good deed done to an animal is as meritorious as a good deed done to a human being, while an act of cruelty to an animal is as bad as an act of cruelty to a human being.
>
> *The Prophet Mohammed (570 –632)*

The first US animal liberation raid was carried out in September 1981 at Silver Spring in Maryland on the basement haunt of vivisector Dr Edward Taub at the Institute of Behavioural Research. The lab had been carrying out research on surgically crippled primates to monitor rehabilitation of impaired limbs. Seventeen monkeys, mostly macaques caught in the Philippines eight years earlier, were being used and were kept in appalling conditions, conditions that were being monitored by an undercover animal rights activist, Alex Pacheco, who was working as a research assistant.

Many of the monkeys were neurotic and would mutilate themselves, even biting off their own fingers. One developed gangrene from a filthy, unchanged bandage and had begun to mutilate his own chest cavity because he was in such a bad state. Rat droppings, old clothes, faeces and urine covered everything in the lab.

It was against this background that Pacheco filed a lawsuit against Taub, who was subsequently charged with 17 counts of cruelty. The monkeys were confiscated from the lab by police and placed in the converted basement of a sympathiser's home. However, a few days later a judge ruled that the monkeys must be returned to the lab. The researchers trucks arrived with police at the address the following morning at 8am to collect them, but there was no one home. When the police broke in they discovered the animals had gone. They had been driven through the night and the following day by a team of four activists to a safe house in Florida and allowed to spend the night outdoors catching flies and enjoying the warm night air for the first time since their capture.

Ten days later, the monkeys were back in Washington under a voluntary agreement between their rescuers, People for the Ethical Treatment of Animals (PETA) and the Police, who said they would drop the case against Taub unless the evidence was returned and gave assurances that the monkeys would not be returned to the lab. Taub was later convicted of six counts of cruelty but appealed so often that this was overturned. Following protracted legal proceedings, the animals were returned to their fate. It was a tragic outcome but this was only the first of a series of spectacular lab raids exposés and legal action in the USA.

Britches

> Cruelty to dumb animals is one of the distinguishing vices of low and base minds. Wherever it is found, it is a certain mark of ignorance and meanness; a mark which all the external advantages of wealth, splendour, and nobility, cannot obliterate. It is consistent neither with learning nor true civility.
>
> *Rev. William Jones (1726-1800) Anglican priest, theologian, musical composer, contributor to the Oxford Movement*

A City of Hope research facility Executive Director, speaking after a US ALF raid during which 115 animals were rescued from his lab, described the act of compassion as one of 'terrorism comparable to the hijacking of planes and the bombing of embassies.' But for those involved in the rescue of animals condemned to suffer and die at the hands of men who become monsters, there is no question as to who are the real terrorists. One of the most dramatic US actions in the 80's was to provide more than ample evidence of this.

Almost 1,000 animals were rescued when the ALF hit the University of California in America in the spring of 1985. Among those liberated were cats, pigeons, rabbits, rats, deer, opossums, and a very special little monkey named Britches, an infant stump-tail macaque. It's him on the front cover of the book. The five-week-old monkey—named Britches by his rescuers—was the gemstone in this haul. He had been kept in isolation, his entire skull and most of his face covered by surgical tape. This was holding in place electrical equipment for a study into the combined effects of sight deprivation and isolation (in a traumatised baby monkey). The weight of the device—from which a constant, loud noise emitted—forced his tiny neck to the side as he struggled to balance. It's not clear what happened to his mother, but she was probably used to produce more babies. He had been taken from her just after birth and given instead a block of wood covered with cloth to which he clung desperately.

He was a few weeks old, blinded by a 40 year old man, his mother was gone and he was trapped in a cage with a lump of wood as his only comfort. But word was out. Someone on the inside had taken it upon themselves to tip off the ALF, or at least someone who might be able to get word out to the ALF. It didn't take long.

Following a brief period of surveillance, masked raiders dressed in lab coats forced their way through the locked doors of this vast basement laboratory by removing them from their hinges, then rifled the labs of all occupants. The tiny monkey was lifted in cupped hands with this bizarre medieval contraption held to prevent it over-balancing his head, and he was gently laid into a carrier. Meanwhile, others wheeled racks of rodents and carried various other animals to the loading bay and eventual freedom. It was an impressive night's work.

It was two weeks from word out, and within hours of his rescue, Britches was in the hands of Betty, a sympathetic vet.

> On this day, 20 April 1985, I have been called upon to administer an examination and follow up care to an infant stump tail macaque, male, my guess approximately five weeks of age. Said infant liberated by the Animal Liberation Front from the U.C Riverside laboratory.
>
> Attached to the infant's head by means of bandage and tape is an apparatus of some sort with what appears to be some sort of electrical cord extending from it. It has been cut (by the raiders). Bilaterally are short lengths of tubing emerging from the bandage. Tape is in direct contact with the face and neck. Bandage lifted totally from the right eye due to excessive moisture and right eye partially visible. Beneath the bandage are two cotton pads, one for each eye. The cotton pad for the right eye has slipped laterally beneath the tape. Both pads are filthy and soaked through with moisture. Bilaterally upper eyelids are sutured to lower eyelids. The sutures are grossly oversized for the purpose intended. Many of these sutures have torn through lid tissue resulting in multiple lacerations of the lids. There is an open space between upper and lower lids of both eyes about one quarter inch and sutures are contacting corneal tissue resulting in excessive tearing, which explains the soaked pads. There are multiple bandage lesions on head, face and neck of infant.
>
> One can only conclude that the suture placement must have been performed by an unqualified or incompetent person and that the infant was not receiving proper ongoing medical care. Such care would also clearly be subject of malpractice given a veterinary or infant practice situation. Infant demonstrates photophobia. Penis of infant is oedematous and inflamed. There are smegma accumulations. Generalised muscle development poor. Skin dry.

Body odor foul. (sic)

What they had done to this tiny creature was tragic, and even the hardest of hearts would and should have been moved by this scene. Betty was finished and stood back, but Britches didn't seem to know he could finally open his eyes. Then realisation dawned. His fingers shot up to his eyes. Betty grabbed them and held them at bay afraid he would hurt himself by rubbing. At first in one eye, then in the other, cracks appeared between Britches upper and lower lids. His eyes began peering out. He was squinting into the light, looking at the world for the first time since his eyes were sewn shut. Fascinated by the experience, two now-twinkling eyes opened fully. His head turned to the right and then the left, then sank back again, it was as if he was saying, 'I can see! Look at that! I can see!' He popped his thumb into his mouth and started sucking contently. The little fella was going to be all right.

When he was fully recovered, he was transferred to a rescue centre where he was introduced to an older lone female, a potential surrogate mum. It wasn't his real mum of course, but it was the piece de résistance in this amazing story to see how delighted each animal was to meet the other. It was love at first sight. Britches was so excited!

The experiment was of course legal and far from a one-off, the rescue illegal and sadly less frequent. One scientist commented: 'Unlike blind human infants, Britches was also deprived of all social interaction, including contact with his mother, and kept un-stimulated in a wire cage since birth. He could not have developed as a normal blind child would. It's rubbish research.' No remorse from the University of course:

> We have reason to believe they [the animals] are in worse hands [than at the University]
>
> *Ted Huller, University Executive Vice Chancellor*

Not very likely now, is it Ted?! Few would dare agree with that statement when presented with the film of this story. As is so often the way when the doors to these places are opened, the term 'scientific research' takes on a whole new meaning.

The Pennsylvania Primates

> Disciples of the Buddha, you should willingly and with compassion carry out the work of setting sentient creatures free. Should you see a worldly person intent on killing an animal, attempt by appropriate means to rescue or protect it and free it from its misery.
>
> *Brahmjala Sutra*

The cruel and hopeless interpretation of scientific research using animals was again exposed to scrutiny as the ALF recovered more disturbing evidence during a break in at the offices of the University of Pennsylvania. Documents taken showed links with Glasgow University in Scotland. The grotesque experiments taking place in these labs were even more unimaginably savage. No animals were rescued—the raiders didn't even see any—but video tapes of head injury experiments taken by the 'researchers' themselves showed in the most appalling and graphic detail the awful truth about the way wholly desensitised human beings behave when hidden behind closed doors. Their invisibility and speciesist bigotry thus assured, they can vent their savagery and perversions on helpless animals, while claiming there may be some benefit from the suffering they inflict on their victims; there's probably nothing they haven't thought of that they haven't turned into a grotesque reality. In our name! This so called 'essential medical research' is so unbelievably pointless and wicked that it's difficult to convince doubters that it is real until they can see it with their own eyes. And then it's too awful for many to watch, so that some will instead convince themselves it must be necessary or people simply wouldn't do it! Presented with the kind of footage recovered here, apologists will ask us to believe this is a one off, the fault of just a few bad apples. They will claim that it hasn't ever happened before and will certainly not be allowed to happen again once there has been a 'review' or internal investigation. It's the same response every time and the conclusion is always the same: business as usual, back to brutality!

When the raiders returned with their haul and started to view their priceless booty they were numbed to silence by what they saw. Nothing they'd seen or read before prepared them for the callous, crass stupidity of these experiments. The footage makes traumatic, sickening viewing, and one cannot watch it without weeping. You really do have to see it to believe it, and even if you are used to this sort of imagery, it's no easier to take with repeated viewings. Baboons were the subjects, their bodies restrained, their heads cemented into helmets with electrical wires attached. The experimenters—students mainly learning how to be awful—are seen listening to rock music, smoking, laughing and mocking the animals as they attach the wires to the 'Penn 2', the hydraulic device that slams the animals' heads to cause brain damage. Not a word of kindness passes their lips as they push the switch, which thrusts the encased heads at a sixty-degree angle at a force of up to 1,000g's. That's plenty fast enough to mash the brain.

Two vivisectors are seen laughing as a small, helmeted baboon struggles with the canvas straps that hold him down. He is strapped to an operating table and probably under the influence of an administered dose of Phencyclidine (also known as PCP or angel dust).

'One, two, three.' Then there is a bang as the Penn 2 jack does its work. Two students attempt to cut some tubing and handle a struggling baboon at the same time. In the melee, a bottle of liquid overturns and spills over the monkey. 'This makes my day,' bawls the first student. 'Why don't you put him in the fucking goddam cage?' yells the second. 'I'm working on it, I'm working on it, I'm working on it. I'm trying to get... Would you cut this? I'm trying to cut this damned thing.' They knock over a bottle. 'What was in there?' 'Acid. It's gonna burn your balls off.' A little later two of them perform electrocautery, an extremely painful procedure for an unanaesthetised animal. The baboon keeps lifting his head, yet the men continue to cut into him.

On another tape, the experimenters are preparing to press the switch for another slam of the head when the baboon manages to turn his body around on the table. 'As you can see, he, uh, is very active, with normal motor functioning. He is quite agitated, also.' The experimenter talks into the microphone as he repositions the monkey. No sooner has he stepped away from the table than somehow the baboon manages to turn over onto his side again, though his legs and arms are now bound more tightly. The baboon is so agitated that he rolls over a total of five times before the researcher tapes him to the table.

In the next scene, you can just make out the legs of a restrained baboon and a researcher bent over him. The man is saying: 'He was banged once at 680g force and quickly recovered. Cheerleading over in the corner we have B-10.' The camera pans to a disabled monkey strapped into a chair in the corner of the lab, brain damaged and drooling. The experimenters laugh; they are having a whale of a time.

'B-10 wishes his counterpart well.' More laughter. 'As you can see, B-

10 is alive.' There follows scenes of experimenters banging at the monkeys' helmets trying to remove them with a hammer. Thrilled with their work they can't help but mock.

'Look! He's moving, he's moving. See! He moves. We have this little string on his tail and we just pull,' says one. The men then try to force the helmet off the monkey's head. 'Push. HHHH! It's a boy!' The helmet comes off in their hands and the monkey's head hits the table. The psychopath with the hammer pulls a face. 'Looks like I left a little ear behind, eeeeh!'

'Why is it so dusty down here?' one student asks another. 'Why? Because they're basically incompetent down here. It's, well, I mean, just in general our procedures are [unintelligible]. They're not. They're not regular in their cleaning at all, and I've called them three times. Ah, when they do clean they're half-assed. Lately the ventilation system's been spewing out some sort of dust. It's the type of thing that I, you know, I complain about, but, you know.' The student agrees. 'I mean, you come down here and it smells like urine. I mean, we have three months of urine down in the bottom of that thing. Uh, urine asphyxiation. We had to get her out of there. She was just filling it up with buckets of urine.'

If this wasn't vulgar enough, experimenters failed to perform sterile surgery. Some wear gloves but no masks, gowns, caps or surgical drapes are used. One researcher rests his surgical instrument on the baboon's unshaven chest and then, after dropping the instrument to the floor, picks it up and places it back in the baboon's head without even wiping it off. They smoke at the operating table around open incisions and in close proximity to highly dangerous gases.

The last two scenes on the film seen on the distribution copy, for the world to see, involve an experimenter tying an injured, conscious baboon to the operating table as he prepares to leave for the night. 'Oh, have some axonal brain damage there, monkey, or else we'll have wasted five hundred dollars' worth of HRP on you, you sucker!' There's a break in the tape, then the dazed baboon appears in shot, held up by a young, female experimenter. The baboon's head has been shaved, and he's covered with stitches.

'Get him closer.' This from a male voice off camera. 'Don't be shy now, Sir [to the monkey], nothing to be afraid of [laughter]. Oh, what's going on here, tsk, tsk, tsk, tsk. Look, there she goes; she's on TV [laughter], holding her monkey. Look! Go! Go! Ta da! Just like a cat! Here kitty, kitty, kitty—look at the cat commercial. Say, over here, say 'cheese.' Looks like he's gonna fall over. You better hope the, uh, the, uh anti-vivisection people don't get a hold of this film.' 'The who?' asks a female student, her grin fading. 'The anti-vivisection people. They got a nice shot of you. They got Larry's name. In the picture. And Karen.' Then, referring to a massive stitched head wound extending the entire length of the monkey's cranium: 'There, look at that part on his head (laughter). Hmm, that's some part you've got there. He has the, uh, the punk look.' 'The punk look is that what you said?' [laughter] 'Friends! Romans! Countrymen! [laughter] Look, he wants to shake hands. Come on. Oh, not again. Put your head down [more laughter].' He mocks: 'You're gonna rescue me from this, aren't you? Aren't you? You're gonna rescue me, aren't you?'

It was beyond apology and explanation but not repetition. Following the release of these tapes and the uproar that accompanied them, grants for this 'essential medical research' programme were halted. Now, only now, some incomparable pain and distress had spread to the cold hearted monsters responsible for this nightmare scenario.

However, a few years later when the furore had largely died down, the men responsible, self-styled head injury specialists (labour MP's John Prescott and Tony Blair have much more recently adopted a strikingly similar stance in defence of such savagery in UK labs, as you will see) Thomas Gennarelli and his partner Thomas Langfitt had their funding reinstated by the National Institute of Health, this time it was for spending on rats and mini-pigs. Langfitt admitted without shame: 'It is our intent to produce prolonged trauma so we can study its effects and we have our own intensive-care unit where they are managed similarly to unconscious patients in hospital.' Sounds lovely. Look forward to the footage.

Gennarelli received over $11 million for his 'research' in the 15 years prior to the raid. This is often the incentive for animal research, public money that in this case could actually have helped patients with brain injuries.

An Incendiary Attack

> The ALF is now so active that Scotland Yard has attributed to it more than 400 incendiary attacks since the mid 80's
>
> *The Times Review November 1992*

Less significant in terms of exposure, but equally important in the eyes of the liberators for every life saved and for inspiring others to act, were the raids occurring elsewhere and being given publicity. The image of the balaclava-clad activist rescuing animals is an emotive and catchy one, and presented alongside the real life story of some unfortunate creature liberated from its prison, is inspirational. In the space of a few months there were 90 rabbits taken from a lab breeder in Sussex; 200 pigeons rescued in Italy; 110 guinea pigs from a lab supplier in Essex; 127 turkeys in California; 264 animals from the University of Oregon; 100 rabbits from the Hylyne Rabbits in Cheshire; 400 mink and 30 pigs in Holland; and 106 chicks in Canada. There were also much smaller-scale liberations involving fewer numbers, but each one was in its own way priceless, though unlikely to affect any business in any great way. That was to change with a little lateral thinking, however.

UK fur traders enjoyed a brief period of hope in 1985 with the imprisonment of Andrew Horbury, when it must have looked for a while at least as though the authorities were getting to grips with the troublesome public. But with the fur trade still very much alive and kicking and a movement agog with its potential, the problems were actually only just beginning as the ALF introduced pocket sized incendiary devices into the equation. Created out of a few household components, their invention signalled a major escalation in the war on fur and took the emphasis away—temporarily at least—from opening animal cages and gluing locks to something far more significant in the bigger picture.

It was December that year when problems began to escalate again for fur retailers and it became clear that, rather than be deterred by the signal sent from Warwick Crown Court, friends of the captive fox liberator and opponents of the fur trade had instead shifted tactics. One ex furrier described it to me as: 'like the second coming.' A cheap, experimental device hidden in the furniture section of the Rackhams department store in Sheffield one dull Tuesday afternoon would, it was hoped, set off the in-store sprinkler system, causing water, rather than fire damage. It did its job and caused over £200,000 worth of flood damage. The device, built into a cigarette packet, came alight as planned at 12.15am and caused a small fire but, more specifically, lots of smoke, which turned on the water to extinguish the fire.

The early hours of Wednesday, 11 December in Rackhams were chaotic and Sheffield city centre was closed off. The sprinkler system did its job so well it poured out water long after the fire was doused, flooding the entire store. Ceilings collapsed, the electricity was cut off, and stock throughout was ruined. Local police, who had been stifling ALF publicity, were desperately trying to keep a lid on things and convince the press that the fire was probably started accidentally by a cigarette end. But journalists were suspicious and were embarrassing the police commanders with awkward questions. It didn't add up that it was gone midnight when the fire started, hours after the 'discarded cigarette butt' should have been all burnt out. Besides which, Rackhams had been the focus of a good deal of attention by many over their dealings in fur and had been frequently threatened.

Conspiracy of silence or not, it would have been impossible to keep this campaign under wraps as over the next four years, dozens of these tiny incendiaries were left in fur stores from Edinburgh to Plymouth, causing widespread controversy and extensive damage. At Debenhams in Luton in the summer of '87, things didn't go quite according to the plan—not that the perpetrators were overly concerned. This high street department store was completely gutted after the sprinkler system was turned off for maintenance the very day the ALF device was put in place to set it off. This was remarkable timing and not quite what the fire raisers had expected. I asked one later if he was concerned that rather than flood the store as planned, they'd burnt it to the ground: 'Ha! We were elated! We were seeking to make a serious statement about the cruelty of the fur trade and we did!' His statement caused millions of pounds worth of damage. The substantial Dingles department store in Plymouth suffered an even more devastating fate including extensive structural damage when the sprinkler system there also failed to kick in and douse the small fire deliberately set smouldering in a display sofa in the December 1988. It took 80 fire fighters many hours to bring the huge blaze under control, by which time there was nothing left worth saving. As was the advice, the top floor was the target of the subversive shoppers in order to cause the water to flood downward through lower floors. Over £16 million damage was caused, half of it through lost trade.

There was of course widespread condemnation of these attacks but there were some brazen enough to suggest that rather than condemning the attacks, store owners should have been thankful that accidental fires hadn't started during opening hours when the stores would have been full of shoppers at serious risk because the sprinklers weren't working properly. In other words, they should have been grateful that the matter had been highlighted! A bit rich perhaps, to suggest the ALF had somehow done these businesses a favour, but still a fair point?

It didn't take an expert in anything to figure out that these actions were going to have the desired effect. Fur in department stores takes up little floor space and the profits aren't large enough to justify resistance and risk just one successful attack of this nature. Any anonymous shopper could deposit a cigarette packet anywhere in a store and any profit would be immediately negated. Very simple, very effective and very naughty. Coupled with occupations, lock-ons, broken windows and so on, it was all too much to take and gradually stores severed links with the fur trade. Naturally, the industry claimed it had nothing to do with the ALF campaign but was simply the result of a drop in sales, a downturn.

Duh! And who forced that to happen! Fur wearers were being turned into social lepers. Animal rights groups regularly picketed fur shops and created an unattractive obstacle, but the most in-yer-face publicity campaign was led by the anti-fur group, Lynx and their slick use of street advertising hoardings, which could but heap shame on the wearers of fur. How about 'It Takes Up to 40 Dumb Animals To Make One Fur Coat But Only One To Wear It' plastered above a model on the catwalk trailing a bleeding fur coat, or the pretty sales girl draped in fox fur offering other wearers the animal's innards in the deal. None of it did anything for the once glamorous image of the fur coat. Rather than adoration and envy, wearers of fur were tending to attract anti-fur stickers, phlegm and chewing gum.

When business went belly up and the market crashed, fur traders claimed it was all down to the warm weather that their product was being shunned. But the word cruelty had become associated with fur and there is now undoubtedly a stigma attached, limiting their attraction. To date, fur sales have not been completely eradicated, and fur has latterly enjoyed something of a revival in the fashion industry. Desperate to maintain a foothold in the market, producers have taken to including fur collars, lining and cuffs in garments—even dyeing real fur to make it look fake! How sick is that? Rabbit skin, or Coney, have in recent times become a focus for campaigners as the industry has infiltrated the fashion market with fur accessories, claiming it to be a by-product of meat production in order to make it less offensive to the mainstream. However, it has fallen foul of campaigners' cameras, which have captured the terrible images of live rabbits being skinned of their fur. Only a few shops still have fur coats on offer, usually in a room out back or under the counter like some dirty porn movie for those so desperate they can't go without.

The Sheffield Trial

> Sentencing at the moment seems to suggest that a woman's body is less valuable than property or the right of experimenters and mink farmers to live in peace.
>
> *Conservative MP Steven Norris 1987*

Not surprisingly, Uncle Arni was soon under political pressure to stop the incendiary campaign. The Sheffield ALF was active and drawing attention, and police had learnt that Ronnie Lee and Vivian Smith had been in the area mixing with known faces. Alarm bells started ringing, activists were put under surveillance and the net began to close in, but no one noticed because they were focused on the fur trade. Police disguised as bin men were taking dustbin bags away from suspect's homes.

Its far from pleasant, nor is it legal, to go rifling through someone else's waste (bad enough your own) but it is one of the simplest ways to gather information on people. Nine times out of ten you will find something there among the beer cans, dirty tissues and animal carcasses to get excited about, as the police did at one address in Sheffield, where there were no animal carcasses, I might add. This foraging led to a permanent observation post being set up opposite and, when the house was empty, a listening device hidden under the floorboards.

Conveniently, the Sheffield crew were all at one address and in the process of modifying the pocket incendiary devices to work using a digital 24-hour timer. They were originally designed to work to a standard watch face with an hour hand, which would allow a maximum 12-hour delay before the circuit was complete. A digital 24-hour delay would make them even user-friendlier, and it meant that they could instead be placed well ahead of ignition.

At the height of this research and development programme, at the Idsworth Road home of Kevin Baldwin, the police interrupted by barging in the front door and detaining all those inside, some with their hands on and surrounded by the paraphernalia of incendiary devices. It was the worst imaginable turn of events for the Sheffield crew but the police had hit the jackpot.

Baldwin (27) Gary Cartwright (30) Julie Rogers (26) Isobel Facer (19) and Ian Oxley (25) were in serious trouble and were duly charged with conspiracy to commit arson. In co-ordinated raids, Roger Yates (29) the ALF Northern regional press officer, was arrested in Liverpool; and in

London, Vivian Smith (26) and Ronnie Lee (35) were apprehended. The ALF Supporters Group office was raided and everything in it retained. All were later charged with various conspiracies: to commit arson, criminal damage and inciting others between January 1985 and March 1986. Elsewhere in Sheffield, Brendan McNally (25) John Hewson (63) Jenny Wall (24) and Neil McIvor (24) were also rounded up and charged with one or more conspiracies. For some this included the theft of an entire pack of hunting hounds, the Ecclesfield Beagles.

All animal rights-related paperwork considered 'extreme' by the police helped greatly make up the case against the defendants. Included in the bundle of 'Evidence' were letters to newspapers, recorded TV interviews, pro-direct action newsletters, information leaflets, and political publications calling for the rights of animals. It all helped to paint a picture of a dangerous global conspiracy at work. Certainly, the ALFsg newsletters would take some explaining, extolling as they did, in no uncertain terms, the virtues of firebombing slaughterhouses and so on. With the exception of Ronnie Lee, the joint editor, who had already been dubbed ALF Commander, all were eventually released on conditional bail.

A year later, the 12 defendants were put on trial at Sheffield Crown Court and billed as the ALF leadership, which wasn't far off the mark. The public gallery was a popular place throughout, and security was overt and hyped for the benefit of the jury and media. The evidence against those caught red-handed was pretty conclusive and included a full transcript of their conversations up to and including the police raid. It was beyond doubt that they had been making incendiary devices. Evidence revealed in court showed that the police had planned extended surveillance and didn't want to raid the address when they had, but because of the rapidly advancing chain of events they couldn't help but capture the moment, and who can blame them! It was certainly just what the police wanted. The arrests weren't the only good news for detectives who'd created an environment where those they hadn't caught red-handed began to make incriminating statements against fellow activists. The Sheffield case turned into a classic example of how to make a bad situation worse.

Baldwin started talking and others followed suit when they realised they'd been fingered by him and that Hewson was talking too. Baldwin & Oxley told how Vivian Smith had been to Idsworth Road, collected a device and had taken it back to Selfridges in London. Smith remained silent throughout. John Hewson told how Ronnie Lee had been in

Sheffield to learn how to construct the new incendiaries, which had been developed by Ian Oxley. Lee had nothing to say to anyone. Incriminating statements were also made against the uncooperative Brendan McNally by the rest of the Sheffield group, with the exception of his girlfriend Jenny Wall and Neil McIvor who also had no comment to make. Julie Rogers confessed to planting the device in Sheffield and claimed Jenny Wall had been with her. Rogers was young and inexperienced and was easy prey for the police who duped her into believing they had both been caught on in store cameras planting the device. They hadn't, but may as well have been because the police now had a full confession to offer the jury.

Most of the Sheffield cell admitted their part in the theft of the 28 hunting dogs from the Ecclesfield Beagles hunt kennels in August 1985. This was an audacious action and the first of its kind. Although saboteurs have been dog napping packs of hounds from hunts for many years, albeit only temporarily to prevent the day's hunting, a whole pack had never before been taken permanently and this upset the hunting fraternity no end! Following the raid, the Ecclesfield Beagles as a hunt pack ceased to exist and later had to be reformed with unwanted hounds from other packs. This certainly isn't something that is desirable in hunting circles because of the loss of bloodlines, history, training and tradition. But short of disbanding, there was nothing else because the original pack had been split up and absorbed into the animal protection movement and beyond. Gone! A similar raid occurred 15 years later with the redistribution by the ALF of the Wye College beagles from their kennels in Kent.

A video of surveillance of the Ecclesfield kennels was found at Idsworth Road, but there was no real evidence to link the defendants to the raid other than their own admissions. As they'd pleaded guilty, it was inadmissible for their statements to be read in open court except for that of John Henson who turned Queen's Evidence under police pressure and screwed Ronnie Lee. He wasn't a typical ALF activist—a 63 year old retired schoolteacher who had been frightened by police with threats that he would never see his wife again and that their home would be repossessed if he didn't help them. Still, he knew to keep his mouth shut when asked to finger others—it's what you do. Kevin Baldwin pleaded not guilty to conspiring to commit arson, and his barrister tried to get the covert tapes removed as evidence due to them being illegally planted. It wasn't to be. With these included, the case was compelling and he was forced to change his plea midway through the trial, which was some kind of just reward for leading the loose talking the others he'd named had felt compelled to follow. Television interviews with Ronnie Lee were shown in court. Evidence against Vivian Smith included a number of items found in her home, such as glass etching fluid, a CIA manual for bomb making, a crowbar, balaclava, a security guard's uniform. She wasn't prepared to account for the whereabouts of £12,000 that had been withdrawn from the ALFsg account, and a police officer gave evidence that he had interviewed her about the firebomb attack on Rackhams by phoning the press office claiming to be a journalist from the Sheffield Star. Roger Yates was accused of being the Northern Press Officer, which indeed he was, and was charged with incitement.

The judge, Frederick Lawton, in his eighties and a favourite for political trials, was brought out of retirement especially for the purpose of dealing with the ALF menace. An armed officer sat next to Lawton throughout the trial and sketched people in the public gallery—deliberately forging the impression for the jury that the defendants and their acquaintances were indeed the dangerous thugs as claimed by the prosecution. There was talk of a General: Ronnie Lee, his Able Lieutenant, Vivian Smith and the Foot Soldiers. This was a stage-managed theatre performance.

At the end of the trial, the only defendant to be acquitted was Jenny Wall. This was despite expert evidence that it was her voice on a tape recording made by a radio station of a woman claiming responsibility for attacking a travel agents selling tickets for the Robert's Brothers Circus; added to this, a shop owner had identified her as having bought glass etching fluid in his shop, and there was additional evidence that she and Julie Rogers had planted the device in Rackhams. It might sound bizarre, but it was plain for observers and defendants alike to see that Freddie had taken a shine to Jenny and she was to be his token gesture, his streak of compassion, his sprinkling of moderation.

He didn't fancy Ronnie Lee though, and gleefully sentenced him to ten years on each of three counts—totalling 30 altogether, but to run concurrently—labelling him, as he went on, a fanatic and a dangerous criminal. Ten years! Vivian Smith and Brendan McNally were found guilty of conspiracy to cause criminal damage and sentenced to four years each. Roger Yates absconded before the verdict was announced and was given four years in his absence for incitement. He was on the run for three years before he was arrested and sent to jail to do his time. The police had distributed his mug shot to the media as an alleged suspect in unrelated offences they were at pains to solve and he'd been recognised by another parent at his kid's school.

Kevin Baldwin and Ian Oxley were given four years for conspiracy to commit arson. Gary Cartwright was also given four years, John Hewson was sentenced to 12 months, and Julie Rogers was sentenced to 2 ½ years for conspiracy to cause arson. The judge decided she wasn't a party to the conspiracy because of her own actions but because of her relationship with Baldwin. He gave the other woman, Isobel Facer, nine months youth custody. She was, according to the old man in the wig, frock and with buckles on his shoes, apparently not in control of her own emotions either. Both women made damaging statements to the police, giving them the lifelong label of 'grass' and bringing the total to five in one case. Trying to save their own skin had little reward for the grasses at Sheffield, which was some consolation for those who were good for their word and kept mum.

Frederick Lawton's olde ideas about how women are supposed to behave were what you'd expect, but then it did get reduced sentences for two of them, so there were no protests. In fact, everyone fared better than they were expecting, even Ronnie Lee, who ran down to the cells whooping, feeling he had got off lightly! The judge telling him, 'You are a dangerous criminal and it is clear there is not much chance of your changing your attitude. You will go to prison for ten years.' Ronnie Lee accepted the silly sentence with some comfort at the time, but everyone else was horrified. Even some of the welfare groups constantly at odds with the ALF over the use of direct action were bold enough to side with the animal liberators and comment that ten years was excessive for altruistically motivated property-related offences. People without any direct interest in the animal rights movement were equally concerned that the law was being used in such a way, especially when in the very same week two men convicted in the notorious Ealing Vicarage rape case, for rape and for beating the girl's father, the vicar, were sentenced to six and seven years.

There's something unsettling about a judicial system that finds it appropriate to exaggerate the sentences of people convicted of offences aimed specifically at damaging property to save life, yet treats rapists and other dangerous social misfits with comparative leniency. Of course, the reality is simply that economics are more important than lives.

Incarceration & Innovation

> In just the first two and a half months of 1986 Dewhurst the Butchers admitted that they had suffered eighty-seven attacks on branches all over the country. It was an impressive measure of how far things had changed since Ronnie Lee and his animal band of thirty acolytes had dreamt up the idea of the ALF.
>
> *David Henshaw, Journalist*

At the conclusion of the successful Sheffield trial, the police claimed that they'd smashed the ALF and others were hoping so too but it isn't as simple as that. What they failed to understand, and still do, is the fact that the ALF is made up of small independent groups, which somewhat puts paid to the theory that taking out some members will succeed in dismantling the entire 'organisation.' Not even the respected figureheads of the ALF would be able to achieve this as long as there are animals in need of assistance. It is animal abuse which drives individuals, not the promise of material rewards or orders from above; the ALF isn't an organisation that can be dismantled—its something that comes from the heart.

It had been suspected for some time that Special Branch were controlling media queries about the ALF and were claiming there had been no reports of ALF activity since December 1987. That was later confirmed by the head of security at Sears Holdings, the parent company of Selfridges, himself a former commander at Scotland Yard, speaking to the London magazine *City Limits* who stated, 'They have been planting bombs all through Oxford Street for years now and they have been very active recently.'

With the raid on the ALFsg offices, the confiscation of the files, and the imprisonment of all those responsible for the newsletters, legal advisers warned that the format of publications had to change from the inciting path they had followed since the SG's inception to one of purely prisoner support. One of the most wide reaching aspects of this legal ruling was the suggestion that to simply compile details of ALF actions was no longer acceptable and editors could face continued harassment and prosecution for doing so. While some articles were unarguably inciting with titles like *'Learn To Burn'*, *'Devastate To Liberate'*, and *'Factories Don't Burn Down By Themselves They Need Help From You'*, it was hard to argue otherwise, though there was a lot more to the newsletters than that but now the shutters were coming down on all unapproved news reporting. In future, editors would have to first consult a lawyer before publishing any material.

The day after sentences were dished out in Sheffield, a team of activists raided the J. Bibby research station on the Wirral on Merseyside; they rescued four piglets and 52 broiler hens, caused some damage and recovered documents. It was a pre-planned raid by an active cell that had carried out spectacular raids in the area during the 1980s causing extensive damage as they went. The Bibby raid was as much a staged symbolic gesture as it was a liberation, intended to send a message that the ALF was still here, was active and organised. A week later, an incendiary device was left in the fur department of the Binns store in Newcastle upon Tyne in the far north of England. Sheffield was safe but there was still a problem.

It wasn't over in the courts either. Following years of remarkable success, 1987/88 was to prove a trying time for the Animal Liberation Movement with trials springing up across the country and a number of key activists imprisoned, albeit for less time than had been predicted.

Angus MacInnes was a 47 year-old former police detective who had long since abandoned a career which involved protecting at all costs the interests of animal abusers and environmental rapists. Working alongside officers with an overload of testosterone and no respect for the values he had was increasingly unpalatable and eventually too much to take. Streetwise, imaginative and mature, he could've reached the heights as a cop, but career prospects gave way to dodging his former colleagues as MacInnes came on side with ALF theory and took up the practical. From one extreme to the other, you might say.

His chosen career reached its peak as he became central to the first ALF trial in Scotland in 1985. Convicted of contaminating a Beechams product by adding urine to Lucozade in a comment on their involvement in vivisection, he was sentenced to 12 months in prison.

Davy Barr (22) and Valerie Mohammed (21) were next before the sheriff. These two deeply committed activists had formed the core of the most active Scottish ALF cell to emerge in a country not best known for its animal welfare agenda. Their detention—for planting a hoax incendiary device in Edinburgh's Jenners department store and for sending threatening letters to the same—impacted heavily on the scale of activity north of the border largely as they were responsible for most of it! Davy was a Scot through and through and could nay hide it if he wanted. So pale, he had no chance of a tan; so pained by animal abuse, he had no chance of a peaceful night's sleep. Though immature and awash with annoying practical jokes and sometimes irritating humour, he was mature beyond his years in his outlook on life and with his views on the way others be treated. He still had a lot of fight in him when he was sent to prison for three years. Ms Mohammed on the other hand, as the name might suggest, always had a tan and was the level headed one of the two. They were an unlikely pair but suited down to the ground as an efficient campaign team. She got nine months inside, served half, and Jenners stopped selling fur.

Davy Barr found prison hard to deal with. Forced to live on crisps and water for two months because the authorities refused to feed him a proper vegan diet, his case was taken to the European Court of Human Rights. Released on parole after a year, he got straight back into campaigning, but had been adversely affected by the experience. The pair tried hard to carry on from where they had left off, but for Barr personal problems and the sheer scale of animal abuse that he, by choice, sought out every day, became too much for him. He wasn't able to wait for it all to come right and on 16 March, 1991, Davy Barr took his own life in his Glasgow flat, aged 24. Five years later, Valerie Mohammed tragically also took her own life. Their passing has largely gone unnoticed outside their circle of friends but a movement screaming out for such commitment sorely misses them.

Three months after their trial, two of the people who had briefly taken over the running of the Supporters Group in Vivian Smith and Ronnie Lee's absence were themselves convicted of conspiring to incite others to commit criminal damage, for compiling and/or distributing the—by now very toned down—ALFsg newsletters and leaflets. Their judge felt that to even speak about the ALF in sympathetic terms was inciting criminal behaviour. Robin Lane (32) and Sally Carr (29) who handled the accounts, were each sent to prison for nine months with a further nine suspended. The authorities were so keen that the ALFsg didn't find its feet again, that even the two people who took over distributing the sales goods were harassed and put on trial for incitement. But some level of sense prevailed in their case and the suggestion that they had incited others to commit criminal damage by merely selling Support The ALF t-shirts and coffee mugs proved a fruitless one for the over enthusiastic animal squad at New Scotland Yard.

Eavesdropping on the flat of Londoners Geoff Sheppard and Andrew Clarke was far more fruitful. Both were arrested after police had begun spying on them in the summer of 1988 and fitted a listening device in the roof space of the flat below.

Alerted to a presence outside one afternoon, Sheppard had approached the front door at the precise moment the police decided to bust it open—in that never subtle manner—and suffered serious gashes to his arm as the door came crashing in and the two met full on, shattering the glass everywhere. As if things weren't bad enough!

When the police made their move, they found all the ingredients for more department store-bound pocket-sized incendiary devices surrounding the men, soldering iron warm. Stunned and bleeding profusely the quiet, reserved Sheppard was violently 'placed under arrest.'

Apart from being caught in the act, which was problematic enough, it emerged that the police had a tape recording of Andrew Clarke phoning the Press Association to claim responsibility—on behalf of the ALF—for previous incendiary attacks. Both men were duly convicted at the Old Bailey of conspiring to cause arson to stores in Luton, Romford and Harrow a year earlier, a three pronged attack, which waterlogged two stores and cost Debenhams in Luton alone £9 million in fire damage and loss of trade.

It was the PA voice recording that consequently led the police to their unsuspecting suspects, and it was then just a case of waiting for the right opportunity to make arrests. The timing, again, was perfect. Incredible as it seems now with excessive political intervention and exaggerated punishment for people seeking to help animals, Clarke was sentenced to 3 ½ years, and Sheppard, who was in breach of a suspended sentence for breaking butchers' windows, 4 years and 4 months.

A random selection of animal lovers was learning painful lessons about contacting the press to claim responsibility for their actions and talking freely inside buildings and cars. The final trial of this era took place in Leeds Crown Court in November that year. Sean Crabtree (26) and George Bogojevic (23) were sentenced to four years each for conspiring to commit criminal damage, arson and attempted arson, following a year long campaign against targets throughout West Yorkshire. Bogojevic had worked in a meat factory near a slaughterhouse and had quickly become aware of the suffering. He stopped eating meat and then turned activist. All in all, considering the hype, the threats, the charges, the new terrorist label and the ten years given to Ronnie Lee, sentences didn't spiral out of proportion. Not yet, anyway. Four years in prison is still excessive for selflessly acting for animals, but arson carries a maximum life sentence and a judge without sympathy for motives or with investments in animal industries could easily impose more years on people he sees as a threat to the status quo.

Sometime before the Sheffield trial began, a publication entitled *Interviews With Animal Liberation Front Activists* was distributed via the local group P.O. Box network to activists and sympathisers throughout the UK and elsewhere. The 52-page document carried in-depth interviews with ALF cells and activists who explain how they go about carrying out particular actions. Also packed with images of abuse and raids, it shared detailed instructions on the construction of the in-store incendiary devices and a modified vehicle version. It served to intrigue, inform, inspire and incite its readers.

Around 1,500 copies of the *Interviews* were distributed. Some were further copied and passed on. They still are. It was largely thanks to the wide circulation of detailed plans for the incendiary devices that led to their wide distribution through fur department stores and elsewhere. No matter how many people were imprisoned and how many copies seized, plans were to hand and stores continued to be targeted and flooded.

Another weapon, newly adopted by the ALF and given publicity through the Interviews, was glass-etching fluid. Used normally for marking vehicle registration numbers into car windows, it comes in small quantities in plastic bottles and its job is to eat glass. It is also used legitimately by artists for sketching on glass, but as with balaclavas and crow bars, their intended purpose is a secondary consideration in this environment. While etching fluid is expensive to buy and meant to be used liberally, it was soon adopted for use in a wider, less careful application to scar vehicle and shop windows. Some targets were once out of reach because of their location and the risk of arrest should they be hit with a brick or ball bearing—fur shops in shopping arcades for example—but with etching fluid there came no sound of breaking glass. It is splashed or painted onto the glass and within a matter of minutes the damage is permanent. The glass then has to be replaced in order to remove the damage. Entire rows of department store display windows were soon being damaged in single, silent walk-by attacks costing the owners thousands and the perpetrator a few pounds. As ever, the news media have done their best to instil fear into the public by suggesting this stuff was being splashed around recklessly by mindless monsters intent on hospitalising children who might come into contact with it as they walked by affected shop windows the morning after. Others have also encouraged this media campaign of terrorism. A good example of this appeared in the *Manchester Evening News* in 1987 after a spate of etchings to fur store windows in the city. According to Detective Superintendent Ian Fairley:

> We have been in touch with experts who say this acid is one of the most horrendous substances. In varying strength, it is normally used for etching glass and ceramic industry. If it comes into contact with skin it causes an irritation but the real danger is hidden because the substance gradually eats into the skin and destroys bone marrow.' And if that weren't awful enough, 'It can travel through the whole body causing permanent injury or death, even in small quantities.

Blimey! Scary stuff, eh? But not quite the truth, the whole truth and nothing but the truth. Despite what it does to glass, etching fluid is quite harmless to the skin and eyes. I know because I've had it there. One ingredient of etching fluid is hydrofluoric acid, a violent chemical that would cause extensive damage to any part of the human body it made contact with, but not diluted in glass etching fluid (the sale of which was being monitored following its wide application as an ALF weapon of choice, and it had become difficult to buy in any quantity without drawing attention). One day a friend gave me a large bottle of hydrofluoric acid from his work. Thinking it would perhaps be useful as it was, or, better still, diluted, I was mischievously excited by this unusual gift, but only until the point I opened it and realised just how volatile the stuff was. It was clearly lethal and put the willies up me, bubbling away in the bottle as it did.

There was no way I was going to be throwing this stuff anywhere except the bin, in the morning. But by coincidence before I had the chance to safely dispose of it, I was arrested at home over some other matter. Having arrived home late the night before, I'd shoved the bottle inside the vacuum cleaner bag until I decided how best to get rid of it. Luckily the police never looked in the vac, and once I was released I dumped the stuff. As I have said, the amount of the acid in etching fluid is so minute as to render it harmless through any accidental contact. To drink a bottle probably wouldn't be a good idea, but the ALF hasn't been encouraging this or selling it to kids to drink, so it needn't come into the debate really, unless you want to scare people.

The authorities are of course well aware of this, yet they will still go to the extreme of calling out fire fighters to hose down shop windows after they've been etched. Apart from the fact that the stuff rapidly dries in, and the likelihood of harm being caused to any passers-by who should rub their hands across etched windows is bordering on highly unlikely, all this achieves is to draw more attention to the damage and of course waste the time of the fire brigade and play on the public fear of 'rampaging fanatics.'

Europe Awakening

> We had a fence and floodlights and we were still attacked. If we put in a video camera they'd only wear masks.
>
> *Slaughterhouse owner*

At the end of the 1980's, West German activists were executing some unmistakably successful raids on vivisection laboratories and their suppliers. Raiders snatched 25 cats and two dogs from a research laboratory at Karlsruhe University; 16 rabbits, 70 guinea pigs, a pregnant cat, a pregnant beagle and three puppies from a dealer in Bochum; 70 beagles and 400 rats from Dusseldorf University; 170 rats from the pathological institute at Bonn University; three beagles from Heidenberg University and six rabbits from Bochum University.

It wasn't all plain sailing; during one operation in which 80 dogs were rescued from a supplier in Beverungen, the owner disturbed the raiders. In a struggle, he tried to use a shotgun but was overpowered by the Animal Peace activists, who broke his nose.

Enquiring about the incident and the bad press coverage I asked the assailant if he felt remorse. He gave me a look of utter disbelief. 'He tried to stop us, Keith. We were there to help the animals and he tried to stop us, so I punched him on the nose. Of course I don't regret it!' Good answer!

The Independent Animal Protection Association took nine dogs, eight cats, 48 rabbits and several rats from the University of Aachen. The Autonomous Animal Protectors in the Offenbach and Dermstadt regions destroyed around 80 shooting platforms using power saws and axes. A spokesperson for the group said when interviewed: 'The hunters love nature like a rapist loves his victim. Hunt and Hunter to the museum!' And arsonists hit a fur farm at Grunemoor near Vechta, setting fire to its offices and warehouse. More than 20,000 pelts worth £600,000 were destroyed along with £250,000 structural damage. Another farmer lost 600 mink to a late night raiding party.

It wasn't all without redress either, as ten activists aged between 20 and 60 were brought to trial. They were charged with forming a criminal association, attempted arson and for raids on various labs and other establishments, resulting in the theft of nearly 50 animals. It was anticipated that some would be given heavy sentences, but, unusually, the judge was empathetic to their reasoning. In court, they were allowed to show the film of the Pennsylvania Primates, which had motivated their resolve to rescue lab animals and the judge later referred to the 'terrible experiments' of which the court had learnt, which 'get under the skin of any person and compel him to give thought to these things.' In his summing up, he said he had been impressed by the high motives of the animal liberators who, he acknowledged, 'had wanted to help the animals and free them from their tormentors.' After imposing sentences varying from small fines to probationary periods of between seven and 12 months, the judge ended the trial by urging the accused to 'continue fighting for tortured animals, but by legal means.' Give me that judge!

Sweden was awakening too. Sparked off by the TV screening of a film about animal cruelty, the Swedish ALF—the Djurens Belfrielse Front—staged their first raid in June 1985:

> Three of us went on our first night shift. One crowbar and a couple of screwdrivers was all we brought. It was late at night and very quiet and we walked around the huge building in order to find the perfect place to break in. We found it, a rather small, rather old door in the basement. This was the first time for us but we really got a good grip of the crowbar and after a short while the door just flew up with a terrible noise.
>
> In we went and ran up and down on various stairs but we didn't get to the top floor. Back down to the basement again and we found a lift. With pounding hearts and a sweat-production that was unbelievable we stepped in, pushed the button marked Top Floor. What would be waiting there? After, as it felt, many hours, the first, second and third keys didn't fit. Lucky for us the steel door had no alarm. Finally the fourth key fitted.
>
> Three very tired and scared people set foot in the vivisection department. The first time outsiders had ever set foot in a vivisection lab in Sweden. At this point we didn't care, didn't understand we were actually writing history. We just wanted to get the dogs we had been working so hard for. We noticed rats in several rooms and finally came to the dog room. Could it be dangerous, big, angry dogs? Slowly we opened the door into the dark room and the barking became louder. By the sound of the barking it didn't seem dangerous. The light went on and we looked at a pack of beagles.

So many and we could only take two. We spent a little time with the dogs. They were all so beautiful but a bit scared. We looked around in the dog room. There were open pens so at least the dogs could be together but there was no bedding, no toys for them. But how to choose which ones to bring? This dilemma worked out by itself. The two dogs that were most interested in us and had the guts to sniff at our hands told us they were the ones. We ran out, into the lift and down and out into the night air. We couldn't believe what we had done when the reality set in.

We were happy but still unhappy for the dogs we had to leave behind. We took them to a safe house and gave them water and a big soft blanket. We could see that one of the female dogs had a metal thing in her mouth instead of teeth. The other one had teeth but her lips were swollen and had a strange colour. Slowly we began to understand what the experiment was all about. Periodontoclasis. The dogs had been given soft food and of course had no bedding and soft toys in order to make them lose their teeth. The metal thing in the dog's mouth was screwed into her jawbone. This required a vet.

Four days later when the dogs were well taken care of and moved away from Malmo, we wrote a press release explaining what and why we had done this. Of course the newspapers had written about this without knowing anything. They actually speculated if the British ALF had come over! We had painted the letters DBF together with ANIMAL ABUSER on the walls outside the dog room. People in various animal welfare organisations condemned the action, saying we had acted as kidnappers and they felt sorry for the dogs and believed the dogs would have a better life in the lab.

It was a modest affair, and illegal, but with it, the Swedish ALF had arrived, as had the animal welfarists, on hand to condemn the activists on the front line for taking the limelight and giving the cause a bad name—the cause about to be made popular by the efforts of the so-called extremists, it might be said! Anyway, unmoved by critics of animal rescue and suddenly up for this getting the animals out thing that people talked about, some of Sweden's animal lovers, the DBF, got to work on with their self appointment.

1985, alone, saw a further 47 dogs rescued from vivisection and re-homed. Since then, tens of thousands of chinchillas, mink and foxes have been released from fur factory farms or had their fur dyed with henna, causing screaming headlines and a lot of damage. Fur farms and outlets have been hit particularly hard, with around 100 farms raided. Farms and suppliers have been sabotaged, breeding programmes ruined and on countless henna raids foxes fur has been stained rendering them worthless. Also dozens of guinea pigs have been intercepted from trains en route to labs; rabbits taken from the Institute of Zoology in Stockholm and from the University of Lund and dozens more dogs from lab suppliers' premises.

Over the next few years a third of the country's fur farms would be forced to close, leaving no fox farms and just six of the original 17 chinchilla farms. In one week youngsters raided two farms, removed all the animals and caused so much damage that the farmers both quit. Dutch enthusiasts rescued around 500 hens from battery units on two farms in Didam and Best, Holland. In the United States, 115 rabbits were rescued from a breeding station in Bloomington, Los Angeles, and fire destroyed a nearly completed farm animal research laboratory at the University of California where the damage was estimated at $3.5 million. Forty rabbits were rescued from a lab in California. The French rescued around 100 dogs, cats, rabbits, monkeys, rats and ferrets rescued from a lab in Lyons. In Japan, 29 wild monkeys trapped for vivisection were released back into the wild, 'ALF' was sprayed about the place, and cages trashed. In Italy, hundreds of pigeons were rescued from a veterinary laboratory and 4000 mink released from a farm in Fordenone; over 1000 mice, rabbits and rats were rescued from an experimental surgery centre in Padova and £40,000 damage caused. Again in France, a private drug-testing lab was raided and 42 dogs taken, lab equipment was smashed and paperwork destroyed. The Salvatore Hospital at Marseille was raided while staff watched a football match and 30 dogs and 23 rabbits were rescued from what they politely described as 'deplorable conditions.'

In the UK, arsonists hit the Pyke Biggs meat factory in Milton Keynes and caused a blaze that roared on to cause damage to the tune of £10 million. In Scotland, extensive fire damage was caused to the Macaulay Land Use Research Institute—which uses sheep, cows and goats in experiments—and the Poultry Research Centre, near Edinburgh.

Car Bombs & Confessions

> We have enslaved the rest of the animal creation, and have treated our distant cousins in fur and feathers so badly that beyond doubt, if they were able to formulate a religion, they would depict the Devil in human form.
>
> *William Ralph Inge*

It didn't sound all that plausible, but the official version of events was that an 'animal rights group' new on the scene had carried out an attack on a British University using powerful military explosives. It was a university well known for using animals and the damage was costly and visually very dramatic and in that sense it was in keeping with strategy but something didn't sound right. Soon after another 'animal rights group' we'd never heard of before planted two car bombs and I mean proper car bombs, to attack vivisectors in another location. It was an odd series of events to say the least. You figure it out.

Bristol, England, 1989.

Early one winter morning, a news agency received a call warning them that a bomb had been placed within the Senate House Bar of the University and was set to detonate at midday. Police and bomb squad officers rushed to the scene with sniffer dogs and carried out a three-hour fingertip search. Nothing was found. Twelve hours later, at midnight, a bomb ripped apart the Senate House Bar, causing extensive damage. If that weren't odd enough Special Branch officers said later that someone with an Irish accent claiming to represent the Animal Abused Society had called claiming responsibility for the attack. Neither he nor they were heard of again. The police duly went on a trawl of known animal rights campaigners' homes but found no likely suspects or evidence. They were looking in the wrong place. They weren't to know that, of course, but there could have been no end of people with motive.

Motive? Here's one: there are millions upon endless millions of victims, sacrificed in the name of humanity—victims who have done nothing other than to be non-human—these give reasonable people reason enough to break the law. Perhaps there are others who object to the collateral human carnage from vivisection. It's different for everyone, of course—that moment when you suddenly realise that this twilight world is a monstrous reality. For me, one of the earliest images I recall affecting my thinking on vivisection and making my blood boil was a scene from *The Animals Film.* The footage had come out of Porton Down in Wiltshire which is where this story takes us and showed a live pig tied upside down by its feet to a frame and blowtorched by men in white coats—the 'researchers.' The pig's skin is burnt to a crisp by the gentlemen who are seen to break bits away and then in a grotesque act of salvation, offer the animal some water as it writhed in agony before them. The government tests better ways of killing people at its secret military testing laboratories at Porton Down. How exceptionally gross is that?

Anyway, a few months after the Bristol bombing, Margaret Baskerville, another vet involved in the disgraceful business of overseeing the devastating demise of healthy animals, was leaving her Wiltshire home to go about her business. Without warning, as the jeep was reversing out of the drive, the bomb attached to the chassis exploded, blowing out all the windows and leaving the car a write off. Incredibly, the driver managed to scramble out of the window and suffered only minor injuries. The attempt on her life was of course headline news and the implication was as it so often is that the entire animal rights movement was to blame! The Movement—all of it—disagreed. Then, before the dust had even started to settle the plot returned to Bristol and thickened.

The following morning a vigilant off-duty security guard had phoned the police to report his suspicions about something under his neighbour's car. He told them specifically that it looked like a car bomb. But he'd called the same Avon and Somerset force that had failed to find the bomb in the university bar, and they didn't even bother to go look for this one! Two days later, the bomb that was indeed attached to the underneath of Bristol vivisector Max Headley's car exploded as he was driving to work along a residential street. Again, miraculously, injuries to the driver were minimal, but a child being pushed along in his buggy by his dad was struck in his back and finger by flying shrapnel and rushed to hospital.

Well this was the stuff of dreams for story-writers and a nightmare for anyone who sided with the animals. Suddenly, everyone who did was a people-hating baby bomber. It was awful that the child had been injured, albeit not seriously, but according to some reports accompanying the media frenzy, supporting animal causes would now by definition encourage more of these attacks on innocent children. You either loved people or animals—take your pick. And some surely did! I remember handing out circus leaflets in a town 200 miles away and being told by one person who wouldn't take one that it was because we were a bunch of baby bombers! There was no reasoning, because he'd had his mind made up for him. Experience suggests that these people are not animal friendly to start with and use opportunities like this to launch verbal attacks on anyone who is claiming it as proof that you must hate people to care about animals and that you are therefore by association responsible for everything that anyone does in defence of animals.

Ever on-hand in blind, almost paranoid, encouragement of any and all animal research and testing, the self-serving Research Defence Society offered a £10,000 reward for conviction of the 'Animal rights car bombers.' It was never claimed. The one positive for the police was the arrest of Roger Yates who had been living in North Wales as a fugitive from the Sheffield trial. His mug shot was widely distributed by the media as a suspect at Bristol and within three weeks, he was in custody.

It didn't seem plausible that anyone active at that time or even since—people who customarily prefer using simple devices constructed from household components to cause fires—would have leaped to this new level and begun using high explosives and mercury tilt switches to trigger powerful bombs attached to cars. Of course, it could have been the work of someone new to vivisection with connections and sufficient anger, but it didn't seem likely, especially as they never struck again. It didn't seem plausible either that both car bomb targets got away only lightly injured by such powerful devices. The wider movement hoped it was the work of someone with another agenda, out to discredit and divert attention. These theories were about to be strengthened ten fold first by the police, who eventually admitted that claims of responsibility widely rumoured to have been made by another unknown animal rights group were in fact untrue. By then, though, the damage had been done. Throw enough mud and it starts to stick.

When a fatal fire broke out on a North Sea ferry travelling from Sweden to Harwich in September 1989 killing two and injuring others, police saw an opportunity and grabbed the headlines by announcing that animal rights activists could be responsible! Seventy-nine beagles had suffocated on board a few days before while en route to a lab, so perversely, some mud was thrown at the animal rights movement.

There was another very good reason to suspect it wasn't animal rights activists responsible for the car bombs. One man, claiming to be an activist, was not so much deterred by the bounty on offer but buoyed on by the widespread condemnation of the animal rights movement.

And a few days after the car bombings, 'animal rights bombers' were at it again. This time it was the leader of the British Animal Rights Society who had called police to claim responsibility for a petrol device packed with nails and attached to a huntsman's Land Rover in a Somerset village. The bomb squad were called and sealed off the area to deal with the latest 'animal rights outrage.' But upon further investigation something strange came to light that proved not everything was as it seemed.

A detailed forensic search of the inside of the locked vehicle had uncovered under the seat cushion a nail identical to those packed into the bomb on the outside. This led detectives to conclude that either the BARS bombers had been inside the vehicle and dropped a nail, which was unlikely since it was locked, or the BARS bombers had. Suspects were few and one man had been acting suspiciously. Arrested for questioning, Alan Newbury-Street, a prominent huntsman and director of the British Hunting Exhibition was soon forced to confess he had bombed his own vehicle and admitted to two similar offences. 'I did it to discredit the animal rights and its associations,' he later told the court. The judge told him to go to prison for nine months to think about his actions, allotting him a unique place in the annals of animal liberation history as the only convicted car bomber. And with a little time to ponder the meaning of the oft-used term 'the animal rights' which has no obvious meaning in the context it is so often used by the ignorant.

It's Not Fur

ALF arsonists are cool, ruthless and professional.

Patrick O'Flynn, Birmingham Post

However bad the news stories were about those 'bloody animal rights', there was good news for activists too. Whoever was responsible for making headlines had people talking about animal rights and vivisection again. Vivisectors were said to be feeling some of the fear they inflict and were having to check under their cars every morning. More importantly the bombers had stirred up a debate. And there was a blood sports fanatic in prison for longer than he would ever get for even the worst acts of animal cruelty! And the news for the fur trade continued to deteriorate.

In excess of 30 fur shops closed during 1988/89 in the UK, including the renowned Edelson fur company that went into liquidation following an intense campaign. The Hudson Bay fur company pulled out of the UK stating: 'It has not been possible to maintain a profitable auction activity in London in the present market circumstances.' The industry magazine, The Fur Review, also called it a day not long after they received one damaging ALF visit and a promise of more. And they were making no excuses for the reason why: 'Our decision resulted wholly from our own experiences of the actions of those extremists who planted a fire bomb on our premises before Christmas and have made other threats since.' Unfortunate that it should have come to this, but refreshingly honest.

Despite the large number of hard-core activists off the scene, the fur campaign peaked with an incendiary blitz at the end of 1988. Stores in Liverpool, Manchester and Cardiff; Harrods, Selfridges and the House of Fraser in London; and the offices of Sears, Selfridges' parent company, were targeted. In December, the House of Fraser announced it was to close the fur salons in all its 62 stores before Xmas, nicely timed to pre-empt a threatened assault on its outlets. Soon after, Harrods followed suit and sold off fur stocks after 100 years of trading for what they called commercial and economic reasons, offering once profitable mink coats for a ¼ of their £80,000 price tag. And Oxfam agreed to ban furs from all their 830 shops. Early in the spring of 1990, Selfridges said they had ceased trading in fur and became the last major retailer in the UK to stop selling fur products. They would years later renege and sneak some products back in as would Harrods.

Working alongside the more radical activists who were still leaving their devices around was an equally determined open civil disobedience drive by animal rights activists, causing shops and departments to be occupied by noisy protest groups and doors blockaded much too often to ignore. In and around the City of Manchester we set up rotas to target the posh fur shops there, one or two a time, so there was a constant display of caged, trapped and mutilated animals on show on the street outside from early in the morning until closing time every day of trading. To begin with, the middle-aged shopkeepers were full of fight from inside their cosy shops, appearing almost enthused by our efforts. They reasoned that it was only a matter of time before we got bored or into something else and left them be. After all they'd been in business for many years and it had always been that way. Protesters had been and gone and the fur was still there. It was usually cold too. Middle of winter in Manchester, sometimes alone, dead animals everywhere, bored with hours to go to closing and no sign of For Sale signs going up. Think of anything better to be doing? Categorically not! We'd made a decision and were sticking with it.

The police were becoming less and less friendly as they were called more and more often by desperate shop owners and disgruntled protesters. Same story, different day. It was tedious for all concerned but we weren't going away. There were enough good activists in the area and others prepared to travel to sustain the campaign and drive these obscene displays from our streets. As the weeks went by, the mood gradually changed and we became enthused by this. We were rooted and they knew it. Customers were becoming few and far between, sales even less, with some shop owners offering to take stock to the customer. These businesses were feeling the pressure and attacks on protesters escalated, which is always a good sign. One angry, ageing trader, who held the record for losing his rag, would chase people down the street just to rip up posters and placards then slink back to the shop with his kill like a victorious warrior returning from a hunting trip.

His life seemed to change after we had been given a job lot of parachute material we had made into banners that just wouldn't tear. He spent ages trying to tear one sweating, puffing and panting, spitting and swearing, twisting it this way and that around a lamppost, under foot, even with his teeth! It was funny but quite sad to watch, as it obviously meant so much to him. He left a broken man, humiliated. It was all too much for him to take, and a few weeks after this very public exhibition, the shop went up for sale.

Above: NALL activists breach security and gain access to the notorious hidden 4th floor Trauma Unit of Manchester University Stopford Building where all manner of freakish experiments take place. The fire escape was removed by authorities soon after. Such places are exempt from fire safety regulations. 1983.

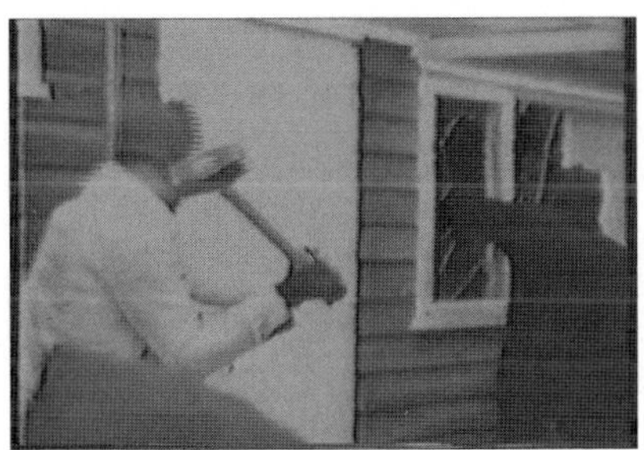

Above left: SEALL raiders film their break in at Wickham Laboratories in October 1984 seeking proof of a pet stealing ring supplying dogs to vivisection.
Above right: EALL raiders storm Unilever. Bedford. 1984.

Fox cub rescued from cage at Cocksparrow Fox Farm in Warwickshire in 1983.

Above: Police line keeping protesters from the fox enclosure at Cocksparrow Farm in Warwickshire. 1985.

Above: CALL raiders wrench open the doors of an Oxford University cat store at Nuneham Courtenay in 1985. Fourteen cats were snatched as alarm bells rang out.

Left: One of the freakish scenes that greeted NALL raiders who stormed the Babraham Agricultural Research Centre in Cambridgeshire in 1981.

Above: Raiders invade vivisection lab in Essex on Valentines Day, 1981.

Above: Huntingdon Life Sciences.

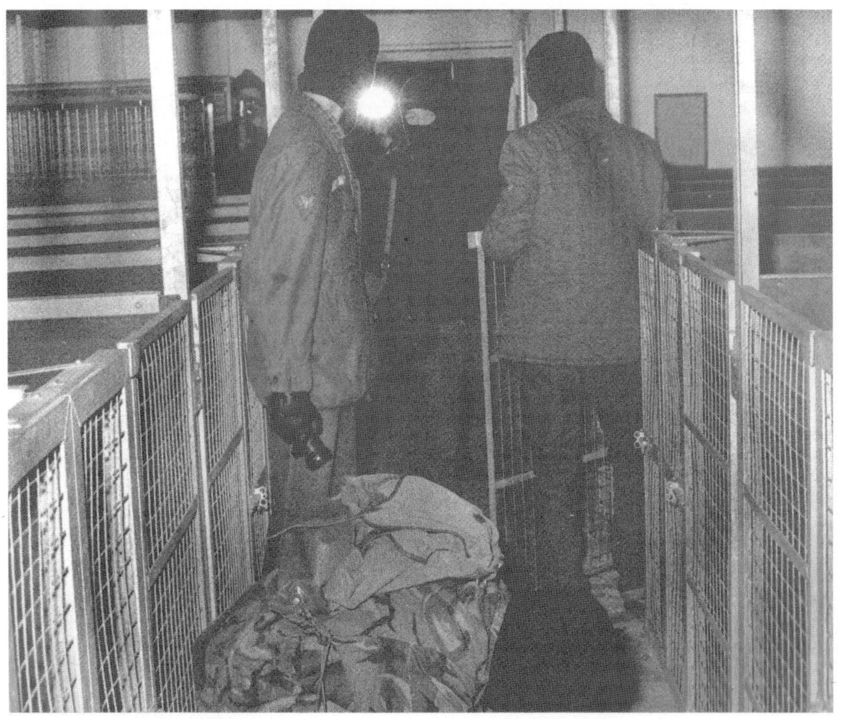

Above: SEALL raiders bagging beagles and collecting evidence. 1985.

Above: Beagle puppies rescued by SEALL raiders. Beagles are a favourite vivisection tool because of their neat size and placid nature.

Above: RSPCA media advert.
Left: ALF raider with rescued Hylyne rabbit.

Above: ALF raider sprays graffiti on the wall of Royal London Hospital animal lab in 1991. Over 100 animals were rescued.

Below left: A group of female protestors are unable to contain their disgust at a worker inside Shamrock Farm in 1987. Behind him hundreds of wild caught monkeys are caged awaiting experimentation. The farm would be forced to close by more radical action years later. (Alec Smart)

Above right: Monkey which has been inoculated with an experimental vaccine. (URSS) Photo drawn from: Annual Pictorial Review of the Scottish Society for the Prevention of Vivisection. (1950's—early 1970's)

Above: Media image of Operation Valentine raid on UK lab. 1982. It seems like a good idea to take the media inside these places but sadly the law protects the exploitation of animals and will punish anyone challenging its propagation as these and other activists would find.

Above: Biosearch laboratories. 1988. What kind of a society does this to such gentle souls? The rabbit's eyes will be injected with chemicals. Not because such behaviour will make products safe but because rabbits have no tear ducts and can't wash them out.

Above: Rescued 'Regal' rabbits. Two of 1,153 intercepted before they were sent to die in vivisection labs in the summer of 2000.

We'd won another little victory and immediately shifted the rota to the next salon. One by one, Jindo Furs, Edelson, Kings, and Glyn & Leinhardt all shut up shop. On top of that, the dwindling industry and fur wearers had to try and ignore the sight of those huge billboard adverts sponsored by Lynx. It was powerful advertising and played no small part in wrecking the image of fur. But Lynx were taken to court in 1990, sued by Swales Moor mink farm in West Yorkshire for trespassing with a national newspaper to film conditions there. A court order imposed to pay the farmer for losses incurred through the exposé bankrupted the anti fur group.

The truth was that twenty-five years earlier, there had been 1000 furriers in England. By the beginning of the 1990s there were only a couple of dozen left. In Holland, sales had reportedly decreased by 90%; in Austria and Germany by 20%. And in Munich a dozen fur shops sold up with the industry blaming militant protest actions and negative film and news reports questioning farming and trapping methods. In Switzerland the fur trade suffered a 75% fall in consumer demand.

According to the Auslands Journal of January 1990, the trade in Greece was on a downward spiral too, thanks to the work of animal activists. And the Chinese authorities dispensed their form of justice for breaking the illegal trade in panda furs by executing five people for handling panda skins. Four others were given suspended sentences. UK government statistics showed that the level of manufacture of fur goods had declined dramatically over the last four years of the 1980s. In 1984, revenue had already fallen to £28 million, a decrease of some 74%.

The fur campaign came alive in 1984 following a devastatingly successful Greenpeace exposé of Canadian seal culling—the heartbreaking sight of cute and utterly defenceless, shiny-black-eyed, snow-white seal pups having their heads caved in by men with long spiked goads, was brought into living rooms across the world and spurred action against the trade in fur products.

The rapid advance of the anti fur campaign revitalised battle-weary activists and, despite the setbacks and the sometimes grim reality of life for participants in the push for happy animals, it gave glaring signals to all involved that there was serious potential for change within reach. Campaigns on all levels of insistence were expanding in initiative and remit all across the animal welfare world. Only a dozen years in for the ALF and the little victories were piling up, something unimaginable only a few years before. And it was showing on the all-important bank statements of all concerned. The police were becoming increasingly involved in animal rights issues and were having to divert excessive resources. Then there were the animal abusers and their many grumbles and bills. There were others with bills to pay, so far not included, who had never even considered that they were of interest to the animal liberators.

Portakabin, for one, were supplying the portable cabins (not surprisingly) used by Glaxo to build on their big research/vivisection site in Hertfordshire and consequently had £50,000 worth of damage done to their property. This was a bit of a surprise for Portakabin. Also for the manager at PBS Cabins, a thus far nondescript no-one-special in the prefab building business who found himself with an incendiary device on his car and the bomb squad in his garden. And the machinery hire company targeted, according to a disgruntled man on the inside, 'Just for hiring a few machines!' Not everyone sees it quite as innocently as that any more and as we will see, no matter how tenuous the assistance given to those who are labelled animal abusers, someone may have an eye on them.

Into The Blue

> Under the pretext of wishing to communicate with dolphins, Dr. John Lilly—who first perfected the technique of implanting electrodes in the brains of unanaesthetised animals to 'stimulate pain and pleasure sectors'—made holes in the skull with a sharp instrument and a carpenters hammer. According to Professor Giorgio Pilleri: 'The dolphin was held down but tried to jump at every blow—not because of the pain but because of the unbearable noise produced by the hammering.' After suffering drug addiction and a mental breakdown Lilly saw the light some years later: 'I was running a concentration camp for my friends', he said.
>
> *From The Rose Tinted Menagerie by William Johnson*

Ever tried to steal a dolphin? Ever thought about it? Anyone who had been inside the concrete compound of Morecambe's Marineland with an open mind about this so-called 'attraction' would have probably considered it. Or is it just the company I keep—people who first think about rescuing an animal in need and then the consequences for themselves? This is a good habit for people to have if you are an animal in need. The performances staged inside those bare concrete walls were a really bad habit, neither fun nor educational. Morecambe is the only such place I'd ever seen, and I knew I'd hate it before I looked, but it was still grim beyond belief once I had. The reality was as follows: there was a dolphin swimming round in an oblong tank of water where he'd been incarcerated for years and just the other side of a wall sloshed the vast expanse of the ocean. If left in the hands of the amusement park owners, it would remain like that forever. Which left theft. Or, to use the more appropriate term when some one removes an animal from cruel captivity, rescue. To rescue a dolphin! Carry him out without anyone noticing? Hmm!

An audacious plan had begun to ferment in active minds. Some might call it stupid or criminal but what would the dolphin think? One man on the inside felt they had no option but to act.

> We decided we had to try something after seeing how bad it was and began to make regular visits to the dolphinarium. Over time we swam with Rocky and became close to him. This was a good idea! He had spent most of his life alone in this tank—even the

sea lions that he shared the open-air compound with were segregated away from him. Rocky's only involvement with humans was when he had to do stupid degrading tricks, for an even more degraded audience, for a reward of a few dead fish! He loved us! He suffered from chemical burns due to the additives in the water and his dorsal fin was deformed and bent due to incessant circling in the tiny pool. Rocky had killed other dolphins that had been introduced into the pool with him over the years—a classic sign of psychotic neurosis brought about by his confinement. His trainer classed him as a dangerous animal but when we swam with him he was as gentle as a baby.

On the day we decided to do a final feasibility trial of the equipment (catching net and stretcher) and then the five of us made our way in a hire car to Morecambe arriving about 5pm. We then killed time until midnight. At midnight, we parked the car in a nearby hotel car park and took what we needed to the dolphinarium. Mel climbed over the rear wall and let three of us in—once over the perimeter wall it was a simple matter of unbolting the door, which was just as well as we didn't want to leave any sign that we had been there because we were coming back. We left a lookout on outside.

After about half an hour we came to the conclusion that despite all our plans and equipment the logistics of moving this 650 lb dolphin just 200 yards (to the open sea beyond the wall) still had us beat—it was back to the drawing board. Tidying up behind us, we locked up and left. We made our way back to the car but before we had time to think there might be a problem there was the problem of a police car cruising into view. Someone had seen something suspicious from a hotel window and the police were on the prowl.

This was really bad timing. We were loaded up with gear and had nowhere to run. We all ran but they had four of us in custody before it was light. One escaped. We were all interviewed on the charge of attempting to steal a dolphin and we exercised our right to remain silent. The four of us were questioned said nothing and were charged with conspiracy to steal a £25,000 dolphin and released on bail early the following morning.

> When we were allowed back to the car we found the fingerprint boys had dusted everything—rugs, the headliner, the boot, all the upholstery, even the engine bay. It took three days to clean up the mess. The funny thing was that the wallet on the back shelf, well dusted but unopened was full of the personal details of the missing man. No one had thought to look inside! It made it all not so bad for a while. But the rest of us didn't stand a chance. Besides the presence of this large net and dolphin stretcher dominating the courtroom for which we had no legitimate explanation and the judge refusing to allow an expert witness to testify to the suffering caused to captive dolphins, thus killing off that defence, the police were lying!

After a five-day trial at Lancaster Crown Court, Northampton men Jim O'Donnell, Barry Horne, Mel Broughton and Jim Buckner were found guilty of conspiracy and fined £500 with £250 costs. Barry Horne and Mel Broughton were given an additional suspended prison sentence.

Rocky meanwhile, oblivious to all the fuss, had started his 20th year in captivity. But the trial had created a lot of publicity and started people asking questions, like why was there a lone wild dolphin trapped in a tiny pool out on a bleak Lancashire pier? Pressurised to break the silence, the business owners argued there was no way Rocky could be released back into the wild as he wouldn't survive without their expert care. This is a regular mantra of those who vivisect animals and those who use dogs to hunt, and it gives a faint whiff of concern for the welfare of animals. It's self-delusion and not backed up by facts. I have had the pleasure of meeting many well-adjusted fugitives living happy lives, bringing me to the conclusion that either these people know nothing of the animals in their custody or they are liars. There is strong evidence to suggest both.

Rocky was born in the wild but captured as a youngster and forced to spend the next 20 years of his life in a fish tank doing tricks. Another dolphin, a female they named Lady, had been shipped from Whipsnade Zoo to perform tricks alongside Rocky. But she was ill when transferred and later became pregnant to the delight of her keepers. Lady was still performing in September 1989 when she haemorrhaged and died in her tank. Rocky, not the luckiest dolphin in the world, was alone again.

But it was no big deal for her captors—they'd seen off 14 of them since they opened in 1965 and there are plenty more fish in the sea, for the moment. There was just too much sadness surrounding this place and the Morecambe Dolphinarium Campaign (MDC) was launched with the specific intention of bringing the business to an end.

Intensive pickets of the site begun during the day, sometimes lasting right on through the night, keeping the pressure on management and discouraging show-goers from paying towards Rocky's continued confinement with their entrance fee.

So successful was the constant presence that up to half the day's ticket sales were being lost after a few weeks of this, sometimes with so many people turning away that shows would be cancelled. These were big victories and signalled the end of a thriving business. It was comparatively easy to motivate a boycott because of the other available entertainment within walking distance of this sad attraction. It wasn't as though families had travelled miles just to see this performance—a common argument put to demonstrators outside some zoos and circuses—there was always the rest of Morecambe to explore, so the kids wouldn't be bored if they gave this place a miss. It helped that there was a long walk for families to make towards the picket line down the pier. Plenty of time to contemplate and turn around before confrontation. For those desperate to see dolphins there were wild ones swimming just off the pier! Any pleasure gained from these pathetic shows performed against a colour mural of the natural world beyond mocks not just the wretched creature but also those enjoying it. Word was out that this campaign was gaining momentum and publicity was growing.

Seven hundred protesters joined a national rally and marched through Morecambe. Amongst others, those responsible for health and safety, the Environmental Services Committee and the local council were all lobbied over something or other. The latter voted to remove all Marineland publicity from council literature and landed a severe blow on the business. This was an entirely legitimate but very effective form of economic sabotage. The campaign was broad based and at times drifted from the subject, the dolphin, and concentrated on other seemingly irrelevant issues like whether Marineland were complying with fire regulations or whether the tyres on their vehicles were legal. But this was pressure and was slowly wearing them down.

Unable to see an end to month after month of such a constant and fluid campaign, Rocky's captors came to the inevitable conclusion that there was no longer good money to be made from displaying this once prized exhibit of theirs. The day after the council made its decision to dump Marineland, management announced that Rocky would be surplus to requirements at the end of the season and they wanted to talk about it! This was stunning news and negotiations began immediately with campaigners. Months of dedication and hard work by volunteers across Northwest England and elsewhere had paid off, but when it came to the crunch the one thing no one had was the £120,000 needed to rehabilitate him. It had to be done though: we had started something and had to see it through before someone fat and greedy got in there first with a business proposition. Beware, beware there is one lurking near beautiful creatures everywhere. It was going to cost a lot for the rehab programme, but money is the one thing the movement lacks so MDC enlisted the help of Zoo Check and a national Sunday newspaper and, sponsored by the Born Free Foundation, the 'Into The Blue' project was announced and the money poured in.

Contrary to self-appointed 'expert' advice that it would not be possible for a long term captive dolphin to be released back into the wild, it actually took this one—who it should be remembered was a baby when captured and had been in captivity for 20 long years—no time at all to readapt to life in the sea and he was soon seen chasing live fish. The first stop was an enclosed 80-acre lagoon reserve of crystal clear Caribbean water in the Turks and Caicos Islands from which the Indian Ocean beckons and whose call he soon answered. Within days, Rocky was seen swimming with a pod of wild dolphins. It was an amazing conclusion to a tragic story and a momentous achievement for human beings with a lot of damage to undo.

Two other captives held at a Brighton dolphinarium were soon to follow suit for the same reasons and via the same route after an intense campaign by activists at the Sea Life Centre opposite the popular resort's pier. Missy was caught near the Mississippi Delta in 1969 when she was a baby, and Silver, a juvenile male, was captured off Taiwan in 1978. Their liberation is a poignant symbol of the genuine strength and compassion of human beings. Or to put it another way, as one man adversely affected by the Marineland campaign did: 'All because of a bunch of layabouts.'

This left just one dolphin show in the UK. What hope for Flamingoland in North Yorkshire? Those involved in organising the Morecambe campaign set to the task of modernising Flamingoland and securing the release of its three captives: Lotty, Betty and Sharky. But those in charge up there weren't willing to give up without the more traditional fight and soon started throwing punches. The forecourt entrance often turned into a battleground, with workers in overalls gathering for a confrontation with protesters. One prominent activist in particular was singled out for a more imaginative campaign of harassment as some of those with a lot to lose here concocted their curious story.

Alan Cooper would be immediately recognised by those who know him in the animal protection arena for his punishing fitness regime, ample blond mop and tireless efforts, particularly in marine life rescue. One or the other got up the nose of someone, who told the police he had witnessed Cooper sexually abusing a wild dolphin! Incredibly, the police rushed to arrest the alleged assailant at home in Manchester and hauled him off for questioning. More incredible still, the Crown Prosecution Service decided to press charges. That it was the very people in the captive dolphin trade who were on the receiving end of the activities of Cooper & Co. that were making the allegations against him made them all the more unbelievable.

The story was fantastic, and so were the police for their response to call regarding an animal in danger. Seldom had they responded in such a way! Incredible still that the case went all the way to trial a year later before the charges were finally dismissed. It was incidental by then though because the damage had been done, not least to the health of Coopers' elderly parents. Some of the mud has stuck and has become a standing joke in the nation's psyche with the accusation more memorable than the truth of 'The Man That Had Sex With A Dolphin.' Being the solid block of resistance Alan Cooper is, he weathered the storm and saw through the campaign until the capitulation of the dolphin traders two years later at the end of 1991, bringing to a close a sordid chapter in this nation's history. Here the moneymen got their way as our three dolphins were sold to a similar compound in Sweden where efforts continue to secure their release.

In the 1970s there were 30 dolphin shows in the UK. Today there are none. For all the deliberate and incidental cruelty, the deaths in capture and captivity and the long-term suffering can there be any doubt that the most valuable thing we've learnt from these shows is how cruel they are?

Into the 1990's

If there be one moral offence which more than another seems directly an offence against God, it is this wanton infliction of pain upon his creatures. He, the Good One, has made them to be happy, but leaves us our awful gift of freedom to use or to misuse towards them. In a word, He places them absolutely in our charge. If we break this trust, and torture them, what is our posture towards Him? Surely as sins of the flesh sink man below humanity, so sins of cruelty throw him into the very converse and antagonism of Deity; he becomes not a mere brute, but a fiend.

Frances Power Cobbe, Rights of Man, Claims of Brute, 1863

Gore 'em Orem

Perhaps predictably, American vivisectors have exceeded all others in their extremes, and in turn, the raiders of the ALF have grabbed the big opportunities. Professor John Orem, in his 15th year of depriving cats of sleep, would connect sleep-deprived cats to a recording device by bolting their heads into a steel clamp and putting metal rods into their ears and mouths so they couldn't move their heads. This is a stereotaxic device, manufactured by some unscrupulous company inside the despised vivisection industry and sold on the open market. Bilaney Consultants Ltd in Kent do the Model 1404 Stereotaxic instrument and offer it as, 'A general purpose, heavy-duty research instrument. Its superior rigidity, large frame bars and precision bearing surfaces assure absolute alignment of laboratory animals for indefinite periods of time. By changing adapters, this modular unit can be used for a wide variety of animals from small primates to cats down to and including mice, with the same ease and precision.'

The bones were exposed around Orem's cats' eyes, and holes were cut into their windpipes. The cats were punished if they failed to learn to hold their breath whenever a tone sounded. The punishment came from a blast of ammonium hydroxide, which made them extremely uncomfortable and burned their eyes. 'Gore-em Orem' had literally carved his career around the brains of live cats. Sleep deprivation was his speciality, and he is credited with devising innumerable ways to keep cats awake, like his ingenious 'flowerpot method', in which he placed cats on a tiny wooden plank inside a water filled drum and where falling asleep meant plummeting into the water. Other ingenious forms of torture he'd concocted included lowering the temperature in their room to below freezing or forcing them to keep running for hours on end on a treadmill that didn't stop. Essential medical research they call it.

Orem's psychology laboratory was housed inside the Texas Tech University Health Services Centre where endless suffering was inflicted on many cats over many years. But on 5 July, Orem met his match when a small team of objectors broke into the lab and took five cats to safety, sabotaging $70,000 worth of electronic equipment and restraining devices before they left. The brains of dozens of other cats were removed from the lab and taken to a final resting place in a field of Texas wildflowers. Only some of these cats had been given names by their killers: Fluffy, Alfalfa, Lady, Pepe. Others were just numbers. One of the rescued cats—Chester to his rescuers—was a three-legged tomcat who had reportedly lost his fourth leg in a laboratory 'accident.' He had a pit in his head where the electrodes had been screwed, and he was on Phenobarbital to control his seizures. Another, a stumpy little orange tiger cat, had stunted legs that the vet couldn't explain. This was to become another national scandal.

Working with the ALF, professional US based shit-stirrers People for The Ethical Treatment of Animals (PETA) and Dr. Kenneth Stoller, a Californian paediatrician whose decision to speak out against the cruelty and waste of resources regularly added fuel to the fire, called a press conference in order to counter claims by the pro-vivisection National Association of Biomedical Research that Orem's experiments had 'the potential to save babies lives.' Overnight, 15 years of go-nowhere sleep deprivation experiments in cats suddenly became Sudden Infant Death Syndrome 'research' to help human babies and, for anyone concerned about these experiments, a chilling choice between a few purpose-bred lab cats and your baby.

'Dr. John Orem has yet to produce a practical application' (for his work) Stoller told reporters. 'I have reviewed his published papers, and whatever he says he has been researching, it certainly is not SIDS. He has been playing with millions of taxpayers' dollars over his career. Now he is playing with the emotions of SIDS families.'

Other physicians and veterinarians who had seen Orem's papers joined Dr. Stoller in his condemnation. Dr. Suzanne Cliver denounced the experimenter's project as 'among the most ghastly' she had ever read. 'I could find no justification whatsoever for carrying out this horrifying work. The gross insensitivity to the animals used is a profound embarrassment to the scientific community.'

Dr. William Wittert wrote: 'The research done by John Orem does not have any relationship to humans' Sudden Infant Death Syndrome. The studies are extraordinarily cruel and the cats are certainly subjected to extraordinary suffering.' It was a painfully familiar story of cruelty, lies and deception.

Them & Us...

> To base opposition to vivisection mainly on ethical grounds, as some societies and speakers are accustomed to do, is on the one hand to neglect the strongest and most vital argument at our command—on the other to postpone all prospects of success for at least 500 years to come.
>
> *The Animal Guardian, London & Provincial Anti Vivisection Society, 1919*

This was a damning exposé, and anyone wanting to end vivisection would want a slice of the cake to air some views. In the UK, the British Union for the Abolition of Vivisection (BUAV) had for many years led the way in publicising such exposés and had generated a great deal of coverage in doing so—something, which the ALF alone wasn't always best equipped to do. Likewise, PETA—the largest animal protection group in the world—have more recently taken up the mantle mainly in the US and have been unafraid to support the efforts of the ALF and utilise to full effect material recovered by its raiders. Other 'respectable' national groups have preferred to side with those in the media, government and industry who use the moment to condemn law breaking and take the focus from the mind numbing revelations exposed to something far less important. All these groups and individuals working together to expose the horrors outlined here give one good example of how to achieve the aims of our movement.

As a consequence of these diverse groupings working in unison against the common enemy, some excellent results have been achieved in creating awareness and exposing the facts, and it's not done PETA, the ALF or, especially the animals, any harm. From an anti-vivisection perspective this makes perfectly good sense; indeed it's the only thing that makes sense. An anti-vivisectionist siding with a vivisector to condemn anti-vivisectionists for their efforts would be absurd!

When Band of Mercy 'thugs' broke in to a federal research facility in Maryland USA, taking with them 37 cats and seven piglets, vivisectors sought to divert attention from their activities by suggesting the cats' health—compromised terribly by the same individuals—posed a threat to the rescuers and to wider society. They sought to publicly shame PETA for their uncompromising stance in support of the rescuers, but PETA's National Director wasn't having any of it: 'PETA will continue to speak on behalf of animals in laboratories through information received from any source, legal or not. Condemn us if you wish. But I believe our great-grandchildren will never shake their heads and say: 'Who were those awful people who broke into the lab?' but rather say: 'Did people really do that to animals?' and 'what did you do to stop it?''

In the UK during the early 1980s, the BUAV was widely admired for leadership shown in the fight against vivisection and stood proudly alongside lab raiders when the labs were breached, but with a change of people controlling the organisation, attitudes were watered down.

During this cooperative era in the UK, the ALF fitted in well alongside the largest and most dynamic anti-vivisection organisation, the BUAV. Founded in 1898 by Frances Power Cobbe, a Victorian journalist who also fought for the rights of women and children, it was set to lead a worldwide movement that was to focus our attention not solely on the cruelty of vivisection but also on the grave damage being caused to human health. With the death of the no-compromise abolitionist president Dr. Walter Hadwen, a strong early opponent of compulsory child vaccination, the BUAV was dragged into a mire from which it never emerged. During the 1960s and early 1970s, people with less radical ideas took control and softened the approach, calling for bigger cages and less experiments as opposed to an end to it all. In the late 1970s, they themselves were ousted when a new fearless generation of activists took control. The membership increased ten-fold and the end of vivisection began to seem a realistic and achievable goal. A generation of activists was educated and funded by the radical BUAV, and the potential for change was easy to see. It didn't last long though, and by the mid 1980s, 'modernisers' (or infiltrators) had begun to work themselves back into control and soften the stance, effectively pacifying the resistance.

In an extraordinary about-turn under the new 'management', the staff at the BUAV, the one-time spearhead of the movement, suddenly began talking not about ridding the world of vivisection, but of pitting their resources against a few cosmetic experiments. They sent out the message that the world's biggest anti-vivisection organisation was opposed to cosmetic tests on the grounds that they were unnecessary. Everything else under the category of so-called medical research was effectively given a seal of approval. The implied, if not stated, subtext was that until alternatives to animals could be found, vivisection in medical research was a necessary evil. The notion was, of course, widely challenged, but the victorious BUAV leadership had already started putting their plans into action, starting by 'challenging the use of animals in warfare experiments and ultimately, medical research.' In a few short years, the possibility that the BUAV would lead a radicalised movement to victory, and bring down the fraudulent institution of vivisection had turned into a false hope in the form of a pink campaign to Choose Cruelty Free Cosmetics. This was turning the clock back. Banning cosmetic testing and changing the profile of the BUAV became a priority over the banning of vivisection. Such was the lack of commitment to achieving the BUAV's founding aim, that a seemingly drastic proposal put forward by the BUAV Committee to call for an annual reduction of animal experiments by 10% was fully supported by the careerists at the helm of this once radical organisation. This commitment on the face of it sounded laudable, but a simple calculation reveals that this meant lab animals would continue to be vivisected on for well over 100 years to come! They must surely have realised this? This was a damaging message to come from an anti-vivisections organisation both for animal advocates and those opposed to vivisection on purely scientific grounds, since it implied that medical research on animals would be tolerated for the foreseeable future and was of some benefit to humans.

Some thought the BUAV had simply been taken over by naïve but apparently enthusiastic, well-meaning campaigners who didn't want to be publicly associated with ALF activists, who had become the media's pet-hate as perpetrators of 'extremist violence.' Others were of the opinion that the BUAV had been infiltrated by drug company agents who wanted to soften it up to suit their agenda of passive opposition to vivisection. The ALFsg had been allowed room alongside the BUAV in its expensive London offices until things started to change in 1984, when the ALF was ousted and the locks were changed. This was guaranteed to please the enemy and give the BUAV some semblance of credibility in media and political circles, where few were moved to campaign to end vivisection. The BUAV's 'assimilation' into society as the 'acceptable' face of anti-vivisection protest certainly made no advances for the cause if we look back on those twenty-odd years. Indeed, the cosmetic experiments, which they were so confident of banning, continue to this day, as do all the other experiments they chose to ignore.

To further garner the approval of the media and by default place vivisection as a secondary issue, BUAV media reps—rather than exposing the scientific invalidity of vivisection when contacted for comment about this or that issue raising incident of direct action—

instead began to join the attacks against the issue raisers! It didn't even need to be related to vivisection, anything unlawful in the name of animal rights could get the BUAV's speakers condemning the activists. The BUAV had become a cruel joke reviled by true anti-vivisectionists and courted by the mainstream media.

The Liberator, BUAV's once radical newspaper, changed its format and its audience, and stopped reporting on ALF raids and other forms of direct action. 'Against All Animal Experiments'—the banner under which the BUAV had grown into the formidable force it became—was supplanted with a new campaigning strategy to 'End Animal Experiments', thus subtly changing and compromising the organisation's abolitionist stance on which it had been founded nearly 100 years earlier. Under their new remit, cosmetic testing (accounting for a few thousand experiments out of the official 3.5 million total annual figure) suddenly became the BUAV's big noise—a PR exercise that made no waves where it mattered, and diluted the vital message of total abolition, which the organisation had formerly been dedicated to achieving. To compound the effects of this shift in position, the BUAV called for a ban on the use of wild-caught primates in favour of those born in cages; once again, it sent out completely the wrong message and further would achieve nothing for monkeys in cages or the advancement of humane medical research. The early campaigners would have turned in their graves. It was the end of the BUAV in the eyes of true anti-vivisectionists and a step backwards for animals in laboratories.

As part of the shake up, BUAV regional contacts' training weekends were axed because contacts were asking too many awkward questions of organisers. Anyone not towing the new party line was weeded out and others resigned. Those now at the top of the BUAV wanted total control. I was one of the former and was treated like a dirty disposable tissue for questioning the amount being wasted on unnecessary expenses during training weekends, which we attended in posh London hotels. I was finally removed from the list of contacts for speaking my mind about the way the BUAV was heading. This had been the first organisation to educate and inspire me with its hard-hitting, no-compromise approach to ending the violent abuse of live animals, and in its heyday it had generated widespread support. There was never a second thought about using documents recovered on illegal forays into laboratories where the likes of the BUAV—or indeed any other body—seldom ventured. The activists did the work, took the risks and sorted the animals out with homes; the useful paperwork was copied and passed to the BUAV to go public. The issue of animal experimentation became such a hot potato because of the material that the ALF and others uncovered and the BUAV publicised. It was a partnership that worked.

The relationship between the unwaged activists of the ALF and the Leagues, and those endlessly vilified for taking home a large pay packet for campaigning against animal experiments, deteriorated gradually after the morning on which the ALFsg was locked out and banished without notice from the BUAV offices. The radical wing of the movement had made the BUAV what it was. Now the media love affair was over, the BUAV had turned nasty and started to publicly accuse its old ally of terrorism and of setting back the movement ten years with each raid it carried out. While the ALFsg found new offices and re-established itself, the BUAV continued its downward spiral in the eyes of the activists, pouring its wealth of animal lovers' money into a doomed political campaign and a cosmetic test ban that never happened.

One hundred years of political campaigning proved utterly worthless when the long-awaited update in legal protection for animals in laboratories through the 1986 Animals (Scientific Procedures) Bill really did set the clock back and made the situation worse. This was described by the BUAV at the time as a Vivisectors' Charter, and so it would prove to be.

When the Bill was steamrollered through Parliament and passed as law by a large Conservative majority, it was backed by Neil Kinnock and his Labour Party. It was the first new law for research animals since the 1876 Cruelty to Animals Act, but it was obvious to anyone who viewed it with even only a passing interest that nothing would change for the better. Not one form of experimentation was outlawed—not cosmetic experiments, not warfare experiments, not even the testing of cleaning products! Instead, those inflicting animal suffering would be licensed and the experiments categorised into mild, moderate or severe projects or procedures, as defined by people with no concept of animal suffering, nor the desire to end it. With few 'projects' defined as severe, vivisection wouldn't perhaps sound so bad, but people can still burn, poison, starve, scald, maim, drown, electrocute, blind, beat and drive captive animals insane in the name of research and testing. Since the 1986 Act, they are permitted to do it to an individual animal repeatedly, whereas previously they could be experimented on only once ('moderate' suffering as described in one application involved a group of marmosets having part of their brain sucked out during surgery and toxins added and then being kept alive in obvious pain and distress and forced to do tasks).

The first damning exposé of this new law was carried out by Mike Huskisson and Melody Macdonald of the Animal Cruelty Investigation Group, who infiltrated the National Institute for Medical Research at Mill Hill in London from December 1989 to April 1990. They captured on film the shoddy experiments, which 89-year old veteran vivisector Professor Wilhelm Feldberg and his assistant, animal technician John Stern were conducting. In the 1950s, Feldberg had been happily injecting morphine directly into the brains of conscious cats. The 1986 Animals (Scientific Procedures) Act was put in place ostensibly to offer some kind of protection to animals in laboratories. The ACIG's footage showed as clear as day what we all knew, that the Act is a sham, and that for those into animal research, anything goes.

During one experiment you can watch a rabbit begin to show signs of early recovery from the anaesthetic that it was fortunate enough to have been administered before the experiment began. It is one of the investigators who has to point out that more anaesthetic might be nice to calm the animal. The vivisector continues to fumble around and display for the world his inability to comprehend anything that is happening in front of, or anywhere else, around him. When he does finally try to give the rabbit another injection, more minded to keep it from squirming than to take away its pain, he can't locate a suitable vein and needs help. Animals are either given so much anaesthetic that it kills them or so little they regain consciousness during the experiments.

The film shows Feldberg—preparing to induce high blood sugar levels (hypoglycaemia) in the animals—position a table lamp 1mm from their little crucified bodies to heat the inside of their abdomens where over a period of 20 minutes, the temperature inside reaches 130°C. Water boils at 100°C. If that isn't obscene enough, so flawed was this research programme that they weren't even using the right anaesthetic on the rabbits they were vivisecting. And lest we forget, such procedures are controlled by 'the most stringent regulations in the world'—at least that's what the Home Office continually claims… But what do these comforting words actually mean in reality?

Such was the embarrassment caused to those in like circles by the incompetence and indifference uncovered in this prize research institute, that the day after the Edinburgh-based group Advocates for Animals showed the Home Office 40 hours of footage, the research was called to a halt and Feldberg's licence revoked. It was the first time this had ever happened and Feldberg was incredulous. He said he couldn't believe what his friends had done to him, but that he didn't care anyway, because he intended to continue his experiments regardless.

Advocates for Animals had supported the 1986 Act, but said they felt 'terribly let down' by it. They could see for themselves that laws and inspectors controlled nothing; it was plain that researchers are a law unto themselves, without any interest in animal welfare. If Advocates for Animals felt let down by the Act, several million animals have without question felt a whole lot worse.

ACIG investigators had tried to interest London-based anti-vivisection organisations to use the footage recovered (in London) but none of them wanted it, so it ended up in Scotland from where it was returned to the Home Office (in London). The official anti-vivisection movement was in crisis.

In an effort to revivify the mainstream movement, radicals made several attempts over the years to put the BUAV back in the hands of the activists. These attempted coups tended to reach boiling point at Annual General Meetings and were unsuccessful. Such was the rot after the 1980s demise that committee documents leaked in 1992 revealed a strategy to eliminate the BUAV's membership structure (down from around 20,000 in 1987 when the CCF campaign was launched to under 5,000 in 1998) to apparently eliminate the threat such a system presented to the leadership; to introduce a proxy/postal voting system without the consent of the membership, breaking the constitution; drop medical campaigns and seize control of the National Anti-vivisection Society (NAVS). A further indicator for those missing what was happening to this organisation came when it transpired that the people responsible for these changes were rewarding themselves with bigger pay packets. Other documents revealed that in 1992, £85,000 had been spent on refurbishing new offices, while grass roots activists struggled to raise cash for campaigns and to print leaflets and banners.

Steve McIvor and Peter Knowles' salaries rose by £5,000 to £25,000 while Director Chris Fisher's rose from under £19,000 to over £30,000 in 18 months, plus a new company car every three years. His pension plan being considered by the Committee made it look far more appealing to him if vivisection were allowed to continue until at least retirement age; he was 32 at the time. And it went on and on and on, fuelling the suspicion amongst the poorly funded, risk-taking activists on the front line that the BUAV was being run by careerists with no interest in the abolition of vivisection.

The ALF has few friends in the higher ranks of the RSPCA either, but then, nor do the animals. In the mid-1980s, during a period of high profile fur farm raids, in which many animals were liberated, the RSPCA placed adverts in national newspapers. Showing a staged, sinister-looking image of a balaclava'd individual cutting a fur farm fence with a pair of bolt cutters, the ad shamelessly appealed to the public for more money beneath a headline, which read:

> Our Supporters Prefer To Use A Pair Of Scissors: Cutting the coupon and sending a donation achieves far more in the end than cutting wire fences.

The many millions of pounds, which the RSPCA has persuaded people to give to the charity appears to have achieved little in the war against the fur trade or anything else, for that matter. Indeed, so twisted is the thinking among the RSPCA ruling ranks, that in 1992, it put its seal of approval to the distribution of its Freedom Food range of animal organs and flesh through supermarkets and butchers shops. The Royal Society for the Prevention of Cruelty to Animals is selling the bodies of cruelly slaughtered, factory-farmed animals reared in secret locations under what they term 'strict welfare criteria.' In reality, these criteria are indistinguishable from those already causing millions of animals to suffer horribly in factory farms and slaughterhouses everywhere. I've been inside some of their approved farms and they are nothing short of disgusting. So fearful of exposure are the RSPCA that their approved farms are kept a closely guarded secret.

Further, according to records revealed in the May 1985 issue of *Time Out* magazine, the RSPCA had money in excess of £8,000,000 invested in such companies as ICI, Beechams (now GlaxoSmithKline) BP, Fisons, Glaxo, Unilever and Boots—all of them relentless users of animals in laboratory tests. And the double standards did not end there, for equally shocking was the fact that there were pro-vivisection Research Defence Society members on the RSPCA National Council and its Animal Experimentation Advisory Committee! (There is more to come from the RSPCA within these pages, and sadly, little of it is constructive: it's a big, potentially powerful organisation with little to show for a lot of advertising and expenditure except 150 years' worth of fine words and a thriving meat business).

Lining up to join the list of nationals preparing to wage war against fellow animal advocates was Animal Aid's one-time Director, Mark Gold, who placed himself in the front line of this internal battle and could always be relied upon to say something unconstructive about animal liberators. Unhelpfully, Animal Aid distributed lengthy defensive reaction to local branches following the 1989 car bombings and the mood was depressing:

> If we are to continue to build on our successes then (we) must exclude from our groups those individuals whose views on campaigning are fundamentally at odds with ours.

It goes on:

> We believe that the ALF as an organisation has behaved irresponsibly by allowing advocates of premeditated violence to operate within its ranks; by publishing articles advocating violence; and through its constant refusal to issue an outright condemnation of campaigns of violence. We therefore urge our supporters not to donate funds to the ALF or the ALFsg as we can have no confidence that these funds will not be used to finance terrorist actions.

Of the ALF fur campaign:

> The ALF campaign was off target, it represented a serious risk to life, and it led to a drop in the effective activity of broad-based opposition to the fur trade. Indeed, if it was not for the tremendous success of LYNX, the ALF fire-bombing campaign would have resulted in the virtual collapse of the public education campaigning against the fur trade.

And that:

> The most effective action against factory farming is not the organising of a liberation raid to rescue a few hens, nor even the filming of the condition inside a pig unit (though we stress we have never condemned such actions), but the regular organising of vegetarian evenings.

The documents then go to great lengths to encourage local groups to sever all links with anyone who supports the ALF, regardless of the consequences:

> We urge every local group to pass the model resolution. If this means your local group will split over the question, that is regrettable but nonetheless necessary.

Split your group! There was even acknowledgement that Animal Aid would likely lose support because of the resolution! So obsessed were they with trying to isolate the liberators, AA management resorted to veiled threats against their own people:

> We also hope that your group will pass a resolution based on the one passed by Animal Aid council as that would make it easier for us to work with you.

This went on and on. A lot of work was put into drafting the document, which was clearly intended to create bad feeling and cause division amongst fellow campaigners. It did actually encourage just that and regardless of the fact that all local campaigning groups are absolutely essential in the struggle for animal rights and are constantly in need of more activists, it stressed the plan was:

> To starve the terrorist tendency of its lifeblood, financial and moral support.

Not only did the ALF have nothing to do with car bombs, but also it has always maintained a strict policy of non-violence, just like Animal Aid, and has never, ever, targeted people. In actual fact, in all the years of ALF activity and the tens of thousands of actions, the number of people physically harmed can be counted quite easily on one hand. I'm certain that if there's any such violence I fail to mention in this book someone will be sure to point it out and I will have no shame in confirming it.

The cost of making a bomb or incendiary device is minimal; anyone could do it. A cigarette is an incendiary device! It's the rescuing of animals that gets expensive and to starve the ALF of funding would seriously affect what it is best known for and best at. The 16-page document mentioned the words 'violence' or 'violent' on no less than 60 occasions, 'terror' or 'terrorist' 16 times, and of course, like in so many of the gutter press diatribes, the IRA are brought into it as some kind of comparison.

This project was unnecessarily damaging and time consuming and had very little to do with campaigning for the rights of animals, an approach a number of welfare organisations have slipped into.

...And Infiltrating The Other

> It is forbidden, according to the law of the Torah, to inflict pain upon any living creature. On the contrary, it is our duty to relieve the pain of any creature, even if it is ownerless or belongs to a non-Jew.
>
> *The Code of Jewish Law (Sephardic compilation of Jewish law) c. 1560*

To be fair to the work of the national groups, it isn't all negative. By the end of the 1990s, Animal Aid were no longer preoccupied with attacking other animal advocates. More enlightened managers took over the reigns and focused on the animal issues though there is still a fear associated with over stepping the line and acknowledging the achievements of the ALF. Without question, some of the money reservoirs we know as 'the nationals' have done some excellent work with some of those resources in recent years, mostly through infiltration.

The BUAV set up Sarah Kite's infiltration of the notorious Huntingdon Research Centre in 1989 and gave the world the first firsthand account of the horrors therein; they infiltrated Denisu Supplies, a business dealing ex-racing greyhounds for vivisection and forced them to close; funded Adam Spare's infiltration of the Royal London Hospital in 1990/91; Terry Hill at Shamrock Farms in 1991/92; exposed Wickham labs in Hampshire in 1993; and placed an infiltrator inside Harlan UK laboratories in Leicestershire in 1998/99 and more recently a number of foreign labs. The National Anti-Vivisection Society (NAVS) paid for Louise Wall's infiltration of St. Bartholemew's Hospital Medical School and the SmithKline Beecham toxicology unit at their labs at Stock in Essex in 1990, and for Adam Thomas to investigate the hidden workings of St. Mary's Hospital Medical School and Toxicol Laboratories in Herefordshire in 1993. The League Against Cruel Sports helped Mike Huskisson's infiltration and exposure of the prestigious Quorn Hunt, and the hunting fraternity's secrets generally, resulting in the most graphic and shocking images of the time from the killing fields of England as compiled in the book *Outfoxed*.

They also funded the now notorious Graham Hall (whom I shall get to later) to infiltrate a gang of badger baiters in Wales in 1990, resulting in convictions and the first prison sentences for such crimes. The National Anti Hunt Campaign infiltrated and exposed fox diggers. Video cameras have remained a favoured weapon of the animal liberator in the fight against animal abuse.

In 1998, Animal Defenders sent an experienced undercover team into the violent close-knit world of the renowned circus empire of the Chipperfield clan. They gathered some truly disturbing footage, which secured various convictions for cruelty against Mary Chipperfield, her husband and their trainer. The NAVS funded an infiltration by Chris Iles into the Charing Cross & Westminster Medical School and the Institute of Neurology between 1994 and 1996 and, along with *The News of the World*, stung the Cambridge-based beagle breeding business Interfauna in 1994. PETA infiltrated activists into Huntingdon Life Sciences labs in New Jersey USA in 1997. They exposed L'Oreal's abuse of animals at Biosearch laboratories, the suffering of the Silver Spring monkeys at the Institute of Behavioural Research, Gillette poisoning animals, poultry slaughter on behalf of KFC, mink farming, pig farming, Wyeth-Ayerst Pharmaceuticals' abuse of pregnant mares for the collection of their oestrogen rich urine, and others. Respect for Animals secured the services of an activist to film and exposé Crow Hill Mink Farm in Hampshire in 1997 and ensure the first criminal convictions against the owners for cruelty. Each was an utterly shocking revelation of suffering and routine, systematic and deliberate cruelty in establishments supposedly monitored by government regulations.

More on some of the incredible findings of these investigations later. But forget all that for now; it's history. Here's a brief, interim reminder about why people do what they do in the name of animal rights...

There are still millions of animals being used annually in laboratory experiments (and that's just in this small, supposedly advanced country alone). Over 700,000,000 are killed for food. Many hundreds of thousands are hunted down in one form or another. A thousand dogs and cats are put to death every week because they're surplus to the requirements of a society that breeds them to order and excess. A whole plethora of species are trapped in the wild and bred in captivity to supply the whims of human society in the name of entertainment and fashion. All of it is unnecessary suffering. For the majority of humans, this suffering is quite normal and utterly acceptable if there are benefits to them, but mostly because few are exposed to the gruesome facts. It's now been acknowledged by officialdom in the US and elsewhere that many of our favourite serial killers began their reign of terror using animals, yet we continue to encourage such behaviour by making life worthless. And we call ourselves civilised. I don't think so!

When vivisectors claim to be concerned for the well being of the animals whom they keep so that they can torture and kill them, they have—by definition—become desensitised to the suffering they inflict. Take, for example, the method used in labs to identify mice in crowded cages: for decades, vivisectors have snipped off one or more of the animals' toes or punched huge holes through their ears. And this is all before the experiments even begin! It doesn't take a trained eye, a great deal of common sense or a scientific mind to work out that the suffering they pass off as minimal is to the animal immense, and no official government statements will change this. The mind-destroying boredom experienced by animals kept isolated in barren cages in labs for their entire lives should be enough to give sleepless nights to anyone responsible for their confinement, but of course it doesn't—only the night creeping activists do that. Aided in no small part by the media.

It is awareness of, and sensitivity to, this suffering which motivates some individuals to give such people sleepless nights. As one man I asked put it when I asked him if he thought he had made the right life decision by joining the ranks of the ALF:

> The images had begun to seep into my subconscious; they were haunting me and keeping me awake. I lay in bed one night looking at the ceiling and thought to myself: I may as well use this time constructively and do some haunting of my own. And sod the consequences. I went out at 3am that night and drove for an hour to a factory farm I'd known about for years since I was kid when we used to mock the birds for the noise they made. I poured paint stripper over their Land Rover and glued some locks and went home. I have to admit I don't necessarily sleep much better but I've never felt so good about myself.

Chickens are still squashed five to a cage in sheds with thousands of others in the most unnatural environment imaginable. They aren't permitted to exercise even their most fundamental behaviour such as laying their eggs in private or bathing in dust, added to which they can hardly move, let alone spread their wings. Their environment is filthy, they get no fresh air, and their food can best be described as boring. Disease, sickness, aggression, cannibalism and neurotic disorders are endemic. Drugs are constantly being created by vested interests to solve the problems inherent in factory farming.

This is classified as veterinary research. To prevent too much damage being done by birds attacking each other, farmers slice off the ends of their beaks—causing intense pain. Some birds, whose nails have grown around the bars upon which they spend their short lives, are pulled out to be sent to slaughter without their legs. Rummaging around a slaughterhouse one night, I saw a battery hen in a crate with loads of others. She had bled to death from the hole torn where the second leg had once been. We tried to get her out but couldn't because the crates were still stacked high on a lorry, and this one was near the bottom. The journey to the slaughterhouse had blown blood down the crates behind her, covering other birds.

Research by Bristol University suggests that a staggering 24% of broiler chickens (bred for meat) suffer broken bones while being manhandled to the slaughterhouse. Even a cursory glance at the way these creatures are handled would back up these findings. It's a poor existence at best, and all they have to look forward to is a violent death. The journey to the slaughterhouse is a nightmare in itself, and all the law can do is offer them a rest period at the place of extermination to recover from the trauma of the journey with the sights, sounds and smells of the slaughterhouse. It's not about compassion—more because the trauma and fear of the journey taints the taste of the meat.

Piglets are castrated and have their tails sliced off without anaesthetic. Dairy calves can no longer be legally confined to veal crates in the UK because the system is so cruel, so it's off across the English Channel they go. Isn't it incredible that this system has been officially condemned for its cruelty and consequently banned, when equally cruel—and worse—practices are protected and given the wholehearted encouragement of the law? There can be no doubt in the mind of anyone who thinks, and hasn't had their vision clouded with pound signs, that to break what is the strongest emotional bond in nature—that of a mother and her offspring—by separating them a few days after birth, can at best be described as cruel. The mourning of the dairy cow is well-documented and pitiful to watch.

My first job while on a Youth Training Scheme at school was on a dairy farm and my only lasting memory of my time there is of the way the milking cows would cry out all day long across the fields in a hopeless search for the babies that had been wrenched from them. The experience of the orphaned calves is something else to be ashamed of: loaded, as they are onto lorries early in the morning, at one week old, they join hundreds of others similarly lost and frightened and without their mothers. They are taken hundreds of miles to Dutch or French veal farms where they spend their short lives in darkness in tiny wooden crates, fed an iron-deficient liquid diet to keep their flesh white. And all for what? To satisfy the human palate and fill someone's pocket. Those who are decimating the animal kingdom and causing untold suffering are the very ones who have the audacity to call their critics monsters. What will our grandchildren think when they look back? Are the vivisectors, slaughter men and politicians right? Do the animals and those who seek to protect them, deserve all they get?

Propaganda & Poultry

> It is estimated that about 1,000 people are disposed towards criminal acts in furtherance of the cause. It is worth noting that most of these people have not otherwise come to the adverse notice of the police.
>
> *ARNI Briefing, June 1988*

The 1980s was a decade of incredible achievement for the Animal Liberation Movement—a decade, which brought up a generation of activists keen to build on the accomplishments of their predecessors. Towards the 1990s, the movement suffered from a lack of direction and unity, and appeared to stagnate. In a sense, this was not surprising. Given the constant reminders of the sheer scale of the task ahead, it isn't a surprise that apathy sets in, as it surely does from time to time. For some people, it can all be too much to bear and they drift from the active struggle. Many people joined and then left, somehow able to move on, as many still do. Others remained on the front line for the duration, learning, teaching and keeping the movement alive.

The 'inciting' pages of the SG had been silenced for a time, removing the public voice of the ALF. The propaganda of the Leagues and the BUAV's once inspiring *Liberator* was no longer worth the paper it was printed on. Gone was the mass participation, and a number of key activists were locked up. The movement needed a right good kick up the arse—a spark that would inspire a revival and reinvigorate the battle-weary. As with life in general, so too with the animal rights movement: there were ups and downs, periods of activity followed by inactivity. That this was a period of relative calm meant only that this was the calm before a storm, and that storm was brewing.

As the grassroots gradually lost grip of the BUAV and others, the local group network began to evolve and coordinate better regionally and nationally and became increasingly effective in campaigning and recruiting. Once upon a time, the big boys at the BUAV and NAVS and Animal Aid planned actions with which the rest of us would join in, distributing 'their' campaign material by the lorry load and spreading their word. But times were changing. The big boys had sold out in the eyes of the activists and had even turned the clock back for laboratory animals. In the eyes of activists on the front line, the BUAV had become weak and spineless. With the Animal Liberation Leagues expired and the ALFsg crippled, there was no leadership to follow, so the activists led themselves.

In a rut or not, it had long since been too late to curb the rise in animal liberation raids. A tried and tested strategy had proved effective in forcing change, and much of that strategy was about attracting attention. With dreams and fond memories a-plenty and lessons constantly being learnt, there were things to be done. Quiet time or not, there are always things going on behind the scenes: plans, meetings, discussions, surveillance. Operation Liberation was plotting the future. With this in mind, 1,500 copies of a document entitled *Into The 90s With The Animal Liberation Front* were distributed anonymously through the movement, for new and old to read, reiterating the sentiments of the more substantial *Interviews With ALF Activists*. The 16-page document was aimed at budding ALF activists and detailed step-by-step 'how to' guides on destroying everything from shop windows and their protective shutters to vehicles and buildings. It carried plans for the construction of incendiary devices and gave pointers for dealing with the press. This was followed by further inciting documents, including *Non Electrical Incendiary Devices*, which was to encourage arson attacks, and *Activist*, another how-to manual for budding ALF activists.

The more mainstream *Arkangel*, was a slightly different publication, designed with a view to promoting unity within the movement. *Arkangel* was the idea of Ronnie Lee, a serving prisoner who, together with the letters of support, which he received daily, also got sent regular details of unreported actions undertaken by activists within the worldwide animal protection movement. The pages of *Arkangel* were filled with reports of actions at all levels from creating road-crossing tunnels for frogs to fur farm arson raids. *Arkangel*, did, of course, keep the ALF's work in the news, as can be seen from the early editions, with direct action featuring alongside reports of naked protests and sponsored parachute jumps. It was a compilation of action at all levels and sought to 'Promote unity, respect and cooperation within the movement.' Much of the first issue, edited by Vivian Smith was dedicated to views on direct action as well as news on the work of no less than 165 local groups; it also carried an encouraging list of national campaigns and international news.

During this period, the Animal Liberation Investigation Unit (ALIU) was established; its designated purpose to march into laboratories, offices, and farms and walk out with whatever paperwork could be found, quite legally. A loophole in the law made it lawful to remove someone else's property as long as its absence wasn't intended to be permanent, which meant that sensitive documents could be taken away from offices, copied and then returned quite legally. So we helped ourselves!

ALF cells had reformed, recharged, and evolved and were plotting. To welcome in the 1990s, the ALF were executing high-profile liberation raids at a rate of one a month. Many small-scale raids were also carried out, totalling around 70 in the first two and a half years of the 1990s, freeing thousands of animals, birds and even reptiles. This was something of shift in tactics after a period more focused on in-store incendiaries, court cases and questionable car bombings.

Activists on the front line were now also handling publicity from raid exposés rather than relying on those in high places who were no longer respected nor particularly interested. The downside was that activists were now in direct contact with journalists once again, and that is a dangerous place to be. The first ALF video documentary was released and circulated; entitled *Animal Liberation—the Movie*; set to music, it mingled footage of raids and scenes of cruelty. It was an exciting and informative new idea—and a new way of sharing the message.

In Daventry, an egg factory farm owned by the Lady of Passion monastery—run by nuns of all people—had become a focal point for some focused activists who had begun raiding repeatedly in the dead of night, causing damage and taking hens. Trying to fathom the workings of the minds of people who want to keep birds in such awful conditions when money is their god is one thing, but local thinkers were particularly drawn to the nuns because they were nuns. With God as their god, you'd expect they'd have more respect for what they consider to be His creation, but not this lot. They were extreme in their objection to any suggestion the birds in their cages were sentient creatures worthy of consideration and were as determined as any animal abuser to continue as normal. Having heard terrible stories of how badly nuns had treated my mum and her sister when they were under their care as kids in Liverpool in the 1940s had long since killed any faith I had in them, but it was still a bit of a shock to see how aggressive and uncaring this mob were.

Junior Health Minster Edwina Currie had done her bit for hens and was made an honorary animal liberator for announcing publicly that it was no longer safe to eat eggs because of the high risk of contracting salmonella. It wasn't the government's line of course, and the industry wasn't impressed. There was a public outcry, and egg sales suffered.

The poultry industry responded by claiming that as long as eggs were cooked properly, there would be no unacceptable risk to human health, but there was mud sticking. The government felt it was necessary to allay public fear by testing the UK's caged flocks and sentencing to death any that carried salmonella. The Daventry nuns' hens were duly tested and found positive for salmonella. Summary execution was ordered, but before the assassins swept through the sheds, an ALF team moved in and took a hundred birds to the safety of an animal sanctuary. The nuns duly sent the rest back to their maker and disposed of their bodies. With the cages disinfected, it should have been all systems go for the next batch of victims, but the steadily increasing pressure, the cost of repairs and the embarrassment caused with each protest at the farm contributed to the nuns' decision not to bother restocking the cages. They had not a shred of remorse over the suffering they'd inflicted, and were comfortable believing it was their God-given right to do as they pleased with his non-human children. Their reasoning for closing their business was because 'The animal rightists forced us.'

Soon after this victory, twenty rodents were kidnapped by the ALF from a Tonbridge Grammar School in Kent. This doesn't sound like any big deal and can hardly be called violent extremism, but in English law it's burglary and carries a prison sentence. If you get caught, that is. The animals were due to be used in dissection displays but in the aftermath the school saw what the raiders were saying about the killing being unnecessary. They ended the programme and resorted to more advanced methods of teaching the inner workings of a mouse. It was a classic ALF action, an example others were keen to follow.

Cocksparrow—The Final Showdown

> The saints are exceedingly loving and gentle to mankind, and even to brute beasts ... Surely we ought to show them [animals] great kindness and gentleness for many reasons, but, above all, because they are of the same origin as ourselves.
>
> *St. John Chrysostom (c.345 – 407) Archbishop of Constantinople*

A few weeks later the final blow was struck against Cocksparrow Farm, the most notorious of the last four remaining arctic fox fur farms in the UK. There had been repeated actions against this farm over the years, with national demos attracting up to 1500 people and aggressive mounted police, not to mention the more impromptu demos with passing groups of protesters who would hassle the owner just by being there.

Often, passing groups of saboteurs who had either been unable to locate the hunt or had packed them up early, would stop by. So gross was the place, locals actually liked to see 30 or 40 scruffy sabs pouring over the fields and freaking out the owner as he ran for the phone. During the 80s and 90s when hunt sabs were mass participation events, it was common practice to complete a day out with an inspection of a fur farm or something similar. In this area it was more often than not Cocksparrow that was visited.

Pacing relentlessly behind the high steel fence beyond the farmhouse, the white foxes had only a few square feet of wire floor to make use of. They could have been anywhere in the world, and indeed they are: Finland, North America, West Yorkshire and here, where few people had cared once upon a time. The caged foxes knew what it was like to suffer; soon it was going to be the turn of the farm keepers. There was a lot of concern about Cocksparrow. Located in an English shire county, the conditions were so bad at the farm that even the pro-everything fur British Fur Trade Association were compelled to disown it. Its owner, Nirbahal Singh Gill, an Asian businessman, listened to what we had to say but didn't see things the same way. His view was that he was looking after the foxes for their fur, so by definition they weren't suffering. He couldn't see that this was part of the problem—he wasn't looking after the foxes!

Gill was a lazy man and a heavy drinker. He was also a creature of habit, and it had been noted that rather than patrolling the grounds at night as today's fur farmer must, Gill was most often found in the pub of an evening, not returning home until some time after last orders, pissed. Some serious activists had noticed this and to use an inappropriate euphemism: he was seen as a sitting duck. Gill's business was clearly faltering under the pressure and he had been approached openly by a couple of local campaigners with an offer to buy his foxes from him. He clearly no longer really wanted them. If that failed, then there was a good chance Gill was going to be ambushed late one night and given a bloody good hiding! Neither option is normal practice, but that's what was going on. The remaining foxes numbered three dozen where once there were as many hundred and they were dying in the cages. The guard dogs ate body parts scattered around the compound. He was unperturbed by the fact that the Environmental Health Department were onto him and had been for some time.

A decision was made to have one final attempt at bypassing the psycho guard dogs. Most attempted incursions had occurred in the dead of night, the dogs would bark, he would come rushing out of the house and his ever-vigilant wife would call the police. It happened with boring regularity but ideas evolved when information passed by a local sympathiser suggested that on Sunday afternoon the place was deserted. A further recce (the next Sunday afternoon) confirmed that the guard dogs were vicious all right; chained to stakes, it was all they had to do! But they were chained to stakes, which meant they couldn't bite anyone taking foxes out of the cages. And barking was pointless, because no one would be listening, as they were indeed out. Job on! They didn't of course know it as the Sunday raiding party made nothing of the perimeter, but the guard dogs were about to be made redundant! It would take an hour, after which all 27 foxes were taken from their cages, bagged up and moved out. They then smashed the cages. In just an hour one sunny Sunday afternoon, the once notorious Cocksparrow fox farm was reduced to a mess of tangled rusty wire as a small pack of seriously miffed straining Alsatians looked on. No further foxes have lived and died inside the now defunct Cocksparrow fox farm.

Bereft of foxes, the misguided Gill later stunned everyone when he made an application for planning permission to set up an intensive poultry farm on the site! Fortunately this was refused. With no animals in cages, he was able to get on with his life unmolested and has since confessed that he is grateful for being forced out of what he now calls 'that awful trade.'

The Season Of Goodwill

> Making good use of the things that we find, things that the every day folks leave behind.
>
> *The Wombles*

The managers of Oxford University Park Farm, meanwhile, may have begun to feel comfortable after four years without much attention. Last visited in 1985, it was New Year's Day 1990 before 'Park Farm's been raided' was again the gossip of the activists and vivisectors alike. With a view to marking the start of the new decade with something newsworthy, motorway service stations were the scene of a dozen covert meetings to seek homes 'for as many beagles as possible.' Few knew the details of the conspiracy, but a lot were in on it.

And fewer would have expected it to happen in broad daylight, but there was a bit of a theme developing here. New Year's Eve 1989 was a Sunday, and there seemed to be no one about at Park Farm. Oh boy! Over the perimeter fence and then the outer kennel, it was then simply a matter of using the dog flaps to access the dogs from their sleeping quarters, bypassing door alarms. Over an hour, 36 were fished out of their kennels with improvised dog-catching poles. It was time-consuming and undignified, but effective, and soon they were being whisked away in the back of vans: the entire breeding stock, valued at £10,000. And it would cost a whole lot more than that to get the dogs back this time, with them scattered far and wide within hours from rendezvous points on the M25, M23, M1, M6…

Since these conspiracies against cruelty began, Christmas, New Year and Easter have all been celebrated by the ALF across the world in the true spirit of peace, love and goodwill. As human society tends to increase the infliction of demand on animal species to celebrate its festivals, it is a good opportunity to make a statement and catch them out. Some who have been: Howard University, Washington DC: 36 cats rescued; Royston, Hertfordshire: 25 battery hens; Martinsried, West Germany: 11 lab cats; Luton, Bedfordshire: three slaughterhouse lorries burnt; UCLA Medical Centre USA: 12 dogs; Ontario, Canada: three cats and a monkey; Nuremburg, West Germany: 114 guinea pigs; Holland: locks of 80 restaurants selling frogs' legs and 'game' glued; Bloomington LA, USA: 115 rabbits; Oxford University: 64 cats; Leyden Street slaughterhouse, London: 77 battery hens; Essex University: 200 mice; Norfolk Cottage Eggs, Dorset: 600 hens. It was Boxing Day when

Sea Shepherd activists sank a Norwegian whaler. And it was April Fool's Day when the activists of Operation Greystoke in France took vivisectors at Gif-Sur-Yvette for seventeen baboons.

Dodgy Shampoo

> The practice of the vivisection of living animals stands condemned by its very inhumanity. The fact that intellectual and educated men are engaged in the pursuit is no evidence of its rightfulness and value. Intellectual and educated men have been guilty of the greatest crimes in history.
>
> *Dr. Walter Hadwen*

As we entered the 1990s, most cosmetic companies had begun to bow to public pressure and one by one announced an end to their use of animal testing methods. Incredibly though, some were still refusing to change from their old ways because they simply couldn't be bothered.

The main offenders then, as now in 2007, are L'Oreal, Gillette, Reckitt and Colman, Colgate Palmolive, Unilever, SmithKline Beecham, Johnson & Johnson and Proctor and Gamble. The start of a campaign of ALF contamination scares against some of these companies began in earnest in late December 1990 when stores selling animal tested cosmetics—mainly Boots—were targeted in a number of towns and cities across the UK. L'Oreal were the main target and following warnings, staff were instructed to carry out checks on their stocks of these products. A few months on, a further coordinated action made a wider sweep and stores from Oxford to Liverpool, Bolton to Brighton were hit. Stocks of L'Oreal products, again sold in Boots stores, were reportedly tampered with. Some were marked with the dreaded X and filled with harmless but alien items, like soil and sand. Others carried the X and a warning to customers to immediately contact Boots and the L'Oreal head office. Using the guise of 'concerned customer', one group then made a series of phone calls to shops reporting glass traces in their purchase. This made the hoax look very real. The intention was again twofold: first to highlight the pressing issue of cosmetic tests on animals and embarrass those engaged in them, and secondly to cost all involved as much as possible. It's impossible to glean whether or not this action was equal to its potential, because those on the receiving end, in collusion with the police, called the bluff of the hoaxers. There was very little publicity—in fact the story only slipped into the news in one area. Elsewhere, nothing was amiss, apparently. Reportedly, stock was taken off shelves in some shops, but in others, soiled goods remained on display for customers to buy.

The number of concerned customer calls must have caused worry at head office, but not enough to cause those in charge to check displays. No products presented an added danger to the purchaser, but it appeared that the decision-makers at Boots on this occasion were prepared to play what could potentially be a very dangerous game. At least a dozen areas were targeted and had contaminated bottles of hair dye and such left on shelves, yet still customers were allowed to buy them. Soon after, the hoaxers struck in Kent where stocks of Vosene shampoo were removed from shelves in Ashford and Canterbury following a warning. In Northern Ireland, days before Xmas, managers at Woolworths and Boots stores in Belfast, Lisburn, Enniskillen, Colraine and Bangor ordered their shelves be cleared after L'Oreal products were reportedly spiked with paint stripper. This was repeated a few months later when stores in Lisburn and Belfast were hit again. Contamination threats are a tricky one for businesses and the police to deal with because to ignore the warnings might one day prove disastrous, something the activists are at pains to consider. Hence the word: hoax.

Huntingdon Life Sciences—Going Public

> Until we have the courage to recognize cruelty for what it is—whether its victim is human or animal—we cannot expect things to be much better in this world... We cannot have peace among men whose hearts delight in killing any living creature. By every act that glorifies or even tolerates such moronic delight in killing we set back the progress of humanity.
>
> *Rachel Carson (1907 —1964) American writer, scientist, environmentalist*

In early 1989, Sarah Kite secured herself a job at the vast Huntingdon Research Centre near Cambridge. Her role was to look after some of the many animals held there while working undercover to provide information to the BUAV that would expose the day-to-day suffering of animals in laboratories under the protection of the 1986 Scientific Procedures Act. She was also there to prove that if the largest contract-testing laboratory in Europe, promoted as a 'Centre of Excellence', was so readily ignoring the strict regulations, then it was a sham. Anyone care? Let's see, shall we?

After eight months in employment working in the rat, mice and beagle units, her opinions on vivisection wholeheartedly reinforced, she handed in her resignation. As a woman new to the world of animal testing, she was considered by her bosses on the job ill-equipped to cope with what was happening in the primate unit, so free access to that was denied. Anything up to 700 cynomolgus, rhesus and squirrel monkeys as well as baboons can be stored on this site at any one time, in the largest primate toxicology complex in the world. According to the Home Office, around 128,000 animals are vivisected there annually with a work force of 900 humans involved. The ins and outs of the primates' lives remained secreted within the locked vaults of HRC and open only to speculation until the efforts of another innovative female infiltrator would expose all a few years later. But the ineffectiveness of the 1986 Act as far as the lesser mortals were doing in 1990 was exposed in a front page/centre spread exclusive in a national newspaper, and further extracts of Sarah Kite's harrowing diaries were published by the BUAV in her book *Secret Suffering*.

Section 3.2 of the basic Code of Practice for those working in animal research states that: 'The aim is to maintain good health and physical condition; behaving in a manner normal for the species.' Mice at HLS were found to be usually bored and frustrated and frantically paced their cages. One technician at the centre admitted the mice often end up chewing themselves for those very reasons.

Section 3.28 states: 'Bedding material should be provided unless it is clearly inappropriate. It should be comfortable for the particular species.' The rats in Unit GO8 at HRC lived on metal grid floors. They were given no bedding or nesting material. The beagles lived on bare concrete floors, save for a sprinkling of sawdust there to soak up the urine. Using any more than that was scorned upon.

Section 3:38: 'All animals must be allowed to exercise. For smaller species, this should normally be achieved by providing adequately sized cages and pens and sometimes play objects.' At HRC, overweight rats were often crammed five to a cage. They weren't even able to move, let alone exercise. In some cages they were so short of floor space that they would have to lay on top of each other! Neither the rats nor the mice were ever taken out of their barren cages for exercise, only to be weighed or experimented on. The beagles were only let into a run for 20 minutes each working day, but on weekends and bank holidays that was restricted due to staff shortages.

Sarah Kite's entire account is filled with examples of the indifference towards animals in an environment where animal care for the animal's benefit is an unknown; indeed, undercover investigations have universally revealed that animals are treated not as living, flesh and blood creatures, but as commodities. She was told not to refer to animals bleeding, but to use the term 'red staining', and to refer not to their death but their 'sacrifice.' The code of practice, like the language, merely superficially cleanses the cruelty. The way animals were referred to and handled on a daily basis says enough: rats described as being horrid and silly creatures, shouted at for squirming when being force-fed or injected chemicals, then thrown back into cages and ridiculed and laughed at, even mocked while having fits. Cages of sick animals were handled roughly and noisily and kicked back into place. These were and are acts of deliberate cruelty whitewashed by the Home Office.

There was no video footage to prove these findings, though this was soon to change. Nevertheless, her diaries caused a national storm. Locally, there was unswerving support for the centre, which is a major employer of local workers with few other opportunities. Many won't talk publicly about what they do and know, but anyone demonstrating in the Huntingdon area will be aware of the undercurrent of solidarity among those who work there. Not everyone in the area can be described as a supporter of the labs, of course, and some are vocal in their objection, but a survey here would surely reveal far more in favour than in the average town.

Within days of the exposé, protesters were on the streets, rallied together by the newly-formed Huntingdon Animal Concern, but this was just a warm up, a taste of the future and there was something unpleasant brewing for the lab and its staff for who secrecy was paramount, the outside world categorically not invited.

Operation Bite Back

> You know, we harvest them, but we like them too, and this kind of thing just breaks your heart.
>
> *US mink farmer following ALF liberation raid*

With the honeymoon period over for UK activists as the authorities closed in on key ALF cells, activists across the Atlantic were flying high, inspired by efforts in the UK. Operation Bite Back was born. It wasn't just our successes that were inspiring more direct action elsewhere but the fact that higher prison sentences in the UK weren't deterring activists. With the very public decimation of the fur trade in the UK, a mood for more of the same took hold. In the US, where of course the trade was bigger and thriving, farm raids there were increasing and activists were planning a more wide-ranging assault on the relative peace and quiet in the fur trade.

The first salvo in this fresh focused campaign occurred in late 1990 when the offices of the US Department of Agriculture, connected to a predator research centre at Utah State University, were fire-damaged to the tune of $200,000 and a dozen coyotes were released into the wild. Thereafter followed a string of highly damaging attacks. In early 1991, the mink research facility at Michigan State University was targeted causing around $125,000 of fire damage and the loss of 30 years of research data. Fire destroyed the storage warehouses of North West Fur Foods, suppliers of feed to mink farmers, in Washington causing $400,000 of damage. Mink were rescued, files trashed and $62,000 damage caused to an experimental fur farm on the campus of Oregon State University. Animal research facilities at Washington State University were hit, offices and two labs were doused with acid and seven coyotes, six mink and ten mice were freed causing $100,000 worth of damage. And on it went.

It was only after the next attack two months later, when fire ripped through the offices of a prominent Michigan State University vivisector with several government contracts, causing $125,000 damage and obliterating 32 years of data, that the FBI started to get busy themselves and attempted to stamp their authority on the situation.

In just two years of the ALF Bite Back campaign, at least two dozen fur farms were raided across North America from which some 38,000 mink, 410 foxes and dozens of coyotes were released back into the wilderness. Twelve coyotes that survived the government aerial shooting and gassing programmes were discovered imprisoned by activists, in Washington State University research station at Pullman. It was the trapped animals' unusually concentrated howls (sounding pained compared to those of the wild coyotes still surviving in the surrounding hills) that led to their discovery in a remote kennel. The trapped animals were being used in Sarcocystis research, a disease non-fatal to coyotes or sheep, but which the former can pass to the latter as they are grazed on public land in coyote country, thereby affecting the economic value of sheep wool and meat, and we can't have that.

Disturbed by the late night intrusion, each animal paced frantically as masked activists busied themselves around the kennels, cutting fences and removing locks. The animals knew they were going to be set free. One by one, the cage doors were opened and without a second thought, each proud beast bounded towards the outer door and fled from the area while others howled in the dark distance, calling to their mates and apparently rejoicing. The wilderness was suddenly revitalised as life returned.

There was absolutely nothing to fear from the last two animals to be released; the first checked himself and, rather than running off as the others had, instead moved back down the kennel block towards the masked raider in charge of opening cage doors. With no other way out, the young man was trapped by this large, wild dog, but he said he never once felt fear. In the end kennel was a young female who was the single-minded focus of the now free coyote, and her eyes were fixed in anticipation on the older male looking in. These two were an item, perhaps a lifelong couple that had been caged side by side and were not leaving alone. As the final cage was opened, the two animals touched noses briefly, then turned and tore off together into the night. It was a magical moment for the dangerous 'terrorist', who glanced tearfully skyward to see a rush of shooting stars welcoming home the coyotes. The punishment for releasing animals from captivity is up to ten years in prison and a $100,000 fine.

From humble beginnings, with the release of 25 foxes from one farm, this hands-on help had grown into a fad! The media didn't warm to it; they saw thousands of marauding predators on the rampage. The reality after the hysteria is that not all these animals stay free, and those that do survive are native to a huge country in need of as many live animals as can be found, given the enormous toll inflicted by the hunt 'em, shoot 'em, trap 'em, kill 'em culture. These releases are doing little more than filling the gap created quite unnaturally by marauding human predators.

Of course, I'm an extremist (ex-trem-ist—someone who wont accept any excuses for animal abuse) and I understand that not everyone sees things the same way. Fur farmers, or 'Ranchers' as they're known in that part of the world, were, they claimed, concerned about the well-being of the missing animals they had been preparing to plunge into the mobile carbon dioxide gas tank or to anally electrocute to death. Hmm, what kind of concern? They claimed they were worried about whether the poor things would be able to survive out there without their regular supply of gruel and their enforced social structure. What they were actually concerned about, of course, was the cost of these raids and the fact that their farms were the centre of attention, which forced them into the uncomfortable position of having to defend themselves against accusations of cruelty. Many ranchers had never even considered it was cruel and more than likely never would. Such was the furore that it soon became international news. The FBI were set on the trail of the raiders and began putting together files on scores of activists whom they suspected of involvement; the majority were college students and teenagers now considered a threat to national security! Freeing wild animals is not really FBI material, if you believe the propaganda, but the FBI protects the status quo as directed. And such attacks were getting serious: if allowed to continue they could wipe out an industry, this being the stated intent, after all.

Ranchers were doing all they could to protect themselves, but for many of the then 450 mink, 100+ fox and 100+ chinchilla farmers that would be costly. More fences, more patrols, more cameras, more lights, less profits. Either spend what you have or risk losing the lot was the message, but not all saw increased security at their farms as sufficient protection for the future of the fur trade and some folded. Arrests were rare, and there was a lot of confusion about who was responsible for these raids, why they weren't being stopped, and who might be next or whether those who'd been done would be hit again. The animals were off to pastures new but the ranchers didn't know whether they were coming or going!

Putting up a $50,000 reward to catch those raiding their farms made farmers feel they were doing something productive, but as life continued as normal and there were no takers—except of animals—they were forced to raise the bounty to $100,000: more than five times the amount being offered for rapists and child abusers! This merely corroborates one of life's recurring themes and one that strongly reverberates through this book and the campaigns that make it: that protecting the well being of animal farmers and associated abusers is a much greater priority for those in power than protecting life.

But it was too little too late to stop the spread of new thinking and salvage the image of an outdated industry. Indeed, such was the strength of the fur campaign in the US by the mid-nineties that on one day of coordinated protest alone, 99 protesters were arrested at 16 different locations throughout the country. Activists locked themselves on to fixtures and fittings in fur stores, occupied rooftops and chained themselves to obstacles to block roads. Enraged by the non-violent protest, police and security guards used physical violence against the protesters, driving more to consider raids and to support those who carried them out. At one Philadelphia store, three protesters had chained themselves by the neck to each other and then lay on the floor in front of the main entrance; the police lifted the three together by their legs and threw them like a sack of coal into the back of their vehicle which then had to take them to hospital. One suffered a broken wrist and they were all considered lucky not to have suffered far more serious injuries.

In two less violent actions, activists slashed over 100 fur coats with knives at a travelling fur sale, and the Paint Panthers did what they do with red paint to 75 fox, lynx, sable, beaver, rabbit and mink coats in New York streets. In the middle of all of this, one of the industry front men claimed that: 'Things are looking up' for the fur trade! No need to worry then!

Imprisoned for between one and seven months at the height of the fur campaign, five young campaigners were determined to make good use of their time in prison by going on hunger strikes. They called on the government to ban the vicious leg hold trap and to end its opposition to the European Union's wild fur import ban. Tony Wong, Stacy Schirholz, Jeff Watkins, Nicole Rogers, and Freeman Wicklund all pledged to go without food until certain demands were met. Tony Wong—the youngest at 16 went for an astounding 30 days, by which time there was a great deal of public interest in the protest and the issues raised. Staggeringly, government agents took control again and for the next 31 days, three times a day, forcibly fed him via the nose with a formula containing dairy products, adding further insult to injury. These were violent assaults on a non-violent young man, but he was empowered by his conviction and many others were motivated too. He had resisted for 61 days and on the day of his release he was back protesting outside the very same fur store, which had led to his initial imprisonment.

According to one farm owner, a raid on his property cost millions. Five Michigan activists were arrested by chance in the early hours of the morning and charged with breaking, entering and mischief at the Eberts Farm in South West Ontario. Two of the defendants gave incriminating evidence to the authorities in the two weeks during which they were held in custody and the support campaign for the Chatham Five promptly became the Chatham Three. One of the former, 25 year-old Robyn Weiner, pleaded guilty to breaking and entering, and possession of stolen property, namely farm breeding cards. She was sentenced to 400 hours community service to be served on weekends, she had her $10,000 bail forfeited to the farmer, and she had to apologise to him. Her 'deal' was struck because she had promised to testify against the others, with whom the judge said he wasn't going to be as lenient because they didn't show any remorse. Not much incentive to! Pat Dobson and Hilma Ruby were each sentenced to 90 days in prison and fined $24,000 after pleading guilty to involvement in the raid. Gary Yourofsky, a Detroit schoolteacher, ran a trial, lost it and was given six months inside where he staged a 40 day hunger strike in protest at fur farming.

The farm owner served them all with a $3.5 million civil suit: $2 million in general damages, $1 million in specific damages and $12 million in punitive damages, plus legal costs. In it he claimed 25 years of breeding information was lost, with 1,542 mink released—42 male and 1,500 female—95% of which were pregnant. From these he forecast 7,125 skins at $70 for a male and $50 for a female. In addition there was the hole, which the raiders had cut in a fence and the damage done to 100 pens, 400 drop-in nest boxes and two gates.

ALF media rep, Rod Coronado, a Native American Indian and leading light in the Bite Back and Earth First campaigns, was also under the cosh and on the run and with good reason to fear for his life. The Feds had been looking for him armed to the teeth and he had received threats from fur industry thugs. After 14 months out of the radar, he was finally located on his peoples' reservation as a result of information provided by an informant who was paid $22,000—a bounty provided by disgruntled farmers, hunters and vivisectors. Led to believe there was an injured hawk in need of help he was ambushed by an FBI posse on arrival. Coronado later pleaded guilty to aiding and abetting the arson on a mink research farm at Michigan and acting as ALF spokesperson for the attack. He was sentenced to four years and nine months and ordered to pay compensation to the tune of $2.5 million. How much is that each week? In an almost civilised gesture he was then given 30 days to put his affairs in order before presenting himself for prison.

Setting up Grand Juries to investigate the ALF in Washington, Oregon, Michigan, Louisiana and Utah, the FBI went to work harassing known and suspected activists and their families and even their families' friends and other loose associates. Grand jury subpoenas were served on dozens of activists across the USA, forcing the recipients to talk or face prison. Most offered what they knew or thought; many others were questioned ad hoc and asked to provide information. Some were offered financial incentives for spilling the beans on the ALF; others were simply threatened with prison for not complying or answering whatever questions were asked of them, however irrelevant, about anything or anyone whom the Feds might want to nail. In ten years of radical action for animals, only a few activists had been prosecuted for minor offences and no one had been imprisoned in the US or Canada, but the authorities and concerned business interests were extremely keen that things were going to change, and, of course, so too were the activists.

During the course of these investigations Jonathan Paul, Rik Scarce, Kim Trimview and Deborah Stout were imprisoned for their principled stand in refusing to gossip about their friends and colleagues in front of jurors. Each served months inside as a consequence and were left to rot until the Grand Jury had expired or the judge concluded there was nowhere else to go and prison wasn't going to force out answers. Darren Thurston had been a key player in a raid on the Canadian University of Alberta's Ellerslie Research Station in 1991 during which 29 cats had been taken and $100,000 damage caused. He was also responsible for an arson attack, which gutted three lorries belonging to the Billingsgate Fish Company.

Convicted on the information provided by Jessica Sandham, another suspect arrested by police, he was remanded in custody on various charges. He spent 15 months inside before pleading guilty in 1993 and was given a suspended prison sentence plus two years probation and ordered to pay $26,725 damages to the university and $47,000 to the fish company. Thurston was released from custody, but the prosecution weren't happy. They appealed against his sentence and eight months later won their argument and had him taken back to prison for two years.

Others were arrested in Canada and one forced into hiding, the same in the US and England. In all, there were probably a dozen activists evading someone else's view of justice. David Barbarash spent many months on remand for the Alberta action and was made to do 200 hundred hours community service after pleading guilty to being an accessory after the fact. Is ridding a community of terrible cruelty not community service? Well, it ought to be.

State repression State Side was gradually taking even more sinister turns and making the Grand Juries look like a walk in the park. Lise Olsen, a Chronic Fatigue Syndrome sufferer, was arrested after placing 21 homemade lanterns around an anti-fur banner that was hanging over a railway overpass, in order to illuminate it for passing traffic. She wanted to take pictures for publicity purposes, however this didn't work out as she intended. In fact, only one lantern lit up for five minutes, then it went out, so she abandoned the idea and went home, leaving the lanterns. Well, wasn't that a mistake! Unable to make any progress with the more able-bodied farm raiders, the police went after Olsen in a big way and punished her severely.

The prosecution successfully argued the lanterns were incendiary devices, even though a military explosives expert testified in court that in his opinion they weren't incendiary devices and whatever, how unlikely that she would be putting incendiaries around an anti fur banner anyway. Still, somehow Olsen was convicted of possessing incendiary devices and the unlawful use of a 'weapon', i.e. more than three teaspoonfuls of gasoline, and was sent to prison for four years! The trauma for this gentle woman, who had never in her worst nightmares expected to find herself on the wrong side of the judicial system, let alone in prison for 'weapons offences', lasted for 14 months before her conviction was reversed by the Appellate Court and she was released to try to rebuild her life.

Olsen was not the first victim to have fallen foul of the system in this kind of way. Some years earlier, agent provocateurs working for the US Surgical Corporation and its security consultants, Perceptions International had wormed their way into the confidence of activist Fran Trutt, and had thus persuaded her to plant a bomb next to a building owned by the company, so that they could discredit her and the movement. Such was the conspiracy, that USSC agents and the police had even rehearsed the arrest beforehand. There had been many public protests over the use of dogs to demonstrate surgical stapling techniques, and company bosses wanted to put an end to the negative press. The agents, paid $500 a week plus expenses by USSC for the 14-month operation, had provided her with advice, the money and the device, and even drove her there! She changed her mind en route but was persuaded by the agent—her 'friend'—to go ahead. The head of the company said he had been hiring agents to infiltrate animal rights groups 'for many years.' With the bomb in place next to the parking space of the USSC president, Fran Trutt was duly arrested as she left the scene, a remote control detonator in her hand.

She was charged with attempted murder; manufacture and possession of a bomb and was initially sentenced to 10 years in prison, but the sentence was commuted to probation on appeal when the sinister facts were revealed. Her lawyer stated: 'This is a scandalous case—a combination of unlawful acts both before and after the arrest of Fran Trutt. It all adds up to one of the most extraordinary cases of misconduct in putting together and going forth with a prosecution that I have ever encountered.'

Raiding Arizona

> We are playing head games with people who are as smart as us for a change. They've been taught surveillance, intelligence gathering and how to get rid of physical evidence—terrorist training without guns.
>
> *FBI research lab raid investigator, The Scientist, Dec 1987*

Sketchy information had filtered through to important people in the animal rescue world that not only were the University of Arizona using thousands of animals in gruesome experiments, but they were also using pound-seized dogs from an animal shelter and greyhounds from local racetracks. As if those dogs—abandoned, over-bred and exploited—weren't suffering enough already. For one of the organisers, who owned two of these wonderful, trusting dogs, the upcoming raid was personal.

The reconnaissance team—not long out of their teens—scoured the area (as students) and learnt a great deal about the campus and the vile operation that was going on at this, one of the nation's top ten animal research campuses, funded by both the federal government and the pharmaceutical industry.

Many hours of surveillance revealed nothing very much but allowed the mapping of security patrols and the habits of students and staff, while police activity was monitored by scanner. In the bins however, documents were recovered that gave the names of experimenters and details of their work and—most helpful of all—maps of the internal layout of buildings! What this also revealed though, was that accessing the wretched dogs was apparently going to be a major problem, although rabbits, mice, rats, guinea pigs and frogs were on offer. Tragic that the dogs who had led them to the discovery would remain doomed.

Weeks of planning and preparation had meant that on any given evening there could be ten ALF activists in position around the university and no one would know it. There was a lot going on; there were some small groups of students carrying backpacks and books and chatting, presumably about their studies; one couple, both wearing swots' spectacles, sitting on the grass pecking each others lips; another drifting slowly along the pavement holding hands, wearing backpacks also clearly happy to be together; a couple in tracksuits and caps who appeared to have been jogging; someone with a problem with his bike tyre. Was the Chinese kid listening to his personal stereo and eating potato chips a potential raider?

The only guarantee was the middle-aged bearded lecturer who had recently caused a stir by his very public u-turn on animal research after 15 years in the game. He no longer believed in what his peers told the public about cures for all ills being just a few more animals away and had begun to pay the price as his name was dragged the way of his career by those fearing his enlightened views. He might not be able to keep his mouth shut and ignore the truth about animal research any longer, but he wasn't the one going to be busting any animals out. He'd be an obvious suspect anyway, and that really wasn't his way.

There needed to be this much activity on campus on the night of the raid in order to keep attention off the raiders in the mingle. If they were going to pull this one off, it was important they blend in, and on 4 April that's exactly what ten of them did. They'd been called in from across North America because they were trusted and able. Between them, they had done a huge amount at all levels to influence change in the way animals are treated, much of it never even mentioned. Whoever it was who chose the team knew what they were doing. They'd been in confrontations together, locked on to buildings and cars, been flyposting and in police cells and had their lives threatened. It is through these experiences that the best team-mates are revealed.

Everyone knew their job and by 9.00pm, they were in position. The Courting Couple headed east to the Microbiology labs, the Joggers went west towards Psychology. There were two lookouts in radio contact with each team, sitting in the parking lot keeping an eye on things. Timing was good and everyone was going about their business, minding their business. The lock on the door at the entrance to the Microbiology labs was forced with ease leaving no glaring tell tale signs but giving free access to the stairwell and top floor lab where an experiment on 100+ mice was about to be prematurely halted by Courting Couple in balaclavas and gloves. It was a beautiful transition.

They set about their duties: while he stood as lookout, she carefully loaded the mice into small boxes, which were then placed snugly into long duffle bags. The couple then left the building minutes apart, carrying a bag each, to rendezvous with a works van parked on campus with false number plates. Inside, two handlers were eagerly awaiting the first of what was hoped to be a large haul.

Progress proved a little slower for the Joggers, now disguised and behind a concrete column at the basement loading dock of the

Psychology Building. They were out of view and trying to tear apart sheet metal ventilation covers using tin snips. A patrol was expected at some point, so speed was of the essence. If it was the older guard of the two guards who patrolled, he always physically checked the door and would therefore see them as there was nowhere to hide. The younger guard could never be bothered to get out the van. It took 20 minutes, but the vent cover finally gave way, allowing clumsy access to the basement where hundreds of rats were held.

They fixed the cover back into place as best they could, and hid up to wait for the security patrol to do their rounds. It was the older one. Damn it! Be just their luck if he noticed the damaged vent cover. In his sixties, he was meticulous about punctuality and was there bang on time but it wasn't his habit to check the vents, and he didn't notice a problem. The moment he drove on, they unlocked the door and called in the rest of the six-strong team, who filtered in from their respective cover all donning masks, gloves and white coats as they reached the basement. Within minutes, there were racks of rat cages being wheeled from various parts of the lab to the loading bay at one end, electroshock boxes being trashed at the other, and the walls being spray painted in between.

With 150 rats waiting to be loaded, the van was called in and was parked outside in no time. There was no excuse to be late: they'd waited hours for this. The moment the doors opened to the outside world, the rats stood up almost simultaneously to sniff at the cool night air for the first time. It was a beautiful sight for their rescuers, but there was no time to savour it. There was no hiding the van parked outside and no explaining it away should anyone come by. It was loaded up and on its way to a safe house as quickly as possible. It was nice for everyone to see the rats enjoy the fresh air but it was really poignant to see them drive away. Only time for a few tears, as there was still a lot of work to be done, and if all went to plan—and there had been a lot of planning—then this was only the start.

With Phase Two complete, they headed off around the corner to Biological Sciences. After yet another door had been professionally forced open, there were soon five Students turning disguise as they gathered on the stairwell before heading up to the fifth floor. One had managed to secrete a five-pound sledgehammer in his bag that even the others hadn't noticed, and he would be making good use of it to force entry through the secure doors. And it worked. What a racket! But they were in.

The conditions in this department were particularly awful. Rats, mice and guinea pigs looked anxiously and cowered in cages at the sight of humans; they had no food or water, and all had shaven skin to which chemicals had been applied to do damage. (No doubt the point of that being that researchers would learn that the test substance was harmful to rodents, and its makers would then make it available for human use. That's what they do!)

Over the next two hours, the team transferred cage after cage from lab to trolley to the foyer outside the lifts. It is a criminal offence to do this and, if caught, would be especially serious for those activists who had travelled across state boundaries. It was an impressive sight to see the flow of white coats trailing behind stacks of animals as they trundled the corridor to freedom. They had to film it! When they'd done, there were hundreds of cages of rats and mice filling the corridor with boxes of guinea pigs, rabbits in cloth sacks, and a number of African frogs. Over 900 animals in total! Over 900 lives saved: how could this possibly be wrong?

There were potentially other people in the building as had been noted during surveillance but thus far the coast was clear. There was still a matter of moving all these animals and cages down to the basement and loading them up, which obviously concerned everyone. Any trepidation lifted when the elevator arrived at the fifth floor with a 'ting', and as the door opened, there stood a totally-at-ease young man who had cried buckets over the last two years at the cruelties he'd learnt of, and so admired the ALF. Here he was in his absolute element wearing a white lab coat with his finger on the elevator control panel and a massive cheeky grin across his face as if to say: look what I found! 'Basement only,' he quipped. They loved it! His facemask was in his pocket. He thought it better to look more like he belonged there than his comrades did in their masks, in case the lift stopped on the way and someone who did belong got in. Once full of animals, there would be no explaining anything away, but it was worth every precaution in the meantime. The kid was smart, he'd been on the ball all night, they all had. They knew they were going to pull this off.

The first load was in and heading for the basement with the two human passengers only slightly concerned it would stop at another floor first. There was no point worrying about it really, but it would throw everything into chaos if someone did call for a lift. As it was, they made it safely down twice with full loads. It was then the turn of the Handlers to feel some of the elation the team inside had felt when the lift arrived safely at the fifth floor to take them all down. Again the van was at the entrance in a flash; they'd been away to drop off the rats and had come back and were in for the surprise of their lives when those double doors swung open. The other side was a picture as five of them in white coats and balaclavas stood surrounded by piles and piles of cages on racks and each other and sacks and more cages.

'Oh my God!' 'Wow!' They gasped in unison. 'You lot have been busy!'

'Not even started yet!' He'd organised it, he knew. 'Let's get this lot out of here.'

Not that anyone was but there was no time to dawdle, there were well over 1000 animals needing relocating. It was early morning by the time they'd done and the van was away for the final time. It didn't have far to go. Everyone else checked their kit for anything missing, switched off radios, dressed down, packed their bags, hugged and wandered off into the night. Just like that! All except for the lookouts who had huddled in cars patiently all night. They were stiff, sore, bored and up for it. They were the final phase of this operation.

One walked with his backpack up to the Microbiology labs, first hit, and put an incendiary device in the centre of the laboratory, carefully setting the timer for 4.00am and surrounding it with flammable material, desks and dissection boards, then casually returned down the stairs and left the building. The two of them then drove off campus to a quiet residential neighbourhood where the Animal Sciences Department headquarters was located. It was filled with computers and records containing vital information and data necessary to every animal experiment on the University campus.

Climbing through a vent into a crawlspace beneath the house, another device was prepared in the middle of the building and set to go off at 4.00am. With that done, they wandered back to the car and were soon out of the area and onto the interstate. They didn't feel they'd done very much, but just you wait!

At 4.40am, university district residents were woken to the sounds of multiple sirens responding to a blaze on the roof of the Microbiological Building. Before the fire could be brought under control, it had destroyed not only the top floor animal research laboratory but water doused on the flames had caused hundreds of thousands of dollars of damage to the labs beneath.

No sooner was the first fire attended than the Tuscon Fire Department received a call to report that the Animal Sciences headquarters was also ablaze. The fire at the residential offices wrecked the computer system and was so intense it caused irreparable structural damage to the building, and it would later have to be demolished. The ALF's Underground Railroad took care of the 1,231 animals rescued and morale was high. It was a massive night out for the ALF.

With attention on the University, another team infiltrated Tuscon once again and recovered four former racing greyhounds from the Veteran's Administration Hospital. Elsewhere, things weren't going quite so smoothly, but still there was good news. Following a multi-million dollar FBI investigation into the burning down of the Utah Fur Cooperative in 1987, which caused $1 million damage, 19 year-old activist named Joshua Ellerman was indicted for the attack on 16 federal counts, including building and possessing pipe bombs which carries a minimum mandatory sentence of 30 years in prison. (That isn't the good news!) However, prior to trial in 1999, Ellerman went on the run briefly, much to the delight of everyone who shuddered at the thought of someone so young and committed to helping animals serving a sentence like that. But it wasn't long before he had changed his mind about a lot of things, not least running for the rest of his life, and handed himself in to US marshals who had offered a deal. They were double chuffed to have him back in custody and keen to do the deal. If he was prepared to grass on his friends, the people with whom he'd carried out the Utah attack, as well as name people involved in fur farm raids, he would have his sentence reduced to seven years inside and they would do 35 years each in exchange.

Ellerman's brother Clinton was in on it too, albeit a bit part player, and also keen to cut a deal. This consequently led to six defendants charged with something serious, four of whom were keeping their mouths shut and prepared to take a severe punishment, and two prepared to do anything to save their skins. One named activist, Alex Slack, took his own life in the middle of all this, partly due to the immense strain of the impending trial, but compounded by serious health problems. Around the world, the movement was kept abreast of the whole affair: from the damaging raid, to the activist on the run, and into the cruel advance of a difficult trial, finally left only to imagine the worst outcome with three committed activists looking at 35 years, two collaborators happy with their deal, and the enemy laughing his socks off.

At trial the Ellerman brothers were good for their word. They stood before their friends in the dock and pointed the finger. And there was a lot of pointing, a bit too much in fact. They were all the evidence there was, and that was the problem. The lads had lied under oath, and the Defence played on not only their self-confessed involvement in the raid at Utah, but also their desperate need to save their own skins. Plus, two of the defendants had good alibis and the jury were suspicious of the conflicting Ellerman story. It was a terribly draining time for the remaining defendants on trial, Sean Gautschy, Adam Peace and Andrew Bishop, not only fingered by two ex-friends, but with a good friend dead and all looking at very heavy prison sentences, however the jury was on their side and returned not guilty verdicts on all 26 charges! Not the best outcome for Joshua Ellerman, who went down for seven years, and Clinton too, to be labelled as grasses and treated by others inside as such. Their only friends are in the FBI, and they sent them down!

From Arizona To Aintree

> These animal rights guys have a point to make but I'm sorry it has to be made this way.
>
> *Victim of ALF arsonists*

And so back across the water...

It had become something of a habit for me and a couple of friends to mooch around at our local hunt's fundraising Point to Point at Aintree racecourse. Since it's a horsey social event designed to raise hunt funds and attract new members, hunt saboteurs aren't exactly welcome, which is why we were there, gathering intelligence and provoking those who hated our endless presence, often using their hard lads, horses, whips and police to stop us interfering with or filming their savagery. We had an odd relationship with the Holcombe Hunt. Years of intense pressure by 'antis' had restricted their freedom and the endless encroachment of urbanisation had engulfed this hunt's former territory so that it was closed by Manchester's suburbs to the south, Liverpool to the east and Preston to the north. The hunt had little room to manoeuvre. With universities aplenty, there were always sabs to hand on any given day, affording this—one of the oldest organised mounted hunts—even less freedom, with only the moors to the north and pockets of land left to haunt.

We knew where they all lived, and they knew it, especially whenever there was any trouble and someone on our side got hurt. In response to a big day of killing, a home visit could be guaranteed; someone's horsebox might get sabotaged or they'd be treated to a Sabbing Special when hundreds would descend on their Saturday get-together and cause havoc! It got to the stage where the thinkers among their ranks began to appreciate the stupidity of trying to beat everyone up, and a situation developed in which it became possible to sab alone or monitor them without fear of attack. I often did and got away with it unscathed. Such was the relationship with the hunt that one or two even went out of their way to be polite and would buy me a drink in the pub at the end of the day. One would even give me the dates of meets if I rang him! He was himself grateful, knowing that although we had his name, phone number and address, he only ever got called occasionally for meet details and at a reasonable hour. He was also respectful and one of a few who never engaged in violence towards us.

Others weren't quite so affable, of course, and were always out for a fight given half a chance; these people (or scum, as they were more often referred to) were called at home all hours of the day and night (more often at night) and regularly had their property at home and work damaged.

The Master of this operation was a nasty piece of work who hated everyone on our side and me that little bit more. As a result, there were many, many confrontations. Sabbing this hunt was made all the more pleasurable by the sight of this vile creature grimacing at our arrival; he pretended not to care but clearly lost sight of his agenda while we were there! He didn't enjoy losing his centre-stage status or being followed by hunt sabs wherever the hunt went.

This day at Aintree in 1990 I became stuck for a lift home. Some punk band was playing in Liverpool that night, and being more into Abba, it wasn't my thing. But the others wanted to go, so I agreed to make my own way back down the M62 to Manchester. I was living a couple of miles from the hunt kennels at Bury at the time and pondered the idea of asking Alex Sneddon, the huntsman, for a lift home. He had come in his horsebox to show off the hounds, so wouldn't be short of room, but why on earth would he want to do me a favour when all I ever wanted was to make his life difficult and see him out of a job? I did ask, though. He thought briefly and said he would but told me to hang around outside the racecourse because he didn't want his Master to see him giving me a lift. This, his most valued servant, assisting the enemy? He would be lynched!

This really was bizarre! Anyway I waited by the roadside as instructed, feeling slightly stupid as no end of hunt supporters filed by. I didn't really think beyond him stopping and never expected him to. So why was I standing there! I imagined them on board laughing at me as they drove on by, me having to wander off to look for a train. But reality reined me in as Sneddon pulled up, jumped out and opened the side door of the horse trailer for me to jump in the back.

This all threw me slightly as I kind of imagined the lift would be in the cab, if at all. It threw me even more to find I had first of all to climb over a huge dead horse lying in the back, one of the victims of the days jollities, and then squeeze in alongside a couple of hunt supporters, the huntsman's daughter, the hunt terrier-man Nigel (to whom we had recently dedicated and regularly played out loud XTC's *Making Plans For Nigel* to wind him up) and a pack of 40 foxhounds.

It suddenly dawned on me that I was surrounded by the enemy and no one knew where I was! Once we set off, even I didn't know where I was. For years I'd followed this truck with no idea of its destination. Now I was inside it with no idea if it was going where it was supposed to be going. Having feigned fearlessness in front of these people for years, it was too late to ask to be let off, so I settled down for the journey. And what a weird journey it was, as I nestled in the straw like one of them, listening to them talk about the things people who carry around packs of dogs and dead horses talk about. I found out where they were hunting the following Saturday—the meet we had on the calendar was changed—and that one of their old benefactors was dead, his funeral Tuesday; and that Nigel was spending his Saturday night down the kennels dismembering the two-year-old horse their lot had shot during the day 'cos of a broken leg and would be feeding bits of her to the pack. None of this was conducive to my idea of a good night out, but I was strangely at ease in the bowels of this particular monster.

An hour later I was dropped off, as promised, near to home. I said a respectful farewell to the horse as I clambered out and parted with the others politely, and was grateful to Alex. We met again regularly over the next two years, argued, fought and exchanged something resembling pleasantries, and neither of us mentioned it again. It was a peculiar experience. He died of stomach cancer in 2005.

But there was more to the Aintree trip than meets the eye. We had talked for some time about confronting the horse racing industry in ways other than breaking a few bookmakers' windows and the talk was: where better to affect a sport consuming 250 horses a year in public events than at a racecourse that hosts not just hunts, but touring animal circuses too? One old activist in particular rekindled the debate each time we met, pestering me to look at Aintree and the possibility of sabotaging the Grand National. We weren't sure then what we were going to do, but the region was awash with eager animal liberators. As the idea fermented and the racecourse was checked out, plans began to crystallise.

The racecourse had been firebombed by the Merseyside ALF during the 1980s. On one occasion, the murderous Becher's Brook and Canal Turn fences had been burnt and £100,000 worth of fire damage had been inflicted upon the old Victorian County grandstand. As a result of these attacks and because of the high profile nature of the annual Grand National spectacle, security was high at race time, with guards and dogs patrolling the course.

We considered it would be a challenge but well worth the reward. At least sabotaging foxhunts allows the opportunity for escape; at Aintree during this spectacle, anyone daft enough to try and interfere would be surrounded by a stadium full of supporters, with no way out. It was a recipe for violence, but we figured it was too public an event for them to resort to the kind of violence you'd experience from blood sports enthusiasts in a remote copse on a Saturday afternoon.

Early on Grand National day, Saturday morning April 1991, we were up and about, packing banners and making final arrangements for a run-on before the big race that afternoon. Pretty soon, we were on the way back down the M62 to Liverpool. Security at night was one thing but it wasn't difficult to get into the course during the day and we duly did, ten of us sneaking in without paying a penny. It would make a successful stunt all the sweeter to avoid contributing to their coffers, and some local kids knew an easy way in, which was all well and good except for the fact it put us in an enclosure at the wrong end of the course. We needed to be near to the start, which we were hoping to delay in front of a purported worldwide audience of 500 million people. Another option was to go for the huge Beecher's Brook fence, which was easier to access without paying for the privilege or attracting attention and was a huge focal point for all the real horror junkies. Press photographers are literally piled on top of each other beside the tangle of tripods in anticipation of the next heap of twisted broken bodies hitting the ground at this hurdle.

At that gruesome obstacle a year earlier, Pete and I had looked on in disbelief as some of the punters crowded round to watch, then broke down and cried as horses fell and died before them. Others too macho to cry winced as these magnificent creatures slammed to the earth headfirst and lay writhing in agony. Not one punter realised it was as much their fault as anyone else's for funding the sport. Two horses died at the fence where they fell that year and five others died elsewhere around the arena over the three-day event. The two in front of us didn't actually die—in the true sense of the meaning—as a result of the fall; they were killed by attendant vets behind hastily erected screens and then winched onto the knackerman's truck for disposal.

What was equally memorable for me on that occasion was the awesome, ground-shaking power of 40 horses thundering by. It would be quite a feat to stop them and you certainly wouldn't want to get in the way. With that in mind, we split up into twos and set off to reach, by fair means or foul, a prearranged location on the inner enclosure where we positioned ourselves as close to the starting post as we were able. There we mingled and waited for the start. Banners were carefully unpacked and the camera set up.

Approximately 30 seconds before the race was due to start, as horses and riders jostled for position and the nation waited 'in anticipation' for the tape to rise, a firework rocket shot into the sky from the inner enclosure. It was ours: the signal to go. It was also something of a distraction and it certainly worked on me. As camera operator, I followed it into the sky, but rather than panning to the fledgling run-on, I couldn't leave the rocket, as it appeared to be heading for the police helicopter hovering overhead. Only in my mind did the two meet, but thankfully the rocket exploded before reaching the height of the aircraft. The two meeting would have been too much of a distraction!

Before anyone really noticed, there were nine people on the course heading for the start with banners unfurled exclaiming 'Stop The Carnage' and 'Ban The National.' Boos erupted from the stands as they realised what was happening. 'Geddem off!' they yelled!

The first police officer to catch up with a protester felt so empowered by the baying crowd he landed a right hook in the face. One down, Sarge! Eight to go! The race was delayed. For the race officials, it was now about damage limitation, about removing the obstruction before further delay. But equally, the obstruction was intent on protracted delay. Drawn to the chase, a couple of spectators and some stewards got involved and all really focused on what was most important to them—pulling down the banners! It's another recurring theme. Often people don't want to be confronted with the truth about their involvement in animal cruelty and find it easier to attack the messenger, aided by media stories about the terrible things the messenger does. Of course they all just wanted to get on with the race!

The crowd loved the rugby tackle that brought down another protester, as in turn, each was apprehended. But even then it needed further reinforcements to remove them from the ground where they'd turned floppy and non compliant. By now there were dozens of people on the track trying to clear it for the impatient queuing riders and fans.

PC 7233 said later in his statement: 'I then took hold of a female and told her to vacate the course. She made no reply and her body went limp, she fell to the floor. I took hold [of her] and attempted to walk her over the course when approximately five yards across she went limp again and fell to the floor.'

Which is where she sat, smiling and intending to remain for as long as possible. PC 7233 didn't find it amusing being so publicly humiliated and didn't want to be seen to drop her again, so used his initiative, grabbed her by the hair and—to the obvious pleasure of the angry crowd—dragged her along like something he was taking back to his cave. The race was delayed for only a matter of minutes, but the damage was done. Everyone was removed and arrested but all were later released without charge. Live TV coverage of the action was censored for the most part, but news editors rallied to cries of extremism tantamount to treason, with only a few making the connection with dead horses.

No horses died during this race, but Ballyhane suffered a ruptured blood vessel and died shortly after. Following the carnage at Beecher's Brook the previous year, the jump had been made less severe but four horses still died on Grand National day itself; Brown Trix and Seeandem died in the big race, Kingsmill suffered a broken pelvis and was 'dispatched' by the vet and Enemy Action suffering a fatal heart attack.

Within weeks an ALF team responded to the carnage. Dropped off early evening near to the site, the three-strong unit—two male, one female—left explicit instructions with the driver for their collection. It was imperative he be there, because they intended to hit the new £3 million Queen Mother Stand with a big fire while they were on site and to leave before being apprehended. They had no incendiary devices to hand, just two large barrels of petrol, a Molotov, an ice pick and a lighter. Oh that lighter! A window had to be smashed to get into the stand, so a slow timed ignition was out of the question, and they all agreed it was better to hit and run.

Having gained access through holes cut in the perimeter fence (which would also facilitate a hasty retreat) the trio had a lengthy trek to the target area across the grass. Weighed down with awkward, liquid-filled containers, they had to keep a close eye out for security patrols which passed by every half hour or so.

Puffed out, sweating and surrounded by pyrotechnic paraphernalia, the raiders took a minute to catch their breath and wait until the next patrol had passed before preparing to do the deed and leg it back the other way, or go to prison for a few years. It would have been ridiculous to try and take back the containers if they were rumbled.

This was mad, but it was too late to back out. With one hefty swing, the back door shattered to the sound of breaking glass and in went the first barrel. The next was poured in after it. There was a seriously strong smell of trouble in the cool night air! The two slower members of the team moved away from the immediate area and squatted out of sight behind an advertising hoarding while the flame was lit. It should have taken a few seconds but the others waited and waited and waited for the whoosh that didn't come. The failed fire starter came back in a panic: 'The fuckin' lighter doesn't work!'

'Wot?'

'LIGHTER!!' He demonstrated.

No one else had one. What a situation to be in! The next 15 minutes were spent desperately trying every scout trick in the book but to no avail. Just when it seemed hopeless, at last a spark turned into a little flicker of a flame and that little flame in turn brought the molly to life. A quick glance around and two of the arsonists took off while the third lobbed in the petrol bomb. In an instant, the entire ground floor was engulfed in a fireball as three figures bolted from the scene sharing a nervous laugh.

As they clambered through the holes in the perimeter, they looked back to see not just the immediate horizon aglow from their efforts, but the blue flashing lights of fire engines heading to the scene. The station was just down the road: they were damn quick and managed to contain the blaze, which still caused tens of thousands of pounds worth of damage. Serious enough, but things were set to get worse for Aintree…

Return To Aintree

That wasn't reckless. I did it on purpose.

Sea Shepherd captain Paul Watson's response when accused of reckless behaviour after ramming a whaling ship in open waters

It was 3 April, 1993, and I was locked up in Walton Prison at the time (just before I escaped) which is just around the corner from the Aintree Racecourse. I was listening to the build-up of the big race on the radio with my cell mate John, in his 40s, who was admittedly a bit of a scally but who had been wrongly imprisoned and did later get released on appeal. Normally I wouldn't listen to the race commentary (out of disgust) but it was a big thing for John having grown up in the area with Grand National day a big local event. Plus I'd been tipped the wink on a visit of something that was in the offing and on which the bookies weren't taking bets. Funnily enough, after we'd talked about the darker side of horse racing, my cellmate was sharing my newfound enthusiasm for today's race and was excited that something might happen to disrupt it.

Punters started to arrive at the racecourse long before the 3.45pm start of the race. Some had flown in especially, others had filled local hotel rooms days before to make the most of the three-day festival of racing. There was a small demonstration outside as always and, of course, heckling from some race goers, aggrieved that anyone might question their right to enjoy their sport. No point trying to persuade a moron whose better arguments in defence of the race that Saturday afternoon were: 'Why don't you just fuck off?'

'Bollocks'

'They (the horses) wouldn't do it if they didn't enjoy it'

'Fuckin' hippies'

'Why don't you get jobs?'

'Can't you do something better with your time?'

Now there's an idea. With intellectual debate getting nowhere fast outside the course and security increasing inside, it was looking rather gloomy for the Objectors, except for the few who had made their way undetected to the start of the race. These brave few were indeed doing something better with their time! With a minute to go before race start with 40 horses and jockeys milling around impatiently and jostling for places behind the electronic start tape, and with security guards, stewards and police keeping an eye on things, a small group of saboteurs appeared on the course, by the Start side of the first fence. One high-ranking police officer saw them and pointed down the course. While reaching for his radio, he was heard to ask of his colleague: 'How the fuck did they get there?' Who's he gonna call? It was his job to keep them out! Tell whomever you want now, officer, but it's too late, everyone's going to know in a minute anyway!

The saboteurs jogged towards the start unfurling the big 'STOP THE SLAUGHTER' banner, which the crowd there had seen before. Well, similar. The police had confiscated the last one 'to prevent any further breach of the peace.' It'll be demonstrations they ban next at this rate! (Ooh, spoke too soon! Keep reading!) The crowd booed and the TV cameras pretended it wasn't happening. You know the script, and so did security staff who charged at the handful of joggers, outnumbering them six to one, and waded in. The race start was delayed again while the track was cleared of non-compliant, bruised protesters and their offensive rip-proof banners.

That done, everyone breathed a sigh of relief that the race could begin. That is, apart from the second group of saboteurs, who, once again, had gone unnoticed further down the track and who were now taking a deep breath before launching themselves into the equation. They were soon also heading for that god-like start tape. Whoa horse! Now everyone is getting agitated, especially the hyped up spring-loaded horses and their squat jockeys, some of whom have waited all their lives to race this race and are starting to feel like they've been at the start line forever. What happened to the bloody security cordon that was supposed to be protecting the racecourse? This was comical!

The race was delayed again while more scuffles ensued and protesters were gradually removed from the course. The start controller then decided that it was time to loose the horses before anything else happened. But in his haste in raising the tape it snagged a couple of horses round the neck that had strayed too close, causing it to rise only enough for half the field to pass. The rest remained behind the tape. Oh dear... False start! That'll be another delay. Or will it? Seeing the problem, the race official standing 150 yards down the course started to wave his flag frantically to signal a false start, but the riders thought the man waving was another saboteur trying to disrupt the race so they ignored him and kept right on racing. *Now* there's a problem!

And so commenced the race that wasn't. Some of the jockeys were so focused on getting round that they ran the whole race before it was pointed out the 1993 Grand National never actually started. The government lost £6 million in betting tax, the bookies lost an estimated £80 million, and five hundred million people worldwide witnessed the greatest sporting debacle of all time. Some blamed the poor flag waver who became the scapegoat, but *The Sunday Telegraph* saw it differently:

> Yesterday the greatest steeplechase in the world was destroyed by animal rights activists.

The following year a £1 million, 6′ high iron curtain was erected around the course and armed police were on patrol alongside hundreds of other officers ready to pounce and presumably shoot saboteurs at the first sign of disobedience. One high-ranking Special Branch officer, whose team put five months of planning into the operation described it: 'As high profile a job as you can imagine.' A horse race!

It was revealed that Aintree later paid £350 plus two free tickets to a couple they'd evicted from the course earlier in the day on suspicion of them being animal activists. Must have been the halo. Might be worth bearing in mind as a nice little earner for anyone fancying a walk around Aintree at race time with a carton of soya milk and a woolly-looking hat. Police in predawn raids on National Day arrested twenty-three animal rights campaigners that year. All were released after the race without charge, and following a civil hearing, £22,000 was awarded in compensation for unlawful detention. A small price for the public to pay to ensure the race went ahead, eh? Similar tactics are used to contain hunt sabs, anti-vivisectionists and others.

Back on B wing the day it all went pear shaped at Aintree, we were glued to the radio. This was the stuff of dreams for me! Sabotage plot executed with military precision right at the heart of bandit territory with a few minor injuries and no dead bodies. We both felt part of it. I knew that everyone around me wouldn't be quite so pleased, especially not the young B wing screw, whom everyone hated—he with the big mouth and some low level humour to contribute to everything including suicide attempts by prisoners. He'd had something to say as I passed him that morning, about how he was looking forward to the race, not really caring if he won his bet, more that there were plenty of fallers. Sure enough, as I passed the servery for food that evening, he snarled at me as politely as he knew how, 'That your half-wit mates acting the twat today, eh Mann?'

Yep! We both knew the answer, but I'd long since deduced people like that are best ignored, so I kept my mouth shut. But I was unable to contain that aura of smugness I had following me. 'Fuckin' idiots' was him concluding our brief one sided debate. Look who's talking—the biggest half-wit in the place!

Within a couple of hours though, the smile had been wiped clean off my smug face as news broke of a serious incident at the closing meet of the Cambridgeshire Hunt. Some incident! According to reports, at least one person had been taken to hospital with suspected serious injuries. Unless one of them has fallen from their horse, this usually means a saboteur has been hurt but it turned out to be far worse than normal.

Hounding Hares & Killing Kids

When I was old enough to realize all meat was killed, I saw it as an irrational way of using our power, to take a weaker thing and mutilate it. It was like the way bullies would take control of younger kids in the schoolyard.

River Phoenix

Ancient Rituals

Foxhunting, as it is recognised today, started over 300 years ago with the training of hounds to hunt, following the restoration of King Charles II in 1660. In Norman England, deer and boar were hunted exclusively by the Royal Family and their guests in royal forests, the privilege gradually extending to all landowners, some who formed their own packs. By the middle of the next century its popularity had increased enormously. While there were always objectors, real opposition took 300 years to really kick in.

The very first coordinated attacks on hunting came with the evolution of the ALF, who had hunting high on the agenda. In August of 1973, the property and vehicles of several hunts in the south of England were attacked. Thirty years and countless raids later, and still no hunt fanatics have yet been injured in the process (which suggests, does it not, that contrary to news stories there probably isn't the intent). Hunting offends around 80% of the population according to repeated opinion polls, and was finally outlawed in the UK at the beginning of the 21st century. The pompous public displays haven't helped win friends, nor has the arrogance. Even given the benefit of all that, they do spin some yarns when trying to defend the indefensible, and there's no hiding the sickening desire for violence. Welcome to the countryside!

There were 347 registered hunts operating in the UK in 1999, made up of 185 foxhunts in England and Wales and nine in Scotland, 18 packs of harriers (hunting—mainly hares—on horseback) 75 packs of beagles (hares on foot) 11 packs of Bassett hounds (hares on foot) 18 packs of mink hounds, three staghounds, 17 draghound packs and 11 bloodhounds.

Hounds hunt by scent and are bred to run with their quarry for as long as possible as opposed to being bred for speed, since this would mean a shorter chase and less fun. Hunt supporters are spies for the hounds, giving away the direction of the fleeing quarry, blocking the way of 'antis' and attacking them when it's quiet. These are not very nice people in my experience, especially the terrier-men. These characters are dangerous, they like to think they are hard-men and often are hard and heartless, threatening by appearance and generally not that bright. They can be seen hovering around hunt meets looking for skulls to crack, usually with a battle-scarred terrier or two at heel or stuck in a box somewhere to use for flushing foxes.

Spades, firearms and iron bars are always close at hand; these are useful tools of the trade for those dealing in death and destruction—often used as weapons against anyone bold enough to try to prevent them being used on wild animals. With a few farm hands thrown in, there's a volatile crowd itching to attack sabs in a secluded valley or woodland somewhere. For some of these people, this has become part of the day's sport.

Everything starts to fall into place when they start to speak and you weigh up the facts. We're been told there are at between 300,000 and 500,000 foxes in the UK (I would estimate more). The hunters themselves say that on average they kill between 12,000 and 13,000 foxes a year. The fox as a species could withstand an annual mortality rate of 70%, yet foxhunts account for only around 2.5% of their number. Hunts are known in certain areas for rearing foxes artificially for the purpose of hunting them down, so it's difficult to establish what percentage of those they kill are purpose bred as opposed to what they call pests, but it's certainly safe to say their efforts are futile. There weren't always foxes on the Isle of Wight, until some fanatics introduced them to satisfy their need to control and dominate something.

The Government's then Ministry of Agriculture Food and Fisheries estimated that predation on lambs by foxes is 'insignificant', unlike human predation. Studies show that even by farmers' estimates, only 1 in 200 lambs falls victim to a fox, whereas between 10 and 24% of lambs die from hypothermia, malnutrition, disease, or are still-born. All the others are slaughtered soon after. Have you heard the one about the fox who enjoyed being chased by 40 dogs with murderous intent? They all do, according to the gentle folk who pleasure themselves with the hunt. Or the one about the quick nip to the back of the neck, ending the chase: nice, clean, painless and lovely? Really? Unlikely! So few hunt riders get to witness a kill that some probably genuinely believe this is how it happens. We are after all taught to believe the strangest things. I've been in at the kill more than I wish to recall and never once did the fox fall asleep with a nip to the neck. Not even David Attenborough has managed to film that!

The sad reality is that saboteurs have recovered more fox carcasses post-hunt than anyone other than the huntsmen themselves, and, without exception, the animal has been disembowelled by a frenzied pack of dogs in an inevitable distressing bloody, violent finale. The only exceptions to this are when sabs have jumped in with the pack and grabbed the quarry before it's killed. It's at this point in proceedings, and at dig outs, where confrontations with hunters often occur. Not as you might think because sabs have attacked hunt supporters in anger, but because the hunters are so frenzied in their desire to recover their trophy or dispose of the evidence. Many dismembered animals have been taken to the press or back to the meet for all to see, but hunts prefer this not to happen.

When I first witnessed this frantic desperation over a dead animal, I was utterly flabbergasted. It was very early one misty autumn morning in Cheshire woodland and as three of us scrambled among the pack for the remains of the fox they'd caught, the huntsman waded into the fray on his horse, oblivious to what injuries he might cause, sending dogs and people scattering. He then leaped off and started throwing punches at the three of us and tried to grab what was left of the fox! He was so angry that we were going to recover the corpse before him. This feverish, psychotic behaviour was for me even more difficult to comprehend than the hunt itself. And he isn't alone: and nor am I in witnessing this sort of behaviour repeated many, many times in this environment.

Battle Scars & Blood Sports

> They are just paid rent-a-mobs. At first we thought they were genuine animal lovers, but now we know they get paid about £40 a day for disrupting things. Most of them are on the dole or on student grants so that is a lot of money for them. It is all politically motivated with someone in the background paying them
>
> *Mrs. Dorothy Cook, Master of the Holderness Hunt in the East Yorkshire, Journal, January 1994*

It was 1984 and I was new to 'sabbin' but learning fast. I was also quick on my feet and energetic, so was able to stay close to the hunt if they were moving, unlike the majority of observers on both sides. This was something I found often landed me in tricky situations and outnumbered by an ever-angry enemy. On one occasion early in my education, at the meet there had been 30 riders and a few dozen saboteurs, four Lancashire Constabulary mounted police and a pack of dogs. A couple of hours in, there were two coppers, the huntsman, the hounds, a hare and myself. The hare is the key player in all this. And they accuse us of putting animals before people! The police seemed to enjoy these events as they talked horsey with other riders, waited in line with hunt supporters to jump the next obstacle and galloped after hounds in cry. Got to be there, may as well enjoy it, eh? Their presence did sometimes help to keep the peace; at other times they just fanned the flames and were to blame for sabs being hurt, animals killed. I may not have been able to save this particular hare, but I desperately wanted to try. After all, that was the point of being there.

She had been hunted for an hour and was slowing down. A hare will run in ever decreasing circles as it tires. As the hounds close in and it has little left, it runs in a direct line. Most of the hunt riders and saboteurs were spread out across country engaged with their own conversations, confrontations, and obstacles. I just had to get in between the hounds and the quarry, a big brown hare with huge legs, ears and eyes, the white of which were increasingly prominent as it looked behind in terror. We could all see what was happening. Sneddon, the huntsman, had had his gallop and could have tried to stop the kill but that would have been too much to ask. I have no idea what the police were thinking, but their actions spoke clearly enough as they did their utmost to stop me crossing into the killing field. I was caught and corralled against the hedge, flanked by two police on huge horses pulling my collar high and threatening me with arrest for action likely to cause a breach of a peace, as the hounds in full cry bore down on the staggering hare on the other side of the hedge. With Sneddon racing in to be there at the kill to collect his trophy or masturbate or whatever it is they feel the need to do, the hare let out the most awful scream as the pack engulfed it in the middle of the field.

This was the desperate last cry of a small animal, a harmless utterly inoffensive individual, and I heard those cries over and over, again and again for months. Most of the hunt didn't even see it, yet it was done in their name! For what purpose? What happened that day changed me forever.

Since the earliest meetings between sabs and hunters there has been serious violence, and the victims have tended to be saboteurs. Hunt supporters—despite the impression given by the media and the hunts—have suffered remarkably little violence in reality. Hunt violence is extensively illustrated on the HSA website. In 1976 in the UK, League Against Cruel Sports activist William Sweet was shot and killed during an altercation with a shooting fanatic. Others have died since and the list of walking wounded is much, much longer, each a shocking story of extreme violence and police and media indifference.

Thirty-four-year-old Eddie Coulston hadn't been sabbing before when he joined hundreds of others at the annual gathering of coursing supporters at the repulsive Waterloo Cup hare-coursing spectacle at Altcar near Liverpool in 1984. Coulston was there less than an hour when his skull was cracked open by coursing supporter Paul Willingale using a shooting stick. Astonishingly, the assailant was later sentenced to just six months in prison. Eddie Coulston had to undergo life-saving brain surgery to remove bone splinters and a clot, and was left afflicted with epileptic fits. The very same day he was attacked, coursers killed one of their own in a drunken brawl. The violence surrounding this event brought home just how dangerous a crack over the head could be—something many hundreds of saboteurs have suffered and narrowly avoided. Many such incidents have been filmed and photographed by sabs, hunt monitors and independent observers, many witnessed by police, yet the number of these thugs sent to prison can be counted on the fingers of one hand.

Here's another random example. Twenty years on, Steve Christmas (34) was awarded £18,500 in criminal injuries compensation, following an attack by hunt supporters whilst out sabbing a cub hunting meet of the Old Surrey and Burstow FH. Considering the circumstances, this was a hard-fought-for but derisory award. Psychotic hunt supporters had been goading the small group of regular sabs for hours, whipping some and making threats of worse to come. Angered beyond words at a group trying to stop him tracking down some tiny baby animals to tear to pieces, gamekeeper Martin Maynard drove very deliberately at the group, hitting Croydon sab Steve Christmas as he tried to flee, then deliberately driving over him with his Land Rover. And all this on land owned by a local magistrate. After the incident, Christmas was airlifted to hospital where he had tubes inserted into his heart, was put on a ventilator and spent four weeks in intensive care with a crushed pelvis, broken ribs, extensive internal bleeding and serious abdominal injuries. Consequently, he had to have part of his intestines removed, a plate fitted in his pelvis and repairs made to multiple stomach hernias. He now suffers from a double groin hernia that is inoperable due to previous operations and he is unable ever to work again. But for his sturdy frame, the attacker would have surely killed him.

There were three good witnesses; they'd all ducked out of the way of the vehicle in time and told how Maynard initially drove off in a panic but then returned minutes later to taunt his dying victim. The police, incredibly, were desperately slow to bring their man into custody. The assailant, even though he was eventually charged with Grievous Bodily Harm, had the charges against him dropped by the CPS because—they said—one of the witnesses had been previously in prison for an unrelated animal liberation offence. An extremely unusual decision under any circumstances, but given the attacker and his vehicle were clearly identified as having nearly killed someone deliberately and Maynard himself had a lengthy criminal record for violence, this decision seemed even more inappropriate. There were tyre tracks in the earth and over the victim; there was a number plate and vehicle description, and even a name to go with face of the driver! Even more perverse was a two-year delay by the police to bring charges against Maynard for driving with no insurance or a driving licence; charges which were brought to bear eventually and only then under great pressure.

Soon after a group of sabs who descended on the hunt kennels to protest following the attack, were attacked by hunt staff with pickaxe handles. The sabs responded by breaking some house windows before scarpering. Comprising mainly young women, they were later hunted down by a squad of six-dozen police who made 18 arrests and later sent them to trial for conspiracy. After protracted legal proceedings those found guilty narrowly avoided prison but were given lengthy community service orders. All as the hunt's supporters continued to attack those who oppose them and their torture of little furry animals.

It was four years and £20,000 in legal fees later before an appeal against an initial decision not to award compensation was overturned. The money awarded for injuries sustained took no account of the substantial loss of earnings of a professional man. This is one of a large number of cases plodding through the courts in which saboteurs are seeking redress for the behaviour of the police and hunt supporters. Many, many others get nowhere near justice.

Some saboteurs can only take the threat of arrest and reality of violence for so long before they decide they have to move on to other forms of campaigning with hardened hearts, or just move on; others seem able to overcome it with admirable dexterity and go on for years risking life and limb to save wild animals. These people are the true heroes of this movement.

Fighting Back

> They really are a dirty and smelly bunch. They don't wash. Apparently most are students paid £35 a day and given a lunch by the League Against Cruel Sports.
>
> *Quorn FH supporter*

I found my feet in this environment with people who had decided early on they weren't going to be compromised in any way by hunt supporters. This suited me fine. Pacifism is a lovely idea, but around hunts, dead, badly hurt or ineffectual is the result. I've seen people kicked unconscious for not fighting back and kicked some more; women and the elderly are treated the same as the rest.

Long before hunt stewards were employed to contain the antis, hunts up and down the country had succeeded in causing some very serious injuries to the young and old, male and female, many of who have never shown any inclination towards violence and have no interest in fighting with anyone. There have been countless permanent physical assaults, many documented injuries, broken bones and fractured skulls, deaths and many near misses, yet despite the exaggerated police presence at many hunt meets to prevent public disturbance or a breach of the peace—the catch all offence for which saboteurs have been arrested wholesale pre-emptively on countless occasions—very few of the many aggressors have ever been taken before the courts and even fewer have been adequately punished.

It was my instinct that the thugs responsible for abusing animals should be challenged at every opportunity long before I realised that they readily attacked those of us who were peacefully trying to stop or monitor them, and their lack of respect for peaceful protesters surely served to fuel my resolve. We had attracted something of a reputation in the Northwest and were often called on to assist other groups when the violence got too serious for them to deal with. National hits were big payback for something serious, a show of strength with 200 sabs to say: you hit us we hit you. It didn't always help, of course, to support these big hits on the local hunt and then leave, because local sabs would later bear the brunt of subsequent retribution. But equally, these raids would have a controlling effect on some hunts. I loved those days when we were able to swamp the hunt and make their day impossible. Maybe catch a few supporters unawares and have them feel some of that fear or occasionally set them up to think we were a few lone sabs, await the inevitable aggression, and then pile into them.

I've seen many anti-hunt activists arrested for being beaten up (me included) some whilst lying in hospital, battered, bruised and bleeding! It always seemed so easy for a hunt rider to accuse someone of an offence and secure a prompt arrest, while the possibility of it ever working in reverse is very slight to say the least. Even if a saboteur was lying on the ground bleeding and the name and address of the assailant was well known, it would be a miracle if an arrest followed. Why is that?

After the 1980s—when many sabs had given up on the notion that taking a beating was an occupational hazard and would retaliate—and win—against hunt hard-men—hired thugs were brought in by hunts. To call them thick-skulled ex-military psychopaths would not be an exaggeration. These 'stewards' or 'marshals', as their employers describe them, act as agents for the landowners and are empowered to use the minimum force they see as necessary to remove saboteurs. The irony is that for years the hunting fraternity had accused saboteurs of being paid to use violence to disrupt hunting, pointing the finger at the Labour Party, the League Against Cruel Sports and even the Communist Party as paymasters (it was actually the police, believe it or not!).

Seeing Through The Lies

> At last week's hunt terriermen were told if they broke a saboteur's leg they would get a bonus of £5. It would be £10 for putting a saboteur in hospital.
>
> *The Mail on Sunday, February 1992*

Lynn Sawyer was in the middle of it. She has an interesting perspective on the subject.

> My hunting career began with the Essex Foxhounds in 1982 when I was fourteen. By 1990, I had hunted with many, many different packs, including the East Essex, Essex Farmers & Union, Puckeridge & Thurlow, Cottesmore and West Kent Foxhounds, the Eastern Counties, Nottinghamshire and Kent & Sussex Minkhounds, the Epping Coursing Club and many West Country foxhound and staghound packs. Those eight years were spent running, or occasionally riding, to hounds; wielding a spade at dig-outs; helping out with hound exercise and doing odd jobs around hunt kennels; stewarding at point-to-points; collecting signatures on pro-hunt petitions and donations for the BFSS stalls and persuading the public at shows and by writing to the press.
>
> From 1984-90, much of my time was spent gathering information for the field sports fraternity on anti-hunt activity. This meant doing anything to gather information including taking vehicle registrations (over 130 on file by 1990!) photographing sabs, delving through animal rights literature and music bought in specialist shops, attending animal rights meetings and gigs, chatting to the police and generally finding out what I could (none of which I'm proud of now).
>
> For several reasons in 1990, I could no longer continue these activities, and I then spent four years trying to ascertain what exactly my feelings were. I spent time with the Shire hunts (the Quorn, the Cottesmore and Belvoir Foxhounds) and revisited the Essex before deciding earlier this year that it was time to speak out in the hope of stemming the tide of grossly exaggerated anti-sab propaganda and the violence it has brought to the field.

I went to great lengths to discuss the issue of hunt violence with the BFSS and other pro-hunting people (including John Hopkinson, Stephen Loveridge, Peter Smith and Nick Herbert of the BFSS and John Swift, director of the British Association of Shooting and Conservation) before, and indeed for some time after, it became clear I could not permeate their rather narrow-minded way of thinking or change or influence any of them without being patronised or being singled out as a trouble maker.

An Open Letter To The Hunting World

This is an open letter to those who I feel have a right to be informed of my recent decision to abandon my position of neutrality on the hunting issue in favour of the animal rights movement. For those who are not already aware, I ceased to be a hunt supporter four years ago because I was very uncomfortable with the way in which I was expected to behave in that role and due to the reaction I received from some pro hunt leaders when I disagreed with their tactics. Four years of sitting on the fence has given me time to reflect upon my past as a hunt follower, a BFSS voluntary worker, a farm worker, a meat eater, etc. Endless hours have been spent studying animal rights literature, keeping up to date via the sporting press, attending hunt meets and listening whilst in the field to the views of a wide spectrum of people from both sides. This decision is probably the most difficult that I have ever had to make, it has not been taken lightly and I am simply being honest with the readers of this letter and with myself. My reasons are as follows:

1. Whilst maintaining my deep respect for the sanctity of human life and dignity, I have extended my concern to ALL sentient beings. I now believe that it is abhorrent to kill, unless in exceptional cases such as euthanasia, or to cause suffering to any living creature for our own benefit. This means that I am now a dietary vegan and I will be boycotting leather, silk, wool etc. in the future. I can no longer ignore my remorse at the large amount of suffering that I have caused, nor can I ignore what is happening in the abattoirs, in the laboratories, in the oceans, down on the farm and out in the field.
2. Whilst I will admit that saboteurs are not all the paragons of

virtue, I can testify that during twelve years of observing sabs active in the field, including six years of information gathering for the BFSS I was treated with courtesy on most occasions, witnessed others being treated in a similar fashion and non-violent, effective tactics. I am fully satisfied that most sabs are altruists and that there is more than adequate legislation to deal with anyone, from either side, who threatens or uses violence.

3. British history is full of cases when people have had no option but to use non-violent direct action unless they wanted their grievances to be totally ignored by a self-serving establishment. The suffragettes were not deterred by prison and their modern counterparts, the sabs, the road protesters, CND, or any other group or individual who refuse to be patronised by the state are not going to abandon deeply held beliefs when they face the same historical fate. The Criminal Justice and Public Order bill seeks to criminalise all those seen by the government as weak enough, unconventional enough or easy enough to brand as a threat to society to use as scapegoats for their incompetence. This endangers the civil liberties of EVERYONE and it obliterates the right to protest effectively, the right of freedom of movement, the right of freedom of association and the right to live in a way that differs from what the government thinks is normal. I suggest that people read this draconian piece of literature and consider its implications very carefully. I cannot maintain a position of neutrality in the face of such a vicious attack on civil liberties.

The instigators of the use of stewards in the field could not have possibly thought up a more effective way of raising the levels of violence to unprecedented levels. It seems rather too convenient that when sabs used the inevitable, time honoured mass hit tactic when faced with large, less than diplomatic hoards of 'the lads', who dragged them off public rights of way under the aegis of the BFSS that Mr. Howard then launched his attack on the less powerful, less influential group involved in the resulting battles. I hope that I am wrong in assuming that this was the desired outcome of those who put the lives of hunting folk, stewards, sabs and police officers at considerable risk by their confrontational tactics, because if I am right then the ramifications of this bill are even more sinister. Once again I cannot turn a blind eye to this sort of manipulation and bullying.

> I apologise to those who will feel betrayed by this change of heart, especially those who have had the decency and integrity to listen. I will never support the use of violence against people and I guarantee that past confidences will remain confidential.

That was 1990. Lynn Sawyer has since then become a deeply committed campaigner for animals who has spent an unreasonable amount of her life in police cells and even hospital for her efforts. Her need to cleanse herself of her past has taken her on an unimaginable journey, more of which you'll read about here.

Partial Policing

> In animal cruelty cases I want RSPCA inspectors to judge whether to alert us to possible child cruelty. Animal cruelty can be a sign of violence in families and can sound a warning bell that children may be at risk. We need to recognise the cruelty connection between child and animal abuse.
>
> *Jim Harding, Chief Executive NSPCC, The Express Oct 1988*

On top of the ever-present threat of violence, hunt saboteurs have as I've indicated also had the police acting as a barrier to effective protest and so strengthening the incentive for more covert direct action. Incitement. For all those police appeals for extra officers, you would be forgiven for thinking their wishes had been met after one or two outings with hunt saboteurs. When an influential hunt master rings for assistance in ensuring a good day's hunting, the local police chief is usually more than able and willing to provide an escort of substance: in vans and cars, on bikes, on horseback, even in the air. And if orders come from above to nick everyone in sight, regardless of what they've done, then that's just what they'll do. As soon as sabs turn up, they'll be bundled into police vans and held in police cells for the duration of the day's hunting. This is Great Britain. It's illegal, but the government promotes it. Like wars and unnecessary suffering. For all the negative contributions from the police throughout this story to the cause of achieving emancipation for animals, not something I want to believe happens, I have to say I have never been so happy to see them arrive as when a situation has got out of hand, and they have probably even saved my life and the lives of people around me more than once, but they have negated this good and the duties they are supposed to carry out, by focusing greater emphasis on calculated bias and indifference.

Such bias was, of course, not a good thing for the wildlife or the sabs in the early days, but because it is still illegal to arrest people for no reason, and because a few sympathetic lawyers have been prepared to challenge the authority of the police, arbitrary arrests became a blessing in disguise for hunt saboteurs. In recent years, countless out-of-court settlements have been paid to saboteurs by police forces relying on the unlawful arrest and detention of law-abiding citizens to appease foxhunters. In one 14 month period alone, one solicitor recovered a total of £80,000 in damages from ten police forces for 80 former detainees, finally substantiating that age-old claim by the hunting fraternity that saboteurs are paid. Told you, it's the police! Hundreds of thousands of pounds of taxpayers' money has been frittered away in this fashion by overzealous police forces over many years, often returned to kit out or buy new sab vans and even to fund ALF raids!

At the end of the 1993 hunting season, *The Liverpool Echo* reported 'Soaring Hunt Control Costs Cause Concern.' A 16 strong police hunt squad, including motorcyclists and video cameramen, had been set up to contain saboteurs who had been disrupting things for the Cheshire hunts for many years. The paper reported that 8,000 hours were now dedicated to policing the county during the 92/93 season costing £120,000. This was not for a few brave but non-violent anti-hunt activists, but for a bunch of arrogant, devious, lying thugs who are stuck in the past and demanding and receiving endless police resources to help them maintain their lifestyle. All of this negativity was conspiring to make hunting an issue for the majority and something to be debated at length in the UK Parliament and eventually banned!

The business of a hunt saboteur is to interfere with blood sports using whatever tactics are available to prevent a kill within ever more restrictive laws. The classic tactic is to emulate the huntsman, who blows a hunting horn to talk to his hounds and direct them where to hunt. Saboteurs do likewise, using hunting horns to tell the pack something completely different to cause sufficient confusion for the hunted animal to get away. Scent sprays like garlic and aniseed are used to mask the scent left by the hunted animal, without which the pack can't make headway as they track by smell. Generally, the only law saboteurs allow themselves to break is that of trespass, which up until the 1994 Criminal Justice Act was passed by the pro hunt Conservative government, was a very trivial civil matter and not a criminal offence. That and other laws, together with preferential policing, have steadily made it increasingly difficult to interfere with the hunting of wild animals and save lives without risking punishment.

It is, then, hardly surprising that there has been a constant trickle of people who have felt they're left with no option but to resort to the clandestine methods of the ALF, when there are armies of hunt thugs and police officers preventing saboteurs saving lives, using behaviour which is more often than not violent and of course criminal. Lawful or not, it was a bitter pill for me to swallow very early on in my career when every effort was used by the forces of law and order to ensure that my local hunt killed in front of me.

Police regularly use their vehicles to block the way, to stop, search and detain saboteurs under the pretext of having to search for weapons or drugs. This has often given the hunters the chance to make themselves scarce and hunt wild animals out of view until their underdeveloped hearts are content. Most people are appalled to hear of this behaviour so it isn't mentioned much. The police are most often there to enforce a law, which has been responsible for putting many anti-hunt activists in a cell for causing harassment, alarm or distress to others, in breach of Section 5 of the 1986 Public Order Act. Far more people are harassed, alarmed and distressed by the killing of wild animals and by hunt supporters than by saboteurs trying to prevent the kill, but laws such as this are created to a specific agenda and in this case that was more with a view to protecting huntsmen and not the general public from harassment.

Baiting Badger Baiters

> First it was necessary to civilize man in relation to man. Now it is necessary to civilize man in relation to nature and the animals.
>
> *Victor Hugo (1802-1885)*

In 1984, the blood sports magazine *Shooting News* (now *The Countryman's Weekly* and still not a nice read for anyone with even a basic level of sympathy for animals) launched a public appeal for funds in aid of three men convicted of badger digging and were sponsoring awards for the best battle-scarred terrier. One article promoting the pit bull terrier as a 'vermin control dog' was written by a David Morphew, who was later convicted for his involvement in a dogfight at Cheshunt, Hertfordshire. Books on dog fighting, badger digging and cockfighting were advertised for the entertainment of the perverts who participated in such practices. In 1988, the paper's then editor, Clive Binmore, called for the badger to have its legal protection revoked and for it to be made again legally available for hunting without fear of prosecution. Attracting the sort of people you'd expect, over the years, numerous advertisers, writers and contributors to the magazine have been found guilty of criminal acts of cruelty.

One advert, for a small black terrier which would 'face any quarry,' is the best recorded case and opened the door for the most revealing undercover operation ever carried out against badger baiting (which we'll get to shortly).

A couple of years earlier, 1988 I think, I had placed my own Wanted advert in *Shooting News,* looking as I was for a fox controller in the Rochdale area. I was out to see what I could tease out of local blood junkies before they realised I wasn't actually looking for a fox controller to control foxes but instead to find out who they were and what they were up to. Well, the applications poured in! I shouldn't gloat because it isn't funny that so many people will kill on request but hey, you have to get the laughs where you can and if it's at their expense, then where better?

These people were startlingly keen. I used our local animal rights group PO Box number, but they failed to notice that, and when the first batch of respondents replied to offer their services—70 of them—I wrote again and asked for references from people they'd killed for previously and any photographs of them and their work so I could choose the best man for the job. Well, not all of them were stupid or keen enough, but at least half complied and sent me hundreds of pictures of them posing with guns and dogs and corpses, all really proud of themselves. They weren't so smug once the penny had dropped and they realised what they'd done! Oh how I laughed, once I got over the portfolio of perversions.

Dimwit Trevor Limb of Benchill in Manchester didn't reply to me, but he was sucked in by another scam, which would have consequences for him and some of his perverted friends. The two men who contacted him in response to his advert looked the part and could stomach eating meat and watching animals being tortured at the same time, yet were on our side!

Not something to be proud of if you ask me, but positive negatives at times like this. Within weeks, they were invited along on a badger-digging holiday at Builth Wells in the middle of Wales. Limb and his four chums didn't seem to mind one bit that their guests brought along a video camera and wanted to take back some moving memories of their trip. It was nothing out of the ordinary, as they regularly took along a camera of their own to record their adventures for viewing later in the comfort of their homes.

What was different and most unfortunate for the intrepid five on this occasion was their new friends intention to show this footage to the world. They were working with the League Against Cruel Sports (LACS) in the hope of securing convictions. The League have had to resort to provide the funding to pursue private prosecutions where there's clearly a case of illegal animal cruelty to answer because the police and CPS have proved all too often they're likely to bodge the job or don't have the motivation to prosecute for acts of cruelty to animals.

The five men in this group were all clearly sadistic monsters; the pub talk alone told of that, but the knives, spades, shotguns and pack of dogs they took along to pit against a few badgers were a big reminder. The whole process from locating active badger sets through to the slow extraction and systematic torture of every animal forced out was captured on film along with the people responsible for it all. With sufficient evidence gathered (mostly coming from the digging of one set housing a family of three badgers, but added to from tapes taken previously by the gang themselves on hunting trips to Ireland and elsewhere) the case was passed to the police and the five arrested.

At their trial at Brecon magistrates' court, the brutal footage of their adventures showed badgers baited by dogs, shot, stabbed and eventually killed. Limb boasted of cooking and eating the leg of one of the badgers he'd taken home to Manchester. Another badger's head was stuffed and mounted but it's what they did to the animals before they died that makes them evil. The footage, which lasts for over three hours, is as bad as it gets. Even the not so hard men in the dock were aware of that, as they sat nervously twitching through proceedings, their backs exposed to a packed public gallery seeking justice. The restraint shown by the viewing public—extremists one and all—as their exploits were screened was admirable.

These types of men are violent and dangerous people who pose a serious risk to society. Historically though, lawmakers in our society haven't viewed those who behave in this way towards other animals as the danger they are, largely because there's a certain empathy between the two, especially so in a rural backwater like this. Inexplicably, those who interfere with inanimate objects are invariably more severely punished by the courts than violent thugs who maim and kill for fun, yet history and the facts demonstrate clearly that those turned on by abusing animals don't usually hesitate in extending their aggression to people. Even badger baiting, which is illegal and probably the most reviled of blood sports, wasn't at this time punishable by a prison sentence—the maximum punishment being a £2,000 fine. Fortunately, the law does protect domestic dogs to a degree, and because the dogs used in this outing were injured in their confrontation with the badgers, the prosecution proved fruitful. One dog in particular—the black terrier offered for sale in *Shooting News*—was badly mutilated, an offence of cruelty carrying a whopping great maximum prison term of six months.

So damning was the evidence that the five were each sent to prison for six months for their part in this savagery, but only because of the injuries their dog suffered. Had it not been injured so badly, they would have walked away with a fine which might have been more appropriate because not only were they going to do no more than 12 weeks inside, they were also going to get a safe escort from the courtroom out into the waiting police van and to prison. Had they been free to walk out of court, some of the people in the street would have probably lost control. They were lucky to get away from an earlier hearing when a smaller number of protesters were observing in front of the court as they were allowed to sneak out the back. They were seen fleeing and ran like wild animals. It was only by jumping from a very high wall behind the courthouse that two of them avoided some of that suddenly less appealing violence they thrived on.

For the next hearing, all entrances were thick with observers and there would be no sneaking away. As it was, the ample police presence was there to see them safely off to prison. Police tried set up a diversion at the back of the court while quickly forming a tunnel of officers from the front into the van parked close by. Word went round that they were coming out the front and the moment they did a roar of anger went up and the crowd—all ages, shapes and sizes—swarmed like a pack of hunt dogs the few nearest kicking out and trying to land punches and verbals as the prisoners were bundled into the van. Injuries were minimal but they got the message. No one likes you, pervert! Justice wasn't seen to be done, and to make matters worse, there was more injustice to come.

Five people were arrested outside and taken before a kangaroo court. One of them, Brendan McNally, explains how these work:

> I was held overnight at Brecon and refused access to a solicitor even though I asked for one and a record of this was made. The next day I was taken to some isolated village court about twenty-five miles away, as Brecon was only open one day a week. Here the magistrates refused to adjourn the case so I could seek legal advice, and I had to conduct my own defence there and then straight from a night in the cells, unwashed and hungry. Incredibly, I was then somehow convicted of obstructing a police officer and fined £100. It was like being taxed! I'd never seen anything like it, and I've seen some crazy things happen in courtrooms in my time! This was a fine they wouldn't see paid.
>
> Of course I appealed and the conviction was quashed at Swansea Crown Court. Then I sued for false arrest, wrongful imprisonment and malicious prosecution and after a lot of bargaining I settled out of court for £5,000, which was put to good use fighting animal abuse.

Firebomb Blitz

> Irish Guards are employed as stewards in increasingly violent clashes with saboteurs. A local saboteur commented, 'It is very worrying that combat-trained troops are being used against peaceful protesters.'

Probably without exception people convicted for ALF campaigns have a history of mainstream animal rights campaigning and/or hunt sabotage. It isn't that the Hunt Saboteurs Association has deliberately recruited for the ALF, or that ALF leaders scout sab vans for talent, as the usual suspects have suggested. On the contrary, I for one was assisted in my transition by the behaviour of hunts and their supporters and police to go for the more direct, less confrontational approach. Oh, and because it worked.

The ALF is on the front-line of the animal protection movement and its activists have more to lose in the courts than anyone else involved, but hunt saboteurs are more often in direct confrontation with animal abusers than anyone else. Some people have preferred to go about their business under cover of darkness instead of risking getting their heads kicked in on a Saturday afternoon. To break the law is very much a last resort for most activists, usually after all the other options have been exhausted. As long as the abusers continue to thrive and to deliver violence with impunity to animals and people alike, breaking the law presents a very attractive practical alternative. It is seldom possible to disrupt the organisation of hunt meets sufficiently to prevent them happening at all, and there is little to compare with the spectacle of taking a pack of hounds away from a fleeing fox; therefore the tried and tested tactic of physical intervention in the hunting field remains a necessary risk for some in spite of the ever-increasing violence. But for others…

In the first in a series of raids early in 1990, ALF activists in Northern Ireland caused £250,000 damage to Dungannon Racecourse where hare coursing meets were being held. Fire destroyed the control box, refreshment rooms, grandstand, Tote building, bar, office and the mechanical hare. 'Bloody idiots. Now they want to save a mechanical animal!' blithered one confused race goer. In fact, the action, I am told was 'For the horses dying during and after races, and for the miserable "waste" greyhounds that no one wants when they cease running fast enough to make money for their owner.'

In England/Wales, a series of arson attacks targeting the blood sports community first saw the offices of *Shooting News* on the Tavistock Industrial Estate in Devon burnt out. The building was badly damaged; the roof was wrecked, computers melted and over £50,000 damage was caused. *Shooting News* represented what are regarded by many as the sewage of the hunting fraternity: terrier-men who dig into the underground homes of foxes, badgers and other wild animals to terrorise and kill them. The rag proudly proclaimed itself as 'Britain's Country Sports Newspaper,' providing books and videos and all the paraphernalia for best dealing with wild animals using dogs, traps and the like. *Shooting News* photographer Simon Everett was awoken very early one morning to discover his van had been torched outside his Derbyshire home. Two weeks later, hunt supporter Paul Hudson found himself short of a horsebox when it, too, was burnt out. Arsonists next set alight to the Vale of Lune Hunt kennels near Lancaster causing £20,000 damage, and in Dorset, an incendiary device discovered at the premises of a saddlers—a business near Dorchester (owned by members of the South Dorset Hunt)—was defused by an army bomb disposal team. The Wessex Fly Fishing School building near Tolpuddle wasn't so fortunate and was destroyed by a fire started by an incendiary, as were two anglers' cabins on the river Frome.

Most of these are obvious targets, but only in preceding years under the guiding hand of the Campaign for the Abolition of Angling (CAA) had the killing of fish become an issue and anglers now have to consider that what they do bothers people who care about animals and the environment and some are prepared to do something about it.

Commissioned by the RSPCA in 1980, The Medway Report focused attention on fish. It remains arguably the best thing the RSPCA has ever done. The conclusion reached by the report—being obvious to even a casual observer—revealed that all the evidence shows that fish do indeed feel pain, a fact with which most anglers and fishermen would disagree. It's a futile stance given that most will happily eat other animals, who it is generally accepted feel pain and are forced to suffer to satisfy the palette.

Keen to swell their ranks, the likes of the BFSS have cynically taken to using the fishing issue to try to galvanise support for their campaign to save their sport from an early addition to the history books and are now more than keen to talk about anglers being in the same boat as hare coursers. 'Join us or you will be next', they plead. There are estimated (by anglers) to be around three million anglers in the UK, and that's a lot of votes if they can convince all those people that theirs is a blood sport too.

One week after the *Shooting News* blaze, the offices of the BASC outside Wrexham in North Wales were visited by ne'er do wells late in the night. This is Marford Mill, the home of the confusingly titled British Association of Shooting and Conservation, which defends and encourages the rearing of game birds for release in front of shotgun-wielding gunmen. (That's the 'shooting' bit understood, but then it gets a bit confusing because although 'conservation' implies the protection of the woods that the organisation and its supporters own and use to rear game birds in, any 'pest' venturing near those places in search of the conserved livestock or excess of feed is very likely to be slaughtered. Or un- conserved, if you like).

A brace and bit were used to drill holes through wooden walls and doors to gain access into the three buildings on the site. Incendiaries were then left inside each building and primed. The main target survived the ensuing blazes as fires failed to take hold, but other buildings and an exhibition trailer were reduced to ashes. In a press statement, the ALF warned that within five years, the job would be done properly and the BASC would cease to exist. It proved to be a hollow threat, although two years later, a 'parcel bomb' disguised in the form of a videocassette was delivered to Marford Mill. It was made safe by the bomb squad. Coincidentally, this was timed to coincide with the dispatch of a batch of BFSS promotional videos, which, according to one news item, 'had the bomb squad on high alert after mysterious packages were sent to huntsmen throughout Britain.'

In May, the offices of the *Working Terrier* magazine were targeted. This rag, as the title suggests, was also big on blood sports and was a favourite of the terriermen. The first-floor office of the unit on the Kirklees Industrial Estate in Wigan was reached using a ladder; an office window was then broken to gain entry, a few 'useful items' were taken and an incendiary device was left behind. The offices were gutted in the ensuing blaze. The magazine editor, Eddie Rowbottom summed up: 'It's sickening. We're going to have to start again.'

The ALF responded: 'What's sickening is that the kind of material they peddled to incite others to participate in this kind of savage, sadistic behaviour is legal. We would advise fat boy (Eddie Rowbottom) and his sick friends to do something less destructive with their time because we haven't finished and we're getting good at this.'

Another Murderous Day

> The righteous one regards the life of his animal but the heart of the wicked is without mercy.
>
> *Proverbs 12:10 (Hebrew Scripture attributed to Solomon, c. 950 BC)*

Saturday, 9 February, 1991. Congregating from across the city at Liverpool's railway station were Mike Hill, a likeable 18-year old lad, and other hunt sabs, all of whom had been there many times before. Sometimes they went on to have a good day out, sometimes not so. A good day wasn't just about getting a group of good people together, locating a hunt meet and avoiding being beating up; it was about making sure the hunt didn't kill. That was the whole point, but other concerns had sometimes adjusted priorities.

There's no predicting it for sure, but it's a safe bet that at most hunts, violence will be the order of the day. For some of the Cheshire Beagle followers, hitting people has been as important an activity as hunting hares and has proved a good substitute where no animals are available for persecution. As a rule (Health & Safety) this hunt is only approached with enough numbers to contain or deter them. There were only twenty saboteurs from Merseyside out today looking for the Beagles, mostly veterans from at least two hunt seasons who were up for a fight if it proved absolutely necessary. The primary concern, however, is always finding a way to use known skills to divert attention from the quarry and take the hunt dogs for an unplanned walk.

Mike Hill and a close friend had made their way into town from work at the Freshfields Animal Rescue Centre, where they gave their time over to mopping up the mess from the local community caused by the endless unchecked breeding of animals and the resulting unwanted individuals: neglect and cruelty cases for whom few others had the time. You could see in Mike's face the hurt he felt at what he witnessed daily. He didn't trash or steal things or get pissed. He was quiet, passionate and committed to making life better for the animals. He didn't want to talk about it. He just wanted to do what he could. He was a good kid. As you may gather he's no longer with us.

When they arrived at the Red Lion Pub at Little Budworth just before 1.00pm, the hunt were still there. An ugly crowd of supporters had also gathered, weighing up their enemy as they drove by in a small convoy of cars and the well-known Liverpool sab van. Their presence wasn't so good for the sabs, but the two usually go together and it was better to know where they were, than not; sometimes they hide and set up ambushes. Everyone in the convoy had hoped to see other sabs—it was a focus of some conversation on the way there—but the ring round the night before suggested they would be arriving later once they'd finished with another hunt out of the county. The one o'clock meets allow for the possibility of sabbing a foxhunt in the morning and finishing off with a hare hunt in the afternoon, which would be a double good day but could equally mean double trouble!

The reality was that there were no reinforcements on the way. One group had become bogged down with a hunt putting up foxes left, right and centre, and the only other group within travelling distance hadn't even made it to their hunt because of van trouble. They van always seemed to break down on Saturdays, as a matter of course!

To avoid any early and unnecessary confrontation before the CB hunt started, sabs waited within sight of the huntsman, Alan Summersgill. He was the one on whom to focus, as he was the hunter; the rest of them just followed on. Basically, when the huntsman moves off, it's time to switch on and lively up. The box trailer towed by the hunt pick-up truck was unlocked one minute before one o'clock. A quick toot on the hunting horn and a flood of waggy, excited beagle dogs poured out and rushed like a river to their leader. They must feel like the Pied Piper to have such control. It was an impressive sight, but it was also a call to action, because it meant some wild animal could be about to die. All but the drivers, who kept the team mobile and ferried them to the heart of the action, were in the field and ready to go in a flash. It is always crucial not to allow a huntsman any ground on you, otherwise he might be able to lose himself for the day. The supporters are happy to miss the hunting fun and for the huntsman to be alone at the kill if they can ensure sabs have other things to deal with elsewhere. That's how it was that day.

Almost immediately, sabs and supporters were within reach of each other. A young female from Toxteth was on her face, shoved violently in the back by a fat, ageing red-faced lout who said he wanted her to 'Get a job.' Eating dirt? If it had been any of his business and he'd bothered to ask, he would have discovered she actually had a job, and quite a well paid one at that. Today was her day off, and she was out to save some lives. No point telling him any of that though, 'cos he wouldn't have been interested. (It's the usual 'lazy-lay-about-with-nothing-else-to-do' remark they make, sidestepping the real issue that hunting wild animals is cruel and unnecessary. And of course if everyone did go get a Saturday job there would be no one to sab the hunts unless of course sabs are paid in which case they are working! Cake and eat it lard arse? And what is it you are doing with your spare time? Hunting the utterly placid harmless Brown Hare with a pack of dogs and a gang of grown men in britches. Hmm!)

Not all the followers were going to engage in attacking saboteurs. Some just weren't up for it: they were either too young or old, but particularly reluctant when their numbers were divided as the day went on and the fit were separated from the not so fit. There were endless scuffles, but not quite enough to keep sabs at bay for long enough to work the scent and track down the hairy little blighter.

For two hours, the hunt was effectively sabotaged on the run with horn calls, voice calls and cracking whips, before the huntsman decided that if he were to get anything out of the day, he'd have to try something else. He called his pack to close quarters, and followers took to milling around waiting for something to happen. It looked like he was hoping the police would arrive and save the day but they were undermanned and slow off the mark with football matches tying them up. Instead, the huntsman decided to temporarily abandon hunting and arranged a rendezvous with the hound trailer three miles from the meet so that they could drive off to somewhere quiet to hunt.

It had worked before, but not this time. A few sabs were occupying the road in front of the getaway vehicle; it was obviously a dangerous place to be. The only safe place was out of the way but that would have been missing the point. Not only was it highly likely he'd run them over if they didn't move, they were now sitting targets for tool-wielding hunters—defenceless, just the way hunt followers like their victims.

There wasn't that much going on for a while, just the usual eyeballing, name-calling and threats. But once the pack was locked back in the trailer, it was time to shift up a gear. The obvious place to be was in path of the thing, but sure enough, Summersgill, who was at the wheel, was happy to drive at anyone whom his followers hadn't been able to remove, followers who were, incidentally, also in the way. Failing to find a gap to move off, he instead jumped out and let loose with a wheel brace, seemingly intent on cracking some skulls. That only delayed things further as more scuffles broke out, which, for the hunt sabs was both very good and very bad! The light was now fading, and time to hunt was running out. Done wielding, the huntsman was back at the wheel and trying again, this time forging a way through the roadblock and making progress, but not before Mike Hill, David Blenkinsop and Pirrip Spencer had jumped on the back of the truck, because, they reasoned it isn't so easy to be kicked and punched when you're up high. And now he'd have to wait for the police because you can't drive around with people on the back like that—it's dangerous and illegal. Right?

Summersgill was in a blind rage now though, and egged on by his co pilot they navigated the roadblock and took off at speed, wheels spinning, trailer weaving, leaving clouds of dust and everyone else behind. What would be the point of speeding away to free himself of saboteurs with three on board? However fast he went, they would still be there at the end, and then the hunters would be outnumbered! Duh! Unless he had other plans? For the next five miles, Summersgill motored at speeds of up to 80 mph, his truck flat out. Recklessly or deliberately he was trying to kill them. This was serious. Soon realising the danger they were in, 'at the hands of a lunatic', according to Blenkinsop, the three clung on for dear life as they tried everything to get him to stop, but they were futile gestures. It was bitterly cold and with their fear mounting that they were in danger of crashing, of being thrown off the back or being driven into an ambush, they knew they had to do something drastic; if he went far enough, they might even freeze to death! 'He had something on his mind and it wasn't in our interest to be a part of it,' Blenkinsop said later. They agreed the best thing they could do was to try to jump from the truck when it stopped at a junction or if it slowed at a bend. Bend! There was one coming up. Mike Hill was the bravest, or most fearful, and he went first. He jumped for the grass verge as they slowed but never made it. He hit the corner of the trailer and fell under the wheels, causing it and its cargo of dogs to bounce wildly over him and back onto the tarmac. The driver somehow kept it on the road, regained control and drove on.

He was well aware of what he'd done but it was only when the rear window of the pick-up was finally smashed a little further down the road that he stopped. He was scared himself now cos there was a fist threatening him if he didn't. Mike's friends ran back to where he was lying and the hunters sped off. Eighteen-year-old Mike Hill died where he lay.

Alan Summersgill was later arrested and spent a few hours in a police station before being released without charge. He wasn't even done for dangerous driving or failing to stop at the scene of an accident! You try and get away so lightly after killing someone! His solicitor helpfully was a good friend and the chairman of the Cheshire Beagles' neighbours, the Royal Rock Beagles. Under normal circumstances, when an incident has occurred—far less serious than the death of a teenager—the police, even if they don't lay the appropriate charges straight away, will lay holding charges in the meantime. This keeps the accused in prison or on bail and deterred from committing further offences. Lesser charges are used to encourage guilty pleas. In a situation like this, one of leaving the scene of an accident would have been a godsend to most people, especially a hunt saboteur in the same boat who could quite rightly be charged with causing death by reckless driving, manslaughter or even murder. Odds on the latter if it had been Mike or one of the others at the steering wheel that day.

Staggeringly, there was no indication that anything close to justice would result and although there were very suspicious circumstances and a dead body, the police weren't that motivated. One witness claimed she overheard a conversation in the police station later that night between two detectives, which suggested that Summersgill had been drinking and was over the limit, but would it have made any difference to anything if he was? These people are renowned for drinking heavily at hunt meets, before during and after. It seems unlikely it was going to matter what Summersgill had drunk because there was quite simply no political will to prosecute him for anything.

When sabs are assaulted on hunts, even within sight of police officers, the normal procedure is that nothing happens, and no one is arrested. This is such a regular occurrence that it's hard to believe this isn't agreed policy. Perversely, there have been thousands of sabs held in custody for the day or over the weekend for far less serious things, like turning up intent on sabotage, being beaten up or blowing a hunting horn. What about standing in a field, walking on a lane or climbing a gate, or perhaps because a hunt supporter demands it! I know lots of good people who have spent more time in police cells for each of the above than Summersgill has for killing an 18-year old.

Were it Summersgill lying dead, all those present would have without doubt been arrested, charged and remanded in custody pending a show trial. The press would have had a field day with the help of the politicians and police, exposing again the violence of 'extremists' and calling for more laws to ban something or other and prevent such a tragedy happening again. This isn't an opinion based on rumour, hearsay, prejudice or anger; this is an opinion based on years of experience.

That hunt saboteurs had warned with every assault that this would happen sooner or later only added to the anger once the widespread shock had passed. Not only did cries for justice fall on deaf ears but also those who should have been listening expressed no remorse. With no action from the authorities, it was left to the rest of us to take some action of our own.

Dodleston

> Wild animals never kill for sport. Man is the only one to whom the torture and death of his fellow creatures is amusing in itself.
>
> *Froude (1818-1894)*

Phones rang throughout the night and well into the following day. We all knew this would happen one day and there was deep despair and an overwhelming sense of injustice. Why the hell hadn't they locked up Summersgill? This was surely an assault too far?

We hurriedly organised a demonstration outside the hunt kennels at Dodleston near Chester, to take place two days later on the Monday. Officially, this was the next day they would potentially be hunting although they seldom did any more. It was imperative that everything be done to highlight Mike's death and the police's inaction, and to ensure that preventive action was taken to stop them from killing again, should they have the impudence to attempt it. The press were informed that there would be a silent vigil outside the home of the person who killed Mike. Granada TV, other local reporters and several national newspapers gathered there alongside 150 protesters. There was no pre-planned conspiracy to smash up the kennels or anything like that but for reasons best known to Cheshire Police, their presence was nothing more than a token gesture. So that's just what happened. Outside the huntsman's bungalow behind a five-bar gate was parked the offending pick-up and trailer, the murder weapon.

Although the demonstration had been billed as a silent vigil, emotions were obviously running high. After a seemingly pointless half hour of silently milling around, the mood lifted when a small group of protesters were seen making their way across fields to the rear of the kennels. A spontaneous cheer went up, hunting horns were sounded—guaranteed to get the adrenalin flowing—and then the thin blue line of eight officers barring entry through the gate was breached by the sheer weight of people wanting in. It was too easy!

What followed was a free-for-all on the bungalow and hound van. No petrol bombs or anything like that—just a few broken windows and some noise. Some demonstrators used their banners to obstruct the view of press cameras; others blocked the gateway to keep them from filming the events unfolding within. The handful of police present attempted to make arrests before concluding it was futile as most were promptly de-arrested by others in a human of tug of war, which the aggrieved were more determined to win. Police reinforcements were heading to the scene but within minutes of the raid the crowd had dispersed, their point made. Just one person was arrested at the kennels—he'd been handcuffed to a drainpipe at the side of the house—and a vanload was detained a few miles away at Chester's railway station.

Three others were arrested later in the day when they called at the police station to enquire about the welfare of detained friends. All were quickly charged with Section 1 of the Public Order Act of 1986, a charge of riot, which carries a ten-year sentence. One was Julie Burgess, Mike's partner. Everyone was refused bail and remanded in custody while the police announced they were setting up an incident room and launching a major inquiry. Not, as you would hope, into their lack of policing of a highly charged demo, or even Saturday's killing, but over a few broken windows! This was a formidable set of circumstances for even the most battle-scarred activist to deal with, several of whom—myself included—were now being hunted by teams of police.

The huge operation that followed to track down as many of those at the demo as possible was breathtaking and caused a lot of resentment and anger. Someone had been accused of killing a young man and there were credible witnesses, yet Cheshire Police were more interested in who'd broken some windows. And how!

Across the UK, the coming weeks saw police forces arrest dozens and dozens of people and eventually charging 41 with riot. Some were remanded in custody with bail only agreed on condition that each provide a £1,000 surety and keep out of Cheshire, Clwyd and the Wirral: Cheshire Beagles hunting ground. There was no desire to prosecute Summersgill but inconceivable enthusiasm to rampage through dozens of homes and to gather intelligence on protesters arrested over those broken windows.

In media interviews immediately before the rushing of the kennels, I had stated it was our intention that this hunt was finished and would kill no more, but clearly the police had other ideas. For this, I was arrested as an organiser. Far from solving the problem, banning so many people from nearing the hunt had the opposite effect as others stepped in to keep the pressure on the Beagles out of deference to Mike Hill. This attracted yet more police resources in the form of mounted and undercover officers together with helicopters and mobile detention cells—dedicated to protecting a gang of thugs and maintain their right to hunt wild hares!

Summersgill was reported to be in hiding and terrified for his life. He certainly wasn't home the night his bungalow was gutted by an ALF fire a week after Mike's death, forcing the hunt to abandon its base and set about the struggle to find somewhere they'd be welcome. They weren't at all welcome in the local community; too much trouble. Ironic that the only people who wanted anything to do with the Cheshire Beagles were us!

By the time the case reached trial at Mold County Court 14 months later, there were 17 people in the dock. It didn't matter that the majority of the arrests went nowhere because there was no evidence, as arresting them had been useful for other reasons. To the 17 remaining, including me, a deal was offered whereby if we pleaded guilty to a lesser charge of Violent Disorder, which carries six years, then the Riot charge, which carries ten, would be dropped. Six defendants who were clearly identified inside the kennel grounds were advised to accept the deal. The rest of us opted for trial.

The single piece of evidence the police themselves gathered at the scene was an invaluable video film of the early part of unfolding events which the camera operator had stashed safely under his patrol car while going to assist colleagues. At least he thought it was safe, but someone had seen him hiding his snazzy camera and while the officer was away it was snaffled. Bang goes the evidence never to be seen again! Unfortunately, in a case of instant karma, one of the occupants of the van detained at Chester who should have known better, had recorded his own version of events, which he still had on him and in fine working order on arrival at the police station. This was, of course, confiscated by the police. This proved absolutely crucial to the prosecution case, which was further complemented by seized press photographs that were scrutinised in fine detail to identify people from clothing and from Special Branch files.

Without any effort, I ended up in the middle of this plot. While our initial plan was simply to demonstrate at the kennels, there's no doubt most of us would have jumped at the idea of releasing some anger on something of Summersgill's, or better still him. We never thought for a minute we'd be given such an invite given the circumstances. Yet here were eight overweight local bobbies, 150 unhappy friends of a dead teenager and the home of the killer a stone's throw away. It wasn't sensible and shouldn't have happened, but it did.

Just before the crowd had breached the front gate at 1pm, two people had been seen approaching the rear of the kennels; one was said to have been me, identified from some grainy long distance photographs showing a wax jacket similar to the one I was wearing. Around the same time, someone had blown a hunting horn—an inevitable consequence of a gathering of hunt saboteurs! The prosecution case painted me as leader of the 'riot' that followed because I spoke to the press explaining reasons for the vigil and then was alleged to have led the charge from the rear. This was pure fantasy, but importantly, it was all helping to deflect attention from a violent killing. As did the story that started to emerge from the police, suggesting Summersgill and his wife had been in the bungalow at the time of the invasion and that he had been nearly dragged out of a broken window when not hiding under furniture from bricks and glass showers.

No one in the grounds that day saw anyone indoors and it beggars belief that they would have been at home given the highly charged situation, which both the police and Mike's killer were aware was developing. Anyway, after two weeks in a packed courtroom, during which some defendants gave evidence and some not, the jury were sent out to consider their verdicts. They were given the option of convicting of Violent Disorder or of using Threatening or Abusive Words or Behaviour or acquitting of both charges. The judge—one Elgin Edwards—was always going to be biased in his summing up. This was indicated in his 'leading' role beforehand, However, he failed to sway the jury.

I was first to hear Not Guilty verdicts on both charges, which really made my day! Five defendants were found guilty of Threatening Behaviour, given three months suspended prison sentences and ordered to pay £250 court costs. Angela Hamp failed to appear at a hearing long before the trial began and a warrant was issued for her arrest. She was, as they say, on her toes. A fugitive. Graeme Wood, John Curtin, Neil Croucher, Martin Eggleton and Alistair Howson had pleaded guilty to Violent Disorder and were sent to prison for 12 months. Dave Blenkinsop, who held Mike Hill in his arms as he died, was sent to prison for 15 months.

No expense was spared in the effort to imprison as many people as possible and no expense was spared on the police operation to ensure that threats against the Cheshire Beagles' existence were not carried out. Summersgill was said publicly by his hunting chums to be terrified for his life and was expecting retribution. He was, we were told, no longer hunting. The kennels were officially abandoned following the fire and the hunt was made homeless, but despite the rhetoric, Summersgill has continued hunting and is known to be particularly keen on the blood lust of terrier work.

A private prosecution was brought against Summersgill, accusing him of reckless driving and failing to stop at the scene of an accident. Despite the facts and evidence, including one independent witness who saw the pick-up careering past her window at a dangerous speed with three men clinging onto the rear, he still wasn't convicted.

Summersgill wasn't at the inquest into Mike Hill's death either, but his sidekick Martin Stonely went along and gave his fanciful version. He told the court Mike had gestured his intention to throw a match into the diesel tank of the pick up—match in one hand, fuel cap in the other—while the vehicle was in rapid motion. The hare hunters were consequently terrified for their lives, hence their erratic behaviour. It was the stuff of fantasy for sure but that's how the story ends.

That Mike's death was officially classified as accidental came as little surprise to anyone. It seemed a foregone conclusion and was the final insult in this awful saga, instilling a new resolve in the hearts of many to fight that bit harder, but cautiously. Hundreds attended Mike's funeral at his birthplace in Somerset and every year since, on the anniversary of his death, similar numbers have descended on Cheshire and disrupted hunting across the county. Mike Hill dedicated his life to fighting animal abuse. It's what he did at the Freshfields Animal Rescue Centre, keeping things in order in the puppy unit, quietly getting on with helping others.

Once upon a time, the popular mantra on marches was:

What do we want?
Animal liberation!
When do we want it?
Now!
Are we going to fight for it?
Yes!
Are we going to die for it?
Yes!

We no longer invite each other to die for it; this has quietly drifted from the chanting since tragic deaths started to happen for real. Instead, 'Are we gonna get it? Yes!' echoes in the hearts and minds of those driven to establish the long overdue enshrinement of a Rights For Animals Act to enable respect and consideration to be showered upon the earth's animal kingdom, with no exception. But die for it we will.

A glance through history shows that political violence, suppression, inconsistent policing and complicity with the one side—the high and mighty—will tend to strengthen the resolve in the other, those driven enough to act. After all, fighting abuse and injustice is what it's all about. For all the pain I feel for animals I will never meet, I am also motivated to act because genuinely decent caring people are so badly abused for their compassion, whilst hypocrisy in power rules, accusing those they punish of violence. Breaking windows is probably a bad thing to do, but there are far worse things we should be angry about.

Mike wasn't the first animal activist to be killed at the hands of animal abusers in recent times nor the last. A few years earlier, in 1985, Dian Fossey was murdered by an unknown attacker at the Karisoke Research Centre, which she had set up to help protect mountain gorillas in Rwanda. Poachers had speared and killed her favourite gorilla, Digit, and she founded the Digit Fund to help protect the remaining gorillas. After Dian Fossey was killed a fund was set up and now strives to protect the last remaining 600 or so individuals that survive in two regions of Uganda and Rwanda.

The same year, the French Government had sent two assassins, often described as secret service agents but more appropriately terrorists, to Auckland harbour in New Zealand on a mission to sink the Greenpeace ship, The Rainbow Warrior, and stop it interfering with French nuclear tests. Greenpeace photographer, Fernando Pereira, was on board at the time and was killed by the explosion caused by the limpet mine they'd fixed to the hull. This classic act of state terrorism served not only to shock the world, but draw attention to nuclear testing and cement Pacific nations to a non-nuclear policy too.

Ironically, the first ever campaign of the Rainbow Warrior had been to relocate the inhabitants of Rongelap Atoll, which had been contaminated by the US through its nuclear experiments on the Islands in the 1950s. The US had ignored pleas for help and now the French were going out of their way to behave incredibly badly by murdering and bombing in the name of power. The two people physically responsible for the murder of Fernando Pereira were later given ten-year prison sentences, but after spending three years in military custody on a Pacific island with their families, the godfathers of the operation, their government bosses decided they'd suffered enough and set them free. Ten years later Greenpeace were back in the Pacific having their boats, including RW II, rammed and impounded by French

Government agents whilst their military experimented with more of their nuclear devices and poisoned more of our planet.

In 1993, Geetaban Rachiya was hacked to death by animal butchers in the West Indian city of Ambavati. She was a strong campaigner against the cruelty of the meat trade and was murdered over a drop in sales.

With a lot to lose and little to deter, be prepared for more of this to come from those who exploit. Without a word of a lie, it's the so-called extremists who are by far the most significant victims of violence in the struggle for animal rights. I will document the deaths along the way on both sides of the divide. You figure out where the true violence lies.

Young Tom Worby

> Compassion for animals is intimately connected with goodness of character; and it may be confidently asserted that he who is cruel to animals cannot be a good man.
>
> *Arthur Schopenhauer (1788-1860) German philosopher*

And so by a circuitous route, we come back to that moment in prison, which should have been, for me, one of jubilation: the Animal Liberation Movement was on a roll and the headline news that afternoon was that the National had been sabotaged. It was 3 April, 1993.

I have never met Tony Ball, but everyone I have spoken to describes him as a volatile, angry man and someone to avoid. The rest is history. Ball had had a crap day out, he'd been forced to pack up early because of a bunch of hunt saboteurs, he'd probably lost on the horses and wasn't in a good mood to start with. For the Cambridgeshire Foxhounds 53-year old huntsman, Ball, a good day meant good scent, foxes to hunt and no bloody saboteurs. He was heading home early at the wheel of his horsebox, and there in front of him, ambling along with others, themselves on their way home having had a good day with very little hunting and no kills, was Tom Worby, who was 15. I didn't know Tom either, but I do know he'd had a good day. I knew just how he felt. It had been his first time out sabbing; it had been a success and the other sabs had been friendly and looked out for him like they do. You have to look after each other. His girlfriend had been out a few times before, so Tom went with her. She knew the score; it didn't take long to work it out.

Country folk will tell you that the etiquette when driving down country lanes is to wait until you are able to pass. Don't drive at the sheep or cows, the farmer will get them out of the way as soon as he can. Don't beep your horn at the hunt riders, they'll get out of the way when they're ready. This is the countryside, townies have to learn and wait. But Ball was impatient. It's his countryside and he was revving his engine to let everyone know it, but there wasn't really anywhere to go to get out of the way. Nonetheless, he was threatening and determined and was heard snarling, 'If you don't move, I'll fucking run you over.'

Revving some more and speeding up the huge truck, he started to force a way through the fleeing groups of two or three. Worby instinctively tried to get out of the way and jumped to the right to get onto the narrow grass verge, but it was on a bit of a slope and there was nothing to keep him there. Everyone could see the danger for all the pedestrians, but there was nothing anyone other than the driver could do about it. The youngster slipped back into the side of the truck, slamming his leg and breaking it as they collided. He caught the wing mirror, which twisted him around, but was able to hang on for only a few second as Ball motored on. With the young man clearly distressed and the road ahead cleared, Ball could have been said to have achieved his aim and should have stopped there and then, but he had become caught up in the thrill of the chase. Fifty yards further on Tom Worby could no longer hold on and fell under the wheels of Ball's truck. He died instantly. The truck continued on its journey back to the kennels.

That there was no major inquiry, no breaking down of doors, no media hysteria about violent thugs killing kids came as no surprise to those of us who have been here before. I have spent the weekend in the cells for far less than murder: blowing a hunting horn and walking in a field being two examples; I have had my front door broken down over the alleged theft of a diary and been given a curfew to prevent me rescuing chickens from factory farm cages. This is standard punishment for those who object to animal abuse.

Tony Ball, like Alan Summersgill before him and others like them, was later arrested, questioned and released without any charge. He wasn't even done for reckless driving or leaving the scene. A curiously similar response to that which accompanied the death of Mike Hill. Far from deterring violent assaults by grown men on women and children, an atmosphere of indifference and even complicity has made these people fearless of the consequences of assaulting people they don't like.

The muted response from Cambridgeshire Police was predicted, but the response of the press was far from understated. Tom Worby wasn't known to the police as a hunt saboteur or seen as a terrorist with a string of criminal convictions, so couldn't be accused of bringing it on himself. Instead, this youngster's death became the fault of his friends and the Hunt Saboteurs Association for ruthlessly educating kids about hunting! *The Mail on Sunday* 'revealed' that the HSA was running a hitherto unremarkable little group called Fox Cubs, for the younger generation of anti-hunt activists, those too young to sab. 'Hunt Saboteurs Target Children', ran the confused headline, as fellow anti-hunt activists were lambasted for behaviour tantamount to child abuse for teaching that hunting is cruel and for coordinating letter-writing campaigns to MP's and so on. And they dug up some dirt on the ex-husband of an older local hunt sab, a man they said was a known fascist. The point? Diverting attention from the death of a teenage hunt saboteur. A middle-aged man with a reputation for violence had been heard to threaten, and then been seen to kill a perfectly innocent, defenceless 15 year-old boy yet it wasn't he who was getting any of the blame! It was the worst kind of gutter journalism and it neatly hid away the truth of what had happened on that dark day.

How the same headline writers scream violence, terror and extremism at the sight of a broken pane of glass or threatening letter yet brush aside a truly violent and unjust killing is beyond comprehension. How could such a story be accidentally turned on its head by so many? It couldn't...

Prison comes into its own at times like this and would have been an unwelcoming place for a child killer like Ball. Not that he was going to end up there. I was though. I didn't know at the time who had been killed; it might well have been someone I knew. Not that it mattered, because he was on my side and he was active against animal abuse. For the first time in many months of incarceration I felt utterly powerless and desperately needed to talk to someone to try and make sense of it all, but phone calls had to be booked days in advance. My cellmate John was sensitive and shared the joy of the earlier news with me, but this was something different. This wasn't just another death but one very personal to me and I needed to speak to someone who could relate to how I was feeling. I was isolated, confused and angry, and the talk show hosts and callers on the radio were more concerned with an aborted horse race and apportioning blame!

There was, not surprisingly, a mood for revenge, but local sabs asked for calm. They didn't want a repeat of Dodleston and to have to take the flak when the dust settled, but how could it get much worse when people were being murdered? Smashing up the kennels in public might not be the most appropriate response, but do nothing? That can't be the right thing.

There was no response from anyone to the killing of Tom Worby, although the police did put officers at the kennels to keep them safe. Other than that, nothing! To have shown so little regard for the death of a teenager was both shameful and provocative. How does one respond? Does it make the movement more mature than the IRA, for example, for turning the other cheek when wronged? Or does turning the other cheek make us more vulnerable, more likely to have casualties in the future? Will we be less or more respected? If those who should care, do nothing, what then? They're killing kids!

Raiding Places

Beagles bred for laboratories can never be rehomed.

Bob Coley, Manager of Interfauna

Interfauna—A Raid & Retribution

Since the hideous Huntingdon Research Centre had been put firmly onto the protester's map, word had leaked to some of the more serious activists that there was more going on in the locality than was public knowledge. Many were already aware of the existence of the huge HRC if not the fine detail from within, but few knew about a company called Interfauna, based just down the road at Abbots Ripton. While Interflora were delivering flowers, Interfauna were delivering animals. A coincidence perhaps? Probably a sick joke. Rumour had it that they were a big supplier of beagles to the voracious lab but weren't overly bothered with security.

Where the potential of recovering animals was concerned, the HRC itself posed a problem because of their security cordon. It wasn't insurmountable—Sarah Kite had proven that—but Interfauna was a different, far more straightforward proposition altogether. Other links in the chain were also revealed including a rodent breeding unit in the middle of an industrial estate at Stukeley Meadows, but Interfauna was the weak link and a veritable jewel in the crown for the ALF. The company was set up in the mid 70s by two vets named Hacking and Churchill. They were ex employees of HRC and destroyers of healthy animals. They had established a way to make a good living supplying their friends and colleagues with the animals they wanted, but someone had taken a look at their seedy little business premises and could see a possible way of getting some of the animals out. It was during one of the demonstrations at HRC that the conspiracy began in earnest as people who knew and trusted each other had a quiet word about breaking a load of beagles out of Interfauna. John Curtin was well and truly in on this and takes up the story.

> With the idea propagated, the next step was to go up and have a look, which I did myself accompanied by another interested individual. Our first reaction on seeing the place—apart from stomach churning disgust—was total shock and surprise at the

distinct lack of security! No barbed wire, no floodlights, no security guards, only an on-site manager and two seemingly docile rottweilers. This place falsely assumed it had one line of security—that it would remain hidden. They were, up until then, secreted away. Security fencing would've only attracted attention—but now their cover was blown! The liberators had landed, and compared to most raids this was gonna be a doddle.

We drew up a few rough plans—it was plain to see that we were gonna require a lot of planning and a lot of people. I approached a number of activists and much to my delight, one of the people I asked, Danny Attwood, had already been hard at work on Interfauna himself. He had drawn up his own initial plans, with the idea of liberation in mind. Great minds think alike! So, after putting our heads together and spending a couple of evenings rooting around the place, it was a case of 'job-on'. One more final recce was needed to put the final finishing touches to our plans and preparations. We had, since hatching the plot, acquired some detailed information from ex-employees, who had resigned, unable to endure the burden of Interfauna's secretive and horrendous trade. The picture they painted was shocking but not outside the realms of our expectation for such a place.

It was decided that an attempt would be made to enter the Interfauna dog units and take away as many beagle puppies as we could. Obviously, we would've liked to have taken the adult breeding stock too. Ironically we were unable to pursue this idea, because upon approach those dogs would erupt into a frenzied din. A prolonged bout of noise from the dogs at that hour would've probably aroused the site manager.

There were, and it should never be forgotten that there still are, something in the region of five hundred beagles imprisoned at Interfauna at any given time. We wanted them all but had to make the best of a bad situation and take what we could. It could never be enough, but better than nothing and for the ones we did get—everything. Two groups made their way to Interfauna, driving onto a nearby field, along the edge of it and concealed our transport out of sight. We trekked cross country to the site and reached the back of the building in which the puppies were kept, and got stuck straight into carving a large hole out of the roof. We knew the doors were alarmed, so gaining entry through the roof was the obvious choice and only took a matter of minutes—although rather noisy in the stillness of the night.

Someone was stationed up by the house to watch for any sign of unusual movement or activity, armed with a walkie-talkie (rather snazzy ones, commandeered by Danny from his workplace, for which he subsequently received the sack!). Meanwhile, the two rottweilers slept on, unperturbed by our presence. Once the hole was made, a stepladder was lowered and within seconds the first beagle puppy was on its way to freedom. From our reconnaissance we knew that we'd be able to make good use of Interfauna's own cages and travelling boxes—they too were liberated and are still being used to good ends. It worked a treat: four puppies were loaded into large cages, and then two people carried each cage across the fields to the waiting transport. We are talking serious hard work!

We began at 9pm, but it wasn't until approximately 1am that we managed to fill the van up, and I mean fill it up—can you imagine eighty-two puppies piled up in cages, in one van? In hindsight I wish we'd obtained a whole fleet of vans and a hundred activists—maybe that way we could've cleared the whole place out! The logistics would have been staggering but certainly not impossible. As it was, we weren't to know the raid would run so smoothly. We never expected to get as many as the 82 puppies that we did, but you can imagine how it felt, amidst the cruel emotional irony of rescuing the 82, only to leave so many more behind.

The van only had to travel a relatively short distance to where the puppies were to be dropped off and dispersed far and wide across the country to previously arranged safe houses and holding units. We literally crammed in as many as we could—in fact to delay any longer would've resulted in tragedy. The body heat alone of the beagle pups would've been enough to endanger them in such cramped conditions—a risk we couldn't possibly take.

So, eventually, the van left the area and took off to safety: eighty-two puppies and two people. Not bad going for a few hours work. But the night was still young. We now embarked upon stage two. The plan being for the van, after the 'all clear', to return, and in the meantime the others present would force entry into the rabbit-breeding unit near to where the puppies had been held. This was a much more secure unit and it was a lot closer to the house and the two sleeping rotties. Hence, it had been decided to leave this until the beagles had been safely evacuated from the area. Again, the initial idea had been to gain access through a hole in the roof, but the difficulty and ensuing noise caused by our cutting attempts meant we had to force the back door instead—which luckily didn't set the alarm off! The smash of the door was nothing, compared to the rabbits kicking out at their cages as we walked in. But still the security wasn't alerted.

We proceeded to rescue 26 adult rabbits, and by the time we'd trekked across the field, the van that had taken the beagles had returned. We managed to find the time to inflict some damage, a 50 yard long, four foot high slogan was daubed across one of the units: BEAGLES BRED FOR TORTURE—THE ALF WILL CLOSE DOWN THIS HELL HOLE THEN SEEK RETRIBUTION. We also took a large quantity of documents, revealing a catalogue of Interfauna's deplorable clientele—which reads like an A-Z of animal torturers. Of course there was HRC, but additionally Boots, Glaxo, Beechams and a multitude of universities across the country.

The raid was over by 4am; the job was done. We were tired but happy. The press correspondence consisted of simply phoning a member of Huntingdon Animal Concern and passing the relevant details of the raid—the rest was left up to the contact there. The raid wasn't done to cater for the whims of the press. As for the beagles, they were transported all over the country to various hideaways. They were in reasonable physical health with a few exceptions, which were treated by a sympathetic vet. Interfauna had been their death row; the torture of the laboratory had been yet to come. It was in Interfauna's commercial interests to see that the puppies were fed and watered and that the 'goods' were fit for sale. However, what surprises me, to this day, is how badly affected some of them were mentally, after spending a relatively short amount of time in there. Most of them were as naughty and lively as you'd expect from puppies, but there were others who cowered in the corner, rejecting any affection shown towards them. One of the reasons beagles are used by vivisectors is the ease with which their spirits are broken—instead of biting back they simply retreat, cower and wet themselves—and it was so, so sad to see this process underway in some of the puppies.

The vet who had helped out many times before with liberated animals had agreed to surgically remove the tattoos from the dogs' ears so as to ensure that, if they were ever to come under the scrutiny of unfriendly eyes, it would be impossible to prove where they had originally come from. It was only possible to do ten or so pups at a time, and so for weeks and weeks we were arranging to pick up puppies from all over the country and taking them to the vet, ensuring that the identity of the vet was known only to us.

The vet kept costs to a minimum, but owing to the number of animals requiring attention, they were, along with all the other expenses incurred, still considerable. People from all over the country chipped in to help foot the bill. The rabbits were in a terrible condition. The adult breeding stock had lived their whole lives confined to a cage on a trolley. They were stricken with brittle bones as a result of their ordeal. The 'incident' reports, removed during the raid, read like a book of horrors, with up to fifty fatalities a day and numerous infections and broken bones. They were given care and gentle kindness, but for some of them all we could do was make their passing away as humane and peaceful as possible. A few died within a few months of being rescued but the survivors improved considerably, regained their strength and soon adapted to their new-found freedom.

Those that do not learn from history are condemned to repeat it: it has to be said Danny Attwood and I dropped some right clangers. But people can only learn from their mistakes. I know Danny would want one of his erased from the history books, but we aren't going to permit that. Everything was running reasonably smoothly and apart from running around getting the puppies to the vet, the raid was behind us. That was until 7am one morning in late April when half of the Cambridgeshire police force arrived on my doorstep. Well, I exaggerated, it was about a fifth; the other four-fifths were busy raiding addresses in Peterborough, Southampton and London. To cut a long story short, following the raid Cambridge police had launched a major investigation, involving static and mobile surveillance, which a month later led to co-ordinated dawn swoops on a number of houses—uncovering a detailed dossier of the HRC/Interfauna companies. Danny, unwittingly, dropped himself in the middle of all of this by leaving the police a good clue as a starting point, which wouldn't have needed the brains of Sherlock Holmes to unravel. At the scene of the crime in a nearby field they discovered a receipt from a cash dispensing machine, with Danny's name emblazoned all over it! The moral of the story here is EMPTY YOUR POCKETS before you go out to play. Goes without saying doesn't it? Doesn't it?

Well, that's Danny's bit of humble pie—now for mine. I hired a van out in my own name, which was to prove my eventual downfall—quite how, I don't know, seeing as the number plates were concealed during the actual raid. The police took possession of it the same day I took it back, and even though it had been cleaned and scrubbed, the forensic scientist had a field day with it. For example, apart from finding dog and rabbit hairs, they took samples from the chassis in which they identified grains of wheat afflicted by some rare disease which matched up with the same variety of wheat with the same disease as that growing in one of the fields which had been driven across by the van. When the police turned my house over, on the table in the front room was a copy of the video taken during the raid. (The 'amusing' thing is that it had been kept safe, but the day before I'd taken it to show someone, got back late and thought it'd be okay until the next morning—which of course it wasn't!) Confucius says: the worst always happens when your defences are down!

The police had been following Danny and had watched him take some puppies to his brother's in London, and then down to Southampton. In the subsequent raids, the police retrieved two puppies, but thankfully Interfauna had already stated that if any dogs were recovered they had no use for them seeing as they wouldn't be able to sell them. Happily, the police passed them to an animal shelter instead. They also took two adult beagles, Derek and Trevor, from Danny's address but these were eventually returned to him, much to his displeasure (Derek and Trevor were inconceivably, unimaginably naughty, beyond belief!). The police also arrested and charged another man, Jim O'Donnell, who was unfortunate to have hired a van from the same hire company on the same day as myself. When it came to court, it was alleged that two vans were used, seeing as they'd found two different sets of tyre tracks, but there was absolutely no proof that this second van had been used.

When I gave evidence, I made it clear to the court that the two sets of tracks were the result of my van making two separate trips—thus Jim O'Donnell was subsequently acquitted. Angela Hamp was arrested in the house with me, despite the fact that there was no evidence to link her to the raid. She was subjected to a hail of personal abuse and threatened repeatedly whilst in police custody. She was charged, but after a few months all charges against her were dropped. Consequently she sued Cambridgeshire Police and received quite a substantial sum in damages, which was then put to good use. When it finally came to trial, three of us were charged with 'conspiracy to burgle' and seven others faced the equally preposterous charge of handling stolen goods—the 'goods' in question being the dogs, valued at £35,000. The fact that they were animals was never brought into the case by the prosecution and had no legal bearing.

On the advice of their barristers, some of those on handling charges pleaded guilty and received fines—but the one who didn't was acquitted of the charge. Ironically, the weight of evidence against the acquitted defendant was far greater than those who'd pleaded guilty. Of the three charged with conspiracy to burgle, Danny, who'd only just been released from prison for his part in the legendary Poll Tax riot, and who faced an overwhelming barrage of evidence against him and therefore wanted to get it over and done with, pleaded guilty after agreeing with my barrister that the jury wouldn't be informed, so as not to prejudice the case against me (which incidentally, the prosecution

> barrister went back on halfway through the trial!) I was found guilty and Jim O'Donnell not guilty.
>
> My defence had been that I acted with honest intentions in that I believed I did nothing immoral or dishonest. I was able to call Sarah Kite to testify about the horrors of what happens to animals supplied to HRC by Interfauna. I also called Robin Webb, who was then on the ruling council of the RSPCA, to testify how woefully inadequate the laws relating to vivisection are and how raids such as the Interfauna one represent the only hope for animals on an individual level. Anyway, for whatever reasons, the jury decided to convict me, but I still think there's some potential in the honest intent defence for any future trials.
>
> Danny received nine months, in the end, I got 18 months. Danny did 4 ½ months and I got out on parole after 6 ½. Neither of us has any regrets, bar one—getting caught. The judge went ballistic over the implied threat in the words painted on the walls of the premises and in particular the promise of 'retribution'. Appearing more upset by that than anything else, he used it as his reason for imposing jail sentences.

Following Interfauna, a string of less traditional raids were carried out. In five raids in four months, all manner of weird and wonderful creatures were released back into their natural environment. Four Scottish wildcats were taken from the confines of their enclosures in zoos at Paignton in Devon and Colchester in Essex and transferred 300 hundred miles back to Scotland where they were filmed being released into the wild. Publicly, zoo staff expressed fear for the future welfare of the cats, cynically doubting their ability to survive outside a cage without the generous care of zoo staff. If I were a wild animal, I would be far happier taking my chances in the wild, like most wild animals tend to be. If they haven't been shot or trapped, they might even have their own families. Happier in a cage? What do ya reckon?

Next the ALF carried out raids on snail farms in Norfolk and Tyne & Wear. At the first farm, 12,000 little critters were liberated and at the latter a whopping 153,000 (3,000 adults and 150,000 young) were kidnapped. After the snails had left the second farm, at Colby near Aylesham in Norfolk, activists set the unit alight, causing £70,000 worth of damage. The business ceased trading in snails and became the fourth cruel business to close down in six months.

And then in Hertfordshire, four guinea pigs, six gerbils, two British toads, two salamanders, four tarantulas, one xenopus frog, a cage of locusts and a cage of stick insects were sprung from Ware College. The college was going to use them for dissection. The college later pledged that no dissection would take place there again.

Boots Butcher Beagles

> Non-violence leads to the highest ethics, which is the goal of all evolution. Until we stop harming all other living beings, we are still savages.
>
> *Thomas Edison (1847—1931) Inventor, holder of 1,093 patents*

In June 1982, 12 beagles were taken in a smash and grab raid on a Boots laboratory at Thurgarton, a small village ten miles outside Nottingham. As a result, Boots became a focus for protest. By the end of the year, the media were reporting on a 'David and Goliath' confrontation, and Boots were in the High Court for an injunction against named groups and individuals known to be involved in organising protests, forcing them to keep away. Unfortunately, after a couple of years, David lost his focus, the campaign collapsed and Goliath was free to impose his wicked way on the animals largely unmolested. There was no co-ordination and no leadership from the BUAV and Animal Aid who were beaten back by Boots' legal threats. Local groups drifted to their own campaigns and Boots won. Only the Bristol-based Co-ordinating Animal Welfare stuck with the campaign, but with little national support. Things did not pick up momentum again until the winter of 1990 when a plan to re-launch the Boots campaign started to unfold.

Boots had been a valuable focal point for the anti-vivisection message because of their High Street profile; their 1,085 chemists sold everything which a vivisector dreams of applying to animals' eyes, raw skin, or, by force, into their stomachs. No other company so involved in vivisection was as accessible to anti-vivisectionists as Boots.

Street campaigning has the multiple benefits of exposing and pressurising animal abusers, raising funds and recruiting new campaigners. Boots gave the animal protection movement the perfect training ground. Those new to the movement and to campaigning could do as much or as little as they felt necessary with Boots and have an impact. Every conceivable method of protest was available to campaigners: handing out leaflets and pledging to boycott, filling up shopping baskets with goods to be tilled up and not paid for on the grounds they were animal tested, occupying the roof, sitting in the store—or something more involved and less lawful.

We only had the word of the Boots PR department that they weren't testing cosmetics on animals because they wouldn't allow anyone access to their two animal testing labs (the second hidden on top of their office headquarters in the centre of Nottingham). Since they were a big, well-known company, one would have thought they'd be really cautious about their involvement with animal experiments. Indeed, their public face was that of a squeaky-clean, cruelty-free company, even down to the leaflets they produced proclaiming their animal friendliness. The only obvious, glaring inconsistency with this was that they were happy to sell their own-brand cosmetic products alongside those of other companies who refused point-blank to stop testing their junk on live animals.

And then, of course, there's that whole thing about the word of a vivisector being consistently shown as worthless. None of these facts inspired confidence. Fact is, they were still unashamedly experimenting on animals for what they and every animal user before and since categorise as 'essential medical research', so it was hardly going to matter to the average AR campaigner whether they tested their cosmetics on animals or not—the problem is animal testing per se.

A preliminary look at the isolated property at Thurgarton late one evening was mouth-watering. The Boots signs all around the perimeter confirmed it belonged to the company; more importantly, though, there were also dogs in kennels. This was no depot or manufacturing warehouse; there was a vivisection lab here with kennels full of barking beagles. Walking a quarter of a mile from the main road through the village and up on to the farmland owned by Boots, the first thing you see is a long, single-storey windowless brick building to the right beyond tall wire fences, sensors and CCTV monitors. At one end of the building, a permanent, uniformed security presence made regular patrols. Beyond the lab, further into the wilderness, stood a network of fenced-in kennels protected by cameras. For a company without secrets, they were cautious. But the ALF 'spies' had seen many places like this lab before, and this one had a good feel about it. It was an awful place for sure, but it had distinct possibilities, something that cannot be said of some other labs, which are just too secure to attempt a break-in.

It was decided very early on to focus on the kennels rather than the lab, since the latter posed a greater risk of confrontation with security. As valuable as entering the lab would surely have been, this was to be about rescuing animals and shaming Boots as vivisectors. Further visits to the site revealed that the security guards gave little more than a cursory glance at the kennels on their patrols. This was crucial because experience had taught that no amount of sweet talk or sweet treats was temptation enough to silence a pack of beagles once they get going. The security guards gave the dogs a wide berth and walked past them quietly so as not to disturb them.

So comfortable was this working environment that one night the security guards themselves were shadowed on their patrol by two men in balaclavas. And so close! They never knew it, of course. This was probably an unnecessary risk, as most of their movements were well mapped out after half a dozen night time recces, but it was described as 'amusing.' All this preparation revealed that there was a camera blind spot to the rear of the kennel block, which backed onto woodland through which there was access to the best place to put a vehicle! On top of all that, the tremor alarm attached to the fence around the kennels was old and not maintained, which had been confirmed while the cameras and security lodge were being monitored.

Although it was taking time, everything was falling into place. It had taken half a dozen visits to work out the best way in and out and though it isn't generally recommended that you go back into the bowels of the monster too often in case you're caught there, sometimes it seems the more you look the more you see. Fortunately for this little conspiracy, Boots' security guards weren't really looking.

When the reconnaissance team did their final check before the raid proper, they cut the fence and waited to see if that stirred Security. It had to be cut at some point, so better to do it sooner rather than later in case a quick getaway might be needed. Spotlights lit the inside of the compound, so there was no need for torches; nobody was paying any attention except for the dogs, and they were making the biggest racket ever! With the camera's blind spot in mind, an appropriate spot in the chain link fence was snipped inside the fence post and eased away from the ground to make a triangular gap that would be big enough to crawl through. No sign of camera movement… A few minutes later, the fence was back to normal—the fence links appeared intact—and soon there was no one around. The barking went on and on and on as the dogs wound each other up long into the night. They are very sensitive, beagles.

That the beagles were so agitated was probably a coincidence, but there was more in store tonight for their allies. There were three lads on site including Getaway Driver sussing his route. On leaving, the wannabe rescuers walked quietly down the lanes, deep in thought. 'How many of the little fellas are we going to be able to get?' 'What of those we don't?' It didn't bear thinking about. And then there was no time to think about anything except getting out of sight. The two chatty security guards were about to turn the corner. It wasn't the best idea to jump into the bushes with the crispy autumn leaves everywhere, but there was nowhere else to go. The guards didn't seem to hear anything, not even the hedgehog in jackboots running around in a panic nearby. Maybe that was a good cover for the noise they just made in spooking the spiky little thing. The guards were too busy talking. No one on the ground was breathing, the curled up activists could see the cold air gushing from the guard's mouths and didn't want any of that! Just as well they'd been talking or everyone would have had the fright of their lives turning that bend and that could have thrown the whole plan!

With the first drama over, back out on the road it was time to hit the dirt again. There was a police car parked behind the getaway car. 'Great!' whispered the Driver sarcastically. He hadn't been to the site before, but because he'd been led to believe this was straightforward, he'd been happy to bring his own car—actually his partner's car. And now the police were onto it! The police knew his own car like they knew everyone else involved in this fermenting plan. Now his girlfriend, whom he'd never wanted to implicate in anything he did, was in on a conspiracy! Great! She was going to get into the sort of trouble her parents had warned her about and he was going to have to sort that out. Suddenly a personal drama was unfolding that he really didn't need.

By coincidence, while the Boots conspirators were nestling in the undergrowth for the umpteenth time awaiting the next police move, a separate chance encounter with them was causing more obvious problems for an ALF team in Cambridgeshire. On the road and on the lookout for some kids who'd allegedly been throwing fireworks at motorists, police had noticed a vehicle parked by the side of the road a mile from Huntingdon Research Centre, and approached it for a quick word with the driver. At the wheel was Barry Horne. On the face of it, although he was an animal rights campaigner, who had—by the by—previously tried to kidnap a dolphin, this wasn't yet that suspicious. No one had recognised him. But close by was a second car with three passengers; all were wearing overalls. While one cop stayed with the first car his colleague approached the second. 'Why are you all wearing overalls?' he pondered suspiciously. Uh oh! They could perhaps explain the overalls, but there were things they couldn't have explained like the contents of the boot. They had been minding their own business and bothering no one but had planned to torch the transport depot of Duncan's who were supplying coaches to ferry workers into the Huntingdon Research Centre. With their plans necessarily now aborted, the drama continued unfolding: once the policeman started to run the driver's details through the PNC (police national computer) it was time to bail out.

Two of the team in the second car took off into the night, but Michael Shanahan and Barry Horne were detained before they were able to make good their escape. All dressed up with nowhere to go! They hadn't been throwing fireworks around—that'd be mindless—but they did have something to hide. The dastardly deed at Duncan's had not yet been done, and the paraphernalia was in the boot, which is where the police would be looking for their fireworks. Needless to say, finding gallons of fuel and a stash of incendiary devices ended the search for fireworks.

Back at the police station, cops ducked everywhere when a random alarm clock rung into life as property was being searched. It was a brief moment of respite for the despondent detainees. The following morning, a long time activist by the name of Gari Allen was arrested at home on the evidence of a police officer that said he'd recognised him at the scene from mug shots he had been shown later. Allen joined the others in custody. Bizarrely, the police never acknowledged there had been a fourth man, and he was never mentioned again by anyone!

Possibly concussed by the alarm clock incident, the police speculated at the bail hearing that the three had been plotting to firebomb a police station. The magistrates couldn't of course risk releasing them to do anything of the sort so and they were remanded in custody and only bailed at a later date. A year on, Gari Allen was acquitted on a legal technicality. There was no evidence he'd been involved since the police officer making the identification had failed to follow procedure. The other two were convicted of conspiracy to cause explosions. The judge acknowledged they weren't plotting explosions, rather to cause fires, but remained unhappy at their lack of cooperation in failing to reveal the intended target and, of course, that they had one! They were each sentenced to three years in prison.

Back at Thurgarton, while Duncan's depot was being given a stay of execution, there had been an anxious hour-long wait for more police to arrive before the police driver returned to his car. He had been in a nearby house, attending to someone else's business and paying no attention to anything else. He jumped in, turned to adjust something on the passenger seat and drove off without a second glance at their parked car. It's bad for the nerves! Relief!

Plans were finalised—the job was on. Three days later, Elderly

Couple in Nottingham were up early, running around preparing a feast fit for kings. They were expecting some special guests. Forget the Queen, she'd not even get a jam sandwich here! An old friend had called round unexpectedly to ask if he and a few friends could hold up for a few hours in a day or so. Despite the age difference, these were the best of friends, bound by years of bouncing off the same police lines and sharing heated debates across the divide with one animal abuser or another. Too old now to climb fences, but they would do anything they could to help the ALF or any animal in need. 'You can stay here for as long as you want. We can go away if you like.' That wasn't necessary, but they insisted they didn't want to know any more than they already did and didn't want to get in the way. They had so much respect for ALF activists and they were honoured that they had been called upon to help.

There was enough food to last months: a feast of lovingly prepared vegan nosh—a bottle of Jack Daniels with a note attached which read: 'Save some for later!' They had even left an envelope with cash in it… These were good people—they made life easier. It was 3 November, 1990; fireworks in the air. Over a period of a few hours, activists—good, trustworthy people—arrived at the house and tucked in. Equipment was laid out, cleaned and packed: gloves and spare (check for holes) new camera battery and spare, spare films, spare footwear, empty pockets (see Interfauna!) check car lights work…

They discussed the plans and reminisced about past events. It was nice to have a bit of time to catch up; everyone was always so busy. A scout car buzzed the area around the lab in the early evening before the safe house was vacated, checking for anything out of the ordinary before dropping off the lookout, who was to keep an eye on the security lodge. He found his roost and settled down for the night. The rest of the team, no longer so talkative, were positioned in the back of a van in a lay-by waiting for word that Security had done the rounds. They didn't patrol to a specific time but they left a good few hours before going out again: a few undisturbed hours were all that was needed to pull this one off. 'You there?' followed by a radio cackle broke the silence. It was the CB radio in the front of the van. Been there for only 45 minutes but it was long enough. They just got back. 'Copy?' There was one excited 'Yes!' and a collective rush of adrenalin. This was it!

The drive to the kennels was a breeze. Once inside the Boots estate, the driver dimmed the headlights; with the windows wound down everyone listened intently for any sound. The van crawled along to keep engine noise down; as it veered away towards the kennels, the lay of the land hid it from sight of the security lodge. Then, with only seconds to go before the van was to pull off the lane into trees just beyond the kennels, disaster loomed. Coming straight towards them from the opposite direction was a swiftly moving vehicle, headlights bouncing. There was a farm down there, but no one had ever used the road before! If it reached the brow of the hill before the van was out of sight, things were going to be really awkward. If the van carried on, chances were that the other driver would want to know what business they had at the farm. If it turned, it would be caught in the path of the other vehicle and forced to drive off site and back to the village. Either way there would be a valuable witness.

There was a moment of panic; this wasn't rehearsed! 'Get the gate! Get the gate!' That was the job of the passenger in the front seat, and well he knew it. The van wasn't close enough yet, but it needed saying and if he were honest, he'd admit that for a moment he wasn't sure what to do. But the quick thinking driver concluded there was nowhere else to go. He'd been here before and knew the lay of the land; he killed the lights, put his foot down and made for the gate. It was difficult to gauge how far from view the oncoming vehicle was; one moment it was near and then not so, as the road wound its way upward. Before the van was stopped the passenger was out of the door and wrestling with the gate. Would you believe it? It was stuck! It hadn't been locked before, but for a minute everyone thought it now was. Well, not a minute, only a few seconds in reality, but who thinks of counting when they're in a panic! Maybe not so much a panic, as dread that the gate wouldn't open. A lot of work could have come to an end right here, but as it turned out, it was no problem: with a little persuasion, the gate shifted and was yanked open.

With the oncoming headlights so nearly in view, the van bounced in and sneaked into the trees. The gate was closed as hastily. Everyone fell silent with the engine. Not that it mattered really, with 200 beagles barking on one side and a 4x4 speeding by on the other! And on it went out of view. That was so close! The lookout radioed through to ask if anyone saw the car that just drove out! Within a minute, the van was empty and covered in a camouflage net and the pre-cut fence was opened up again. The dogcatchers squeezed in with their homemade catchpoles and crawled along the camera blind spot to the furthest accessible kennels. And that's when the fun began!

Beagles can be difficult dogs at the best of times. These ones had been destined from birth to live and die in a vivisection laboratory. All they knew was what they had experienced in their prison. Suddenly, while fireworks periodically filled the sky in the distance with lights and explosions, people in balaclavas were crawling around in excrement in the kennels, trying to lasso the dogs and remove them through the dog flaps from the relative safety of their sleeping quarters. It was described as like a very difficult, very messy fairground attraction with a beagle as the prize.

The animals were neurotic. They either cowered in the furthest corner or bolted from one side to the other. It took quite some time to get the loop over a dog's heads and onto the neck but once that was achieved there was no way back for the captive captives as they were dragged unceremoniously, whites of eyes prominent and fat toes spread in protest across the slippery floor and out of the flap. The first was down the ALF conveyor belt within minutes: out the hole, over the fence and over to the van where the Puppy Pacifier was waiting to settle the new arrivals down for the journey home.

It was all going to plan when something really cruel happened: the radios packed in. With dogs leaving the kennels only slowly, it was going to take some time to fill up the van, so contact with the lookout was essential. The next six dogs took over half an hour to catch, which was just seven in nearly an hour on the job. Some were just too terrified and slippery to catch. It was all taking too long. And then someone noticed a camera above had started to pan the site. This had never happened before either! Everyone was out of range but for one catcher. She had just pulled a dog through when told to stay put. The camera was slow and seemed thorough, but it couldn't see under the overhang above the kennel. It passed over the catcher and her prize, who ran towards the hole before she got pinned down by the camera returning. It was a sure thing that Security would be on their way to check. With one eye on the cameras it was time to get in the van and leave.

By the time the lookout had been prised from his post and returned to the van, it was too late to do anything about the fact that Security had apparently no idea anything was amiss. The lookout couldn't understand the fuss. Security hadn't shown any sign they were concerned, although they or an alarm could have alerted the police. It mattered not now, enough of the job was done. It wasn't a huge haul but it was significant. All eight passengers were female. Within an hour, they were safely hidden away for the night, and early the next morning they were taken to a proper vet for a once over and to have their ear ID tattoos dug out. It transpired that the ones who were hardest to capture had been experimented with already and had areas on their skin shaven.

The raid was press released and well publicised in the local and national media and throughout the movement. This was the beginning of Phase Two—that being to put Boots back onto the agenda. Forget the secret labs tucked away in the middle of nowhere, this is where the issue needs to be—free for all the general public to see! These gross tests are supposedly done for us and we have a right to know everything about them. Three days after the raid, 12 large display windows of the four Boots stores in Bolton were smashed with bricks and others soon followed suit. A week later, the lab at Thurgarton was breached again, this time during the day and by 43 activists operating under the banner of the Animal Liberation Investigation Unit. This was the first action of the ALIU, taking example from a case three years earlier in which four raiders were acquitted of burglary after admitting they intended to take documents, photocopy and then return them to the London School of Tropical Medicine where they were arrested. As the prosecution were unable to prove they intended to deprive the lab of its papers permanently, the case failed to a principled public interest defence. A significant result, but sadly there was no rush to exploit this loophole, which was rather a shame in my view.

We thought we should try it out at Boots. Our plan was to invade the complex en masse, to rush in and run around, occupy the roof and cause as much confusion and disruption as possible whilst collecting our documents. This wasn't intended as a return to the suicide daylight raids of the early 80's and no laws were going to be broken. The main intention was to remove papers that would be photocopied and returned.

I was driving one minibus, but that broke down just outside the city and left me stranded. My passengers piled into other transport. Now, because timing was ever so slightly out, the plan had to be altered at the last minute and everyone headed instead for the kennels where experiments were also carried out, rather than the main lab as intended. Ten people took to the roof of the main building and unfurled banners exclaiming 'Boots Mutilate Beagles', a statement that would soon spread far and wide. Others had a nosey around with video cameras and took pictures. Those on the paper chase set about recovering documents and boy were they good! They did such a good job in fact that it was impossible to move it all with any speed—bit like the hand in the cookie jar—and by the time the first vehicle was leaving the site the police, who were by now alert to this flashpoint, had started arriving.

The police were in good time to stop our motorbike as it attempted to leave the area, its hefty load and driver detained, as were all the other vehicles and the rest of the raiding party. The police response was incredible. All those present had witnessed police overkill on hunts but never anything quite like this. Within around 20 minutes of the alarm being raised, there were no less than 60 police vehicles—cars, bikes, riot vans—and twice as many officers. Forces from all over Nottingham had been scrambled to Thurgarton. It would have been an impressive show if hadn't been for the fact that it was designed to prevent the rescue of some dogs.

The consequence of the police's swift reaction, their inflated numbers, and the sheer volume of paperwork that had been removed, was that only a small amount of information was actually recovered. The bulk of it—literally the entire contents of the filing cabinets—was returned to Boots. Everyone was arrested and taken to one of three police stations around Nottingham and, following court appearances, all were eventually released on condition that they didn't go near any Boots stores or any animal research establishments. The request was made but they wouldn't supply a comprehensive list of these, unhelpfully.

All were initially charged with three counts of conspiracy to burgle, which was silly, given that the press were informed of their intent and invited along, and all 43 participants carried a document explaining that they had no desire or intention to break any laws, only to do what the law says is acceptable and borrow some paperwork. Before the case reached trial, all charges were dropped with no case to answer, as predicted. Boots didn't want to be in the limelight any longer and anyway the police had to concede that no laws had been broken after all, save trespass, and that wasn't a criminal offence.

So it was now confirmed that it was lawful to rifle filing cabinets and take what you want as long as you don't intend to permanently deprive the owner. This was great! According to solicitor John McKenzie after the case: 'You can certainly say this is a major victory. It will be a real poser to establishments involved in animal abuse.'

The inspection had caused more unwanted publicity for Boots. A film of the labs and photographs soon went public and were used to good effect to put pressure on Boots to stop their experiments. Just what was this animal-friendly company doing with a treadmill and hundreds of terrified beagles? The wider industry was openly perturbed by this new development and concerned about its potential. We later came by an internal circular warning all staff at the Wellcome labs in Beckenham to observe a 'clean desk policy', to keep all doors and drawers locked when not in use, and to keep paperwork hidden away from prying eyes: 'From the anti-vivisection point of view it has much to commend it; it is a fairly simple matter for them to walk into any laboratory site en masse; they commit no criminal offence by merely doing so and thus, without facing the prospect of imprisonment or fine, they can gain much publicity.'

Within months, the first national march against Boots was organised by a coalition of groups now actively muddying Boots' clean image. Around 700 people attended and let the people of Nottingham know what dirt lay beyond the apparently squeaky-clean facade of their celebrated employer. Activists everywhere literally hit the roof. In Nottingham, several went up onto the city centre store for the day, draping a huge banner. 500 protesters marching through the centre of Manchester against the university's abuse of animals laid siege to shut down the city's big Boots store for the afternoon. Police snatch squads moved in there and accounted for 25 demonstrators. Another 18 activists were arrested after two hours on the roof of the Birmingham branch. The campaign intensified when arsonists attacked the Boots distribution depot offices at Rochdale. Within sight of the police station and working 24 hours a day, the company probably felt relatively comfortable here, and there was no reason for them to expect such an attack.

There had been no precedent since the beginning of the campaign, just lots of annoying low-level actions. But you never can tell what's around the corner and tonight it was two suspicious figures with a suspicious package. They crept into the parking lot as discreetly as one does with a Molotov cocktail and a five-gallon barrel of petrol. With workers occupied loading and unloading at one end of the site, the raiders smashed an office window at the other with a brick, emptied the fuel inside and lit the petrol bomb. Enthusiasm is one thing, but it's sometimes better to take your time, especially when handling a naked flame near a room full of petrol fumes! What was later described as a 'wall of fumes where the window once was,' rushed forward and engulfed the molly as it headed through the hole, engulfing our arsonists in a whoosh, like a Venus Fly Trap closing in on its victim. Situation serious! But only for as long as it took to singe four eyebrows and force a hasty retreat from the flaming scene of crime.

Caught up themselves, albeit only in the publicity that followed this upsurge in action against them, Boots denied they were party to any animal experiments. No one ever is unless it's the kind of stuff the animals quite enjoy! No, apparently we were confusing them with a subsidiary company called Boots Pharmaceuticals.

Thinking that the burnt offices, the high street shops and the vivisection labs are all owned by the same Boots company that use the well known Boots logo—the same one found in the Boots shops and offices up and down the country, like the depot in Rochdale—it is an obvious mistake to make. Sadly for Boots, there was little real confusion around, but there were a few arsonists, and things were hotting up. Luckily, a passer-by saved the Boots store in Lancaster after petrol was poured through the air conditioning system there, but others wouldn't be so fortunate.

By the end of 1991, according to *The Guardian*, Boots had suffered up to 70 attacks per month, and 50,000 people had signed pledge forms vowing to boycott Boots. Campaign T-shirts, posters, badges and stickers were churned out as fundraisers and sold like hot cakes. Within the first six months of 1991 over 100,000 leaflets were distributed by the ALIU and many local groups produced their own. The London Boots Action Group alone distributed the same number outside London stores and organised the regular picket of annual general meetings and any other Boots-sponsored events that came to light. Completed petitions piled up and banners were photographed hanging from the rooftops of Boots stores up and down the country. Whether or not they like to admit it—and of course they won't—things took a turn for the worse for Boots in November 1990. The combined effects of the backlash from all of the publicity and activity, and the failings of Boots' crude research methods finally led to the abandonment of their involvement in the research and development of drugs just a few years later.

In August 1992, the Boots drug Flosequinan, marketed as Manoplax, was licensed for the treatment of chronic heart failure. The release of Manoplax followed ten years of experiments on cats, dogs, rats and guinea pigs. In one experiment, beagles had their kidneys surrounded in a rubber latex tube. After being left for between nine and 17 months, each had flesh on their necks removed and the carotid artery pulled away from their throat (dogs liberated by ALF ten years earlier had had their carotid arteries similarly exposed). The hole was then sewn up with the artery left outside the neck so that it could be punctured to measure blood pressure. Manoplax was then administered and the blood pressure measured while the dogs were suspended in slings. They were of course killed once they'd served their purpose and the results noted.

In another experiment using cats and dogs, Flosequinan had a different effect on the two species. Again the results posed the question that won't go away: that if such species differences exist between cats and dogs in the same lab, how can we hope to predict results in the ailing human in the real world? The fundamental problem with relying on animals to teach us about humans is that they don't react the same and even the subtlest of differences in DNA can cause fatal contradictions. Even more important is the fact that animals do not suffer from the same diseases as humans so these have to be artificially induced in them. Hardly good science! Dogs are said to be man's best friend so perhaps we should rely on the result they give us rather than cats? Which species do we rely on when the results conflict? Is it guesswork? Oh yes!

Interestingly, in August 1992, *The Pharmaceutical Journal* said of Manoplax:

> There are no data yet from large studies on whether treatment with Flosequinan will prolong life. One early trial found more deaths in treated patients than in placebo groups.

In trials, side effects observed (in humans) included: headache, dizziness, palpitations, tachycardia (abnormally fast heartbeat) symptomatic hypertension (low blood pressure) nausea, vomiting and diarrhoea. The world market for this kind of heart treatment was estimated to be worth $2 billion a year in the early 1990s. The UK market had been predicted to bring in around £10 million per year and US approval could've meant £100 million within a few years. That's why proving it works in an animal is so important.

Manoplax was to be Boots' wonder drug. A drug they hoped would do wonders for their profits. For the year ending 31.2.92, the Boots Company made a profit before tax of £374.2 million. Income was further supplemented by the NHS, which was placing 11% of its orders (prescriptions) at Boots outlets. Unfortunately for Boots, Manoplax proved to be a monumental disaster and in April 1993, just seven months after its UK launch, Boots issued a press statement explaining that preliminary results from a clinical trial had suggested that patients

Above: Lynx anti-fur advert. Used to great effect this ad and others sought to shame fur wearers from the streets.

Mink freed from Swedish farm.

Above left: Riot police escort waste dairy industry calves out of Shoreham for European veal farms.

Above: Horses rescued from Laundry Farm in Cambridge, 1991.
Below: Some of the 79 beagle puppies rescued from Cambridgeshire based Interfauna in 1990.

Above: Swedish activist releases farmed fox back into the wild.
Below: Protesters and riot police discuss the future of the Hill Grove cats.
World Day 1997.

Above: Still from video of Beatrice, a 15 year-old rhesus monkey used in arthritis research in a Birmingham University lab. Bereft of human contact but for surgery and injections, she was delighted to be taken from her cage during the rescue and would never part with the blanket she was given to keep her warm during the journey away from the lab.

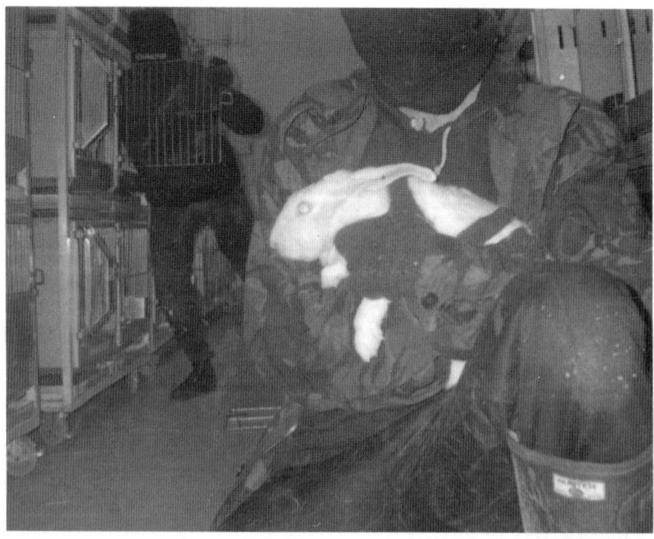

Above: Oxford University Park Farm raiders rescuing rabbits.

With extreme violence key to the hunt supporter, why are such vast resources spent on imprisoning and investigating hunt saboteurs? Here a sab is kicked in the head and left badly injured by a supporter of the Chiddingfold, Cowdray and Leconfield hunt in West Sussex on 17/2/05, the day after hunting was banned by law in the UK. Hunts and their supporters boasted proudly of 91 foxes killed this day during which several saboteurs and hunt monitors were arrested and/or violently attacked. Hunt saboteurs also saved a number of foxes, hares and domestic animals.

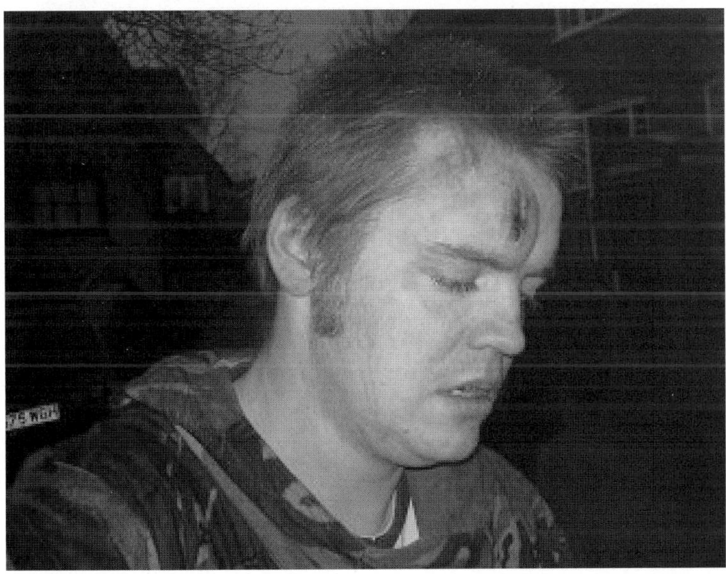

Above: Cat restrained in stereotaxic device. These grotesque contraptions are manufactured specifically for the purpose of clamping live animals so that their working brains can be fiddled with.

Above: A sad day for decent people and wild animals in the killing fields of England. (Mike Huskisson/LACS)

Left: Hunt saboteur Debbie Marsh occupies a foxhole to prevent the hunt digging the fox out. (Simon Wild)

Right: An ominous development in the early 1990's was the deployment by UK hunts of 'stewards' to deter any public opposition to bloodsports. Not just hunt supporters but football thugs, and former soldiers were persuaded with a wage to beat up hunt sabs and monitors.

Above: Mounted hunt riders use their horses and whips to attack a group of saboteurs. These violent attacks take place every week in the UK yet the assailants are seldom arrested and almost never convicted despite the wealth of photographic evidence available to police.

Above: Here Portman Hunt supporters welcome a group of hunt saboteurs to Dorset in November 1997. The assailants remain at large.

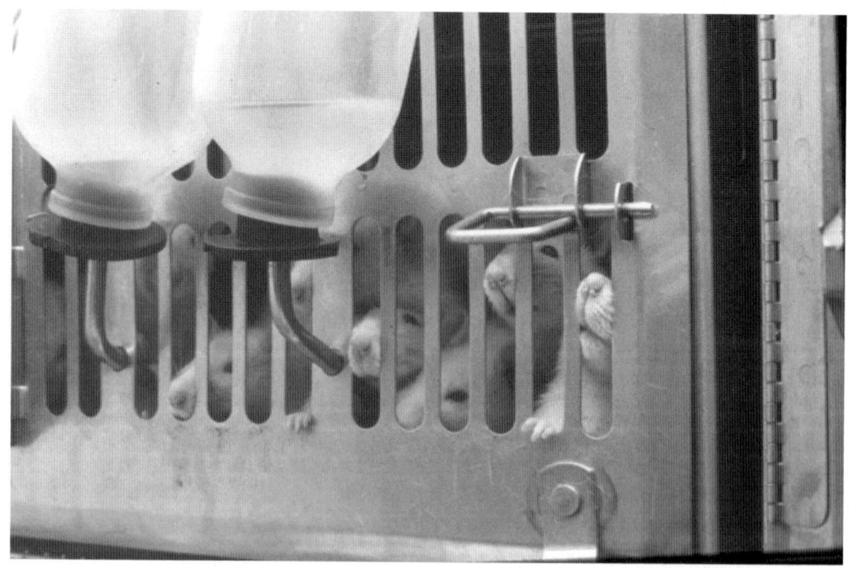

A British miner once saw two large rats proceeding slowly along a roadside, each holding one end of a straw in its mouth. The miner clubbed one of them to death. To his surprise, the other rat didn't move, so the miner bent down to observe it more closely. It was blind and was being led by the first.

with severe congestive heart failure taking 100mg of Manoplax a day had a 'significantly increased risk of death compared with those not receiving the drug.' What on earth?! A few weeks later, unmoved by tests on vulnerable trusting humans, a spokesman announced: 'We have every confidence in its prospects' due to results seen in some other animals!

Three months later, ten months after the drug was first put on the market, Boots announced they were withdrawing it following the outcome of a two year study of 3000 human patients in the US and Scandinavia, their statement concluding: 'In view of these data, the continued use of Manoplax can no longer be recommended.' Once again, it had been clinical studies (tests on people) that showed the tests on animals to be worse than useless and so dangerous.

Boots went on to abandon their drug development arm and sold their laboratories, but they remain a focus for boycott due to the endless supply of animal-tested products in store.

Ours Is Not To Reason Why

> Animal experiments lack any scientific validity and reliability in regard to people. They only serve as an alibi for the drug manufacturers, who hope to protect themselves thereby.
>
> *Drs H&M Stiller, Munich 1976*

Here's a brief recap of some of what we know about the pharmaceutical industry, drug testing, money, profit, human health and of course, animal suffering. It is perhaps the cruellest irony of all that because vivisection is so vile, many believe that it must be necessary. Surely no one would do these things to living creatures if it were avoidable? Those who perform these experiments in secret argue the same. Let them prove otherwise by opening up this supposedly invaluable yet still highly secretive method of research to full public scrutiny, something only the industry are keen to prevent! As things stand, the market is awash with dangerous toxic products, and who knows how many potentially beneficial treatments have failed animal tests? Penicillin is surely one of the most glaring examples, one of our most valuable drugs delayed for a decade for application for human benefit, due to the fact that it doesn't work in the rabbit. It kills guinea pigs and hamsters. Blood transfusions were likewise delayed and people died as a consequence of animal tests failing to produce the result needed.

By choosing the correct species of animals, product manufacturers can prove absolutely anything they want. If, for example, a company wanted to market arsenic as a medicine, it could provide its safety certificate by testing it on sheep, which can tolerate considerable amounts of the poison. Fortunately for us, penicillin wasn't tested on guinea pigs because it kills them, but they can eat strychnine, which is one of the deadliest poisons for humans. Belladonna should be avoided too, unless you're a rabbit or goat. Digitalis has helped many human patients with heart conditions, yet wasn't thought at all helpful after laboratory experiments on dogs showed that it raised their blood pressure to a dangerously high level. Chloroform isn't good for dogs either; its toxic effects on them mislead us so it wasn't employed as an anaesthetic for humans when it was really needed. Morphine calms and anaesthetises humans and causes manic excitement in cats and mice, but dogs can tolerate doses 20x higher than people. And the list goes on and on and on, taking with it the list of human animals that have suffered and died because of the results of experiments on animals, which—if they have proved nothing else—is that data from animal experiments doesn't extrapolate accurately to humans.

Drug companies bolster their profits by continually flooding the market with new and 'improved' preparations and promises we don't need. The World Health Organisation has estimated that of 30,000 to 40,000 drugs on the market, only 220 are of any real benefit. Health Action International has stated that: 'Most of the tens of thousands of drugs on the world market are either unsafe, ineffective, unnecessary or a waste of money.' Ciba Geigy, one of the world's largest pharmaceutical companies, once admitted that 95 percent of all drugs passed as safe and effective on the basis of animal tests fail when entered for clinical trials on people. Quite a staggering fail rate. Tossing a coin would be far more reliable method giving a 50% return and would be far less dangerous and destructive, but not so good for the wheels of industry.

Vivisection isn't just about drug testing on rats and mice of, course; that's just the party line. In 2003, 4,799 primates, 7,094 dogs, 8,879 horses, 25,326 rabbits, 121,611 birds and 14,985 amphibians were experimented on, amongst others—8,007 animals were killed to test food additives—6,008 animals were injected into the brain and another 25,470 had their brain interfered with—109,000 animals were killed in poisoning tests for pollutants, agrochemicals, industrial chemicals and household products—16,596 were deliberately subjected to psychological stress—18,929 were physically traumatised or burnt—10,341 endured radiation experiments—1,691,897 animals were given no anaesthetic for most or all of the experiment. Plus there are the warfare experiments. There's the testing of new methods of farming and breeding, experiments to test theories and to satisfy curiosity and the repetitive experiments. But it's the search for new drugs that sway the argument in favour of 'animal research', yet drug companies know that animal experiments do not prove the safety of their product in people, the environment or even in non-target animals, and are carried out for legal protection rather than medical comparison.

When Roussel was taken to court charged with producing misleading advertising for its product Surgam, its own defence expert witnesses testified that data from animal experiments could not be extrapolated safely to patients. An American girl, who suffered eye damage from a shampoo she'd used, tried to claim damages on the basis that the product had proven to be an irritant when tested on animals. The court ruled in favour of the company on the grounds that there was no evidence to show the tests done on rabbits could be used to predict what could happen to humans. These are random examples, but this is standard legal judgement.

Each year in the UK, tens of thousands of people die from coronary heart disease, something that costs the NHS hundreds of millions of pounds every year. As the British Medical Journal stated way back in 1980: 'The control of coronary heart disease necessarily depends on prevention, since treatment so often comes too late. Mass medication is potentially dangerous, and it would be better if risk factors could be controlled by changing habits.'

But there are no massive profits generated by changing habits and keeping people healthy. The main causes of heart disease are recognised as smoking, high blood pressure, diet, obesity, stress and lack of exercise—all of which are best dealt with without the need for expensive drugs. We're told repeatedly that saturated fat in the diet raises levels of cholesterol in the blood, which is a direct cause of heart disease. Most Britons (Americans more so) eat too much animal fat and so have too much cholesterol in their blood with around 60% of fat consumed coming from meat and dairy. Before 1925, heart disease was uncommon. Since then it has increased steadily with our consumption of animal products. So we have evolved into a species that inflicts complete confinement, uses torture and mutilation on farm animals that we then kill cruelly to eat, while killing off any wild species that competes with or preys on this bounty of livestock. Our consumption in turn leads to degenerative illness, so we torture other animals in a desperate search for miracle cures! How would visitors from another planet view this behaviour?

Langford

> One may not reach the dawn, save by the path of the night.
>
> *Kahlil Gibran*

Just three weeks after the Boots beagles were rescued, activists took ten dogs from Langford University College in Bristol and introduced them to the joy of life amongst extremists. Amongst its other vile excesses, Langford's speciality is experimenting on 'farm' animals to test new drugs to counter the side-effects associated with factory farming: so-called veterinary research. Langford is the place where factory farming meets vivisection in a gruesome contradiction of what humans should be achieving.

For years, campaigners had protested and asked nicely for the release of the ten beagles who had been kept there for some secret long-term experiment. It's not clear if this was related to farm animal research because no one was admitting anything. No can do, said Langford; they were contributing something essential to human health. Unconvinced by the unconvincing arguments coming from the University, a small group of young people took it upon themselves to sort out the problem. Late one night at Langford:

> We didn't know whether we would be able to get all the dogs out before the night watchman arrived, but we weren't going to be able to live with ourselves if we didn't at least try. We were being haunted by our knowledge of what was happening to the animals at Langford; it wasn't just the cruelty and indifference, it's all so completely and utterly unnecessary. The security wasn't what we expected, there was just one door between us and the dogs and they sounded so pitiful. We expected the door to be alarmed but we hoped to be able to grab all the dogs before being disturbed. As it turned out, the door wasn't alarmed, or the alarm wasn't working if it was, and then if it was, no one was paying any attention to it. Either way, it was good news.
>
> We drove right up to the kennels, jumped out of the van and forced the door open with a crowbar. The dogs were apparently excited that something was happening. We had expected them to cower with fear, but this was an adventure maybe they'd dreamt about; it really was as though they knew it was their turn to be

rescued. Within ten minutes we were loaded with our friends and on our way to somewhere safe. The three of us were over the moon, the ten of them in heaven: never before had they seen anything quite like this, nor had we. What a sight! Here were ten tubby beagles who we were expecting would be defecating in the back of the van and cowering in a corner, instead they were tumbling about having a ball and queuing for a sniff of the cool invisible fresh stuff that was blowing through the open window. They weren't 100% sure about us, but it wasn't going to take long to persuade them we were good people.

All the dogs were fairly old and showed signs of mistreatment. One in particular, Ramble to her friends, was—without exaggeration—covered in wounds, scars and shaven patches, some healed, some not. Some looked like cigarette burns. They were all taken to a sympathetic vet who carried out full examinations but was unable to say with any degree of certainty what they had been subjected to. Langford weren't of course prepared to say what they had used the beagles for, neither before nor after we took them. It was never going to be explained why some didn't have identification tattoos either, not that it mattered to us. At least it kept the vet bill down and meant they didn't have to have the ink in their ears scraped out.

Five days after their magical mystery tour, they were all delivered to their new homes. In every case it was hard to decide whether the dogs or their new families were the most excited, but then that didn't matter either. All of a sudden all that mattered was that we had done something for them.

The Christmas Cat Nappers

> The cats were staggering about with terrible wounds. All were suffering horribly. I have been brought up in a fairly rough school but I must say that had it not been for the gentlemen (there)… I would have smashed the whole place up.
>
> *Ex-MP John Bromley following a visit to a London laboratory*

Christmas Eve is traditionally spent celebrating the birth of Jesus, or at least that's the underlying reason for celebrating. Whatever the reason, whatever our beliefs, most of us find it a good excuse to seek pleasure with our families, to chill out and to treat others with a higher degree of respect than normal, and gorge ourselves on the body parts of other animals. I was always slightly uncomfortable with religious teachings when I was younger, but it was only when I grew up and learnt more that I became utterly cynical. How does the idea of an all seeing, all benevolent god tie in with the concept that we must pay homage to this father of creation by massacring, on a massive scale and with exquisite cruelty, his furry and feathered children? Any time of the year is the wrong time of year to take life, but to celebrate the birth of the son of the father of creation; we massacre millions of small creatures! Are we evil or merely misguided? The answer I think lies in whether we are able to alter our behaviour.

The good thing about this time of year from a purely tactical ALF perspective is that while the abusers are busy sharing their version of peace and goodwill, they won't be expecting anyone to break in!

Officially in the UK, a few hundred cats each year are subjected to what are some of the most vile experiments imaginable but only a few have ever been rescued from laboratories and suppliers in this country. Early enquiries by budding cat nappers into key cat places weren't productive, just a lot of talk about security guards, prison and how 'you'll not be able to get in there.' This was from people who had been there years before. One of those now had a wife and two kids and was super paranoid about the police being led back to him. For what: telling people not to bother doing anything! The other mused over how he 'Ant done owt for ages.' It was the last arrest that did it. Nothing serious, but it nearly cost him his job and relationship and it caused a lot of stress. While he was taking a back seat, not wanting to risk anything while on bail, he got more into work and was promoted. Once the trial was over a year later—not guilty of stealing a dozen hens from cages at a battery farm—he was too far removed to return to the campaign trail he'd once called his life. He felt guilty but he'd get over it, he had to. He offered good luck and he meant it. He hadn't been told very much but could see that his visitors meant business and were probably going to do this anyway; it's how he once was himself. 'If you do it and get any out, be aware they might be pretty messed up, some have been in there for years.'

These people had already made their minds up; being told it wasn't possible just strengthened their determination to try. There were at least two known breeders of cats in Oxfordshire and work on them began simultaneously one night, deploying two teams to ascertain a) security arrangements b) number of cats c) anything!

There were only a few archival newspaper reports to go on, which contained their approximate location and other snippets including the motivating factor: two dozen examples of the kind of things being done to cats in the name of science in Oxford and elsewhere, some translated from scientific reports by a particularly bright spark in the Uni.

The drug company SmithKline Beecham in Essex used at least 100 cats to test the effect of drugs. They were anaesthetised, maintained on artificial respiration, and had tubes inserted into their blood vessels. A hole was then cut in their skulls and an electrode was inserted into their brains. Its position was checked by seeing that their jaws moved and that they dribbled when an electrical current was applied through the electrode to the brain. Changes to blood pressure and blood flow following injection of experimental drugs were then measured.

At the National Institute for Medical Research, Mill Hill, London, Feldberg and Sherwood injected a number of widely different chemicals into the brains of cats. They reported that one substance either: 'Produced a peculiar high-pitched cry or the cat retches or does both.' Another substance caused: 'profound motor impairment.'

The injection into the brain of a large dose of Tubocurairine caused the cat to jump 'From the table to the floor and then straight into its cage, where it started calling more and more noisily whilst moving about jerkily. During the next minutes the cat fell with legs and neck flexed, jerking in rapid movements, the condition being that of a major (epileptic) convulsion. Within a few seconds the cat got up, ran a few yards at high speed and fell in another fit. The whole process was repeated several times within the next 10 minutes, during which the cat lost faeces and foamed at the mouth.' The animal died 35 minutes after the brain injection. *The Journal of Physiology* recorded this scientific exploit for posterity.

Farmer Brown's remote farm at Witney had potential, but he and his family lived on site, as did B&B guests in their farmhouse and there were a hell of a lot of cats—a lot more than at Oxford University's outpost in the quiet little village of Nuneham Courtenay. Probably too many to consider rescuing all in one go. Both farms had been broken into before, the former in the early 80s when 11 raiders were barricaded in by the farmer in his tractor and arrested, the other during the reign of the Central Animal Liberation League when steel doors were wrenched open in a smash and grab raid at Nuneham that resulted in the hasty rescue of 12 cats as alarms rang out. Security would surely be tight around such a sensitive university facility, but at first glance it didn't appear to be so. There was no one on site; there were no high fences, no lights and apparently no perimeter security.

Partly relying on its anonymity, partly on the fact that its alarms had rung loud and long the last time the only doors had been forced open, the farm had thus far avoided being too much of a focal point for ALF's attentions. To look at it, one wouldn't have thought that there was anything awful going on here in the converted hay barn standing at the entrance to a field beside a little-used side road. On the other side of the lane was a row of houses. From the floor to the roof of the barn it was breezeblock, broken only by a sprinkle of extractor fans, which provided the only clue to the goings-on within. Two solid steel doors at one end were the only entrance. There was no fire exit, such places being exempt from the statutory requirement for most buildings to provide a fire escape; the most important thing here was not the safety of people, but the protection of secrets.

The arched roof was made of the same corrugated asbestos sheets from which it had been constructed; it was crucial to the plan. Indeed, roofs had begun to prove increasingly important in thinking through and facilitating these break-ins. Doors and windows are alarmed as standard on most buildings but the roof seldom is. The other alternative to bypassing any alarm system should the roof have been alarmed would have been to ambush the unit manager when he arrived in the morning to see to the cats and to keep him until the cats were safely away. This would've solved any access and alarm problems, but if he resisted, it could've got awkward and turned a simple cat rescue into a kidnapping and robbery and this one was meant to be as much about good publicity as a rescue.

Using ladders, it was possible to see in through one of the extractor fans that there were a few cats running free, rather than caged, but the view was limited. There was the smell of cats too, but it was not clear how many were there. Up on the roof it proved straightforward enough, if not precarious, to unscrew the panel fixing bolts and ease out one of the panels. This was the tricky bit. The roof was well weathered, old and covered in moss. As this was only a dry run, it was imperative that trespassers left no damage or any sign of having been there.

The roof shape meant it was impossible to climb onto, but leaning against two sets of ladders on the wall, two people could work a panel out and walk it to the ground. Very carefully! The gaping hole revealed a plasterboard attic floor to the prize below; it wouldn't stand being walked on, but was no deterrent to those with an arsenal of tools for the purpose of forced entry! Most importantly, the roof was not alarmed.

Through very tiny holes in the floor it was possible to see a surprisingly large area beneath. There were 16 x 10'sq rooms below, all with cats. Only very young ones with mothers were in cages, the others presumably free to breed more cats for the local animal research community. To have learnt so much and got so close to so many cats in a place such as this was cause for some celebration for the exploration party, but replacing the roof panel and sealing the cats back to their fate killed that notion. Some might be selected to die before their rescue was arranged—perhaps at the hands of the creepy Colin Blakemore, the notorious stitcher-up of kitten's eyes—but there was nothing anyone could do about that. These negative thoughts spoiled an otherwise exciting night.

The next two weeks were spent finalising plans, collecting cat carriers and meeting with trusted friends. Those chosen—eight in all—had usually complied with social tradition and spent Xmas time touring pubs, smoking pot, eating to excess and lounging around watching TV repeats. And the Boxing Day hunt. This year they were about to risk spending the new year in cells for spending Xmas Eve inside a secret Oxford University field station, a cat lab known to only the tiniest number of people, the inside of which even fewer had seen. It was an exciting undertaking in the repertoire of an animal rights activist. If only more were willing to celebrate their Christmases at these places…

And what of the vet on stand by? He was completely respectable, but unlike many in his profession, he was one of a tiny number prepared to risk imprisonment and his career to remove tattoos from the ears of stolen animals in order to make them anonymous and to treat any illness or injuries. He didn't want paying properly—he just seemed happy to ensure that no animals could return to whence they came. (It seems ironic that in this nation of so-called animal lovers, its easier to make contact with ALF volunteers when animals need this kind of help than it is to find a vets who can be trusted!)

The ladders had been stashed in a nearby woodland but were soon back up against the wall again. It was 9.05pm on 24 December, and for the second time in two weeks the panel was off the roof and on its way to the ground. Everyone got on with their jobs and within minutes a hole had been cut with a cordless drill and hacksaw above the first holding room. It was dark inside, but it was easy to count 15 pairs of cat's eyes gazing skywards. Merry Christmas everyone! The young ones were easy to catch, but the older ones knew better than to trust humans, even if they were wearing balaclavas and one was dressed as Santa Claus. Improvised catchpoles were on hand to negotiate the problem of catching those clinging for dear life to the top wire partitions. It wasn't nice, but force was the only way to get them—clawing and spitting—into the carriers; once boxed up, they were passed up into the attic and carried carefully over the rafters. They made a mental note—To Organisers: A guide rope tied at each end of the attic would have proved handy.

A few cats out and suddenly everyone was told to hold everything. 'Shush!' One of the lookouts had heard someone leave one of the houses opposite, but couldn't see where they'd gone. She crossed the lane to take a closer look but saw nothing. Car headlights appeared up the lane, heading towards the site, forcing her to sit tight… This didn't feel right. Slowing by the houses it pulled up close to where she was hidden, headlights full beam. The driver stepped out of the car wearing a pair of brown leather POD's—he was standing that close, she could read the tag—then sparked up a cigarette. Meanwhile, the rest of the team waited anxiously for word.

Oblivious to what was going on around him, the driver finished his smoke, calmly stepped back into his car, drove it into the garage next to his house, locked up and went indoors. No one else was calm! After a 15-minute wait, they were given the all clear: cats started to move along the conveyor belt again, out of the roof, down the ladder and into the van parked in the field. Four hours into the raid, one young kitten from the last cat room to be vacated panicked and managed to escape from a carrier as it was being moved across the attic. He disappeared just as the last of the headlight torch batteries began to fade, and patience was beginning to wear thin.

'Are you sure one got out?'

'Of course I'm sure, I nearly broke my bloody neck trying to stop it!'

Only asking! It was not what anybody wanted at 2am on Christmas morning with the job all but done. The first search revealed nothing but during the second sweep, the pathetic cry of a frightened kitten revealed his location down in the dark all alone. It took about ten seconds from catching his eyes in the torchlight peeping from under a table, to getting him out back in a box and on his way to somewhere nice. He was passenger number 64 and his arrival signalled the exit of the van and its precious cargo, which was pushed from the field. Safe driving and good fortune saw it arrive an hour later at a safe house outside Oxford.

Spending Christmas day with these cats was the icing on the cake for the driver and her passenger who'd spent the previous night in a hedge, but boy it was worth it! Ever played Name The Kitty? There was Postcard, Chippy, Blown-up, Virus, Lettuce, Notice, Germs, Toothpaste, Tears, Lemon, Sweet Stuff, Palm Tree, Stolen, Fruit Juice, Lemigo, Treetop, Willow, Whisper, Apache, File, Boots, Wallis, Scatty, Peanut, S'curity, Elbow, Squeak, Light Bulb, Friday, Shifty, Pistachio, Arapaho, Scheese, Post box, Max, Roland, Peapod, Marbles, Timepiece, Altcar, HusKiss, Pebble, Dove Top, Sherbet, Secret, Nina, Wenonah, Blackfoot, Sortie, Snakebite, Black, Foolscap, Freedom, Mushroom, Breakdown, Treacle, Scally, Liberty, Switch, Dynamite, November, Liquorice, Garlic and Lakota. It was a fun gesture, as most of these cats would soon be dispersed, renamed and never seen again but it was a little something to welcome them to the vegan world where respect is God.

Some had serious problems, which needed urgent veterinary attention. Some of the older cats were showing signs of ill health and for six, that was as close as they got to freedom. So riddled with cancer after years of forced breeding, they would have had no quality and very short lives, so were allowed to pass away under anaesthetic. All were taken to the vet in batches. If they were up to it, they were spayed or neutered and their ear tattoos removed before being homed. Sixteen were pregnant; six of the pregnancies were terminated. The other ten were so far gone they were left to give birth. There would normally be no rejoicing in more unwanted births, but it was too late anyway and these cats deserved the chance to keep just one litter. In all, nearly ninety cats were saved directly and hundreds, possibly thousands of others that would have been bred from them will never know how lucky they are.

All the healthy cats were homed soon after leaving the vets, and it didn't take them long to adjust and adapt to their new lives. Even the wild ones learnt to trust people and were indistinguishable from any other cat within days. Typically, the University demonstrated their complete lack of understanding of these animals and their welfare needs, claiming that the cats would die once outside their 'sterile environment.' A spokesman for Thames Valley Police duly concurred, adding 'The cats have no immune system and will die in a very short period of time in the wild.' Not so!

That police make such statements without authority is one thing, but how, one wonders, do these researchers really expect to be able to extrapolate the results of invasive experiments on healthy cats to sick human beings if they don't even understand the basics of the animal? Unless of course they were lying—a recurring theme in this mind numbing world of cruelty and deceit.

The Nuneham site was never used again and stands empty to this day, with no trace of the horrors that befell countless of its former detainees. As ever, there is little evidence that this or any other raid has had any immediate effect on the numbers of animals used each year in experiments. Indeed they are on the increase once again, and the cruel stupidity is no different. But as costs rise, so does the paranoia. In a way, I am in awe of the depth of imagination these people have when thinking up new ideas for experiments. Cats in particular have occupied the deepest, darkest minds for decades and yet despite the determination and complexity of this 'research', have revealed very little about the workings of the cat or the human, aside from the disturbed mentality of the individuals inflicting this damage. That some people find cats' weird or threatening is for them to deal with, but using it as an excuse to inflict torture is something for the rest of us to deal with. And deal with it we must. Here are some more of those facts that remind us why.

Dr. Richard Ryder, the British clinical psychologist who performed many experiments, which he later recanted, reported in his book *Victims of Science* that in British universities, cats' brains have been isolated and maintained alive, still attached to the animals' body. These unanaesthetised and apparently fully conscious brains were then observed for their reactions to the injection of various drugs. The same Dr. Ryder once told an audience at a conference in Toronto of an experiment where 'Cats had their tails cut off and were blinded, then they were put into a revolving drum to see how long they could stay awake before they died.'

In 1949 at the Royal Naval Laboratory at Alverstoke, cats were exposed to 100% oxygen until they convulsed or died. The lucky ones convulsed and died after three days of continuous exposure. One was removed after 67 hours, suffering convulsions fifteen times before being killed. Another died after being intermittently exposed for 52 days. One journal describes experiments on pregnant cats after mutilation and other revolting experiments with their eyes. There is also a description of the construction of a window in the chest wall of a cat and the insertion of a light bulb so that observations might be made during experiments.

Fifty years of human evolution and medical progress later, vivisectors hiding in a Newcastle University bunker purchased eight cats to investigate how nerve messages from the skin on their feet might affect control of their leg muscles. The cats were anaesthetised and arteries in their necks were tied. Most nerves to their left back legs were cut below their hip and two recording wires were pushed into one of their leg muscles. The cats were placed with their heads held in a frame over a treadmill with pins in their hips and clamps on their left back leg. Part of their brain was then removed and the anaesthetic discontinued. Some local anaesthetic was applied near the pins and to the cut skin on their legs. With the treadmill running to make the cats' legs 'walk', the reaction to electrical impulses applied to a nerve from their foot was then measured.

More recently at Bristol University, ten cats were used to investigate the structure of a part of their brain. Electrodes were inserted into their brain to identify areas into which fluorescent tracers were injected. The wounds to their skulls were closed and the cats were allowed to recover from the anaesthetic. Painkillers were provided for the first 24 hours only. Two weeks later, the cats were again anaesthetised and killed by pumping preservative fluids through their blood vessels via a needle to the heart. Parts of their brains were then removed and thinly sliced to allow the areas marked by tracer to be identified.

And the conclusion of decades of such research projects? The scientific community has lost its way. Check the various medical websites referred to in this book for a fuller assessment of the scientific opposition to experiments on animals. Ignoring for a moment the animal abuse, there are serious issues here to be addressed for anyone genuinely concerned about human health.

There are plenty of examples available for scrutiny if you look past the hype about 'extremist activity', all as nice or nasty, as you want it to sound. Vivisectors and their PR retinue talk repeatedly of 'scientific procedures' (vivisection) being overseen by 'ethical committees' (vivisectors) who are governed by the 'the most stringent regulations in the world' (which have been set out by those in the industry). And still there are no miracle cures… Animal research is irrelevant to the understanding of human health and there is no proof to the contrary. To make matters worse, most of the details of these procedures are never even published because the experiments are so gross or futile. You would do otherwise, wouldn't you, if you were proud of your invaluable, honourable endeavours?

Through my school years, I grew up with some kids who had a profound problem with cats and would shoot at them with catapults and guns, trap, kick, brick and throw them in rivers or to dogs, expressing the most vicious hatred without a sliver of remorse or concern. All I could do then was watch and pretend not to care or risk losing my friends. But I grew up and gave up caring whom I fell out with. In fact, I've got so many more friends now I speak out against the slaughter of the innocent.

Some of those sadistic little morons went on to become sadistic big morons. One, many years later, had become so deeply involved in blood sports that he was threatened by my stance and left a fresh cut fox tail on my doorstep as a joke. Sicko always had a thing for rats too and would torture them before killing them, just like vivisectors who pride themselves on the huge number they put to death and the surgical tricks they make them do. Another was serving time for rape. I would never have known it had I not I met him in the gym at York prison where I was working as Orderly while serving time for my ALF activities. He recognised me, knew my story, told me how he respected me for all I was and how he regretted what he had become. I felt a little smug he had turned out that way, just as I'd expected. He was scum, he acknowledged, but now vegan! Trying, he said, to do his bit to repair some of the great damage he had done to people and animals since those early days of animal abuse…

Oxford University Park Farm

> There are no alternatives to vivisection, because any method intended to replace it should have the same qualities; but it is hard to find anything in biomedical research that is and always was, more deceptive and misleading than vivisection. The only genuine alternative to vivisection is therefore abolition.
>
> *Prof P Croce MD, former vivisector*

The Park Farm we stayed at as kids was a happy place with a pond where chickens and ducks pottered about happily with sheep and lambs. The Park Farm at Northmoor in the Oxfordshire countryside was a lifeless estate of small buildings, full to capacity with different species bred for research, all within a chain-link perimeter. The dogs lived at the far corner, presumably so their barking didn't disturb the farm managers. Other buildings housed cats, rabbits, guinea pigs, sheep, goats and monkeys. Not for the first time, Park Farm at Northmoor was under surveillance by the ALF.

The kennels were becoming increasingly secure with each raid and the primate unit was always secure with alarms linked to the police, as much to keep the animals in as the public out. There were a number of other outbuildings on site, housing all types of animals apparently less valuable to the owners. With no electronic security within the perimeter, it was easy to move around the site, figuring out what was where. The primate unit, managed by a vet, was obvious from the old oblong cages on wheels rusting outside, big compared to most but tiny for a wild monkey, with crude crush bars in the middle to enable the user to squeeze the terrified captive to the front of the cage to facilitate the administering of injections. Housed here were a hundred monkeys shipped in from their jungle homes a million miles away, held in storage in a field in Oxfordshire awaiting shipment to a laboratory and their turn to be tortured.

And it wasn't hard to work out who had been eating the cat food from the empty tins in the bin outside the newly dubbed 'cat unit'... Two other buildings were less revealing until access was gained to the roof and guinea pigs and rabbits could be seen through the skylight in the unit below. It was agreed after this first recce to return within the week. There was no shortage of keen volunteers; they had learnt long ago that matters such as this were on a 'need to know' basis. Everyone agrees it's the best way, it's just that some forget to practice it.

It was pure coincidence that the whole area was shrouded in fog the night of the raid in February 1991, which meant it was possible to park in the field right next to the perimeter fence, by the farmhouse. Although this would have cut the workload greatly, it would have been embarrassing for all concerned had the fog lifted midway through the night. So, as planned, the vehicle was stashed a field away, out of sight, beyond a hedgerow. That meant quite a trek to and fro across a ploughed field, but it was safer that way. Too many people had cut corners in the past to make the job easier and fallen foul as a consequence.

There were seven people on the job, hoping to clear out the three units containing rabbits, guinea pigs and cats and to move them all into the concealed horse trailer, commandeered as it was a week earlier from a rider at a hunt elsewhere along with a car borrowed from the same sad individual who had left it parked unattended, keys in situ, while he was out hunting. The person asked to look after the stolen traffic wasn't at all put out when he was told its history. 'Yeah, course I will,' he said: 'It would have been rude of you not to take it.'

For once, there were no concerns for the owner/hirer of the getaway vehicle, because this one wasn't traceable. Everyone unloaded as many cat baskets and boxes as they could carry and set off across the field towards the perimeter where they were piled up. While some returned to collect more, others spread out to a) keep an eye out for the farm manager who lives on site or b) cut some holes. First, a large hole was gouged in the fence, then a series of drill holes cut into the side wall of the cat unit, which would be linked via hacksaw to create a hole big enough to climb through, avoiding alarms. But it wouldn't cut like it should have, because it was made of metal rather than wood—it was like trying to open a tin can with a screwdriver—a bit messy. The door was wood though and not as solid as it first appeared. In fact it turned out to be nothing more than two sheets of balsa wood inside and out, with a hollow interior. A few minutes of drilling, chopping, peeling and sawing and bingo: access! Early fears gone, it was easy. Too easy!

At first glance in torchlight, there was painfully little for anyone to get excited about. While the bins outside were full of cat food tins, there were only five cats in the building. By a cruel twist of fate, the majority of the cats that had been inside had been shipped out in the previous few days. How cruel! No matter how many times they were counted, there were still just five. Word went round and the team's spirits sank, but saving five cats from a fate worse than death is still something to be proud of.

Four of the five were friendly enough and soon in baskets. The fifth, a big Tom, would have taken on the world to stay put, and indeed started with the two raiders wrestling with him. But before he could inflict any damage on them, he was in a blanket then boxed up and on his way across the deep plough with his girlfriends. The doors to the other units were far sturdier, solid hardwood, and they weren't about to peel away without some serious persuasion or 'bloody hard work' as someone noted. Forcing the doors with a crowbar would have been the easiest method but setting off alarms wasn't a choice so it was going to take slow, patient drilling. It took four men, each taking turns, over three hours and two drill bits to drill a square of holes and push out the middle in the four doors. This was hard, physical work that made the lookout's role suddenly seem appealing. The other option was carrying fat cats, rabbits and guinea pigs in the dark across a heavily ploughed field using cat baskets with a wire handle in the middle that aren't designed to be carried with any comfort at the best of times.

Everyone shared duties in turn so once full access was secured and another door was being cut into, some animals were being boxed up while others were lugged back to the trailer. In all, 250 cats, rabbits and guinea pigs were taken through the course of the night from Park Farm. Many of the guinea pigs were at various stages of pregnancy and started giving birth within 48 hours, which went some way to explaining the huffin' and puffin' emanating from within the carriers in the mist! For the first time, these oft mocked, much maligned and heavily abused little guinea pig mums would be allowed the pleasure of rearing their young rather than have them removed for experimentation. Within weeks, there was a whole generation of ex laboratory-bound guinea pigs playing in the gardens of 'extremists' up and down the country, and the vivisectors had to look elsewhere.

Documents recovered on the night revealed Park Farm's intention to upgrade its primate unit to bring it into line with the basic requirements of the Scientific Procedures Act. They estimated they would need just short of £100,000 to replace old cages, to be met mostly with grants but also UPF profits, overestimated at £15,000 for the year 1989/1990 and now taking into account the view of police Inspector John Crossley that 'A considerable amount of structural damage has been done' during the raid. The new caging would see them shift their stock levels from the current:

57 Breeding Female Rhesus

9 Breeding Male Rhesus
3 Experimental Rhesus (Ex Dept. Physiology)
13 Experimental Cynos
17 Imported Cynos (plus 22 to be delivered at the end of July)

to:

40 Breeding Female Rhesus
9 Breeding Male Rhesus
18/20 Stock Rhesus
32 Imported experimental Cynos
8 Experimental Cynos (in isolation)

The Thames Valley Police investigation that followed the UPF raid was no less determined than the one six years earlier, when they returned rescued dogs to their cages. This time, however, they weren't so successful. The raiders sent footage taken during the raid to various news agencies including Central TV, who broadcast clips in news reports the following day.

TVP were desperately keen to view this tape and promptly contacted Central TV demanding a copy of the video under the 1984 Police and Criminal Justice Act—not so they could watch the rescue of desperate animals of course, but so they could be assisted in apprehending the rescuers. Central TV refused to comply, so the police then took them to court where the company's lawyers argued that they had the right to protect their sources and that there was nothing in the footage they hadn't transmitted that would help the police identify anyone. The judge agreed. The lawyer for the TV company said afterwards he had defended around a dozen such cases for the BBC and others but this was the first that he had succeeded. The police were no nearer tracing the missing bunnies or making arrests. But they weren't going to let it go that easily. Although I had nothing to do with it, I was to become a suspect for the Park Farm raid and, for once, it turned out to be in my interest that the police were so keen to solve the terrible crime.

Eighteen months after the UPF raid, Thames Valley Police were in Manchester seeking answers. I was in prison at the time, awaiting trial on other matters, which I'll get to later. I had just been moved for the umpteenth time to the most notorious police station in the system, The Bridewell in Liverpool, which had a reputation second to none in the world in which I was living at that time surrounded by hard men, none of whom wanted to spend any time there. The Bridewell was used as a dumping ground, as punishment for prisoners who were either too difficult to handle, too mouthy or had political views that weren't welcome.

Prisoners who had carried out a massive revolt at HMP Manchester, better known as Strangeways, in response to years of abuse by out-of-control prison officers, soon rendered the entire prison uninhabitable. Suddenly, the prison estate was short of 1,800 places and as a result, inmates were detained in police cells for many months. Some were relatively cushy, but others, like the Bridewell, were worse than prison. I spent nine months being shuffled from one police station to another during this period, constantly hoping to spend more than a week somewhere with my property arriving before I moved again, to somewhere 'cushy' hopefully.

Our destination was always a secret for security reasons. They reasoned that imparting this information would enable us to send a message to colleagues on the out who would arrange a hijacking. It was not unusual to be told at 9am to pack and be on the road in the back of a sweatbox within an hour. I was being moved to the Bridewell from the Central Detention Centre above the courts in Manchester where I'd been for a week. The only place worse than one was the other. It was pouring with rain and I hadn't seen my property since I arrived in the Manchester cells because they didn't allow such privileges there, but at least my bags were with me on the bus. Arriving at Liverpool and watching out of the darkened window of the sweatbox I saw the cop they called Matty, whose reputation preceded him—he was all chest and snarl and full of steroids, constantly looking to pick a fight with prisoners.

It conjured up images of a Neanderthal man with his kill as I watched this lump drag my property bags from the bus along the wet floor only to bounce them up the stairs to the main entrance. The rest of the morning revealed this was Matty at his best. And he wasn't alone; there were half a dozen coppers strutting around barking instructions and squaring for a fight with anyone daft enough to look them in the eye, step out of line, answer back or ask a question. The cellblock was a foul stinking dungeon from a bygone era. There were no windows in the cells, just a boarded-up hole high up the outside wall and a bench along one side big enough only to lie on sideways if you were small enough. Falling asleep and turning over was a wake up call! The ceiling was high, the floor cold damp cobbles.

I was allocated a cell alone. I think everyone else had to share. This suited me fine, preferring as I do my own company. Stuffed under the bench was my mattress: wet, stinking and covered in stale urine c/o the previous occupant or possibly someone from many months before him. I wasn't about to ask or complain. Outside the cell, the large Scouse bouncers were spitting and swearing at a young Salford kid who'd made the mistake of straying over one of the yellow lines they'd painted on the floor over which inmates weren't allowed to cross until told to do so. For the additional offence of pleading ignorance, he was throttled against my door. He was right of course. No one had told us the meaning of the yellow lines, but I figured that saying so wasn't a good idea. Not usually good at keeping my mouth shut, I was impressed with my restraint.

I'd expected to end up here and had decided that I was probably going to spend the next 12 months in this pit. Not punished, I don't think, because of my offences so much as for my endless prison 'protests' for vegan margarine, the return of lost property and lots else. But thanks to the determination of Thames Valley Police to capture the Park Farm burglars, I was only there for three hours when one of the Bridewell Massive came to the door and told me to get my kit packed 'cos I was on the move! Odd, it was usually a week at least before the next move, but nice to hear. I wasn't sure it was for real but it still sounded good and gave me hope of better scenery! My kit was still lying in a sodden battered heap with everyone else's by the reception desk where it would remain until someone could be arsed to process it, so it didn't take me long to pack nothing. The process of sorting property never actually got going and wasn't likely to be that productive when it did, judging by events thus far. When an older con asked to take a book to his cell that he'd been reading at the CDC and on the bus to the Bridewell one officer replied 'I don't give a fuck if it's allowed at Happy Holidays, Sonny. This is the fuckin' Bridewell.' And didn't we know it.

I'd gone from the centre of Manchester in the morning to Liverpool for dinner and then back to Manchester's Stretford Police Station where TVP were waiting to arrest and question me about a number of matters including Park Farm. They'd found themselves a facial mapping 'expert' called Richard Neave at Manchester University who specialises in reconstructing the facial features of people with serious injuries caused by fire or decomposure. Neave also claimed to be able to identify faces from under balaclavas by measuring distances between facial features and so on. During a meeting between the two parties, Neave was shown photographs of UPF raiders and others in action and photographs of suspects such as Angela Hamp and I. His conclusion was that we were both in raid photographs at UPF and at a London lab that was broken into.

The consequences of this were enormous if all of a sudden the anonymous activists of 30 years of ALF raids were about to have their masks removed and their pasts catch up with them. Neave and his team are certainly highly respected in their field and appear to be worthy of accolade, but surely this is ridiculous? Given that there was no legal precedent for measuring this as reliable evidence and they never bothered charging, I guess so. A conviction secured against an armed robber in Manchester in 1989 made legal history as the first case of its kind using the facial mapping technique. However, the conviction was overturned after he'd served two years of a nine-year sentence when the Court of Appeal ruled that the methods used to identify him were unsatisfactory. Neave conceded under cross-examination that the method he used might not be 100% accurate, but he liked to think that it was. Still, if the police have the money to spend on the mapping technique, the potential is there to confirm their suspicions about raiders which, of course, is far from ideal if you are one and has led to eyes being smudged out in many of today's raid publicity photographs.

I was questioned about various offences, maintained my right to silence and was released from TVP custody back to HMP c/o GMP without further charge. Off the Bridewell residents list, I spent the week in Stretford before being moved to Cushyville in Cheshire where my property finally caught up with me and life was more relaxed and pleasant, but I would soon be heading back to Stretford for yet more questions and no answers and the most incredible turn of events.

Lancashire Polytechnic

> As raids go, they sound more like the imaginings of a Disney film scriptwriter than the operations of a commando war machine, but they have one thing in common. They are performed with daring, skill and surprise, and executed with such finesse they still have the police guessing.
>
> *Australian journalist's account of British liberations*

It was a local animal rights group discussion about the rights and wrongs of breaking windows that set the wheels in motion for the next raid. One opinion was that this was a futile tactic because it saved no lives and got negative press. The debate became briefly heated when someone asked angrily, 'Well what have *you* done to save any lives this week? You can be proud you haven't broken any windows but what have you done?' He had no answer. A student at Lancashire Polytechnic in Preston, he'd spent all week studying—in fact, he'd actually spent weeks studying and had let his motivation slip, while others, however misguided he felt they might be, were at least doing something. Festering over the conversation, something changed for him that night. He didn't have far to go because there was something on his own doorstep that he was beginning to think he could do something about. Words are cheap and everyone who cares has an opinion on how best to bring an end to animal abuse, but how many actually act? A first look at the Poly labs revealed little, but a search through research papers confirmed that this was indeed the place to look for animals: birds, possibly frogs, but mainly rats. Having two rescued rats at home, he knew how individual, intelligent and loving these animals are.

There was nothing much to see beyond the bars on high frosted windows. Helpfully, the guy in the university security office was in a hurry as the reconnaissance team was leaving, which gave them the chance to take a quick look at the alarm panel in the office. There appeared to be little security around the labs suggesting that there were either no animals there or little reason for not breaking in and get out any that were. Eager to establish which, they were back the same night and got onto the roof of the Biology Department where it was immediately obvious from the smell of sawdust rushing out of the air ventilators that there were indeed animals inside. How often this helps!

They were able to get a limited view inside through a skylight on the flat roof, which was helpfully only overlooked by vacant buildings. No one passing at ground level would be able to see them. The security office was a safe distance away. The only problem anyone could foresee was removing animals in cages via the access point, which would have to be the skylight—itself a limited space—which was partly blocked by security bars. This was, however, a secondary concern, the first being the successful liberation of the animals.

Ten days and two further visits later, a five-strong team were hiding out on site and keeping a lookout, awaiting the go ahead. Vehicles were parked out of the area. On the roof—armed with tools—were two people sporting baseball hats, their faces hidden by scarves. They set to work teasing out the bolts holding in the plastic skylight bubble, and hoped they'd find no wires or sensors beneath that would alert security or the police to the break-in.

Half an hour in, the skylight was lifted out of the way and placed to one side and they were able to start cutting one of the steel bars using a heavy duty hacksaw blade, which they'd been advised by the man in the shop would cut through anything. Apparently so, for the bar was out of the way in minutes—it was enough to cut one end, and then force the bar back. For the time being, this was room enough for a couple of activists to drop through, and depending on what they found inside, and whether there was an easier exit point, they might have to cut another. There were no alarms on this point of access, so they went in, updating the rest of the team. Initially, and to their dismay, they found only two guinea pigs, one rather overweight rabbit and a load of empty cages, but a further foray revealed cages full of doves, rats and mice, all peering inquisitively out of their cages at this intrusion. The solid fire door opened outwards and didn't appear to be alarmed, presumably because the animals wouldn't be able to break out (well, at least not on their own, but with a little helping hand…!).

As soon as they had assessed everything, the escape committee began to move the little prisoners to the fire exit. With cages on racks, cages on cages and cages on the floor, the corridor was soon clogged up. Though new to rescues, the team worked well. Meanwhile, the getaway van was brought in and manoeuvred into place. The offices were ransacked of every bit of paperwork, which was loaded into five sacks. Time to open the fire escape and start loading. Opening the fire escape could still set off an alarm, so they knew they had to be ready to load quickly.

But the dreaded sound never came. Since there were so many bulky cages, the van filled quickly and had to be sent on its way. A second vehicle had to be commandeered from a fellow student living nearby. He didn't ask and wasn't told what for! Once that was loaded with everything else, it too drove away. Meanwhile the lab was trashed. All done, the rest of the team wandered off into the night. It was as easy as that, aided of course by not having to pass the animals out via the skylight.

170 animals were saved, including 43 ringdoves, but the local press weren't impressed. One headline told how 'Pet Dies As Masked Raiders Bungle Poly Raid At Start Of Terror Drive' and revealed how a mouse, apparently a lab worker's pet, had been trampled underfoot by the cruel raiders. It was headline news, but not a word about the brutal daily exterminations taking place there. I think they call it double standards.

The raid organiser later said that the whole experience had been an eye-opener for him. Having once complained of his revulsion at the smell of dead animals and those buying their body parts for consumption, he realised that he could achieve a lot more by acting himself than by questioning what others were doing. Two weeks later, he broke a local butcher's window for the first time: he said it felt like he was fighting back.

The documents recovered from the lab were an eye-opener as they usually are. There were loads of personal details of staff including names, addresses, telephone numbers, vehicle registration documents, diaries and even photographs showing smiling animal technicians posing with various animals and reptiles. Well they wouldn't be smiling now, with the ALF in possession of their happy snaps and the rest of the above. As it was, there was no follow up terror drive but the media did a good job of instilling that fear.

More importantly the papers revealed the cost of animals to the lab when their own stocks run short—and the profits earned by the suppliers—at £9.65 for a guinea pig and between £4.30 and £6.50 for a rat. Entries in one diary showed that not only were staff aware of exactly what day Home Office inspectors were due to visit the lab but at what time, rubbishing again the oft touted claim that unannounced inspections ensure there is no cruelty.

On one visit an inspector found the rat room to be overstocked and the atmosphere far from ideal due to failings in the ventilation system. He made recommendations that they either repair the system or reduce the number of rats held there. Lab staff opted to kill off 50 of the rats so the remainder could breathe easier before they too were sacrificed on the Altar.

Proposed 'projects' were first put to the in-house Ethics Committee for approval, but the Ethics Committee weren't overly concerned with ethics. They appeared to be very friendly with the researchers with whom they were on first-name terms and applications were rubber-stamped without question.

One project involving 24 rats—according to its applicant Malcolm Edmunds—was to determine: 'Do rats become ingestively conditioned?' i.e: to determine whether they prefer food they are used to eating, rather than novel food. Not particularly horrid by vivisection standards, but the rats were still imprisoned in crowded cages for their entire lives and killed at the end of the experiment. Why did an ethical committee not reject this out of hand as unnecessary research? After all, in their own words, all research should be 'Compatible with the pursuit of legitimate scientific ends.' Even by their interpretation, how little of it is!

Some of the mice used at the lab were disabled dystrophic dy/dy mice engineered to carry the genes responsible for muscular dystrophy, an animal, which vivisectors say: 'most closely approximates the human condition.' Yet as long ago as 1971, it was claimed that the dy/dy mouse was not likely to be a good model for the human condition and even today, the only progress in this field has come from clinical studies.

Another revealing detail came out of this raid. Only one in every four of their offspring can be used in experiments; the healthy ones are killed off. Darrell Brooks at the lab wanted 80 such mice for one project, for which they were killed and their tissue used. But neither the 80 mice he killed, nor the 240 unwanted siblings who were killed because they were rejects have to be covered by a Home Office licence. The law does not require that their contribution as a carrier of a serious disabling disease be added to statistics: their short lives are not afforded even the scant protection of the Act supposed to protect animals in their position. Many other animals were shown to have been bred and killed in the lab so their organs could be used in experiments—for example 500 rats, 350 frogs, 142 guinea pigs and 44 doves—none of which the Scientific Procedures Act even bothers to mention. If proof were needed that the true number of animals killed to satisfy an industry is higher than they admit then here it was in black and white again exposed by the ALF.

The National Anti-Vivisection Society (NAVS) were handed copies of all the relevant documents and compiled a detailed 30-page analysis exposing the failings of the 1986 Act, which apologists' claim protects animals from abuse. It showed that University vivisectors were wasting lives in experiments (and described Lancashire Polytechnic as 'operating in a scientific backwater')—the sort of experiments that had long since been replaced in other institutions with more appropriate methods. It was yet another example of wasted lives, crude research and pointless cruelty—a shamefully familiar story.

Sky Commercial Rabbits

> There isn't a single genetically manipulated mouse that has been used to produce a drug that cures a disease.
>
> *Kathleen Murray, director of transgenic services at Charles River. New Scientist, February 2002*

Another northern ALF team was active just across the Pennines drawing all kinds of publicity. John Dawson had never met them but knew they were at it. He, like scores of others, was in the business of growing rabbits in rows of cages in sheds for use as fur, food or to be the subject of experiments. His business was Sky Commercial Rabbits operating from the village of Meltham near Huddersfield, West Yorkshire. He'd didn't like the ALF and they had a problem with what he did.

> Around 1964, I commenced renting some land, which is on the railway embankment off Near Lane, from British Rail. I built a shed on the land in order to keep poultry and over the years have added to this shed and built others so that I eventually had a shed approximately 100 ft in length and 19 ft wide, a shed 48 ft long and 10 ft wide, a shed 24 ft long and 10 ft wide and another 5 ft long. The majority were wooden. Some of them had PVC corrugated roof panels.
>
> Around 1967 I started to keep and breed rabbits. This was a business with the rabbits being sold for either meat or as pets. The types of rabbits that we kept were 'New Zealand Whites' and 'Californians'. These were sold for their meat to butchers, or to wholesalers alive for the animals to be slaughtered later. The business was doing quite well and at one time I was keeping 7-800 rabbits. I would keep the rabbits for approximately 12 weeks before sale. I was advertising in the *Yellow Pages, Yorkshire* Post newspaper, *Huddersfield Examiner*, a magazine called *Fur and Feather* and *Farmers Weekly*.
>
> The trouble first began around six years ago. I recall it was New Years Eve when I received a telephone call at home, the caller wished me a happy new year. He told me they had broken into the shed and taken some rabbits. I checked up on this and

discovered that a hasp had been broken off and around half a dozen rabbits stolen.

From that point on I received a number of telephone calls, anonymous, from people acting on behalf of animal rights groups. The advertisements seemed to attract a large proportion of bogus telephone calls and I consequently stopped the advertisements. This had an effect on my business so I wound up the limited company around a year ago but carried on trading as 'Sky Rabbits', keeping around a hundred breeding stock and a few which I had for fattening.

Around the beginning of December 1990 I went to the sheds one day and discovered the word ALF sprayed on the gate and words to the effect: 'These rabbits are bred to die' and 'ALF' sprayed on the shed roof. The words were in large block capitals in white spray paint. The rabbits had been sprayed with red paint. This made them useless for sale.

Around 3pm on Thursday, 17 January 1991, I tended to the rabbits and then left the sheds locked and secure. At this time everything was in order. There would have been eighty rabbits in the shed. Around lunchtime on Friday, 18 January 1991 I went to the sheds to tend to the rabbits. On arrival I saw that the padlock and hasp for the main shed had been broken off and there was extensive fire damage to the wooden structure, virtually leaving nothing of the portion of shed which comprises of the main shed 100 ft x 18 ft. This section housed all the rabbits. All the rabbits were missing.

I estimate the cost of repair to the sections of the shed to be approximately £2-3,000. The cost of replacement of the rabbits would be £800. I should also mention that I found in the debris one or two skeletons of rabbits, which had been killed in the fire. I have been shown by the police a photograph of a hooded figure holding a white rabbit. The rabbit is a New Zealand White, which is identical in every respect to those that I kept. After this I was shocked and distressed at what had happened. I eventually went over to the sheds and started clearing up, intending to try to start the business again.

> On Sunday 3 February, I think in the afternoon, I visited the sheds and whilst there was the previous damage as I have described, everything else was in order. At 10am on Wednesday 6 February the police called at my house and informed me there had been further damage to my sheds. I accompanied them round to the sheds and saw all the sheds had been destroyed or damaged by fire. I estimate the cost of replacements of the sheds and contents at around £10,000.
>
> I have continued to receive malicious mail addressed to me and calling me 'Mr. J. Chan', 'Mr. N. Shed', 'Mr. J. Blaze', 'Mr. K. Burnt' and 'A. R. Sole'. These are obvious jibes at what has happened. The latest correspondence I received on 9 August 1991. In total there must be in the region of a hundred malicious letters for loans, life insurance and the like. There have also been parcels with goods I've never ordered; in fact there was a van come with a wheelchair I hadn't ordered. At this moment in time I'm not trading, I cannot afford the capital to start the business up again.

And that was the end of another chapter. Hardly the downfall of a multinational and no big headlines, but a significant marker in the liberator's notebook and 80 rabbits free to boot. These raiders are usually vegan of course but they were feeding off each other! 1991 was off to a flying start. A myriad of animals and birds were finding a helping hand lift them to freedom. From one end of the country to the other, like-minded people were on a mission to rid the world—or at least part of it—of caged animals. These people must be stopped!

A Glorified Zoo

By and large a lot of this damage is going unreported.
David Henshaw again, Public Eye 1991

There was no under-reporting what happened next. It was genuine interest in the work of the Highland Wildlife Park in the hills at Kincraig near Inverness in the wilds of Scotland that caused A Concerned Citizen holidaying in the area to approach an animal rights information stall in the High Street to talk about this place. They thought it was a wildlife refuge, somewhere that sick, injured and orphaned animals received tender loving care before being rehabilitated back to the wild and where endangered and rare animals and birds were bred and released. Err, no, apparently not. Set in a 264-acre enclosure in the vast expanse of the Highlands, there could be no problems with space for the captive animals, which were wild after all. Part of the problem with this kind of set-up is having the Zoological Society as management. Zoos traditionally concern themselves more with raising money from exhibiting animals and selling them to the lucrative vivisection market and few can show genuine desire to care for the needs of their captives or release them back to the wild. Wildlife parks likewise.

The tip-off about the Kincraig park had been passed on 350 miles away in the south of England and it wouldn't have been surprising if it had been forgotten about with so many stories of cruelty sloshing around. The sheer numbers can be overwhelming, and there aren't the hours in any one day to check them all out. This was near Inverness!

It can take a protracted period of surveillance and a degree in trickery just to work out how badly a dog in a back garden is being treated and, if needs be, how to get it out. This wasn't even really that bad in comparison, so it had been put on a back burner for a while. By chance, a couple in their sixties—long time animal campaigners—were on a walking holiday in Scotland and remembered the name mentioned at their group meeting so they went to see for themselves.

'It's incredible,' he said in a phone call south. He was wondering what could be done. What can you do? Talk to the owner? The lady at the stall had done that. She'd been told it would be too expensive to make the enclosures bigger and people wouldn't be able to see the wildlife. It was a well-rehearsed response. He explained: 'There's this big area of land inside a wire fence surrounded by rolling countryside far beyond the eye can see but these magnificent creatures are confined in tiny pens, or big cages if you like. They could easily double their area but the cages are designed to show off the inhabitants.' Is that a reason to keep perfectly healthy wild animals in captivity?

He'd wanted someone to contact the press to expose the place, but that would, he agreed from experience, be futile. He was told to go back and take more notes with a view to DIY problem fixing. He returned to England and explained that there was no security and to release the animals would indeed be a doddle.

'Are you going to get them out?' he asked of his younger friend in anticipation.

'If you think it's feasible and that straightforward, I can see no reason why not. You're welcome if you like.'

Music to his ears! A month later, when the weather had improved, a group of six activists including the reborn OAP set up camp in a field a couple of miles from the park. As night fell, they wandered onto the site cutting the gate lock then, armed with plenty of wire cutters, set about systematically dismantling all the cages. He excitedly re-lived the story years later:

> There was an excited atmosphere, the animals and us. I'd been involved in rescuing animals before, but not for some years as age was catching up and walls and fences were now formidable obstacles. Our little raids were always exciting, usually nerve-wracking and often rushed to get the animals out before anyone turned up; there would usually be someone not a million miles away in a security cabin or house. But there was no one for miles around here, no security patrol, no fences to climb, no farmer, no passing dog walkers, no one but us and these amazing creatures and a million stars. How could they walk away at the end of every day leaving owls penned in like that with freedom just a snip of wire away?

Good question. But they did. No one wanted to leave the site, which is another odd thing to happen at a centre of animal abuse. It was no big job, but it took the raiders four hours to cut open the cages of native red and arctic foxes, eagles, owls, badgers, polecats, pine martins, wildcats, grouse and otters. Some, like two of the foxes, couldn't wait. It was as if they'd been planning where to run, because the minute the activists had finished cutting and stood back to watch, the couple took off in a straight line heading for the patch of trees way up on the hill.

Some animals and birds waited till there was no one around, others were just too institutionalised to know what to do and were still sitting there in a cage full of holes the following morning when shocked staff arrived for work. The brown bears and the wolves were the only animals left caged as they had been found. They wouldn't have had much chance of surviving the hysterical overreaction that would follow them into the wilderness. 'Not that anyone wanted to take their chances releasing a couple of pissed off bears!' the gent said later. Every trigger-happy have-a-go-hero in the country would be volunteering their pest control services to wipe them out again as others had hundreds of years earlier. The last wolves were reputedly wiped out in Scotland around 1743; bears had long since been eradicated by the tenth century. With messages painted all over the visitor centre in a horrible green gloss paint, there could be no doubt about who had called and why, and what a reaction! Bears on the prowl or not, there was widespread—if largely unfavourable—media coverage of the raid, but the raiders were remorseless, pledging to return to give those animals that were recaptured another chance.

Not releasing the wolves would come back to haunt the liberators years later when it was revealed that following the death of the pack Alpha male, the others had begun to behave unnaturally so were massacred by the park keepers. Scotland's wolves had been wiped out once again…

Operation Lance

> Over the past ten years the ALF has become the cutting edge of an increasingly militant animal rights lobby, emerging as a small but ruthless organisation.
>
> *Patrick O'Flynn in the Birmingham Post, 1991*

Some of the ALF activists in Manchester and elsewhere were pushing their luck. While most were also working on other projects in other areas, impatience and over-confidence springing from being in the company of like-minded individuals was a dangerous combination. It led to the tactical error of trying to do too many things and being unable to resist the somewhat lazy and risky temptation to shit on one's own doorstep.

Arrests in the coming months for breaking windows turned out to be specimen charges in relation to the overall conspiracy the police were concocting. There was another good reason why the police were going to find it relatively easy to pinpoint those responsible for these raids, the arson attacks and so on. Many of those responsible were friends who attended demos and went hunt sabbing together. Some had been around for years and were well known to the police, others were new on the scene but were regulars who hung around with the movers and shakers. I don't expect many activists have joined the ALF ranks without having first pursued the ordered path of protest, and experienced the inevitable disillusionment and anger that follows; sadly, this inevitable trend often gives the police a head start in identifying the perpetrators.

In addition, it appears that only a handful of activists are responsible for a considerable amount of the damage occurring over any given period. Investigations led the police to believe that 201 Clarendon Road in Whalley Range was a good place to keep under observation. Inside the flat, little-known animal rights protesters associated with well-known activists. In the early summer of 1991, an observation post was set up on the upstairs floor of a house opposite. It was staffed between 7am and 7pm, at which time the police apparently left. This Op was part of Operation Thermal, itself an arm of the wide-ranging Operation Lance. Pretty much all of the crimes under investigation by this squad of detectives, who were announcing publicly they were going to clamp down on the ALF, were being committed after the hours of darkness and certainly after 7pm at that time of the year, but it was nearly two months before observations were extended into the hours of darkness. But there was a bigger plan afoot.

From the outset, the intention of the police was to create a conspiracy by association rather than simply to seek the conviction of individuals for the less serious criminal damage or arson charges. Activists weren't only caught in the act but were also taken out of their homes merely for associating, and were placed under tight bail restrictions once bail had been granted. The long-term aim was to set up a show trial with a view to securing lengthy sentences for as many activists as possible. The short-term goal was to monitor and disrupt active cells.

This part of the operation set out to prove that whenever two or more of 12 key suspects were together in the premises they were probably conspiring. Three of them lived there. Twenty-four hour observations began in August, and two weeks later a listening device was fitted into the wall of the flat next door where it recorded conversations for the rest of the year. In addition, further observation posts were fixed overlooking at least half a dozen other suspects' homes in the Northwest, and the occupants' movements were monitored. They had Operation Illustrious, Spear, Sabre, Foil, Sword and Blade. Operation General and Rocket kept tabs on the Manchester Animal Protection Group and ALIU offices in the city centre. The net was closing in.

With 201 Clarendon Rd under daytime observation and safe from burglars, the burglars operating from the address were using the cover of darkness to burgle, if you see what I mean.

In a copycat raid to that at Kincraig, various wild animals were cut free from their cages at Riber Castle Wildlife Park at Matlock in Derbyshire. It could—at best—have been described as a zoo, but the owners preferred it to be called a wildlife park. Unconvinced, the ALF called one night and granted the inhabitants free reign of the Derbyshire countryside. Overnight, the Riber zoo was to become a shadow of its former self as the Tawny, Little, Eagle and Snowy owls, the foxes, doves, wallabies (already long established in the area) polecats and Geoffrey's cats were set free. Two-dozen domestic rabbits and the rat collection were boxed up and taken away for re-homing. 'ZOO'S OUT', 'ALF' and 'KEEP WILD ANIMALS IN THE WILD' were left in paint around the place. The very next day Terry Helsby, who lived at 201 and was well known to the police and Alison Mckeon were filmed cleaning out a hire van on Clarendon Road.

Zoo spokesperson, Fern Millard, of course thought they were

actually doing the animals a favour: 'The animals are happy with their enclosures. If they weren't happy, they wouldn't breed.' Content with life in captivity and wanting to raise a family, or forced by instinct, boredom, rape and artificial insemination? It's a similar argument used by others who exploit animals. The zoo closed a few years later.

While police monitored the Manchester scene, some of those on their watch list were in view but others were elsewhere. Some were in Cambridge plotting. Wherever they were, they showed no respect for the ineffectual system of checks and balances protecting animal abuse. Only a determined state offensive against its determined opponents was going to stop the slide into a society free of animals in cages.

The Cruel Conspiracy

Whilst there are slaughterhouses there will be battlefields.

Tolstoy

When Cambridge University's outstation at Laundry Farm was raided in 1991, masked activists broke into the stables, led three horses out, and loaded them into transporters. Once they had been driven away, the bold raiders made a determined effort to break into the fortified dog unit, which set alarms ringing, forcing them to abort, but not before material was recovered, which once again suggested that there might have been stolen dogs being used for experiments at the farm.

The use of stolen pets is a legal matter under the 1986 Animals (Scientific Procedures) Act and if someone is found to be peddling people's pets then the powers-that-be should act. The reality is of course that they don't care very much where animals come from as long as they are generating income and there is not much point directing any concerns to the self-serving Home Office or Research Defence Society, and the police and the RSPCA really don't give a shit either.

With all this in mind two weeks later, the ALIU arranged an overt inspection of Laundry Farm to see what could be uncovered. The Government, RDS, RSPCA, the media and the police have condemned this approach but we've all seen time and again the failings of these official bodies and people are sick of talking about it. According to the Home Office figures for 2003, there were, for example, just 26 of their inspectors monitoring well over 300 labs, over 4000 licence holders and an excess of 2.7 million experiments. It would be a physical impossibility for these people to properly monitor all these experiments even if they were under strict instructions to do so and without first warning they were coming! A huge number of animals, thousands of men and women mentally equipped to do the most awful things to them, and the inspectors can still find not one serious breach of the rules? No cruelty? Anyone smell something rotten?

From May 1990, of the 18 members of the Animal Procedures Committee (the body responsible for overseeing animal experiments) 13 were one-time or current vivisectors, including two representatives of pro-vivisection lobby groups, the RDS and the Animals in Medical Research Information Centre (AMRIC). Three others were appointed as neutral and two were said to be 'concerned with animal welfare,' a description animal researchers, more than most, attach to themselves when courting public opinion. Nonetheless, this token, hardly animal-friendly membership—however corrupted by self-interest—instilled fear in the hearts of the pro-vivisection lobby.

By 1999, the committee had increased to 23 members, supposedly to weight the balance more in favour of an animal welfare influence—a contradiction in itself to many observers, not least those even less well represented, who were concerned with the scientific invalidity of vivisection. Today, it remains a pro-vivisectionist government-appointed body, beloved of the RDS, who refuse to question even the most obviously cruel and ludicrous animal experiments. From their perspective: 'This group of appointments, with its concentration on working research scientists, made a welcome change from the previous round of appointments, which increased the proportion of animal protectionists.' Ha!

With committees such as this run—and made up—by members of the 'in crowd'; with government-funded inspectors appointed to inspect experiments from which the government itself generates income; with vast amounts of tax payers' money being poured by the government into the vivisection industry—in short, with all of these government players in the field encouraging, upholding, perpetuating and defending this vile practice and ensuring its expansion, it can safely be said that the odds are stacked against the animals. And all of this, let's not forget, from the same government that threatens to apply Section 24 of the 1986 Scientific Procedures Act (peddled as the saviour of laboratory animals) which carries a two year prison sentence for anyone who dares to reveal the inner workings of vivisection laboratories without government permission.

Laundry Farm

82% of UK doctors don't trust results gained from animal testing.

Europeans For Medical Progress

Wearing ALIU hats, equipped with the layout of Laundry Farm and geared up for the possibility of a publicity coup, some public-spirited activists were empowered by the idea that—in line with a clause in the Theft Act—they could remove property, as long as they did not intend to permanently deprive the owner thereof. Government lawyers will, of course, interpret this differently in a courtroom, but it remains a sound defence, inviting people to test the law where it has the potential to expose animal suffering and thus hopefully prevent its continuation.

Organ transplantation—for which many of the animals at Laundry Farm were destined—is frequently cited as a banner example of scientific progress through animal experimentation. Hundreds of thousands of animals have suffered and died at the hands of researchers and surgeons experimenting with transplantation, and the Anti-Vivisection Movement has seen evidence of that suffering a-plenty, with witness accounts documented by activists and investigators alike. These experiments did not remove obstacles to successful transplantation in humans—indeed, they often introduced new problems. Fuelled by the images of such suffering, an action such as that of Northamptonshire based activist Angela Hamp (very much in the loop of suspects under regular surveillance) during the ALIU incursion, was emotion and instinct-driven; she had this to say of the inspection:

> Within a minute of entering the premises through an open, unlocked door, we came upon some of the dogs. The main housing unit for the dogs was locked but these ones were held in what appeared to be a loading bay—they were today's chosen few for delivery to one of Cambridge's torture labs. Roy Calne's Addenbrooke's labs are one likely destination, for experimental transplant surgery. I held in my arms a small collie cross, mostly black in colour with a white flash on her chest and on the tips of her toes. I passed her to someone as I climbed over the small perimeter fence and as she was passed back I saw in her my own little collie dog when she was young.

The pup was approximately four months old and she showed no

fear as I talked to her, reassuring her gently as she licked my face. We'd been able to grab eight dogs before having to leave and we headed with them across the fields away from the farm towards my van. We had several fields to cross and as I started to tire I passed her to a colleague. She was only a little weight, but I needed to rest a little. After a minute, I took her back. I wanted to keep her safe and was praying for everything to be all right.

My vehicle was parked at the bottom of an old track road at the edge of the field. Seven pups were placed in the back of the van, there was a beautiful bundle of fluff, from different litters and none older than six months—black and white collie crosses and red, white and yellow Labrador crosses. One dog went in another car. As I pulled out onto the road I passed the first police car, at the T-junction I turned right and passed the second. They were onto me and it started to look like I had little chance of getting away but had to try. The pups were in the back playing with each other on their little adventure. They had no idea of the seriousness of it all. All that I could think to do was get the dogs as far away from the hellhole as possible.

The police were intent on stopping me as soon as possible. There was a chase on now. I was calm and I drove well, even though on one occasion tears came to my eyes and I heard myself call out loud to no one in particular, 'please help them.' If there was a god, they wouldn't have been there in the first place. I didn't care what happened to me, I just wanted to get the dogs to safety. I went for around 17 miles before the police forcibly stopped the van. I then jumped in the back to be with the dogs and see they were okay.

They were fine. They playfully pounced on me and I kissed and cuddled them all, tears pouring down my face. I kept repeating to them that it was going to be all right. All I had now was the knowledge of what happened to the dogs the police recovered after the Interfauna raid. They went to the Wood Green Animal Shelter—not far away from where we were—pending the court case and were later re-homed. Moments later the side door of the van was opened and I was dragged out violently by my hair. As I struggled free my arms were twisted and I felt myself being punched and kicked as I was forced into one of the police cars. When I was in I was elbowed in the stomach for good measure. From then on I was totally silent. Tim Walker, my solicitor's clerk, phoned the police station every hour to check I was all right and the doctor was called out twice to witness my injuries.

I had no idea what had happened to the pups. I was told by the desk sergeant that they would be okay. Little did I know that at that moment they were in fact being driven back to be used in some hideous experiment somewhere in Cambridge. I'll never forget those little pups for as long as I live, particularly the little black and white collie I carried. I still have nightmares. Those pups will be long dead now, I hope, out of their misery, but I'll fight in their memory until the day I die.

Angela Hamp was held in police custody for three days and then charged with burglary and driving offences. For her, like a number of other campaigners, the charges were starting to mount up and prison was looking like a grim reality. The eighth dog, a young Labrador, tattooed as AP24, made it to safety and was immediately re-homed by her kidnappers. The plan to trace the home roots of AP24 were hampered by his high profile on the police's Most Wanted list. Their obsession with recovering him and tracing other raiders forced him out of the headlines and into a quiet new life. There was dismay in the usual circles and anger at the decision to return alleged stolen property to its (questionable) owners for them to dispose of, rather than have it held safe pending legal proceedings as is standard police procedure, but the raiders persisted.

Pigs. In There?

> Atrocities are not less atrocities when they occur in laboratories and are called medical research.
>
> *George Bernard Shaw (1856-1950) Irish playwright, winner of the Nobel Prize for literature, socialist, feminist*

For someone wanting to uncover something grotesque, Oxford's vivisection labs are the place to look. Riddled as it is with such sites, the options around Oxford are wide and varied; some places are more secure than others and the animals more or less accessible depending on the funding of the institution in question. The Churchill Hospital Research Institute, owned and run by the University hadn't given much away over the years and wasn't about to start—not deliberately anyway. The best information is always leaked, however, and the key to this one came through a root through their waste bins at the back of the complex. Hardly the most socially acceptable practice, but nonetheless productive.

Of course the institute had either lied or denied what they were doing, but during a hopeful exploration of the site, someone had found interesting documents that elevated the status of the Churchill in the anti-vivisection annals of crime. Hundreds and hundreds of pigs and rodents had apparently lived briefly and died there in some freaky experiments involving radiation. Getting in to prove it was not out of the question but wasn't going to be conventional.

It wasn't long before a raiding party was on site and heading for the roof. Working a way onto a lower roof was easy going. They went from there to the air extractor, which was spewing Eau de Rodent into the night air from second floor walls. Alarm boxes were filled with a spray expanding foam to jam them up, and work began on punching a hole in the flat ground floor roof. The asphalt-coated compacted chipboard surface easily gave in to repeated stabbings with a crowbar until there was a big enough hole to squeeze through. Two agile volunteers lowered themselves in to explore. Below, there were half a dozen experimental pigs penned in concrete stalls all looking scared and uncomfortable, which wasn't surprising given they had been assigned to re-enact a human nuclear disaster!

Cockroaches scurried everywhere. They weren't being experimented on here—that's elsewhere. Here, they just hung out feeding on nuclear waste. They couldn't even attempt to rescue the pigs—they were just too big and there was no easy way of getting them out. Not being able to do anything to help these incredible, intelligent animals was heartbreaking. All the activists could do for them was to capture them on film and to spend a few, brief compassionate moments with them to go with the last scraps in the food barrel—pigs go for that! Their bodies were scarred with what looked like large square cigarette burns. Given the wealth of data acquired on irradiation from the study and treatment of the human victims of nuclear accidents, tests and bombings on our planet, these crude tests were not just cruel, but totally surplus to requirement. But then, futility and cruelty were the reasons the raiders were there!

While someone filmed the pigs' condition and living quarters, someone else was drilling a hole through a first-floor fire escape door. Half an hour of drilling away in a sheltered part of the roof gave access to a vacant area of the institute, a boiler room, which in turn led up via a service ladder into the attic space above the offices and labs. By removing roof panels it was possible to look down into each room below. By again descending into one of the offices, the intruders had free rein. The rodent smell pervaded the complex but there wasn't a live one to be found anywhere, not even a cage, not even in the cupboards. A frantic search revealed 200 vials of irradiated rats brains in one of the fridges, their discovery merely adding insult to injury.

For the rest of the team, the wait for their colleagues was to be a long one. There was nothing happening out there. It was a nice enough night if a bit cold and there was no one about but the wait was frustrating. Suddenly the sound of breaking glass got heartbeats racing. At least now they knew there was something happening. The others had been so busy looking for their rodents they'd forgotten to tell those outside what was going on. Freezers were opened and broken; books and encyclopaedias torn and soaked in acids and dye mixtures; scientific and electrical equipment broken; sinks blocked and taps turned on. Or a mixture of the above! All the useful documents were bagged up and passed out for later scrutiny. It wasn't all they'd hoped to return with, but at last there was something for others to do! There was a lot of anger released inside those labs. In ALF circles, 'trashed' is the boast.

The Daily Express reported how, 'Work worth thousands of pounds has been lost after a raid by the ALF. Files detailing painstaking research were stolen and ransacked.' They claimed that, 'Scientists were exploring ways of helping cancer sufferers by reducing the impact of radiotherapy on human skin.' What recovered documents actually showed were details of ongoing radiation experiments involving pigs, hamsters and rats supposedly meant to mimic the effect of a nuclear accident involving humans. Funded by the Cancer Research Campaign (which later merged with the Imperial Cancer Research Fund) and British Nuclear Fuels. This was priceless!

The activists passed a copy of the video footage to local media contacts. The film showed the pigs' injuries, their living conditions and the facts surrounding the research, which was comparing animal experiments with unpublished data from the atrocities carried out on Nagasaki and Hiroshima. Having been thus exposed, the CRC later confessed and announced that they would be dropping the radiation experiments on the pigs claiming it to be 'part of the CRC's ongoing commitment to reduce animal experiments.' Curiously, not so altruistic once exposed to public scrutiny.

The Royal London Hospital

> Today's medicine is at the end of its road. It can no longer be transformed, modified, readjusted. That's been tried too often. Today's medicine must die in order to be reborn. We must prepare its complete renovation.
>
> *Professor Maurice Delort, French physician, 1962*

Six days later, where Jack The Ripper had stalked the same streets of the East End of London over a hundred years earlier, some animal activists were looking to stop some perverted violence.

An older local activist, Sheilagh, had taken note from circulating missives about the usefulness of looking for information in the waste bins of animal abusers. She knew most of the London labs and had been looking around to see what she could find. Unfortunately, many labs are hidden in universities or hospitals and their bins aren't as obvious or as accessible as the more remote labs or 'farms' outside the City. The Royal London Hospital is, as you'd imagine, quite a large complex and finding the vivisection laboratory without insider knowledge would be difficult. She had got that from a chance encounter with a delivery driver who was offloading boxes of mice one afternoon; to all intents and purposes, she was temporarily 'lost' while herself 'delivering' to the hospital. Back then she had been a fish-eating 'vegetarian' who had called herself an animal lover. She recalled:

> Eating more dairy products and fish to make up for the fact I wasn't eating meat wasn't reducing animal suffering at all, and calling myself an animal lover wasn't exactly saving lives either, but this was the attitude of the farm animal welfare group I did fundraising for. They did tireless work, but some weren't even vegetarian and only one was vegan, and they would go on about the activists doing damage to the cause every time there was anything bad in the news. It was the final straw for me at a group coffee morning. A couple of them were talking about prison being the only place for the people who had broken into a breeding farm and released a load of animals 'to die'. They went on about what they'd heard but had no idea what they were talking about. For me, even if the animals were merely released into the wild and were going to die, it was still a less horrific end than what was coming to them. It's their torturers who should be in prison.

> Another agreed the experiments probably aren't nice, but because the government regulates them there would be no suffering! I had been quiet up until then but lost it, told them what I thought and never went back! It wasn't like me at all and they were gob smacked, but I felt liberated, like a big weight had been lifted from my shoulders and I was now able to speak my mind and do my own thing.

It was brewing anyway, and her instinct was more with the ALF than with what was considered the 'right way' to achieve animal liberation, but this encounter was the catalyst for more direct action. She quickly eliminated dairy and fish from her diet as she learnt more from the literature and videos coming through the post and from her first visit to the big annual London Vegan Fair. It was here that she had made contact with one of the people she thought might be interested in the window they left open at the rear of the Royal London hospital. She was right. Once she had been afraid of what the ALF stood for; now she treated the ex-prisoners and those she knew who were involved in direct action as she would her own children—better in fact. She looked nothing like a stereotypical ALF activist so was able to wander around the hospital labs for longer than many of the youngsters could. She was curious. She didn't really know what it would achieve, but if she got near enough to any of the animals, maybe she could pinch one or two. It had happened before but her thought was more hope than anticipation.

Liam lived miles away, but like a lot of others turned up annually to see what new goodies were now on offer at the vegan fair. He used the day not just as a rare opportunity for self-indulgence, but equally to catch up with those he knew from years of active service but seldom found the time to catch up with, due to other commitments. Always too busy! Here was an opportunity to combine the two.

Paula was living outside London and wrapped up in various campaigns around the capital and found little time to organise forays into laboratories and farms to rescue animals as she once had when living on the south coast. Life now was more mundane and less immediately productive, but London being as populated as a small country, there was a pressing need for the vegan influence to promote a different way and expose animal exploitation. The two of them had worked together on a variety of ALF projects in the not too distant past and both had sailed dangerously close to prison more than once but they'd drifted for personal reasons and seldom met up now. It was the fluttering of long dark eyelashes, her smile and butter wouldn't-melt voice that had drawn Liam to her in the first place. And it was that, that had saved them early one morning, when they were stopped by a police patrol a mile from a transport depot they were intending to firebomb with a boot full of the required material. Had they searched the car, they would have been going to prison for a long stretch, but because she was dressed well and had flirted with the fat copper and wrapped him up in some story about her ailing elderly mother, he didn't even give her a ticket for the dodgy rear light. It was a reminder that it wasn't just the quantity of their raids that was important but more so the quality. Failing to check the lights were working could have easily ended their reign there and then, had he been driving. Liam wasn't so good at dealing with police!

Persuaded by the information from Sheilagh and the rare opportunity to spend the night together and catch up, they altered their plans and took a walk down to Whitechapel that night. Being as they are, located in built-up areas, removing animals from city labs is more of a challenge than out in the countryside and there were clear obstacles. For one, the entrance to the hospital containing the animal labs was on a main road. And directly opposite there were people in the building. One glance across the road would clearly compromise a team of raiders loading up boxes of animals.

Not itself a major thoroughfare, Ashford Street is largely deserted at night with just the occasional vehicle driving by and not many pedestrians, but the activists were used to parking their getaway vehicle in a field somewhere where no one wandering by would see it even if the job took all night. If this raid was to happen, they were going to have to be really brazen and really quick. Or find a helicopter.

It was the busiest time of night as they wandered casually hand in hand towards the hospital. They walked straight past the entrance the first time, noticing the alley Sheilagh had referred to which led to the rear of the hospital and would see them out of sight. They crossed the road and walked back, checking out the area. A couple of cars drove by in the time it took and another courting couple walked the other way, none paying much attention to our couple who were able, at the third pass, to duck into the alley without being noticed.

The window was, as promised, unlocked. Wow! Without needing to consider the consequences, they raised the window, climbed in and, carefully looking around, walked up the stairway. It was all just as Sheilagh had said, to the last detail! There was no way of knowing for sure if there were animals in the rooms along the second floor corridor, but there was a whiff and an atmosphere that suggested so. That these doors had no glass in them and were secured with digital card entry locks was another clue. All at once, all their combined weekly plans for rescuing trapped pigeons, school talks and homes checks were thrown into disarray. But this was what they did as a priority. The other stuff was far less risky and could be done anytime.

Preparations were few but the excitement aplenty as they popped out of the alley and sauntered back down Ashford Street. They closed the window behind them so it appeared shut just in case anyone noticed and locked it. By the end of that week, preparations were complete. Research suggested the brave vivisectors at this lab were predominantly into mice. There was nothing they could do about the risky loading situation should they recover any, but they were just going to have to take a chance with that, or 'blag it' as Liam would say when he wasn't quite sure he could pull it off. He didn't like to say no because it wasn't straightforward, and he'd much rather risk it than err on the side of caution. These things usually worked out eventually.

Driving slowly down Ashford Street the van pulled up on the opposite side of the road with its lights off, but engine ticking over. In a flash, the rear doors were open and the proverbial courting couple were back on the pavement. There were two of them tonight, couples, of a sort, something of a family affair. From the van they pulled several bundles of flat pack cat carriers and a bag of the tools and a camera they might need inside. They first headed away from the labs as the van drove away to park up as they checked the surround then crossed to duck back down the alley beside the lab and out of sight.

Paula was briefing Emma and Wink in the second floor corridor when Liam joined them. They were meeting at a hospital vivisection lab late at night and no one knew they were there! How cool is that for an animal liberator! It was something of a miracle given the sound of crunching and splintering wood that was echoing around the deserted corridors as electronic swipe cards gave way to Liam's crowbar. He was in his element. 'Sorry!' he muttered unnecessarily after the first loud crunch.

'It was hardly going to open quietly with that thing, was it now!' Paula half jested. This was part of a hospital after all. There were people around all night and it would take only one witness to alter the course of events. Having calculated the strength of the obstacle, the door was torn open in one last certain assault, causing enough noise to make each conspirator grimace and tense as they imagined the great distance it would surely travel, seeking people as it went. The sound reverberated forever, then died away and was followed by silence. Complete silence. They stood stock-still, listening. There were no shouts or footsteps or the sound of doors opening (apart from this one) no alarms. Just a long beautiful silence and a hole where the door once was! Good boy!

Paula trotted business-like through the broken door and its broken frame and into the animal lab to find wall-to-wall mice everywhere she looked. Stacked high on moveable racks, innumerable white plastic trays with wire lids were home to countless tiny white creatures, who were in all likelihood going stir crazy. Some had stitches in their bodies from operations to remove their spleens. There is nothing for them to see or do in these tiny prisons as days, weeks, perhaps months of hopeless boredom, psychological torment and physical brutality are drawn to a close by death. Even the diet consists solely of bland processed pellets. The cruelty of the existence forced upon them isn't much discussed, yet it is palpably clear to anyone with even a modicum of knowledge of the inquisitive nature of these energetic little animals, that their sense of deprivation must be immense. Their life is spent in a tiny plastic tub, lined with a scattering of sawdust and shared with perhaps half a dozen other mice. That is their entire world...

One defence is that they're only mice and bred for the purpose of exploitation, so we needn't worry ourselves. Indeed, those who use these animals in vivisection proudly declare that rodents make up around 80% of the total headcount. That just means 80 monkeys a week, 120 dogs, a dozen cats, and 300 rabbits etc, etc. The smaller animals aren't even recognised in US statistics, and they of course process a whole lot more than anyone else. Worthless yet irreplaceable mini human beings in the same breath! Brilliant!

The activists discarded the empty cages and lids in a heap as they went and tipped in sawdust and water bottles for good measure. Not so smart as it turned out as some mice escaped the roundup and legged it to safety under the disorderly tangled heap. It took over 2 ½ hours to collect up all the escapees. 'Earthquake Hits Tower Block in Mousel!' was Paula's take on the news headline! She found room to joke in the direst situations, this not being one of them. Since they had already filled all the boxes, the remaining mice were taken in their cages and stacked by the stairs ready to ship out.

Across the corridor another locked entrance door was forced open, once again in dramatic fashion. Beyond a second door was a cage-partition—home to four bemused-looking beagles. They were as surprised as the raiders who'd expected more mice. The floor was splattered with sloppy droppings and the only decor in the clinical white room was a large ghetto blaster hanging on a wall. To drown the sound of them barking? It was such a small room with so little else it seemed unlikely there were people here much. The beagles—as lab dogs tend to be—were characteristically wary of men. Paula and Emma used their endless patience and experience of working with disturbed animals to win over the dogs' confidence and tease them into improvised dog leads. Liam and Wink with knowing enthusiasm began collecting from the offices and computers what they, and the people responsible for these animals being there, wanted. And trashed things!

Getting the dogs into leads was one thing but persuading them to walk quite another, as the first to go walkies begun to spin by its neck on the spot in some kind of an exhibition of a doggy break dancing routine. Paula said she needed more time than was available to make these fellas believe leads were a good idea, so they had to be carried like the big babies they were and secured to the stairs on the landing.

Liam nipped out for the van to prepare for the final stage. This was the really risky bit. The street was quiet but there were still lights on over the road. It could all so easily go to pot now if someone were to see them as they loaded up. 'Wait by the front door. I'll pull up outside when the coast looks clear but don't come out until I open the rear doors of the van. Then start loading.'

It was as much good fortune as good timing that no one drove by, walked by or looked onto the street while the van was being loaded. It was a nervous few minutes scuttling in and out to the van with boxes and cages, looking up and down the street with each pass hoping there was nothing new to look at. On CCTV it would have looked sleek with the four of them moving freely at all times doing exactly what they needed to do to load the precious cargo as quickly and safely as possible. No panic. No need. It was 1.00am Sunday morning.

With everything loaded, the dogs were tossed in and held onto in the back. It was raining but in the van it was snug. Emma and Wink were London activists, a perfectly matched couple busy all the time. Been around a while, been together longer and could be trusted not to boast about their exploits. They weren't organisers, but were the best company to have along, were always ready when needed, never complained and just got on with things. You warm to that. The van was away. Far, far, away. *Chirpa chirpa cheep cheep* was playing on the radio, which came on with the ignition whether you wanted it or not. They were singing out loud and rhythmically in the front of the van, 'last night I heard my momma singing this song...' A time to relish. In the back, the music was drowned out, but no matter—they were happily occupied making all manner of childlike noises and faces to the once-cautious and excited dogs in their care. It's one of those moments you don't forget.

A lapse in concentration and the heavy rain now falling nearly threw everything into a cauldron as Liam ran a red light driving through London at around the same time a police car passed going the opposite way. 'Fuck!' He realised late. 'Idiot', he called himself, feeling slightly nauseous while trying to see behind him through his mirrors. 'Don't worry. It'll be fine,' said Paula, as comforting and positive as ever while checking the wing mirror. 'Watch the road.' The patrol car carried on. He squeezed the steering harder with both hands to prove he was in control. It was cars that most often landed activists in trouble. Dodgy headlight, speeding, parked in a country lane, number taken. Too many been there, done that, and here was nearly another silly mistake.

The safe house was an hour away, but it was an otherwise smooth run. There were no immediate neighbours here and room to organise the animals. It was gone 2am and there was still a lot to do before anyone could relax and think about what they'd just done.

By that time exactly 1,070 mice and four beagles had been sexed, fed, watered and sorted. It had been a good night's work. Sheilagh was going to be so pleased. No point in acting innocent to her! It'd be a rare opportunity to tell the story to someone who wasn't there on the night. Some mice were blind, others' little bodies were scarred from surgery. Spleens removed. Soon be off to new homes, somewhere safe to live out their lives.

The lab calculated their losses and came up with 15 years of research and 400 mice. Can these people really be so wrong about so much? Stationed just minutes away at Scotland Yard, ARNI's organisers were on the scene in a flash (it'd be wrong to invite anyone else) and had been doing some calculating of their own. Things weren't adding up right for them either. Detectives soon begun to suspect things weren't quite as they should be at the Royal London Hospital and the plot thickened considerably when they discovered a member of staff in the animal labs was actually working undercover for a national anti-vivisection group.

The Morning After

> If [man] is not to stifle his human feelings, he must practice kindness towards animals, for he who is cruel to animals becomes hard also in his dealings with men. We can judge the heart of a man by his treatment of animals.
>
> *Immanuel Kant (1724-1804) German philosopher, pre-eminent modern ethicist*

It was 7.00am Monday morning in the Pathology Room and Adam Spare, trainee animal technician, was washing cages. The senior animal technician, Janet Jury, who carried out experiments, came in and asked him, 'Have you heard what's happened?' She revealed there had been a break-in over the road; she didn't seem particularly shocked, though she hadn't seen what had happened and was heading over. Adam dried up and went too.

The first indication that anything was amiss was a lot of sawdust spilt at the bottom of the stairs, while the walls upstairs had been daubed with: 'YOU'VE BEEN ALF'D' & 'THEY CAME THEY SAW THEY STOLE YOUR ANIMALS—ALF.'

Up the stairs ahead of Adam he could hear Janet cry out: 'Oh God! Oh God!' Bit more than a break-in then, Janet. When Adam reached her she was standing, holding her hands up, crying and asking: 'Oh God, oh God, what are we going to do?' But God was probably quite chuffed with what he saw and kept out of it. She was in the office that was normally used for splenectomies and which staff also used for their lunch, even whilst experiments were being performed there. It had been devastated.

Machinery was all over the floor, telephones had been ripped out and slogans had been sprayed everywhere. Adam couldn't help himself and started to laugh and was forced to hide his face. Meanwhile Janet's condition deteriorated and she became hysterical. Too much to deal with, Adam left the office and walked down the corridor to the animal house. The door was open and there was no one in! It was completely empty of animals and vacant cages littered the floor. The walls were covered in spray paint and the rooms were very, very quiet. He was floating; this was like a dream for him; he couldn't say that to anyone of course, not even his handlers at the BUAV, who would probably be as horrified as Janet, oddly.

Security arrived in the shape of two uniformed guards and a man in a suit. They looked around and said that no one should touch anything—a little late arriving and a little late with the advice. Richard Rowntree, the head of Pathology, turned up with police. He was in actually quite a jovial mood; his only apparent concern was whether ARNI had been informed. But Janet wasn't coping and Adam was asked to take her away for a smoke because she was in such a state. He took her to the tearoom. One of the missing dogs had left a pile of shit at the top of the stairs before it left, and the police believed there was a footprint in it that might be useful, so it was dutifully scooped up for forensic analysis. Exhibit A: one squashed turd. Other workers started arriving and were sent to the tearoom so statements and fingerprints could be taken. The police then sealed the lab shut and kept it that way for three days. They didn't bother with those statements or fingerprint after all.

Later in the afternoon, an elderly researcher, Rosa Vasquez, arrived. She was the Splenectomy Queen of the Royal London Hospital animal labs and had been experimenting on mice with a specific genetic status and it had taken about 30 years to build up the strain, which was no longer around. Adam said later: 'Everyone was worried because the lab was all she had in her sad life. All of her animals had been taken. Janet took her to a room and told her what had happened. She couldn't take it and was still in denial later in the day. She could have been using human cells but preferred animals. The project was completely halted by the ALF raid and hasn't been resumed.'

Not all the people at the hospital were as concerned by the raid as one might have expected. Nor were they about other incidents. Adam had been working there when the ALF raided Surrey University months earlier. Soon after, someone on the clerical side had approached him saying: 'Have you heard? Surrey University has been raided and all the animals taken.' He was actually pleased, which was an odd reaction within the world of the Animal Technician. These people are at the sharp end of medical research and scientific advancement, where recruits are often teased with 'a career working closely with animals' and only need Maths and English and one science subject at D grade or above to qualify. Adam believed this person, who used to cry when he saw the dogs in the lab, would have been promoted if he wanted to get involved in vivisection, but he refused. He had no greater qualifications than those thoughtlessly handling the animals in their care, he'd simply thought about it. He was pleased the hospital had been raided but was concerned whether the dogs had been taken to good homes. Adam, himself an activist, knew they would have but didn't say anything.

With the lab closed and nothing for them to do, at 3.00pm workers were told go home. Two weeks later, Adam Spare was arrested there. The police had figured out he wasn't quite what he said he was and that he'd got himself the position some months before with the intention of relaying lab secrets to the BUAV for them to do an exposé. It was surreal for him, one of very few lab workers to be pleased the ALF had been in. It was the one organisation he so admired but had never had contact with. Here he was in enforced unemployment, and he loved it!

Adam's handlers at the BUAV weren't so chuffed, however. In fact they were downright miffed. They had been effectively gazumped and were suspicious their man was somehow implicated in spoiling their investigation. Adam was duly ostracised by the BUAV—a bit like gaining street credibility amongst the ranks of the radicals. The police put Adam under surveillance and were of the opinion, though lacked proof, that he was the inside man. They gathered no proof of this but later charged him with conspiracy to burgle, theft and obtaining a pecuniary advantage by deception.

Nearly two years later, his trial and that of Nancy Phipps, who was charged with providing him with the false reference he needed to get the job (the pecuniary advantage) started and was duly stopped by the judge at the end of the prosecution case. Because there was no case, no physical evidence, the judge said he would feel uneasy if he were convicted. The footprints in the doggie doo were neither use nor ornament.

The seven-month BUAV investigation revealed that dogs had been kept in pens with no daylight or bedding; that there was a lack of veterinary care; that one dog had died from blood loss following a fight because no vet was available, and other animals had suffered painful and fatal complications following massive invasive surgery.

Ex-breeding beagles sold by pharmaceutical companies were being used by the lab in research before being killed. Two were ten years old and had had 13 litters each before their awful existence was finally brought to an ungrateful end in a hospital lab. Glaxo had sold Molly—a five-year-old ex breeder and a favourite of Adam's—cheaply to the hospital. He saw she wasn't in her pen one day and later found her bound and cut up in a bin bag in the freezer. Being driven out of this world by the ALF was the best thing that could have happened.

Hylyne Rabbits—The Start Of The Rot

The Animal Liberation Front—The Provisional RSPCA.

Jasper Carrot

An old haunt of mine was Hylyne Rabbits in Cheshire, one of the largest rabbit breeding farms in Europe, churning out 250,000 rabbits a year for vivisection, meat, fur or anything worth a penny. The company headquarters by the Thelwall Viaduct at Lymm were home to Edwin and Eileen Sutton. Their offices and their main rabbit-breeding centre had featured in ALF literature repeatedly over time and had been raided regularly with at least eight big raids on the site during the 1980s and many smaller ones. Eighty-seven rabbits were taken across the Manchester Ship Canal out back one night by boat, an ingenious idea rendering useless the cameras scanning the road out front.

A couple of years before that, over 100 rabbits were taken in one night's work, and on another occasion, the offices were cleaned out of paperwork during a burglary, which had revealed a wealth of documentation on the many laboratory customers of this leader in rabbit production and supply. I was later charged with the latter offence after police took from my home—during a forage over some other matter I can't recall—some supply catalogues from Hylyne they said had been taken in the raid, but which in fact Hylyne had sent out to me as they would have done to anyone with an interest in breeding rabbits.

I was found not guilty of burglary but fined for handling stolen documents. Anyway, in early 1994 the owners' car was burnt out and empty rabbit sheds followed soon after. The pressure was building when the Justice Department sent them an exploding poster tube, which the bomb squad dealt with, and they were then warned by the police to check under their car every morning. (A wave of postal devices marked a brief escalation in violent activity by this previously unheard of group around this time). Then the local Manchester Animal Protection Group (MAPG) announced they intended to launch a campaign against Hylyne, increasing the number of demonstrations there. It was too much from too many and it all came to a head in June 1994 when Hylyne issued a public statement:

> Due to recent severe firebomb and parcel bomb attacks on Hylyne Rabbit Farm at Lymm, Cheshire, the company has been forced to cease trading and go into liquidation. The company has no desire

> to subject its staff and families to further fear of harm and harassment. Several recent attacks have destroyed staff vehicles, burnt down rabbit breeding and nursery units and in the most recent incident caused severe problems with newborn baby rabbits and lactating females. Many rabbits have been stolen.
>
> Hylyne Rabbits Ltd have become known worldwide for the development of modern rabbit farming technology, improvements in housing standards, animal health and environmental enrichment. Visitors from all over the world have visited the modern rabbit maternity facility at Lymm and attended training courses held at the farm. The business was founded in 1955 with a capital of 30p, has traded worldwide and more than once been considered for export achievement awards. Several large export orders will be lost and staff jobs curtailed due to the closure. The Continental rabbit industry gains as very little Animal Liberation Front activity exists in other European countries. This will be a sad loss to British agriculture, which is constantly seeking methods of profitable diversification.
>
> Coney Europa Ltd, the associated rabbit marketing company, has also been placed in liquidation as their housing has also been burnt down only months after complete refurbishment.
>
> RIP Hylyne rabbits.

Unfortunately for Edwin and co, the European scene has mushroomed since then and is far from a safe place for animal abusers to do their thing. 'What about the rabbits?' was my first question down the phone from prison to a local friend in the know.

'They're all safe. The RSPCA have got them for now but we're working on it.'

I dislike what the RSPCA is and don't trust those in control to put the well-being of animals first, and nor did she, but I have to say their statement gave us all some comfort. The liquidators had given the RSPCA care of the animals while they sorted financial affairs. If the RSPCA is good for little else and perversely promotes meat eating and vivisection, they would at least ensure the rabbits wouldn't be subjected to any suffering and certainly wouldn't be experimented on. Imagine the headlines if they were: '600 Bunnies Passed By Nation's Favourite Animal Charity to Rabbit Dealer for Use in Cruel & Pointless Tests!'

Sadly the headlines didn't follow the rescued rabbits' fate because that, staggeringly, is the reality of what actually happened. No one knows their exact fate, or at least no one will say, but a happy ending it wasn't.

The RSPCA couldn't afford to do a deal to save the rabbits? Surely a miniscule percentage of the organisation's vast accumulated wealth could have satisfied the liquidators who only wanted rid of the farm stock? Following the closure announcement there was only silence and apparent disinterest from the RSPCA in the rabbits' future leading to deep concern at the way they were dealing with the matter, so the ALIU sent a team into Hylyne in July to try and establish what was going on.

The ten-strong team swiftly accessed the farm offices, loaded up, and left again before the alarm could be raised. All the rabbits had gone but there were plenty of documents to be had—which were copied and returned—including six months of invoices for the sale of rabbits. The trade with vivisectors included not just live rabbits but also their heads and even ear mites, which were ordered by a pesticide and rodenticide manufacturer in Cheshire. Large recent customers included Liverpool and other universities, and dozens of laboratories and commercial companies were found to have received rabbits, their heads, or ear mites, and orders showed that deals for laboratory rabbits were still being done three weeks *after* Hylyne went into liquidation and *while* the RSPCA were looking after them. It was devastating news. No longer shocking but still hard to comprehend. How could they?

One Butcher's Too Many

> Even though I'm a butcher I'm all in favour of vegetarianism. I think it is a good thing, because vegetarians don't live as long as meat eaters, and the more vegetarians there are, the fewer old people there are to burden the country. That is why the Japanese armies always lost against the Chinese—because the Japanese only ate rice and vegetables.
>
> *Butcher Paul Jenkins showing signs of BSE infection in a ramble to the Kent Evening Post*

Marbles & Windows

It was October 1991, late at night in a Derbyshire town south of Manchester and the police were pulling over motorists. A large number of windows in the county had been potted that night as on many previous occasions and as the three passengers in one suspect vehicle were being searched, a couple of marbles, some ball bearings and three catapults emerged. No innocent explanation for their presence immediately sprang to anyone's mind! It was a good result for the police, which would have been complete had the three not been suddenly reduced to two as the third suspect made off into the night before he had been securely handcuffed. Manchester activists Alistair 'Brench' Howson and Rhian Thomas were charged with conspiracy to cause criminal damage to 17 shop windows. Since he was out on bail at the time for the incident at Dodleston during which he'd been cuffed to a drainpipe and she for hammering windows at Liverpool University's notorious Devil's Tower vivisection laboratory, it came as no surprise when they were remanded into custody pending trial.

Like the rest of us, they were aware that the police were putting evidence together of a big conspiracy, and that they were in the frame for it. They were clearly involved in their own thing as well as team work with others whom the police had on their radar, but because they weren't logged entering through the conspiratorial doorway at 201 Clarendon Road, they were left out of it. After four months spent in police cells as a result to the Strangeways fallout, the two pleaded guilty at Derby Crown Court to six counts of criminal damage amounting to £8,570 and of going equipped to commit that damage. Rhian Thomas was sentenced to 12 months, suspended for six and Alistair Howson received 15 months, with nine months suspended, most of which he had served while awaiting trial. These were still long sentences for what they had done, given that drunken thugs and burglars were getting non-custodial sentences for far worse crimes and others 12 weeks for breaking every bone in a dog's body (in a lab you'd even get paid for it!).

Howson and Thomas were released within days, while others, who had been to 201, settled in for a long slog to trial, imprisoned at home and attending the police station daily. Mark Power was the next to fall foul of the rout of 1991. Nowhere near the Manchester scene, he was none the less wrapped up in a conspiracy of his own making.

> At exactly midnight on 3 November, the police stopped me outside a butcher's shop in Birmingham. In hindsight, it was evident that they had been watching the area for some time. The policeman who arrested me called for assistance, and despite the fact I offered no resistance, no less than four squad cars sped up and I was taken to Smethwick police station. The police held me there for five days and interviewed me on three occasions. Throughout the interviews I said: 'No comment' to each of the questions. I went to court on the second day and was remanded to police custody. I quickly got in touch with a solicitor, not the duty solicitor as they are notoriously unreliable and appear to take little interest in their clients.
>
> Eventually, on the third day I think, I was charged with conspiracy to commit arson, possession of items with the intention of committing arson, and arson. Nine counts of criminal damage to butcher's shops were added later. On the same night I was arrested, the police raided my flat and took away stacks of printed material and all sorts of household items and tools. Eventually, most of the documents they confiscated appeared in the depositions, including leaflets/literature from such innocuous organisations as the NAVS and Campaign for the Abolition of Angling! They even confiscated an ALF T-shirt. They took away a hammer and were later able to match fragments of glass found on the hammer to that of a shop window that had been smashed. The forensic scientists were apparently very thorough; the police were obviously determined to get a conviction.

On the fifth day in police cells, I was taken back to court and remanded to Winson Green prison. At the same time I learnt that I'd been suspended from my job as a psychiatric nurse. The whole thing was a bit depressing to say the least. While I was waiting in the reception of the prison, a loud aggressive-looking screw came up to me and demanded to know if I was responsible for firebombing eight meat trucks in Kenilworth, which were torched the day after my arrest. When I said no, he glared at me and told me to go fuck myself! Charming!

I was sent straight to the hospital wing for observation and stayed there until the end of December. Finally I was transferred to an ordinary wing where most of the people I met were very sympathetic to the ALF. Many were vegetarian and a few vegans. I went straight into full time education, although the facilities were very limited but at least it got me out of my cell and I did quite enjoy some of the things we did. The conditions in Winson Green are very bad. It isn't so much the fact that it's dirty, and that most of the prisoners are allowed only one shower a week, it is the totally uncaring indifference that you are met with each day. A lot of inmates have some very genuine problems that need sorting out and are given no help whatsoever, unless you can get the ear of a sympathetic screw, which isn't very often. Another major problem is the macho atmosphere of prisons where there is a great deal of male posturing and the type of moronic attitudes towards race and gender that go with it.

The following March I was sent to Wolverhampton Crown Court for sentencing. I pleaded not guilty to the conspiracy charge, but guilty to other charges because of the overwhelming evidence against me. The CPS accepted my plea. I was given a four-year sentence, and to be honest it was a relief. From the way the judge had summed up, I was expecting more. He described me as a terrorist who had tried to intimidate the Birmingham business community. I've always regarded myself as the least intimidating person I know! But at least the whole thing was resolved and I knew where I stood. All I had to do then was bide my time and look forward to release. I don't regret what I did, I just wish I hadn't got caught.

Some argue that the ALF are freedom fighters and deserve reward, others compare them to the IRA and believe that ALF sentences aren't nearly heavy enough. Most people, though, agree that animal abuse is unacceptable and while they won't do much about it themselves, they understand why others do. Sadly, the lawmakers and judges aren't influenced by Joe Average but by the businessmen who use animals and demand ever increasing punishment. They are not so much concerned with whether people are hurt or not, but with protecting their investment—this being precisely what the ALF is targeting. In reality, money is power, and life is expendable.

Ultimately, legalised animal abuse must end before opposition to it ceases; only then can human beings lay claim to being civilised and fully evolved. It is down to the 'extremists' to ensure that this happens sooner rather than later. Historically, radical social change has always come as a result of radical action, where reasoned debate and political procrastination have merely served to prolong stagnation: the status quo, after all, has never favoured change.

The combined effects of ALF action and of strategic campaigns by others do work, as we are seeing, and keep the struggle for animal rights in the spotlight. Despite huge media bias and prejudice, there are many people who feel such extreme rhetoric and imprisonment of animal rights campaigners is wholly unjustified. Sadly we have quite a long way to go before the will of the people is translated to the remit of the police.

Given the scale of activity, it came as no surprise that Special Branch were called in to defend the reign of institutionalised state terror. By the beginning of 1991, Manchester, surrounding areas and further afield saw Special Branch engaged in the biggest police operation yet mounted targeting the ALF—and there was no shortage of targets. Now everyone was flexing their muscles!

The UK of the 1990s saw many liberation raids, arson attacks, hoaxes and so on, as well as a number of other imaginative actions. Increasingly, those arrested—when not remanded in prison—were forced to exist in virtual isolation through strict bail conditions, the effect of which initially was to shift the centre of activity and get others involved. One tactic that grew in popularity was the catapulting of shop windows. Positioned as they are in vulnerable locations, the highly offensive, bloody displays of the butcher shop windows have fallen victim to the opportunistic/drunken activist late at night for many years. More of us than are prepared to admit it have lobbed something heavy at one of these when under the influence, and not always successfully! It's not so much to do with bringing down the industry—it's more a gesture to all those murdered to satisfy the human palate.

Catapults, which are subtler than bricks, but just as effective, were causing extensive damage, particularly to butchers, pet shops, animal research 'charity' shops, fishmongers, bookmakers and Boots chemists. The damage is so subtle that it's often undiscovered until the following day and is initially insignificant. But a small hole in a pane of glass such as that left by a ball bearing tends to spread over time, sending tentacles across the window, which becomes unstable and needs replacing. Once word spread of the potential damage that could be done with a bag of marbles or ball bearings without even having to leave the comfort of one's own car, the damage spread. This tactic was particularly employed by activists in the Northwest who relentlessly potted shop windows in Merseyside, Lancashire, Cheshire, Manchester and Derbyshire, causing damage to dozens in any one night and no less than 1000 in one eight-month period alone. Shops in West Yorkshire and Northants were also hit hard. Other regions suffered but less intensively.

One butcher in Northampton devised an ingenious method to prevent the spread and save the cost of replacement or the need for shutters. Gluing squares of cut glass over the holes did seem to work for a while and stemmed the flow of current holes, except that it looked ridiculous after a time and probably added unhelpfully to the weight of the weakened pane. And the more he stuck on bits of glass, the more he encouraged the local catty crew to pot his windows! At one stage there were 15 holes in one pane of glass. These mini campaigns become a battle of wills. Arguably, an unnecessary amount of attention was focused on small meat outlets with so many other bigger suppliers in supermarkets and so on but it was as much about the principle.

It got to the point where police surveillance was laid on to protect targeted shops. For the owner, it's of course about protecting his livelihood and maintaining a way of life. For some of the activists it was probably more about egos than tactics. But such concentration has also led to some imaginative thinking, which can't be a bad thing. Undercover officers set up observation positions overlooking numerous potential targets, rather than simply follow suspects who were wreaking havoc with bags of marbles and who had actually managed to pot shop windows without their tail knowing. One particular target in South Manchester—a big fronted shop called Andrews The Butchers in

Chorlton—had had steel shutters fitted following repeated attacks. The owner was confident his insurance premiums would level out but the police didn't think that was the end of the story, and how right they were!

Andrews was especially in-yer-face and both the owner and the gross display of exotic body parts had become something of a magnet for local radical vegans, whose views Mr Andrews of course rejected.

The police don't like to admit to the extent (or even the existence) of surveillance operations, but a large number came to light during this regional deployment of resources. They were engaged not just in watching rows of shops, but were also eavesdropping on homes and offices and tracking individuals and vehicles, the end game being to stamp out those harbouring radical ideas.

Detectives may have been watching shops for months on end, and it would've been exceptionally boring for the most part, but one incident changed all that. Police film of unfolding events from a lookout post located further down the street from Andrews' is grainy and may have failed to pick up a catapult firing at a window from a passing car, but the butcher's windows were shuttered anyway, and they weren't about to be catapulted. For what was planned instead, the camera would do just fine.

A yellow Escort can be seen to brake as it drives by the shop, which excites the surveillance team. The three men get out. The car's stolen. They mill about suspiciously for a moment as if they're waiting for something to happen. Then one of them returns to the car and makes it happen. Next thing you see is the car starts moving, but instead of driving on down the road, it cuts across and heads in the direction of the shop. Surely not! It mounts the kerb, crosses the pavement and slams front on into the shutters. On collision the shutters are buckled, the windows broken and the street suddenly comes alive. The surveillance team couldn't believe their eyes. The most they could have possibly hoped for was someone on foot with a spray can or one of those sharp T-shaped metal rods some smart-arse had devised to force through shutters and break the protected glass on the other side. Everyone's suddenly running. The police were up and at 'em in a flash.

The driver of the car wasn't wearing a seat belt and had lost his glasses on impact so was slower leaving the scene than he needed to be. Trying to recover them, he got wrestled to the ground by the first officer to arrive. Now he was in trouble; his activist career temporarily but severely curtailed. In minutes there were dozens of officers swarming the area hunting the escapees, on foot in cars and in the air. One later recalled how he had hidden amongst the refuse sacks in the rear yard of a terraced house nearby and waited to be arrested as the aircraft slowly scoured the area, its beam of light sweeping along until it lit up the yard like a floodlight. 'Fuck! Where am I going to run?' he asked of himself, annoyed he'd got himself into such a predicament. Should have kept running! But there were men chasing him, he could hear them shouting and he wasn't that quick anyway. What he should have done is not ram a car into a shop surrounded by police! Oh hindsight, wherefore art thou? He'd run as far as he would now he just had to remain totally motionless and hope. Incredibly the craft did eventually start to drift away and the voices went quiet. He couldn't believe his luck and remained in the rubbish for a good hour before heading home for a bath and to mourn his absent friend.

Just the one arrest and that was a lucky one. Oh for those contact lenses he'd been thinking about getting... John Hughes was charged with conspiring to commit criminal damage and unlawfully taking a motor vehicle and remanded in custody. He was bailed weeks later to an address out of the area and told not to return. The warning signs were there for everyone to see and we knew the police meant business. There was no question that activists in the area were under observation and that there needed to be a shift in the modus operandi, but where some people do drugs others pick up their own bad habits.

One observer, Pippin Took, summed up the situation at the time in a letter to *Arkangel*:

> Those who participate in the preparatory stage of a guerrilla movement must have an extra-ordinary capacity for self-control and sacrifice'. The words belong to Inti Peredo, a Bolivian guerrilla of the 60s. Yet they could apply just as well to the ALF of the 90s. Nobody can doubt the personal sacrifice and commitment of today's animal activist. Faced with the full array of state suppression, the ALF have become the most effective non-violent underground guerrilla movement in Europe according to many sources. Examining the reasons for this success, paramount must be the ability to strike randomly where and when we choose and on our terms. Obviously this is the keynote of any guerrilla campaign—Through The Door When They Least Expect It, as CALL slogans went. And this is where Peredo's insistence on self-control becomes so important.

I know little of recent events in Manchester so maybe I'm wrong, but I feel that the continuing action in the area is fast becoming a prime example of an instance where self-discipline and the rules of underground warfare are falling by the wayside. A series of admirable actions have led to a massive security clampdown and surveillance operation—only to be expected, and an important signification of the activists' success. The immediate instinct of the guerrilla should be to 'go to earth' and lead a normal and ordered life in a 'clean' house for as long as needs be. The funding of any police operation is severely limited, especially if it has a negligible success rate. One of our greatest allies is time, while police man-hours are under severe pressure.

Knowing when to keep your head down requires self-control and good sense, but how long can the authorities afford to watch nothing happening? If ARNI want to stake out butchers' shops or activists' homes let them sit there and play with themselves 'til their superior officers get fed up picking up the tab—they won't be so quick to subsidise such an operation in future.

So why are major ALF actions taking place in Manchester and activists being picked up on the streets? When does courage become foolhardiness? Maybe when our personal pride says, 'those bastards aren't going to stop me taking action,' and maybe that is precisely when we stop playing by our rules and start playing by theirs. Continuous action is one sure way to be caught and we must resist the call of the ego to 'keep fighting at any cost.' The animals need their defenders free and underground, not in prison. Perhaps it is the same pride that drives hunt saboteurs to attend violent hunts expecting confrontation and little sabbing, rather than attend an easily-sabbed hunt. Obviously this is a gross over-simplification, but how often have we heard 'we can't let those scum get away with chasing us off!' It is personal ego speaking, and it does no good for the animals. It was human ego after all that enslaved them in the first place. We have a duty to be where we can be of the greatest service to them regardless of our feelings. There is no place for the glory of going down in flames. If we can keep our keep our egos in check, maybe our activists' careers will last a little longer.

This is not intended in any way as a criticism of any Manchester activists, and I hope it will not be taken as such, but please remember: He who turns and runs away, lives to fight another day.

Melting Meat Trucks

> At 10.40 this morning I did receive a phone call from a child who stated it was pleased to hear our lorries had been burnt and it was National Vegetarian Day. I put the call on hold in an attempt to trace it and they rang off.
>
> *General Manager of the Fresh Meat Company*

Not so much thinking about slowing down, the raiders were stepping up a gear. Setting something alight will generate more 'concern' that someone might be killed than any other tactic regularly employed by the ALF, and more attention. Fires naturally scare us, and it's true they can't always be controlled, especially if you have left the area! That said, there have been hundreds of arson attacks on slaughterhouses, laboratories, department stores, meat transporters, cattle wagons, intensive battery units, hunt kennels, fishing boats and so on and yet there have been no serious injuries caused to anyone. I can find endless reports of lorry drivers who would be dead had they been sleeping in their lorries when they were burnt and others of people being evacuated from the scene and one fireman being overcome by smoke. But compared to crossing the road, playing football, drinking water, spending time in a police station, walking in a thunderstorm or eating beef, it seems that firebombing empty buildings is a safe thing to do from a health & safety point of view. You wouldn't want to be caught doing so of course and I don't seek to encourage anyone to do so but the fact remains.

It's an unspoken rule among activists that unusual care is taken to reduce the risk to life in these actions and if it's considered too dangerous to set a fire because there's a chance that it might spread elsewhere that hasn't been targeted, then no fire will be started. In reality, only a minority of ALF activists commit arson, but those that favour it tend to have a preferred method.

Incendiary devices are a mystery to many and few, if asked, could describe one. An incendiary device is by definition something that can be used or adapted to ignite a fire (so, for example: a complicated, wired construction with a detonator or a timer, or a sponge and candle would be considered to fit into this category). Non-explosive incendiary devices are the sort mostly used by the ALF, and they are designed simply to start a fire at a set time i.e. when the arsonists are out of the area. They don't 'blow up', as is often suggested in hysterical media reports; instead, they ignite or burst into flames. The purpose of the exercise is to generate publicity for the cause and to push up the insurance costs of the targeted business.

When a handful of meat lorries were firebombed one night early in 1990, the media reported the beginning of a campaign against the meat industry. This was slightly off the mark because that had started many years earlier, but it did indeed signal an intensification of one aspect. There were stories about how, now that the 'loonies' had finished off the fur trade, they were turning their attention to the meat industry. Again, only slightly off the mark. While a few arson attacks are unlikely to devastate the meat industry, an ongoing campaign pushes up insurance costs, and of course, the cost of the product, while media publicity from some actions makes animals a talking topic, at least 'til the heat dies down…

I've read a lot while researching for this book about concern over the potential loss of jobs if we adopt a cruelty-free lifestyle, suggesting, it seems, that we should forthwith abandon all attempts to behave like civilised human beings because there will be some poor souls left looking for alternative employment. The same self-serving argument was used to defend the interests of slave traders, of those who used to send children up chimneys, those who deal in porn, and men out on the vast oceans harpooning whales and bludgeoning seal pups on ice floes. The hunting fraternity have used the same argument and have even had the arrogance to cry crocodile tears over their proposal to kill off redundant horses and hounds. It is unfortunate that some might lose their jobs as society turns away from barbarism, but that is the price of progress—progress, which in its turn would create alternative employment possibilities in the new businesses that would inevitably be created. They wouldn't stop fighting crime just because success might eventually lead to the redundancy of a police force and prison officers, though of course that's precisely why crime is a good thing for the economy. And glaziers, car repair businesses and security services are doing rather well out of the ALF, thank you very much.

In July 1991, activists in the Northwest of England set off a series of incendiary devices in a coordinated attack on two slaughterhouses in the Greater Manchester area. Lorries were badly damaged at the Strivens slaughterhouse and the R&J Taylor depot, None were guarded with anything other than basic security and wishful thinking. Spring-loaded centre punches were used to break side windows and bottles of fuel dancing to candle tunes were left to burn on upholstery. Ironically, the unwanted intruders on site that night claimed to have saved the slaughterhouse from far more serious damage. They said they'd had enough devices to do the whole site, but instead only targeted the fleet. Some vehicles were also ignored due to the close proximity of buildings housing animals awaiting slaughter. This might be seen as something of a contradiction given the extremely cruel way that animals are killed for meat; perhaps being overcome by fire and smoke might have been a better way to die—who are we to decide? It would doubtless have been a far greater prize to raze the entire slaughterhouse, but this is hardly the instinct of the average ALF arsonist.

Four refrigerated vehicles were burnt out at R&J Taylor, three at Strivens and, an hour or so later, a cattle transporter was similarly done. Local media covered the attacks extensively, and the damage was estimated to be around £500,000. The local Labour MP expressed his concern that '...this sort of action will turn the tide of public opinion against them. I am very anxious that these militant methods are being used. It could easily result in a death. This kind of terrorism is not the way.' There was no advice forthcoming from the meat-eating politician on what kind of terrorism would actually be 'the way' forward, nor, indeed, did he even pledge to set the best example of non-violent direct action by removing dead meat from his diet! As ever, there were sound bites and objections but no solutions.

In what was to become a sustained campaign over the coming months, meat lorries were attacked by fire all over the country prompting calls for depot owners to consider parking vehicles away from buildings and from each other in order to minimise the potential for damage. Over a period of 12 months, the ALF in the UK burnt out no less than 100 meat and animal transporters. Ten articulated tractor units (the main at the front) were attacked at Europe's biggest slaughterhouse—Midland Meat Packers at Crick—causing £500,000 damage. Drive-by security guards with roof-mounted spotlights had this place apparently secure, but the activists simply waited until the guards had driven by, then crawled under the high fence and primed each vehicle to ignite. Security returned to a scene of devastation. Soon after, another ten vehicles were hit at the Great Harwood Frozen Foods slaughterhouse and meat processing plant near Blackburn in Lancashire, affecting three separate companies. I met an old lag in prison a few years after this incident who joked with me how 'Your sort deserve bloody locking up' for carrying out these raids. Or this one in particular. He explained how one night he and two mates had been on their way to nick a couple of fully-laden meat wagons which they'd had an eye on, but en route, a convoy of speeding fire engines had forced them to pull to the side of the road. With this, the wannabe thieves had joked that the emergency might be at their meat plant of choice 'if the bloody animal rights lot have been at it.' It wasn't quite so funny when they got to their destination to find a scene of frenetic activity, flashing blue lights and flaming meat wagons. They'd been gazumped! Another six lorries were torched at the Fresh Meat Company in Kent, five at the British Bacon Company in Huddersfield. Weddel Swift had four attacked in Rochdale, three in Nottingham and two in Wolverhampton, and Snelsons of Kenilworth lost eight in one night, worth another £500,000. There were 17 multiple attacks of this nature claimed between June and August of 1991.

Industry workers were in uproar, fearing for their futures and talking of victimisation—an ironic gripe coming from those who make a living from the victimisation of those weaker and less able to defend themselves, but still understandable. The meat industry wasn't the only industry caught up in this escalation of direct action against animal abusers: others with blood on their hands were also in the firing line of this growing public disquiet.

Public Relations—The ALF Press Office

> It could be a pervert, a psychopath, an animal hater, a hunt saboteur or someone with a grudge.
>
> *Anonymous police spokesman commenting on a wave of assaults on horses, as reported in The Daily Telegraph, 1993*

It is still somewhat surprising that however gentle and genuine the perpetrator, however altruistic and measured the action, the animal liberator invariable gets bad press. It wasn't always so: as the BoM and ALF emerged in the 1970s and then beyond, into the early 1980s media coverage of actions was broadly sympathetic and the rescuing of animals regarded as a decidedly English phenomenon. But underlying the quaint Englishness of this novelty, is—as we know—a very serious message. It was not merely a question of alerting the public to the plight of animals—it was also a question of exposing their abusers who, it should be remembered, get away with what they do because they do it in private. The Animal Liberation Front changed all that: the graphic exposés were accompanied by sympathetic press coverage; the ALF ranks swelled and actions increased. It was not something any society, no matter how animal friendly it purports to be, would encourage or tolerate and certainly not one with an economic structure built on animal exploitation. Given that investors in this huge market area advertise their wares using the same media outlets that report the news, it's logical they will influence the reporting of that news.

It would do no good for egg producers to do nothing to stem the tide of negative reporting from inside their egg farms. For example; typically images turn Joe Public from buying battery eggs, take the profits from producers and kill the advertising. Better to have a rich and powerful company on side if you are a news editor than a bunch of law-breaking but well-meaning animal lovers with nothing to invest in advertising and no high profile contacts. Today, the rescue of animals from unimaginable cruelty is condemned as criminal, cruel and even dangerous by the government, the media, by businessmen, police and white-coated scientists. Even some animal welfare charities who are keen to fit in and be seen as respectable go out of their way to condemn the liberators; more often than not, only the words of an anonymous ALF communiqué tell the animals' side of the story.

In its early days, the ALF posed no obvious threat to the status quo. Public speakers could thus not only speak openly about animal cruelty and the motives behind raids, but also refute the opposition's frequent claims that liberated animals cannot survive outside their cages. As ALF actions increased in frequency and effectiveness, so too did fear surrounding what they were doing. This, combined with the formation of police squads to tackle the animal rights threat, filtered through to the media, ensuring that the cause would no longer be able to get a fair hearing via media outlets; indeed, association with the media has become difficult—even dangerous—for activists.

With the imprisonment of Ronnie Lee in 1986, the voice of the ALF was silenced. Others brave enough took over briefly but soon went the same way, leaving the position vacant. (Roger Yates, northern press officer, had absconded during the same trial as Lee and was sentenced in his absence. Their successor, Robin Lane, was arrested in May 1987 and also served a prison term. The primary charges in all these cases were of conspiracy and incitement. Clearly, the role of any ALF spokesperson was a difficult one at best).

For several years, the task of dealing with the press was left to ALF activists themselves, thus forcing them to compromise their anonymity and risk their liberty twofold: first by organising and executing their raids and then by talking about them and breaking the first rule. On more than one occasion in my dealings with them, journalists have compromised me and those directly involved in an action. Given this trend, it was hardly surprising that some activists would simply ignore the media, and refused to respond to false claims made by the police and those targeted.

It became clear to all concerned that a public voice was needed, someone confident and articulate who was not involved in direct action but who had a good understanding of it, and would not be afraid of standing up to defend ALF actions in the face of a media and police onslaught.

There were few takers. Just the one in fact. Enter Robin Webb—perhaps the least likely of candidates—a 47-year-old silver-haired welfarist, well known in the movement as a member of the RSPCA council and of the Christian Consultative Council for the Welfare of Animals. He was at home in a suit and involved in nothing illegal, nothing he was admitting to, anyway. He certainly didn't fit the stereotype, but he did fit the profile.

Webb was in a prime position to weigh up the effects of 150 years' worth of RSPCA campaigning against the ALF's 15. There were, of course, far greater career prospects within the RSPCA. 'It's not a career I want, to spend my life promoting bigger cages and better treatment for animals in captivity awaiting their demise. I want animal liberation and I want it now,' was his unequivocal response when I asked him for ideas where we might look for a spokesperson. 'I'll do it!' The ALF immediately gained and the RSPCA was set to lose an asset, but then the RSPCA isn't short of those. The rest of the RSPCA council—under the patronage of the all round animal-abusing Queen of England—weren't impressed at Webb's support for the activists. So?

We arranged a press conference to announce the new post at a venue in October 1991 in central London and sold it as 'The Animal Rights Media Event Of The Decade.' It was the chance to offer the media an opportunity to obtain proper replies to burning questions, but also to allow the Animal Liberation Front itself to make a major statement about future aims and activities. The press release read:

> Those hosting the press conference consider it a unique event—it is unlikely that they will ever again be available as one group for the media. The conference will, however, establish a communications pathway between the ALF and the media for future use. For security reasons we are unable to give any further information prior to the press conference, but if you have any queries please telephone… We look forward to seeing you there.

Unfortunately the press conference never happened. 1991 proved a busy year for all players and in the blink of an eye between issuing the press release and staging the event, only Robin Webb was available for comment (and he was soon watching his back) while of the others fronting the conference, one was on the run and three were in prison! The Press Office however had been officially established.

The RSPCA suits were furious to hear what their man was doing and called for him to be expelled from the council, but he pre-empted the vote and resigned, so allowing him to stand again in future elections should he see fit. Horrified at the prospect of having the ALF front man on the RSPCA council (and Webb was especially keen to be on the council, if only to give the RSPCA a kick up the arse and take a look at itself) they moved to expel him from membership of the society on the grounds that he was working with an organisation whose methods—and indeed, many would say, goals—were contradictory to theirs. Given some of the characters the RSPCA has courted that was a bit rich. The latest appointee in 2006 was Sussex Police Assistant Chief

Constable Nigel Yeo, who had previously ordered the destruction of a police dog he dismissed as 'a piece of equipment', after it bit a teenage lad. His new job: the charity's South East regional manager. Yeo also gave the green light for hunts to break the law by refusing to police the legislation! Other's I will get to.

The Great Lucozade Scam

> The Utopians feel that slaughtering our fellow creatures gradually destroys the sense of compassion, which is the finest sentiment of which our human nature is capable.
>
> *St. Sir Thomas More (1478—1535) author, attorney, Lord Chancellor to Henry VIII from Utopia, 1516*

Before the roast lamb lunch had gone cold at RSPCA HQ, Robin Webb was in full flow, wrapped up in media frenzy about Lucozade and its link to vivisection.

It was 4.30am on a silent, bitterly cold mid-November morning on a housing estate somewhere in Coventry. The peace was about to be shattered. Gathering in a back street was a gang of 20 fearful-looking blokes tooled up, dangerous and ready for a riot. This was the anti-terrorist squad about to flex its muscles publicly for the first time against animal liberators. Other gangs were gathering at locations in Northampton, Hastings and Manchester, waiting for the word. Their warrants had been issued to search for salt, vinegar and rat poison. Police claimed to have proof of a serious contamination plot afoot. It was a slick operation and by 4.40 that morning, ten suspects were in custody, shaken, rattled and rolled out of slumber. It was a rude awakening!

The warrants were quite specific in their detail but the police were apparently not so bothered about that. It was claimed that information had been received that suggested those arrested (mostly the usual suspects who were picked on at random and not necessarily always innocent!) were about to contaminate a Smith-Kline Beecham's product with the listed condiments. Finding rat poison in any of the houses raided would indeed have set alarm bells ringing, especially amongst their peers for whom it is symbolic of the cruel, routine, thoughtless destruction of small animals that some call pests. There was no poison anywhere. Apparently disinterested in recovering the necessities for flavouring a bag of chips from the kitchens they searched, detectives instead settled for any printed publications referring to the rights of animals.

With no clue to the alleged source of intelligence, nothing resembling evidence and no admission from the detainees, the case for the Crown looked rather shaky, but there was a big story in there somewhere. One conspiracy theory suggests that the police were keen to rack up media hysteria to coincide with the trial of the Brampton Three (arrested with incendiary devices near HLS a year earlier) due to conclude at Crown Court. There was certainly some hysteria in the media's response to the police press release, with one national paper screaming the headline 'Animal Fanatics Pile On The Pain' and another warning of 'Poison Coup By Animal Rights Fanatics.' It was a big story but one completely without substance, if judged by the unconditional release of all those arrested, one of whom was also meant to be in the dock in the Brampton case. He was duly acquitted in that case too, the other two receiving those three-year sentences.

If there was a police conspiracy, it failed terribly, then backfired. The police never explained the reason for acting as they did and each of those arrested later received between £3,000 and £4,500 in compensation for wrongful arrest. But most significant of all was the rather unnecessary withdrawal of all five million bottles of Lucozade on sale throughout the UK with all suspects in custody and no sign of any conspiracy. Someone may or may not have talked about contaminating Lucozade, but either way, SKB lost £3 million through recall and sales. Overnight, £130 million was wiped off their stock market value.

Scotland On Fire

> I was a Labour voter all my life and I was so excited about the future for the animals and all of us when we got them in that we had a party. We made them what they were and look at what they've done. I'm ashamed. Politicians have lost all credibility. The ALF is the only hope the animals have.
>
> *Nancy Phipps*

Robin Webb was finding the ALF lot far more happening than the conference room-cum-talking shop at the RSPCA. Soon after the Lucozade affair there was a fierce blaze in a Bolton Lucozade factory followed by an unprecedented series of arson attacks on targets in Scotland. In a brazen two-week-long assault there were no less than ten substantial fires. The first night saw three laboratories set ablaze on the Bush Industrial Estate at Penicuik near Edinburgh. The Tropical Veterinary Medicine Centre, the Scottish Agricultural College of Genetics (and breeding unit) the Ministry of Agriculture Food and Fisheries and Lassulade Veterinary Centre all suffered serious damage. Next, six incendiary devices seriously damaged the Henderson abattoir at Linlithgow, West Lothian. The following night, £300,000 damage was inflicted on the Institute of Terrestrial Ecology at Banchory and two days later fire wrecked a horsebox used by the Lanarkshire and Renfrewshire Hunt. Next day, the Nastuiks meat factory at Falkirk was hit. And two days later offices of the J. Hewitt tannery at Currie, mid Lothian, were destroyed by fire. Next hit was the Ross Breeders Poultry Research laboratory at Newton, West Lothian, and finally the Marshalls Chunky Chicken factory at Bonnyrigg. Both were badly damaged. The next day, at Southport in Lancashire, the eleventh shrimping rig in four days was burnt out.

Trials & Tribulations

It was a slow day in heaven, so God phoned Satan to see what was going on down there. 'It's a slow day down here too', said Satan.
'Well,' said God 'How about a dog show, that might be fun?'
'Sounds good', said Satan. 'But why are you calling me when you've got all the dogs up there?'
'Of course,' acknowledged God, 'But you've got all the judges.'

Running Out Of Luck

It was a busy summer, and during the same week in which Scottish targets were hit, activists made their mark in the East Midlands city of Nottingham, where in the early hours they set light to a fleet of refrigerated wagons belonging to Masons Brothers Meat Wholesalers, causing an estimated £500,000 damage. The lorries and their full loads were wrecked. That they were full of meat was a significant detail but that was not as much of a deciding factor as the fact that they could burn safely in their location: they had only been parked temporarily at the city's cattle market, away from their secure compound during rebuilding work.

Next arsonists struck at the city's Pork Farms depot, causing £200,000 damage. A lorry and a van, both brand new August issues (with no mileage on the clocks) were destroyed and another car badly damaged by the heat, which buckled the steel girders along the roof. Again, publicity was extensive and anguish in the industry reached new peaks as a week later, in an apparent coordinated action, raiders struck fleets of trucks in three counties.

But luck was starting to run out for the moonlighters, and SOCO (Scene of Crime Officers) had begun to compile quite a collection of complete and partial incendiary devices like those found at The Pig Improvement Company. (Situated at Kingston Bagpuize outside Oxford which rears and 'improves' pigs for profit to create the industry's dream of faster-growing, less disease-ridden piglets) the company owns a fleet of pig transporters, which had attracted a couple of ne'er-do-wells who had crept onto the site one night equipped with half a dozen improvised incendiary devices. It all went wrong when a small fuel spillage prematurely ignited one device and the vehicle in which it had been left which meant that the other devices—and plans—had to be hastily abandoned.

In Lancashire, Mayfields Chicks was targeted the same night. This company is a major supplier of the day-old chicks that intensive poultry farms need to fill their sheds. Broilers, or table birds, are white chickens that are packed in 50,000 at a time or more. For a week, life is possibly bearable, but they grow so big that by the end of their life at the age of six weeks, they can hardly move and their legs start to give. By this time they have become drug-filled freaks, regarded merely as meat worth a couple of pounds. Their death is a blessing of sorts, since it releases them from their suffering, though the road to it is a terrible one. Catchers bundle them off for their journey to the slaughterhouse, where their ending will be a violent culmination of the brutality and contempt they have been shown from birth to death. 41 days of life in a dark shed is seen by the industry as far too long, and they want it shortened as much as possible by more 'veterinary research.' To maximise profits.

Ten vans from Mayfield's bird transport fleet were set alight; the local fire crews who quickly arrived on the scene saved half. (Four years later, the arsonists returned, causing £200,000 worth of damage).

That same night, three activists fled after they had set out to burn a fleet of meat wagons at York House Meat in Bedfordshire. By chance, the story goes, an off-duty police officer had overheard the sound of breaking glass and phoned colleagues before going to investigate. Using skill and great daring he disabled the bombs left inside vehicles before they blew; at least, that was according to the news reports that followed. The reality was that he blew out three candles attached to plastic bottles of petrol, but then the truth doesn't always make such good reading. Nor does it sound quite so terrifying, an essential requirement of reporting animal rights actions and keeping people scared.

The Bedford raiders were a part of the wider network of committed activists who were either involved in direct action or knew who was. Many were already known to the police and had been in custody for something or other. As ever, that was part of the problem, along with the fact that they were involved in as many legal campaigns as illegal ones. Immediately following the Potton incident, detectives monitored the addresses of likely suspects in the region. It was enough of a coincidence for the surveillance team at Abingdon Avenue, in Northampton, when just after midnight three people were seen to pull up and go into number 11. The police had been there often enough to know it was an address very much in the loop and, as three people had been seen leaving the meat depot just a county away an hour earlier, it was worth another knock. Many of the previous police raids had been 'fishing' trips to see what could be learnt, or if there were any animals to be 'bagged' that weren't legit and might be returned to the cruel environments from whence they came. At least they were the threats, though it never actually happened. But better than finding a fugitive beagle or bunny, this time there were three key activists in the bag and evidence to link them to Potton. Angela Hamp found herself back in custody with Annette Tibbles and a man from Oxford.

There were still tiny bits of glass in their clothing and on footwear that was later forensically matched to the site of the attack. It was initially sufficient to remand them in custody pending trial charged with conspiracy to commit arson, but when the police ran out of time to present their case, they were released on bail six weeks later.

Back in Manchester, the efforts of the Boys From Lance were again bearing fruit in their quest for the marble maniacs who were wreaking havoc. It was a black Vauxhall Astra estate cruising slowly past one row of shops under observation that first started alarm bells ringing, not to mention the fact that its rear window was blacked out and it was known to the police as being owned by a hunt saboteur. The rear window had previously been smashed by hunt supporters in Cheshire but had been adapted to hide the unlawful acts of sabotage originating from within the vehicle. It still needed an officer on the ground to check for damage to confirm suspicions but the car wasn't going to get far before being stopped.

Inside were John Marnell, Clare Rush and Max Watson and a catapult and some marbles. All three were regular faces at 201 Clarendon Rd and all were arrested on a charge of conspiring to cause criminal damage. By the next morning, reports had come in from elsewhere regarding windows with holes causing damage totalling an estimated £13,500. It wasn't the biggest of crimes in the wider scale of things but a big deal in the world of animal exploitation and something the authorities were keen to tackle. Where offences were such that extended periods of custody before trial weren't appropriate, the use of strict bail conditions was employed to full effect and, in the judge's own words, ensured that suspects became 'internal exiles.' These three were successful in their applications for bail some weeks later but first had to find a £2,500 surety to get out of custody, then leave their homes in Manchester to stay with relatives elsewhere. They had to sign on at a police station daily, observe a 7.00pm—8.00am curfew and keep away from each other and other animal rights activists—their friends. They were also banned from leaving the country, restrictions that were to continue for the next two years before a trial was convened. Further observation continued, including at the parents' address of one where a police observation post was discovered above the butcher's shop opposite, keeping a constant eye on their man, the vegan across the road. They didn't trust him to behave.

By the autumn of 1991 Manchester was a risky ride, but Terry Helsby and John Hughes, who were well known to the police (Hughes bailed to an address in London and banned from the North West, Helsby living at 201 and someone who had been of interest to the police for some time) were up to no good in Liverpool. Observation logs at 201 had seen them leave the address earlier in the day and then disappear from the radar.

Some hours later they reappeared when spotted by chance potting a window by an observant beat officer. He had stopped in the shadows of a shop doorway to see the passenger of a slow passing car lean out of the car as a butcher's window was hit with something. He took the number and ran it through the Police National Computer, and that set those alarm bells ringing. Soon after, the car was stopped leaving the area and both men arrested on suspicion of causing criminal damage. They were later charged with causing £3,000 damage to six butcher's windows that evening. Helsby was released into a state of internal exile a few days later, but Hughes, who shouldn't have even been in the area let alone breaking windows, was remanded in custody. The prosecution were so busy tying themselves into knots in trying to create this mammoth case and working overtime withholding from everyone the extent of the ongoing operation that their warnings that it might be some way off completion meant that defendants were being allowed home on bail to await trial. And that included Hughes four months later.

The Huddersfield Four

> We have enslaved the rest of the animal creation, and have treated our distant cousins in fur and feathers so badly that beyond doubt, if they were able to formulate a religion, they would depict the Devil in human form.
>
> *Rev. William Inge (1860-1954) Anglican priest, Professor of Divinity, Oxford, Dean of St. Paul's Cathedral*

Those who knew Denise, Gavin, Richard and Daryl (a close-knit team who kept to themselves) were gutted to hear they had been arrested for arson but, worse still, caught red-handed. Daryl was quiet, and a bit of a lightweight in appearance although this was deceptive; Denise (whom I'd met at a group meeting in a local Rochdale pub some years before these events took place) stood out a mile with her massive spiky red hair. She was a punk and proud of it (that must surely go without saying) and was passionate and keen to be active. I'd never been keen on the punk look when campaigning, especially not the leathers many wore, but during the 80's they made up a large portion of the movement. Many of the Rochdale group, though vegan for the most part, were older and more sober in appearance, and not at all radical; indeed, they were keen to avoid association with those who were, believing as they did that it was not good for the image.

It soon became clear that Denise and I were of a like mind, and we drifted away from the 'fluffies' who weren't as active in the AR field as with other noble causes. Denise was always available and we often did as many as four or five stalls a week together. She was keen on hunt sabotage—something I had tried to get others into without much success—and together we experienced trauma and joy in equal measure in the hunting field and outside the circus, as we battled with and outwitted large men with sticks and guns. Some days were good, others not so good, but she was always prepared to give it a go and not afraid of a beating. Afraid yes, and admittedly so, but more afraid of playing safe and as a result doing nothing. As worthy as they are, it was a lot more exciting than those vegetarian evenings, and also far more likely to lead to trouble!

Denise later moved to West Yorkshire and I migrated the other way into Manchester, but we still met up, albeit less often, on cross-border hunt sab hits and demos, where the chances were that someone with a gun or spade or 4x4 would lose it and try to kill her, me or someone else. It was out of necessity that we mixed with like-minded people, but we were obviously far more likely to get into trouble this way. It would have been a miracle, given the extent of police surveillance at that time, that they would think anything other than that we were amongst those involved in direct action, but it was still something of a surprise to discover the scale of the surveillance work in Yorkshire, even though there were few more likely suspects than this little crew.

Unlike across the Pennines in Manchester where the reaction of the police had been a warning, there was little to indicate any such interest in the remote converted church home of two of the group. They were all known to the police as hunt saboteurs and protesters but nothing more. It might have simply been a casual conversation overheard which had referred to 'Denise' or 'Richard' doing this or that which provoked deeper police interest in the group; perhaps it had been the sighting of one of their cars somewhere suspicious, or increased ALF activity in the region. Whatever the reason, the police had many known vegans under observation and few had fully expected it. The property landlord had given police access to the rooms above the target flat where they fitted a listening device under the floorboards to record conversations in the rooms below.

It was August of 1991 and it had become clear to Special Branch agents working on Operation Fox that their suspects were planning something big. In fact, so informed were they of the next ALF raid that they poured in resources and physically ringed the Rafiq's poultry slaughterhouse at Holmfirth with arc lights, dogs and camouflaged police, packing firearms in anticipation of the team striking there. There was even a force helicopter parked in a field over the hill ready for the ambush.

The slaughterhouse was a grotty criminal operation, known as a particularly unpleasant place where birds were slaughtered the halal way, and where every moral code and many criminal laws were regularly being broken. Perversely, the focus of Operation Fox was to prevent any interference in this. At 1.30am on a pleasantly warm morning in late August, the four of them crept onto Rafiq's slaughterhouse premises to check there was no one about. It was dark and deathly quiet. Since they were planning to burn it down, they wanted to make sure! They were fairly certain the place was empty but were nonetheless cautious and kept close to the buildings. As they quietly slid open the barn door, blinding lights came on all around them and suddenly all hell broke loose!

There was so much light and so much noise it was disorientating. Men were screaming and running, dogs were barking and there was a helicopter above the rooftops! They'd all run into the unexpected before and had had to scarper—it goes with the territory, but this was different. This was bad. Really, really bad. Before she knew what was happening, Denise was lying face down in the dirt with a rifle to her head. 'Keep still or I'll blow your fucking head off!' bellowed the camouflaged gunman above her. 'Move?' she reminisced later: 'There were loads of them running around with guns and truncheons screaming commands and just screaming—it was all I could do to not shit myself! For a brief moment it was a almost a relief to find it was the police and not the monsters running that place, but that soon gave way to the awful truth of what was happening to us.' Still, everyone agreed, it was reassuring to have been given a choice of whether or not to die. Richard, polite, thoughtful and never looking to fight with anyone, didn't feel able to rationalise anything as he was punched to the ground and was soon surrounded by snarling police dogs and policemen. With Gavin a quivering disorientated wreck felled by a truncheon whilst other dogs were wrestling with Daryl, what should have been a coup for this likeable group had somehow turned into a rout.

Battered, bruised and humiliated they were arrested for attempted arson and were taken to separate police stations around West Yorkshire where they were held for the next 36 hours and questioned repeatedly. None of them were any help with enquiries. They were later charged with burglary with intent to commit criminal damage, burglary with intent to steal, going equipped for burglary and possessing items for use in criminal damage, and were remanded in custody for seven days.

Incredibly the police had a problem with their case. Of initial concern to the four was how the police had come to know what they were up to that night when only they had any knowledge. It was becoming obvious they'd been bugged. The primary concern of the police was to keep them in custody and to do that, they had to a) admit to the listening device and reveal what they knew, or b) provide the court with more than they had done in order to prove the alleged conspiracy to raze the slaughterhouse. As it was, as hard as they searched, the police had failed to recover any incendiary devices from the four or the surrounding area despite the conversations they'd overheard, which had made clear reference to them. The police were, as is often the case, reluctant to admit publicly to using electronic surveillance, especially with so many associates under similar observation, but this only turned the tables and left them with a conundrum and the defendants with a Get Out Of Jail Free card.

All four were dressed in dark camouflaged clothing when arrested, they had gloves on and a lighter each, and socks over their shoes. They'd referred to plans back at the house, but the police later searched all their homes and their two cars, which had been tailed to the scene and promptly impounded. There was nothing hidden in the area around the slaughterhouse but for a bag containing a pair of bolt cutters, a crowbar, a bradawl, an automatic centre punch, some tin snips, a damp rag and a Stanley knife. One was carrying a torch with a red filter over the lens, but there were no incendiaries anywhere.

All animal rights-related paperwork police took from homes was recorded as 'ALF Literature' though clearly it wasn't. Added to the incense sticks in the cupboard, empty plastic bottles in the recycling, petrol canister in the garage, gaffa tape in the stationary box, pot of weed killer in the shed, they collected together letters from friends (one or two in prison) referring to this or that demo or arrest or whatever and planted for good measure a copy of *Into The 90s* with its incendiary diagrams. On the face of it, it all looked like proof of something but when analysed there was still that something missing.

Desperate to prove an arson conspiracy at the bail hearing, the police told magistrates the rag was soaked in accelerant. This was another lie. It was in fact water, and clearly so, used for deadening the sound of padlocks cracking. Still not the highly organised incendiary attack the police were claiming to have foiled so they came up with a logical explanation. Enter the Invisible Man. They claimed that there must have been a fifth conspirator: someone no one heard speak, heard spoken about, or saw during weeks of surveillance but who was in on the job, carried the devices and was able to escape with them without anyone seeing. So desperate were the police to detain the defendants, they were happy to make themselves look ridiculous!

At the next hearing—to everyone's amazement—all were granted bail with the obligatory restrictive conditions attached, including being banished from their hometown of Huddersfield and banned from communicating with each other. The listening device was left in place for three weeks after the ambush in the hope of solving this puzzle and perhaps revealing further plots from others associated with the defendants. The plot thickened considerably for the police when I turned up at the address to meet a mutual friend to sort out prison visits and other essentials. We were very wary and as was shown in recordings, which were later revealed, all conversation would be taken for a walk.

A year on, Special Branch were boasting publicly that because of a series of police operations targeting the ALF, a number of trials had begun involving 30 defendants and that exemplary sentences would be handed down upon conviction. It was touch and go when things started to hot up in Leeds Crown Court with Denise Booth, Richard Anderson, Daryl Cavanaugh and Gavin Robinson on trial for conspiracy to commit arson.

The case began with prosecutor Roger Scott introducing the State side of the story, calling the least significant witnesses, then boring everyone to sleep by playing hours of tape-recorded conversations which they now had to rely on to prove their case. The quality varied from very clear to poor, with interference. The evidence was played on digital audiotapes via an infrared amplifier that sent out a signal to headphones.

Everyone except the viewing public had a pair of these. An explosives expert from the MOD and Home Office Research Laboratory came next. He was intent on proving that snippets of conversations recorded on the tapes were of people making incendiary devices. To be even more specific, he was sure that they were devices based on an ALF manual: Non Electrical Incendiary Devices. Because of this, each member of the jury had a copy of the pamphlet, along with copies of Into The 90s, despite the fact that none of the defendants were found in possession of these. This witness was perhaps the high point of the prosecution case, although despite being an 'expert' he had to concede he was unable to make a device ignite outside during his trials.

Court cases often have unusual and unexpected twists. In this case, one of the major twists came in the shape of a certain Mr. Mohammed Rafiq, the owner of the slaughterhouse that the four were accused of attempting to rid the world of. For some reason Mr. Rafiq left the country in late October to go to Pakistan, fully aware he was to be a prosecution witness. His statements detailed what happens at the slaughterhouse and the layout of the premises. When it was discovered he was unavailable, the prosecution thought they could proceed without him, but the defence for good reason had other ideas.

Mr. Rafiq, deemed a key witness by the defence, was ordered back from Pakistan by the court and appeared on 18 November. Speaking through an interpreter, he was guided through his statements by Mr. Scott for about half an hour. The defence then cross-examined him for two days. During the cross examination, which concentrated upon previous breaches of laws by Rafiq, Judge Saville interrupted enquiring: 'What issue is at stake? How is that an issue in this case?'

Defence barrister Jonah Walker Smith replied: 'It goes directly to the defence.' It was at this stage the defence was revealed to all. The Criminal Law Act 1967 Section 3, reads: 'A person may use such force as is reasonable in the circumstances in the prevention of crime.' Exactly what is deemed reasonable is for the jury, and not the judge, to decide. The defence was very specific to the conditions and history of Rafiq's slaughterhouse, especially with regard to previous prosecutions and crimes committed there. However, it still caused a stir when it became apparent that one of the lines of defence would be that this 'criminal and terrorist' conspiracy was going to be argued as legally justified!

Mohammed Rafiq and his son, Shafiq, were cross-examined for a total of three days about the slaughterhouse. They were bad witnesses for the prosecution, often asking questions back, calling barristers liars and generally being evasive. For reasons best known to themselves, the prosecution didn't care about this, seeming to be sure that they'd get a conviction regardless of how bad the conditions were proven to be.

The defence tore the Rafiqs to bits, producing countless letters from Environmental Health officers, RSPCA officers, press cuttings of Rafiq's convictions, etc. Basically, the slaughterhouse was shown to be a Grade 1 shit-hole for chickens and workers. Staggeringly, Rafiq's slaughterhouse didn't have a licence to slaughter chickens. This means it was an illegal slaughterhouse. There is an exception to this, if poultry are reared on site for 21 days prior to being killed. The Rafiqs were normally killing in batches of up to 2000 chickens at a time within three days of delivery and were therefore operating illegally. During cross examination, reports from visits by Environmental Health officers revealed: '…chickens kept in crates outside overnight; …never had a veterinary visit; …neighbours stood in a garden feeling sick; …no water in drinkers for chickens in shed; …dead and decaying birds in with live birds; …mould and algae growth in slaughterhouse; …employees paid £40 a week for nightshifts; …no toilet or washing facilities on site for employees' etc, etc. For all this, the Rafiq's blamed the 'health people' for allowing their crimes to continue!

The prosecution then began calling the police witnesses. These were treated very carefully by the defence in cross-examination, attempting to keep the focus of the case upon the conditions at the slaughterhouse and away from a conspiracy. That said, they were given a hard time whenever the errors and holes in their statements were exposed. Most striking was the revelation that a detective sergeant had copied, word for word, parts of a detective inspector's statement. All of the cops told lies under oath; some did only that, and their story about there being other suspects at the scene who had evaded arrest became all the more ludicrous as time went on. Another amusing aspect of the police secrecy about techniques involved in their surveillance operation was their refusal to specify what kind of vehicle they had been using when making a mobile observation; they also tried to disguise the fact that some of the police in the ambush had been dressed in full camouflage clothing (and were probably hiding up trees). One did let slip and described the detectives in camouflage as 'Crop Men.'

The way a court case develops is very subtle. What may seem like an insignificant point can often be turned into a crucial issue with clever cross-examination, and that was precisely how things developed, forcing the prosecution's allegations about the ALF to wane gradually as the trial went on. Everything was steered by defence barristers towards the bad conditions at the slaughterhouse. Even the questions put to the defendants during their interrogations in police custody were brought up. This had the general effect of turning the prosecution's own evidence against the very picture, which it had been trying to paint.

Presenting the jury with gory photos taken by Environmental Health visitors to the premises and even photos taken by the forensic scientist meant that gradually, during the case for the Crown, the jury received masses of defence exhibits. Two days prior to the start of the trial, the *Times Saturday Review* ran an article about 'animal rights', or more specifically, an article which had nothing to do with animal rights other than some individuals' opinions on the morality of killing vivisectors. It was headlined '*They Shoot Scientists, Don't They*?' (a parody after the film: '*They Shoot Horses, Don't They?*') which was rather a strange question, given that none has ever been shot… Timed to coincide with Ronnie Lee's impending release from prison, it included a small paragraph at the end about the Huddersfield case and referred to the nationwide ALF conspiracy police had been working on and the number of key arrests they'd made. The result was that each jury member was asked before being sworn in if they'd '…seen last Saturday's *Times* or read any part of the *Times*.' Any juror who had would not be involved in the trial and those who hadn't were invited not to read it because of its potentially prejudicial effect on the defendants. The prosecution team cynically opened the paper so the jury could see and glanced at the article repeatedly.

A further twist in the trial was the decision by all of the defendants not to take the stand. It was believed that the prosecution were counting on cross-examination of the defendants to seal their convictions. The decision not to give evidence was therefore kept a tight secret. By avoiding tricky questions on what exactly was going on that night, the defence still left it for the prosecution to prove a conspiracy and to prove that these mysteriously non-existent incendiary devices ever existed. Instead, the defence case was to call Kirklees Metropolitan Council employees to talk about the slaughterhouse, again shifting the emphasis of the case away from any guilt on the part of the defendants, to guilt on the part of the council for allowing an illegal slaughterhouse to continue operating.

An animal inspector was called to describe the ugly conditions she'd found on an inspection of the premises. Next up was a top-ranking bureaucrat who, despite trying to pass the buck down the ranks, was shown to be inept at doing anything about an illegal slaughterhouse. The inference was that if the council were unable or unwilling to do anything about Rafiq's, then who would do something about it?

The case for the defence ended with glowing character references being read out for each defendant. The prosecution had spent about four weeks trying to show that the four had conspired to damage Rafiq's slaughterhouse by burning it down. The defence had taken a day or so to say, effectively, so what? At the end of the case for the defence, all parties sum up their side of the story: the prosecution, the defence and finally the judge. The prosecution in this case believed very little had changed since the start of the trial. They continued to emphasise that what could be heard on the tapes was a conspiracy.

Mr. Scott argued that since the crimes at Rafiq's were not armed robberies, murders or serious house burglaries, then arson could not be seen as a reasonable way to stop them. He even went so far as to suggest various options that could be used against the slaughterhouse such as writing to the council, holding demonstrations etc. The prosecution didn't try at any stage to defend the slaughterhouse, since it was clear that the conditions there were quite simply indefensible. Instead they said that the Rafiqs were irrelevant and tried to discredit the defendants. To do this, Mr. Scott used a publication called *Animaliberation* found in one of the defendant's homes. This, he said, categorised '…the way these defendants think' and concluded, 'They're not particularly balanced.' He then went through various snippets of the transcripts pointing out references to security and insinuating that one of the four was the leader. In Mr. Scott's opinion, 'It was run as a military affair.' He was, unfortunately for the prosecution, snide and far too confident in his assertion that 'The case is simply overwhelming.'

The defence summing-up was long and passionate. It opened with the assertion that 'Mr. Rafiq is a liar and an animal abuser. Like father, like son.' Mr. Smith for the defence stated that it was both morally and legally right to destroy the slaughterhouse. To illustrate the morality he used a quote from the *Animaliberation* publication: 'To let evil thrive, it is only necessary for good men and good women to do nothing.' The legal justification was that nowhere in the law does it state that 'under no circumstances should a person build an incendiary device or damage a building by fire.'

Placing the blame on the local council, Mr. Smith argued the reasonableness of any action by saying that, 'No-one else was going to put a stop to it. This is an exceptional case, concerning individuals in respect of specific premises. That they took precautions is common sense.' The next defence barrister, Mr. Peter Hall, pointed out the holes in the prosecution case, presenting the ideas of 'persons unknown' being involved as pure fantasy: contrived to cover the fact that no incendiary devices were found and that elements of the police's transcript of conversations were also based on fantasies and assumption.

Mr. Terry Munyard then went on to say: 'Treating a living being in a bad way is not a trivial offence. So can you write Mohammed Rafiq's breaches off? Anyone with pets knows of the revulsion of seeing them mistreated and knows how they can suffer. It's not surprising that a caring person would want to stop this cruelty.' The full scope of Rafiq's crimes was then brought up again. Michael House, the last defence barrister, consolidated by saying that the 'Rafiqs were involved in a long term criminal conspiracy and by setting fire to the slaughterhouse the conspiracy would be stopped.' The jury were then asked to decide what is reasonable, one fire or nine years of sickening conditions. 'It's clear nothing short of physical force was needed to stop this operation.' Mr. Scott's assertion that the four should have demonstrated was answered with: 'Do you think that would've had the Rafiq's shaking in their shoes? Fat lot of good demonstrating would've done.'

In Crown Court procedure, the judge is the last to sum up, and what he says can often carry the most weight, not only because he is the figure of authority, but because his words are the most recent in the minds of the jury, who are probably by this point numb with boredom. It's his show, in a sense. The judge calls the shots, and an opinionated judge enjoys making everyone know who's in the right and who's in the wrong. In political trials, like this one, the judge's speech is a nightmare prospect, particularly if it's clear he's on the opposite side of the fence to the defendants, as will likely be the case. Convictions are overturned on appeal when judges have been biased in their summing up so they do have to be careful, but there are ways they can make their feelings known without saying as much.

The Huddersfield Four expected no favours from Judge Saville and got none. He went through all of the evidence, concentrating on what he thought was relevant, particularly in regards to sections on the tapes. To help the jury make their minds up he prepared four questions: 1. Are we satisfied there was a conspiracy? 2. Are we satisfied each defendant is party to the conspiracy? 3. Are we satisfied the purpose considered was not to be used to prevent crime? 4. Are we satisfied that the force is unreasonable in the circumstances? Towards the end of the speech, which was carefully worded to avoid appeal points, Saville asked: 'Would there be any danger to nearby buildings, any danger to firemen?' At no point other than this was it even considered there could be danger to either. Saville was later forced to withdraw this statement, but once something is said it is in the minds of a juror it is not going to be dismissed when considering their verdicts. He concluded by saying: 'Mr. Scott says that a person has a means, albeit limited to demonstrate and lobby, without recourse to the violence of the conspiracy.' The jury then had—some weird court procedure—two hours and twelve minutes to reach a unanimous verdict.

The jury returned without having reached a verdict. They wanted to hear various sections of the tapes again and to be instructed on exactly what a conspiracy was. They then retired again and left everyone else to go back to pacing the cafeteria. As the day wore on, it seemed clear that at least some of the jury members were on the defendants' side. At teatime, the judge told the jury that they'd have to spend the night in a hotel and return a majority verdict (ten agreeing) in the morning.

The next day, there was still no clear sign as to when or whether they were going to reach a decision. Everyone was called back into court, for the umpteenth time, to hear some questions the jury had. They wanted a dictionary, but instead the judge asked what words they wanted defining—they were 'reasonable', 'unreasonable' and 'terrorist.'

The word 'terrorist' strikes fear in the hearts of most people. That some members of the jury clearly thought that the four people in the dock were terrorists demonstrates the insidiousness of media sensationalism and misrepresentation surrounding damaging animal abusers' property. For the prosecution, establishing a link between ALF and terrorism was a key factor in the trial. For this reason, it was understood from the beginning by the defence that any association—however tenuous—with the ALF would be dangerous. Indeed, thousands of leaflets seized from the defendant's homes (ranging from ALF Supporters Group leaflets to RSPCA and hunt sab literature, to be used for information distribution on stalls) were used by the prosecution to promote the idea that these all inferred terrorist links! As far as the defence were concerned, the more they could distance the issues from pro ALF connotations, the better their chances of a successful conclusion to the trial.

Aware of the law, Mr Saville told the jury to: 'Ignore the word 'terrorist' as it is not an issue in this trial.' No doubt this knocked a few heated arguments on the head in the jury room. Around this time another worrying potential result, other than prison sentences, was looming: that of the jury being unable to reach a verdict and the need for a retrial. Go through all this again! The prosecution, obviously aware of this possibility, approached the defence with an offer for a deal. Should the jury fail to reach a verdict and the defendants plead guilty to the conspiracy to cause criminal damage charge, there would be no retrial on the arson charge and the bugging evidence would be ignored. It was a tempting offer, since it was unlikely that custodial sentences would result from this plea.

Towards the end of the second day of deliberation, and of endless fraught anticipation in the court foyer, the jury were called back in and asked if there was any chance of them reaching a majority verdict. Most shook their heads, the foreperson said no and they were all thanked by Saville and discharged. All the time just a nod away from a long prison sentence for the defendants. This is the most traumatic of experiences.

It was up to the defendants whether or not to accept the prosecution's offer. It was too much to risk a guilty verdict next time and not at all attractive going through all that again so the deal was done and the case was adjourned for pre-sentence reports. Suddenly the curfew was lifted, putting an end to fifteen months of home detention.

Three weeks later, the four received 120 hours community service each as punishment, for effectively embarking on a scheme to be of service to the community by ridding society of Rafiq's slaughterhouse.

The judge told them that had they been convicted of the arson conspiracy he would have sent them down for a long time. The police, desperate to salvage something, or maybe just to be vindictive, made an application to keep the defendants' cars, which they'd already had for fifteen months. Amusingly they failed here as well, and the cars were freed! So, four people walked free from a court case that seemed a foregone conclusion to most. Very few observers thought the Huddersfield Four would get off. They themselves had prepared everything for long prison sentences. It just goes to prove that there is always a defence and the show's not over 'til the fat lady sings.

So what? What did this case show that warrants its story being told in such detail? What was special about this case? Perhaps not much; after all, its defence was incredibly specific to Rafiq's slaughterhouse and its history. But the trial was defended as most animal liberation trials would ideally be defended. It concentrated on the cruelty inflicted, it demonstrated that *this* was the crime, not any potential damage to the slaughterhouse.

Again, legal circumstances were exceptional because the crimes at Rafiq's were illegal under British law and because the judge was forced to allow the defence to explain this. In most trials, the crimes of the animal abusers are not illegal under British law, so the section 3 defence couldn't be applied. Although that is a legal point; the crimes of the Rafiq's are no worse than those of the huge chicken processing plants which churn out 'oven ready birds', 'fresh farm eggs', 'chicken nuggets' and the like. At least five people on the jury thought it was justifiable to burn down a slaughterhouse after seeing the extent of the cruelty there. That's five ordinary people, which surely speaks volumes.

The trial cannot be left without mention of the subject of racism. Mr. Rafiq is an Asian and his chickens go to the Asian community. It was always a fear of the defendants that some would see racist motives behind their plans for Rafiq's. But nothing could be further from the truth. That slaughterhouse was a disgrace by any standards regardless of race, colour or creed. What is also interesting was the prosecution's attitude. It was clear that they didn't give a toss about Mr. Rafiq or his son (their own witnesses). They never helped them in the witness box and openly laughed at them. At no stage were they defended by the prosecution. In the private words of one defence barrister: 'I don't think they (the prosecution or police) would've cared if fires had been started at the slaughterhouse, from racist motives as much as anything else.' One detective reinforced this in an overheard remark to a colleague outside court: 'There's so much shit coming out in there. Mind you, any Paki can lie for England.'

They never really cared for Rafiq or his property; they just wanted to nail the Defendants, which is one of the things that made this trial political. The state lost what they were after, which makes a pleasant change, and it cost around half a million pounds. And despite the inhuman environment of their courthouse, despite a formidable use of their rules, their laws, their evidence, on their terrain, 12 people found themselves unable to convict a group of individuals who never really denied conspiring to burn down a chicken slaughterhouse.

The Stonegate Ambush

> Animals are my friends—and I don't eat my friends. The worst sin toward our fellow creatures is not to hate them, but to be indifferent to them. That is the essence of inhumanity. A mind of the calibre of mine cannot derive its nutriment from cows.
>
> *George Bernard Shaw (1856-1950) Irish playwright, winner of the Nobel Prize for literature, socialist, feminist*

It was beginning to reach the end a chapter for me around the time of the raid at Rafiq's. I'd never made any secret of the fact I favoured criminal acts over violent exploitation, even speaking publicly to that end. I have little respect for the prized possessions of people who abuse or exploit other people, animals and our environment. Not then, not now, not ever. I rejoice at every action taken in defence of the weak and downtrodden. Surveillance teams watching homes in Oxford, Northampton, Manchester, Kent, West Yorkshire and elsewhere had seen me come and go. I had attracted a police following and I knew it. They were watching my home, monitoring my phone and following my car and friends were being arrested all around me. I had a number of curious experiences involving police surveillance that didn't result in my arrest. Some I dismissed as coincidence or a one-off, others spooked me.

Rather than be careful, I needed to stop what I was doing. But it never felt like a hobby, something to come back to when there's the urge or a spare moment. It's deadly serious and those who care need to give it their undivided attention, and now. For me, the way animals are treated is like a wound I have that won't heal. There is always some guilt there for not doing more. It was, and remains, my view that those of us who are fighting fit, young and able should use those assets to improve the world the best we can. I've felt most comfortable and at my most productive with the direct life-saving tactics of the ALF. Walking the streets and leafleting houses helps me fill gaps (and colour in my street map) but doesn't save the animals that farmers around and about are sending to slaughter tomorrow, or those suffering in lab cages or chained on concrete in back yards. Nor is it likely to affect their income much. I can't put aside the terrible suffering of the sublime animal kingdom, much as I'd like to.

It was October of 1991 and I was off to Kent to help Vivian Smith work on the *Arkangel* edition she was putting together. She was struggling, so I offered we spend a few days together and blitz it. It was one of those essential but tedious jobs and Viv felt burdened with it, but it gave me something useful to do while keeping me out of trouble for a bit. She had been around a while and was well known to the police from her involvement with the ALF, the SG and Ronnie Lee. Intelligent, articulate and respectable, someone who had would have otherwise been destined to a profession as a lawyer or similar, but had been exposed to animal abuse and did not wish to or could not stop her battle with it. Working mainly as the full-time editor of *Arkangel*, she always took time out for a spot of direct action. It helped her to relieve the pressure that inevitably built up as she sat for hours in front of a typewriter or sifting through endless news cuttings for the International News section and demo reports for the Local Group section. She needed to get out there and do something more hands on.

It transpired some time later that police had seen me enter Piccadilly train station in Manchester and order a ticket for Folkestone in Kent. A team of detectives didn't happen by me and travel there along with me because they had nothing better to do; it was rather that I was under observation by a team of detectives with nothing better to do. Funny that. I didn't think I was under such close observation at that point but wasn't particularly wary, because I wasn't necessarily planning anything illegal (although it could have happened spontaneously, as has been known on occasion…)

As it was, Vivian was under surveillance following a string of arson attacks in the Kent area, in which meat depots and the egg supply chain had been targeted and claimed by a woman with a regional accent. Once I arrived on the scene, two and two began to look more and more like four. Our arrangements were made over the phone so that kept the detective work to a minimum. Vivian had commandeered the use of a friend's house at Hythe while she was away. Sandra owned a neat semi-detached cottage that backed onto the English Channel. Detectives, meanwhile, had commandeered one for themselves and were firmly rooted upstairs in a house across the road from where they were monitoring all our movements. Operation Igloo was up and running, cameras and listening devices were in place. It was then just about patience, which neither of us had. Once our movements began to take in potential targets, their boredom lifted in line with ours.

One night, taking a break and looking around the area to see what we could see, we drove by a huge 150,000-bird egg farm owned by Stonegate Farmers at Stelling Minnis outside Canterbury. The farm is a

Using a drill to bypass door alarms.

Right: Shamrock Halloween demo in 1999. Sitting on this grass hill opposite the farm would soon be an arrestable offence.

Cat with electrodes rescued from Texas Tech Lab. Many horrors were exposed. For example the bones were exposed around some cats' eyes, and holes were cut into their windpipes. The cats were punished if they failed to learn to hold their breath whenever a tone sounded. The punishment came from a blast of ammonium hydroxide, which made them extremely uncomfortable and burned their eyes.

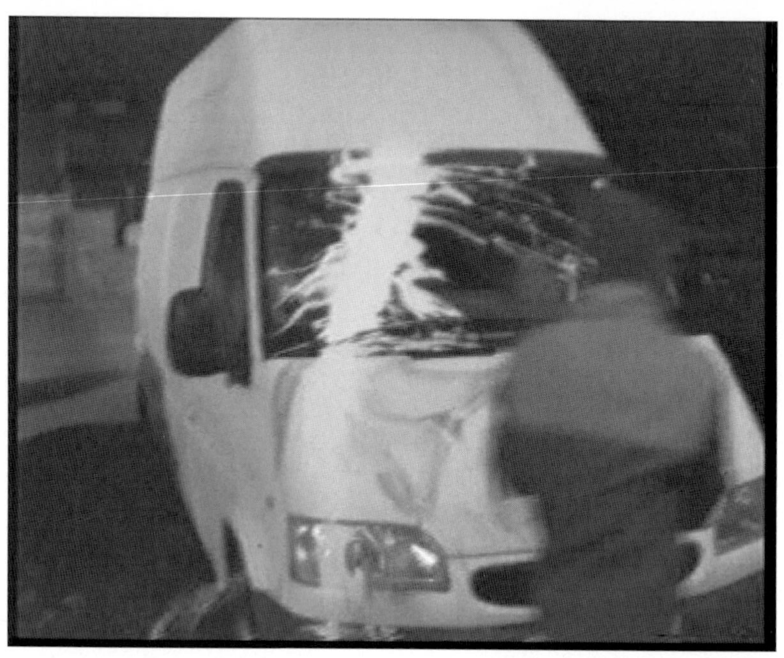

Above: Video image of ALF raider throwing paint over vehicle at vivisection supply company. 2003.

Above: Monkeys in restraining boxes.

Britches. Infant macaque monkey subjected to sight deprivation experiments at University of Riverside in California. He was rescued by the ALF in 1985. Here this so called scientific research is exposed to the world as an ALF raider shows him off.

Britches eyes were stitched shut with coarse thread and he had a sound-emitting contraption attached to his head. After his rescue he was treated by a sympathetic vet and later placed in the care of a surrogate mother at an animal sanctuary where he lives out his life in peace.

Above: Protesters block the traffic during World Day For Laboratory Animals march London. 1993.

Above: Protesters use steel tubs to lock on together and obstruct access to fur sales.

Above: A battery hen rescued from waste pits below the cages. These birds are often left to rot and become unable to move as waste builds up on their legs and solidifies.

Above: An activist attempts to breach the security of a vivisection lab during a public protest.

Above: Gambling with the lives of majestic animals: hundreds are maimed and killed every year. (Animal Aid)

Above: Civil disobedience. Dozens of activists lock on at HLS supplier using concrete filled barrels. UK 2001.

Above: Jill Phipps, killed while protesting against live exports.

Above: Two campaigners lock on at a vivisection supply company. Two years on both would be sent to prison for separate unrelated incidents after taking their protests one step further and becoming ALF activists.

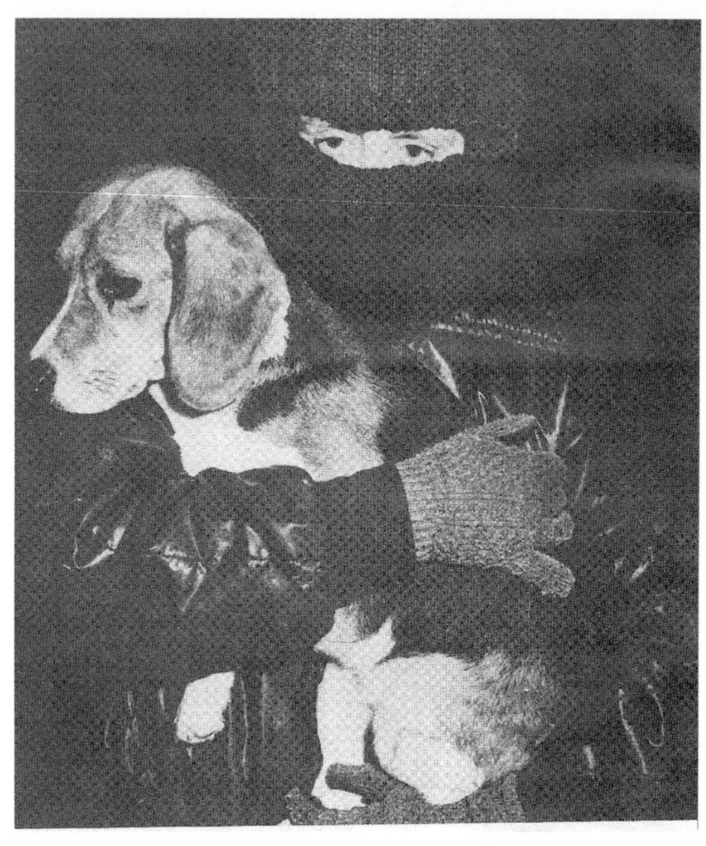

Above: Popular media image of female raider posing with a Wickham beagle. 1981.

Above: Female hunt saboteurs occupy the underground refuge of a hunted fox to prevent the huntsmen digging it out.

series of industrial warehouses packed to the rafters with caged birds, looking every bit like what it was: a concentration camp for chickens. We'd seen the lorries delivering eggs around the county, and the company had a reputation for the scale of their operation, so we decided we'd have a look. We parked up out of the way, grabbed a camera and walked onto the deserted site. The units were outwardly indistinguishable from warehouses on industrial parks and could have contained anything from cotton to car parts.

Inside, the difference was striking. Without a doubt, such places must count among the worst living environments on earth. The conditions were awful, but the story was much the same as it always is. Here the waste pits underneath the cages had not long been cleaned out, so it was possible to walk from one end to the other. Unusually, there were no birds dying in the pits. They'd probably been removed only a day or so before, scooped out with the waste and spread on the fields or firmly locked back in their cages. The sense of desperation of 50,000 traumatised birds crammed in cages was almost palpable, and you could taste the ammonia.

It had become something of a regular habit taking hens out of the cages at such places when the opportunity arose; it's a logical, rational, humane thing to do in my view. Most people who have a shred of decency are unhappy to see the way these birds are kept. Birds aren't meant to live in cages! The European Union have accepted the cruelty of the current battery system and intend to outlaw it in 2012, albeit allowing it to be replaced by something equally cruel but with slightly more leg room… There will still be rotting hens in the waste below the cages post-2012 and, of course, plenty in the cages. Profits will be affected and the price of those so-called fresh farm eggs will go up but there will still be endless numbers of birds in cages.

It felt pathetic just to take some pictures and a mere handful of birds from the stacks of them surrounding us. To do so was a proverbial drop in the ocean, but we were supposed to be focusing on the magazine. We couldn't help but notice the firm's fleet of ten refrigerated egg lorries parked at the far end of the site away from the bird units. Asking for it, you might say (well I might!). They weren't a priority at that moment because of the magazine… That's why we weren't finding homes for a load more hens. But it was a naughty thought for another time.

Well that idea stayed with us for the rest of the evening. Not only did the dreadful smell from the stinking bird prison stick around long into the next day, but also the dire situation of all the birds we'd left behind. The new arrivals at the Kent allotment were a delight to watch as they adapted to their new life in no time at all. They always do, bless 'em. They soon overcome what they've been through, however poorly they are. Fragile but hardy and quite ferocious too, when they taste blood. Not to mention their craving for dog poo, rotting flesh and slugs! They'll eat anything, and fight like gladiators for it!

Our attention was diverted. We started to reason that it would take no time at all to go back to Stonegate one night—sooner rather than later—slip some incendiaries under the wheels and get back home before the computer switched to hibernate. If one of us went out and bought what we needed while the other got on with the paperwork, then we'd lose no time and we might even get it done before we planned! No logic in this I know, but you can convince yourself of anything if you want. We were reeling from the fact we had been so close to the sadness in those units. We wanted to do something about it and it looked like a doddle.

Our guard was down at the wrong time altogether. There were now any number of target locations in the Kent area under observation in the hope of catching us in flagrante delicto. The police's suspicions had been further aroused from observing our movements. Being under suspicion was nothing new to either of us and wouldn't have mattered much had we not got side-tracked, but we had and were back at Stonegate a couple of days later with a rucksack full of incendiaries and some ill will. It was 9.30pm when we parked out of the way on a country lane, walked across the field, stashed the bag and sneaked onto the site to find to our surprise that there were cars in the car park, a large poultry transporter with its lights on by the sheds and workers dragging birds from the cages for slaughter. It was too late to do anything for them now and not the right time to be firebombing wagons.

However, quite why I don't know, we sat there in the bushes for an hour and looked on in silence. It would have made sense to call it quits there and then, but instead we decided to watch as the gang of men carted out by their feet a dozen distressed birds each with every trip, six in each hand. They'd appear in the light of the doorway and throw the birds into the compartments of the transporter like they'd been bad. They were so brutal. Rather than feeling empathy for the birds when they shrieked with pain and distress, they became inflamed and angry at them and handled them even more roughly. They laughed and shouted at the hens and apparently seemed to generally enjoy themselves. If life for the chickens had been cruel so far, then they were in for a truly terrible experience. As common as this kind of scene is, I'd never witnessed it personally, but it was as awful as it could possibly be. We were in a good position to film it but didn't have the camera. It was as much out of curiosity as despair that we stayed so long, hoping that maybe they'd finish soon and leave us to it, but these men will work through the night clearing out places like this.

An hour of this forced our hand. We whispered our options and persuaded ourselves. These people had no idea we were there, and the lorries were parked a good distance away from them. It would mean something of a kamikaze mission, but it would be possible to set on fire the whole fleet before the workers knew what was happening. The candle fuses would be abandoned. Instead, I would light the accelerant soaked sponge attached to the bottle of fuel and drop it into the vehicle. Petrol bombs rather than incendiary devices, but the result is the same and it would mean they would have no opportunity to intervene before the fires got going. It wasn't my preferred option, but it seemed like a good idea at the time. We'd come too far. Viv could keep an eye on that lot while I lay a device by each vehicle in preparation. That done, I'd centre punch a window and drop a burning device in the furthest one away, running from ten down to one, meet Viv and then be gone! By the time they realised what was going on it would be too late to do anything but watch, and we would be back home doing paperwork. What a great idea!

I'd got as far as placing the devices and was about to head back to start them off, when I noticed something move through the window of the up-and-over shutter of the loading bay. At first it looked like a head, like there was someone looking out! I squatted out of sight and looked again to see what looked like two heads, but this was some distance off, and with the shadows it was hard to tell for sure. With my next look across, it appeared there was nothing there. This was all too weird. I couldn't carry on without satisfying myself I was seeing things, so I ran across the car park, jumped up on the ramp and looked in. I prayed I'd been seeing things, but there were two figures crouched down in the dark behind the shutter. Fuck! It was time to leave. I turned and ran towards my escape route, radioing Viv as I went to tell her to go, leaving behind another ten incendiary devices for the burgeoning SOCO collection. We met on the jog back to the car, where I told her that I thought that workers or security guards in the loading bay had spotted me.

We were a little startled and keen to move on, so comforted by the racing of the car engine as we left the scene of the crime, safe at least in the knowledge that there would be no forensics on the devices we'd abandoned and were free to fight another day. We hadn't of course sussed this was a police ambush in the making and were having to improvise a way out of it. It was a disastrous night out for us, but we figured no one knew who we were and we were out of it. It was all we had to hold on to.

But once we started driving, car headlights came on in the lane behind us with its full beam lighting up the night. It couldn't be anything to do with us because the farm was ahead of us so we assumed hopefully that it must be a local off to the pub. That faint hope was dashed when a second car's headlights illuminated the dark night ahead of us and as it drew near, it was clear that it was blocking our way out. No doubt at all now that there was something very wrong here. I was about to bail out as we were forced to a stop. The passenger out front had jumped out of the car and was running towards us. But there was a gap in the road and Viv managed to ease the car out beside theirs by mounting the verge, somehow avoiding gouging the sides or running him over. We were racing away and they were reversing, one running. Some security team, this! It still hadn't dawned on us that we had run into something far more complicated than that. But there was no time to think about the detail. Escape was paramount. That they'd seen our car was a concern but something we could worry about later! We just had to get away from them for now.

'Left, left, left' at the junction, onto the road and past the farm gates. Suddenly not just one, not two, but five or six pursuing cars all quicker than ours. We were in a lot of trouble here and with little to hold on to but escape on foot. For me, there was something in that idea but Viv was quietly less hopeful. She wasn't a runner, but she certainly wasn't finished yet. Where to go, where they wouldn't be able to follow? There was nowhere within reach. But you have to try! Got to first get off the Roman road, which is as straight as a die for miles.

One of the pursuing cars was able to overtake after five miles at 90 mph, but before he could manoeuvre to bring us to a halt she was around him again. Next time we weren't so lucky. There's only so much weaving you can or should do at this speed in an Astra van designed more to carry goods than win a race. The second car that got past was able to slow us down before forcing a crash at which point we were trapped between cars in the middle of the night in the middle of nowhere. Happy days! Before we stopped, I had bailed out and was on the run. Viv followed very soon after, but I heard her yell out as one of her pursuers caught up with her and wrestled her to the ground before she had got far from the car.

I'd gone up the embankment and over the stock fence into the ploughed field like my life depended on it, and boy was it ploughed deep and boy did my life depend on it. I enjoyed my life and I wanted to keep it as it was. This had not been part of the plan. They weren't going to kill us, but spending years in prison is something worth avoiding. Running was hard, and to make things worse, torch beams were bouncing light off the dirt around me like in some wartime prison camp break out. Somehow I dodged them. The early sprint had slowed me down but had got me out of their immediate grasp. Not, I figured, far enough to lose any dogs they might set loose to track me down, but enough to give me time to think.

As quickly as I could, and quietly, I headed in a general direction over fields, through hedges and down into town. I had to cross over a dual carriageway at one stage and wait for traffic to pass. As I did, I watched one police car drive by with Viv in the back! There were a few of them but that one stuck out. It felt like someone was rubbing salt into my wounds. I felt so sorry for her. This was not how it was meant to be. And what about the birds? They'd be on Viv's mind too. It was great for me to be running free and I was obviously over the moon that I'd got away, but there was very little to be happy about when I sat and allowed myself to think about it.

The hens were what all this had all been about and we'd probably only delayed the final cut, if that, prolonging their agony. Would men still be dragging them from the cages in which they'd spent the first year of life? Would they still be breaking their limbs and terrorising them in the process, or had the police called the bomb squad in and sealed off the area because of our devices? I felt such sadness... Yet in comparison with the birds and Viv, I was having quite a pleasurable experience marching purposefully across open country in the middle of the night.

Physically and psychologically, I was comfortable working my way back home, although I didn't have a definite idea where I was, having only been near the area once in my life, and never on foot. And it was dark. Very dark! Over the next couple of hours, I made my way via hedges, power lines and road signs back to the address in Hythe where we were staying. I had no money on me and I'd got nowhere reversing calls to the two numbers I could recall that could help me, but the safe house was still safe and I had to go there to sort out things. Or so I thought.

I was so glad to make it back I didn't think enough about what was going on around me. I thought I was wary of everything and everyone but walked smack bang into the trouble I'd gone to great effort to evade. The lights were on. Sure we turned them off, I thought to myself. Sandra must have come back early. Or maybe we did leave them on. It was unlikely to be someone else, unless we'd been burgled! 2:1 against by my reckoning! I lost. I opened the front door and walked in. There was a policeman. Not an obvious one in a uniform but he looked more like one than a burglar, and the penny had finally dropped. He was as surprised as I was.

'Who are you?' he asked, knowing full well.

'Martin,' I blurted hopefully, smelling of petrol and not feeling much like a Martin. With the door behind me locked in place it was time to do some cute talking.

'Who are you?' I knew I didn't need to ask but it was a reasonable question, and whatever I said would've been futile now!

'I'm Detective Sergeant blah, blah, blah. I believe you are Keith Mann and I'm arresting you on suspicion of blah, blah, blah.' I heard detective sergeant and arresting you but the rest was just a blur of words. I knew it was time for me to stop talking. It was a rotten end to a rotten night.

Next stop Folkestone police station. In my experience, by far the most civilised of them all. The next five days were filled acclimatising and slowly acquiring decent food, clean clothes, stuff to read and being questioned about all manner of offences. Barry and Taff were in charge at Folkestone and probably the nicest policemen I have ever met. They were polite and honest, with no hidden agenda and the only coppers to whom I felt compelled to send Christmas cards from prison! Detectives, meanwhile, were raiding various addresses linked to both of us in Kent and the Northwest and collecting together anything useful to them or us, including the almost complete *Arkangel.*

It never did go to print. We were both initially charged with conspiracy to cause damage by fire at Stonegate, but this was later amended to include a series of similar but more damaging attacks around Kent. We were remanded in custody.

One address raided was Howarth's Farm and its outbuildings on a hill in south Lancashire, owned by Marilyn and Gerry Fahy. I had met this couple some years earlier while stalking the hare-killing Holcombe

Hunt. The police had closed public footpaths to bar access to fields that were being hunted in order to allow the hunt to do their thing uninterrupted and Marilyn was not impressed.

The Fahys were country dwellers, not at all like most of their neighbours who were silent when it came to the issue of hunting across their land so as not to stand out. Marilyn was particularly outspoken and hated what the hunt did, and with land in the middle of pro/tolerate hunt territory she was able to do something about it. We were well used to having our path blocked by the police and rather than enter into futile, time-consuming debates with them, simply got on with finding a way around but she had been utterly incredulous. 'Don't speak to me like that, officer! You should be bloody well ashamed of yourselves. That lot are leaving the dismembered bodies of wild animals around while you lot are treating these people like scum for trying to stop them!' To have such passion and anger on your side is empowering.

We were protected farm side for once, the gate keeping us in, rather than out! It had been a delight to see how flustered the police and the hunt were when told in no uncertain terms over the farm gate that sabs were permitted free access and were encouraged to blow horns and shout as much as was necessary and that the hunt and police were banned! 'Step one foot on my land,' was a very real threat that sent them away sheepish but thoughtful. Marilyn had officially become a hunt saboteur that day and made many new friends. It was the beginning of a fruitful association that would serve to assist many animals and activists in need of refuge before police came back to try and put a stop to it.

Now, years later, they'd found three rucksacks in the hay in one of her barns plus some tools and a few other items they thought suspicious and wanted to link to her. She was arrested and later charged with possessing items with intent to cause criminal damage and elevated to the imaginary position of an ALF Quartermaster in the Manchester Conspiracy hierarchy. It was some transition from a vegetarian housewife who had never been in any kind of trouble before, but she had no problem with this. Feisty as ever and tirelessly angry at the effort put into attacking animal activists, she growled on release from custody, 'Let the bastards prove it!' Swearing was new to Marilyn but they'd brought it out of her. They'd been trying to prove it; like a lot of others passionate about animals, she had been under observation for months and had had men sneaking around her farm, hiding in fields and gathering evidence of links to the ALF and campaigns that were so effectively highlighting animal abuse. The truth was they weren't her things but had been left there by unknown others for safekeeping.

Ballies In Bandit Territory

> Our lives begin to end the day we become silent about things that matter.
>
> *Martin Luther King, Jr*

By coincidence, on the night we were arrested in Kent, the core of the ALF in Northern Ireland was being detained under the Prevention of Terrorism Act. There were six being held in the notorious Castlereagh Interrogation Centre in Belfast where they were questioned about various ALF attacks in the province. After four days in custody, they were all charged with a variety of offences from criminal damage to arson and planting explosives. At the High Court, five of the six were granted bail on condition that they didn't communicate with each other, didn't enter the countryside, didn't ride in a vehicle unless with a member of the family or workmate and that they reside at a permanent address and sign on once a week at the police station.

The alleged ringleader, David Nelson, was already in breach of a suspended sentence and so was remanded in custody. At this time, the laws in Northern Ireland were different to those in England and there was no right to remain silent. Suspects under those laws, as with UK laws today, could remain silent, but to do so would infer guilt and anything a suspect failed to mention during questioning which was relied on later in defence would be seen as proof of guilt rather than a human right. ALF literature has always advised detainees to remain silent when questioned, as most of the evidence the police gather to prosecute usually comes from what those arrested tell them, but there had been little coordinated ALF activity before then in Northern Ireland, so this aspect hadn't been adequately addressed. Consequently, some of those arrested were duped by police who had used intelligence gained during eavesdropping to convince them that friends had grassed on them and so they made admissions, which not only implicated themselves but others too.

Given the situation, you wouldn't think it prudent to go sneaking around fields and farms late at night wearing a balaclava, but that didn't prevent the factory farming and blood sport communities from feeling the wrath of an ALF cell whose main focus was economic sabotage. A few months after the initial police raids, two more names were added to the conspiracy, making the Belfast Eight the fifth ALF case to come out of 1991, with more on the way.

The Manchester Conspiracy

> I am in favour of animal rights as well as human rights. That is the way of the whole human being.
>
> *Abraham Lincoln (1809-1865)*

Special Branch successes and ongoing surveillance were still having little adverse effect on the scale of action other than moving it around. Back in Manchester, the police carried out a series of raids, for no good reason and with no apparent evidential reward, but four more local campaigners who had been seen at 201 were detained and remanded in custody. Rhian Hopkin and John (Fran) Morgan were arrested at their homes on 10 December 1991. At Fran's house, police told magistrates they 'found' some OS maps, a catapult, some marbles, incense and some freezer food bags in various places, none of which were illegal or linked to any crime but could in some way be... perhaps. (Echoes of endless animal research papers describing the experiment's possible outcomes, which may on the face of it benefit human patients, but never do).

At Rhian's, they found nothing at all about which to make wild claims. The two weren't specifically accused of anything, but Operation Lance was being wound up and anyone on the list of targets who was not already in custody or exiled was rounded up for trial. To the disbelief of all (even the police were surprised, albeit pleasantly) Fran and Rhian were both remanded in custody, which is where they spent the next ten weeks before a judge agreed there was no evidence against them and that all the talk of terror plots and anarchist conspiracies was wearing thin and promptly released them on bail.

In court, you would have been forgiven for thinking that the police had smashed an international terror gang (or 'Britain's most successful band of urban guerrillas' according to Thomas Quirke on the ALF in the *Times Review*) and that the defendants were involved in arson, conspiracies, fanaticism, threatening behaviour, organised crime and the breakdown of society as we know it. Yet there was no evidence of anything of the sort! The police said they had detailed evidence of all this and that they would prove their case in due course. Merely hearing the police's considered opinion is often enough for a magistrate to decide to remand someone in custody; by playing safe, they ensure their own reputations, avoiding the possibility of making a wrong judgement by granting bail to a re-offender.

There was no need to manipulate the case against Max Watson and

Clare Rush, who had been arrested at 201 for breach of bail. He was supposed to have been in Newcastle, she in Oxford. But they had been in Manchester for a court hearing, which was permitted, but had outstayed their welcome in an attempt to spend a few days together. She was pregnant with their baby and they would have got no other chance before the trial. Her mistake had been to phone home to explain she'd be a day or two late. The police were listening and were wholly unsympathetic. They insisted magistrates lock the couple away for Xmas for their little indiscretion. And so it was. It was a vicious thing to do and caused a great deal of resentment amongst their friends and colleagues.

I was settling in to life behind bars and was relatively content in Canterbury Prison, when in early March 1992 I was arrested in the prison by Manchester's ALF squad and driven north for more questioning so they could reveal their hand. They had driven all that way to arrest me and weren't happy that I then initially refused to leave my cell at their request, as was my right. I refused to go voluntarily to reception to be arrested, so they had to spend the night in Kent before successfully obtaining a warrant for my arrest the following morning, something I was then unable to resist. These little victories made prison life bearable.

Back in Manchester, the case the police had been preparing unfolded. There were ten defendants singled out for trial on conspiracy charges and the documentary evidence complied by the prosecution was extensive, filling ten large ring binders and referring to four hundred witnesses and over 25,000 exhibits. Over time, the allegations, dates and details were altered so often we seemed to be served with a new set of these papers with each appearance in court. It appeared as though the prosecution didn't know what they were doing. We were half expecting something really juicy, concise and specific, but for the most part it was meaningless drivel except for a few snippets of real hard evidence. Even then, little of that could be deemed serious.

It was really quite a simple matter for them in many cases—where people were arrested breaking windows, for example—should have meant simply presenting factual evidence to link individuals to those offences. But there was something far more complicated afoot, a real burning desire to create something much more serious and make the whole thing far more threatening than it was. I was charged with:

1. Inciting others to pursue the aims and purposes of the ALF by destroying property by fire between 1988 and 1991.

2. Inciting criminal damage over the same period.

3. Damaging three lorries to the tune of £6,000 belonging to F. Strivens slaughterhouse in Oldham. This related to a hand written claim of responsibility I had sent to a local newspaper, which forensics had linked to me and was the most damning piece of evidence against me in the entire conspiracy.

4. Conspiring together with Rhian Hopkin and John Marnell to pursue the aims and purposes of the ALF by damaging property in Yorkshire, Cheshire and Derbyshire. The owner of a battery farm who disturbed prowlers breaking into one of their sheds detained Rhian Hopkin on site. Others made off, but John Marnell and I were arrested a little later in a restaurant nearby. Previously, hens had been rescued, but this time only the alarm system and a padlock had been damaged.

5. Conspiring with Hopkin, Helsby, Hughes, Marnell, Watson, Rush and Morgan to pursue those aims in Greater Manchester, Merseyside and Lancashire.

6. Conspiring with Marilyn Fahy to pursue the aims by causing damage. She was additionally charged with having in her custody or under her control three canvas bags, wire cutters, a hammer, two pairs of bolt cutters, plus two packets of incense sticks and two theatrical maroons (used in the theatre to simulate explosions and in some incendiary devices to cause a fire) without lawful excuse and intending the same be used to destroy property.

7. Terry Helsby and Alison Mckeon were accused of damaging property belonging to Riber Castle zoo. They'd been seen cleaning out the hired transit van on the morning after the raid on the Riber Castle zoo. Plus there was a statement from the hire company manager who said he saw a bag of tools in the back of the van when it was returned. The forensic evidence linking a pair of wire cutters found at 201 to cut fencing at the zoo squared the circle on this offence.

8. John Marnell, Max Watson and Clare Rush were charged with conspiring to damage property in Greater Manchester following their arrest for potting windows.

9. Terry Helsby and John Hughes were accused of conspiring to damage property in Merseyside on the night of their arrest. John Hughes was additionally charged with conspiracy with others unknown for driving a car into Andrews butchers.

10. Fran Morgan was accused of having in his custody or under his control a quantity of incense sticks, some plastic bags, a catapult and a quantity of marbles and ball bearings with intent to cause damage. The

case against Fran Morgan was created by the fact that incense sticks and catapults have been used by some in the ALF, coupled with his association with other animal activists.

There was a lot to think about and a lot to plough through, but very little to worry about. There were endless promises about more evidence to come; damning stuff that would apparently see us all locked away for years, but it was slow in coming. The total cost of these offences was really quite small, but the general conspiracies and incitement charges were designed to give the impression of something far more substantial and worthy of greater sentences than one would expect for rescuing a few animals from a zoo or breaking some windows. But fitting them all together was far from straightforward for the highly motivated ALF team at the Crown Prosecution Service.

There was a comprehensive spreadsheet setting out the comings and goings into 201, showing when each of us called, for how long we remained there and who else was with us during the eight month observations on the address. It was somehow impressive, a huge project in itself that must have taken an enormous amount of work to compile but not worth the vast amount of paper it was written on. It proved nothing alone, but coupled with the evidence they would present of conversations allegedly overheard inside the flat, it would make the case watertight. Allegedly—now there's the rub!

There was, yet again, great police reluctance to reveal that electronic surveillance had been used, but without it, they could not begin to prove the great Manchester Conspiracy and months of surveillance would have been wasted. For reasons better known to themselves, detectives had destroyed the recordings they had made during the many months of eavesdropping on 201 due—they said—to their poor quality. Instead, they intended to rely on hand-written transcripts they said they had made of conversations, which they said they had (allegedly) overheard. These, the prosecution claimed, would be clearer than the poor quality recordings and would better further their case!

We thought that a bit weird. The bugs could arguably have been useful evidence, but relying on hearsay was not going to further their cause in a court of law, which didn't seem to leave them with much of a case. Undeterred, they prepared with vigour.

It would be hard to believe that the ambit of their listening devices was the problem, given they had had so many months to sort it out and replace them with something better. More likely, there was nothing in the recordings to prove their case. Their problem was possibly due to the fact that early on in their operation, we had got wind that there were observations on 201 from sightings made of different couples entering the flat next door and a tip off from a neighbour about police enquiries. When the transcripts finally materialised, there was clear indication of the fact that we were wary of police surveillance and some of the visitors to 201 and residents had even engaged in overt verbal teasing of the snoops and occasional banging on the listening wall!

Throughout the transcripts the police noted: 'Music turned up loud, unable to hear.' There was a conspiracy going on within those walls, it is true, but mainly aimed at keeping private conversations private. One or two written entries did suggest suspicious conversations were taking place but only teasing snippets were logged: 'Some conversation re. 'Burning down' (not able to make out clearly what is said).' And then at 12.10pm one day: 'Green' was overheard to says something about …sabbing…' and went on to say: 'You like making firebombs.' Peculiarly, this incriminating sentence, or what there was of it, was actually the pick of the crop but was scribbled out after it was written. It was what someone said, or wasn't it? We never did find out. Harris on another occasion is said to ask: 'Have you got some?' Unidentified Male replies: 'Yes.' Harris again: 'Firebombs?' U/I male: 'Yes.' Nothing else is heard. Late one evening the spies in the wall note the music was put on very loudly but odd bits of conversation could be occasionally heard, the most helpful being Carl's enquiry: 'Where would be the best place to plant one?' It's not known to what he was referring, whether it be begonias, tomato plants, hunt supporters or those incendiary devices everyone was talking about in the bugged flat. Given the number of so-called extremists living and visiting the centre of the conspiracy, all of this really was a bit of a poor show.

And that was it as far as evidence of the global conspiracy went. Oddly enough, it was people not involved in the final line-up that allegedly contributed those more interesting snippets. The best the police got from the suspects in the trial was personal baggage, the kind of things people say to each other in private and the arguments. Following a row between one couple, the officer with the headphones used his pen to note, 'This looks like the end for Max and Clare,' then added further snide comments about their once private lives.

The allegations of incitement in Counts 1 and 2 were the most serious for me and were made up of wads of material that they suggested proved that over a number of years, I had encouraged others to break the law. Investigators had used a voice expert and a hunt supporter whom I knew well to identify my voice from a recorded interview with four masked men in a *World in Action* documentary during which, amongst other things, explanations are offered about the department store firebomb campaign. There were no claims of responsibility made during the interview, only some comment about the attack and the reasons for it. It was on that basis that I was charged with incitement to commit arson.

While I make no secret of the fact that I consider the saving of lives paramount and the open discussion of issues about animal abuse fundamental to consciousness-raising, there was nothing in the evidence to prove that I had actually encouraged anyone to do anything. It is my overwhelming view that it is animal abuse and a corrupt system that incites law breaking to help animals, nothing else. Certainly every activist I have spoken to was driven to act by what they saw, and not because of something they had been told to do.

Amongst the piles of police 'evidence' against me, there were a handful of copies of *Interviews With ALF Activists* which the police had found in Kent, and which they alleged I would have distributed although they had no substantive proof of this. There were many animal rights magazines, material related to *Arkangel*, news cuttings and videos—all taken from places I'd been at, together with recordings of numerous interviews in which I could be seen speaking in support of direct action. These apparently all pointed to my 'state of mind' and my intention to incite criminal damage, which was key to the prosecution's case.

They said that ALF actions were reported in some of the publications that may have been in my possession and may have been passed on to others by me. The story was that I was therefore central to a wide range of offences and told to expect between 15 and 18 years in prison! Me! What on earth had I done to warrant that? What had any of us ever done that would earn us the terrorist label that many have pinned on us? To my knowledge, all that any genuine activist, including myself, has ever done or attempted to do is their utmost to address very serious issues of animal cruelty. Any suggestion that anything they have done comes close to being as awful as that cruelty, is derisory.

There has always been little if any comprehension of the fact that we are driven to act because we are—not to put too fine a point on it—grief-stricken by the appalling suffering we have witnessed. There is little chance of any income from this career choice, little satisfaction for those seeking personal glory or the comforts of material wealth or possessions. Activists are and always have been drawn together simply to better the lot of animals, but those prosecuting claimed we were professional, dangerous, organised and ruled by a command structure with generals and foot soldiers and a Quartermaster! There were a lot of claims but understandably (given that they were the fabrications of delusional thinking) little substance to back them up. Originally, the Manchester trial alone had been predicted to drag on for two to three months, but there were other considerations for the newly ordained CPS ALF Coordinating Committee, whose role it was to cripple the ALF through nine separate cases involving nine police forces and 21 defendants. The added bonus of a successful outcome for the prosecution was of course that it would show their 'men' in a favourable light: the bigger and better organised we had been before we were crushed, the greater the glory for all concerned on the prosecuting side. And of course those industries that are the focus of ALF attention will be assured that the problem is being resolved.

The Committee's duty was to manage the complexities of each case and decide the correct use of evidence that overlapped across cases and ensure it was all kept simple. That was the theory, but we witnessed something completely different unfold, beginning with the immense amount of work they had created for themselves by producing endless bundles of evidence in succession. It was chaotic and disorganised and driven by obsession. There was little rational consideration of the facts, just pressure to put to trial as many people as possible and lock them away for as long as possible. As a movement, we may be poorly funded and sometimes poorly organised, but it's little wonder compared to the way this operation was conducted that the Animal Liberation Movement has those watching over it so flustered! There's no excuse for highly paid civil servants to mess things up so badly and it isn't really funny, although in this instance we did laugh!

Initially, Kevin Goodwin, the possessed CPSALFCC prosecutor, had wanted all his eggs in one basket, with one huge trial involving all twenty-one defendants—including me at centre stage—and him at the helm of the proceedings. Goodwin, or Muppet as he became known, intensely disliked everything we stood for and saw the promise of great political capital in our downfall, and the resulting delights of seeing his name in lights. We were able to monitor this sickness through our legal representation coupled with his erratic public performances. However, those working with him—who were also of course striving to secure convictions and heavy sentences—could see the error of his ways and vetoed his grand plan for something more manageable. The only viable link in all of this was the fact that all of the defendants were vegan and active in animal protection; investigators could not prove any other connecting principle to make this conspiracy look good. To Goodwin's dismay, the Committee decided that six separate trials should be held at crown courts in Derby, Maidstone, Manchester, Leeds, London and Northampton. As a result of further complications, the Manchester trial was subsequently split into two, with the various conspiracies going to a jury in September 1993 in Manchester and my incitement charges put to trial the following spring at the Old Bailey in London.

The monstrous show trial, which some had envisioned, based on the evidence the police had laid before the prosecution, looked less and less likely at every court hearing. It was not what Muppet Kev had wanted, and he wasn't a happy man.

In Maidstone Crown Court, things were moving quickly. Suggestions that we were responsible for similar attacks had been rubbished during the cross-examination of the forensic expert, who on paper appeared to be saying that devices used in various other attacks in Kent were constructed by the same people that had built the devices found at Stonegate. When questioned by the defence at the committal hearing, he agreed he was unable to confirm this with any degree of certainty and that the makers of the other devices could have simply used the same blueprint. In the absence of any further evidence, there was nothing to link us to anything other than Stonegate, and the conspiracy was dropped in exchange for guilty pleas to a charge of attempted arson. A not guilty plea was to complicate matters further, as the Kent case would be joined to the Manchester conspiracy. As the evidence was strong, in order to limit the damage we pleaded guilty to the one count to claim a reduced sentence.

But Judge Felix Whaley wasn't a happy man either. He didn't care for deals or giving credit for guilty pleas and he really didn't like those who did these kind of things to help animals. He was persuaded by legal argument to let my sentence be deferred to Manchester so that I would get just one sentence all in one go, which would apparently benefit me, but that was as reasonable as he got. He then became completely unreasonable towards Viv and let rip about those of us 'waging war' on our fellow citizens. He was absolutely disgusted by our behaviour. So disgusted, in fact, it left little room for him to be any more disgusted about anything anyone else did to fellow citizens. His view was that people had the right to do what the hell they liked to animals if the law said it was OK to do so. These crimes were as bad as anything he'd ever seen. And so on and so forth. He was angry. His opinions were forthright and after half an hour, quite irritating. How appalled can one man be at what we tried to do? Very! When he'd finished, he gave her a massive six years which was as excessive as his rant and he gave her no credit for pleading guilty.

In part, this was because she'd had a four-year sentence previously, at Sheffield, and clearly hadn't learnt her lesson, so he wanted to see if six would sort her head out and send a message to others. This was a bit of a shock and the second biggest sentence ever for an ALF activist at the time. A reduction on appeal was predicted by observers due to the extent of his rant and his over-concentration on warning other people, but it wasn't to be.

The legal complications in Manchester, meanwhile, were immense, but for us, something to gaze on in wonder. We were able to enjoy the little courtroom victories that shone some light on dark drawn-out proceedings. We wanted access to all the unused evidence, but the police weren't prepared to show it. The judge, a man called Alliot, was a nasty aggressive little creep, into sheep farming and county pursuits and he didn't like any of us one bit. He and the prosecution agreed that we shouldn't be allowed access to any of the 50,000-page deep, mountain of unused documents. This made a mockery of the process. He claimed he was 'shocked' by what he'd seen in this material laid before him by the police and denied it to the defence. But shocked by what? No one had done or been accused of anything that would shock a High Court Judge, so what did they show him that was so terrible? Whatever it was, it made him hate us all the more.

We wanted access to the missing tapes or other recordings that might completely disprove the conspiracy theory. After celebrated cases, (such as those of the Guildford Four, the Birmingham Six, the Bridgewater Four, Judith Ward and Stefan Kisko who had all served the equivalent of life sentences before being exonerated) in which people had been wrongly convicted due to police withholding evidence, the laws had in theory been changed so that all evidence could be made available to defendants. Of course, and probably inevitably, given the political climate we live in, the rules have since been altered again to prevent this free access to all potentially relevant police information. At the time of this case, however, there were still ways for the police to get round this 'problem', and naturally, regardless of any changes in the law, there has been and will always be a system in place that can ensure that information can be withheld from the defence.

The prosecution here were readily granted Public Interest Immunity (PII) certificates by the judge, so they didn't have to release a whole mountain of unused evidence. They sought to protect any informants, observation points, novel or unusual surveillance techniques, ongoing investigations and national security, amongst others things. To support their claim to retain certain documents, they argued it would be impractical to disclose everything because of the amount of unused evidence in the Lance investigation. They said they didn't want to burden us any further by giving us what we wanted!

This all took years of preparation and planning, and many months of legal wrangling, and for months after my arrest I was in custody somewhere or other with lots of time on my hands—so much time, in fact, that I began to start work on constructing this book, the growing material for which followed me throughout my incarceration. I had other plans too!

Escaping From Custody

> True benevolence, or compassion, extends itself through the whole of existence and sympathizes with the distress of every creature capable of sensation.
>
> *Joseph Addison (1672-1719) British poet, playwright, member of Parliament*

One of the most unsettling aspects of my punishment was to be moved around the prison system with great regularity, sometimes not staying in one place for more than a few days. Messing up my visits, losing contact with friends and losing property were all part of it. This didn't help the preparation of my defence either. I had so much property, a lot of it legal documents, that this tactic caused headaches for prison staff and me. Some officers are incensed that inmates should be allowed anything other than bread and water and bloody well enjoy it, let alone luxuries like a radio or Game Boy. Some literally frothed at the sight of my haul and would throw things aside in anger—'Can't have this... Can't have that.' I had a massive amount of legal documents, material for this book, books, food (if you are strict vegan you hoard and take what you can wherever you go) and toiletries that they wouldn't provide (ditto) letters, tapes and clothes. I was on remand, and since I had not yet been convicted, I was therefore allowed all of it in my cell. Sometimes my property went with me on a move, other times it followed on: days, weeks or months later. Once I got someone else's; he was with mine 200 miles away in Yorkshire.

They would want to search and document everything at every stage of the journeys, and it got to the point where I didn't even bother to unpack when I got allocated a new cell somewhere. I'm sure they started to monitor this and left me places just long enough to get settled, start spreading things around the cell and make it homely before carting me and my stuff off again! Some staff refused to help anyone with more than a handful of belongings to move them. They'd spend an hour making a five-minute trip getting me to or from reception, watching me relay my bags from one locked gate to the next and the next rather than offer any kind of help to speed things up. It was their protest, but I was in no rush, which wound them up; the more they got riled, the more I clung to my precious comforts.

Not that I had any choice when they ghosted me in only the clothes I wore; such was the rush to get rid of me one time I was wearing just a pair of shorts when they took me out of my cell! There was one Home Office rule that said prisoners should be permitted to take legal files when ghosted but, like most others, this was ignored at will. It was something of a battle to keep on top of anything when moved eighteen times in as many months from one end of the country to the other, and the early book draft in particular was a constant cause of stress once it had started to take shape, and quite how I avoided losing it during this enforced nomadic interlude is still something of a mystery! Like I said, I had other ideas on my mind as well, and juggling the two projects kept me busy.

My intention had always been that if I were ever imprisoned, I would seek to escape and from the day I was arrested that was on my mind. Prospects were not looking so good for me: one attempt at arson—worth a couple of years—had grown into a series of broad-based conspiracies worth double figures. Any hope of bail had evaporated with the hysterical overreaction following each successive appearance we made in court, where we were presented with new, or even rehashed, allegations. Being held in a modern prison makes the notion of escape a dream, but when one is on the move to and from police stations, the idea isn't so unlikely. After an initial period in prison custody and a court appearance, I found myself locked out of the prison due to a cell shortage (between leaving for court in the morning and returning that evening my cell was taken by someone else) and instead taken into police custody.

And there I was to be traded for months as the forces cashed in on the Home Office compensation scheme for the care and containment of its cell-less inmates or Operation Container, as it was known. The more inmates they got through the door the more they got paid. Not all police custody officers were as security-conscious as they should be, and most weren't versed in housing prisoners for long periods. That was something myself and others were keen to exploit before the inevitable happened and we ended up back in the prison system. Having said that, whilst Viv and I were being transported to and from court each week from our respective prisons early on in our remand, we had every opportunity to leg it every time we walked from the police station at Folkestone to the vans out in the yard. But we were being escorted by either Barry or Taff who didn't want to handcuff us and had treated us with so much respect during our stay that it just wouldn't have been right to leave them in such a predicament. Given the effort I made later and the circumstances of my detention, this sounds an odd thing to do, but I would react the same way again put in the same situation. Respect is a trait not to be abused.

By the spring of 1993 I'd been locked up for well over a year and I hadn't been to the dentist for about 11 years, purely out of fear. I'd had a bad experience with the gas as a kid and never come to terms with it. On one occasion while at school my mum tried to take me back, but we got as far as the door and I legged it. I decided while held indefinitely in a police station that it was time to overcome my fears. They were good at responding to reasonable requests at this place. I told them I had toothache and they booked me an appointment with a local dentist. My teeth were fine, but out of necessity the dentist had become my friend and may give me an opportunity to make a break for it. Two officers in civilian clothes escorted me, top half anyway, but you could still tell they were coppers! I was handcuffed all the way but was expecting to be let off at some stage. Then I would make my move.

I was handcuffed all the way there and in the chair was still cuffed to one officer with the other cop hovering nearby. I told the dentist where the pain was, he prodded and poked and found no sign of decay, and so that was that. Still cuffed. I started to think I was going to hit a brick wall if there were nothing in need of attention, so I asked him about these two fangs I had that had grown over the first set in the front of my mouth. They were supposed to come out years before, but that meant going to the dentist, so they had just grown in front of the others instead and weren't really a problem. He poked and prodded and then said to me 'I could pop them out now if you like,' which filled me with utter dread. No one 'pops out' strong healthy teeth, they use force and pliers to yank them out, leaving gaping holes and blood. But that wasn't what I was here for, I was going to escape before it came to that and I expected the dentist to want me unshackled whilst he worked. 'OK,' was my nervous reply. With that said it dawned on me that there was such a fine line between freedom and an extraction!

The Dentist began to prepare the instruments of torture and told my man on the right arm that he wanted the cuffs off because he needed to work from that side. Bingo! They um'd and err'd for a brief moment and asked the dentist if they could cuff my left wrist instead. No, don't do that! 'Yes, that'll be OK', replied the dentist. Er, no it won't! With the dentist on my left side, the other cop came to stand by his side and took hold of my free arm, while the other undid the cuffs and transferred them to him, just like that! A feeling of panic started to set in now. Extraction! I was trapped and about to be tortured. I um'd and err'd to myself, thinking of a way out of this that wouldn't leave me looking like I'd lost my bottle, but before I could think of anything that wasn't the truth I'd closed my eyes and been given a completely painless injection. I nearly enjoyed it! He yanked two huge teeth out minutes later and within an hour I was back in my cell with a mouth full of tissue and somehow seeing a silver lining in my flawed plan. It was good to have overcome my fear but that wasn't what I'd set out to do.

The next bid for freedom presented itself when I managed to get an appointment at the optician to get my eyes checked after a year or so in lighting conditions that are far from ideal for reading and writing. I hid on me some cash I had smuggled in, phone numbers I needed and I had prepared two friends to be expecting a call from me, one to pick me up and another to safe house me. There was no guarantee that I could get away then either, but I was certainly going to try. It was out of genuine concern for my eyesight that I had asked for a check up, but my eyes could wait if I got a chance to leg it.

Three uniformed officers escorted me from the station in Staffordshire and on leaving the reception area, their sergeant reminded them not to lose me and he notified me of my status in his nick. He had no inkling of my motives—it just isn't good practice to lose prisoners, whoever they are. I was handcuffed to one policeman at the station and still attached whilst walking into the opticians in the centre of Tamworth. In the van they took them off but locked me in. In the town centre, he draped a jacket over the handcuffs to disguise the fact we were cuffed together, but that would have only fooled those who thought we were holding hands! In the Opticians we were shown through to the examination room out back. My co-joined went in first, then I followed with the second officer and third, and finally the lady optician coming in behind.

Attention to detail, eh? With hindsight it's easy, but in the time it took to seat everyone and arrange the removal of the cuffs (the essential ingredient in my plan) I'd switched off and it suddenly dawned on me that I had no idea whether the door behind me was now locked or merely shut. The optician was opposite me and seated at the furthest end of the room were my escorts who were no longer on edge, with the lady and I talking eyes and all of us shut in. I think their calmness threw me a little and I assumed the door must have been locked behind us. I could have gone through that door at any time over the next half hour. Had I known it was open, I would have done just that, and they wouldn't have seen me again, but I didn't want to get myself returned to a secure prison cell as an escape risk by running at the door, pulling it and finding it was locked. And it must be, or one of them would have surely stood in front of it! How stupid would they look back at the nick telling their sergeant they did just what he told them not to! And how stupid would I look and feel stood there, handle in hand, door in place, appointment cancelled! My best opportunity thrown into confusion by a brief lapse of concentration!

Focused as one can be on a closed door, I cursed myself mercilessly when the thing slid open without complaint, coercion or key at the conclusion of my eye test. We were heading back to nick and Curly Larry and Mo were attached to me again and on high alert. I was gutted, I felt so stupid. What was I thinking? I'll tell you.

What I was thinking about as we walked in and I noticed the testing equipment was whether I was going to get to look at one of those coloured pattern cards I was shown as a kid, the ones that reveal colour blindness. Lots of circles with numbers written in them in subtle colours. I remember I wasn't very good at it. I had trouble with reds and greens and have wondered if I'd do any better or worse if I was tested again but never have been. My eyes were OK but for a touch of short sighted in one, but my head was in a spin that night back in my cell as I mused over what had just happened. Or not.

Sometime after this non-event and after some deep consideration of circumstances, not to mention the help of the same friend who was on call to assist me in my non-escape, I managed to acquire the tools which, believe it or not, were to enable my cellmate Dean and I to dig our way out. (Steve McQueen, eat your heart out!) I had moved again and this police station was one of those that employed very green rural bobbies with no idea of the rules of the jungle. Most of them were easy going and polite but not meant to be in charge of tricky customers who wanted to be elsewhere. There wasn't much crime in the locality and there were just a few cells in the cellblock. We were allowed to have food brought in from outside to supplement the menu and sometimes the duty officer didn't even bother to check it. Amongst the treats we'd have delivered were Bacardi in the coke and hash in the dried fruit handed to us by the police! There was, it has to be said, a good atmosphere and no risk of a riot, but for security reasons, this was clearly not acceptable.

One night I was handed one such box of goodies, delivered to the front desk by 'Someone called Dave.' Dave was my mate who wasn't called Dave, and Dave had been shopping for food items that might allow someone to secrete a hacksaw blade and/or screwdriver, down the inner edge of a carton of juice for example or whatever. There were two possible ways out of here: one was through the cage on top of the exercise yard; the other was through the brickwork in the wall under the bench in the cell. It was one floor up and led onto a back street outside.

The fat greasy copper, the joker of the duty crew whom no one trusted, had handed me a sturdy vegetable box full of treats, from Dave, including the means to put to test an escape plan. The greasy one, incidentally, used to sit in the corridor outside the shower cubicle, arms folded, and watch prisoners come and go in hand towels. Others when on duty would sit facing the television, not at all interested in wet semi-naked men, but he was and he wasn't fussed who knew it. He was not someone you'd warm to but had given me a box containing not one but three tungsten carbide hacksaw blades and two screwdriver shafts, so I didn't care in the slightest if he'd seen my butt.

The tools were pushed, evenly spaced, into the corrugated lining of the box, which was itself full of vegan goodies. My cellmate told me he was a car thief, though I later discovered this was not the whole truth. He was a nice enough kid on the face of it though, and someone I was happy to escape with. Not as if I was ever going to see him again once we hit the street. I had loads to eat and drink and the makings of a way out. Like him or not, he was a meat eater and not sharing my food but we had a good night in together!

As you would imagine, we were straight to work the next day. A teaspoon was commandeered for use as a key for the Allen lock locking the hatch under the bench and the hacksaws blades dealt with the small welds permanently sealing it. I'd borrowed the spoon before and knew it worked. Inside, there was a dusty crawl space and water pipes before the outer wall and an air vent to the outside and freedom. The mortar around the bricks was old and crumbly and it was possible to dig it out, but we only had a couple hours each night between lock down at 11.00pm and the night staff returning around 1.00am to play table tennis upstairs. We could hear them, and they would surely hear us scraping away.

For four nights we dug away at that wall around the vent. It was hard going, but we were confident that with one more night's work we'd be able to kick out the bricks around the vent and drop to freedom. One chipping away, one listening at the door for the sound of a key swinger. If one came along to do a head count it'd be out by the legs, up with the hatch, lock it, then drape down the blanket on the bed. We'd be lying there reading: one on the floor, one on the bench, like we'd been there all night. It'd go something like:

'Evening lads.'

'Gov. Alright Boss.'

'Everything OK lads?'

'Yes thanks.'

It would be if you weren't here! In a minute he'd have checked every cell and be back watching TV or looking at porn in the office and we'd be working the tunnel. It was dark in the hole, but using a mini Casio TV wrapped in a sock and powered by a PP9 battery we had ample light. When we'd finished we'd seal everything up like new, with no sign of anything untoward: the tools stashed away, the welds replaced by blu tac and dyed with colour crayon.

What was perhaps most amazing about all of this was that other prisoners in adjoining cells knew there was something going on, but no one said a word. In prison there is little loyalty and a lot of inmates would do anything to gain favour. Telling tales on someone they don't know, or care for much, would be no concern to the majority in return for a cushy number or extra fags.

By early Wednesday morning, we had the things we were taking with us packed and ready to go. We were planning to break out the following night. A couple more hours chipping away and a hole would appear with a little pressure. How it came to be that at 10.00am we had two uniforms at our door repeating those immortal words, 'Get your kit packed lads, you're on the move,' I don't know. They weren't suspicious at all and could see the dismay in our faces, knowing we were happy to be detained in their cushy nick and added, 'Don't worry, you'll be back Monday.' The cellblock was going to be redecorated over the next few days so we would have to wait a few more days even if we had to bribe our way back into our cell when we returned. I offered that we could do the decorating, but there were contractors booked, friends of the duty sergeant by the sound of it.

Whatever the real reason, we ended up in some dive in a Yorkshire village and never went back to our tunnel, which was lost forever with the closure of that cellblock some years later. Dean, the car thief, I discovered some months later, was moved to the sex offender's wing at Strangeways, convicted of rape. The silver lining in another failed plan was that I wasn't responsible for his liberation.

I'd had a number of other opportunities to escape but for one reason or another, I couldn't quite fashion it. An idea Willie and I had in Wandsworth was to clamber up the bars of windows overlooking the exercise yard, onto the roof, down a drainpipe, then between the razor wire on top of a high wire fence and onto the perimeter wall. It looked straightforward enough if we could create enough of a distraction to get up onto the roof before whistles started blowing. Irish Willie was only five foot in boots and doing life for killing someone. He deserved to be there for what he'd done, but he was a good friend and good for a laugh. He was also something of a handful for screws to deal with. We thought about it for only a week. It did seem a bit obvious and we weren't sure why no one else had tried it. Then on the morning of New Years Eve, with my side of our wing locked up and Willie out on the yard without me someone else did try it!

There was a roar outside and everyone migrated over to watch as a young inmate followed our route and scaled those bars like Spiderman. Willie was outside my window, jumping around, pointing and going on. He was as mad as the screws. And why? It was his idea, it was a good one, he was doing life and he was probably now staying. However, it turned out the kid who'd spoiled our party was too. He made it to the perimeter wall but broke both his ankles as he landed outside. He was only free briefly and in a lot of pain and a more trouble. Sorry mate, but that was my silver lining. Happy New Year!

I spent months in police cells and nearly two years in total in custody before the conspiracy trial was finally listed for October 1993—two years after my arrest in Kent. It would be a relief to get on with it and know for sure, either way, what the outcome would be.

I was finally moved back into the prison system and found myself at the charming HMP Liverpool where I'd been before, where property allowance was at a minimum, where there were buckets for toilets, and from whence my escape opportunities were about to be whittled down to zero.

Since I'd first been imprisoned, I'd had issue with being doubled up with people who smoked. The bulk of cells are doubles in most remand prisons these days, apart from those of escapees or high-risk prisoners. I don't smoke and it was unpleasant to say the least to be locked up with someone who did and in prisons that's the majority. At one stage I was locked in a windowless police cell, 23 hours a day with a drug smuggler who also had in his possession hundreds of extra-long duty-free Benson & Hedges which were legit and he was allowed to keep and which he got through in a week! I'd never smoked a single cigarette in my life and I was ill. It was something of a joke for the odd unhelpful screw in charge to deliberately double non-smokers up with smokers. I was going through the complaint procedure but that is painfully slow. Prison is unpleasant, but lung cancer is an excessive punishment and breaking point came for me when the 50 roll-ups a day warehouse burglar left and a chain-smoking, drug dealing hippy moved in.

I asked to speak to the prison governor again and again but he'd already lied to me repeatedly and was too busy to talk to me. 'Put in an application,' was the usual response and then to ignore or lose the application. I'd put in plenty and all that was happening was the situation was getting worse. I'd had enough and made my mind up to get myself categorised an escape risk and put into a single cell. I told visitors on the Monday my intentions for later in the week and asked for the press and my solicitor to be contacted. I was going to tell my mum on the Wednesday visit that I was only going to dig out a superficial hole in the wall of my cell, let them find it and nick me for attempting to escape. She was and always is incredibly supportive and proud of me and would always worry herself silly and beg me not to anything likely to get me into more trouble. Too late for that though, my mind was made up. The reality is that there's no easy way of digging through the strengthened walls of the modern prison with the tools and time available, but I would be able to get my way with a little hole. But before I set about my plan the strangest thing happened.

22 June 1993 was a Tuesday and set to be just another unremarkable day behind the door writing and reading letters, books, the paper, with perhaps an hour in the gym thrown in and maybe ten minutes on the phone. A shower if it was Friday. Maybe. Food wouldn't be anything special, but it was something to look forward to all the same, and broke the day up three times. Other lads would hand me their fruit knowing I ate loads and because they didn't eat any. That's a good day in Walton. But I hadn't even had the chance to get out of bed when this escort screw opened the door, which was now attached by chain to his trousers like a shiny jingly umbilical cord, and asked with knowing sarcasm if I was packed and ready for court. Duh!

He was now telling me to pack my kit so I could cart it to reception to be rifled through and documented again and thrown onto a van for a court hearing I knew I didn't have, in order to bring it all back again that evening and go through the whole performance in reverse and often having confiscated something that was permitted previously. I'd been there before and done that and would rather not, thank you. I got up and located a wing screw I knew to question my appointment, he told me I was going to court cos the computer said so and would be back that evening. He agreed that I could leave my things if I wanted after I reminded him of the amount of stuff I had.

Court listing or not, if your name appears on the prison service computer, then its desire is your destiny. My destiny was Reception, where it transpired there were a number of Manchester detectives lurking, waiting to arrest me over another matter. Not safe anywhere!

Some of my prison musings had found their way into their hands and they wanted to talk to me about them—as if they didn't have enough to be getting on with! Well, greed is the downfall of man and so it was for the Boys From Lance. It was back to Stretford police station for yet more questioning, which was procedural but pointless because I wasn't going to say anything to assist these people fixated with doing me harm, and well they knew it.

I was booked in to Stretford and had my laces taken for the first time in all the time I'd been in custody—I was told so I didn't try to hang myself. What were they going to put me through? It wasn't that bad last time I was here! As it was I spent the day bored, locked in a bare cell with nothing to read so I fashioned myself some laces for my trainers and was questioned briefly before being charged with attempted incitement. At 5.00pm, I was told by PC Smith to pack my things as they were taking me to the Central Detention Centre above the magistrates' court across the city for yet another appearance the next morning for the latest charge to be added to the list. The only request I had was that I be able to call my mum to tell her to cancel her visit for the next day because more than likely I wouldn't be back in time, but they wouldn't allow or make the call because they were in a rush to get me out of the way before rush hour kicked in and told me to ask at the CDC. I'd been there before too and done that and there is not a hope in hell.

This got my back up. I wasn't cooperating much before but I wasn't even going to bother being polite now. It was bad enough my mum going through the visit procedure at all, but she did insist and I didn't want her going there for nothing. But PCs Smith & Morby were in too much of a rush for their own good, and the visit was about to be cancelled.

PC Morby recalled later: 'My police van was parked in the secure yard (sic) at Stretford custody office. PC Smith escorted the prisoner MANN out into the yard while I locked the adjoining gate.'

PC Smith: 'I then walked with MANN to the rear of the police van, taking hold of him by the right arm. As I opened the rear doors, MANN turned away from me, breaking my hold on his arm.'

PC Morby: 'I next heard PC Smith shout, and saw the prisoner on top of the gate which leads into the car park and then out of the police station.'

PC Smith: 'I turned and saw him jump onto the gate which he climbed over.'

PC Smith: 'I climbed over the gate and chased after MANN onto Talbot Road where I saw him turn into the North Trafford College. I lost sight of him then. At the rear of the college I saw him running into the bushes at the rear of Trafford Town Hall. During the chase other patrols were made aware by use of my personnel radio.'

MANN: 'Puff pant. Hee hee! Puff pant…'

Informing other patrols didn't prove very fruitful, as it was nearly a year before he saw me again! And that fixed my passive smoking problem! I had noticed the lack of cover on the secure yard previously: three walls, a camera and a twelve foot iron gate but no roof cover. That wouldn't have mattered if they'd handcuffed me, as is procedure. It says so clearly on the wall on the way out of the door: All Prisoners Must Be Handcuffed Before Leaving The Station.

When I landed the other side of the gate, one of my improvised shoelaces broke, and I lost my training shoe (a brand new one at that) but it didn't stop me running. Nothing much would have. I didn't have a plan worked out, it must be said. I had no money, and safe phone numbers I could call were few and far between. I could recall none at that moment! PC Smith last saw me disappear through a hedge, which cut my face and arms but gave me the extra time I needed to lose myself. I ran through a works car park, across a main road and past the Old Trafford cricket ground, then over another big steel fence into another company car park where I thought my luck was in on spotting an unlocked bike in the cycle bay. It was an ancient iron thing but it beat walking. Except that once I got moving I realised there was nowhere to go because of the security barrier at the entrance to the car park. I cycled, instead, to the furthest corner from the road and climbed the chain link fence onto rough ground, which took me onto a railway line and ultimately Manchester city centre. The bike was more of a hindrance now, so I dumped it and headed away from the mainline down a disused track heading east.

It was still light; looking like I did and considering what I'd just done, I figured I needed to be somewhere out of sight until it was dark.

There were going to be a lot of people looking for me, some with dogs, but the scent wouldn't be good around all that traffic and the various obstacles should have helped. Apart from car drivers at the traffic lights on the main road, no one had seen me since the hedge behind the Town Hall. A mile on in various directions and I was able to hide up under an old railway viaduct. I was thinking fast, but there was a lot to take in and I didn't know the area very well. Tuesday had exceeded all expectations! I hadn't stopped running and needed to sit down and rest. I was a bit giddy and rather pleased with myself, not least because I had only one trainer on and they still didn't manage to catch me!

I had a lot to do before I would be safe, but at least my life was back in my hands. I was anxious not to be spotted and was suddenly really excited about my prospects. I stayed there for the next five hours, buzzing on adrenalin. I became calmer as time passed, chuckling intermittently to myself as I took stock of what I'd just done.

They'd be feeding tea at Walton! Chips with that vegetable stew from Monday now wrapped inside pastry. The lads on the wing would be pleased for me and stealing my stuff if they got half a chance. If not, the staff would have it. That'll be goodbye book transcript for sure. There would be the same mixture of joy and horror amongst friends and officials on the out. Lovely!

I heard the police helicopter overhead panning the area not long after I settled, so I sat huddled under the concrete viaduct, confident I was safely hidden. Sure enough the thing soon floated away. I was in the best place I could hope to be, and staying put. After I found an old Dr. Marten boot in the bushes, it dawned on me that this was absolutely meant to be. It was what I was looking for! Not quite, but similar. This was old. It was soggy, rotting and it had a hole in the sole the size of a 50p where it had been worn away through years of use; it was home to numerous insects, it was a size too small and for the wrong foot and it was leather, but I loved it and it was all mine! It was an improvement on the dirty wet sock I had on. I gently evicted the occupants, apologising, and laced it up using half my good lace and it was perfect in its own way.

I sat there waiting for nightfall, thinking about all the things I'd dreamt about doing one day and now suddenly I could, at will. I watched a plump dog fox walk past beneath where I was sitting, going about his business oblivious to my presence. He walked by a few times and I held my breath in case I scared him away. When it was sufficiently dark, I set off in the direction of Manchester via the railway line. I had to head north to find sanctuary and to keep out of sight while doing it. The police knew what I was wearing and my face would be public again as they searched for me, so it was a case of keeping to the back streets, parks and so on. I nearly came a cropper before I even reached the city centre and got the shock of my life as, with the wind blowing into my face, an express train came hurtling from behind. I didn't hear it until it was virtually alongside me and let me tell you my feathers were ruffled and it shook me out of my aura of smug complacency in a flash! Being splattered by a train would've have been a dreadful conclusion to my escapade and I didn't come close twice.

I kept my wits about me and moved quickly towards the city, hoping the train driver didn't report me. Once there, avoiding traffic as best I could, I found a phone box and tried to reverse the charges on the one safe number I could recall, but there was no one in. Instead I made my way across the city streets and parks looking for someone I could ask for a bus fare. Oh, that would be something, a warm bus ride home but no one wanted to help this scruffy beggar so I gave up on that idea. I grew up around here, so I knew the safest and quickest way to get where I wanted to be, and appreciated it would be a trek of eight or nine miles and take some time using the back streets, parks and alley ways.

As indeed it did. It was around 6.00 am and light again when I rested up for a while near my destination, close to Bolton, finding nourishment in a field of strawberries and water from a reservoir. It was all I had eaten since dinner the day before and I like to eat constantly if possible. Recharging, I watched the street for a little while to make sure it wasn't being watched by anyone else and then tentatively approached the front door ready to sprint off at the first sign that someone might be looking for me. I knocked and Joanne's 70-year-old father answered. We'd met before, he knew what I did and knew I was in prison and probably deduced from my appearance that something wasn't as it should be, but he didn't ask. 'They're not here, Son,' he apologised. 'They're on holiday in Turkey.'

He was house-sitting and invited me in anyway, but I declined. It didn't feel right to compromise him. 'I'd better not, thanks anyway.'

'OK. Take care Son.' An hour later, the police were at the door asking after me as they had been at a lot of other places, but he hadn't seen me for years, he told them. His daughter and son-in-law were occasional protesters and he was appalled at the way they and others were treated by the authorities and had changed his view on the police's role in society. He was both ashamed of the fact it'd taken him so long to realise they were too often used for political ends and proud of himself for having it within him to change. I never saw him again as he died soon after our meeting.

I headed off to try Plan B, a mile away. I was by now very tired and anxious to get off the streets. Mavis lived here. I'd met her a couple of years before while re-homing dogs. We got on well and we met periodically over some animal or another, us helping her with her horse problems, her us, when we had rabbits or hens or something to evaporate away. We were both well chuffed to see each other. She assumed, as you would, that I'd been given bail or something traditional like that, so didn't wonder why I was on the doorstep again at an odd hour. She had been used to that. All she had to say when I told her I'd escaped was: 'Bloody hell! Good for you! Well let's make sure they don't get you back.' That was my intention and the message I got loud and clear from my co-defendants in Manchester who could see clearly the beneficial connotations of me not being in the dock with them in October. That could really mess things up for the prosecution case!

Within an hour I couldn't eat anything more and was feeling tipsy from the wine and was about to get in the bath when Mavis's daughter rang to tell her that I'd escaped and was on the news. She met my glass with hers and drank a toast straight after a convincing 'Has he really?' down the phone. We laughed heartily. Those critical of our efforts to liberate animals are right—people are important too, only they usually mean just themselves! I'd liberated myself and it felt great.

Later that evening, I was picked up and taken to another safe house for the night. This was safer still. There was no link with me to this contact. She, like Mavis, was older—of the animal welfare school—not vegetarian or that inclined to be one but a hundred percent with those out there rescuing the animals and had resources on offer to help. Bit weird if you ask me but that's people for you. I later discovered this safe house was in the same street as the home of one of the detectives working full time on Operation Lance. He was presumably out during my stay! I'd never met this lady before, but she'd supported the ALF financially, knew about me and was so pleased she was able to do her bit, and how excited she was that it was with something like this!

She was a bit naïve, perhaps, hypocritical even, party to the cruelty, certainly, yet essential to the struggle. We chatted lots, met on some things, disagreed on others. Different generation, different all round, but on a path to something together. She kitted me out with new clothes and fed me (as awkward as it was for her to fix something for what she thoughtlessly referred to as 'a vaygan', there were plenty of goodies in the kitchen for a vegan to eat; a dozen meals in the making). I was wined some more and given cash and a spare room whenever I wanted it and early the following morning, was taken to an animal sanctuary in Wiltshire where the absent Angela Hamp (or Sam as she was now known) was holed up and awaiting my arrival.

On bail for sabotaging meat lorries, damaging hunt property and rescuing dogs from Laundry Farm, she'd gone underground 18 months before and was living under an assumed name. She was in her element, self sufficient in a lovely self-contained chalet in the middle of a rescue centre surrounded by animals, regularly carrying out home checks and rescuing strays. We'd planned this reunion back then when she visited me on remand in prison and told me her plans, which had finally met mine somewhere in Wiltshire. We'd made a grand plan and to our delight we'd pulled it off. It'd taken nearly two years but it was well worth the wait. It was back to business for us, not fugitives for the sake of it, but with every intention of making the most of our youthful enthusiasm and health and, of course, avoid the inevitable as for long as possible.

Greater Manchester Police, meanwhile, were in a bit of a mess. How embarrassing that everything for which they had worked so hard had disappeared into the rush-hour traffic. There I was—gone—the central character in their drama, missing. They'd based their case around me and if I wasn't back there in time for the trial then the plan was kaput. Over coming months, detectives were found desperately trying to bribe people for information about my whereabouts, with offers to clear debts, pay for holidays, redecorate houses, even arrange the outcome of legal wrangles, as well as of course 'doing Keith a favour.' The essence of their approach was that grassing me up would help me get back to prison to finish my sentence so I could rebuild my life away from animal rights extremism. But for them, the trail ran dry behind Stretford Police Station and I settled back into normal life, although I understand they did receive quite a number of calls suggesting sightings in places as diverse as Toxteth, Inverness and Sweden, which they would no doubt have followed up!

The day I escaped, there was cause for celebration elsewhere for three activists in the loop and working on the Campaign for the Abolition of Angling (CAA); they had been arrested in early February in a car near Reading in Berkshire which contained a number of incendiary devices. Yet more for the SOCO haul! Marianne Macdonald, Ed Sheppard and Sam Remington were charged with conspiracy to commit arson and remanded in custody. But this clear-cut case that had reached trial remarkably quickly was then abandoned to everyone's amazement with even greater haste.

Despite the seemingly damning evidence against the owner and driver of the car, at the very least, the prosecution were told by the judge that in the interests of justice the little matter of the informant, who had allegedly tipped off the police that it might be worth them stopping the car in the first place, needed resolving and that they should disclose more information about that person. The defendants were claiming they had been set up and that the informant had put the devices there, but the police weren't for humouring the judge by revealing any more information about this individual. That meant there was no credible evidence and all of a sudden no case to answer, so the charges were dropped, the defendants released and everyone went their own way to try again.

Not wanting to miss out on the rush for the door, Vivian Smith, who was by now two years into her six and had had both her appeal and parole refused, was attending college outside Holloway Prison and failed to return one night. A warrant was issued for her arrest. That was the summer of 1993 and she hasn't been seen since. For the ALF Destruction Squad, it was another bloody nose and things weren't getting any better.

The End Of The Road

> They want everyone to stop eating meat, it's a democratic society we don't stop them eating vegetables.
>
> *Anonymous Cambridge butcher*

Whilst a satisfactory conclusion to the Manchester Conspiracy seemed far from imminent, other trials were coming to court. The next one, though not on the Co-ordinating Committee agenda, was the Belfast trial in Northern Ireland. The defendants—who were on serious charges—would have had enough problems, which were greatly exacerbated by incriminating statements made in interviews. Still it was clearer here than anywhere else that the loosely used term 'terrorism'—when viewed in the context of a society in which bombings, shootings and knee-cappings were the norm—clearly couldn't be reasonably applied to the ALF.

At Downpatrick Crown Court in May, a deal had been struck and after some charges were dropped, the eight defendants pleaded guilty to a total of 23 others. These related to several minor incidents of window breaking and paint daubing, plus nine bigger raids including an arson attack on a battery egg farm, two arson attacks on broiler sheds, the burning of six angling boats and a fishing club office, arson and criminal damage to a hare coursing club near Dungannon, criminal damage to the North Down harriers point-to-point course, attempted arson to a gun and tackle shop in Belfast and the attempted arson of a huntsman's car. Dave Nelson was convicted on twelve charges, including four counts of arson and one of attempted arson. He was sentenced to 3 ½ years in prison and was as flabbergasted as everyone else, having expected much more. Alistair Mullen was convicted on eight charges, including three of arson and one attempted arson; he got two years. Graeme Campbell was convicted on four counts of arson and one attempt. He also got two years, reduced on appeal to probation. Kerry McKee, Michael Kerr, Chris Roberts, Kenny Burns and Gavin Gourley were convicted on the lesser charges and given community sentences. For all the hype, the ALF appeared to be something of a relief in a society rife with violent religious conflicts.

The next trial to reach court was in Northampton for attempted arson at Potton. With Angela Hamp unavailable, there were just two defendants in the dock and it was a close call that this case wasn't dismissed when it was disclosed that a sealed exhibit bag containing an item of clothing from one of the three had re-emerged from police stores knotted rather than security sealed and contained tiny slivers of glass from the crime scene. The defence suggested this was potentially tampered evidence, but the judge wasn't convinced and allowed the evidence. The trial went ahead; Ricky D and Annette Tibbles were convicted and sent down for four years each.

October in Manchester County Court was a rather muted affair. There were still prison sentences in the offing, and there's no fun in that, but with people in the foyer sporting 'Where's Keith, Mr Goodwin?' T-shirts and no likelihood of a major show trial, one couldn't help but laugh! I did when I heard! John Hughes was nowhere to be found either and to cap it all, before the trial began, the 2 ½ year old conspiracy charge was abandoned with a monumental prosecution u-turn. The police were still clinging to the contention that a lot of people would be going to prison for a long time, but that was wearing a bit thin and all they had to cling to was the judge, the gruesome Mr Justice Alliot. Only he could save the day with some whopping sentences and he tried his level best, even after deals were agreed upon.

Clare Rush, Max Watson and John Marnell saved the need for a trial on their charges by pleading guilty to conspiring to cause £15,000 damage to 27 butcher's windows. They were sentenced to two years, three years and three years respectively. Terry Helsby pleaded guilty to causing £21,000 worth of damage at Riber Zoo and to damaging six windows in Liverpool. He got three years for the first offence and six months for the second. Alison Mckeon pleaded guilty and was sentenced to two years for aiding and abetting the damage at the zoo by hiring the van that was used.

The custodial sentences Alliot gave to the women were particularly excessive given none of them had any previous convictions and both played very minor roles—neither was convicted for actually committing any damage. Worse still, Max Watson and Clare Rush had had a baby in the time it took to get this thing to trial. Daniel was 15 months old with no parents to look after him. Up until two days before sentencing, when he was discharged, Clare had spent a week in hospital with her son, where he was seriously ill with gastric flu. It would surely take a cruel man to send a young mother to prison under such circumstances when all she had to answer for was sitting in the back of a car from which some windows were broken to protest the violent death of millions.

There was outrage at her punishment, even from other judges. Such was the injustice that soon afterwards, three Appeal Court judges agreed that she and her son had been punished enough and converted the sentence to 21 months in prison, suspended for two years. She was free to bring up her son, a 'terror tot' I suppose you could call him. Fran Morgan, Rhian Hopkin and Marilyn Fahy wanted their day in court. Marilyn Fahy was duly acquitted of any involvement due to an absence of proof that she knew tools were hidden in a barn, which was used by other people. Fran Morgan was convicted of being in possession of a catapult with intent to use it against unspecified targets and was sentenced to six months in prison, suspended for two years. Rhian Hopkin was convicted of causing £800 damage at the Devon Eggs battery farm and was given a conditional discharge. Alliot was livid at this; he wanted desperately to send her to prison but she'd been there for ten weeks over Christmas and there was no more time available for the minor offence she'd committed, so he couldn't. He sulked and grumbled at a 'quirk in the law' that allowed her to 'escape proper justice.' Weirdo.

Alliot had allowed himself to become possessed by his anger at what we represented. He had his moment and let all his emotions erupt. He had a serious preoccupation with me, something really unhealthy that caused him to froth with anticipation at the prospect of me standing before him for sentence one day. I was advised repeatedly by those who witnessed his rants not to let this happen. I was trying!

He talked a lot of 'extremism' and 'single issue fanatics' upsetting other people's traditional way of life. He blamed me for most of the defendants being in the dock and my lack of conscience for putting them all there and for showing no remorse. Every defendant was, of course, very much there of his or her own free will for doing what he or she thought the right thing. What he failed to acknowledge was that it was precisely because I wasn't there that these people weren't going to be facing a lengthy trial and sentence!

But single issues they aren't. It's about changing the way we treat the weak and vulnerable in our society and removing the day-to-day violence. It's about our human right to have safe and effective medical treatments. It's about our democratic right to protest; its about lying politicians and a failing democracy. It's about wild fur-bearing animals in cages being fed on fish, a rapidly diminishing life form, herbivores fed other animals and antibiotics as routine, it's about pus in milk and the damage dairy does to human health, it's about rain forests felled to provide land to rear farm animals, it's about creating a clean environment. It's about behaving responsibly, honestly and allowing free access to the facts. It isn't just about animals; animal exploitation has wide ranging connotations for us all. You judge a society by the way it treats its animals. Alliott was too blinkered to see any of it.

Everyone fully expected him to be unhappy with the outcome. The sentences were harsh but not nearly harsh enough and there weren't enough of them. At the conclusion of a very involved multi-million pound operation with the line up of twenty-one defendants, six were in prison serving less than four years, four were on the run and the rest were without restriction. On the face of it, the conclusion was nothing to get excited about if you were involved in the prosecution and anticipating more exemplary punishments. But equally, we had little to boast about. There may not have been dozens of activists in prison for decades, but the authorities had been successful in disrupting some very effective cells and sending many of those who'd come close to prison into retirement from direct action. Some did find other outlets for their energy in the same struggle and have kept their heads down. Others thought it prudent to take a break for a while and have become wrapped up in their lives, lost contacts and are unable or unwilling to rejoin the frontline. Some got work and a mortgage or have had kids, others went to ground to re-emerge when the time was right. It's something of a game, a battle of wills; serious but seldom deadly. Meanwhile, for the animals, it's deadly serious.

Back To The Big House: Justice For Keith Mann!

> Kindness to all God's creatures is an absolute rock-bottom necessity if peace and righteousness are to prevail
>
> *Sir Wilfred Grenfell (1865-1940) British physician and missionary*

It was a few weeks after Tom Worby's death that I escaped and nearly a year before I was arrested again. It was now 1994 and there was a lot more to come from the animal liberators.

Life as a fugitive was great for me as 'Ian.' Every day I was supposed to be in prison was a bonus, but it wasn't just about delaying the inevitable, It was also about making good use of that time. 'Sam' and I had options for places to stay and we tried a couple out. We'd tried to chill out and take a back seat as we'd been advised, but we both needed to be busy with what we did and that, for now, meant sanctuary work. Simply living on the run and keeping our heads down indefinitely was not going to happen. After a few weeks, we moved on from Wiltshire to Sussex, to another place we had heard was looking for helpers. We had contact with a couple of good friends who kept us in cash and in touch. We were lucky and we knew it, but we also knew that it was only a matter of time before we were tracked down or otherwise detained. Unable and unwilling to find 'proper' jobs, a regular income wasn't high on the agenda, but working at a sanctuary has the added benefit of reducing living costs. While few have enough income to pay wages, many will at least provide shelter and meals and are an obvious hideaway for animal activists on the run.

Some animal sanctuaries are of course better than others and to our delight the one that Celia Hammond ran outside Hastings was one of the better ones. Not only was it well-established and well funded, it was in beautiful countryside and there was no one else there for the most part, certainly no one that knew who we were. Celia had been a supermodel in the 1960s but had given up the seedy catwalk to do animal rescue work and is now widely respected for her energy and compassion as opposed to her tits. Seeing a cat trapped in a derelict house from the top of a bus while travelling in London, her attention was first drawn to the plight of feral cats during her modelling career. Haunted by its silent cries and oblivious to her career commitments, of which there were plenty, she didn't think twice about getting off the bus and going back to the house, which she was forced to break into to rescue the cat from where he would otherwise have died. It was a life changing moment. All those modelling sessions with *Vogue*, social events with pop stars and actors, interviews and photo shoots became irrelevant. She had found a huge gap in the market for a woman with talents.

There is no money in it, nothing in comparison to the earnings of a supermodel. On the contrary, it was going to cost her everything she had to care for others, but none of that mattered once she'd uncovered the needs of large numbers of wild cats struggling to survive in the back streets, factories and building sites of London. With that one rescue, all she had became worthless compared to her desire to do something to help those particular animals.

I have to say, neither of us had any idea who this Celia Hammond was when we were told about her; in fact we were wary she was going to be some pretentious luvvie like so many people are when they become wrapped up in their own self importance. Given the status she'd had, it wouldn't have been a surprise if she was, but nothing could have been further from the truth. We arranged to meet at her sanctuary and immediately warmed to her. And it was mutual. It was weeks later after we'd moved in, during an attic clearing session that we came across some of the portfolios of her past life. This girl had been big! But there could be no doubting her commitment to help cats, she was totally focused on that and her past was very much behind her. That she had made the time to meet us was something of an achievement as it turned out because she was completely preoccupied with catching stray cats!

We moved in to the large detached farmhouse called Greenacres as Sam and Ian, and for the next few months ran the sanctuary as our own, looking after three hundred cats and various other animals. Celia didn't know who we were and wouldn't have cared if she had, as her priorities were with the animals' welfare, although it wouldn't do the public image much good to be associated with the like. For the most part, we were allowed to do as we saw fit, not that she was there much to question. If she wasn't setting traps in building sites and cellars in the East End at all hours, she was trapping cats somewhere else.

Fearless of the dangers of wandering around the squalid parts of London at 2.00am and oblivious to the need for sleep, she was saving lives daily, returning to Greenacres only to drop off cats for re-homing. Others would go to the veterinary clinic she had established in London to be spayed and then when they were well, if it was safe, returned to the streets. It wasn't just to remove cats from danger that motivated her but to reduce the huge over-population of feral cats struggling to survive, something which as an RSPCA council member, she struggled endlessly to get the charity to support. There wasn't only indifference to such a logical approach to a huge welfare problem, but even physical resistance from some local vets and even the profession's governing bodies.

A number of vets were quite aggressive towards her, at being a woman with ideas of her own and determined to set up a low cost neuter clinic on their patch. These would enable people on low income to prevent their animals from breeding more unwanted animals. One or two vets even made threats against her because they saw cheap neutering as affecting their income. These vets, and some high-ranking officials within the RSPCA, tried everything to hamper her efforts, including raising the money needed to outbid her on the premises she wanted! She was utterly focused though, she courted the sympathy of the property seller and she now runs two clinics, with a third in the offing, doing what the biggest national animal welfare charity with all its wealth has never been driven to do. Shameful. They don't deserve their legacies.

Having failed to stop her setting up the clinics, these people had to make do with ensuring hers were restricted to neutering only and would not be licensed to perform operations or carry out any other treatments. With 'friends' like that, the animals don't need enemies.

I'd been out for nearly a year and Angie a lot longer when our world caved in at Greenacres. The police had tracked us down and were there en masse very early one morning. The first signal that we had a problem was the sound of breaking glass at 6.00am followed by men in heavy boots screaming and shouting. It's a dead giveaway. It's police. Jumping up and looking out of the window I could see there were plain clothed coppers in baseball caps with dogs standing out in the field, surrounding us. I knew then it was over. I turned to Angie, sat up in bed; she knew. It was a good thing at an end! I felt sick. We had been so happy with our lot and had no desire to swap it for anything else.

Them smashing the doors around the place was unnecessary as they were always left unlocked, even at night. They could have simply opened them and walked in, arrested us in bed! The fact that they didn't give that a go, gave us the chance to pull on some clothes while they were streaming and screaming through the house. Yelling 'POLICE!' 'POLICE OFFICERS!' as they went, they somehow missed our room downstairs, which gave me the opportunity to bolt again. Angie was instinctively more concerned that the animals were all right. The cattery was full and we had animals in various rooms isolated from the rest: cats with flu and leukaemia, others recovering from operations. And then there were the dogs—Angie's babies—all sent fleeing by this rampaging mob tearing through the place, barging and breaking doors as they went. Some cats were never seen again.

Fully aware of what the police were there for, I couldn't believe my luck when I opened our door and saw that both the kitchen and outer doors were open and there was no one in the way. In the rush for the upstairs bedrooms, they'd missed the one room they were looking for! We rushed our sad farewell and I took off. There were others in the house: a couple of helpers, one a girl over from Holland, Carolien, here to learn about animal care and see how we do things in the UK, and Celia, back from London with a couple of strays only an hour earlier, catching an hour or two in bed before heading back. She, like everyone else, was growled at, threatened, handcuffed and arrested. I ran through the house and out the back and was heading for the woods when I heard someone shout 'STOP! POLICE!' I figured it was a policeman, which could be a problem; he had a dog. There was no chance I was stopping, until a few hundred yards further on when this Alsatian bounded past me. It was big and woolly and my thought was it should have brought me down, teeth in arm and all that, but for some reason, it ran in front of me and stopped as if to give me the choice. On my side but with a job to do, kinda vibe. I had nowhere to run as the dog stared at me, willing me not to. I was again under arrest and soon in very secure custody.

Almost all on the RSPCA Committee considered Celia Hammond an extremist anyway, for her commitment and self-sacrifice, but they must've struggled with the fact there were now two members closely associated with the ALF. Robin Webb was deliberate, Celia just sort of happened.

Everyone but Angie and I were released without charge after 24 hours. We were both questioned about various other offences and I was later charged with possession of explosive substances under suspicious circumstances due to items they found. These included a tub of sodium chlorate weed killer, fireworks and names and addresses. Angie was sent to Holloway in London to await her various hearings and I was taken to Strangeways in Manchester, which had been refurbished following the riot. Finally, I was given a single cell as a Category A prisoner and Escapee and made to wear yellow banded prison clothes. I said all along I'd get my own place!

Over the coming months Angela Hamp was threatened with and offered various options to resolve her complex legal situation, all of which meant a lengthy prison term. Five months after arrest, she reached court. Bearing in mind her co-defendants had been given four years each for attempting to burn meat lorries, and they hadn't absconded, plus she had three other charges to answer to, four was a likely starting point. But unlike the others, she had pleaded guilty to attempted arson and was given due credit: three years. For a guilty plea to a reduced charge for Dodleston, she got a further six months, plus six months for breach of bail making four years in total. It was a good result, all things hyped.

Burglary charges for the ALIU inspection of Laundry Farm were dropped, despite the fact that she'd admitted it and was in fact caught red-handed; remember the car chase? It was thought Cambridge Police and the University were happier to see this affair forgotten about. All things considered, it proved to be in her interest to have absconded 2 ½ years earlier.

I wasn't to be allowed to escape again, and if I did, I'd stand out a mile wearing this outfit! That being the idea, and to humiliate. Bit like the yellow star forced on Jews by Nazis. In HMPs, however, it is something of a status symbol and my uniform didn't half fit me well, unlike the rest of the clothing they issued. Category A prisoners are those classified by the authorities as highly dangerous and a threat to either the public, the police or the state. They would never say which it was for me, or how, but it meant I was escorted everywhere and I wasn't allowed visitors unless they were first cleared by security, the police and the Home Office and that often took months. All my friends of old were immediately rejected, regardless of whether they had criminal convictions or not. There was no explanation why, just the all-encompassing 'security reasons' they would claim a thousand times over coming years, to justify all manner of behaviour. To get round this, I got a friend to invite 'the banned' to visit on his visiting orders for the same day. We'd then pull the tables together and have one big visit. This went on for months and no one figured it out or cared!

I did very little for the next few months, while the police tried to work out how best to deal with me. Lying there in yet another cold barren cell, it didn't take long to conclude I was in for a long stay, but this was what I had chosen over a passive existence. I was worried about Angie, Celia and the others arrested and how many more charges there might be. How did they find us? Would they plant something? Would the animals be all right? Those poor dogs… We'd had so much fun on walks, they had always been with their mum and all of a sudden she was gone and how! Not seeing them for years would be the worst punishment for Angie. And how the hell was I going to get out of this one! Lots of questions, but no answers. There was very little that would likely happen that could have made me feel worse, but there was good news to soften the blow over the next few weeks, which I consumed with relish.

An ALF raid on the Tuck-owned lab-breeding station at Battlebridge in Essex saw the liberation of 100 guinea pigs, an action that was dedicated to Angie and I. And £10,000 damage was done in our names at a meat depot in Lancashire. Better than a Get Well Soon card or a bunch of flowers; even better than a box of vegan chocolates. Just! Months later, avoiding the increased security patrols, raiders returned to Tucks and rescued the entire stock of one unit, a total of 470 guinea pigs. Also rescued were 15 rabbits, 98 rats, 54 hamsters and 52 guinea pigs by raiders breaking in through the roof of the North East Surrey College of Technology labs. Awful crimes? Few kids think so.

Carolien was clearly always going to be an asset to the animals and extended her stay indefinitely to take care of everything for us and at the sanctuary, with the help of the old friends who could always be relied on. Nameless, but priceless. Carolien eventually went home, went on to establish the Dutch ALF Supporters Group and currently works on primate rehabilitation projects. An extremist to some but a gem to society.

Ronnie Lee was released from prison having served six years and eight months of his ten-year sentence and was looking for campaigns to engage with. No one before had served such a long sentence for ALF actions, and yet he emerged from prison as strong, determined and uncompromising as when he went in. He was an inspiration to others worried about the effect prison might have. I was in court when he was sent down and ten years seemed like forever, yet there it was done! I knew I was away for a long time, and it helped to see his light at the end of the tunnel. Today he is working on greyhound rescue initiatives, tidying up some of the mess the racing industry creates.

Then the last UK dolphinarium released its captives from Flamingoland in Yorkshire following a concerted campaign. There had been increasing pressure applied by activists in preceding months using all manner of tactics to persuade the management of the site, who typically resorted to violence. That only made matters worse, of course, and guaranteed that another focused campaign was going to resist until the bitter end. It was becoming a habit. Stick it out and see 'em off!

And in a storybook sensation, Brazil's last performing dolphin was released back into the ocean and returned to the same pod—his mother's—from which he had been taken by fishermen nine years earlier.

In November 1992, the Today newspaper ran a story of two ALF arson attacks at Driffield on Humberside, one on a pig farm and the other on seven refrigerated lorries belonging to a chicken factory, alongside a picture of the wreckage at the latter. All of the lorries had been empty bar one and that contained chickens. Dead, frozen ones. The headline? 'ALF Torches Chickens' followed by the story of how these birds were 'burned alive.' Oh, how they spin!

The ALF had also raided kennels in Lincolnshire and removed 11 dogs that had been used to fight badgers. They were going to be returned—courtesy of the courts—to the badger baiters from whence they came. In London, 150 hens were taken from the Leyden Street halal slaughterhouse and creosote and oil was spread around the place, taking the number of birds rescued from the place to over 300 in four visits. Fifty-seven dogs and seven cats were rescued from a puppy farm at Lampeter in mid Wales and another 87 rabbits were taken by the ALF from Hylyne Rabbits in Cheshire, where this was becoming something of a bad habit.

My case, meanwhile, had been booked into the Old Bailey for December 1994, the judge was still called Alliot and he was straining at the leash. I was being told to expect between 12 and 18 years by my lawyer! The prosecution wanted to avoid a lengthy trial and I didn't really want to go through one either, so there was room for some improvement on that. It would have been a task for the police to get all their witnesses to London to testify; most of them were based elsewhere with evidence years old. There was a lot of potentially revealing material to come out, but at the same time it would have caused me problems, especially if convicted at the end, as was likely. So after lengthy discussions with my legal team, I agreed a deal. It was, with hindsight, probably a mistake.

Part of the deal excluded Alliot from sentencing. I made it clear I wouldn't even attend the trial if he was in on it. I had few cards to play by this stage, but those I could, I did. We prepared a dossier of the reasons why he shouldn't judge this case, including the fact he had interests at odds with mine, namely his love of hunting, shooting and fishing, and the fact he was once the master of a pack of beagles. And, how intriguing is this? A month before my date with him, during an IRA trial he was presiding over, Alliot interrupted the defence questioning of an anonymous MI5 agent when the witness was asked about the future of the secret service if peace came to Ireland: 'I can make a good suggestion', says Alliot, 'The Animal Liberation Front needs a good deal of attention: that is my next major trial.' He was unimaginably preoccupied.

He was presented with this compelling dossier and rejected it, as is his privilege. I'd agreed to plead guilty to possessing explosive substances—a £10 tub of weed killer, two fireworks, some white spirit, firelighters and sugar—diagrams for incendiary devices I was experimenting with and names and addresses of abusers, attempted incitement, escaping from custody and of causing £6,000 damage, if he was replaced by another judge for sentencing. The prosecutor persuaded him and the other charges were dropped. In open court, Alliot announced he was stepping down for a prior engagement; the truth of the matter was that the trial date was arranged around him and he would have moved heaven and earth to finish it and me off.

19 December 1994, below Court 1, Old Bailey. Some serious characters had trudged this dank path before me. What the hell was I doing here?! Alliot's replacement was Justice Stephen Mitchell, described to me by my barrister as 'a fair man', but that wasn't my view by the end of the day. Optimistically, and because I could, I asked him to look at Hans Ruesch's book *Naked Empress* and the images in particular, in the hope he'd understand some of my motivation for keeping lists of the people and places responsible for the horrors graphically depicted.

He took it, looked at it for a while, then put it aside and got on with his lecture.

> All these offences were committed in pursuance of a cause, the cause of animal welfare and animal rights, a cause which you must know is close to the hearts of millions in this country. Unlike you and those who think like you, most who want to alleviate the suffering of animals work tirelessly within the law. Some, admittedly, in their enthusiasm do stray into criminal activity, but you and those who joined with you deliberately and persistently have opted for tactics, which often bear the hallmarks of

> terrorism. Many would say that in so conducting yourself you have betrayed the very cause you sought to further. These are grave offences. You and like-minded people must understand that however worthy your cause, for offences such as these very severe sentences will be passed if you are caught.

He said he had taken into account my pleas of guilt and that he recognised no one was injured; also that he'd read the various letters of character witnesses, including Celia Hammond, which were impressive. He said he wasn't sentencing me for being a leader but that he was satisfied I was a 'dedicated, ruthless, full-time activist whose goal was the infliction of severe economic damage upon legitimate business' and sentenced me to 14 years in prison!

'Animal Rights Chief Given 14 Years For Campaign Of Terror.'

Grave offences? Really! I put my views on paper, thought about burning things, terrorised three meat lorries and escaped from custody. What is it these judges do every day? Is there no violent crime any more? I was expecting to be punished, so it came as no bolt from the blue to me. If anything, it was a compliment. For all my efforts, this was the best proof of the impact of our efforts. It was an outrage but I was rapidly working out release dates, possibly four years away with a couple of years off on appeal, but it did send shockwaves around the movement. Would the sentence achieve what was expected of it? Would it serve as a deterrent for others with objections to animal abuse and no other outlet but to break the law? Apparently not...

I lodged an appeal against the sentence and the Justice for Keith Mann Campaign sprang up, the support for which was incredibly heart warming. There was widespread public support for the campaign, for me, a vicious thug who terrorised neighbourhoods! Clearly, for all the headlines and scare stories, the propaganda wasn't working. So many people came together from around the world and a broad social spectrum, to offer their support for and demonstrate their disgust at, this sentence and they filled my cell with correspondence.

The JFKM Campaign coordinated a fantastic show of support and did the movement proud, as did the ALF Supporters Group and Vegan Prisoners Support Group, formed specifically to assist Angie and I with ongoing and endless dietary issues. The VPSG has gone on to serve all animal liberation prisoners and improve the diet and access to non-animal tested toiletries.

Two major demonstrations at the Royal Courts of Justice in London prior to my appeal a year later drew between 400-500 hundred people, with a similar number at my appeal. It made me very, very proud to see and hear so many supporting me outside the courts (and nearly as many police to ensure I wasn't sprung!). This support was priceless.

Michael Mansfield QC represented me, Celia Hammond spoke on my behalf, as did probation officers, a 6000-name petition, the Bishop of Dover and others. The appeal judges said they didn't consider I was any longer as described by the sentencing judge just a year before, and called 14 years 'manifestly excessive' but still only reduced it to 11 years. Before I discovered animal abuse in its many awful guises and was driven to act, I would have moved mountains to avoid prison but here I was in a way rewarded for my actions and happy with 11 years!

1995 And All That

> We are all entitled to our opinions. We are all God's creatures even down to the good old tomato that gets chopped in half and thrown into the frying pan.
>
> *Butcher with a broken window rationalising the way he treats animals with the way we treat tomatoes*

Live Animal Exports—A Truly English Objection

Over a period of six weeks during the winter of 1994, three significant events rocked the movement, uniting its various elements into a single powerful force. The first was this groundbreaking judicial backlash at the Old Bailey, followed two weeks later by a huge uprising against the live animal export trade. Flaring up from a small spark at the southern port of Shoreham in Sussex, an evening of determined protest led to the most remarkable ripple of events across the country, involving thousands of people, many of whom had never even protested before. And then there was another violent killing. Again the so-called extremists were on the receiving end.

Live animal exports were traditionally the domain of the RSPCA and Compassion in World Farming (CIWF) and fronted by the likes of Joanna Lumley and Celia Hammond; not an animal liberation issue, but a welfare one. What was once considered a secondary issue regarding the perceived benefits of animal killing in UK slaughterhouses over death elsewhere had become a raging battle for the entire movement. Naturally, I take issue with the 'niceness' of UK slaughtering, as does anyone who has experienced our way of killing animals for food. I have no aspiration to see any animal killed here first and then be shipped out dead for human consumption to spare them the horror elsewhere as the welfarist demands. This strikes me as a logical stance, believing as I do that slaughterhouses by definition are cruel places where no animal should ever be taken under any circumstances.

To have 'welfarists' on the one hand publicly and tearfully objecting to the export of live animals for slaughter, whilst on the other consuming the products, taking money from Slaughterers and Co. for advertising animal products smacks of hypocrisy and double standards and will never bring an end to animal exploitation. One of these media babes—who describes herself as an 'animal lover' and courts the label—

advertises dairy yoghurts with added gelatine, while in the ranks RSPCA inspectors have been caught on camera munching on animal body parts while tracking the horrific journeys of UK 'farm stock' across Europe for slaughter elsewhere. With representatives such as this, what chance do the animals have?

This astounding hypocrisy amongst animal welfarists is commonplace: the CIWF are happy with UK slaughtering to continue ad infinitum and suggest in their Compassionate Shopping Guide that consumers should 'favour organic or free range meat, milk and eggs' to 'help increasing numbers of farm animals enjoy fresh air and sunshine,'—that is, of course, before they are loaded up and carted off for slaughter. (Unsurprisingly, at the beginning of September 2006, CIWF apparently endorsed the potential resurgence of British veal, claiming that it is humane, especially the organic version). When does it dawn on organic and free range meat eaters that in actual fact it's all been a big lie and there is still terrible violence associated with the habit, that animals aren't good converters of food, that slaughterhouses suck, and that meat production badly degrades the environment?

The RSPCA go one step further to baffle and bewilder, by promoting their Freedom Food animal products, which, they say: 'Improve the lives of as many farm animals as possible'—animals that are living short, miserable lives and are dying a brutal death. You can help by choosing the recipe of your desire from their Freedom Food Celebrity Recipe collection which is packed full of disgusting meal ideas for your animal friends to become. As one P.D.N. Earle, President of The Country Gentleman's Association rightly said: 'Instead of turning into a wholesale slaughtering organisation, it would be better if the RSPCA took the more positive line of preventing over breeding … the RSPCA also has been totally ineffective against the ever increasing scandal of vivisection and experiments of doubtful validity on animals…'

So how did the Animal Liberation Movement get dragged into a massive nationwide battle over live exports? How come some of its more radical activists ended up fighting on the streets alongside the welfarists ostensibly demanding animals be killed in UK slaughterhouses?

It was the third day of January 1995 when around 200 people, including many locals, staged a protest at the port of Shoreham on the south coast. This issue would not be ignored for long with so many people witnessing scenes reminiscent of 1940's Europe, as huge truckloads of baby calves were driven along the Brighton sea front to the docks through the traditional heartland of the Animal Liberation Movement. 'Big black noses and sad eyes follow you, seeking solace as they peer from every hole in long convoys of trucks as you make your way to the beach' isn't a sentence you'll find in the brochures, but you couldn't miss these forlorn orphans as the trucks trundled by.

This protest in itself wasn't remarkable as there had been a low level of opposition for some time, largely orchestrated by the likes of the South East Animal Rights Coalition, East Kent Animal Welfare and CIWF, but there was something brewing that no one could have predicted. For some time the race had been on amongst the welfare groups to track the longest journey from the UK of our animals; such trips are a well-documented nightmare. The thousand strong, CIWF-sponsored, lobby of Parliament following the release of a World in Action documentary exposing surveillance footage of the terrible journeys to which these animals are subjected to for days on end without food, water or rest or any degree of comfort, and the headlines that followed were perhaps a hint of public feelings—not to mention the 400,000-signature petition which was presented to the Ministry of Agriculture. There was consternation that the banning of veal crates in the UK on welfare grounds was merely causing more animals to be shipped abroad and it was revealed that William Waldegrave MP, head of MAFF, was himself involved in the trade in baby calves.

There were only 50 police on hand to control the first protest at Shoreham, which suggested they'd missed the signs too. They were ill equipped to clear the road being blocked by cold, angry protesters as the first wagons arrived that night. After half an hour of this stand off, with police outnumbered and protesters empowered and determined, the wagons were turned back; police announced there would be no attempt to try again that night. Forget the petitions, live exports had finally been stopped! Playwright & welfare campaigner Carla Lane was right: 'These people have done more in a few days to bring this cruelty to public attention than people like me have done by peaceful discussion over years.'

Word went round that there had been a victory at Shoreham and the ranks swelled. The next night, well over 300 people turned up, all ages, shapes and sizes. Sussex Police had only doubled their numbers, which meant they were again unable to prevent a repeat performance, which was by this time being reported in the media but described as an anarchist riot with yobs attacking ill-equipped bobbies. A balaclava-clad activist on top of a truck full of calves was photographed smashing its windscreen with a house brick, and splashed over the news the next day. Rather than scare everyone off this served as a rallying cry! The news editors may have preferred to focus on the 'thugs', but the animal lovers, welfarists, vegans et al were focusing on the animals, who were leaving our shores for the slaughterhouses and veal crates of Johnny Foreigner. This is what really mattered.

CIWF surpassed themselves by siding with the media version and denounced the violence of a couple of glass smashers and the trickery of those out-manoeuvring the police and exporters to stop the cruel trade. Terrified of being associated with these images, they took away their placards and said they weren't going to have anything more to do with the organisation of the demos. They asked their supporters not to attend; to not campaign against live exports! Local campaigners responded to this confused message by calling for more and bigger protests while asserting these protests were nothing to do with CIWF in the first place. This was borne out the very next day as numbers swelled to over 1000 activists determined to stop the wagons. Suddenly the campaign against live exports had become something significant. And why?

After three days with no live exports and extensive media coverage, the police had the measure of what was happening at Shoreham and had block-booked local hotels and shipped in 1500 officers from other forces to balance the numbers and ensure the wagons kept rolling, at a cost of £200,000 a night! They then surpassed themselves with what they did next.

Imagine riot police punching elderly ladies, throwing kids into walls, wading in feet first on families sitting in the road; a dozen motorcycle outriders in front and behind and riot cops marching in tight formation alongside huge convoys of wagons full to bursting with baby cows; a police dinghy with divers in the harbour to ensure the smooth passage out of territorial waters... These were real scenes that many will never forget. The Metropolitan Police had a lesson or two for the Sussex force in how to deal with dissent and there seemed to be no shortage of officers in reserve to take over from their exhausted colleagues as the battles raged for hours, then days, then weeks then months, leading to over 300 arrests and many people being injured. This was a wake up call for Middle England.

And it went beyond Shoreham to every location from which live animals were exported: Brightlingsea in Essex, Plymouth in Devon, Dover in Kent and Coventry in Warwickshire. If Shoreham was a revelation, then Brightlingsea was the second coming. The tiny Essex town rallied the majority of the 2000 people who gathered to block the port there, which, from a population of only 8000, is quite remarkable. So, too, the scenes plastered across TV screens worldwide as Essex Police, with an aggressive reputation second only to the Met, waded into civilians sitting in the road trying to prevent cattle trucks from leaving the country. So overt and aggressive was the violence that one tabloid saw it as it was, describing police as 'rent-a-thugs' in its front-page headlines.

Derrick Day, an elderly veteran campaigner, collapsed and died of a heart attack during one public meeting between protesters and Essex Police soon after giving them a dressing down for their brutality.

Seventy-six-year-old Roger Sear found his forte with the coming of the Shoreham protests. With his home overlooking the harbour, it meant he was able to keep a vigil over the water for the veal ships arriving and then alert others. It was an important role he played and was acknowledged by the farmers who threatened him. Undeterred, he responded: 'I had to do something—I couldn't stand by and think what might happen to those calves. A man called and threatened to poison my cats. But cowards like that won't stop me.' The threats didn't deter him, but they did frighten him and probably contributed to the pneumonia that killed him suddenly a few months later.

But this wasn't just about cruelty to animals. It was about upholding our right to protest, about challenging the realms of our so-called democracy and about the rule of law being broken and violently by police officers. There was also an element who so intensely disliked the idea of some backwater Spanish slaughterhouse killing our animals that they were prepared to face the wrath of riot police so the animals could instead be sent to one here.

There were of course plenty of vegans on these protests as one would have rightly expected—people who object to the practise of making cows routinely pregnant so that humans can drink their babies' milk; people who are not prepared to be party to the deportation of their baby cows to a living death in Europe, spent in tiny wooden crates, being fed a nutrient-deficient diet to make their flesh anaemic, ready for the day they are sent to slaughter a few weeks later to be cut up and sold as 'veal.'

Yet there were also vegetarians and meat-eaters at the protests who were among the consumers responsible for the calves' fate, and for their suffering and that of their lactating mothers. Of course, some had never made the connection and would change their dietary habits in due course, but others remained set in their ways, quite prepared to be sent to prison or hospital but not to change their eating habits! News editors, finding it hard to perpetuate the myth that this was some kind of anarchist riot, instead rounded on these people for their hypocrisy. In using the time-honoured trick of draining public support by portraying peaceful protesters as violent thugs, they created their headlines. In some reports it was claimed there were, for the most part, only NIMBYs blocking the traffic; locals not wanting the animal cargo trundling through their town, or 'back yard.' Some claimed with successive news headlines that at Brightlingsea a 'police officer has been stabbed by animal rights protesters.' It transpired, the officer caught himself on a lorry wing mirror, but how many of us hearing the earlier shocking news story were given the benefit of the actual truth once the lie died? It was a footnote and stabbing police officers was now up there on the loony agenda with poisoning babies, terrorising neighbourhoods, burning chickens alive, killing animals in labs and on release, poisoning and blinding hunt horses and hounds and holding back medical research. Come and join us!

However diverse the motivation of the protesters, the state was single-minded in its approach. In the middle of this muddle over infant cows and a trade said to be worth around £200 million a year, there was a break out from the top security Parkhurst Prison on the Isle of Wight just across the water from Shoreham. This was a really serious incident that ultimately led to a very public, very damaging conflict between the Home Secretary and the Prison Service, which suffered enormous upheaval, the downgrading of Parkhurst from Category A to B, the sacking of the prison governor and acute embarrassment for all concerned.

Three category A life sentence prisoners (two doing time for murder) were on the run for five days, yet there were considerably more police resources ensuring that calves were successfully shipped out to the Continent than there were looking for escaped murderers. It was only bad luck that the escapees had been unable to steal a light plane as they'd planned and were arrested on the island five days later when spotted by chance by a prison officer. There had been 200 police officers searching the 22 x 12 mile island but over 1000 at the tiny port of Shoreham and it was ultimately the bill for policing the protests, estimated at £4 million and which the Sussex force was footing, that sealed the besieged Shoreham Port Authority's decision not to renew shipping licences from the port the following year. The main ferry companies had been encouraged to pull out by supporters of every group from the RSPCA to the Justice Department, who we'll get to shortly (most persuasively by the latter, sadly) and airlines backed out too, for fear of being targeted by British activists. This was a victory for people power but failed to kill off the trade that today circulates through the port of Dover.

What makes an even greater tragedy out of this tragedy of live exports is what happened next...

A Young Mother Slain

> Forbear, mortals, to pollute your bodies with the flesh of animals. There is corn; there are the apples that bear down the branches by their weight; and there are the grapes, nuts, and vegetables. These shall be our food.
>
> *Pythagoras, 582 B.C.*

With the closing down of routes for the traffic of livestock, new ones were sought by dairy farmers. Justice Department parcel bombs had sent them, and protesters, to Baginton Airport in Coventry. The enforced decision by shipping companies to bar live animal exports from their ferries caused exporters to try flying the animals out instead. It was here that the most significant human tragedy occurred.

The Phipps family, whom you may remember from the chapter dealing with the Unilever raid in the 1980s, were passionate about many issues, and were regularly to be seen at protests around the country, so it wouldn't have taken a degree to figure out they'd be out in numbers at the airport just around the corner from home. The youngest, Leslie, was there with her sister Jill and her 68-year-old mum Nancy, whose catch phrase to the bad guys was: 'You lot ought to be ashamed of yourselves!' They would usually be accompanied by anyone whom they could persuade to come along, like Gurjeet, usually, a family friend and a stalwart of the local group who'd unfortunately been imprisoned for doing his bit to force the exporters from the ferries so wouldn't be there this time.

Jill Phipps had been spared a prison sentence ten years earlier at the Unilever trial because she was pregnant at the time with her son Luke. She was devoted to him and he'd taken up much of her time in the intervening years. But she was there on the front line again, just like they'd been in the old days at Cocksparrow and other places. Flying baby cows out of their hometown was incitement to act.

A permanent camp sprang up at the main entrance to the airfield. The exporters thought the calves could be flown out, but what they hadn't bargained for was they still had to be driven to the airport through a small group of those who'd stopped their progress to the docks.

Jill—one of the bravest of the group—was at the remote airport every night for six weeks, braving the elements and the police. She was a pretty woman, with a natural ability to disarm men, which she used in diffusing confrontations with the police, but she was no pushover. As the mother of a young son, perhaps she felt the plight of the motherless calves more passionately than some—in any event, it was her empathy with them that spurred her on.

It was 1 February, 1995. If anyone could wriggle a way through the police lines to intercept the wagons, it was always Jill. The police knew her well and so did the drivers, who'd stop for her or whoever while the police cleared a path and gave the go-ahead to continue. They were there primarily to see the wagons through but also supposedly to stop them should anyone be at risk.

In a way, it was perhaps predictable to all who knew Jill that it was her at the centre of unfolding events that winter night on that barren airfield. There was no great motion to the wagons as they approached the airfield—that was why she'd been able to stand before them a thousand times, arms raised, pleading for them to stop. There were a hundred officers on duty that cold February, supposedly keeping three dozen protesters from obstructing the flow of wagons carrying a thousand calves a day. Outmanoeuvring the police, Jill and a small group of friends did their usual protest, but the driver just didn't stop for her this time. He had plenty of time to see her and it wasn't as if he was moving too fast to stop, but he did exactly the opposite and slammed into her, forcing her under the wheels.

Jill Phipps died cradled in the arms of her mother Nancy on the tarmac at Coventry Airport. She was 31 years old.

No more poignant destiny could have befallen this gentle, loving family, and the irony of their loss could not have been lost on many, given that the Phipps women—both of them mothers—were fighting to protect the lives of orphaned calves severed from their mothers at a few days' old. They believed—as all right-thinking people should—that it is a travesty to deny generation after generation of mother cows their natural right to fulfil their maternal bond with their new born.

As she lay on the tarmac the police worked really hard to keep the other protesters from the scene, and they kept the wagons rolling. Two days later, as the movement struggled to come to terms with this latest tragedy, the inquest into Jill's death was opened and adjourned and her 70-year old father, Bob, her partner, Justin and younger sister, Leslie, were arrested at the airport with 45 others as they tried to stop the flights. Justin had locked himself to the wheel of the plane on the runway and succeeded in preventing it from taking off, causing it to be grounded for safety tests. That night, ALF activists broke into a

Cambridge University lab and rescued a number of cats that were being prepared for spinal injury experiments and dedicated the raid to the memory of Jill.

As has become the norm, the gutter press rounded on the activists. The gentle Jill Phipps was blamed for what had happened; she was called a 'law breaker' and an 'obsessive' who should've been at home tending to her son, not out getting herself killed over animals. Only a few journalists honestly reported on the very real tragedy that had happened here. The final insult was saved for the inquest. It had clearly been the duty of the police to ensure no one got hurt at the protests (and presumably to tell the truth about the events later). But the version of events presented at the actual inquest left witnesses to the facts reeling. Staggeringly, police claimed that Jill had placed herself under the wheel of the moving truck with the intention of getting herself crushed! One PC David Toms said that having moved one protester from the path of the lorry, his 'intention was to go back and do the same with Miss Phipps. She turned and lay on her back and shuffled under the lorry with her stomach directly underneath the wheel. It was my opinion from what I recall that it was a purposeful motion.' This presentation of the story exonerated both them and the driver and put the onus on Jill Phipps for committing an act of reckless stupidity; but although the word of other witnesses who had seen the unfolding tragedy contradicted this, the outcome, it seemed was a closed book from the outset. The inquest verdict returned was one of accidental death. This made a mockery of the killing of a young mother.

It wasn't the first time the police had confused the facts when dealing with Jill Phipps. Four years earlier, during a trawl of Special Branch dossiers, they had somehow concluded she had been in Cheshire, protesting at the kennels of the Cheshire Beagles two days after the killing of Mike Hill, when in fact she was collecting her son from school in Coventry 200 miles away at the time. Yet she found herself targeted by detectives, arrested and held at a police station near home for the day, before being taken to Cheshire to be questioned and later charged with riot! She was then held in custody for two days pending the clearance of a bail surety before she was released to find her own way home. She spent eight months on bail before the charges were dropped due to a lack of evidence and the police and CPS apologised for the way they had treated her. Sorry, I made the last bit up. They didn't at all. Perhaps one day they'll acknowledge the wrong done to this gentle soul who was never able to collect the compensation she was eventually awarded years later for the wrongs done in Cheshire.

Those who had turned on Jill Phipps had condemned the idea that her funeral service was to be held at Coventry city cathedral, claiming that her memorial service should have been held in a back street with little fuss and that the cathedral was the preserve of those who had died for their cause in wars, not for the likes of an animal protester. Clearly, many disagreed as over 1000 mourners packed the historic cathedral and crowded outside to pay their respects.

As for Phoenix Aviation—the company responsible for the flights out of Coventry—well they struggled on for another five months of intense pressure before being forced into liquidation. It had cost the taxpayer another half a million quid to keep the runways clear, and over 200 people were arrested trying to block them. Company boss Christopher Barrett-Jolley insisted: 'This is not a victory for the protesters. They have not influenced our decision one bit. The cessation of our animal flights operations was on purely economic reasons.' (Same thing, dummy!) He added: 'Although the company is owed a lot more money than it owes, the situation with the animal flights has become impossible, absolutely impossible to continue.' There were guards at the home of Barret-Jolley 24/7 after it was repeatedly attacked, but the problems were only just beginning for the delightful Mr Not So-Jolley.

First, in March 1993, one of his pilots was convicted of smuggling cocaine and heroin. The following June, Phoenix Aviation were flying dairy calves to Europe and firearms to South Yemen to fuel a vicious civil war, which was tearing that country apart. Questioned about irregularities in the paperwork, Jolley insisted his weapons were going to save lives. At the same time, he was flying arms to Angola, where right-wing rebels had re-ignited a war that would cost a million lives and last ten years. In August 1994, he was sued for stealing fixtures and fittings from Packenton Hall, which he was renting. Then in December, when the company's ageing five-crew Russian cargo plane was returning for more calves, it slammed into waste ground dangerously close to a housing estate near Baginton Airport, killing all on board. The assessment was that this had been due to pilot error or fatigue, but it was more ammunition for the terror journalists who, unbelievably, suggested the plane might have been sabotaged by animal rights activists.

A day earlier, the same plane, whose ancient navigation equipment wasn't able to read the airport navigation aids, had narrowly missed a passenger jet en route from Brussels to New York. In January 1995, Jolley was arrested after shooting one protester (whom he wished to prevent from filming) and attacking another with a crowbar. He was also prosecuted for defrauding the Norwich Union, but all of this paled into insignificance in comparison with the trouble he and his co-pilot got into when they were caught dropping five suitcases of smuggled cocaine worth £22 million from his plane as it landed at Southend from Jamaica in October 2001. The pair were convicted amid a flurry of desperate lies, including once again, with staggering audacity, trying to blame 'the animal rights'; Jolley even claimed in court he was working for a CIA agent codenamed 'Mr J Phipps.' It was probably the name that came first to mind when he was being tangled up in the dock (haunting him one hopes); it didn't help his cause that Nancy Phipps was in the public gallery at the time and promptly told the court what she thought of his desperate falsehood. Jolley and kin were sentenced to 20 years each.

Curbing The Burning Desire

> The more you say about these people, the worse it is. You can't beat them. The insurance people pick up the bills and it comes through in increased premiums.
>
> *UK Butcher*

I was told in my early days as an activist that I would/should grow out of it and get a job. It was a similar theme in prison: that's it now—done your bit—get a job and settle down. But it doesn't work like that: animal abuse is still there and I feel no different about it now than I did the day I discovered it. It must be stopped, whatever the obstacles. That's my view and I'm not alone in it. If anyone thought that killing activists and dishing out sentences in double figures was going to silence objectors, then read on, because there are a lot of like-minded people springing up in all kinds of places, and they are impossible to track if their luck is in. It isn't always though.

A big message had been sent out during the 1990's in Cheshire, Cambridge, Coventry and at the Old Bailey: mess with our systems of animal abuse and your punishment will be severe. But the response was everything but muted. What seemed to be happening is rather than deterring this stuff they call extremism, they were making matters worse.

The bearded thirty-seven year old Dave Callender had been around as long as any in animal rescue circles: a calm mover and shaker with John Lennon specs, he was often to be found leading the charge in defence of animals. Based in Liverpool and a natural hunt saboteur, he was well known to the Cheshire packs but he'd backed away from the leadership role and was living and working at the Freshfields Animal Rescue Centre from where Mike Hill had travelled on that fateful morning in February 1991 and never returned. One an ageing hippy, the other just out of school, they were united in their abhorrence of animal abuse and content to do the messy jobs few others will. They tended to wounds, cleared up animal waste and dealt with morons who'd turn up with an ultimatum at the perennially overloaded sanctuary to dump a litter of puppies (because they'd messed on the carpet): take the puppies or we'll 'throw 'em in the canal.' They would drive miles to collect a recently homed dog that the new 'owners' had decided they didn't want after two days because it moulted—and they managed to remain calm and polite—admirable qualities! It is always something of a personal blow if an animal in need of a home 'bounces'; to place one, then have another five dumped is like running on water. Callender, like other rescue workers coped and copes with this because it helps the individuals, but the death of his young friend was a huge blow to this gentle man and forced him to act.

Since an earlier brush with the law in Cheshire, following the NALL raid on ICI in 1984, Callender had kept his head down, allowing himself time out from the never-ending animal welfare work to try and save some wild animals in the killing fields of Cheshire and beyond. He recalls: 'I still remember my first ever sabotage in June 1978 of the Kendal and District Otter Hounds, the last season of legal otter hunting on the River Crake, running out of Lake Coniston in Cumbria. That was the day I first came face to face with perverse pleasure. The hunters' attitude, aggression, alcoholic intake, and capacity for bullying guaranteed my lasting obsession to oppose blood sports.' Indeed.

To describe these forays into the countryside as a rest from the endless terrible cruelty witnessed daily at Freshfields and places like it would be inaccurate. Hunt sabotage in Cheshire is dangerous, especially for someone well versed in sabotage techniques and well known to hunt supporters. There are few sabs alive who haven't been beaten up or attacked and Callender has had more than his share over the years. But it's also fair to say that he has managed to get his own back and felt things were reasonably even until that is they killed Mike Hill. For many like him, this was one death too many.

Callender was working towards some sort of retribution, in the pursuit of which he purchased sixty tomato-shaped kitchen timers. That they were tomatoes is not the point; the quantity and the fact that they can be used as timers for incendiary devices, was. Had he opened a shop in the centre of town selling kitchen accessories, there would have been nothing suspicious about this purchase, but when the police were alerted and discovered who it was that had collected the order, alarm bells started ringing, as it were.

Working from a safe house in Birmingham, Callender and Greg Avery (who had re-emerged following a close call with prison in the 1980's) had embarked on a campaign to draw attention to and then launch campaigns against various establishments involved in animal abuse. The Animal Health Trust, the Cambridge Hunt and the Milk Marketing Board were some of the sites they recce'd, and they'd intended to use inert hoax devices as a launch pad—hence the timers. But all that the police saw were the timers and Dave Callender: they put two and two together and set up surveillance.

It was exactly three years earlier to the day, detectives in Kent had prematurely revealed themselves to me during a surveillance operation. The same thing happened in Cambridge: just forty-eight hours in, an undercover officer accidentally found himself face to face with the man he was supposed to be watching covertly. Callender and Avery—albeit suspicious—dismissed the incident; the man in the field could have been anyone: bird watcher, perhaps pervert. As they were taking a break from cycling a few hours later by the side of the road in this vivisection-rife county, the joint Cambridge/West Midlands police operation was brought to a head early. The police decided it was too risky to assume their man had been dismissed as an innocent field dweller, so their targets were arrested, questioned, charged days later and remanded in custody. Subsequent searches of the safe house unearthed plans of sites to be targeted and other material for making some kind of devices, but nothing remotely explosive or incendiary was discovered.

And there the case rested. At trial months later, several defence witnesses testified at great risk to themselves, that the dummy devices they were privy to were indeed intended to be nothing more than elaborate—illegal—hoaxes, designed to draw attention to the institutions concerned and cause some disruption and financial loss. They were categorically not intended to cause fires or explosions. Even the prosecution forensic expert agreed the devices recovered could well be harmless dummies. It was an intriguing, if slightly implausible, defence but for reasons known only to the judge, Peter Mathews, the evidence of these witnesses was allowed to be used in favour of one defendant and not the other. Consequently, Greg Avery was found not guilty of conspiring to plant incendiary devices at the end of the five-week trial and went home, but Dave Callender was found guilty. It was a peculiar ruling.

In March 1996, after spending many months on remand, Dave Callender was sentenced at Birmingham Crown Court to ten years for conspiracy to commit arson. Once again, supporters rallied and hundreds demonstrated at the Appeal Courts in disgust at the trial and long sentence and called for a retrial. The calls fell on deaf ears. At appeal, ten years was simply reduced to eight and on the fourth anniversary of his capture—to everyone's surprise except his own—he was released on full parole, as he had always known he would. He went back to working at Freshfields.

Michael Green and Melanie Arnold were also wrapped up in animal sanctuary work; a couple of animal lovers whom you would never think to accuse of firebombing a slaughterhouse but in their spare time, they were, in fact, doing exactly that. Undeterred by the endless threats of prison, they were trying to relieve some of the emotional pressure on themselves and animals not yet lucky enough to make it to sanctuary life. Mel Arnold explains:

> You would never guess Ensor's business if you drove past uninformed, for the office block at the front of the building belies its true purpose. But the smell! The smell will always give it away. It was chosen for its location. Situated in an obscure part of Gloucestershire, it was isolated enough to be safe to burn without danger to life, but not so isolated that our presence in the vicinity, if disturbed, could not be explained.
>
> Michael and I hid on the premises one night and once the whole compound was empty we did a preliminary recce. We inspected perimeter fencing, escape routes, the surrounding land; we covered the lorry park, the animal pens and various out buildings and vehicles. Everything was observed, checked and memorised. Next we made a more thorough check of the slaughterhouse itself; we scaled the roof for possible entry points as the front was alarmed. A closer inspection brought us to one of the many large shed doors at the rear of the building. It had a large metal bin against it, which we moved. And in we went. What we entered was a pitch-black maze of corridors and side rooms. The silence was eerie, but an unmistakable, almost tangible atmosphere pervaded the building,. The stench of fear and blood filled the place. Echoes. Echoes all around.
>
> I walked into a room containing two dead cows strung up from their hind legs, their open throats swinging over a grate in the floor. Metal bins nearby held the blood, organs and skins of our animal friends lying like shrugged off coats in their own juices. We spent two hours there that night. We retraced the doomed animals' footsteps starting from where they would be herded in from their pens, up to the drover's ramp to be prodded and stunned (or not) and then through to where they would be hoisted up, cut and bled. We went up to the first landing, to the

kitchens, toilets and offices and then back down to the main slaughterhouse in silence, both deep in our thoughts. We left without a trace.

A fortnight later, I had bought everything we would need, and early in the evening we dropped off our tools, petrol and the devices at the compound and drove off to park the van somewhere inconspicuous. We walked back to the compound like a courting couple then slipped through onto the lorry park. We checked the lorries, the building and the surrounding area for any sign of life. Finding none, we continued. A hole was cut in the fence at the opposite end of the compound to where the police or security would enter so as to ensure we wouldn't have our escape blocked. We then smashed each vehicle's side window, relatively nice and quietly with a centre punch. We then withdrew and waited for any response. There was none. We left an unlit device by each vehicle ready for the correct timing and we moved onto the building.

We doused the whole top floor with copious amounts of petrol, dragging overalls and paper towels from the locker room out onto the landing and down the stairs, to form one long snaking continuous fuse. Next we attempted to blowtorch and cut our way through to the chilling/processing section through two huge iron gates. No luck there, so we concentrated on what we could get to. I climbed onto some corrugated roofing and left devices together with a trail of petrol leading to the drover's ramp, which I set on fire.

Machinery was hoisted together, splashed with petrol and then a device placed next to it. The devices were a potassium nitrate and sugar mix, sealed in freezer bags. The bag was attached to a bottle containing a detergent and petrol mixture. We had twenty-six of these devices and a further twelve large packets of the nitrate/sugar mix on their own, in addition to the petrol. Basically, we meant business! Next, the vehicle devices were lit and they were placed through the smashed windows and left on the upholstery. Back inside the building we manually activated another fire and began throwing devices into it to encourage it to spread. The explosive mixture with the petrol shot blue flames 8ft

> into the air which began to creep dangerously close to us over the petrol soaked floor. We ran out just as two of the lorries exploded into flames. We slipped away into the night.

Sadly for them, the police were just as determined to see a result and got lucky when they turned up at the sanctuary where Michael Green was working to see if anyone there knew anything. He arrived for work at the wrong time and walked straight into them. Arresting the three people there, they later found sufficient circumstantial evidence to link him to the crime and force an admission. Further investigations led them to his partner in the raid, who was arrested and unable to explain away the forensic match between bolt cutters in her possession and a severed bolt at the site of the attack.

Since the fire service had got to the scene quickly, the slaughterhouse itself was saved from extensive damage but boss Robert Ensor said: 'A lot of vehicles have been damaged but thankfully no product has been damaged. There is a lot of debris and some structural damage but it could have been much, much worse. The current situation is that we are back in production, we are slaughtering and everything's OK.' Of course, that is a matter of opinion.

After spending 15 months on remand in prison, Michael Green was sentenced to a total of five years, 3½ for the above and a further 18 months for attempted arson at a cattle transport depot in Northampton. Melanie Arnold got 3½ years for her attempt to raze the slaughterhouse. While hardly praising them for their efforts, the judge did put things back into some sort of perspective with these sentences and ignored prosecution calls for eight-year terms.

By the mid 1990's, direct action was mushrooming in Holland, as well as in much of Europe, spurred on in part by the seemingly endless stream of UK activists hitting the headlines. The Dutch ALF—the Djurens Belfrielse Front (DBF)—had been busy acting against the meat trade and would have continued indefinitely were it not for a stroke of bad luck with someone in the wrong place at the wrong time. While the DBF had been becoming more confident and active, the police had been slow to react, a detail that is in no way a criticism from me. (Take all time you need, I say!)

Detectives had been tracking a gang of drug smugglers who were living in the same neighbourhood as a very busy DBF team. That wasn't the problem so much as the fact that they were all using the same phone box and the police had bugged it. Still, not a problem, except that the animal liberators were using it to claim responsibility for their actions. Blissfully unaware they'd walked into someone else's surveillance operation, the net rapidly closed in.

That meant that two lots of suspects were now under surveillance and a great deal of suspicion, and it wasn't long before arrests were made and excuses were thin on the ground. Frank Kocera and Eric Van Der Laan had no choice but to confess to painting the walls of a butchers' training school, and three arson attacks and two attempts, which were all linked to each other by the similarity of devices used. The ALF had claimed responsibility for 14 arson attacks between 1993 and 1996, including the destruction of an entire meat factory, plus a lot of lesser damage and graffiti which added up financially. Given due credit for their cooperation, Frank Kocera was given 28 months in prison plus eight on probation and Eric Van Der Laan got twenty months plus ten on probation.

It was a mark of how far things had progressed in Holland when representatives of the meat trade turned out in force for the sentencing, confident their troubles would be over once this prolific team was off the streets for a few years. Their celebrations were short lived, however, curtailed as they were by the sight of an even larger turn out in support of the defendants', lower than expected sentences and a new wave of devastating arson attacks even before the cell doors had clanged shut. One Dutch activist described events as 'Sad for the two men in prison but proof that the Dutch way of seeing animals is changing for the better.'

There was a similar show of solidarity in a German court two weeks later, when well-wishers crowded in for two nationals who had been working with three Swiss activists from across the border. They had been arrested following a high-speed chase after being disturbed trashing a slaughterhouse at Westerheim. After they had been convicted of the raid, 90,000DM (£32,000) was seized to compensate for the damage they had done, and they were also fined 2,000DM each, given four months suspended prison sentences and had their car and other property confiscated. All told, things got rather expensive, especially for the Swiss to whom the judge took a particular dislike for border hopping.

Sledgehammers And Nuts

> While we are the living graves of murdered beasts, slaughtered to satisfy our appetites, how can we expect ideal conditions on this earth.
>
> *George Bernard Shaw*

Another legacy of the live export campaign was the longest criminal trial in animal rights history, which, despite the fact that it lasted a massive 22 weeks, little has been written about it.

The petrol bombing of the White Hart public house in the village of Henfield in West Sussex at the height of the live export campaign was at the centre of one alleged conspiracy involving several defendants. The story goes (and the full story is hard to find) that two brothers who were key figures in the trade, were known to frequent the pub. After the pub had been closed one night, a flaming device was lobbed through a downstairs window. The landlord and his family, who were upstairs, were forced to flee. The ground floor was gutted. Following the attack, one of those allegedly involved was heard to brag about it to others. He was said to have still smelled of petrol the following day. Soon the police were making arrests for various offences and soon after that most of those arrested—one whom was only 15—were making statements to the police implicating not only themselves, but each other too. There was something of a mess back at the White Hart and local protesters—to whom direct action was a complete unknown—were totally bewildered by the whole affair.

There was also a problem with a police informant in the area, someone who—whilst operating in the Midlands some years earlier—was known to have set up two activists who had been—it was then claimed—trying to obtain a gun. Both men had initially been remanded in custody charged with conspiracy to murder but had later been acquitted of all charges. Mick Roberts, an unlikeable, overweight middle-aged man, had somehow managed to immerse himself in the live exports campaign in Sussex. If he wasn't trouble enough, the local back stabbers and gossips were making themselves busy adding to the mess, and they were a vocal minority who were arguably the most dangerous of all. It wasn't long before the main topic on the minds of many Shoreham protesters was speculation about who might have been responsible for the burning of the pub.

That secondary targets are legitimate in the struggle against animal abuse is largely unquestioned in today's campaigning, though there was a time when even the homes of abusers were out of bounds for protest. With the evolution of the movement has come the introduction of a broader, more inclusive sweep, which has taken in other, not so obvious areas. Today, vivisector's homes are considered a primary target, as is a firm that might profit from business with, say, a vivisection lab—for example, even the sandwich delivery firm. The thinking behind this is that by profiteering by association from animal suffering, one is both condoning it and perpetuating it.

Tactically and morally in this case, however, the problem was considered by many to be the indiscriminate nature of the action; it wasn't so much the fact the pub had been frequented by the two exporters, but more that there had been innocent people upstairs at the time of the attack. The targeting of a business over its use by a Hunt or even because of a customer's attendance has been a legitimate tactic, but not the targeting of innocent tenants. There are other banners under which people operate which are less restrictive than the ALF's unofficially agreed code of ethics. These appear to encourage physical attacks on animal abusers, according to the likes of The Justice Department, The Hunt Retribution Squad, or The Animal Rights Militia and conspiratorial landlords would certainly be seen as targets in some circumstances. In reality, of course, someone acting alone or without title can do what the hell they like in the name of 'animal rights', indeed there is proof animal abusers have done just that in order to discredit the movement, and of course the State machine will do just that as and when they feel the need, which is why a boundary needs to be clearly drawn. Such a position was sought following this affair but it proved very divisive.

In September 1995, at Lewes Crown Court, 35 year-old Barbara Trenholm and 18 year-old Justin Wright were sentenced to ten years and five years respectively for their part in the arson attack on the 400-year-old White Hart public house. Both always denied any involvement in the attack.

The White Hart episode caused a serious dilemma for the ALFsg. For the first time in its history, it was faced with having to deal with an action, which had crossed the defining line between that deemed acceptable and unacceptable under the ALF 'statutes.' A great deal of energy was expended on the debate that followed the attack and arrests, and the SG members narrowly voted that financial support should not be offered to the defendants, though moral support should. It was later taken into consideration that the convicted arsonists—if indeed guilty—had acted (in their view) in the interests of animals and should therefore be supported. It was a confused compromise.

The firebombing of a public house (under any or no banner) occupied by an innocent family was seen, quite rightly, to cross the boundary. Despite the enormous amount of rhetoric there is about 'violent animal rights thugs', not a single one of the cruellest monsters targeted has ever been killed. There are few with any genuine desire to take the movement down that path as this completely opposes it's fundamental opposition to violence, though some would possibly rejoice at the killing of an animal abuser, and the ensuing news coverage which would panic others. In a wider social context, rightly or wrongly, attacks on perceived perverts and paedophiles are met with celebration and it's interesting to note how some newspapers gloat over attacks on alleged sex offenders, even giving them their tacit approbation, while calling animal liberators all manner of names for doing the same to inanimate objects.

As a result of this debate, it was generally agreed that such drastic action should not be undertaken lightly—if it were indeed a pre-planned action by genuine animal activists—and whilst it is accepted that public houses are legitimate targets for protest action if they provide entertainment or refuge for animal abusers, publicans who don't really care what their customers do in their own time shouldn't be. Had there not been people in the pub at the time, there would have been far less concern, but a mature debate about the validity of attacking a secondary target in this way, whilst initially painful, was a necessary process.

The live exports protests in the UK attracted a lot of new blood to the wider campaigning spectrum at all levels, including quite a few genuine loonies, as other activists have described them. They also attracted some violent policing and taught people new to all this just how badly the guardians of law and order can behave. There were huge crowds of decent, men and women of every generation, entire families—'normal' people, if you will—and 'Rent-a-mob', the animal liberators who started it all off and who will be there at the end, opposing the shipments of live animals (or dead ones for that matter) by abstinence. Some spectacular and innovative tactics were used to stop the wagons and ferries and there was a huge amount of media coverage; it all seemed to point to a positive change in society's attitude to animal abuse. But inevitably, as is usual where a large number of human beings are drawn together in a struggle—there were problems with egos, personality clashes and *agent provocateurs*.

Three years after the campaign erupted, six people from the Shoreham area were serving sentences of between two and ten years and many more with lesser sentences for a range of offences and alleged offences. And that isn't all it is to be remembered for. So many defendants made statements implicating each other, and there were so many rumours and hints about police infiltrators and grasses, it seemed there were as many people working for the police on their side of the thick blue line as the other. More than anywhere in England, the south coast has had a reputation for attracting grasses and informants, not all of them genuinely so, but there have been a handful of undisputed cases. Three of four confirmed were Ros Loescher, Kristine Sinclair and Graham Ennis (alias Innes, Cameron). Shoreham was a breeding ground for naïve young activists with little experience of the ways of the police, and of the need to keep one's mouth firmly shut. It made them easy prey for the likes of Loescher and her cronies.

At the conclusion of the lengthy conspiracy trial at Lewes Crown Court, Mick Roberts (real name Michael Suorot Ali, and affiliated to the above-mentioned unsavoury crew) was somehow convicted of conspiring to cause criminal damage and sent to prison for six years. Joe Taylor, age 27 got four years and 18 year-old Kevin Chapman got two. Tony Daly, 35, also got four years, having pleaded guilty to damaging lorries. His wife received a suspended sentence. Appeals were immediately filed against these convictions. The Appeal Court was asked to consider the defence's arguments that evidence, which was unrelated to the charges, had been used to convict the defendants. For example, during their trial, repeated references were made to the arson attack on the White Hart public house and to the Justice Department's postal devices, none of which bore any relation to the allegations of criminal damage with which they had been charged. The Appeal Court judge set a precedent by concluding that when the charge of Conspiracy to Commit Criminal Damage is used, it has to specify exactly whether it relates to arson, arson with intent to endanger life, criminal damage, criminal damage with recklessness, criminal damage with intent to endanger life or whatever, as the law—Section 1:1 of the 1977 Criminal Damage Act—covers all of these and is too wide ranging and unspecific. The Appeal Court decided that because it was unclear whether the jury had been swayed by references to arson and so convicted them of arson as opposed to criminal damage, the convictions should be overturned. Tony Daly had his sentence reduced to time served and the others were released unconditionally after several months in prison.

The day before the live export demos kicked in, the Sunday Express ran a story prompted by 'police and intelligence experts' warning that animal rights extremists were about to escalate their campaign to include the assassination of vivisectors, who it claimed, faced 'a terrifying new threat from doorstep assassins.' A high-level police source added spice, as did a couple of vivisectors with tales of periodic harassment, which were causing them to live in fear. Pressure from the industry was increasing, demanding more resources and laws to deal with the menace of public objection. Ten years on, there are no dead vivisectors, just a hat trick of deceased activists, a few close calls and many, many serious assaults on campaigners. On the other hand, in all these years, only a couple of guns have nearly found their way into the hands of activists, offences which were later dismissed by the courts for the suspicion that surrounded them, one man hit with a baseball bat and numerous others threatened. Yet still the laws have come thick and fast to curtail lawful protest, including, in response to the aforementioned claims of a new threat, the formation of a new national police unit under the direction of Scotland Yard's Anti Terrorist Branch. Not the friendly sounding adversaries once set against the animal people in the form of Uncle ARNI, today we have to outwit something called National Extremism Tactical Coordination Unit (NETCU), which sounds more like a Romanian centre forward and doesn't really make sense unless the police are admitting to being extremists, but is a serious development, and signals the extent to which government will go to protect the interests of business from those of us with issues.

NETCU shamelessly promote links to the RDS and other pro vivisection organisations on their website, claiming that: 'The Research Defence Society works to promote understanding of well-regulated, conducted humanely, animal research. It also works with welfare groups and Government to promote good practice in laboratory animal welfare and the development of non-animal replacement methods.' The Government care not to hide the principle reasons for their arrogant and dogmatic defence of all things done to animals: their remarkably close relationship with the animal testing industry and their lobby groups, such as the drug-industry funded Research Defence Society (RDS). The growing integration between government policy-makers and these vested interests is blatantly financial. The Department of

Health even recommends the RDS in its response letters to public inquiries into animal testing! Thus, the Government basically regurgitates the propaganda of the RDS.

The last Conservative government tried using the power of the law to contain people who want change. First they introduced the 1986 Public Order Act, partly with the intention of making hunt sabotage impossible. This was billed as the death knell for hunt sabotage, but it came too late, didn't work as hoped and cost the police dearly in mass compensation claims for wrongful arrest and illegal detention. Attacking the animal liberators was again part of 1994 Criminal Justice Act. This contains clauses which makes trespass a criminal offence for the first time; it took away the right to silence; gave the police power to set bail conditions, which were used to ban saboteurs from returning to a hunt for months, or protesters from returning to a lab to demonstrate and gave power to stop and search people attending protests—amongst other things. The law of 'aggravated trespass' is defined as doing anything on private land, which is intended to disrupt a lawful activity. Anyone convicted is liable to three months in prison or a £2,000 fine. This law was also badly drafted and wasn't as effective as was intended in stifling opposition. Although some forces have used this law, many haven't and of arrests made, very few convictions have been achieved, with an early acquittal rate around 90%. In seeking to diminish or destroy protest groups, these new laws, especially under the CJA, have brought together the dissatisfied—anti war, pro animal, environmental, travellers, party-goers…The battle lines are being drawn.

In June 1997, new legislation was added to the excess of laws available to the police to prevent people from protesting. Under the Conservative government, it was open season on public demonstrations, partying, picketing, hunt sabotage, living on the road, health care and so on. Better things were expected under New Labour, but we know now we were taken for a ride. The 1997 Protection from Harassment Act passed through Parliament on a tide of media 'concern' about a growing problem for women being stalked by men, reinforced by a small number of highly publicised court cases showing just that. There was some concern voiced by protest groups and civil liberty watchers, but a fat lot of good that's going to do when civil liberties are precisely what the government is after. If protecting women was the real motive for introducing this law, then it was a jolly coincidence that it would quickly go on to stifle protests by women against the cruelty and abuse inflicted by the same kind of men who introduced the new law. Similarly, there is the 1992 Trade Union Act, the 2001 Criminal Justice and Police Act and the 2003 Anti-Social Behaviour Act, all readily available and regularly used to deal with animal rights protesters. One woman was arrested and had her house raided in 2004 for sending polite emails to companies involved with poisoning animals in lab tests, the police deeming her actions to be harassment when one recipient received two of her e-mails. The charges were dropped because of the time it took police to get their case to court. Others are being arrested and harassed for displaying images of animal abuse. One small group was moved on by police from outside a circus because circus workers living in the caravans were said to be harassed by the protest. These are increasingly common incidents and are being documented at the Nectu Watch site.

In 2005, the Labour government rushed through the Serious Organised Crime Bill, which defines just about anything as harassment and can be used to ban even the distribution of leaflets. Section 121 of the bill prohibits people from 'pursuing a course of conduct which involves harassment of two or more persons' in order 'to persuade any person not to do something that he is not under any obligation to do, or to do something that he is not under any obligation to do.' Harassment can involve 'conduct on at least one occasion, in relation to two or more persons.' In other words, you need only approach someone once to be considered to be harassing them if you have already approached someone else with a similar leaflet that a police officer, or force, might object to.

In recent years, police have taken firearms with them on house raids, as they did whilst looking for evidence to charge someone for breaking a pet shop window; they were also well equipped for serious violence at the Rafiq's slaughterhouse. CS spray and batons have injured many other unarmed protesters. How long before they make a 'mistake' and offer to hold an internal inquiry into the untimely death of an animal rights advocate? Before or after increasingly violent hunt supporters kill someone else? Anyone care? All in all, there does seem to be a lot of violence surrounding 'animal rights', apart from the animal abuse itself, and the abusers and the police are getting away with dishing out rather more of it than they're receiving.

Early in 1995, masked men connected with the Cheshire hunting fraternity smashed their way into the homes of known saboteurs in Liverpool and Manchester and in one case beat a female occupant and her dogs. Others were out of the house, so escaped injury. The assailants found a second house empty, having broken down four doors to get in and were unable to gain entry to a third property. The woman who was attacked was told that if she ever attended another hunt meet, they would be back. More recently in Milton Keynes, a device was found under the car of a well-known saboteur. It was not the first attack of that nature, but of a pattern and increasing severity: vehicles have been burnt out and mutilated animals left as some kind of sick calling card. As always, there are regular stories of the violence associated with circus workers, including a protester shot on one occasion and another stabbed, though fortunately no one has yet been seriously hurt in that arena.

Undeterred by the threats and the violence and in response to the attacks in Liverpool, two transport firms contracted to Milk Marque in Cheshire were sabotaged by ALF arsonists who wrecked over 30 milk tankers and other vehicles in a massive two-pronged attack, which caused around £2 millions' worth of damage. I supposed it goes without saying there were dairy calves at the heart of this attack also. The first ignited in Macclesfield at around 2.00am and 12 vehicles were wrecked by devices placed around the wheels. Twenty minutes later, a further 20 large vehicles belonging to Wincanton Distribution were targeted at the second site. Assistant Chief Constable of Cheshire, John Dwyer said, 'If their objective was to cause a lot of damage it certainly achieved that. Most of the vehicles were a write off.'

The Grass, The Turncoat And The Spy Who Loved Us

> You can't stop change in society, and that's what we are seeing now. In ten years fox hunting will be banned. In the next century, animals won't be treated as they are now. Our problem isn't with the aims of the animal rights movement—it's with their methods.
>
> *Special Branch officer speaking to The Observer, November 1995*

The ALF Press officer had been busy for three years, clearing up confusion and keeping animal abuse as the central talking point whilst making no apologies for the actions of the ALF and others. In return, the authorities were keen to shut him up by using whatever means necessary. With the emergence of the Poultry Liberation Organisation in early 1994, they seized their chance. It was Webb's prerogative as a member of the National Union of Journalists, and of course as the elected ALF Press Officer, to report on breaking news stories. So when the PLO sent him a press release claiming they had contaminated battery eggs at Tesco's supermarkets throughout the south of England, he decided it not just important, but imperative, to share it. More PLO actions followed and so did arrests, including that of Webb, whose house was searched from top to bottom. He was accused of urging people to shun battery eggs by issuing the press release. It was an incredible accusation, effectively silencing him, or anyone else for that matter, who had anything unapproved to say as a journalist. The press office's material was confiscated, and Webb was bailed pending further inquiries.

Two weeks later, Robin Webb found himself in custody again after Special Branch officers pulled his car at Hove in East Sussex expecting—they said—to find a shotgun! Webb had been visiting the area, and travelling with David Hammond, a prominent Sussex-based ex squaddie who had 'ALF' tattooed on both his temples. A couple of dozen detectives closed in on them and both men were arrested.

If there had ever been any doubt that a concerted effort was being made to silence the voice of the ALF, it was dispelled the moment the police opened the boot, where there was supposed to have been a parcel containing bolt cutters, but most certainly not the gun they found there. Good intelligence or a set up? Police told magistrates at their bail hearing days later that, acting on a tip-off, they had found a shotgun and 22 rounds of ammunition in the boot of Webb's car and a bullet in the glove compartment. They were also reminded that Webb was already on bail for another serious conspiracy. It all seemed really convenient and straightforward and, given the level of harassment he had been experiencing, kind of expected. But there was much more to this than the suspected police set-up.

One of the men's friends, it transpired later, had become an active police informant, and it was she who had handed Webb the parcel with the 'bolt cutters.' Problem number one. Problem number two was that Hammond had a close personal relationship with a second, well-established police informant (not involved with animal rights campaigning) who used the name Graham Ennis. Added to this, Hammond himself was a rather hot and cold character, prone to angry public outbursts and other erratic behaviour. He was opinionated and not particularly popular, but he was motivated and not averse to taking risks, not unlike Webb. All things considered, there was no way this pair were going to keep out of trouble for long.

What the police didn't explain was why—if, as they'd alleged, they were dealing at the time with two potentially dangerous gunmen—they approached the two suspects without being armed themselves. It is fairly standard procedure that when dealing with armed and dangerous political extremists or criminals, the police send in armed officers. That is what their guns are for, after all. But not even a water pistol did they take! The police weren't forthcoming about this minor discrepancy—they were simply happy they had bagged themselves the ALF front man for something so big. As far as the two arrested were concerned, the weapon had been switched with the bolt cutters while they were away from—and the police near to—Webb's car. They were unaware that they were surrounded by double agents. Both men were initially remanded in custody but granted bail weeks later with strict conditions. Webb wasn't to travel more than 20 miles from his home in Cambridge and had to sign on at his local police station daily, a 25 mile round trip from home where he had to live and sleep each night. With the material of the press office in police custody, his role as Press Officer was severely curtailed. That—needless to say—was the intention.

Ruffled but not frightened off, Webb continued his work as acting Press Officer, engaging in endless interviews over the phone and elsewhere within his zone until, that is, he returned to answer bail a few weeks later for issuing the earlier PLO press release. One detective in a designer suit told Webb that 'bail conditions have failed, so we're going to lock you up to shut you up.' And so it was that he was charged and remanded in custody for six months before legal delays allowed him another bail application, which was granted after a lengthy legal battle. He was duly ordered not to speak to the press, not to write articles for publications or speak at rallies. He was told 'Not to be party in any way to any publicity for or on behalf of the Animal Rights organisations or any other body with similar aims and objectives.' The 20-mile restriction was lifted on appeal only to allow him to travel to London to see his solicitor by prior arrangement and on those days he was allowed to miss signing at the police station. They called this relaxing the conditions!

Locking him up had been the police's favourite option initially, because being on bail didn't stop Webb from talking and writing with relative freedom. But the new release conditions effectively gagged him and were therefore a suitable Plan B. There was no longer any pretence about the notion that someone out there pulling police strings was desperate to silence the Press Office, which, given the wealth of information that the ALF has released into the public domain over time, and the issues that have been raised, should be viewed as unfortunate to say the least.

After three years of curfews, remand and signing on at police stations, the shotgun trial was finally scheduled. The opening two days comprised legal battles at the end of which the judge ordered the two suspected ne'er-do-wells be acquitted of all charges and the case dismissed due to a lack of evidence. Both defendants persistently denied any knowledge of the gun. The prosecution had alleged that the police were tipped off about where a gun could be found. The defence argued that the informant—the all-seeing, all knowing witness—was a potential suspect and should be cross-examined about the mysterious appearance of a gun where none had previously been. The judge agreed. The police refused to disclose the identity of their informant, who did not want to be publicly identified, and chose to abandon the case.

Something funny was definitely going on and the police were anxious no one could put their finger on it. Paranoia among many is preferable to prison for a few but it's as disruptive to a cause when close friends have to be viewed with caution just in case. Hammond's odd relationship with 'Ennis' continued long after his role in working for the State had been exposed, for example in one statement in 1996 he told the police: 'I've been using him (Hammond) as a source of information on various terrorist matters that have been going on inside the animal rights movement and it's been very useful.' But Hammond was in denial and losing face amongst colleagues; he finally became persona non grata within the movement after the disclosure of peculiar activity detrimental to the cause, and the misappropriation of £2,000 from a prisoner support campaign fund of which he was in charge.

Once a hardworking activist, Hammond turned first to backstabbing amongst himself, drawing childlike caricatures on his new website, New Vegan Liberation, where he mocked the ALF and individuals with whom he had fallen out or disagreed. When the web server pulled the plug following complaints, he turned totally weird and went to the press for support. Taking his story to *The Sunday Telegraph*, he revealed: 'Why I quit the evil animal fanatics.' The 'story' from the former soldier purportedly spilling the beans on the vicious, sinister side of the ALF, but that's been tried before and since, and there's not really a lot to tell! This article was really just a mishmash of his views. Having whet our appetite as much as the PR man for the Bognor and District Morris Dance Troupe might do, it concluded that he had moved to a secret address in France to write his memoirs of his time inside the ALF and would be appearing in a *Dispatches* documentary of the same title that night. The memoirs never materialised and he probably wishes *Dispatches* hadn't.

The Express gleefully spiced up Hammonds story, *'Inside The Animal Liberation Front'*, in which it was claimed he had seen the error of his ways. The strength of the story rested on a claim that he had occasionally been phoned by Robin Webb for his views on campaign material ideas and slogans. His view of joining the ALF was: 'If you have led a boring life, you suddenly have a purpose. You become someone.' It was really quite sad, terribly unrevealing and his 15 minutes of fame served only to lose him his job as a school groundsman, his credibility as an animal advocate and left him with few friends either side of the divide.

Smack bang in the middle of this 'south coast problem' was the woman called Sally Jenkins, or—as she is more disparagingly referred to—Fat Sally; the gun-runner, if you like. She had, it seemed, also changed her mind and turned on her friends and against the animals. Whilst no longer around to confirm the speculation, it appears that this once brave and active campaigner had been sufficiently intimidated by police threats to turn informant, passing to them what information she had on the plans of her one-time friends.

A rather round woman, Sally Jenkins wasn't really designed for climbing fences and over rooftops, but she was committed to doing what she could for the animals. She was apparently fearless and always on hand to do the driving, no matter what was planned. She and her puny husband Henry were a somewhat mismatched couple; she definitely wore the trousers, dominated him in public and enjoyed humiliating him.

She was active for three or four years at all levels and there was no reason to doubt her commitment; indeed she was, on the face of it, probably the last person to worry about. Others would talk about the ALF and speculate about who they were, but she was the ALF. That was the problem, though; because she was so deeply involved in campaigns and raids she was beyond suspicion. But it turns out she wasn't quite brave as she thought and when the spectre of prison loomed, she sold out the animals and her best friends to the devil.

It all seems to have stemmed from an arrest over the alleged contamination hoax of battery eggs. She and others were suspected and arrested and probably could have been charged, but the police were after bigger things. They told Sally: 'We have enough evidence or can make up enough to send you down for years. You won't see your animals again, you'll lose your job and your house and someone your size will have a hard time in prison. Or you could help us.' The overwhelming majority of arrestees have heard something similar to this and accept prison as an inevitable consequence of their actions should the worst happen, but Sally was suddenly very afraid. Perhaps she had never considered the consequences. It's thought the police may also have offered her money.

Sally was a self-motivated activist and was considered trustworthy and reliable; at one stage, she even almost took over the running of the ALFsg. She genuinely wanted to help animals. Webb and Hammond likewise. They had all known of each other for some years. People who didn't know them personally respected them for their commitment; it was how they felt about each other. To invite someone like this round after a meeting or demo would be nothing unusual.

What the long-term goal of the police was will never be known for sure, but when they saw that Hammond and Webb were drawn to her, perhaps they recognised she was potentially a weak link. She wasn't the smartest tool in the box, but she was very much in the right place at the right time. She was able to travel the country and pop in to the homes of other well-known activists, she was that sort and if needed she was there and would help out.

Thirty-four-year-old Gillian Peachey has been around animal issues for years and has always been involved in something or other. These days the government badger extermination programme in Cornwall keeps her busy. She had known Sally for years and trusted her more than anyone else in their group. They went on demos together, did prisoner support and other legwork. The two of them and others in their all-girl cell had been busy over that time against a variety of targets in the Hampshire area and weren't averse to popping out to leave an incendiary device or two around the place of an evening. There were countless times when, as the driver, Sally took the greatest risk and they could have gone to prison for years for their actions, but instead she'd turned weird, really weird.

No one could put their finger on it at first, but they had noticed a number of odd things happening in the area, like the police appearing to have prior knowledge of events. Naturally, fingers started pointing, but fingers were pointing in the wrong direction. It was no coincidence that Peachey and Jeanette McClunnan were arrested outside Botley Grange Hotel in Hampshire, moments after Peachey had left a hoax bomb in the women's toilet. The Hursley Hambledon Hunt were due to meet there to hold one of their balls and undercover police were in the majority in the lobby, bar and car park. They weren't there because of the hunt, in spite of an ongoing campaign against it, but because Sally had tipped them off that two of her team would be around. Funnily, the initial plan had been simply to check out the hotel with a view to invading at a later date but it was Sally that suggested the girls should leave something behind. Sally made her excuses and stayed home.

Although it was unclear how they were detected, it was clear why both of them were arrested. Something else that didn't add up was why Gilly Peachey was remanded in custody for six months and Jeanette McClunnan was released after a week. The latter did have children at home as mitigation, but was also on bail at the time for other offences including police assault. All of a sudden the assault charges were dropped and she was out! Meanwhile, others in the team were finding themselves under increasing surveillance and rumours were rife that there was a grass among them. To Peachey, Sally and others in the loop, McClunnen was the most likely suspect—an idea fermented by Sally. Peachey ignored warnings that Sally might be the problem; she felt her friend could do no wrong. It simply didn't make sense, as Sally was far more an ALF activist than McClunnen.

To test the theory and with Peachey out of prison, the group set up McClunnen to believe something was planned one night, then sat back watched and were unusually gratified to observe greatly increased police activity in the area. Excuses were relayed via Sally (who was at the time helpfully arranging prison visits for Robin Webb) to McClunnen as to why plans had been aborted and the date changed, and the performance was repeated. Again it was as clear as day: McClunnen knew of their plans and so did the police. Twice.

Of course, none of it had anything to do with McClunnen, and Sally and her handlers must have been wetting themselves. This was the stuff of dreams: they had a well-placed informant and were making significant arrests, and the blame for it was on another genuine activist who had become a target for the ALF! McClunnen was harassed by her one-time comrades and put through what she describes as months of 'sheer hell' while Sally plotted her next move. Peachey was sentenced to 21 months, suspended for two years and fined £1,800 for planting the hoax device. McClunnen was found not guilty. See the pattern developing here? It wasn't McClunnen's doing and while it was good for her, it was making others very suspicious. It was something of a relief for Peachey to have not only avoided the three years she was expecting, but also to have identified and isolated the problem. Sally was pleased too, to not have to spend any more time sorting out her friend's affairs whilst she was inside. She was a rock, genuinely! The kind of person you need on the out when you're locked up. Peachey was empowered. Utterly unmoved in her conviction that the best way ahead was through direct action, she was back in the fold in a flash and plotting her next move.

Any further conviction over the next two years would give her a sentence starting at 21 months, with more added accordingly, but she was happy she could avoid that particularly now the grass had gone. The fact was, there was a lot of stuff going on in the area, much of it their doing. A suspended sentence is meant to serve as a deterrent for someone keen to avoid prison, but to someone like Peachey, it wasn't a straightforward consideration. She was very much of the view that actions speak louder than words.

The girls around her were keen to crack on too, especially Sally. It was Xmas Eve 1995 and the four of them felt pretty safe, one for a different reason from the others, of course. The police would be busy with drunk drivers and drunken brawls, giving arsonists the opportunity to go about their business uninterrupted. The master of the New Forest Staghounds who was about to be caught off-guard and have a costly, disrupted Xmas day. Sally, of course, was privy to the plot and knew what was in the car with her three good friends. But Sally wasn't in the car with her friends as they went out that night. She'd made good her excuses again and gave her friends a wide berth.

Funny as it might sound, all things considered (it was over a year since the shotgun incident) the penny still hadn't dropped when a marked patrol car stopped their car just minutes from their intended target. Happy Xmas, officer!

Police must find some interesting things but how often is there a stash of incendiary devices in the boot? A terrible, collective sinking feeling swept through the car, which always accompanies the blue lights and siren in these situations. You don't have to have been there. At first you aren't sure if it's just a traffic offence they're pulling you on, one that can be resolved in a minute and have you on your way with an exchange of the season's greetings. But luck was not with Gillian Peachey—the spectre of Sally Jenkins was. It was the detective going to the boot that brought on the rush of sickness. Trapped like wild animals and no way out.

There were so many of them rushing in they knew what they wanted. One wide boy, Detective Constable Avinagoodnight, shoved his face into Peachey's to offer his own greeting and snarled: 'Got you now you little bitch,' even before he looked in the boot! They certainly had. All she could do was avoid throwing up.

Five days and lots of house searches later, Gilly Peachey, Gaynor Ford and Sandra White were charged with conspiracy to possess explosives and cause criminal damage on 24 December and with arson at Webbs' poultry farm on 5 December. They were remanded in custody. It was a clear-cut case, you'd think. Those in custody were still to wonder if their downfall might be because the car had been bugged or perhaps someone's house? Any one of them might have said something, or been overheard somewhere. Others were looking at Sally but for Peachey; it couldn't be. No way. She was still around offering support and helping out with things. It was only when her and Henry quietly moved home and disappeared some months later that the penny finally dropped.

The ease with which the police were locking people up was one thing, but difficulties arose when the trial judge insisted the informant be made available for cross-examination by the defence, who successfully argued that there was potentially an agent provocateur at work. There was no way Sally was having that. She had been partly responsible for the planning and was probably embarrassed by her double life and the damage she was now doing to the animals cause and ashamed to stand up and spill the beans publicly. She'd done the dirty and run away.

Without her, and with other complications, two trials had to be aborted and the third trial collapsed. Sandra White and Gaynor Ford were acquitted of all charges. But for the ill-fated Peachey, the police would have had nothing to show for their efforts. Due to the seemingly damning evidence against her, not least incendiaries in the boot of her car, she had made the decision early on in proceedings to cut her losses and plead guilty in the hope of a sentence reduction. But the judge showed no mercy and sentenced her to a total of six years and nine months, including 21 months for breaching her suspended sentence. Her co-defendants went home.

Gillian Peachey was to be the final victim of the mess of informants and loose-talking activists operating in the South East during the mid-1990s. Robin Webb, on the other hand, had more to come from the police.

Gandalf

> True benevolence, or compassion, extends itself through the whole of existence and sympathizes with the distress of every creature capable of sensation.
>
> *Joseph Addison (1672-1719)*
> *British poet, playwright, member of Parliament*

Just five weeks after Robin Webb was cleared of allegations regarding the unlawful issuing of a press release to a news agency regarding the PLO contamination of eggs, Hampshire Police were at his door again and he was arrested along with a number of other people and charged: 'that at Hampshire or elsewhere on days unknown between 1-1-91 and 17-1-96 you jointly (with the other defendants) conspired together to unlawfully incite persons unknown to commit criminal damage.'

At the case conclusion, three of the accused had been sent to prison for three years each for simply reporting on acts of sabotage and animal rescue without condemnation; more than that, however, it exposed as a myth the notion of free speech of which we boast so proud.

From the outset, it was clear that this case, which was to become known as the Gandalf Conspiracy, sought to link the people behind the ALF Press Office and ALFsg newsletter with the editors of the *Green Anarchist* newspaper: GA aND ALF. It was a scandalous attempt to stifle free speech and cut the information exchange on radical thinking between those fighting for change. There was never any threat, perceived or real, from the GA; without doubt their main target was Robin Webb. Whatever it took, they were determined to get him; the others were there to make up numbers. For the rather obsessive Hampshire detectives of Operation Washington and a DCI Desmond Thomas in particular, this was to prove an expensive, fruitless and time-consuming cock-up. But it seemed to matter little to Hampshire Police that they were unlikely to actually convict Webb of anything, as long as he was gagged and kept restricted on bail.

Right at the beginning of the final court process, after a week of committal proceedings, the magistrate ruled that the case against Robin Webb was oppressive and he released him. End of story? Nah. The others were committed to the crown court for trial. The evidence, which committed Simon Russell, was now even more dubious. He was the hardworking editor of the ALFsg newsletter at that time. Because he had taken the ALFsg newsletters to a barrister for legal approval before publication (as had become normal practice to protect editors and the SG from incitement allegations) they suggested he therefore intended to use it to incite. Some kind of weird logic! They were additionally relying on his close link to Robin Webb, who was now in the eyes of the law not guilty again!

The prosecution argument was that the five defendants, Saxon Burchnall-Wood, Paul Rogers, Steven Booth, Simon Russell and Noel Molland, were involved in publishing newspapers, knew the others were doing likewise and were on the left hand side of the political divide. The gist of it was that to publish the details of direct action constitutes incitement and if there are others doing likewise, you are part of a conspiracy with them. Saxon Wood's contribution to the GA was writing the music reviews and an article on technology. To confuse matters further, Paul Rogers sacked his barrister because they disagreed on tactics and had his case deferred to a later date. This left four.

One of the allegations against Simon Russell was that he had created a website on the Justice Department. The person who actually did—Canadian ALF activist Darren Thurston—travelled to the UK to give evidence in court to that effect. The police felt this gesture unhelpful to the flow of justice so he was detained upon his arrival at Heathrow airport and questioned about his reason for travelling to the UK. His reason was verified by Simon Russell's solicitor, yet they promptly sent him back to Canada—because, they said, of his ALF convictions. After a great deal of legal argument, the court finally agreed to accept a written statement from Thurston. Only then did the police drop their ill-conceived conspiracy to blame Russell for something with which he had clearly not been involved. To add to the weight of his defence, his own solicitor gave evidence in court to stress the deliberate effort Russell had made to keep the ALFsg newsletter within the confines of the law.

After a 46-day trial, the jurors were finally sent out to consider their verdicts. They acquitted Simon Russell but convicted Noel Molland, Saxon Wood and Steven Booth. Three years each. The magnitude of this assault on free speech was largely ignored by the mainstream media, which is somewhat ironic given the wide-reaching implications such a precedent could have for those very journalists if such political prosecutions go unchallenged and the State machine is allowed to shut down whatever news media it dislikes.

At the Appeal Court six months later, the same argument was used as in the Shoreham trial: namely that the defendants were convicted of offences other than those with which they had been charged, i.e.

conspiring to incite criminal damage. Here evidence was introduced in relation to arson attacks and Justice Department actions, which had it been admissible, would have been more serious and would have required additional charges. It was easy for the judges. They debated a retrial but were persuaded it was a bad idea due to spiralling costs, and the amount of time that had elapsed since the arrests over two years earlier. The Appeal Court quashed the convictions, not, unfortunately, on the grounds of free speech but because of a legal point. His Honour Lord Justice Henry stated: 'The events that flawed their trial were too fundamental to be described as a technicality.' It was noted in the ruling that even if the defendants were properly convicted, their sentences were excessive. There were no national newspaper reports of this newsworthy trial, which should have had far greater public interest than David Beckham's latest haircut.

Normally, the police would accept such a rebuttal as part of the game (especially given the fragility of their case) and would go away and think up something else. However, obsessed with pursuing their multi-million pound campaign against the Press Office, they sought a judicial review to appeal against Robin Webb's acquittal at committal and then had the charges against him reinstated. The charge against him and Paul Rogers was amended in light of the appeal to include the word 'arson.' They now sought to pursue the men on the same evidence that had previously been used in court and thrown out. Some of this had been used against Robin Webb on four different occasions. Legal principle forbade evidence used in one trial be used in a second, but that seemed not to apply just now!

The prosecution had tried to argue that, as the first Gandalf trial had been quashed on appeal, it had never really happened and so they could use all the evidence again. After three weeks of legal wrangling the defendants were finally acquitted of all charges and free of bail conditions, but it wasn't over for Webb just yet.

Branded A Liar

> When I was a young man I observed that 9 out of 10 things I did were failures. I didn't want to be a failure so I did 10 times more work.
>
> *George Bernard Shaw*

Graham Hall had earned his stripes in 1990 for his audacious infiltration of a gang of badger baiters, which resulted in their trial and subsequent conviction at Builth Wells, mid-Wales. In this case, no prison sentence or long active service history was needed to earn the respect of the Animal Liberation Movement. When you've been undercover in the dangerous world of the badger baiter and had a few locked up for your efforts, you are in there. What many in the movement failed to grasp was that for Hall this was just a job. He busied himself on other unrelated business projects in the intervening years but when he re-emerged on the animal rights scene a few years later, few were suspicious of his interest in becoming involved with the ALF.

But Hall was up to no good and in cahoots with Hampshire Police and Channel 4. Not so keen to fight animal abuse as one might have expected from someone who had apparently taken such fantastic risks to help animals, Hall was now out to entrap some of the activists siding with the animal kingdom and with hidden camera in tow, was conducting a tour of willing activists. It was remarkably good timing on his part that he latched onto David Hammond during his big tantrum. He also fell into the arms of the loose-tongued Gaynor Ford and was introduced to Robin Webb, potentially the biggest prize. Hall, a rough-cut brummie, was good at fitting in and was able to convince some of his new friends that he was good for a bit of direct action. Having made a career out of subterfuge, it mattered not to Hall whom he trapped as long as he got his footage for Channel 4's *Dispatches*. The police of course wanted Webb.

Inside The ALF shows Gaynor Ford apparently wooed by Hall and his gifts of flowers and hash. She even took him—and his hidden camera and microphone—on a driven tour of places she claimed to have targeted in the Hampshire area telling how she funded her actions with public donations. It certainly looks from the film as though she had talked herself into a lot of trouble. But this documentary, like so many, isn't all it appears to be. For all her apparent admissions, even the enthusiastic ALF bashers of Hampshire Police weren't minded to arrest, let alone prosecute her. Nor, indeed, were they interested in the loose cannon Hammond, who was, at this time in his life, not sure if he was an activist or not.

Apparently in a bid to seek credibility, Hammond played the reformed activist, so appalled by the behaviour of his former colleagues and the violent agenda of the 'ALF elite' that he had to tell the world all he knew. But Hammond was making it up to get himself noticed and, as he saw it, punish the movement for disowning him. He saw Hall as an activist, and an ally and, while cautious of what he admits to his new friend while chatting, it's clear that, far from being reformed and appalled by the imaginary 'ALF violence', he talks of how he would still like to see animal abusers hurt.

Hall went to great lengths to get Webb to demonstrate to him how to make an incendiary device and appeared to substantiate the claim that the press officer was 'heavily involved in inciting terror.' But with some neat splicing of footage and manipulation of the facts, you can prove anything. That the police weren't interested in his claims about Webb either really does speak volumes! The Channel 4 documentary was seeking to prove for the umpteenth time, that the ALF is a dangerous terrorist organisation intent on murder. Hall had reportedly spent 'seven months undercover inside the highly dangerous and secretive world of the Animal Liberation Front,' whose inner workings he said had never before been exposed, yet all he had to show for it was that the ALF exists! But he didn't finish there.

The plot thickened considerably when Hall reappeared a year later on the front page of *The Mail on Sunday* in another Exclusive, which ran to two pages, presenting a horrifying story of how the ALF whistle-blower was subjected to a night of terror at the hands of the fanatics whose evil agenda he'd exposed on television.

This time, just to prove once and for all those endless unfounded claims that the ALF is hell-bent on violence, he bravely revealed the wounds inflicted by the people who had kidnapped him, held him hostage for a terrifying twelve hours and used a hot branding iron to burn 'ALF' in four-inch letters into his back. Hall claimed later: 'Even I underestimated them. They are highly organised and totally obsessed—they'll stop at nothing. That conflict is now out of hand and ready to explode.' Hmm, really!

West Mercia Police, who weren't even made aware of the alleged assault until the story appeared in the press, hinted at their view of Hall's claims: 'Wasting police time is still an offence.' According to Hall, a professional con man, he was so traumatised by the attack that he had wet himself, but he was able to re-enact the terrible event for the newspaper cameras. It was a fantastic story, which many, including the police, found hard to swallow and it started alarm bells ringing among other journalists, who had heard similar claims of kidnap and torture from Hall years before, then said to be the work of dog fighters who had tarred and feathered him.

Many allegations of Hall's trickery have come to light since including the embezzlement of £10,000 from one animal welfare organization for which he was supposed to have been doing undercover work under the guise of UK Animal Watch. He was even accused of staging animal cruelty to record on film for another group. He has also served time in prison and has an extensive criminal record including burglary and theft.

Hall's ALF branding story centred around the staged and much vaunted 'Picture that shocked England.' The timing was impeccable and the media loved it, coinciding as it did with a highly dramatic hour-long storyline on the hospital soap *Casualty* about animal rights bombs going off in hospitals, and, coincidentally, yet another government announcement of the introduction of more urgent legislation to deal with the increasingly violent urban terrorist threat from animal rights extremists, confirmed the following week in the Queen's speech!

Live Mink & A Dying Empire

> In the killing of animals there is cruelty, rage, and the accustoming of oneself to the bad habit of shedding innocent blood.
>
> *Rabbi Joseph Albo (1380-1444) Sephardic philosopher*

The growth in direct action against the fur trade in the UK during the 1980's and the rapid sequence of victories that followed with the closing of outlets, farms and department stores, together with Labour pledges to ban fur farming, contributed to the overall picture of a dying fur trade. But as other campaigns took on a life of their own, there was a slow downturn in the campaign to force the fur trade out of existence. Consequently there has been something of a resurgence in the sale of fur as the industry has, on the quiet, sneaked its product back onto the high street—albeit mostly in the form of fur lining, cuffs and accessories. What is especially obscene for this industry boastful of the beauty of natural fur, is that this has been achieved in no small part by disguising real fur as though it's artificial 'fun fur' and selling it that way, whilst all the time claiming that a demand for the real thing has returned. To all intents and purposes (industry profits aside) it may as well be artificial fur. That it isn't, is being addressed by the Animal Liberation Movement.

Personally, I took the view that the fur trade was all but done for and wouldn't be able to re-establish itself and have focused for the most part on other issues. But others have continued the battle elsewhere. In the UK, we are once again getting to grips with an industry that is hopeful of a return to the good old days and a market opening up to their cruel exploitation. But things have changed since the time it was viewed as just an English problem to be overcome; word has spread not just across the Atlantic but the other way also: into the heart of fur-farming Scandinavia.

In early summer, 1995, Finland saw the first raid of its kind when over six hundred foxes were freed from their cages after raids on four farms in the west of the country, a county boasting the world's largest captive fox population, contributing over two million skins a year. This was a significant enough development in itself, but it was the trial of the three young women responsible for the liberations that was to draw the industry into the limelight and ignite a campaign that was to spread across Europe during the 1990's.

Of the three 20 year-olds arrested, two said nothing to the police when pressurised, while the third told them everything. With her evidence, they were all convicted. A promise of leniency for Kirsi Kultalahati turned out to be her only reward, as she fared little better than the others at the conclusion of a month-long trial. Mia Salli and Minna Salonen were given suspended sentences of 2 ½ years whilst the talkative one got two years suspended. They were between them fined 850,000 Finnish Marks—around £135,000—to cover farmers' losses and increased insurance. It was a hefty sum in any currency and a price that had to be paid under Finnish law.

Media coverage of the story and exposure of fur farming made regular headlines and inspired others to act. Elainten Vapataus Rintama, the Finnish ALF, had arrived! By the end of the year, the police estimated that one fur shop a week was having windows broken, and locks were glued even more often. That autumn, two more farms were raided, and 200 foxes were released into the wild. The hundreds left behind were dyed with red henna and all breeding records were stolen. Soon after that, a huge pelt processing plant owned by the country's second biggest fur farm and feed supplier, and housing 20,000 polecat and 2000 fox pelts, was set ablaze causing extensive damage. At another farm, 50 foxes were dyed red. Two months later in a first of its kind, several meat trucks were burnt out and on Xmas Eve there were three more in flames. To prove this wasn't the preserve of a small number of objectors, 200 activists protested at the International Fur Auction, a hugely important event for fur traders. Sporadic actions around the event gave the appearance of a siege and resulted in over 40 people being arrested by the end of the day.

And all this in no time at all, in a country that had hitherto played a negligible part in the growing Animal Liberation Movement. At the end of this year of unprecedented direct action, carried out predominantly by 19 and 20 year olds, scores of fur shops had closed down and rather bold predictions were being made by activists about the imminent collapse of the fur trade in Finland in the next few years. This was a rallying call to all involved in the industry to stand up and fight back. That meant not so much defending the practice of fur farming and extolling its virtues, but more violence.

Those on the front line of the industry were quick to issue their own threats to activists to the effect that if any were caught by the farmers, there would be trouble. Sure enough, it was two years on, but for the fur traders it was worth waiting for to prove they were good for their word. Alerted by recently installed movement sensors and silent alarms, five young raiders were rumbled late one night by the sleepless farmer as they entered a fox farm that had been raided three times before. As they ran from the scene, he emptied his shotgun into them.

One was hit in the lower back, one five times in the arms and legs and another was hit in the lungs and took another nine puncture wounds. All survived and considered themselves to be very lucky, even though they were arrested in their car en route to hospital and had their homes searched. One injured woman was remanded in custody for five months and questioned repeatedly and was only released after going on hunger strike. The farmer told a pack of lies and was allowed to go about his cruel business armed and dangerous until some time later, following public pressure and threats of civil proceedings, police invited him to have a less cordial chat. He was then arrested and charged with assault, an unlikely charge in the event but a step in the right direction. As media interest grew and the police were forced to see through the gunman's story, they upped the allegations to three counts of attempted manslaughter and two of reckless endangerment. The activists were charged with disturbing the domestic peace.

The raiders were convicted. At the wounding trial, the farmer argued that there had been no other way to detain the prowlers save by shooting them and was duly convicted of aggravated assault and reckless endangerment. Everyone then exchanged money. He had to compensate the three people for their injuries to the tune of four thousand Marks and pay their hospital costs and got 18 months probation. They had to pay him and his wife one thousand Marks for emotional suffering and serve four months probation.

The amount of public sympathy generated for one man and his gun, and indeed the wider industry, was a wake-up call for the enthusiastic fledgling movement—a reminder that there was some way to go to make Finland fur farm free. A thousand farms have closed in ten years with another 1,500 still operating.

During legal proceedings, it emerged that just one of the 50 foxes freed in another raid on the same farm had remained unaccounted for after the roundup, a statistic that has been repeated elsewhere. In the UK following a release of 150 mink from Fairwood Mink Farm at Darcy Lever in Bolton in 1984, 145 were recaptured, three died and just two remained free. Other raids have resulted in larger numbers of animals avoiding the round-up and all have resulted in wider implications for the farm owners.

Results of tests carried out by the Finnish Fur Breeders Union on henna-dyed pelts confirmed there was no way the damage could be undone, rendering sabotaged pelts worthless. Worthless pelts mean worthless animals and worthless animals don't live in cages. Over the next ten years, in the region of 100 fur farms were raided in Finland releasing tens of thousands of animals and causing huge damage to pelts and equipment with no end in sight.

A series of raids on mink farms in Germany saw 300 mink released, pelts wrecked and a variety of buildings burnt out. In Austria, two raids saw 150 mink potter off to pastures new from recently established farms. In Italy, 2,000 mink were released from their cages. In Norway, a fur trader's offices were attacked, dozens of windows broken, locks glued and equipment sabotaged. 110 foxes were dyed with red henna at a farm in Telemark where a car was also damaged, graffiti was sprayed around the place and breeding books were taken. In one night, five separate farms in the Rogaland area lost 20-25 mink each. Fur outlets have typically been targeted too. In Sweden, the DBF burnt five buildings at an unoccupied fur farm processing plant and offices, causing $600,000 damage.

In America there were plenty less outrageous actions affecting fur traders, but an incendiary device thrown through a window of the two-storey Alaskan Fur Co. warehouse at Bloomington started a blaze which went on to cause $2,750,000 worth of damage. Also one million dollars-worth of damage was caused to the main office area and four trucks belonging to the Utah Fur Breeders Agricultural Cooperative; and destroyed by fire was a one-ton truck belonging to a company that manufactured a pelt cleaning solution used by furriers.

There were, and still are, all manner of less newsworthy activities pressurising the fur trade in these and many other countries. Harrods in London have again begun to sell fur coats and attracted a regular animal rights presence, which has cost the business tens of thousands of pounds in legal injunctions alone in an attempt to restrict the protests.

In the UK in 1976, when the first foxes were deliberately freed from a farm in Scotland, it heralded the beginning of the end for fur farming. (But not before some controversy. You just can't abuse animals these days without there being some controversy! It's inevitably become an essential ingredient in the crusade against animal abuse). Where there had once been 600 fur farms operating, by the early 1980s, there were only 68 mink farms and a handful of fox farms left, including one in Wales and eight in Scotland. And the majority of these were closed down during the 1990s, down from 52 in 1989 to just 13 in 1999.

While its fair to say that much of the movement had gone slightly soft on the fur trade, there were some activists who had kept their eye on what was going on at the dozen or so remaining mink farms still operating in the UK. They'd also set aside an evening or two to remind the rest of society that there were wild mink in cages. There has been an hyper sensitive reaction to the deliberate release of captive animals into the vast expanse of the USA and in Europe but the backlash was unprecedented in the UK when 6000 mink were released into the New Forest in the autumn of 1998. It was in the middle of what they call the silly season for news reporting, and along with the mink, the ALF unleashed a swarm of human prejudices.

Reasoning that there was no point complaining or feeling angry, not even much point voting, one rescue team headed into the New Forest early one evening, aiming for Crow Hill Farm, they got dropped off half a mile away and walked through the pitch darkness to the back of the compound, masked up, then negotiated the ageing mink-proof fence.

Tucked away in a valley, this is an ideal location for something you want to hide, but access is good through the trees from the back if you are reasonably agile. The guard dogs were locked up at the front of the site. The night was young. It wasn't hard to persuade the mink out of the cages. Most didn't even have nest boxes attached in which to hide—something even the fur industry now accepts as a necessary extravagance. Two hours later, in a slick operation, the raiders retraced their steps, called transport and left the county. Six thousand mink had the one chance they'd get to do the same.

Within hours of daybreak the following morning, MAFF had a 14-strong team dressed in camouflage clothing hunting down escapees across the New Forest—all 93,000 acres of it. Farmers and landowners were granted free reign to exterminate any that surfaced. Every trigger-happy, gun-toting moron stirred. The Hampshire Mink Hounds were empowered! The do-gooders were out stalking mink, believing they were doing something for society. Everybody was out there trying to get the poor things back into their miserable cage existence. Wanted Dead or Alive! It's not their fault! The liberators who created this state of near hysteria among so many must have been stunned by the over-reaction to their simple act of sabotage. Suddenly, bored journalists, 'conservationists', apologists, hunters, editors and policemen were all qualified to comment on the impending demise of the New Forest. It looks and sounds like a totally reckless act and who would dare to say otherwise? I will!

Local residents armed and protected themselves; they were warned to be vigilant. Some kept themselves and their children indoors as the murderous mink 'rampaged' across the Hampshire countryside, as you might envisage a swarm of locusts, devouring everything in their path. One woman reportedly barricaded herself in and blocked up the chimney. It would be funny if it weren't quite so serious. For the hated mink: small, cute, furry meat-eaters, who are far less scary and dangerous in the real world than the big unattractive hairy ones that keep animals in cages, even the RSPCA were rounding them up. Even! Given their track record, this should have come as no surprise.

So, back into the filthy, stinking hole the captured mink went with the RSPCA inspectors. Back to where animals had been dying of septicaemia from huge open untreated wounds, where live animals existed alongside dead ones, displayed stereotypical behaviour, had limbs missing and broken. Crow Hill Farm was a wretched factory farm festering with the living, the dead and the dying mink packed into cages with maggots, flies and shit everywhere and the most unbearable stench in the air.

An RSPCA inspector had previously visited the farm and found nothing wrong, while animal rights activists were on site covertly monitoring. MAFF officials had made routine visits and found nothing that bothered them either. You would have to be asleep to do this! It was only after video evidence was personally delivered to RSPCA headquarters that someone there finally acted, but it was too little and too late.

The horrors that befell so many beautiful fur-bearing creatures in that place and others like it are too awful to put adequately into words. New Labour politicians knew of the situation, said they would act to end the trade and then, of course, didn't. I don't vote for any of them and that makes me feel very angry, so how must those feel who voted for their promises feel? And to whom should they complain? And what about the mink? That was a primary concern for a few deep thinkers.

This obviously wasn't some 'mindless act of terrorism' as it was referred to by some. 'It was planned a long time ago. We were waiting to see what the government would do first. If politicians won't do what they're told to do then its time people stopped talking to them,' said one of the unrepentant raiders when quizzed. His theory was that while the released mink would surely predate on any other suitably sized wild creature they could catch, there would be a lot more suffering and death in the long term if the cages weren't emptied once and for always. This was about forcing the issue; it was a mindful act. Shocking.

It wasn't the ALF that had caused the growth of the population to around 100,000 wild mink in the UK. Ask the fur farmers—they brought them here from North America at the end of the 1920s. It was another 20 years before mink settled the British countryside and began to breed in the wild. Some made their own way out of the farms, while others—shed loads of them—were deliberately released by their erstwhile captors when the pelt profits dropped off. With otters struggling due to modern poisonous farming practices and hunting, and polecats persecuted to near extinction by gamekeepers of the nineteenth century, there was a niche in the countryside. So not only have mink been forced to live here where they clearly aren't wanted, but in cages! Can't be right! The government agreed the practice should be banned, then did nothing. This kind of unhelpful, erratic behaviour, or lying, doesn't instil confidence and encourages people to force the issue, usually by controversial methods.

What of the 'Ecological disaster' which *The Sunday Times* forecast or the RSPCA's 'Environmental disaster'? *The Guardian* said the mink were threatening eighty square miles of countryside and *The Mirror* ran the headline: 'Mink Go Wild in the Killing Fields' which it qualified with absurd notions about mink on a 'countryside killing spree', leaving a trail of destruction up to five miles away from the farm. The police warned: 'Young children, especially babies, should not be left alone, certainly not outside. They will attack babies, young children, cats, dogs, chickens and they will go for the throat.'

Eek! In *The Independent*'s view, the released mink were: 'The Four Letter Word Striking Fear Into The Heart of Hampshire... stalking wildlife in the New Forest, slipping over the border into Dorset. The mink have no shame, and no mercy.' Blimey! Interspersed in this storytelling was the token sprinkling of 'concern' that not all the poor creatures were equipped to survive in the wild and would die. Was it really lost on them all that the very purpose of the animals' confinement was to facilitate their premature death? At Crow Hill prior to the raid, one of the workers was covertly filmed swinging mink by the tail and smashing their heads on the ground to kill them.

One of the papers carried the story of Ian Sturrock, who had apparently watched in horror as a mink had leapt onto his 18 month-old son's buggy. Strangely enough—given the fact that that Sturrock had feared for his baby son's life—the article was accompanied by a photograph taken by Sturrock of the moment the mink—if that's what it was—lay down next to the baby. Surely a doting dad would have leapt to the rescue of his son, if the animal were so dangerous? Was the photo worth a few quid? Or 15 minutes of fame? And dead or alive, was the animal actually doing the child any harm? Obviously not, yet the clear inference was that our children were in danger. Why? Any previous mink attacks to learn from? Another one of the more fantastic stories—and there were bundles to choose from—came from an angler who claimed he was attacked by a gang of mink while he sat peacefully trying to impale fish on his hook. 'Mink Mug Angler For His Bait' was the story in *The Telegraph*. 'Suddenly these dark shapes sprang out of the bushes nearby and jumped on me. They were all over me. There were at least four of them, if not more. They were running all over my legs, my feet and trying to climb on my seat. I was screaming. I picked up my landing net to try and beat them off. I hit a couple but it didn't seem to affect them. They were fearless. I battled with them for about a minute', alleged fearless fish hunter John Stone, an hour or so after taking the magic mushrooms. The maligned mink's reputation was sealed, it seemed, to be regurgitated ad infinitum.

Some mink were shot and killed or trapped and returned to the farm. Only a minority escaped; perhaps a few hundred survived the initial break out and not all would have made it thought the winter. Some mink are probably still free and making a better job, I'll warrant, of living in harmony with the countryside than most modern humans.

There was so much forced concern in these news reports about the mink killing other animals and then taking over the world, that the message in all of this was forgotten. The double standards were unfathomable. Presumably it didn't take a mathematician to work out the equation: the released mink had been fattened in their cages on the bodies of other animals, killed cruelly by people far more ruthless than the four who'd opened their cages, not to mention the fact that the mink themselves were destined for slaughter if they stayed. All of them! At one Devon fur farm alone, 26,000 caged mink were fed eight tons of chicken, fish, cooked cereals, vitamins, liver and wheat germ every single day. That is a lot of suffering and a lot of waste: worth a few angry comments, surely? And what of the utterly senseless carnage by gamekeepers on three hundred shooting estates where millions of animals and birds are blasted with shotguns, caught in snares and poisoned for a sport? Let's talk cruel killing!

Mink on the one hand were allegedly on a rampaging killing spree throughout the countryside, or, conversely, starving and fighting to death. So moved were the raiders by this hysterical media reaction, that a week later they returned to Crow Hill Farm and opened a load more cages to release 1000 more mink. Or was it simply that there were still mink in cages to be released? Sometimes there are far more important things to worry about than what others say, but the fact that so many people were talking about mink farming was primarily important because, for all their pre-election wooing promises, the government had stopped talking of banning fur farms.

Very few of the many who had complained about the mink liberation had actually done anything to stop the cruelty and suffering in these farms, and the barrage of criticisms was an obscene exaggeration of the true impact free mink would have on the countryside. Happily, there were one or two voices of reason in the hysterical onslaught of terror tales following the raids. Perhaps not an obvious commentary point but Ben Sharratt of *Motor Caravan* magazine (Jan 1999) was considered in his opinion: 'I was under the impression that the mink was a small but aggressive carnivore with a penchant for voles and young birds, before I read in the paper and heard on the telly that it is in actual fact a baby-killing, dog-slaying fighting machine with mean eyes, a cold heart and relentlessly thuggish tendencies!'

John Vidal, *The Guardian*'s environmental correspondent, agreed that: 'The mink got a ludicrous reception from the press. They are solitary animals that mark out territory a mile apart from each other and can travel miles in a day in search of food, ensuring a well dispersed population. They aren't stupid!' He quoted a New Forest District Council report, two months later, which stated that only 1000 mink were still on the run and that these had all gone to ground with little damage reported. Anyone else notice that?

'Mink are the victims of fashion, economic pressure, political expediency, scientific theory, conservation policy, moral principle, ignorance and prejudice—all ideas with guns. We should show these creatures some respect,' so said Paul Evans of the British Association of Nature Conservationists in 1998. Lots of studies have been commissioned into the mink population and its effects on other wildlife. These have repeatedly shown that mink have not caused a demonstrable impact on other species. Not even to the endangered water vole, whose biggest problem, as always, is man, who continues to wreak destruction on their habitat by overgrazing, grubbing up hedgerows, removing reedy river edges, setting up flood defence and drainage schemes, building houses and roads and hunting the river banks for mink with dog packs. The same goes for the 'game' birds, whom many gun-toting farmers are keen to protect from mink. The biggest threat to the lives of these and other birds is man, whose keen observation has led him to decide that rabbits are vermin too, and therefore must be exterminated! Somehow, their keen observations missed something: rabbits are preyed upon by the mink and of course the fox and the occasional raptor and if left alone, would maybe, just maybe control their own populations. It's radical, almost extreme thinking, I know.

Finally moved to act, an RSPCA inspection team visited Crow Hill Farm, with the police in November 1997. Equipped with nine hours of footage filmed covertly by Respect for Animals over a 19-month period, they were availed of every detail they needed to facilitate their tour of the 4000 cages in the numerous sheds. They had the exact location of cages with dead bodies, the injured and mutilated mink and of the overcrowded cages containing up to seven fully-grown mink, which were meant to hold two or three animals. Post-mortem reports from dead animals taken during the investigation revealed their awful suffering. One caged mink had a bare bone for a back leg, the result of a fight. Another taken for post-mortem had nothing but sawdust in its stomach. Others had died from untreated severe injuries. The RSPCA took more bodies for post-mortem examination and killed off the more seriously injured animals. Intriguingly, a break-in occurred at the veterinary surgery where the corpses were being stored over the Xmas holiday and a number of them were stolen, the evidence thus removed. Nothing else was taken. Who on earth would have wanted to do that?

It was all there in black and white for the officials to sort out. They had, of course, each been at Crow Hill Farm before to inspect the conditions about which so many had complained, but somehow, each time, they'd missed the endless trail of horrors they were looking for. How is this possible? Even a cursory look at the footage or the farm itself would tell a moron that things were far from 'acceptable', or even legal, but it took the animal liberators to expose what the RSPCA and government inspectors had failed to see. Or maybe just refused to see. This could not be passed off as incompetence or an accident.

And therein lay a way out for MAFF, ironically. They couldn't be seen to rely in court on evidence obtained illegally by the animal activists so they cut a deal with the farmer, who initially had 29 summonses issued against him. The conclusion was that 73 year-old

Terence Smith, who had farmed mink for 50 years and described himself when interviewed following the ALF raid as 'an animal lover', got off with little more than a scarred reputation as the 29 charges against him were dropped. He pleaded guilty on behalf of the company T. T. Smith (Mink) Ltd to 15 counts of cruelty and breaches of animal welfare rules and was fined £5,000 with £15,000 costs. The fall guy, Ian Stroud, 43, the ogre employed by Smith to do the killing, pleaded guilty to six counts of cruelty to mink after he was filmed smashing their heads against the cages to subdue them when they resisted his attempt to gas them. He was given no more than 150 hours community service and told to pay a token £100 costs by New Forest Magistrates, who said without a whiff of irony that: 'Society in this country is always going to treat very seriously cruelty to other living creatures.' Allowing him to walk away with a smile after inflicting such terrible suffering and receiving no deterrent punishment is not the way to persuade those drawn to the ALF to down tools now, is it?

Two weeks after the sentencing of the Hampshire farmer, and while the mink furore rumbled on, it was stoked some more when Kelbain Mink Farm at Onneley in Staffordshire, one of the more secure of the baker's dozen left, was visited by ALF raiders. Here they set about 3,500 cages with bolt cutters, freeing 8,000 mink, 3,000 of whom made good their escape from the compound. Four days later, around 400 were said by the farmer to be still unaccounted for. He estimated a street value of £50,000. Just a few days earlier, breeding cards had been removed from cages, but the intruders were disturbed before completing the job. Returning the night following the liberation raid, the farmer's wife's £18,000 Audi and his van were doused in paint stripper outside their house.

'It is still horrendous out there,' complained Len Kelsall, the ruffled 60 year-old farmer and Chairman of the Fur Breeders Association, 'It looks like a battle field.' We've been telling them this for years! 'It is just starting to hit me how bad this is.' Len went on. 'It is terrorism and cruelty at its worse and the government must act to stop it.' Indeed.

In a monumental meeting of minds, both the Chair of the FBA and the liberators had come to agree that the Labour government was to blame. 'They made an election promise to abolish mink farming but have done nothing more,' sulked Len, who was sounding more and more like his adversaries with every comment but also had his eye on compensation. Conversely, Mark Glover, a serial ALF-basher of the group Respect for Animals who documented and exposed the awful scenes in Hampshire, claimed that the liberation of the mink had been, 'an extraordinary thing to do', given the Government's pledge to ban fur farming. The ALF raiders said they considered it their duty. He reckoned the outcome for the mink was, 'equally as bleak outside' as in the cages on the farm, somewhat ironically echoed in a statement by Robert Morgan, Chief Executive of the British Fur Trade Association (explaining in *The Observer* in June 1997 why mink, who naturally spend 60% of their life in water, are better off in wire cages) 'If mink have access to swimming water then they would get wet and probably get cold and die.'

So give them hair driers. Sure, out there there's no regular serving of gruel and no terraced housing, but wild animals tend to struggle through and, given the option, few would choose a brief frustrated life in a cage and a certain brutal death over taking a chance on reaching their second birthday in the countryside.

By the following spring, Labour MP Maria Eagle's Bill to outlaw fur farming in the UK had gained cross party support and had the backing of the National Farmers Union and even the Fur Breeders Association. All but one of the remaining mink farmers were happy to be bought out of business with compensation payments and be spared the hassle that modern life was bringing. Such an opt-out would also save them the cost of a proposed legislation forcing farmers to spend big money on increased security measures. This was a move, which had been prompted by the recent raids, which also saw the Government ratchet up the cost of farm licences from £115 to £630 a few months after.

As would be expected, Conservative MPs, who tabled over thirty amendments, talked the Bill out of time. But in early 2003, the legislation finally reached the statute books and made what was left of the fur farming industry in the UK illegal. There are no longer any mink or fox farms operating in the UK. A significant milestone. And not the only one.

The Death Knell Of Hunting

> Until we have the courage to recognize cruelty for what it is—whether its victim is human or animal—we cannot expect things to be much better in this world… We cannot have peace among men whose hearts delight in killing any living creature. By every act that glorifies or even tolerates such moronic delight in killing we set back the progress of humanity.
>
> *Rachel Carson (1907—1964)*

The 1996 Wild Animals (Protection) Bill was introduced to finally put an end to hunting with hounds and give protection to all wild mammals from specific acts of cruelty—the first such legislation of its kind in a country with a reputation as animal lovers… But before any protection for wild animals would be agreed, the clause in the bill that would have banned the hunting of wild animals with packs of dogs would have to be removed so the rest of the Bill would be allowed to proceed through Parliament. Otherwise, pro-hunt MPs would scupper the entire thing.

There had been previous attempts—in 1949, 1970, 1992, 1993 and 1995—to improve the protection of wild animals, in particular banning hunting with hounds. In April 1996, some wild mammals (excluding birds, reptiles, amphibians and fish) were generously awarded some weak legal protection from those who would: 'mutilate, kick, beat, nail or otherwise impale, stab, stone, burn, crush, drown, drag or asphyxiate' them 'with intent to inflict unnecessary suffering.' Under the terms of the Act, anyone caught and convicted of the above, faces the prospect of a 12-week prison sentence and/or a fine of up to £5,000. Animals left on the quarry list that are caught and injured during hunting sessions with dogs, guns and snares should be killed in a 'reasonably swift and humane manner', whatever that might be. If they aren't, and someone can prove it, the offenders can face prosecution under the Act.

The first prosecution was recorded nine months later. In Great Yarmouth, a youth was found guilty of kicking, beating and stabbing a hedgehog and given 120 hours community service and ordered to pay £50 in costs. In other cases, two Hampshire men, Richard Smith and Paul West, were convicted of blowtorching and kicking a hedgehog to death. They were ordered to do 80 hours community service and pay £75 costs. In Salisbury, a £75 fine and £45 costs were imposed upon school chef Simon Bundy, who kicked a hedgehog around the street while drunk. Hedgehogs, like cats, are a favourite toy for sadists. The fact that creatures such as hedgehogs are finally recognised as living beings is a huge step forward. The fact that these people are being convicted of anything is some sort of progress, but such sentences are hardly a deterrent. I doubt the animals would be fired up for partying in the meadows in celebration if they knew the rate of our society's slow evolution.

It is perhaps understandable that pro-hunting MPs (read Conservative MPs) would scheme to protect their sport, but what possible explanation could they have for aborting a Bill, which was seeking to regulate the cruel practice of farming puppies? Not to outlaw it totally, by the way, as imperative as that is, just to monitor, control and regulate the degree of abstract squalor and degradation endemic in the mess of farms from which this industry pumps out an endless supply of puppies for the open market.

That Bill, put forward by Liberal Democrat MP Diane Maddock and backed by the RSPCA (hurrah!). MPs of all parties and at least one national newspaper (one that had waged its own war against puppy farming for some time) would have brought in compulsory inspections of breeding premises and imposed fines of up to £2,500 for any infringements of basic standards of welfare and care. But two MPs, Sackville and Ottaway, felt that this wasn't in the public interest, nor in the interest of the countless offspring that will be born in barns, sheds, outhouses and back rooms without restraint. It was notable that the wealthy RSPCA added its support to this Bill, since the national organisation has done little else to help combat the huge problem of domestic animal breeding, which has been left to animal sanctuaries, its own local rescue centres and the single-handed efforts of one of its own Council members to clean up.

Further attempts to bring a ban on hunting with hounds brought together hare coursers, gunmen, fox and hare hunters and other blood junkies to be known collectively as the Countryside Alliance (CA) and they have organised some impressive mass protests. The CA is an amalgamation of organisations, which present themselves as the defenders of traditional country life, although broader countryside issues appear to be poorly represented. It incorporates the likes of the pro-blood sports British Field Sports Society (BFSS), who feature prominently amongst its ranks. In reality, the CA is a pro-hunt show of strength formed to lobby against the then newly elected Labour Party and its promises for a better deal for animals.

Better than a press release, they launched themselves into the public arena with a huge march and rally in London in the summer of 1997. Cleverly, they predicted they would get 100,000 supporters and, right enough, most reporters saw exactly 100,000 pro-hunt people in Hyde Park for the first Countryside Rally. It was an impressive sight, whatever the true figure and the cause and they were mostly there to demonstrate their opposition to the Mike Foster Bill to outlaw hunting with hounds, although some didn't realise it and others didn't want to be there. The CA had used its inherent accumulated wealth to charter planes, trains and coaches to ferry the simple folk into the city, a place of wonder for many of those who had never seen the like before. So many really were fish out of water. There were even threats distributed among the bumpkin ranks, warning that if they didn't attend the bash in London they might as well forget hunting next season because they wouldn't be welcome.

Members of the Oakley Hunt in Buckinghamshire, for example, received the following advice from their hunt committee instructing: 'You should arrange to take a day off work, or pretend to be sick or whatever.' Sick behaviour shouldn't be too much effort. It further instructed boldly: 'Keep the children back from school and be there! If you simply cannot be bothered then please do not bother to come hunting with the Oakley next season either.'

Ooooh!

Similar sentiments, albeit less forcefully expressed, were repeated in *Horse and Hound*. The National Secretary for rural workers at the Transport and General Workers Union commented: 'I've had a number of phone calls from people being forced to go. Tenant farmers have been told by their landlords, agricultural workers by their employers. It seems to be fairly common.'

Buoyed by the publicity they generated and desperate to stress their point, the 'Countryside', as they described themselves, arranged another gathering in the big city—The Countryside March. This time they wanted a quarter of a million there and they duly invited everyone. According to Janet George of the CA, 'It's a chance for anyone who wants to, to voice a gripe.' Ramblers demanding the right to roam, landowners wanting them banned from doing so, pensioners wanting improved bus services to rural communities, anti-hunting families protesting about housing development on greenbelt land, cattle farmers complaining about the handling of the BSE fiasco and other workers wanting their rural jobs protecting. And out-and-out blood junkies, of course. This must go down as the most confused protest in history! Of course, the CA claimed that they were all there in favour of hunting, but then they would do. They boasted how activists had been flown in from Ireland and the US and 'virtually every country in Europe.' Well, at least they weren't out hunting! As on the previous march, tenant farmers were ordered there and employees 'encouraged' to go or face losing their homes. The British National Party were there on fertile territory, recruiting supporters to their 'traditional British way of life', with 20,000 copies of their special edition newsletter. Organisers, with little contradiction from the media, claimed there were a few short of a quarter of a million marchers.

However, a comprehensive survey revealed the true figure to be less than 163,000. Then, soon after, all the confusion created by pro-hunt activists hijacking the CA to promote their cause over the other less controversial issues led to the group turning in on itself. Some organisers felt the pro-hunt lobby had too much influence and that the other issues were being sidetracked. They called a meeting and duly sacked over half the board members, including the Duke of Westminster, Earl Peel, Lord Steel, the Earl of Stockton and Janet George. The Duke of Westminster, one of the wealthiest landowners in the country and an enthusiastic bird blaster, gave an estimated £1 million in advance of the Rally and later demanded it back! Lord Steel was exposed for failing to declare to parliament the £94,000 he was paid to lobby for hunting by the Countryside Movement.

Hunt supporters were so vexed at the primary value of their issue being questioned that they discussed plans to disrupt the meeting. Reputedly, they couldn't work out how to do it, which slowed down the revolt somewhat. Confounded and cornered they turned instead on the RSPCA over its anti-hunt stance, 'Eighty-five to ninety percent' of whose policies the BFSS said it supported, which is less shocking than in should be. BFSS executive director Peter Voute suggested that: 'Animals cannot have rights because they do not have responsibilities.' It's a common excuse for abusing animals, interestingly placing them somewhere between toddlers and the seriously mentally ill.

Under the banner of the Country Sports Animal Welfare Group, pro-hunt activists had been affiliating its membership to the RSPCA in order to influence policy and protect their interests within a wishy-washy welfare society seen to be dominated by 'animal rightists.' If the RSPCA scare them, then they do have an awful lot to fear from the rest of us. Members were asked to 'Join the RSPCA and start to play a part in steering the RSPCA back onto its traditional role of caring for animals and away from animal rights and political campaigning.' Up to 3000 were said to have joined the RSPCA in 1996, just prior to its AGM, but were unable to vote because of a rule that states you must be a member for over three months before becoming eligible. The plan was flawed! Phew! The animals could breath easy.

Resolutions to keep the society's anti-hunting stance were backed by nearly 500 votes that year at the typical London AGM. Three years on, a number of prominent pro-hunt Council members had incited an incredible decision to move the AGM to traditional hunt country in Leicestershire, much to the delight of newly enrolled pro-hunt members, five hundred of whom gathered at the animal welfare meeting. There were around a quarter of the number of normal members present.

The RSPCA has since regained some control of its polices, expelling some of those whose actions are counter to its founding aim of promoting animal welfare, but that's it. By 2004, it was necessary for Council rules to remind officials 'That no animals are to be eaten on RSPCA premises such as RSPCA HQ or premises where RSPCA meetings are held.' It's some sort of progress but the RSPCA has a long way to go before it will be the animals' favourite charity.

Here's why: So obscene has been the RSPCA's accumulation of wealth, that by the end of the 1990s it stood at over £100 million and the Charity Commission was forced to step in and tell them to reduce the available booty by over half to £45 million. No wonder animal abusers want control of this—in the right hands, animal welfare would indeed be advanced! The Animal Liberation Movement has missed the boat here. The RSPCA duly complied with its obligations, but rather than spending it directly on animal welfare initiatives like solving the country's stray animal problem, or for example by promoting the benefits to all of the vegan diet, the Council set about pouring money into wages and office 'improvements', including splashing out a staggering £21 million on new office headquarters. They have also spent money extensively to promote animal industries through their Freedom Food range of meat, eggs and dairy products. The justification for this travesty in the words of RSPCA Director General Peter Davies to BBC Watchdog: 'We have to have intensive farming in this country because of the demand for protein meat products and dairy products. You could not do it from a backyard system—it's impossible. Freedom Food is one of the most important things we do, in my view.' Says it all really.

Since the New Labour government announced it was proposing to make time for legislation to outlaw hunting, hunt fanatics have been forecasting the end of the world as we know it. They predicted it would create mass unemployment, the disintegration of the countryside and the increased massacre of foxes, horses and hunt dogs by hunt supporters. And endless belly-aching about an oppressed minority in need of the help of the rest of society. It was worth a moment's thought, but it is, of course, just themselves for whom they weep. The hunting set has traditionally shown utter contempt for minorities and anyone with a conflicting opinion, politics, or gender.

They predicted that if hunting went, then fishing and shooting would surely follow. They tried to encourage the reported three million-strong angling community to join the struggle and 'resort to extreme tactics.' (Not my words; as far as I'm concerned they've always been extremists). Not simply attacking their opponents physically as is their wont, they threatened to adopt the tactics of revolution, of civil disobedience and sabotage, flouting the rule of law en masse. They pledged to burn down woodlands so the 'little red devil' would have nowhere to hide up while planning his next sortie into animal farming territory. They threatened to block artery roads and motorways with their horse boxes and 'poison the waterways' until they're allowed to hunt down foxes again. Janet George again: 'There will be a riot in the countryside. We will have to show we will not be messed around with.'

The Daily Telegraph columnist Auberon Waugh would have been sent to trial for incitement, were he animal-friendly as he called on fellow extremists to block main roads if hunting were banned. He called the ban: 'A declaration of war on rural England.' All for the lust for blood. In that pursuit, while very much in the majority on their march in the big city waving their shooting sticks and threatened by no one, and while shedding tears for their human rights as an oppressed minority, hunt supporters still managed to put two anti hunt observers in hospital, one with a broken arm and the other with a broken jaw.

A week after the second gathering in London, the National Anti Hunt Campaign held a march in the City which attracted a smaller number of protesters, totalling only a few thousand. The comparatively poor turn out could probably be blamed in part on the efforts of the national animal welfare organisations operating under the umbrella name The Campaign for the Protection of the Hunted Animal, which united the RSPCA, LACS and IFAW. Members were urged to boycott the march because it was unnecessary and confrontational. The LACS arranged their Devon sanctuary open day to coincide and encouraged their members to go there instead. John Bryant of the LACS added his bit for unity and the hunted animal by informing the public that: 'The London demonstration is being organised by Niel Hansen, a man with a serious animal rights terrorism record. We campaign peacefully.' What did the terrible terrorist do? He sent some cat litter to someone involved in vivisection and paid his debt to society for it with a three-year prison sentence.

But what was the point of bringing this up and exaggerating so? It is true that the LACS have monopolised the political campaign against hunting and have done a good job of it; it's also true the LACS have exposed hunting for what it is through undercover investigations, most notably with Mike Huskisson and his book *Outfoxed*, but being anti-hunt is not the preserve of a clique. Whatever their reasons, the CPHA had helped pour fuel onto the flickering fire of blood sports. One supporter claimed with glee that this was proof of 'a dwindling interest in anti hunt protesting.' In reality there was never any mass interest in anti-hunt protests as such; opponents preferred instead to stage token protests at meets and disturbances at hunt balls. The real opposition has always been in the field in the form of direct physical intervention and in the hearts and minds of the majority of non-participants who wanted hunting banned and should be encouraged to demonstrate their feelings at every opportunity. Likewise, opposition has been less concentrated on property sabotage than in other areas of animal abuse and more of the democratic political process, which needs, more than ever, to be seen to be working.

The wealthy International Fund for Animal Welfare (IFAW) was under the leadership of its founder, Brian Davies, who was earning around £115,000 annually for his work with IFAW and was paid off handsomely when he left their employ. IFAW was exposed on the *Here & Now* programme in April 1994 for having moved thousands of pounds into a trust called the Brian Davies Foundation where £30,000 of animal lovers' money was invested in lab animal suppliers Bausch & Lomb; £60,000 invested in US Surgicals who kill countless animals to 'test' their medical staples; £20,000 invested with Glaxo, Merck, Abbot & Upjohn—all massive users of lab animals; £63,000 invested in cigarette manufacturers Phillip Morris, who have a long history of animal testing and last, but by no means least, £40,000 invested in McDonald's.

In March 1998, MP Mike Foster's Wild Mammals (Hunting with Dogs) Bill was again talked out of time by animal-abusing MPs, as is traditional. Earlier in its (non) progress through parliament, it gained an all-time record of 260-majority in favour—411 votes to 151—but time was running out. The Labour MPs, for whom this issue had long been a priority, were striding forward confidently, if not for their own animal welfare considerations or to appease the animal lovers who had voted for Labour because of their promises to widely improve animal welfare laws, then because of their political leanings to pay back for what the miners had suffered under the Conservatives. By now the majority-led progress of the hunting ban had gathered too much momentum to be stopped. After years of political shenanigans, MPs were allowed a free vote on a complete ban or some kind of hunt licensing system and again voted overwhelmingly for a ban. Tony Blair's one time anti-hunt stance shifted as hunt supporters became more vociferous and threatening. He instead became a fan of the Middle Way, the licensing scheme that would allow most hunting to carry on as normal but would ban coursing and stag hunting. Unmoved by their leader's attempt to do a last minute deal on a ban, the Middle Way lost the way by 362 to 154 votes but Parliament was still hindered by the remnants of the powerful, un elected, very pro-hunt House of Lords who held back the will of the majority. The Government was now forced to enact the seldom-used 1949 Parliament Act to bring about a ban, a full eight years after New Labour promised a free vote in Parliament. At midnight on 17 November 2005, hunting with hounds was banned in England and Wales.

Practically speaking, this ban has done little to ensure the safety of wild mammals, as angry animal-killers who once claimed the kill has never been important to them have very publicly continued killing wild mammals using whatever means are at their disposal. Indeed, as a show of strength, over 250 hunts met as normal just two days after the ban and shoved two fingers at democracy and the police, who have continued to arrest hunt saboteurs. Some were hunting artificial scent, others 'exercising' hounds. The police, for the large part, have declared they no longer have hunting as a priority, claiming they haven't the resources suddenly. Eh? There were endless resources just weeks before when hunt sabs were present. Some police speakers have even suggested that anti-hunt activists would be better off taking out private prosecutions with the evidence they gather. The Chief Constable of Suffolk and Police and Rural Affairs Spokesperson for the Association of Chief Police Officers, Alistair McWhirter, was a voice in the wilderness but delivered some hope speaking in the *Mail on Sunday*: 'Be under no illusion, police are going to enforce this legislation.' It hasn't happened though.

At the end of the first day's illegal hunting, the CA publicly boasted that 91 foxes had been killed by hunts, but not one arrest was made. They claimed over 150 the following week and so on and so forth. Indeed, the Joint Master of the Old Surrey & Burstow FH proudly boasted on 18 Feb 2005: 'We killed four foxes today, a lot of fun.' There were many who were obviously proud of the head count, but it was still less than the average Saturday kill rate. Suddenly all the claims about tradition, socialising and enjoying the countryside had been superseded by an overwhelming desire to publicly prove a capacity to kill as many foxes as possible.

Still, for all glaring failings of the New Labour Government and the lack of police will to actually impose the rule of law, this is a monumental first step towards consigning hunting with dogs to history. It has immediately affected hare coursers and some mounted hunts reliant on Forestry Commission and MOD land, some beagle and fell packs too and mink hunts. Evidence gathered by monitors over the coming months showed repeated incidents of criminal activity—certainly more than enough for the authorities to have acted upon by now! Yet there is little official interest in these crimes. The effect of a lack of political will to properly deal with illegal hunting will almost certainly see private prosecutions being brought against those openly breaking the law, and further, see the political process stripped of the last semblance of credibility and more power to the elbow of the ALF et al.

Getting Serious?

> They'd daubed paint on the wagons and smashed a few windows and they'd put sugar in the tanks. But I never thought they'd go to these lengths, never in a million years.
>
> *Slaughterhouse manager*

The Animal Rights Militia

In the pursuit of animal liberation, some groups have tried to take the struggle one step beyond the stated non-violent aims of the ALF, and in doing so have courted controversy a-plenty. That said, dead bodies still don't figure in the equation.

The Animal Rights Militia (ARM) is one name we've heard periodically; a group not so much prolific as dramatic, it would be considered to be on the more extreme fringe, if you like. The ARM first emerged when the group claimed responsibility for sending parcel bombs to MPs in 1982. This did seem an odd tactic at the time and there's very little to suggest this was an activist thing at all, but the name was adopted years later and has been used sporadically over the years to claim some of the more dramatic actions, including the planting of car bombs.

In late September 1985 in south London, incendiary devices wrecked the cars of Drs. Sharat Gangolli and Stuart Walker, both animal researchers for BIBRA, the British Industrial Biological Research Association. Neither man was injured. The ARM told *The Sutton Herald*: 'We will go to any length to prevent these animal abusers' murderous activities, if it means killing an individual, we will not shy away from such action.' A few months later, one night in January 1986, car bombs were placed under the vehicles of four well-known vivisectors, one in Harrogate, one in South London, one in Staffordshire and one in Sussex, all timed to go off at hourly intervals. This time—the last time according to the ARM—warnings were given and an army bomb disposal team was able deal with what were described as viable devices.

The next attack was apparently intended to kill Dr. Andor Sebesteny, a vivisector with the Imperial Cancer Research Fund (ICRF) but he saved himself after noticing the device attached to the bottom of his car. No warning had been given.

Three activists have since been imprisoned for ARM actions. Paul

Scarce was sent down for a year in 1988 for sending razor laden letters to people on his Hit List and Niel Hansen in 1995 for sending that litter bomb via taxi to the public relations officer for Glaxo in Hertfordshire. That's right, a litter bomb: a hoax device containing cat litter. He was initially charged with conspiracy to kill but this was later revised to something less ridiculous, though he was still given three years. And there's one other, a much more significant one.

The ARM was back in the headlines following a string of incendiary attacks on high street stores, the like of which hadn't been seen since the fur department store sprinkler campaign of the 1980s. There wasn't so much emphasis on the sprinklers this time, more wholesale ruin of everything by fire. Nor were targets so specific either.

In the early hours of 6 July, 1994 reports started to circulate of fires in the Cambridge branch of Boots and in the Edinburgh Woollen Mill in the city centre. The two floors of the large Boots store were gutted in a blaze that raged for more than four hours; the wool-clothing store was badly damaged and the entire stock destroyed. A third device was found smouldering in a sheepskin coat pocket at the Marrs Leather shop and a fourth discovered in the Eaden Lilley leather shop. The centre of Cambridge was cordoned off and many places evacuated while a search was made for further devices. The ARM claimed to have planted six, four to go off the previous night and two at midday the following day. It caused huge disruption.

A month later Oxford was hit. This time the C.H. Brown Saddlery and leather shop was gutted and the Edinburgh Woollen mill suffered minor damage. Three other incendiaries were recovered, hidden in two leather shops and a fur shop. The police, well aware of what had happened down the road in Cambridge, promptly searched all potential targets after the first device ignited and prevented the situation getting any worse.

Two weeks later, there was nothing Hampshire Police could have done to control the blitz that spread across the Isle of Wight, although they could have prevented it! An incendiary device had accidentally been discovered in a fishing tackle shop just before closing time when a customer who was trying on a jacket found what at first appeared to be a packet of B&H cigarettes in one of the pockets. It looked nothing like that upon further inspection, of course, and so the police were called. The sale was lost as the jacket was seized for forensic tests, but it was an incredible stroke of good fortune that the thing was discovered at all or else the shop owner would have lost an awful lot more than that.

Police duly contacted all other fishing tackle shops on the island advising them to be on the alert and left it at that. For the arsonists, who weren't exclusively targeting fishing tackle shops, good fortune had returned.

Incredibly, a further four incendiary devices were left unchecked to tick along to ignition in the early hours at shops in Ryde and Newport. One device was discovered at Halfords, a subsidiary of Boots, and detonated in a controlled explosion, but at 2.00am stock in two leather shops and the Imperial Cancer Research Fund shop started burning. The main Boots store was also soon ablaze. So widespread and severe were the fires that the island's hundred fire fighters and 19 appliances were stretched to the limit and extra help had to be ferried across from stations on the mainland but not in time to prevent extensive damage. The island Council later called for the Home Office to address the under funding of the service and demanded an explanation from the police as to why all likely targets weren't searched.

Placing incendiary devices in shops is a very public thing to do and of course tinged with danger for all concerned. To endanger life is never the point, but to make a public statement is, and in that respect, these were strikingly successful acts. There were witnesses who formed a photo-fit image of a man they thought responsible for leaving the devices, which the police made public. In response, they received over one hundred calls, many naming Mark King, the singer and bass player with the band Level 42. Wrong! Not only did he have an alibi, but also he had no motive. The trail ran dry and just five days later, the ARM struck again.

Following the first fires, Boots had issued repeated warnings to its 1100 stores to be on the alert, but it still didn't prevent extensive damage being done elsewhere, most notably to stores at the other end of the country in York and Harrogate in North Yorkshire. Boots in Harrogate and Fads, another Boots subsidiary, were both extensively damaged. The Lindsey Brothers gun/blood sports shop and the Imperial Cancer Research Fund Shop were also burnt. In York, the newly refurbished Boots shop and Fads were hit, although the damage this time was less severe. In all, the damage caused by the fires averaged £2 million in each location, with any amount added in lost sales and increased security.

The police, it was reported, failed to properly assess their intelligence again and responded with blind enthusiasm, soon after, to posters advertising an ARM Meeting at Boroughbridge, North Yorkshire. Only out of sheer desperation could they have thought the ARM would publicly advertise their meetings and hoped to catch the bombers red-handed sitting round the table in their balaclavas with devices at the ready. Instead they found the Association of Radical Midwives discussing babies! There was more to come from the ARM, but the police were wising up. Meanwhile…

The Justice Department

> A million years from now the earth may be filled with creatures who strictly deny they ever descended from man.
>
> *The Irish Digest*

As the final big trial of the early 1990s concluded, a message was sent out to demonstrate that the radicals, rather than be deterred, were still very much at large. Describing their devices as 'experimental', the Justice Department announced their arrival on the front line when they posted a batch of parcel bombs to leading organisers in the blood sport fraternity and to Frank Evans, the UK's resident bullfighter. When one of these exploded prematurely in a postal sorting office north of London the area was sealed off, mail searched and six others were subsequently discovered and disabled.

While the details are sketchy, it seems these devices were more than a hoax, not designed to do any serious physical harm, but rather to shock the recipient and cause fear. The JD were undeterred by their failure to reach the intended targets or by the inevitable condemnation of something so reckless as sending bombs through the post. With blood sports fans on the alert for suspicious packages, devices were next sent to two men notorious for their involvement in other forms of extreme cruelty, dispelling any complacency about the devices being a one off or just to do with blood sports.

Colin French was only a farmer, albeit one who had notched up 92 convictions for cruelty to animals under his care and for breaching court bans on keeping them. A *Daily Star* headline article observed that: 'The Law Cannot Stop Him.' When he was first banned from keeping cattle, sheep and goats for 15 years, he had employed his stockman to 'own' the animals should anyone have asked. He was also fined a total of £70,000. When his stockman was similarly banned for cruelty, they turned their attention to other species of exploitable animals and on it went. One RSPCA inspector branded the French farm 'A concentration camp, a Belsen for animals. I can't think what animals would have to go through for anyone to be worse than him.' A donkey had been found lying beside the maggot-infested body of its dead foal, while an emaciated goat had been tethered so tightly that a rope had acted as a tourniquet. Many of the animals were so hungry they could barely stand. French was sent a JD device.

Christopher Brown was a farmer too and responsible for breeding and supplying thousands of cats to laboratories worldwide from his farm in Oxfordshire. Years earlier, he had become a hero to his peers when he successfully trapped a group of animal liberators inside one of his cat sheds—rescuers who were after snaffling some of his cats. They weren't able to free any cats and were all arrested, but he wasn't so lucky this time. Disguised as videocassettes, both these devices exploded on opening, causing minor injuries but massive distress. For both men there was plenty more of that to come as the Animal Liberation Movement tracked their careers to a satisfactory conclusion, Brown out of business and with no cats to sell and French rotting in hell.

Over the next four weeks, a further five packages were dispatched: two to furriers, two to blood sports fans and one to a mink farmer. Not surprisingly, the first thing the blood junkies did upon receipt was phone for the bomb squad. The mink farmer too was suspicious. But Haydon Noble of Noble Furs in London mistakenly thought his was some promo video from the British Fur Trade Association and had it blow up in his face. Rosalie Noble duly left hers for the bomb squad to sort out.

The early Xmas post of 1993 brought something similar, this time built inside two-foot-long poster tubes. Thirteen explosive devices were en route and set to explode on opening, sending HIV-infected needles into the recipient, or such was the grand claim. Various researchers, breeders and others in the vivisection community were targeted. The JD explained the action was designed 'to return the virus to the people who created it.' A frequent target for protest action for their links to Shamrock Farm, a supplier of primates for vivisection at Vet Diagnostics in Small Dole, West Sussex was first to receive one with the result that four workers suffered burns, hearing problems and shock when the device was opened with the morning mail.

Special Branch officers were quick to warn other potential targets and sorting offices to expect devices, and eleven were intercepted. Which left one outstanding. Terry Hornett received it; he was climbing the top of the vivisection ladder and had become the manager of the Glaxo laboratories at Hereford, a council member of the self-serving pro-vivisection Institute of Animal Technicians and a member of the RSPCA's animal experimentation advisory body—this being some kind of sick joke, both its existence and pro vivisection involvement in it. Anyway, he'd missed the warnings of trouble in the post and opened the package, which exploded in his face albeit causing little lasting harm. If that weren't an unpleasant enough experience, days later Mr. Hornett died of Weil's disease—something nasty you can catch from rat pee—something with which he apparently came into regular contact while doing his vivisection thing with them.

Xmas Eve saw a shift in tactics as the same group used a less violent, but more financially damaging, incendiary device at the Boots store in Northampton, causing a fire and extensive flood damage. Boots were soon to be under attack from the JD, ALF, ARM and various others. Days later, the JD hit Boots stores in Cornwall, placing on shelves devices built into the company's own brand hair dye products. They were so skilfully disguised that a shopper bought one from a store in Liskeard and took it home from where she later called the police to report the suspicious contents. Boots issued yet another alert to all their eleven hundred stores to be on guard. The police advised shoppers who had bought Boots hair products to be on their guard too and instructed that any suspect packages should be placed outdoors.

The Justice Department publicly stated their desire to inflict injury on their targets, something that hardly needed stating, as parcel bombs tend to go with physical injury. Whether it was bad fortune or a tactical risk that shoppers would take home incendiary devices with their shopping isn't clear. It does seem an odd thing to do deliberately, but one consequence would be to create a fear or mistrust of Boots products and it's one thing to have to keep an eye out for suspect packages, but searching inside every product for suspect material only increases the inconvenience to the target company, something which was next compounded by hoax bomb calls to stores and a general state of paranoia about 'suspect packages.'

Next came primed mousetraps with razor blades attached, which were apparently designed to trigger as the package was opened, slicing the fingers of the recipient. Over the coming months, dozens, possibly hundreds, of these things were dispatched to a whole variety of named animal abusers including Charles Windsor, the Prince of Wales. Whether they were successful in their aim there is unknown. JD activists next burnt out two speedboats belonging to the notorious laboratory puppy breeders at Garetmar kennels (formerly known as Cottagepatch) in Hampshire, from where the ALF had previously rescued ten puppies. They followed it up with two further video devices, one aimed at the Boots store in Cambridge, which was dealt with, and a second to the British National Party HQ in South London; the second causing injury to Nazi activist Alfred Waite.

The next round of devices, whilst apparently increasingly sophisticated and random, realised fears over the chance targeting of explosive devices when secretarial staff at Stena Sealink were injured as they opened the morning mail. The targets in Gloucester, Oxford, Edinburgh and Kent were linked to the live export trade. Such was the impact that ferry companies involved in live exports pulled out soon after out of fear for the safety of their staff. With exploding parcels, combustible hair dye and mousetraps aimed at numerous targets, these were far from single-issue fanatics!

With so many exceptions to the rule gracing the rampage of this fringe group, it was maybe only a little surprising to see SO13, the Anti-Terrorist Squad, raid the family home of a Sikh man from Coventry during TV news coverage of the attacks the following evening. Only Gurjeet Aujla was paying a great deal of attention; his parents barely understood the news they were watching as they spoke so little English.

The animal rights movement is made up predominantly of the white working and middle classes, which isn't healthy and needs addressing. There are few campaigners from our established ethnic groups, as can be seen on the marches and even fewer in the ALF or any more radical group. There are a few who stand out, especially in the countryside where Gurjeet heard it said, with just about every attendance at a hunt meet or demo, that he was a 'Paki bastard' who should 'Fuck off home' to where he belonged. To Coventry! Gurjeet could not hide under a balaclava! He was well liked by those working with him, a quiet, generous and trusted friend who had broken away from the tight-knit family fold to join something in which he believed passionately, but which was alien to his family. He was the black sheep, so to speak, like many of us. His sisters were keeping tradition going by working in the family business; they were good children. Gurjeet was bad. Very bad, although the parents didn't know it and would never have guessed.

Best not to tell them too much was his view and many of us have felt the same, either because there's no point as they'll only try to talk you out of what you do, or they won't understand. His arrest was a significant development in the search for the JD bombers and in Aujla's bedroom police found all the clues they needed to link him to the devices. He was charged and remanded in custody as a Category A prisoner alongside the notorious, albeit still untried, serial killer Fred West, who was also awaiting trial. It was some transition from the cosy life with the loving family he had left a few days before. He was in big trouble.

The week before Aujla's trial, the storyline in ITV's prime time drama *London's Burning* portrayed animal rights extremists sending parcel bombs through the post and causing a great deal of carnage in the process. Gurjeet Aujla wasn't accused of anything quite so horrendous as depicted in the fictional drama, but he had been sending parcel bombs and the police were asking for six life sentences should he be convicted. Aujla negated any potential negative jury influence by pleading guilty in the hope of cutting his losses.

The judge accepted his mitigation that his campaign started and finished with the six devices sent to ferry companies shipping live animals and that he wasn't responsible for other JD devices. The judge also accepted that the devices had been intended to cause disruption and fear rather than serious physical injury, and he further accepted the plea that the defendant was frustrated by the lack of political action to curb the cruel trade in live animal exports, an issue that had drawn large sections of what they call Middle England into unprecedented protest.

Not so much swayed by Aujla's guilty plea and his genuine remorse for the injuries and fear he caused to innocent people, it was the impassioned contribution from his family that had the most profound effect on the judge. Their son had never been in trouble before and, according to his father, in no way fitted the picture being painted by the prosecution. He was a loving, caring son with a future in the family business who had been led astray by his beliefs. Aujla knew he was a lucky man and indebted to his family when the judge gave him six years, the lowest sentence he said he was able to pass under the circumstances. It was indeed a good result, as many would say was Fred West killing himself in the cell next door to Aujla on New Year's Day 1995. Aujla has proven good for his word and since being released kept himself on the right side of the law.

Derailing The Vivisection Gravy Train

> In the UK, more than 10,000 people a year die from the side effects of medicines prescribed by doctors
>
> *British Medical Journal, 2004*

Explaining why the Government has failed to keep to its promise for a Royal Commission into vivisection, the Prime Minister Tony Blair said in December 2004:

> We pledged to ensure better welfare and better safeguards in animal experiments, and we delivered on that pledge. We have made sure that all the experiments that are conducted are conducted according to the tightest possible regulations. It is for precisely that reason that we are in a position to say to the animal rights extremists that we have tough measures in this country, so there can be no justification whatever for harassing and intimidating people who are going about their lawful business.

The promises made by the Labour Government prior to their election proved to be a bunch of lies, and worse than that, there's been an increase in the number of animals killed in laboratories. The true agenda became apparent when they started to play host to the pharmaceutical and vivisection big guns and to publicly defend the proliferation of animal experiments and the development of new experimental facilities. One man's mission to force the government to keep at least one of their pre-election promises would end in his death following a heroic struggle from behind bars and reignite this struggle and take campaigning and policing to new extremes.

The Hunger Striker

> It is far better to be happy than to have your bodies act as graveyards for animals. Accordingly, the apostle [St.] Matthew partook of seeds, nuts and vegetables, without meat.
>
> *St. Clement of Alexandria (c.150-c.215) Church Father*

In July 1996, 44 year-old Barry Horne was arrested while in possession of—and in the process of planting—pocket-sized incendiary devices in shops in Bristol City centre as part of the ARM campaign. Shops associated with vivisection and other forms of animal abuse. He had been in and out of the cells for a few years for one thing or another and had been under surveillance on and off for some time. Barry had become aware of animal abuse issues nine years earlier and had taken himself to a local group meeting in Northampton where he was to find himself in good company. There had long been a healthy quota of radical thinking activists operating in the area, people really determined to make a difference who didn't care about what others might say; people prepared to take risks for the animal kingdom.

Over time, Barry learnt the benefits of working alone, particularly given the amount of police interest in activists in the local area. There was no shortage of trustworthy people but the police knew them and might very well have had them under observation. Barry was happy with his own company. He felt he had a better chance if he went out alone to 'do stuff.' We talked about our activities, usually in the pub or Labour club; it tended to be general chat, with few admissions of anything in particular, but you kinda knew who'd done what for the most part. It was important to know your friends were busy at it—genuinely dedicated people doing something to ease the animals' suffering, to salve the conscience, to inflict some damage and maybe inspire others to make inroads of their own. There is a sense of comfort to be had from the fact that we are together working towards a common goal.

Barry Horne could perhaps have been called something of a loner but he still needed to be around like-minded people who were deeply moved by animal suffering, and with whom he could share some of the nightmares he'd witnessed. There are many who are unwilling to listen but you have to let it out somewhere so we soak it up between us. He enjoyed a pint and when he was ready, sharing an anecdote or two. He was not shy, but reserved. He wouldn't set the pace but was good for it once he got going, and a pint of beer certainly helped release the wicked sense of humour he possessed, which many seldom saw. He could have been called moody at times, but a lot of men are, especially when their hair starts to recede! He wasn't vain, but bemoaned the fact that as he got balder, it left a bit in the middle: 'It's pointless,' he'd say. 'Looks daft.'

And let's be honest: he did have an awful lot to be moody about. The indescribable cruelty either eats away at you, you ignore it, or you do something about it. We saw the videos together, read the horror stories. These are good conversation-killers in a room full of vegans. Barry would be last to rejoin the good mood as he took in what he'd just learnt. It always did his head in.

He didn't try to be forceful or demand anything in the way of material possessions. Just to get by was good enough, except where animal abuse was concerned: this demanded much more attention. It came to him late, but it came to him, and that was all that mattered. He was older than most ALF activists tend to be when they're at their bravest and most confident, with least to lose.

The police had deduced that he was up to something and they were right. It wasn't rocket science; he always was up to something. A suspect for involvement in previous ARM incendiary attacks, detectives were now watching him intently. They knew he was largely off the scene, not showing at many demos and bored of the meetings but seeing the usual suspects socially who were all known to be at it. Two and two were adding up to four. They could've picked up from someone else's loose chat referring to 'Baz working alone.' They had a reasonable description of one suspect they wanted, not that he fitted it particularly well, other than being white and male. It narrows it slightly, but there aren't really that many people who have been prepared to build and plant incendiaries in shops, not even within Animal Liberation Front circles. During the fruitful fur campaign between 1984 and 1987, around 40 in-store devices were placed by only a small number activists, mostly unknown to each other, but all had been working on a simple plan to get fur off the streets.

Less technical devices were and have been used much more often, but still not by any great number of people. Put simply, it isn't something a lot of people do and those that do so once then lose the fear, and go on to do most of that work, prepared to continue until the inevitable happens. Those that do are also invariably known to the police for other activities. Barry had been arrested with a team in

Lancaster in 1987 while attempting to free the dolphin Rocky. The police judged them rightly as being hard core. He was arrested again with another team of well-known activists from the locality together with a collection of incendiaries a few years later. There were other arrests and less dramatic incidents—they are ten-a-penny tales around any activist dinner table—but the point is that he stood out above the rest and was on the radar. He didn't necessarily fit the stereotype, but there are less and less who do as this movement grows.

There is something to fear for those who might feel complacent about government promises of clampdowns on protesters or the imprisonment of key players, because this movement has spread tentacles far and wide to people who can step over the line and make a difference with no fear of intelligence-led detection.

But Barry had been through the motions and was known. That pervasive sinking feeling begun to rush through his body the moment the man grabbed his arm—tightly—as he left the Halfords store in Bristol City Centre. Suddenly, in that one brief moment, his world had caved in. As far as he was concerned, he was going about his business and no one knew but him what that was, but he was wrong, tragically wrong.

It was a Boots-owned store in which he had just placed his incendiary device and he didn't have time to hope this was someone merely drawing attention to something he'd dropped or perhaps knew him and wanted to say hello. He knew the moment he heard 'Barry Horne', followed by that blur of words beginning with 'I'm arresting you on suspicion of…' that his life had not just changed dramatically, but was nearing its end. He was held tightly, rapidly surrounded by detectives and handcuffed. They were obviously out to get him and knew exactly what he'd been up to. Suddenly, it was painfully clear.

On the face of it, it would appear Horne wasn't going to be very active again for quite some time and he knew only too well that if he were arrested again for anything serious like this, his career as an activist would be seriously curtailed. But he had bigger plans, a trump card that would overshadow even firebombing high street shops.

For the rumours or loose talk of any suspicious movements on his part that might have led to his arrest, it mattered not a jot, for the evidence now was compelling and Horne was duly remanded in custody as Category A. After his arrest with incendiaries in 1990, which resulted in a modest three-year sentence, Barry had decided he wasn't going to serve a long one again; too much time wasted. Nor was he deterred—just hurting that bit more for failing the animals for the year he wasted inside. It wasn't about being afraid of prison for what it is, or being unable to cope with the tedious routine and the retarded outlook of those running the system, it was the enforced inactivity that bothered him: being unable to do anything to help improve things for the long-suffering animal kingdom.

He wanted to do more, he wanted everyone to do more. Although a man of few words, he certainly made that much clear. Charged with possessing incendiary devices in Bristol and with the ARM blitz on the Isle of Wight in August of 1994, he was never a candidate for bail. While in prison, he realised he was severely restricted in what he could do to further the cause, but there was one thing that he could do, and that was go on hunger strike. That it doesn't take many people to make a difference is something friends in Barry Horne's circle knew only too well from the numerous initiatives in which they'd all been involved. It was all too often the same old faces, albeit often hidden behind a mask, the same people planning things. It doesn't really take many: history proves again and again that it's the determination of a few that moves mountains. Of course there has to be a popular will to change society for the better—it was this that added to the driving force which banned the slave trade and gave votes to women, but the igniting spark—the effective catalyst—has always been the preserve of a few wilful individuals who have badgered, cajoled, exposed and broken all the rules.

Thirty years ago, a ban on the well-rooted establishment penchant for hunting wild animals seemed completely out of the question, with only a handful of objectors prepared to take the punishment for trying to change the status quo, yet today, the vast majority of politicians and voters are clamouring for the ban to be enforced.

Banning vivisection has been an even more unlikely goal, up against the might of the Pharma giants, but it is something that must happen at the earliest possible opportunity. This is human behaviour at its very worst. Not the necessary evil described by those who partake in it, but simply evil. It is torture for every single white mouse, not long weaned, to be crammed into a plastic tray with loads of others, then drowned in fluid, injected with poison or burnt on a hot plate. Barry Horne said to me once that the only good that will come from these experiments is the inspiration they give to those fighting them. 'We shouldn't be inspired by public speakers but by every little life taken.' Numbers he felt were unhelpful in the debate: 'It doesn't matter if it's one or three million every year, it matters that they tortured an animal. Every one is an individual,' He'd growl at someone quoting the number of animals killed for this or that. He was annoyed by the fact that we talked like them, turning the victims into statistics. He wasn't hoping to reduce the number tortured over time, he wanted them to stop it now and couldn't get to grips with why anyone would demand anything less. Some people don't even demand it—they just asked nicely that the cages be made bigger or have someone pop along to observe the torture, then describe it as 'regulated' or 'monitored.' 'Who the fuck do they think they are calling themselves animal rights activists?' was Barry's response.

Mocked by a screw when he arrived at Full Sutton prison 'just for a few animals', as opposed to stealing something off someone or doing drugs, he retorted by saying he would have done exactly the same for just one animal. It was for him very much a war—a war in which the only victims are countless millions of animals undergoing horrific suffering, countless millions of animals whose lives are extinguished without a care. He was quite prepared to be a casualty in this war, though his ambition was to work to disable the mechanics for as long as possible. He had a simple long-term strategy that had focused on vivisection and would cause maximum damage to the industry or any part of it until he could do no more.

Some say he should have done his time and come out to carry on the fight and indeed he would have been out by 2006, but for Barry there was nothing greater he could do in the war than offer his life. Is that not what we expect of our young men? He did what he did for others, in a gesture encapsulated in the famous line: Greater love hath no man than this, that he lay down his life for his friends (*John 15:12,13*)

In January 1997, whilst on remand, Barry Horne began what were to become the most spectacular string of protests the world has thus far seen in this struggle. US activists remanded in custody for fur protests have used hunger strikes in recent years to good effect and gained publicity. Other animal liberation prisoners have used them to demand dietary improvements. Barry Horne wanted to highlight the plight of animals in laboratories, to inspire the rest of us to commit more than a few hours of our time to the struggle and to force the government to end its support of vivisection and do what they had promised. In his words to 'Protest at the government's continued support for, and encouragement of, the vivisection industry in this country and to call on the Government to give a commitment to end its support for the vivisection industry, both financial and moral, within a period of five years.'

He got his first wish and the second, but he was dealing with the same right-wing government, albeit not with Margaret Thatcher at the helm, that were more than happy to allow ten Irish political prisoners to die rather than accede to their demands. It was a tactical error that meant Barry Horne was up against it, but the movement rallied to ensure the government, vivisection community and the public took notice and for that, he could be reasonably content.

Only a few of Barry's close confidants were aware of his plans. His idea wasn't something he would boast about but he would occasionally sound out. People talk about hunger strikes and how far they could go; some engage in them for a short time but rarely do we expect they will be seen through to the death in our society. It is something people do to draw attention to issues and themselves and when that's done, or if it looks hopeless or their nerve goes, the protests are abandoned before any physical damage is done. There are of course exceptions. It does take the seriousness from the protest when so many start and don't end a hunger strike, not that I question the decision individuals take in this, but for Barry this was as serious as anything he had ever done and he wouldn't be talked out of it for anyone. His priority was serving the vast and hidden world of earth's animal kingdom who are incarcerated by the fraudulent, moral malpractice of vivisection.

He was not willing to take anyone's advice regarding the last remaining freedom he had left. He was only interested in what people were going to do in support of his demands. The Conservatives were in charge at the time and had been seemingly forever. They seldom even pretended to care, but their days were numbered by an impending general election. This made any political action on their part even less likely than if they'd had another term to look forward to.

While it took some time for the first hunger strike to pick up momentum within a sceptical movement, helpfully he was in Oxford's Bullingdon Prison when he stopped eating and Oxford equals vivisection. This was useful, as there was plenty to do nearby to make the point for the hunger striker. As campaigners latched on to the idea, many seeing it as another stunt worth exploiting as opposed to the hopeless means to an end it could become, a series of pickets were organised, both at the prison and at local laboratory and animal breeders. At the first demo outside the prison on the thirteenth day of his fast there were over a hundred people in support. Action was

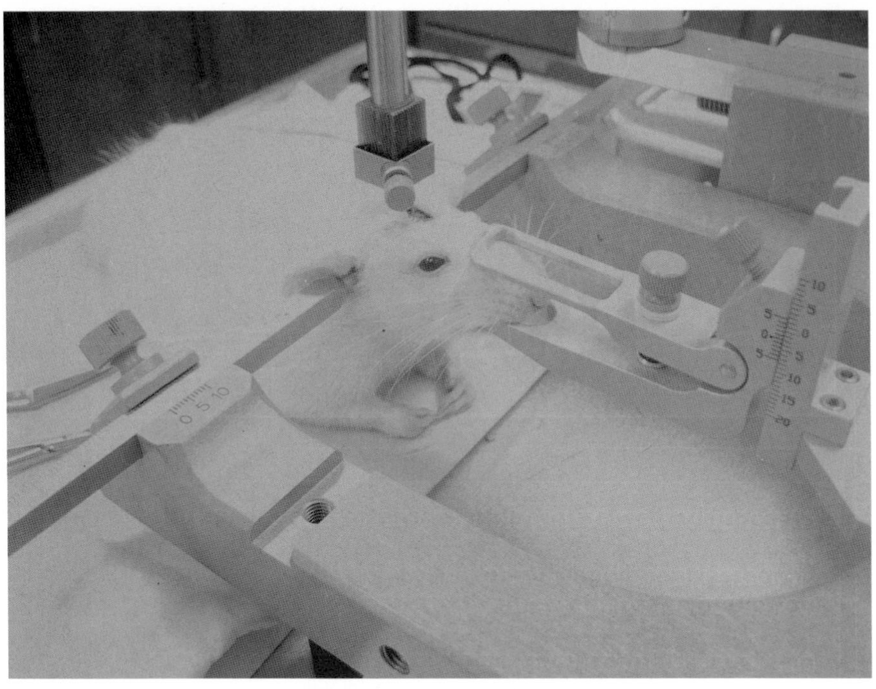

EXTREMIST VIOLENCE

Above: Rat clamped into stereotaxic device undergoing brain experiment.

Below: Monkey torture.

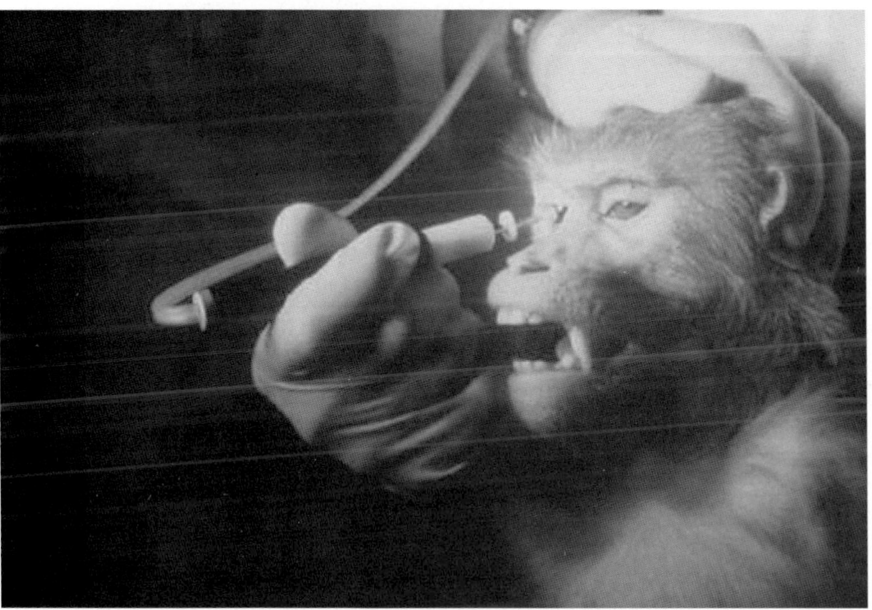

Above: A 'Justice for Keith Mann' demonstration.

Above: US activists on home demo of HLS supplier executive. 2005.

for animal abuse

William Pitcher

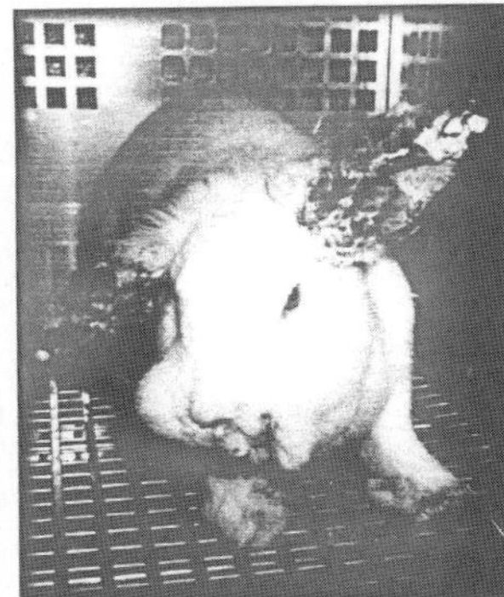

"THE BUNNY BUTCHER OF BOOKHAM"

From their farm at Chapel Lane, Great Bookham, William Pitcher and his partner Caroline Smith breed rabbits for cruel and pointless vivisection experiments. Phone them with your objections - ask how on earth experiments on rabbits can help people, or pay them a visit and demonstrate your opposition to their vile business.

SABOTAGE AND VIOLENCE

Below left: Milk lorries burnt out. Oxford 1999. Right: A mouse tied down and sacrificed.

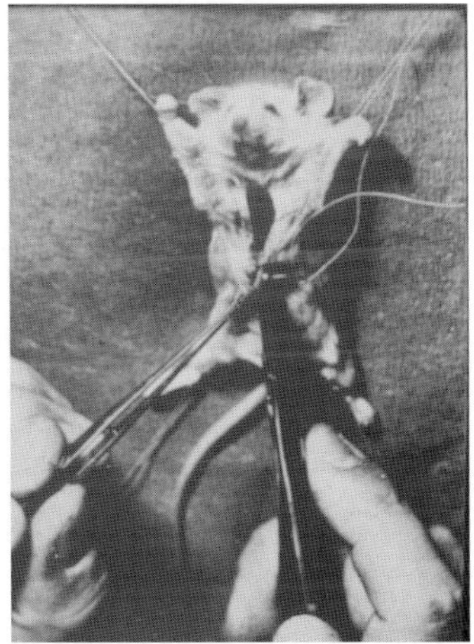

Above: People for the Ethical Treatment of Animals anti-fur advert.

Above left: The anger builds in Europe against Huntingdon Life Sciences. 2006
Above right: The author while serving time in HMS Full Sutton prison for Animal Liberation Front activities. 1995.

Above: Activist scales the fence of beagle breeding compound in Cambridgeshire.

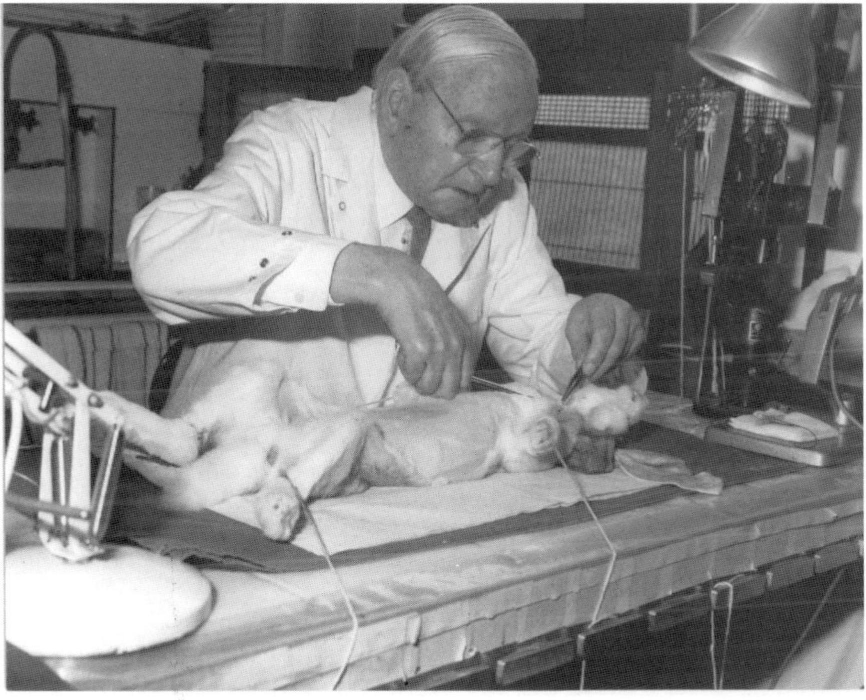

Above: The 89 year old vivisector Wilhelm Felberg seen experimenting on a rabbit at the National Institute of Medical Research at Mill Hill in London, 1989. Incorrect anaesthetic was used and animals were seen to recover consciousness. (ACIG)

Above: Young and old alike hit the streets of Shoreham to oppose the export of live animals. 1995.

Above: Pre-raid recce to rescue Rocky the dolphin from Morcambe's Marineland. 1988. There are no captive dolphins in the UK today thanks to the tireless efforts of campaigners.

Above: Hunt Retribution Squad publicity stunt in response to hunt violence. 1984.

Barry Horne.

Barry Horne's funeral.

Left: Mike Hill.

Below: Tom Worby.

Above: These two teenage 'extremists' were killed by middle aged animal abusing men while attempting to save animal lives in England in the 1990's. Both killers are known but neither was prosecuted.

Above: Hunt Supporters greet saboteurs to the New Forest.

inspiring itself.

After a short rally there in the morning, and in order to avoid disrupting afternoon visits at the prison, people then moved on to two breeding facilities outside the city, Harlan-Olac at Blackthorn and the Hill Grove cat farm near Witney. At the first complex, full to the brim with all varieties of rodents, the sparse police presence inspired the desire to spill over into the site. Three sides of the perimeter fence were dragged down, doors and windows smashed, and other damage done.

The police had seen and heard the bricks but couldn't stop them, or the disappearing crowd. But they had caught the mood and soon had a helicopter scrambled and roads blocked, but a little too late to prevent a similar outpouring of anger a few miles away at the site of Christopher and Katherine Brown's cat breeding farm to where some of the number had headed. On arrival, all the doors and windows were smashed causing thousands of pounds worth of damage and 14 cats were snatched from one of the sheds. The police were catching up and managed to collar three people and some of the cats in the vicinity. They were arrested and the cats returned to the farmer and their fate. The befuddled Christopher Brown, who had bred cats since the 70s and was raided last in the early 80s, said of the raiders, 'They are completely misguided and misinformed. They have pretty evil minds and seem to think people doing medical research have no respect for their animals. Vivisection is a bad word. The correct terminology is that they are used for medical research. Cats are not now used as a laboratory animal except for veterinary research.' In fact, Mr Brown neither knew nor cared about his cats or their destiny, be it within the UK or anywhere else in the world he sold them. Vivisection is a bad word indeed and a bad practice, not good for the animals or medical progress.

By the time the brief spontaneous assault on Hill Grove was over, it was blatantly clear that police chiefs had coordinated their forces and any other attempt to rattle Oxford's vivisection community further would have to wait. Most of Oxford's police force was on guard at roadblocks and at laboratories, private homes and breeding facilities. Police had been drafted in from other counties to provide added protection. It was a massive reaction to some broken windows. In all, 26 people were arrested.

Some were held overnight, but all were released pending further enquiries. It was a signal of what was to come in a new push for some domination over the monster called vivisection. Or if you prefer the interpretation of one businessman targeted, it was: 'Nothing short of anarchy. Just a gang of mindless thugs intent on destruction.'

Days later, a candlelit vigil was planned outside the prison. The police weren't having any of that and used their CJA Section 60 powers to stop, search and harass citizens entering the area. Many believed to be vegan were turned away with threats of arrest should they proceed to engage in their democratic right to protest. Fifty people still made it through and lit candles in the wind to the open disdain of Thames Valley Police who weren't trying to make friends even though they went a long way with some protesters after the vigil, tailing cars across several counties and even home to the doorstep a hundred miles away.

The police were as excitable and resourced at the next demo outside the Consort beagle breeding kennels at Ross on Wye in Hereford, but somehow missed what was happening. They weren't alone in missing the action, as there was a new private security firm on site to make darn sure the defences weren't breached, yet they were. While that keen team on security were goading the demonstrators out front, a number of resourceful individuals managed to find themselves a blind spot out back, which led them to a puppy pen from where they spirited away ten baby beagles—in broad daylight! Even the now-obligatory animal lib spotter chopper failed to see the puppy pinchers as they slinked out of the area with the priceless booty stashed under jackets. Management Note To Self: Better Security!

Early next morning, incendiary devices ignited seven refrigerated lorries at a Buxted chicken processing plant at Brackley in Northamptonshire, causing tens of thousands of pounds worth of damage. Following that, action moved north and several hundred earthworms were taken from the University of Central Lancashire research labs and reunited with their rightful home, while computers and other equipment were damaged. These actions, and more, were carried out in the name of Barry Horne who was, whether those involved could see it or not, being in turn inspired to starve himself to death.

Hunger strikes, whilst deployed more and more by desperate people, are often seen as a futile form of protest. Trying to persuade a right wing Conservative government in a capitalist society to act on animal abuse is surely futile, but there was nothing futile in any of this, in Barry's view. Certainly he had reminded the movement and put vivisection back high on the agenda from which it had slipped with the rise in live export protests. Clearly the Home Office was getting rattled by the reaction his protest had generated and, stuck for the best way to react, decided to punish him and shift the problem from Oxford to somewhere less likely to cause a breach of the peace on a daily basis. At week four without food, he was made to pack up his cell and, handcuffed, lug his belongings to HMP Bristol.

The national media in the UK had kept a virtual blanket silence on the hunger strike and assorted protests, but elsewhere in the world where solidarity actions were being carried out it was a different story. It was a story! Union Jack flags were burnt outside British embassies in protest. The rest of the UK's animal liberation prisoners, 18 in all, staged 48-hour solidarity fasts, Geoff Sheppard carrying his for 21 days. Never good without food, I was not a nice person to be around by the afternoon of day one of my token 48-hour solidarity fast. As the final hour approached, I was to be seen with a curry and chapattis wrapped in towels on the heat pipes in my cell. I was focused only on my stomach as I had been for nearly 48 hours: Spinach and potato with chapattis and rice…I can still taste it.

The ARM threatened that if Barry Horne died, five vivisectors would follow him. Predictably, the government refused to act and instead made threats to use force to keep people indoors and to silence them, but the proverbial cat was out of the bag and making the biggest fuss. The Tory administration was reaching the end of its term in office and New Labour officials were in contact with the campaign, reminding the movement of their stated commitments. It seemed likely that Labour would be taking over at the election in May and since they had made promises to set up a Royal Commission into vivisection and to ban various practices like tobacco, alcohol and weapons testing on animals, Barry Horne chose a tactical retreat.

A week after his politically-motivated prison move, with the movement abuzz with renewed vigour, excitement, energy, and the government and the vivisection community aware of the potential of a bigger reaction should Horne die, he suspended his protest after 35 days without food. This was a huge effort, enormously empowering, and it was just a trial run. A bit like dipping a toe in the water. One wrong move from the next government and he knew he could take this protest and up the ante.

Far from being ashamed at my lack of extremism in this endeavour, it inspired me immensely to know what Barry was able and willing to do and he will always command the utmost respect from me and many others. Just leave me out! It's no joke of course, and this was as serious as cancer. What if he had gone all the way? It was a question asked more as the days had ticked by, and it had looked to everyone like he was serious. Deadly serious. What few people realised was that Barry Horne was deadly serious and far from satisfied despite what he had so far inspired. It was of course back in the hands of the politicians, who were at first slow to act, but then stopped and went into reverse.

Consort Beagles—The Rot Sets In

> Tests on animals have led to around 100 drugs being thought potentially useful for stroke; not one has proved effective in humans. You don't need to be a balaclava-wearing animal rights activist to question the value of animal studies in this area of medical research.
>
> *The First Post. 25 January 2007*

Empowered by Barry's incredible campaign, the demise of Hylyne Rabbits, the Boots u-turn, the emptying of the dolphinariums, the live export uprising and the massive upsurge in action across Europe, the movement was thriving and hungry for more.

In a field off the A49 between Ross-on-Wye and Hereford, The Consort Biosciences beagle breeding kennels were crammed with howling beagles, a thousand or more by the sound of it, and all wanting out. Consort had been subjected to intermittent levels of protest action over the years, had been raided periodically and dogs and cats had been liberated from the complex. In 1991, Charles Gentry of Consort had said, following the closure of a number of other animal suppliers: 'These are indeed hard times for animal suppliers in our industry and we can only hope that market forces which have created this situation will change for the better.'

The insidious spread of the horrors of animal exploitation into so many areas of life has, left those exposed and opposed to all the cruelty desperate to find a quick solution. On the one hand, it isn't a bad thing to have individual animal abusers on the defensive and forced into dealing with the spiralling costs of increased security measures, but this hasn't for the most part reduced the animal suffering. There is a school of thought, which says focusing too much energy on one target, such as the Consort kennels, leaves others to get on with making their killing whilst even perhaps benefiting from the misfortunes of those targeted. This is a potential long-term problem for a movement fixated on simply closing places down, which may send the cruelty elsewhere rather than focusing on and forcing education and in this case an independent public inquiry into the failings of vivisection. Whether or not focused campaigns are the way ahead, presently there are few in the business of vivisecting live animals who can claim they aren't fearful of the present and the future because of this kind of protest action and many people are now talking about the wider issues.

The powerful vivisection industry is, of course, a bigger proposition altogether than a few dog kennels, but at that moment, there were a lot beagle dogs wanting out, and no one else likely to get them out. For the first all-nighter at Consort, nine security guards greeted three-dozen demonstrators. They'd never had that many on guard before. It was a good sign! They goaded protesters through the fence about the dogs and their future and bragged about the extra work they now had and the 'nice little earner you lot are!' Their disgraceful attitude didn't help their cause.

Consort was an independent venture with no Big Brother to bail it out at times of need and security people needed paying. And clearly more of them would need paying in order to keep out the adventurous few who breached the cordon during the vigil, accessed the kennels and smashed windows. Existing Security secured nothing. It was clear that this was going to be an issue for Consort.

Over the winter of 1996, and through the following spring, the kennels were the main focus of anti-vivisection attention, the end game being their closure, to be achieved either by making all the workers leave, or just by making it too expensive for them to operate at profit. The timing was perfect. Barry was starting to recover from his hunger strike and, like every one of us, was closely watching for signs that the new government was beginning to work towards fulfilling the promises it had made to the electorate in December—namely, that it was 'committed to seeing a reduction and an eventual end of animal experiments.' It was one amongst many other progressive pledges made by Labour, but as time passed, the pledges turned to dust and we all began to realise we'd been listening to a pack of lies. Again! How much more will people take of this? Who else is there left to vote for? Can we believe the Green Party might be any different under the present system? Do politicians lose the high moral ground in these circumstances and forfeit the right to dictate tactics? Of course they do!

So infuriated was one impatient activist that he used New Labour's glossy pre-election leaflets *New Life For Animals* to start fires at a meat depot. 'They weren't even much good for that!' he complained in disbelief. Meanwhile, Consort had another 21 all-night vigils to look forward to and an almost daily presence at the entrance for months. The security situation was a big focus for all concerned. There were also home visits—extras, if you like. That two workers resigned immediately after the activists hit home base did nothing for their kith and kin, for whom life was destined to only get worse. There were public meetings (not that the wider public cares that much for such meetings) and regional demos drawing people in from all over the country to have a look around. It made it personal. Being able to see animals in the environment where they're held captive is a sure way of making such matters personal.

The local police helped too, by winding people up with their pettiness, which usually helps stimulate public interest. The protests were never huge or overpowering, nor even remotely aggressive, but there were people there almost all the time—some new faces, many of the same old faces—but they were there and they didn't look like they were going away. Imagine the scene for the widely publicised annual World Day for Laboratory Animals gathering for April 1997 as five hundred people turned out to a national shout on the grass verge outside the entrance to the kennels. (Incidentally, 24 April has gone from having initially been a World Day to a World Week for Laboratory Animals and April is now World Month and a call to action. In 1991, the World Day march organised by the National Anti-Vivisection Society attracted 20,000 people. More recently, events have been organised at a more local level, attracting less numbers but achieving more than a walk through London).

There was no shortage of police officers on duty, but there were more were tucked away in reserve inside the compound than at the gates and around the perimeter. There were vans in side streets too, full of police waiting to join in. They were expecting a large turnout and some trouble but were looking to confront rather than prevent it. Ill-equipped to keep out so many wannabe liberators, the original stone perimeter wall had been extended a hundred yards all round by a temporary steel fence ringed with barbed wire. With a dozen or so officers inside the new bigger perimeter, it seemed the beagles would be safe from the outside world. Right? No way in past the fence, right? The barbed wire would keep 'em out; had done for years.

Among the crowd gathered outside Consort was the usual mix of radical 'grannies' and older men on the frontline; groups of teenagers and school kids and families. There were moderates who rigidly adhere to the non-controversial approach; those who were simply there to help in any way, and the masked, darkly clad find-a-way-in posse looking for points of access. Within minutes of the official meeting time for the national demo, the police had been outmanoeuvred and the new police boundary had been shown the contempt it deserved. At the very least, one should have sight of the place one's shouting at! Everyone expected the fence to be breached, but perhaps not quite so soon. Seeing the fence coming down, police inspectors began to mobilise their forces, but not in nearly enough time to prevent a handful of protesters crossing the dead zone and going over the compound wall. That razor wire-covered obstacle was more formidable than the temporary fence and injured some who challenged it, and it kept most of the in-pouring protesters between the two fences, leaving them to be confronted by a heavy police presence using sticks to force them back out.

The police temporarily regained some control of their zone, but they lost it again soon after two masked men appeared on the roof of one of the single storey buildings inside the police-filled kennel compound, holding a beagle they'd managed to grab from the kennel block. This was hugely symbolic and raised the crowd. This was animal liberation! The two were desperate to get back out with the dog but that meant getting past the gathered force of riot police they'd tricked to get in. In the struggle that followed, on the one hand to keep the dog in and the other to get it out, there were now a number of flashpoints where scuffles broke out and the fence came down.

Initially, the focus of anger had been about causing chaos and upping the ante and about feeling some power over the immense forces of 'law and order' congregated there, but suddenly it was all about saving that one dog's life. The stage couldn't have been better set; there were film crews aplenty capturing the moment, with the police helicopter missing very little from its permanent position above the kennels. Even the moderates couldn't help themselves on seeing the beagle and the desperate attempts by others around them to get it out. It was one little animal among many, but that was the whole point.

What was slightly baffling here, as has happened elsewhere, was that the police allowed a situation to develop where protesters were able to get their hands on a £200 beagle and display it for everyone to see. A recipe for disaster, exacerbated by the officers ringing the immediate area with fifty riot police who beat away anyone that tried to get within reach. One moment we could have a beagle if we tried, the next categorically not!

A woman friend in the crowd told me later: 'One of them sprayed me with CS gas, and then another hit me with his stick while I was blind and on my knees. Others ran over to stop the police and got really angry with them. Billy punched the one with the stick full in the visor of his helmet and sent him flying.'

'Billy' had never punched anyone before in his life. He is a big lump and obviously capable of hurting anyone he wanted, but he's a gentle giant. It wasn't just seeing them protecting the business of breeding beagles, but the fact that they were attacking a defenceless woman for trying to help these animals that sent him over. He really regretted what he did in hindsight but felt he had no choice.

Although he wasn't arrested, he vowed he'd never do anything similar again, but everyone agreed he had done the right thing. He had been provoked. There's doing your job, and doing your job, but beating innocent people up for trying to save a little dog holds no sway. (And lest it's not obvious from the above, there's a moral to the story here, and that's if you don't want to be responsible for keeping animals inside labs where they're tortured, don't join the police).

An hour into the melee, with the lines between the them and the us clearly defined, between keeping the dog in and getting it out, one of the two dog handlers had moved to another building and found a blind spot where the police were less prolific and aggressive, and managed to lower the animal to someone on the ground who was surrounded by a crowd of maybe forty, shielding and protecting him from angry riot police. As word went round that the dog was down and the mood lifted among protesters, the police became noticeably more volatile. Incredibly, the activists had managed to get the dog out beyond the heavy cordon. The men on the roof disappeared back into the kennels to grab another! But the first one wasn't away yet, and it was going to take the bravest and most agile to sort that out. There were hundreds of police on alert by now. This wasn't subtle or very efficient, but this was animal liberation and for those dressed in black, just what they'd set out to do.

Breaking back out through the police line then splitting into smaller groups, people ran in various directions with their coats under their arms as though carrying a bundle of beagle. The odds were stacked against them, pursued as they were by groups of police, their dogs and the force helicopter. This dog was hot! Aided by the eye in the sky and detaining individuals as they ran off over the fields away from the compound and searching them, the police huntsmen and women finally isolated their man two miles away from the kennels. He wouldn't volunteer the dog for all it was now worth and was soon joined by a dozen other protesters. They crowded in, only to be thrown violently out of the way by police, who were determined to recover the stolen 'property.' Everyone on the dog's side was then arrested. When the dog finally emerged from the scrum, she turned out to be a very excited pregnant bitch—one who would be returning to the kennels where she was destined for vivisection.

An American woman visiting the UK to take notes on how we did things here found herself handcuffed in the back of the police car with the dog on her lap heading for the cells. Unable to even stroke her, she cried for the little beagle, trying not to let her see how upset she was. Her image of our cops was in tatters. Back at the kennels, meanwhile, CS spray was thick in the air as the battle raged for another hour or so with fires breaking out in outbuildings and workers cars set about after the front gate was breached. Regularly changing clothing to hinder identification, people were using corrugated roof panels and even a bathtub to try and get over the boundary wire. This was done again occasionally, but no more dogs were recovered and the batons soon won through. Several protesters needed hospital treatment for the effects of gas spray and baton contact. The random use of this nasty stuff was the cause of dozens of complaints over the course of the campaign.

Throughout the day there were two-dozen arrests made for offences of theft, burglary, criminal damage and assault. A Consort man who went to the police station that night to collect the little dog (who had been enraptured by all the attention she had received) had to be escorted away with her by police. Taking her back at all was an act of arrogant stupidity by Consort management, who had become so blinded by the worth of every wretched creature, they couldn't see the damage they were doing to themselves by winding people up this way. That evening, three employees and the manager received home visits and their property was trashed.

The pickets continued for weeks after but were less noteworthy than this dramatic demo. A few people stood outside in all weathers, being abused, spat on and CS-gassed periodically. But it was more the daily slog that protesters endured that put paid to the business than a bit of a disturbance and a few broken windows. The lesson about pressure had been learnt and was being put to good use here.

Ten months of 'You will never close us down,' but by the beginning of that July, rumours had started circulating that Consort had had enough and were considering closure. Within a week, these were confirmed in a fax received by Central TV. It was what so many people had waited to hear. It was a victory for people power, not a great concern for the wider industry—not obviously so—but a massive achievement for the movement.

This just left the little matter of several hundred beagles to be resolved. Just 200 were made available at a cost for re-homing, these were taken into the caring arms of campaigners and found good homes. There was no comment on the rest. Within days, ongoing monitoring of the site had revealed a number of vans leaving carrying this bankrupt stock away. Where to? Attempts were made to follow but the police blocked the way. They weren't being moved to the safety of an animal sanctuary, that much was obvious. One rumour was that Consort might relocate in Scotland where the English problem wouldn't readily reach, but that was soon laid to rest when the awful truth was revealed.

Huntingdon Life Sciences has a long tradition of animal abuse. Records over 30 years old prove it, and here's just one example: A veterinary surgeon, assisted by other scientists, poisoned three pedigree Beagle dogs with the weed killer sodium chlorate. These experiments were performed at the Huntingdon Research Centre. The animals were force-fed the weed killer by stomach tube over a period of five days. The scientists noted 'marked loss of appetite and body weight with lassitude, vomiting and blood streaked faeces... urine contained blood on day three. Death occurred on day four (Vet Record April 1972 pp 416-18).

By the time Sarah Kite blew their cover in an undercover investigation in 1989, nothing had changed, and Huntingdon were still torturing animals—except that the Kite report had shattered their cosy little operation and brought it into the daylight. It was exposure they didn't need or welcome. As a consequence of the exposé, there was a 'shake-up' in management, creating a refreshing new image at the 'Centre of Excellence', where animals could look forward to their stay. Actually, it wasn't so much a shake-up as a cover-up. Taken in by none of it and privy to another more recent and more public exposé that had shocked the nation and forced a criminal investigation by police, an awful lot of people were distraught to hear that the Consort breeding beagles had been taken there, to a contract testing laboratory poisoning to death 500 animals every single day. There could be no worse destination for a beagle. A Channel 4 investigator had been inside HLS with a hidden camera and just before the World Day demo at Consort in 1997, C4 had screened the documentary *It's A Dogs Life* on national TV as part of their *Countryside Undercover* series. The UK once again ridiculed for pretending to have the most stringently regulated research in the world.

It's a Dog's Life showed that life for the animals at Huntingdon Life

Sciences Research Centre in Cambridgeshire was—as we already knew—a daily routine of violence and death on a massive scale. The company's profits depend on the perpetuation of that selfsame violence and death. It's all about money. It always is. Perversely, it was 'good' to see four-month-old beagles being punched in the face for refusing intravenous weed killer through a tube and being shouted at and shaken so violently they wet themselves; it was prime time TV and it didn't just upset the 'extremists' who know about these goings on, it upset a lot more besides, who would thereafter be known as extremists too. Some of the comments I've heard from the average person on the street, who to this day still make reference to this footage, wouldn't bear repeating in public—they'd be put on trial. The surge of emotion provoked in someone possessed of a compassionate sensibility when faced with the brutal realities of vivisection is the very reason why it's so secretive. Yet this was just someone punching a small, terrified dog in the face. And, believe you me, it gets so much worse than that.

With the uproar that followed the screening, the Home Office had no choice but to ask the police to investigate HLS for possible offences under the 1911 Protection of Animals Act. This was a landmark decision because, incredibly, it had never happened before! As a consequence, two members of staff were charged with cruelty offences and their imprisonment eagerly awaited. It was to be a long wait! Animal Technicians Robert Waters and Andrew Mash made legal history in September 1997 by becoming the first ever vivisectors to be found guilty under the 1911 Act for cruelty to animals and have their licences revoked. They admitted cruelly terrifying dogs and were given a derisory 60 hours community service each and ordered to pay £240 court costs. In addition, the licence was revoked from a third and two others were 'admonished.' This is maybe similar to euthanasia, or being sacrificed or dispatched, but I doubt it. Three days later all the windows in the Mash residence were smashed.

Under great public pressure, the Secretary of State threatened to revoke the HLS licence to vivisect after considering all the evidence, unless basic conditions of retraining and so on were met, which the Home Office would set and assess. Bit like the Guild of Paedophiles setting the rules on child abuse. They were given nine months in which to comply with the so-called 'stringent conditions' and were duly given permission by the Home Office to continue as normal, two months ahead of the deadline. With a pile of cheap breeding beagles to soften the blow of being told off and exposed to the world, things weren't looking too bad for HLS, but life never would be quite the same again, neither profitable nor peaceful.

Hill Grove Farm

> Another visit from the Home Office inspectors. This time I see them outside in the corridor. A technician tells me to sweep the floor, I sweep it, but they don't enter my side of the laboratory. I've now seen them arrive twice, but I haven't seen them look at a dog yet.
>
> *Zoe Broughton, 1997, inside HLS*

The victory at Consort didn't give licence to take on the rest of the world. It was a two-bit affair compared to HLS, ICI, Proctor & Gamble and Porton Down with their vastly superior resources and influence; this was nothing in the industry—just one small link in a big chain. But viewed from another perspective, every broken link weakens a chain. It was obvious where to go next. What about the Oxford farm breeding cats for vivisection? A large number of individuals had been part of the Consort campaign and some had agreed to set about the Hill Grove Family Farm as a full time venture and stick with it 'til the end. It would take time no doubt, because people don't give up their wealth easily and don't like change, but in the campaigners' favour was the fact that they had no full-time job, no mortgages to weigh them down, and not too many family commitments to get in the way of this project. It enabled some to focus single-mindedly on closing down this gross business. A honing of tactics was now dictating campaign strategy. It had a lot to do with self-belief and perseverance, about putting in as much time as those who put their energies into a successful business enterprise. It was about certainty that what you're doing is right. It was no longer a question of being there for a demo today, elsewhere tomorrow; this was it. It was time for action. Time for leaflets, posters, stickers, t- shirts, a newsletter… all about Hill Grove.

Since the 1970s, 'Farmer Brown' and his Family Farm had been the contact point for the supply of caesarean-derived cats to laboratories, with regular adverts in all the right places. For such a venture to thrive in a country such as this, with its attitude to animals, not least cats, is something of a miracle. And something to be ashamed of.

The last time there had been any incident of note at Hill Grove was in September 1981, when Brown had used a tractor to imprison a number of daylight raiders inside one of his sheds. All 11 had been arrested and put on trial and had run a defence of justifiable cause i.e. what they did was right because what he was doing was wrong. 10

were convicted, fined and given lengthy suspended prison sentences to deter any further such behaviour. One defendant said on leaving court 'If they think they have stopped us they have another think coming.' Then in 1993, a JD parcel bomb arrived at the farm and was briefly unsettling for the business. But in 1997, the movement arrived en masse.

The Browns had other irons in the fire beside the cats. They also grew arable crops on the 340-acre farm, ran a campsite and had Bed and Breakfast accommodation in their farmhouse. These were advertised with the Caravan Club and in holiday and the British Bed and Breakfast guides. To an outsider, it would have appeared that the outbuildings housed nothing but farmyard paraphernalia. Certainly you'd have no reason to suspect there would be hundreds of live cats awaiting experimentation! You just wouldn't!

Christopher Brown came from nowhere special; far from the yokel his accent betrays, he's a scouser, not that there's anything particularly wrong with that—so's my mum! His wife Katherine was an ex-vet nurse born into a family of vets, suggesting to some that she'd respect animals in their own right rather than for their financial worth. But as we see with just about every reference to cruelty, there's always a vet on the pay roll, giving the cruelty some credibility. The grim reality is, some vets are cruel and heartless and just in it for the money. Just see how she turned out! It was her father who, in 1970, had heard that vivisectors wanted access to more cats and developed the idea to diversify into cat farming and got on the gravy train. Christopher married into it. And what a good idea! Some of their ilk at the time saw the burgeoning market for more animals amongst their colleagues and invested. The vivisection industry found a way of turning animals into profits by investigating them for cures to every ill and to provide test results, reports, papers and statistics. Here was a way to prove anything was possible using animals and to make money from it! Most of the bigger suppliers of the 1990s were a consequence of this revolution in torture techniques and deceit; some turned to breeding, some to pet stealing and others became importers in a network of secretive, seedy deals involving countless millions of animal lives.

As with the movers and shakers in any walk of life, the men responsible for the majority of the animals available to vivisection are but a few who have shown themselves to be utterly ruthless and committed to what they do. Animal Fanatics, I suppose we should call them. Thirty years later, Brown had a colony of cats, which were worth £100,000 a year. Not bad for a few happy cats, which would go on to live a life of luxury in state of the art accommodation courtesy of Oxford University and others—lucky enough to be monitored by the Home Office. Or so the vivisectors and their vets say. Brown could never say exactly what use his cat might be put to but maintained that they didn't suffer and even if they did, it was regulated. Boy, does that word bring out a big sigh of relief. Besides, there was no one else; he had the market cornered and was in fact doing cats a favour: 'I love animals. If it wasn't for me this market would be filled by back-street cowboys who stole animals off the street,' was what he told the *Big Issue*. His public statements came thick and fast in the early months of the campaign, almost as if he was relishing being in the limelight and soaking up the moment before it went away.

From the minute the announcement was made that Hill Grove was to be the next campaign to occupy the movement, Brown displayed absolute arrogance and indifference. A thick set man with suspicious eyes and an aggressive smile, he'd seen protesters come and go before and he'd laughed them off each time. One elderly lady had sat up there at the farm gate in her wheelchair holding a placard all alone some days before others became interested. She represented the animal protection movement and he laughed at us. His ten-strong work force did themselves no favours with this attitude either, more than happy to throw abuse at protesters on the soon to be never-ending picket line. Laughing at them, laughing at the cats. Come again any time was their attitude, too: 'You make our days more interesting.' It's what they all say, to begin with.

Brown had a panic button installed as the pressure built up and the protesters stayed and not only had the rule of law on his side but the government was with him too. And, most significant of all, he secured the total commitment of Thames Valley Police, who set up Operation Stile to protect the business and even stuck a police radio mast on his chimney. Cat lovers were on side, drawn in by the extreme visual horrors that cats are subjected to in laboratories. They were working hand in hand with the campaign hardened regulars, who didn't care what the species was, or the excuse. They were all liking the pattern of protest. Driven to it, in fact. One woman, pretty, blonde, well dressed, thirty-something, attending her first ever demonstration had just learnt of the cat farm and had fully expected not just the RSPCA to be there but the police as well, to aid in the cats' removal.

'I was walking down the lane with my cat basket and my friend when the police stopped me and asked me where we were going. I told them we were going to get some cats. Obviously! What did he think? I was taking my cat basket for a walk? I thought he was having a joke when he said, 'Don't go doing anything stupid like that, love, or you'll be getting yourself arrested.' I found out he wasn't joking. He was serious! To get down there and see them surrounding the cat farm like they were, bowled me over. I just stood there and sobbed.'

She went on almost immediately to become an ALF sympathiser and soon an activist, paint-stripping cars, making silent phone calls and stealing animals. She said at first she didn't blame the police but what they were doing to protect this place changed her life.

There was a heady mix for the arrogant farmer to contend with. That some campaigners had set about working on this project full-time would be the key to its success. This was aided in no small part by the central location of the farm, making it accessible to many. And the lesser contribution of so many was utilised to the full as the campaign to Save the Hill Grove Cats intensified. The extreme contribution of Thames Valley Police didn't just protect the farm but deterred protests and intimidated protesters, and actually made the situation worse and played a big part in assisting the campaign. The Browns' problems had, of course, begun months before the official start date with an impromptu raid by activists supporting Barry Horne's hunger strike, when a number of cats had been rescued. Some were tracked down and returned by police. Nine young activists were arrested nearby and some were later prosecuted; this only compounded the sad news but cheered Brown no end. He remembered that the last time that happened, all opposition had dried up. To make matters all the worse for Brown, the trial of Kievan Hickey and two others for a commercial burglary and handling stolen property didn't focus simply on those minor offences but more so on the Hill Grove cats and Christopher Brown.

During the nine-day court case, invaluable information was revealed which was to help in the undoing of the cosy business of the Browns, as his workers and him were called by defence lawyers to give evidence on the day-to-day workings of Hill Grove Farm. To explain in public for the first time why records showed that the mothers killed a staggering 10% of all the kittens born into the stress of cage life at Hill Grove was, for Brown, awkward. And how was it that some of those that did survive were taken from their mothers and sold at just six weeks of age for experimentation? That can't be right! A list of the kittens' injuries was read out in court; there was page after page of mutilations. These were supposed to be happy cats, yet were engaged in infanticide.

Brown didn't like to talk about how he tattooed the cats' ears using pliers and no anaesthetic either.

It was looking like Brown and the police were going to get a resounding slap in the face when the three defendants were cleared of burglary and nineteen-year-old Kievan Hickey alone was convicted of handling stolen property, a gentle cat called Margaret, who had been used for breeding and who had in any event been returned to the farm. But the impossibly-named Judge Tickle caused ructions in court as he played to the press gallery and did his bit for Hill Grove's cause by reasserting Brown's claims and accusing the raiders of causing suffering to the cats by rescuing them. He then sent Hickey to prison for a year, suggesting he should choose his targets more carefully. He couldn't have chosen better as it turned out.

Arriving at HMP Oxford, Hickey got into a row with staff over his diet. One said they didn't do a vegan diet, so he responded by reminding him they'd not long since had Barry Horne there who was also vegan. To that there was an easy retort. 'Yeah but he didn't fuckin' eat anything.'

Brown sealed his fate in the eyes of some by announcing in court that Margaret had been killed two weeks before the trial began, because, according to the self-appointed animal lover, 'She had come to the end of her breeding life.' At that point, he rewarded those he vowed he loved, by killing them for being physically worn-out or sending them away for experimentation. Pebbles was another from whom Brown had extracted 12 litters of kittens since her birth at Hill Grove eight long years before; she had also had a brief taste of freedom at the hands of her would be rescuers only to be returned and put to death.

With the campaigners scrutinising everything Brown did, lapping up his every word and sharing them with the world, it wasn't long before all reference to Hill Grove Farm as some kind of get-away-from-it-all holiday destination in a lovely stone farmhouse in the idyllic Oxfordshire countryside began disappearing from the literature. There wasn't just the distasteful nature of his other business to consider, and many of those contacted certainly did. For those who didn't really care, there were now the resident activists to contend with and they were making their presence known and an awful lot of noise, both day and night. Few holidaymakers would come back for a second night of air horns, fireworks and the Thames Valley Police helicopter!

As that side of the business empire started to fail, it became clear there is indeed more than one way to skin a cat killer. The cats might well be secure in those units but little else was. After months of this pressure on his other interests, Brown stupidly let his guard slip and told *The Oxford Mail* 'It's pretty grim. These people are very misguided. They are unreasonable people. It's not fair on people coming here for a break. These people have no consideration for anyone and make noise all night.' Not so cocksure and unfazed all of a sudden.

It was as much the arrogance as the indifference of the man that inflamed his opponents, and the more he spoke, the more he wound people up. He didn't look like a nice man and he didn't sound like one either. Not that he cared much about that. Brown was, however, given some sense of security by his influential friend Jack, who lived nearby in Witney and with whom he attended church on Sundays. Yes, church on Sundays. The two of them had been put out by the regular protests in the area, which had been made so much more disruptive by the police imposing banning orders and blocking all the roads to keep protesters away from the farm. Jack was even able to fix up a five-mile exclusion zone around Witney to keep protesters from bothering his friend on the next big rally—only the second time these special powers have been used on the British mainland. With this intervention added to the Prevention of Terrorism Act, the threats, intimidation and arbitrary arrests, one PC commented gleefully as he manned the thick police barrier to lawful protest: 'This is it. Your demonstrations are finished.' The folly of using this draconian act was demonstrated an hour later as a thousand disaffected protesters took the day to the city centre of Oxford instead and awoke a county! Compared to standing in a field in the middle of nowhere, this wasn't a bad idea! The police were trying too hard to keep this one man and his vile business afloat to the detriment of not only peaceful objectors and the democratic right to protest, but other citizens of Oxford who had never before seen so many police. The police soon spent all available local resources and had to go cap in hand to ask for extra funding from the Government to sustain their campaign. This £100,000-a year cat farm was quickly becoming not such a good proposition, after all. Indeed, according to Superintendent Davies of Thames Valley Police, commenting on January 1998, the police were 'de facto becoming a private security firm' for Brown. It had been noted.

The government and its erstwhile Home Secretary and Witney resident, Jack Straw, were going all out to backtrack on pre-election promises and prove to a jittery industry that neither the government nor protesters were going to interfere with the smooth running of their vivisection empire. Coincidentally, the Protection from Harassment Act was passing through Parliament to protect women, so we were told, from stalkers. With it came the token concerns of civil liberty groups who worried that the new powers might be misused and instead applied to protect men like Mr Brown. Ask your average protester and there was no doubt in anyone's mind that this would be the case. Sure enough, barely four weeks after the Act became law in the summer of 1997, Christopher Brown was granted a restraining order at the High Court which effectively placed an exclusion zone around him and his property. It banned 'Anyone holding himself out to be an animal rights activist' from communicating in any way with him or from demonstrating on the land surrounding the farm, including, 'For the avoidance of doubt, all public footpaths crossing the land.' Also included was a ban on any advertising of demos or protests aimed at his business, 'Whether within the land or at all.' The punishment could be a five year prison sentence, a fine, or seizure of assets. For protesting! The rules and the mood were changing in the English countryside.

Acquiring this order cost the Browns £5,000, to add to an annual bill of £30,000 for private security. But whilst able to force the few named personally to keep away, there were a lot of others not so named who worked the loopholes. Time was running out and costs increased with every legal letter and new bundle of documents added and it was starting to prove unworkable. But it wasn't an entirely lost cause and had established a precedent for others with greater resources, a new law and a similar problem to follow in the future, as we shall see.

With Thames Valley Police using every trick in the book and some not written to keep the protest numbers down, their bill went up to £1 million in a year. To protect a cat farm! While the large number of animals being vivisected might not bother everyone in Oxfordshire, the fact that their taxes were being poured into protecting it certainly did. Few actually wanted a cat farm in their county. It hadn't been that good for the local economy before the campaigners arrived, and it had, since then, become downright detrimental, and impacted heavily on policing. The police service had no choice, of course. Individuals do. Had the police not been there, Hill Grove wouldn't have lasted a week. But they were increasingly under pressure locally to do more for the other citizens of the county who weren't making big profits from tormented cats. With this in mind, the crucial advice that had been given to activists on the ground (namely: not to allow the police to become the enemy no matter how badly they behaved and to keep the focus of energy on the defeat of the animal abusers) was upturned. It was still not advisable to get into fights or cosy chats with the police, but time to think about how best to inflate their spending. Essentially a publicly-funded protection service for Hill Grove Farm and TVP's blind obsession with protecting the business at all costs may be the key.

With this in mind, extra demos were advertised to the 8000-strong mailing list of supporters, inviting different regions to pick a day to organise to travel to Oxford and spread out! Coupled with mass protests every two months, local demos almost daily, the inevitable visits to workers' homes and the night vigils, the police were finding their workload increasing when it should be, in their experience, decreasing. The Chief Constable of TVP, one of the largest and most experienced forces in the country with a history of 'dealing with' large-scale protests (like those which greeted the builders of the Newbury by-pass and foreign troops at Greenham Common) claimed that over time: 'The numbers of protesters will dwindle and fade away.' His view was that people would lose interest and join other causes. But he had misjudged the mood and determination, aided again by the less vocal but more honest Mr. Brown who told *The Independent*: 'It's been horrific. Devastating. We're existing, not living. And you can only withstand so much. But yes, I'm stubborn. I'm not going to give in just yet. I just wish I could see a future.' He would never admit it, but he was talking himself out of selling cats. This was music to the ears.

From the start of the campaign, Christopher Brown was unequivocal that he wouldn't give up his sordid business to 'Mob rule'—not for love nor money. But a year on, his attitude had changed and he'd started to waver. He was now saying he had stock worth £100,000 and would consider shutting up shop if paid £200,000. There were no takers, though Thames Valley Police might have considered it a sound investment had they not had other ideas.

On World Day in 1998, the 2000 people who headed for Hill Grove Farm on chartered coaches from across the country were left breathless on arrival. The isolated farm had been erased from view by the TVP's piece de resistance—a 10' high steel cordon that had swallowed the farm and all its secrets! With defensive watchtowers on the corners for Evidence Gatherers to look down and film protesters, it could've been Northern Ireland or the West Bank. But this was Witney and the stage was set. That the police had put this thing there, further burying the cats—without planning permission as it turned out—was like a red rag to a bull and of course inflamed the situation further. Not even a house to shout at to release some anger—just a solid steel fence. If that wasn't incitement enough for the hotheads, there was this big pile of rubble left just outside the fence. Had no one noticed ammunition aplenty?

That day, as on most others, coaches and minibuses entering Oxford were stopped at police roadblocks, drivers' details taken and vehicles searched. Burly, overdressed police officers with video cameras and powerful spotlights marched onto vehicles, ready to film everyone and pile into anyone with anything to say. Those who objected and hid their faces—old people, young people, big ones and little ones—had their faces forced into camera shot. Aside from making people late, this is guaranteed to make them very angry. The earlier mentioned young woman (this time, less cat basket) had lost all sympathy for the police once this happened to her a second and third time. If this wasn't their fault, whose fault was it? Are we not all responsible for our own actions? Once off the coaches there was then the police cordon to contend with around the site of the protest, through which officers corralled protesters, stopping each one so they could be filmed and photographed. So many photographs!

Whatever the reason they gave for wanting to shove cameras in faces all day long, such intimidation, the massive security fence and the pile of rocks they left outside the cordon made for the most dramatic and devastating protest of them all at Hill Grove Farm, as the police looked on and filmed! There were three hundred riot police between the house and cat sheds and the steel fence. They remained there throughout the long afternoon, ensuring no cats were saved. They clearly weren't too bothered about the house, as over a period of two hours that was pounded by several dozen protesters, transferring the rocks and anything else likely to do some damage into the house, smashing eighty windows and much of the roof. The fence was pulled down in part for a time, but sheer weight of police numbers prevented anyone getting inside. Others used an improvised battering ram, and some tried to tunnel under, but the cordon held firm. The cats would be safe but the house was trashed in front of 300 police.

Could it be that one of the biggest and most protest-hardened forces was really outmanoeuvred so easily on a day for which they were amply resourced and prepared? It was soon widely believed that this event was a stage-managed 'disturbance' to allow the police to make arrests later. Certainly that was what happened and there was no shortage of willing participants. Despite shelling out £70,000 on one day's policing, the huge mass of men and metal made no effort to save the Browns' property. It was smashed to bits, with curtains ripped and blowing in the wind through shattered windows, and more holes than tiles on the roof. To have affected Brown this way was a morale booster for many seeking his downfall.

It wasn't long before the police had compiled a list of names and addresses they intended to visit over this disorderly conduct, and they weren't subtle about it, to say the least. People were arrested at their homes during early morning raids over the coming months and at future demonstrations by specialist police teams with protester portfolios to hand for making on-the-spot identifications. Court cases were two-a-penny and prison sentences too, for those who fell into the police trap and hadn't been sufficiently disguised. The trashing of the Hill Grove farmhouse makes dramatic footage but it was costly for all concerned.

However, too much momentum had gathered to stop what was happening to the business now. It had become personal for too many people. One night the Browns' Range Rover was burnt out in front of their house and windows were broken. Their phone lines were repeatedly jammed during co-ordinated national phone-ins, which served to disrupt business and generally harass. They received tens of thousands of calls during the campaign. Their telegraph pole was cut down. They were subjected to firework displays early in the morning. Workers resigned and they all received piles of unsolicited mail. Day after day, they were confronted with having to deal with something new.

In late July 1999, gum-chewing, tooled-up policemen made twenty random arrests at a national rally in Oxford, including the public speakers and those who were standing close by. All were later released 'pending further inquiries.' It was an unnecessary action that, once again, served only to inflame the situation further. So it was by no coincidence that later that night, the ALF struck twice in the county, torching four Tadmartin Poultry trucks and then 17 belonging to United Dairies, causing £1 million damage.

The bill for protecting the farm had reached almost £5 million in two years. Over 350 people had been arrested and at least 21 imprisoned, Kievan the cat napper for the longest. Brown had been living with this pressure for 19 months when he claimed: 'It's just anarchy. Terrorism. I've been beaten up, I've had letter bombs and so have my staff. But I'm not going to give up. If I did, we'd have mob rule.' But adverts for Hill Grove cats were conspicuous by their absence from the Laboratory

Animals Buyers Guide of 1999. By August, a key event had changed his mind and he no longer wanted to sell cats.

Christopher Brown had done all the talking and kept his wife out of the limelight throughout. One small conspiracy concluded that it might be an idea to include her some more; after all, she was a Director and Secretary of the business, and he a Director and Mouthpiece. Soon after these private discussions, Kathleen Brown was accosted while out walking the dog one evening in the woods at the rear of the farm. Good for the dog to have a regular routine but not her; someone had noticed. Unhurt, but petrified and blubbering, she was left tied to the fence with a clear warning about the consequence of dragging things out any longer. Two months later, it was all over.

This incident and police hints about the damage Brown's business was doing to the local economy influenced the final decision to quit, or, as the cruel king of contradiction put it, 'retire.' The rumours were everything and sent an adrenalin rush around the movement coming as they did late one night in August 1999 from a sympathetic RSPCA worker who'd been put on call to accept 800 cats. The source was kept a secret, but no one else in the country had that number of cats. This was a massive day for the Animal Liberation Movement. This wasn't just a cat farm or about dethroning a stubborn unhinged farmer—it was symptomatic of something far greater than that.

Under cover of darkness in a secret operation on 10 August, 1999, 30 RSPCA staff took the Hill Grove cats in sixteen vans to re homing centres. Ironic really, that the RSPCA was the only animal welfare organisation not to call for the closure of Hill Grove Farm, even speaking out against the campaign, yet were now plastered over the newspapers the next morning 'rescuing' the Hill Grove cats. Christopher Brown's parting shot was: 'They were lovely cats, and I greatly enjoyed caring for them. I hope they will be appreciated in their new homes. I would be upset if anybody were to treat them badly.'

Despite the forceful nature of this campaign and the state's reaction to it, Save The Hill Grove Cats was a perfectly legitimate campaign with police on the mailing list, a postal address, newsletters and a phone number. That some activists took things further remains an inevitable consequence of state restrictions on lawful protest. The reality is that many of the more standard methods applied by moderates to achieve the alleviation of animal suffering or the closure of an abusive establishment did not succeed in their objective. Petitions and polite requests pale into insignificance are often ignored compared with more radical objective-driven strategies. And would simply not provide enough material to write about.

Apart from Mrs Brown's moment in the woods, the only people who were physically injured in this campaign and the one before were protesters, many of whom needed hospital treatment for various injuries. For all the violence that was reported in the regular local and national coverage of this campaign, it was protesters who were mostly hurt. Anyone care to write headlines about that? That our most radical thinkers are able to restrict their efforts to economic sabotage and threats is, I think, a great credit to the self control of people whom the media loves to accuse of being violent and extremist for ignoring protocol and standing up for animals. We should praise not condemn this movement for its restraint.

In the middle of the battle for Hill Grove Farm, the Conservative government lost power to Labour after eighteen years. Reasonable Britain was living in hope that a lot of things would change for the better. Certainly the promises were there. Lots of promises. Barry Horne was still in HMP Bristol awaiting trial and had regained his strength after refusing food for over a month. He was empowered by the Hill Grove story and looking forward to starting, or stopping, again. He didn't, in reality, have a lot to bargain with that time, as the Tories had never promised anything and didn't give two hoots about either him or animals in laboratories. But he believed like many that the Labour Party, New Labour, was different.

They'd promised to abolish the LD50 test, a crude poisoning test in which a batch of animals are fed or injected poison and observed for days until half are dead, at which point the rest are killed. They'd promised to ban tobacco, alcohol and weapons tests and experiments on primates, all of which the Research Defence Society defend as routine to maintain the status quo and keep vivisection off the slippery slope. New Labour said they were going to ban these practices and prove there was no need for any slide into ALF methods of protest to affect change. Instead, they were soon to become very public bedfellows with the very people whose vile excesses they had vowed to limit, even ban. But that, as a government spokesperson was to say of their broken promises, was a thing of the past: 'December was a long time before the election.' A day, after all, is a long time in politics…

That Hunger Striker

> All should remember this, that I do this now not for myself, not for the movement, not even for the cause, I do this for the animals.
>
> *Barry Horne*

In tandem with the increasingly violent police response to lawful anti-vivisection protest, political promises of action turned into excuses for inaction and the political rhetoric began to swing definitively in favour of vivisection. Barry Horne was refusing food again. It was August 1997.

Barry Horne's efforts once again sparked a huge worldwide reaction, including blockades of laboratories and breeding facilities, large-scale sabotage, rooftop protests, office occupations and daytime liberations. Four hundred marched on Shamrock farm, three hundred on Wickham Laboratories. Labour Party offices were picketed and 150 people converged on the home of the Home Secretary, Jack Straw. Police in boiler suits and with no numbers on show greeted activists here. The force helicopter was airborne for around ten hours, with roadblocks in place to prevent anyone else getting near. Within days, the ALF had hit five Oxford vivisectors' homes. Just when Thames Valley Police thought it was all over!

And it had spread. The inner workings of Huntingdon Life Sciences had again become a focus for campaigners, with the lab besieged by angry locals and the Huntingdon Death Sciences campaign. Camp Rena sprang up on land opposite the lab beside the A1 in Cambridgeshire. A permanent protest camp was of course seen by the professional animal poisoners as something of a joke. 'A pathetic futile little protest,' as one called it as he breezed in through the gates to 'poison some nasty little rats.' But a joke it wasn't. Aside from the fact that the tents and their occupants were stirring the sensibilities of HLS management, who didn't like to have visiting customers and staff constantly reminded that there was opposition to what they did, it was a focal point for activists. It was a strange sort of refuge of hope in an area blighted by the grim network of windowless buildings that make up the sprawling laboratory complex that is HLS, which stands in barren, borderless, intensively-farmed Cambridgeshire countryside. And there weren't just tents, there were tunnels. Not tunnels heading under the fence, just tunnels to prevent a smooth eviction should it come.

Lawyers for Huntingdon noted:

> The immediate background to the present situation is a hunger strike presently being conducted by Barry Horne presently in HMP Bristol. Mr Horne's hunger strike is at an advanced stage and may continue to provoke serious incidents of harassment. Although his hunger strike is directed at the government, in support of a change of legislation concerning animal research, it is clear from the documentation being produced in the name of 'Barry Horne Support Campaign' that his supporters are using his strike to direct a campaign of harassment against the plaintiff (HRC).

Yes—in his honour and name and due to the fact that the plaintiff was torturing and killing 500 animals a day.

There were actions taking place every day in the UK and elsewhere. In Staffordshire, in September, the ALF raided the Newchurch guinea pig farm and rescued 600 guinea pigs destined for places like HLS and labs abroad. Supplying 10,000 of the 80,000 used each year in the UK, the thriving family business was in the process of expansion. It was one of the new units, not yet alarmed, that the ALF team were able to access by drilling out door locks. Film and documentary evidence recovered revealed the terrible conditions in which the guinea pigs were forced to live, including the alarming mortality rate amongst the newly born. The raid was a precursor to a focused campaign that was already well planned and was to kick in over coming weeks, armed with footage and facts recovered by the raiders. It was to become a campaign that would pile on the kind of pressure seen elsewhere and lead to some of the most imaginative tactics thus far employed in the battle to drive vivisection out of the UK.

Barry Horne had written a living will, which meant that in the event that he lapsed into a coma, no one could interfere and keep him alive. He was utterly serious about this. His physical condition deteriorated quicker than on the previous fast, but his determination remained immovable throughout. On the fourth day of the hunger strike, the prison put him on a punishment regime which isolated him from other prisoners and saw him locked up 23 hours a day. A soon-to-follow press release issued by the support campaign generated intense media interest and persuaded the prison authorities that they'd made a mistake and that refusing food wasn't a punishable offence after all! He was back on normal location a few days later. The (BHSC) campaign answer phone and website were updated daily and regular bulletins and press releases were issued to keep supporters and the media up-to-date with the rapidly changing situation.

After six weeks without food, Barry's health, and in particular his eyesight, had markedly deteriorated. The press ignored events, largely, no doubt as a result of the untimely death of Princess Diana in Paris on 31 August. But there was a lot of talking behind the scenes with government officials, who were being bombarded with letters, emails and phone calls. Lord Williams of Mostyn, then Home Office Minister, phoned the campaign to discuss Barry's demands and agreed to hold talks with three representatives. Previously, they'd refused to so much as look at anyone to whom their legal system had given 'criminal convictions for violent offences relating to animal welfare issues,' which was downright stupid, somewhat narrowed down the field and stalled all talks. In due course, they acceded that 'crimes' relating to animal welfare issues were political and not criminal. Official recognition that the Animal Liberation Movement represented something other than a bunch of lunatics was indeed a step in the right direction. The foresighted Barry Horne alone seemed to accept this as an inevitable consequence of the hunger strikes and felt he achieved his aim.

His hunches vindicated, and happy in mind and body, he called off his second hunger strike (this time after 46 days without food) to the relief of his weary supporters, who had been gearing up with trepidation for a deadly conclusion. His friends and supporters were not the only ones to breathe more freely—there were clear indications that the industry and government felt similarly, but for very different reasons. Hunger strikers have died before reaching this point, but a few days into recovery, Horne was already reaffirming his allegiance to the cause, promising that he was ready to go the course again and would take it to the bitter end if they weren't good for their word…

The signs were ominous from the start, as later the very same day the government granted HLS full licence to vivisect again. Days later, the police and bailiffs moved in to evict the protest camp at HLS, although it took several days for them to negotiate with the various human obstacles such as one woman locked to a safe, deep underground. Within six weeks of HLS reclaiming their Certificate of Designation to vivisect, the *Daily Express* exposed another leak of damning documents, courtesy of Uncaged Campaigns—the biggest ever leak from a UK laboratory. These documents revealed that not only were HLS involved in the grotesque transplantation of genetically modified pig hearts and kidneys into wild caught baboons on behalf of drug firm Novartis—known as xenotransplantation—but that the shoddy experiments caused so much suffering, they were deemed illegal.

Animals were wrongly reused in experiments and, on hundreds of occasions, scientists failed to record results, especially where they were negative. One monkey was killed because the pig kidney he had been given was accidentally frozen. Another, a female, had to be killed off after she was given a quadruple overdose of a powerful drug. The leaked documents revealed that many higher primates were being used in shoddy pig-to-primate organ transplant experiments conducted at Huntingdon Research Centre from 1995-2000 by Imutran, a subsidiary of Novartis. The macabre research involved the transplantation of hearts and kidneys from genetically engineered pigs into hundreds of macaques and wild-caught baboons. Some of the most horrific experiments involved researchers implanting hearts from transgenic piglets into the necks of baboons. One traumatised animal was seen holding the swollen red transplant, which was seeping yellow fluid, for most of the last days of its life.

The research was widely condemned by all comers, except those in Government who had misled Parliament in order to protect HLS and co and the misleading promises on offer of a new life for organ-dependent patients. (See the Uncaged website for all campaign details including the mammoth court battle won by Uncaged which eventually enabled the leaked documents from Novartis to be published on 'public interest' grounds very much against the wishes of those involved who went to extremes to impose gagging orders).

The greatest success of this research programme was that one baboon survived for thirty-nine days with a pig's heart. Others lasted an average of ten days. Their suffering and the failings of this programme of experiments were described by scientists later advising the Government on the programme as research 'leading up a blind alley'—comments which were not made publicly available until the documents were leaked.

Yet another exposé a few weeks later from within the second HLS' lab in the UK, at Occold, revealed that staff were routinely drunk whilst working with animals, that there was drug-taking on site, gross incompetence and flouting of safety regulations, and—as if that's a surprise—extensive animal suffering including that of one monkey whose leg had been broken as a result of mishandling. For all the fine words of Government Ministers, the reality for animals living inside HLS and elsewhere was and is a gross indictment of our society, yet the corrupt systems that operate to uphold it wield so much power that they seem to be able to deceive the majority into believing that the world of vivisection is squeaky clean and suffering-free. George Bernard Shaw was certainly right when he said that: Whoever doesn't hesitate to vivisect won't hesitate to lie about it.

At the end of 1997, Barry Horne was convicted of several counts of arson relating to the ARM blitz on the Isle of Wight which had caused £3 millions' worth of damage three years earlier—allegations for which he continued to maintain his innocence. He had pleaded guilty to several counts of attempted arson and possession of articles with intent to cause criminal damage following his arrest in Bristol city centre. Judge Simon Darwall-Smith sentenced him to a massive 18 years. The IOW conviction rested on the similarity of devices used on the island and those in his possession, but there were also differences. It was as likely that they simply came from the same blueprint, which was available to a wider audience. Horne was put through 14 ID parades but picked out on none; other suspects were also arrested, but this was now a minor issue to him.

Government representatives talked and were given a year in which to take some action, to make some convincing public statements, to do something—anything—for animals in laboratories. These were simple requests made by members of the public who had been pledged action by elected representatives prior to their election. So nothing impossible, unacceptable or unreasonable, then? Barry Horne waited patiently—as did the rest of us—for something to happen, but nothing did. In meetings with senior civil servants, a timetable for action was refused and the same worn-out rhetoric about their 'commitment to animal welfare' was repeated and more talking urged to allow the government time.

They talked, but said very little and did even less. They were playing a dangerous game. The people were conned again! Stupid! Blind faith, they call it. Patience isn't something society should be promoting whilst others are suffering and dying. If nothing else, exhausting the political process so publicly has fuelled calls for more direct action and forced some to take this course. It's a historical norm. With politics, there are usually only dead ends. Horne, like the rest of us, had been down them before and he was back in the same old mess with no way out.

The government made a very big public song and dance about ending a few hundred cosmetic tests, which in any event should have been banned with slavery and proved to be another lie. Yet overall, the number of animals was rising again, for the first time in years, by tens of thousands.

Following sentencing, Barry was transferred to the long-term Full Sutton Prison in York. While recovering his health only very slowly on the prison diet, he was no less determined that the Government wouldn't be allowed to get away with what it was doing and he had only one thing on his mind. The problem now would be to persuade an already cynical movement that another hunger strike was a good idea. The media, too, would be even slower to show interest until it was probably too late for Barry. Many in the movement and beyond thought it a futile gesture that would reap few, if any, rewards in the political arena; they asked him instead to do his time and return to campaigning. But for Barry, there was a lot more to this than forcing the political hand. It was as much, if not more, about forcing the hand of activists who were playing the protest game. He wanted the movement to rise in up anger, if not about vivisection, then about his death. He was putting his life on the line to inspire others.

Less than a year later, on 6 October 1998, he announced the start of his third hunger strike, and wrote outlining his position:

> This decision taken by myself alone but with the support of the Animal Liberation Movement was not arrived at easily. It followed months of soul searching by myself as to whether, should another hunger strike become necessary, I had the required determination and resolve to carry out what would be my third. During those months, the situation—as regards the government desire to limit and decrease the activities of the vivisection industry—deteriorated. The decision was made for me by events beyond my control.
>
> The fight is not for us our personal wants or needs. It is for every animal that has suffered and died in the vivisection labs, and for every animal that will suffer and die in those same labs unless we end this evil business now! The souls of the tortured dead cry out for justice, the cry of the living is for freedom. We can create that justice and we can deliver that freedom. The animals have no-one but us, we will not fail them. Believe me, the best is yet to come.

His demands were for:

1. An immediate and final end to the issuing of all new licences to vivisect.
2. An immediate and final end to the renewing of all currently held licences to vivisect.
3. An immediate and total ban on all vivisection carried out for non-medical purposes.
4. A genuine and unconditional commitment to adopt and implement policies that will bring a final end to all vivisection, for whatever purposes, by a date no later than 6 January, 2002.
5. An immediate cessation of all animal testing and experimentation at Porton Down warfare research establishment, and a genuine commitment to make that cessation permanent.
6. The immediate scrapping of the Animal Procedures Committee, the Government sponsored front for the vivisection industry.

Although these demands were asking for far more than the government had offered, and much more than they would agree to, it left an awful lot of room for negotiation. In truth, if the Labour Government had agreed to ban the LD50 test and set up an inquiry into the rest of it as they had pledged, it would have been the biggest step forward ever and would have given Horne a victory he deserved and got him out of this cycle. But the government was under commercial pressure to ensure nothing changed.

Barry Horne wrote:

Day 5: A very strange five days it's been. The first hunger strike I did the first few days were no problem at all. Likewise my second hunger strike, more or less the same. Seems like I might be paying for that on this my third such protest. I don't know, maybe it's the damage to me from those two previous hunger strikes, but these first five days have been rough. I'm feeling exhausted all the time, weak, nauseous and light-headed. My concentration has been affected, I cannot be bothered with anything and my stomach feels like a hard lump, which is uncomfortable.

> Day 6: I feel quite a lot better. Hopefully that means it's just an initial reaction and things will improve from now on. Whatever, I've no problem with it and my morale is high. As is my determination to see this protest through to a successful conclusion.

He was on D Wing in Full Sutton by now. He had renewed the living will he took out on the second hunger strike and was being messed around. On day ten without food, he was told he had an appointment in the hospital block. Escorted there slowly, he sat in a cell to wait for his appointment, only to be told he had in fact just been relocated from D Wing to the hospital wing, without his belongings. These took five days to get there, from just down the corridor. Unable to tell anyone what had happened, he was located in the 'hunger strike cell', the only one in the hospital without proper furniture, no toilet or sink, just a cardboard table and chair. He had to pee in a plastic bottle and could only go to the recess to wash and clean his teeth when the door opened in the mornings. Having been on Full Sutton's punishment regime myself, I can attest that this *is* a punishment regime. Once again, it was only after intense pressure from outside that the prison authorities were forced to move him to a normal cell. This made life a little less uncomfortable for VC2141 Horne.

> It's day 19 (25 October) as I write this and I've been in the hospital for 9 days now. During that time my condition has deteriorated a little. A week ago I felt really good, but now I'm feeling more and more tired and having to move more slowly. My weight is now down to 11st 12lbs, down 1st 5lbs on the start, and I'm getting thinner and looking a bit gaunt in the face. Sudden movements are no longer a good idea as they make me dizzy, and I'm out of breath very easily. Plus my body temperature is falling and I'm feeling the cold more and more.

> Day 26. I'm feeling quite rough as it goes. Very nauseous and cold, dizzy and tired. Having to be really careful and not move too quickly as my head spins if I do. From past experience I know that this sensation is the prelude to blackouts, so I'm being careful about that. But I'm not too bothered about how I feel today, as with anything there are good days and bad days and that's particularly so on hunger strikes. All in all feeling good and

taking it one day at a time.

Cosmetic testing on animals banned.

The Guardian, 17 Nov

All through he said he found the third hunger strike mentally harder, 'much harder', and put this down to the exertion of the previous two and the knowledge he'd have to go further still to gain anything from the government.

Jail protester near death.

The Guardian, 23 Nov

On day 43, he was read the last rites in Full Sutton prison hospital. The Prison Service now acknowledged publicly that he was in danger and the international media had started to take notice and begun to contact the campaign for details and to create their own stories. It had taken seven weeks and his health was deteriorating beyond the point of no return, but things had started to happen. Three days later, whilst waiting for a visit, Barry was rushed to York General Hospital suffering from dehydration following a week of constant and violent vomiting. A permanent vigil and the press pack followed and set up camp outside. The story was getting the attention it deserved. He'd lost 25 % of his body fat and stood a 30% chance of dying. He had already gone without food for longer than previously. Suddenly there was a flurry of interest in the hunger strike and Barry Horne was headline news.

Police fear backlash if animal activist dies.

The Daily Telegraph, 26 Nov

Things had started to shift politically and the Home Office wanted to talk again, and urgently. They were really worried by now that he might take this all the way and get the public reaction he wanted. While many media commentators were calling Barry names, some were calling on the government to compromise. Another two-hour meeting brought nothing but hints of more lab inspectors and a reform of the heavily pro-vivisection Animal Procedures Committee and vague promises about the possible formation of an independent body to investigate vivisection. It was meaningless waffle and it was widely agreed it was pointless talking to these people. What they had to say was too little too late.

An animal passion with murder in its heart.

Sunday Times, 6 Dec

He'd gone for over eight weeks without food and was dangerously ill. He knew his body was starting to shut down and pain had become constant. A tape recording of the latest round of talks and several detailed documents outlining Government proposals were taken to the hospital for him to study. Unable to make sense of the situation, and with failing eyesight, it was at this stage at day 52 that he decided to stave off a coma and stabilise his condition overnight by taking small sips of orange juice and sugared tea, although he had great trouble keeping these down. Two days later, it was his conclusion that the government was being intransigent. As they were refusing to negotiate in any meaningful way, the hunger strike continued with water intake only, but with a compromise on offer. From six demands down to just the one, the one that will in the eyes of many see an end to all vivisection!

I want to die. It's the end.

The Observer, 6 Dec

If the government agreed to set up a Royal Commission as they had promised, he would end the protest. Simple as that! This was a clever move and it caught the government on the hop. They were now very publicly apparently going to let someone die for simply calling on them to keep their word. While they wasted more time, Barry's condition deteriorated. He should have already been dead. The Government didn't care for him and they had made clear they had nothing to offer then or in the future, except the hospitality of the House of Commons for future meetings! Oh, and an appeal against his 18 year sentence to tempt him off, which wasn't exactly above board as his appeal had been rejected some months earlier when he was told he had no right to appeal and would do his 18 years. The games they play, eh!

Animal activist on edge of coma.

The Independent, 7 Dec

As can be seen in the final paragraph of correspondence from the

Home Office after the second hunger strike ended: (the Home Office) 'will not allow this programme of work to be dictated (in timing or content) by the protest action of the Animal Liberation Movement.' And that remained their line. As their programme of work—relating to the use of animals in unscientific procedures—did then and continues to only increase the number of experiments, what else is left but for the Animal Liberation Movement to force the agenda? Nothing will ever change otherwise.

> Dying for nothing.
>
> *The Mirror,* 7 Dec

Still a Category A prisoner in the hospital, Horne was allowed daily visits but was under constant watch by three prison officers, and at great public expense, as sections of the press were at pains to point out. Except for the time he struggled to a window to wave for supporters and a film crew camped outside the hospital. Prison bosses didn't like that! Nor when a visitor breached security and sneaked in a couple of cameras and a camcorder to capture the hunger striker on film looking gaunt but as determined as ever at this advanced stage in the protest. That footage went around the world, generating widespread exposure and causing that visitor to be banned.

> Defiant hunger striker on verge of coma says he wants to live.
>
> *The Guardian,* 7 Dec

There were protests everywhere: Downing Street, Parliament, the Prime Minister's Durham home, Jack Straw's constituency office and at his home in Oxford. There was a permanent camp outside the hospital and people picketing the Home Office, Labour Party HQ and regional offices. Demonstrations were held in numerous cities outside British Consulates in the US, and in numerous other countries around the world. People were outside labs and breeders, and government buildings were occupied. A hundred and fifty marched on BIBRA labs in southwest London to be greeted by a large police presence. Two hundred staged a noisy protest at Windmill mink farm in Dorset and at a ferret breeder in Hampshire, where a large amount of damage was done. In Finland, 400 foxes and 200 raccoons were freed from a fur farm. The offices of the RDS in London were invaded and there were innumerable other actions carried out throughout the hunger strike and claimed in solidarity with Barry Horne.

> Unmasked, the deadly fanatics who exploit our love of animals.
>
> *The Daily Mail,* 10 Dec

The super-secretive, toothless APC met to discuss the hunger strike and were making some noises about becoming more accountable. They even issued a press release to this effect, the first one ever recorded. It was a token gesture and an admission they needed to change but never bothered.

> Royal Commission is unnecessary, says government adviser on animal testing.
>
> *The Guardian* 10 Dec

In hospital, he had a TV in his room and was able to watch things develop. By day 60 his condition was such that his judgement was impaired and his eyesight got so bad he had to have his mail read to him. Barry was being visited daily by a small number of close friends, probably as close to being 'extremists' as the label dictates, but none wanted Barry to die. At the same time none wanted to tell him the truth about what was on offer, which was nothing, which meant he would die. He didn't want to die, he wanted the government to help the animals.

> Time to stand up to animal rights terrorists.
>
> *The Times,* 11 Dec

By the 63rd day he was dangerously ill. He was deaf in one ear, blind in one eye and his liver was failing. At this point, the body begins to consume its own organs. He was in considerable pain and discomfort but still remained strong and determined and was still thinking with remarkably clarity about the best thing he could achieve for laboratory animals, albeit sinking into a confused state more and more frequently. He'd analysed every word in the papers and the recordings brought in, desperate for something. It was never about staying alive but about getting something for the animals. Call him what they may, he never hurt anyone, he was consistent and he cared beyond the comprehension of those who judged.

He could manage 18 years fine as long as there was an inquiry carried into the efficacy of vivisection in the meantime. That the filthy word equals a scam and that a proper independent inquiry would show it to be so and in turn cost the government and drugs industry dear, is clear for many to see. No government wants an inquiry. The pharmaceutical industry certainly doesn't want an inquiry. They all say vivisection works and so it does, period. It makes them all an awful lot of money, that's undisputed. But they could have at least offered one again and saved their prisoner before it was too late.

The animal rights 'hero' who doesn't care about humans.

The Daily Mail, 11 Dec

The Government had no intention of doing anything of the sort and were instead playing with words, which he was finding it hard to interpret. He had been the orchestrater of the whole shebang and was always in total control in spite of one media spin claiming his 'so-called friends' were using him. But for the whole thing to work, someone needed to tell him there was nothing of any worth in any of what the government said and that put simply, he would have to die. It was his friends who were unable to tell him there was nothing doing and that he needed to get on and die, but how? There was no room for emotion now, but there were a lot of high emotions, no one really knowing what to do for the best when a firm decision was needed. Then something occurred which was nothing short of outrageous.

On day 65, further documents were faxed through to the campaign for Barry from various MPs and the Home Office regarding another 'offer' from the government. By then it was impossible for him to understand any of it, so a meeting was arranged in the hospital for the following day at 12 noon for him and his visitors to assess the content. This would be make or break. If there was any substance to the waffle he would accept and call off the hunger strike. If not, he would be dead within hours. But before that could happen, at day 66, as millions waited for the news that the critically ill Barry Horne the hunger striker was dead, the patient was smuggled out of hospital and taken under cover of darkness by Home Office prison officers back to the Home Office-run Full Sutton Prison. He'd been kidnapped!

Hunger striker sent back to prison

The Independent, 11 Dec

The Home Office had taken full control of Barry's life. His next of kin didn't even know anything about it. By now, he was hallucinating and his memory was in a bad state, so bad that he couldn't even remember why he was on hunger strike. The move had a serious additional impact on him physically and mentally. The Home Office gave no credible explanation for this other than to say that, since he was refusing treatment, there was no point in him remaining in hospital. Yet he had refused treatment from the start of the first hunger strike, as he was when they moved him from prison to the hospital. Was there something sinister afoot? Why would you risk moving a critically ill, dying man back to a prison? The hospital hadn't wanted rid of him and the prison could do nothing for him whatever state he was in. If he changed his mind, they'd only have to take him back to hospital and risk his condition deteriorating further. Two days later something really odd happened. Not an inquiry, it'll clearly take more than one dying man to force that from this government.

Hunger striker 'drank juice'.

The Sunday Times, 13 Dec

By day 68, two days after the move, Barry was in a terrible state, his thinking utterly confused. He had confounded medical opinion and was at the point of no return when he called off the hunger strike and rescinded his living will. He was immediately transferred back to the hospital where a recovery programme was implemented. The media went wild with almost universal condemnation and vitriol for a man who, they claimed, had fooled everyone by pretending to starve himself, his friends exaggerating his condition. They had turned the three days of Barry attempting to stabilise his condition with the tiniest sips of sugar tea and juice into 68 days of feasting. No matter what the press releases said, the newspapers weren't going to change the story. On Monday he was a dangerous ruthless terrorist prepared to kill himself and anyone else and on Tuesday he was a cowardly con man afraid to die for his cause. Nothing like having your cake and eating it, eh? Or not, as the case may be. The propaganda machine was in overdrive.

Whatever happened between him leaving the hospital and returning to prison may never be known, but all those close to him suspect something did and he was never the same again. Which in itself is hardly surprising given what he put himself through, but something else wasn't right. Aside from the unacceptable explanation for such an act of crass recklessness in moving him, nothing but the government's acceptance of his demands for a Royal Commission into the efficacy of vivisection was going to change Barry Horne's mind. As sick as he'd become and for everything he lost, he never lost his determination. The outcome was ideal for the Government, its Home Office and the industry. It was the worst for all others concerned, not least Barry who never recovered his physical or mental health and first went through excruciating agony during the early recovery period and then suffered constant pain in the aftermath.

> Horne ends 'sham' hunger strike.
>
> *The Daily Telegraph,* 14 Dec

He later went on to carry out countless hunger strikes in prison without any clear, cohesive motive or strategy or the incredible outside support he had previously inspired. It got to the point where no one but prison staff knew whether he was eating or not. For visitors, there was even less chance of reaching him than when he was himself. It was his own choice, but who could tell him in all honesty that there's a better way?

The government had repeatedly said they weren't prepared to act on Barry Horne's demands because in their view he was blackmailing them. The alternative view is that they are kind of obliged to do as they said they would, prior to being elected.

> A fanatic, a sham hunger strike and a publicity machine stuck on overdrive.
>
> *The Daily Mail,* 15 Dec

Many years on, no one is blackmailing them and nothing has been done. In fact, according to Home Office statistics, the opposite is happening. There are now more experiments, not less. More propaganda, with government ministers such as John Prescott extolling the virtues of opening and damaging the brains of tiny marmoset monkeys in the quest for cures for brain disease in humans. And the leader of the party can't contend enough that vivisection is essential to human health—scientific experts, none of them—saying the same things but not prepared to put the theory to the test in public. That suggests to me they are lying and vivisection is a scam; prove to the public otherwise!

Barry Horne's courageous and selfless protest rattled a lot of cages and gave the movement a hugely positive impetus to act en masse, reigniting an almighty battle whose fires are still smouldering. That there is no desire in government for any kind of independent inquiry is suspicious to say the very least, but more like a deliberate ploy to maintain the status quo and keep rich industry happy. At the end of the day, all Barry Horne wanted was for the public to be allowed to assess the real facts about vivisection. How many of us are going to be labelled extremists or allowed to die, perhaps on a protest, or as a result of something they tested on animals, before we get some answers?

As a direct result of political action taken in response to the hunger strikes and all that came with them, the pro-vivisection Animal Procedures Committee still rubber stamp all manner of vile research projects, but report to the Associate Parliamentary Group for Animal Welfare. This is made up by Government officials of 'Over 100 MPs and peers with an interest in animal welfare and 40 associate members from the animal welfare world and from both ends of the spectrum of debate.' Sounds like happy times ahead for animals in laboratories to me. According to the head of the group, Ian Cawsey MP, it would make: 'a real and independent impact.' Err, when?

Public Government statements about the voluntary ban on cosmetic experiments that they'd worked on with cosmetic companies grabbed the headlines at the height of the hunger strikes in November 1997, belching the party line that 'Blair Halts Animal Tests,' and 'Beauty Testing On Animals Banned Today As Make Up Firms Bow To Pressure from the Government.' Yet within just a few years, this was exposed for the lie it is following a break in at Wickham Laboratories. Documents I recovered that night proved that cosmetics are being regularly tested on animals in large numbers using the LD50 test, which the public had also been assured was being phased out. We revealed that the LD50 poisoning tests were being extensively used to test the increasingly popular cosmetic Botox, or Botulinum Toxin, by proving it unsafe for animals to use! It's a painful death for the victims, as I witnessed for myself that night.

It took just two weeks from the Home Secretary announcing that discussions seeking an industry-wide voluntary cosmetic test ban were under way for it to come to pass. But, incredibly, it is still legal to test cosmetic products on animals in the UK in 2007. Given the lack of restriction, the lack of commitment and the loopholes, there seems to be little to deter even cosmetic testing, which if we are to believe the lie is essential medical research because that's all we do in the UK.

Not suckered in enough to the lies we are being told? In 2007 there have been no more prosecutions under either the 1911 Act or the 1986 Scientific Procedure Act (claimed as a saviour of lab animals) than there were in 1997 when the only ones ever recorded were instigated by an infiltration of the UK's animal testing centre of excellence.

In the wake of this announcement, the Government also announced a ban on the use in experiments of our closest ancestors, the Great Apes. (It is a ban that prominent vivisectors in 2006 have publicly stated they would like to see lifted). The ban accounted for only a tiny number of animals used in preceding years anyway and fails to address the failings of vivisection which are surely compounded by using less of the mammals that are similar to humans and using more of the rodents that bear less resemblance, if we are to follow their logic.

Such examples are not singular; the horrors continue unabated in laboratories around the world, justified by palliative language that is meant to reassure the public that the suffering is necessary, and vital for our well-being and thus morally acceptable. It is the sort of atrocity that Barry Horne fought to extinguish, as do the rest of us in the thick of the struggle, refusing to bow to the pressures brought to bear upon us by lying politicians and self-serving multi-national corporations.

Barry Horne died on 5 November 2001 in Long Lartin Prison of liver failure during a short-lived hunger strike, and as a direct result of the punishment his body had taken from his earlier efforts at forcing change. He was 49. It was a tragic, untimely passing, mourned by many who knew him and many who hadn't and was marked by none of the publicity there would have inevitably been had he died following his public hunger strikes. There was some relief amongst his friends that his suffering was finally over, but deep sadness at the way it had ended. It wasn't meant to be like that. He was buried in his hometown of Northampton by hundreds of friends under an oak tree in a woodland cemetery, wearing his Northampton Town football shirt.

Barry Horne was ahead of his time. He died because of what he believed. He believed neither in a god nor that money rules, but that vivisection is an evil. He believed in the power of the individual and that his elected representatives should do as they pledge or lose the right to dictate the rules. Barry Horne's beliefs are not unique, but he was a unique man, possessed of immense courage, and he will not be forgotten.

The Monkey Farm

How many more people have to die before we admit there is a problem with animal testing?

Dr Ray Greek

Those who are self taught about the use and abuse of animals in research know only too well that monkeys are victimised in many long term experiments so pointless and misleading as to be risible were it not for the suffering that these sentient creatures have been forced to endure. Pick any number out of a hat or watch the videos, if you can stomach it, and you'll find an example that proves the rule: vivisection is not only immoral—it's scientifically invalid.

Dr Albert Sabin, the inventor of the polio vaccine, regretted that the vaccine was 'long delayed by the erroneous conception of the nature of the human disease based on misleading experimental models of the disease in monkeys.' Heart-valve replacements, penicillin and many other therapies were similarly delayed because of misleading test results in animals. People died as a result of those delays. Smoking cigarettes and eating lots of cholesterol were given the thumbs-up by animal experimentation. Probably no two mistakes have cost as many lives. Now millions of women on hormone replacement therapy are at twice the risk of breast cancer and heart disease, thanks to tests in monkeys, which predicted the opposite.

Monkey business was on my mind as I neared the end of my sentence. I had spent most of the 1990s in prison, inspired and strengthened by the incredible support I received from many in the movement. I was released on parole in March 1999 and moved to Brighton. I had applied for a Judicial Review to take the Parole Board to court for refusing my first application for political reasons, but I had been released before we got to court for the second application. A never-move-me northerner, I was suddenly—well, eight years after that doomed train journey to Kent—firmly rooted as far south as I could be. It was during weekly prison visits that my friend Kate and I had discussed the idea of bringing Shamrock back from the dark and giving the south coast a focus. She lived and was active in Brighton, which to all intents and purposes was the centre of the universe, with a healthy collection of worthy activists well within shouting distance.

Shamrock Farm had been situated a few miles outside Brighton since the 1950s. It was outside the village of Small Dole, from where they'd supplied British and foreign laboratories with monkeys, either bred on site or imported from the wild all of which had provoked sporadic opposition for some time. It's the same old story really. Shamrock Farm stood alone in the UK trade as the place from which monkeys could be purchased, either caught in the wilds of the Philippines, China or Mauritius, or bred on site in Sussex. Other animals were acquired from UK zoos and documents recovered from Shamrock exposed this excess stock trade during the late 1980s, including 83 macaques from Longleat, 32 from Woburn and various species from Ravensden and Robin Hill on the Isle of Wight.

In just one year alone, Huntingdon Research Centre, Shamrock's main customer, took 373 cage-bred long tailed macaques, 440 wild caught animals, eight squirrel monkeys and 37 baboons. During the 1990's, Shamrock delivered just short of 50,000 monkeys to universities, government research centres and hospital labs. Realistically, a head count closer to the truth would have been 250,000, taking into account the documented number of casualties of capture and shipment. Mostly rats and mice they tell us!

Shamrock Farm was pivotal in the demise of huge numbers of monkeys and key to a lot of users' needs. Most of the men in the import trade had at one time or another been employed by Shamrock. With the end of Hill Grove imminent, it was the right time to launch another campaign, not wishing to dilute the pressure in any area too much by creating too many targets on which to focus. Besides which, there were busloads of people travelling miles from Sussex past Shamrock Farm to protest against animal cruelty elsewhere! It was an opportunity being missed. Kate did the rounds, canvassed support from those who could commit and ended up with quite a formidable team who understood the need to stick this out until it was done so we wouldn't have to be doing it forever.

Shamrock Farms (GB) Ltd once supplied other animals too, but had for years specialised in monkeys, held in rows of windowless Portacabins on their site in a field in East Sussex. Up until the time they were infiltrated by Terry Hill during 1991/2, they also bred animals. In the aftermath of another dreadful exposé, they were forced to change the way they operated and began instead to import from 'captive stock.' Then, acting as the middleman in the monkey chain, they quarantined and 'conditioned' the captives before delivery to a laboratory, perhaps back across the Channel to Europe. Using the offspring of animals recently taken from the wild (as they must, to keep a healthy gene pool) they held them in cages calling them 'captive bred' intending that this signified less cruelty than using wild caught ones. Not my idea! The good it did, though, was to increase costs.

I'd been strongly advised by my probation officer to keep away, not just from demonstrations, but also from other activists. It was something of an issue that the person I was moving in with who had given me a roof over my head, and collected me from the Isle of Wight was, herself, very much an activist—an 'extremist' who shunned animal products and was pained by cruelty. The Parole Board and my probation officer were concerned that this association might lead me into trouble; it was the view of officialdom that if I kept away from other activists, I would be able to follow the straight and narrow path to animal liberation, or better still not bother trying. Not an option.

None of them were ever able to explain to me how that would get me where I want to be. As often as we discussed the options available for achieving animal liberation, for closing places like Shamrock Farm and all the others, for just getting politicians to listen, no one ever came up with a viable alternative to taking risks, pushing the boundaries, forcing the issue. I'd explain the futility of writing to MPs, who they agreed lie and often have a vested interest. They—like so many people—would just shrug their shoulders at this as though it's something we have to accept. No we don't! I'd explain the dangers of simply protesting when the police were so aggressive and able to restrict those protests so as to make them ineffectual.

Having spent so long in prison, the last thing I wanted was to be going back, but even before I got out, it seemed to me inevitable whoever I hung out with or if I hung out alone. Rather than join me in my revulsion of animal exploitation, the same advisers were consuming animal products and telling me to be passive about it! The Parole Board didn't want to let me out because of my 'continued strong commitment to animal rights', which in their view would lead to law breaking. But why should it, if the political process works?

Was I to be denied my views in order to remain a free citizen? They did mostly agree with my point of view but couldn't for one minute say so, because their job was to advise on the right way to behave and think. So the more these people told me to stop and water down my concerns, the less likely I would be to listen. Hence my leaving prison and joining the Shamrock campaign. I'd been away for nearly seven years and it was good to be back, to be involved in something worthwhile. I'd made good my time in prison and got really fit. I'd educated plenty of people while inside, read and written as much as I could and made progress for the vegan diet within the prison system. But this was all just filling time until life returned to normal. Not that it could be, with the restrictions placed on me by the Parole Board and the observations placed on me by the police. But stuffing envelopes and putting leaflets through doors was a step in the right direction. This, of course, led to increased police surveillance and harassment, but they weren't able to intervene just yet. I tried to keep away from the gates of Shamrock to avoid confrontation with workers and arrest, so that was left to others, but I kept my hand in on things and a watch over others. Shamrock's location at the foot of the South Downs afforded a good opportunity to keep the place under observation with a long range lens, from a high vantage point out of sight of the police and workers in the undergrowth on the hill opposite.

The isolation of life in a cell is good training for this kind of work where for hours and even days, very little of interest might happen. From here we could compile a comprehensive list of those attending the site. They would in turn be contacted by Save The Shamrock Monkeys and the extensive accompaniment of agitators and educated about the fine detail of the company's involvement and asked to pull out. Some did straight away. Some didn't care for our endeavour to stop the supply and importation of these animals and so found themselves with a mini campaign of their own at their doorstep. This can be very persuasive and over time, one by one, suppliers and contractors pulled out. Each was only a small victory, but fuel to the campaign and more aggro for Shamrock.

We talked a lot about the best way to go, fully expecting the campaign to be a long, drawn-out affair. Not just because this was more than a family run operation, but also because of the increasing political pressure on the police to stop the rot. Shamrock's owners, the American-owned animal supply company Charles River, have breeding and storage sites all over the world, feeding a greedy industry with the lifeblood of the trade. They wouldn't bow to pressure from the likes of us moaning about animal cruelty, no matter who else we chased away. We were reminded of this by a number of workers: they'd obviously talked about it and felt secure in their employ.

From the outset, STSM set a target of two years to close down Shamrock. Even though this was a bigger concern than previous targets and with more backing, we believed it would be possible with some tweaking of tactics being used elsewhere. We met often and discussed the way ahead, deciding on whether to focus on removing contractors, supply services or getting workers to leave. All were equally important to the wearing-down process, but we were especially keen to get someone on the inside and an ideal opportunity for this presented itself in the regular turnover of staff and visitors. They were paranoid enough as it was, having been infiltrated and rudely exposed ten years earlier, and they were extra vigilant as a result of everything else that was going on. But we were still confident we could either get someone inside or get at someone inside and persuade them to help us out. One on the in is worth fifty on the out.

Sadly, it wasn't long into the campaign that the efforts of the police to intimidate those involved started to have an impact. Where there had originally been eight of us organising things, there were soon four involved in the admin and run-around. The police knew whom to target and duly did so, knocking on doors to ask for a chat, even parking vans outside on the morning of demos, then following close behind all day like a close protection squad (in reverse) whose presence was there to intimidate and make an arrest at the first opportunity.

One Saturday morning I took a video camera out to the vanload of police parked in the road outside to film them filming me as I asked them what they hoped to achieve by intimidating citizens to whose views they objected. I was polite and a lot more talkative than they might be used to, but they wouldn't say a word to me! They weren't even prepared to look me in the eye. There was one filming me, while a vanload of others stared aimlessly out of the windows waiting for us to take them on a demo. Some kind of weird role reversal going on there!

The police interest in the core of this campaign was more of a problem for me because with any two-bit allegation I could find myself back inside for a parole violation, doing another year of the sentence I'd finished. In fact, it would only take the police informing the Home Office that they thought I might be up to no good for them to recall me. The alternative to taking this risk would be to walk away and have nothing to do with the campaign, but that wasn't likely to happen, since I had spent several years looking forward to once again making just such a contribution towards creating a more civilised society.

We held public meetings and we leafleted the whole county and did stalls, night vigils, phone blockades, leaving few people in any doubt about what Shamrock did and what we were going to do. When the police blocked the roads to our demos, protesters went to the centre of Brighton or elsewhere and blocked roads. To have hundreds of people in the centre of town repeatedly meant no lessons had been learnt in Oxford.

Conversations we overheard, disposed-of litter we read, or gossip from locals, kept us abreast of the inner turmoil we were creating inside Shamrock. Some days would be slow with only a few in number on the early morning picket line and little to see by way of reward for our efforts until we collected the mail to find another leaked document or letter of resignation from a worker. What a turn up to get a polite letter from someone who, for the first few months could only manage obscene gestures, imitate a monkey and make threats as he drove into work past elderly ladies, but was now asking if we would be so kind as to leave him alone as he was leaving his job!

One woman made her own way from Kent to stand there every week to see them in and out and tell them what she thought. Seven of the eighteen staff contacted us in the first eleven months and at least three of these moved houses. One moved following a series of home visits but continued in his job until he was tracked down two weeks later and had his car messed up by the ALF. He left his job soon after and moved again. From the beginning of the year, we tried to work it so there was a presence at the farm almost every morning to see the workers in and someone there every evening to see them out.

This was an invaluable tactic that enabled us to monitor the changing behaviour of the workers and management as the campaign progressed, but was hindered at times by the work commitments of protesters, sometimes leaving a small core to fill in the gaps or for there to be gaps. Over time, bravado tends to dissipate among workers under such circumstances, and the 'not-bothered' façade fades. As hardened as many are to the suffering of the animals, perhaps there is some sense of guilt about what they do which is expressed in anger as they're reminded that once they leave the electronic gates behind them they are no longer invisible. One worker would park in a lay by a mile up the road and phone in first to see if there were protesters at the gate. If there were, she'd wait in her car for the all clear. She realised we'd spotted her one day, panicked and just stopped going in at all!

As the mood of the workers began to have a knock-on effect on management, the police were called upon for assistance—needless to say in little need of encouragement—to, in turn, harass protesters. As the campaign progressed, the police were called more frequently to both the site and various related addresses we attended; their mood changed and became far more aggressive towards us. The press likewise turned on us. It wasn't as though the demos at Shamrock had escalated as they had elsewhere, except for the odd home visit which saw a window broken.

The local *Evening Argus* stirred up an immediate response from the police when reporting their version of events in the 'war of terror' being waged against Shamrock Farm and staff by campaigners 'that will stop at nothing.' This story followed a thousand-strong national demonstration at the end of January 2000, which saw a dozen people arrested and two hospitalised by the police. One was a pregnant woman, the other an elderly man who sustained a fractured hip during his arrest. The injury required emergency surgery and he was unable to return to work. He had been sitting alone on the bottom of the hill opposite the track to the farm, minding his own business, when several police dragged him down and arrested him. This was the day's theme; there was no violence from protesters, no windows broken, nothing. Yet Sussex Police set up a special squad to 'tackle the terror' in response to anti-animal MP Howard Flight's call for them to deal with the violence that had been reported in the paper.

There was in response wide criticism from local people, many of whom had heard it all at Shoreham and were once again being accused of being violent thugs hell bent on anarchy with no justification whatsoever. Why was this large public rally ignored for an out-of-date exaggerated feature on Shamrock workers who claimed they were under siege in their homes? The outpouring of anger from readers later led to a confession from the paper's editor who wrote: 'You won't have missed the maelstrom unleashed on us in our letters page last week. And with good reason. We pride ourselves on balanced and accurate coverage. However, on Monday last week we let you down with our lop-sided and half-hearted reporting of the protest and the ugly clashes with police.' It fell short of an apology, but at least it acknowledged a wrong had been done.

What about the MP: did he have any remorse for dispatching his soldiers to war on a rumour? Or the police: did they disband their special operation following the editorial about-face? Asking too much! Operation Impact was here to stay and soon in overdrive increasing its harassment of those with objections to voice about Shamrock Farm. The change of mind by the paper was as unexpected as a guided tour of the cabins at Shamrock, but the wider effects of campaign pressure and the slide of opinion in its favour were to have an even more surprising impact.

One morning, seasoned campaigners Toni and Claudia were at the farm track entrance at 7.30am for an early morning shift awaiting the arrival of workers around 9.00am. Once all the workers appeared to have arrived (without a police escort on this occasion, which was unusual) Toni and Claudia had walked down the farm track to the main gates to see what they could see. They were greeted by a couple of workers who embarked upon the usual round of abuse and derogatory remarks. Whilst arguing pointlessly with them (one of whom was Andrew Bradwell, the second in command) a car pulled up alongside which had to stop to wait for the gates to open. 'It was a rare opportunity to get so close to this endangered species,' Toni quipped later.

It was Lynda King, a vet and Managing Director with another female worker. As was usual, the pickets started verbally haranguing the occupants of the car, trying to force a proper debate and get some sense of understanding from the person responsible for holding captive hundreds of monkeys in cages just a few feet away. King drove defiantly through the electronic gates as they opened. While she parked up, they told her in no uncertain terms that she was a disgrace to her profession and an animal abusing monster. Suddenly, something happened to Lynda. Was it that her conscience had pricked her, perhaps? Who knows, but as she got out of the car, she dropped all pretence of calm. She stormed down to the gates where she proceeded to launch into a hysterical rant, gesturing and spluttering and going on about how she was 'fed up' of all the hassle and of being accused of torturing animals, which she never did. Then she told them to come in and see. 'Come on!' She insisted!

They were stunned into silence. Not easy for these two, especially around people like her! We'd been trying to get inside this place for months! We'd put forward so many different ideas—some a bit wacky, some we were working on—but we'd never even entertained this one! Seeing their disbelief and getting no response, she repeated the offer, adding that she wanted them to see with their own eyes that she did not torture animals, that no animal torture happened on site and that the animals were, in fact, quite happy with the government's minimum requirements and Home Office inspections. In total disbelief, they warily accepted.

King ordered the gates to be opened and they followed her into the complex and to a back office, where she told them to leave their coats and change into protective gowns, gloves, masks, hair caps and shoe protectors. Why she continued the guided tour with them still having a go at her is anyone's guess, but they said they couldn't help themselves. She of course responded, claiming they were helping to save human lives and that sacrificing animals for human benefit was a 'necessary evil.' She stated categorically that she supports vivisection and that was why she chose to be involved in this particular aspect of the business. She came out with all sorts of arguments about how pharmaceutical companies are here to serve the rest of us, that there is no alternative, that her son was an asthmatic and had to have anti-asthma drugs and what did they expect her to do, take him off and watch him gasp for air! The usual drivel.

She was utterly convinced that a billion tortured souls had just about solved everything and refused to listen to any alternative viewpoint. It was another pointless debate, as she herself acknowledged. She said the only way she would be put out of business would be if all the staff were made to leave, or if we blew her up, which she imagined would be the most likely conclusion to all this and what everyone wanted to do to her. Throughout, she was on the verge of absolute hysteria and desperation, shaking, screaming and shouting—hardly the actions of a confident Managing Director with nothing to feel ashamed about!

After about a quarter of an hour of this, she took them to the monkey cabins. First of all they were shown to the newly delivered cages, which were as yet unoccupied. She announced proudly that they'd paid for them themselves and said they were bigger and better than the cages that government regulations stipulate as the necessary minimum. Clearly she hadn't been listening to what people had been yelling at her for the past year and long before about the failings of vivisection and about cage sizes being immaterial to caged animals! The debate continued as they questioned how she, as a vet and therefore someone supposed to help sick animals get better, could work in an industry such as this that deliberately traumatises and kills healthy animals. She was immovable and truly believed she was doing nothing wrong because her cruelty was legally sanctioned and fully 'regulated' by the Home Office. Her by-the-book arguments brought once again into stark focus the great divide between the 'them' and 'us.'

Doris the cleaner wandered by, looked over and checked herself. She was getting on a bit and had a bit of a hunchback and a scowl. She looked like a nasty piece of work and she was one. She'd been there for years and was one whose anger at the protesters outside the gates had never abated. On one of the few occasions I went, I was attacked by

Doris, who stopped her car on the way in with another old bag in the passenger seat and both jumped out with aerosol cans of polish to spray at us. We backed away, laughing at them, but they didn't find it funny. We were supposed to be the angry ones, angry at being attacked and at the cruelty, yet here we were faced instead with the wrath of two haggard old women.

Back in the farm, Doris insisted Lynda 'Get them out!' while Linda shouted to everyone to leave her and her visitors alone. This was her way; she was in charge and she had invited them in to show that nothing inhumane went on in there. Bradwell stood by most of the time, though didn't contribute much to the conversation. He kept reminding his boss that it wasn't a good idea to show the antis the monkeys and asked her what he thought she was going to gain by this. It was a good question and he should know. He'd been there for ten years and had been out to the Philippines to set up Siconbrec, a monkey-holding station and a secure supply line for Shamrock. Described by an ex-worker as 'the filthiest bastard that worked there,' it was more than just a job for him.

A man of low intellect, Bradwell was right about one thing: Lynda was entirely missing the point by banging on about regulations and cage sizes and was going to change no minds here. She seemed to be rethinking what she was doing for a moment, but they pulled her back by pointing out that they thought the worst of her anyway, so she really had nothing to lose by showing them more. Lynda wasn't thinking! Outside the cabins, the cages could be heard rattling and there was a horrible smell, like that in a dirty pet shop. She let them in through the security door and they stood in the observation area looking through a glass panel in the door, which separated them from the monkeys.

There were no outside windows, only bright, fluorescent lighting down the middle. There were two rows of cages on each wall with 40 or more little monkeys in them, some peering out nervously at the door. The cages were small and bare—no bedding on the bottom—and some monkeys were obviously distressed and were screeching. Some were dashing frantically around the cage, others were cowering, cuddling each other. Some cages just had tiny little hands sticking through the metal gates, hanging hopelessly. The girls stood there at the door for a few minutes and just stared on in disbelief. The reality was worse than imagined inside the cabins. These were two brave, clued-up activists who had seen it all before, yet this, one said, 'had the feel of a house of horrors.'

So near, yet so far from help. It was heartbreaking. One of them broke down and had to go outside. Lynda stood quietly in the corner, not saying anything at all. What was she thinking: 'Oh, they're gonna think I'm an OK kinda gal now they've seen this'? Outside, she got a feel of their mood from the silence and the cold shoulder from there on out. She'd achieved something then, she'd shut them up! How could a woman and a vet think there was nothing wrong with this nightmare prison camp? She actually seemed to calm down for the first time now, almost as if from relief that she had made a confession. What she had done was to strengthen Toni and Claudia's resolve; they hated her and everything she stood for. Lynda King's tour was an act of desperation and said a lot about her state of mind. It was an odd thing to do. Perhaps part of her was looking for some sort of absolution.

Bradwell wasn't happy either. Soon after he called the STSM to say he'd resigned! He was the eighth worker to go since the campaign began. Others were steadily dropping out of the equation too. MBM Services read the information they were sent regarding Shamrock and immediately contacted their one-time customer to advise, 'It is with regret that we have to send this letter to you, but give notice to terminate our contract with you. This is due to the nature of your business and the unwillingness of our engineers and staff to attend site.' It was a good week.

Over the Christmas holiday, the Kings and others received home visits on Xmas Day and New Years Eve. With a steady build-up of pressure and a lot of enthusiasm for the coming new year, during which we were planning to focus fully on the closure of Shamrock within the year, things took an unexpected twist.

In the early hours of the last day of the following February, a fire tore through Lynda & Colin King's garage at their home in Worthing. Colin was the boss at Vet Diagnostics, also in Small Dole, the company responsible for testing the blood of the monkeys arriving at Shamrock and was one of those who had been targeted by a JD parcel bomb in 1994. Their garage and cars were wrecked. The following afternoon, a posse from Operation Impact arrived at our doorsteps intent on gaining access. They'd decided on the basis of available intelligence to make random arrests, admitting to one solicitor they didn't even know at the time whether the fire had been deliberate.

Not that random really, given the paraphernalia from the STSM campaign, which was found at both the houses that they raided and in view of our involvement in the campaign, but we weren't responsible for the fire. We were working on a series of demonstrations we had planned for the coming weekend and had just collected the newsletter from the printers (which was elsewhere) the inserts, thousands of plain envelopes, petition forms and so on. It was supposed to be a hectic time but we were locked up instead. They searched everywhere, took all the above and our cars, computers, office stationary, tools, everything—little of which was likely to be involved in any way in starting or planning a fire. None of which was. We thought at the time we were being set up and I fully expected to be kept in custody merely because of their suspicions. As hard as I'd tried not to be, I was in trouble again!

Thankfully, we were all released the following day pending further enquiries. The police kept everything they had taken. I had kept in the background of the campaign, had done things 'the right way' as instructed to keep out of trouble, filling out my petitions, writing letters, and leafleting. And I had still got arrested, locked up and had all my pens, computer and petitions confiscated! I had only just recovered the toolbox from Manchester Police, which they'd taken in 1991. (Buy your own bloody tools!) To add insult to injury I was put back on weekly reporting by my probation officer, having had it reduced to once every three weeks due to good behaviour; I was also reported to the Parole Board with a view to them recalling me to prison!

We met the next day to get the newsletter out, discuss the situation and made plans to broaden the campaign. We'd had offers for replacement vehicles and computers etc. and pledges for numbers for the demo and home visits pouring in, which was a response to the police's attempts to hamper a legitimate campaign. How unfortunate that this fire should be the most effective tactic to affect Shamrock Farm in 40 years. Workers still thought they were safe in their jobs and safe beyond the gates. Some would probably want to be buried there, but higher up someone didn't like the way things were going and less than two weeks after the fire, Charles River surprised everyone with a press statement issued early on 10 March, 2000. We were stunned.

> Shamrock (GB) Ltd announces its primate facility, located in Small Dole, West Sussex will be permanently closed in the coming weeks. The effective date of the closure will be dictated by the professional care required to tend to the humane relocation of the animals residing in the facility.
>
> We regret the loss of employment in Small Dole resulting from

this difficult decision. Some within our small staff have been with us for more than 25 years. We are entering into generous severance arrangements with our employees, and we thank them for their dedication and perseverance. Shamrock is also deeply grateful for the gestures of support and kindness by many local citizens, and for the assistance of the local authorities over the past months. There will be no further comments from Shamrock on this matter, and no spokesperson will be made available.

Well! This was incredible news. Added to which, neither the workers nor the police knew until we told them! I was in the printers at the time trying to do a deal on a print job when I got the call. I cancelled it and sped to the farm and stood there alone trying to take on board what was happening. One minute there was so much to do and all of a sudden apparently nothing! I phoned my mum to tell her. She would prefer I had a steady job and a mortgage and was settled down so that she could sleep easier and not worry, but she is proud of all my friends and me, and the news meant as much to her as it did to me. It was a long, long overdue chat and by the time we'd done, almost everyone else I called already knew. Good news travels fast. Soon others would start to arrive. There were lots of hugs and tears and some disbelief and no idea what 'humane relocation' meant. Was it possible we were going to be given control of the future of the 2-300 animals still inside Shamrock? That would be awesome!

We had discussed the possibility of this happening long ago but were aware that most of the Shamrock monkeys were shipped in to order, so actually already belonged to the likes of Oxford and Manchester University and HLS, not to Shamrock itself. The likelihood, of course, would be that the RSPCA would be called in if there were any surplus to requirements and with us being accused of bombing Shamrock into submission it was unlikely they would want to be seen to be cooperating with us. Despite what was a monumental victory, the mood was soured with concern for the animals left behind.

Whilst at the farm, I spoke to the RSPCA to find out what their involvement might be. They weren't that interested and told me 'We aren't getting involved whatsoever,' which was as much help as we could expect and maybe even a good thing after what happened at Hylyne. We had made enquiries months earlier to find places for as many homeless traumatised lab-bound monkeys as we could in anticipation of Shamrock's closure. The International Primate Protection

League were keen to help as were some less well equipped rescue centres. Monkey World were flatly uninterested. One wealthy supporter offered to buy the monkeys for £2,000 each, £400 above their commercial value.

Shamrock management weren't interested and how stupid were we for entertaining the possibility that their interpretation of humane was anything like ours. This not a concept that most animal exploiters can understand. It took some time to get clarification, but as big a blow as it was, it came as no real surprise to find 'humane relocation' in vivisector-speak means awful fate or 'to be sent to a vivisection laboratory.' Every last one of them was sent off to labs for vivisection; some possibly remain alive to this day.

The animal-hating workers leaving that night had got over the shock and were as foul-mouthed, abusive and smug as ever. And they had good reason. Not only did they know the fate of the animals still on site, but knew that they were in for redundancy payments and had beaten us in their eyes by sticking it out to the end. Those who had stuck it out and had remained loyal to their employers after many years in the business, were in for a big pay off. And as far as some were concerned, they were still very much an asset to a hungry industry.

It took some weeks for the last monkeys to be moved out of Shamrock and be driven to their fate. As the cabins were emptied, the bulldozers got to work demolishing them, leaving nothing recognisable. The site was then sold on. This was good to watch. It had taken 40 years to get this show on the road and there was no way I was going to miss the final curtain. Forcing the closure of Shamrock Farm had seemed for years like an unachievable goal to the Animal Liberation Movement, especially repulsive because it had incarcerated our closest relatives in cages, yet here it was, going, going, gone!

But it wasn't all over quite yet. With one eye on Shamrock and while we were planning our next move, all kinds of interesting details began to emerge. In March, the RSPCA wanted nothing whatsoever to do with Shamrock Farm or the animals inside, but by April they had employed as their Assistant Chief Veterinary Officer, a man called Paul West who had been Shamrock's main man at the time of the undercover investigation in 1991/2. This was a man who for eight years had been responsible for supplying monkeys to vivisection, a man in charge of a system of widespread abuse, neglect and cruelty, whose tenure was condemned even by a Government report as inappropriate, insensitive and incompetent. This was the man who on the film jokes as he yanks the fur from the legs and arms of a terrified monkey, before slapping her to locate a vein and shoving in a needle in excess of 200 times to try and draw blood.

A man who sent monkeys for torture, complicit in the collapse of wild monkey populations, was being promoted as second-in-command in the veterinary department of the country's largest animal welfare charity! What on Earth is going on there? Such news doesn't really come as a shock, but it caused some serious swearing!

Somehow, we were at loggerheads again with the RSPCA! They knew precisely what Paul West was long before we put out a press release telling everyone who wanted to listen. This was latched onto by the national media and as a result of the adverse publicity, the RSPCA 'invited' him to resign.

We were under no illusions that the closure of Shamrock would kill off the primate trade and had considered the alternatives available now, but what transpired exceeded all expectations. Key workers from Shamrock were kept under surveillance and a pattern gradually began to emerge, starting with the reappearance of a couple of their specially converted monkey import trucks. Even more suspicious were the journeys they appeared to be making. Sadly they hadn't been converted to move furniture or sold on to carry fruit—not a hope. They were still clearly up to no good with these vehicles. The first occasion a surveillance team were out to tail a target vehicle early one morning was aborted. They were caught out by its premature appearance; they hadn't had time to fuel up before setting off in pursuit and lost sight of it on the motorway an hour later, as their car ran out of gas. 'We were gutted,' said one. 'We'd been looking for them for weeks and finally caught up with them only to lose them again as we rolled to a stop on the hard shoulder and they disappeared into the distance.'

They'd been heading towards Kent—which had been their old route out of the UK—to collect animals from Paris Airport and then bring them back to Shamrock. As it transpired, little had changed. A month later they were tailed out of the country via the Channel Tunnel and what was uncovered can best be described as an underworld trafficking operation second to none in its ruthless, blind devotion to the cause of supplying vivisection with the maximum number of primates possible. Ex workers were bringing in regular shipments of the essential ingredient to make profits for themselves, the trappers, the users, and the clients. Whilst Shamrock wasn't best known for sourcing healthy animals from forests around the world (often not even live ones) they were keen and were blessed with the contacts needed to get at least some live samples into the labs. With a bulk buyer in the UK able to quarantine the animals themselves and trappers in the forests capturing them, it only needed a man and a van to complete the chain. The supply to others would be hampered, but for HLS, in the aftermath of the Shamrock closure there was hope that they could be kept well stocked. This ex Shamrock gang had moved in and taken over the remnants of the south coast monkey trafficking operation.

The specially converted Shamrock transport trucks had originally parked inside the Shamrock compound just outside Small Dole when not en route to collect monkeys or en route to a lab to deliver them, but they had disappeared from the radar during the summer of 2000. Soon after, they were traced to Oxcroft Farm, a storage yard in Small Dole, a mile along the road from the old Shamrock site. There were three men, with two vans on call to collect animals from Paris and deliver them to their fate at a phone call's notice. It was a nice little earner for the gang, just for driving into France and then Cambridge once a week and no protesters sneering at them at every turn. One of the mens' wives had been a sales manager at Shamrock for 19 years; he himself had been employed as a general handyman at the site and had been abusive towards protesters for nearly as long. Another gang member's father had worked there long before him. It was definitely a family affair.

Word got around there was still something suspicious going on in the Small Dole area, and before long the ALF were in on it. Late one night, they took out the vehicles with a series of incendiary devices, causing a fire that wrecked everything in the vicinity. Police and fire officers spent four days investigating the incident and concluded it wasn't suspicious. So it was an accident then.

So that, for the time being, was that, but this is unlikely to be the last word from the dregs of Shamrock Farm.

Soon after we got the news about Shamrock we were looking elsewhere to make ourselves busy. We had a number of places in mind; we'd snooped around most of them or knew someone who had. By this point, there was a serious campaign brewing in Staffordshire focusing on the guinea pig breeder of Newchurch, and Huntingdon Life Sciences had also caught everyone's attention, including that of the team who had focused so much attention on Hill Grove Farm and Consort. Elsewhere, others were taking a less public, more direct approach to mark the end of a millennium that will be remembered for the terrible, terrible cruelties human society perfected and the ecological damage we did. But it will also be remembered for the new consciousness that had begun to flourish to see our non-human kindred as equal in status to our species, and to take action to secure that status.

Interfauna

> It is a denial of the fundamental principles of evolutionary biology, modern-day molecular biology and genetics to continue using non-human primates as models for human neurological diseases.
>
> *Europeans for Medical Advancement (EMA)*

While the likes of columnist Carol Sarler were declaring in the *Sunday People* that the country was 'going animal crackers—and I don't just mean the monstrous blackmailer Barry Horne (may he rot in hell)' others were getting on with trying to make a difference. Information and animals were pouring out of everywhere and activists were sadly spoilt for choice as to who should be targeted next. The Newchurch site had been raided in September and the huge Harlan Interfauna beagle-breeding site at Abbots Ripton in Cambridgeshire was hit again that November.

Interfauna is one of those places which, once seen, cannot be forgotten, and one that inspires anger in all who know about it. There are windowless buildings lined up close to the side of a remote road in Cambridgeshire, and if you get close enough to the perimeter fence, you can hear the muffled barking of some of the thousands of tormented beagle mothers and their young inside. Since being exposed 10 years earlier, Interfauna had become the focus of a great deal of passing attention from protesters targeting HLS down the road; its extensive security, designed to keep out raiders had proved something of a deterrent, and certainly, at first glance, the ten-foot-high fences, razor wire, alarms and patrolling guards were daunting, but as is often the case, things aren't always what they appear to be.

An extensive and long-drawn out period of information gathering had revealed gaps in the security routine: whilst there was at least one guard with dogs on site at any given time, he wasn't minded to keep an eye on things constantly but patrolled the inner perimeter every two hours, checking the kennel doors and the main gate, after which he would return to the comfort of his TV. Happy the beagles were secure, he would lose himself in nonsense until his next inspection. What he hadn't noticed was the pair of eyes watching his every move from fields just outside the fence and no matter how many times he checked those doors, he was about to fail in his duty to keep the puppies inside.

The patient observer was happy to watch him do this patrol a hundred times, and indeed he was seen to do the patrol a hundred times. By the hundred and first time there weren't just two pairs of eyes watching him but 20! As regular as clockwork, he returned to the lodge as predicted and settled down as masked figures began to emerge from the undergrowth and set about quickly constructing a frame that would traverse the high fence and allow access to the inner compound. That this worked was a surprise to everyone. It was homemade and haphazard, but it worked!

Accessing the roof of the single-storey kennel block nearest the rear of the perimeter further from the security lodge was easy, but removing the roof panel caused the first problem. The cutting tool that would cut around the fixing screws in the corrugated roof panels failed to do anything of the sort so it was back to plan B (which is usually plan A): the crowbar. Noise could have been an issue, but dozy-nuts in the security lodge was too wrapped up in his goggle box to notice the roofing panel being broken apart one crunch after another, until there was a hole big enough to drop in through. Before the noise finally stopped, everyone was expecting the guard to appear. As it was, he heard not a sound.

In the kennel they had, though, and there were many pairs of eyes looking skyward, wondering what the hell's going on?! They soon found out. With a chain of rescuers formed, puppies in sacks were passed out through the roof and away out of the compound. There were sixty pups and some older dogs in the unit. The pups loved the whole thing; they bounced around wanting to play with the balaclava'd raiders and continued to play even after they had been dropped into the sacks, while they were leaving the compound, and for the rest of the night! Some necessarily anonymous humans were very lucky to be part of this special once-in-a-lifetime experience that night.

In the kennel, the older dogs were, by contrast, terrified of human contact and would have nothing to do with anyone walking upright. It's anybody's guess quite what they must have experienced to be so terrified by the sight of humans that they wet themselves, cowered in corners and bolted whenever anyone approached them. This meant that since time was limited, a certain amount of force had to be used to catch them, the last thing these dogs needed and not something undertaken lightly, but it's one of the few occasions when it's acceptable for a vegan! Outside the perimeter, the dogs had to be hauled the distance to waiting vehicles, which took time and effort but was enormously rewarding for all involved. (NB: Just being vegan isn't enough for this—

you have to do exercise too!) All escaped.

Seventy-one beagles and the tattoos in their ears just disappeared. A good vet shifted the tattoos, and the movement shifted the beagles into the welcoming arms of sympathisers hungry for more. You can always home an ex-lab beagle puppy! Some of the older ones came out of their shell in their own time, some didn't; never have, and never will. They will go to the grave haunted by what the monsters inside Interfauna did to them.

Beagles safely in the bag, two weeks later, 140 male chicks were rescued from BIBRA laboratories in Surrey, where activists once again broke in by dropping through the roof. In America that August, rescuers broke into the premises of lab supplier Bio Devices Inc. in California where they found 46 beagles in various stages of ill-health, many of whom had been surgically mutilated, others with eye problems, and all extremely—and characteristically—nervous. A separate team of raiders released 3000 mink from one farm in Wisconsin, 3,500 from a second and caused $1.5 million damage to the United Feeds (mink farm supplier) Co-op. In September, raiders freed 100 foxes from a farm at Minnesota, the 62nd such raid in four years. In August in Sweden, five beagles were rescued from breeders at Orkelljunga, 2,500 mink released from a fur farm outside Falkenburg and 24 hens released from a battery farm at Morarp. In Holland, 12,000 mink were freed in two raids and a poultry processing business in Ermelo was reduced to ashes. In Belgium, a McDonald's store was burnt out causing a million dollars damage, the latest in a string of similar attacks. In Norway, 70 foxes were freed from a farm at Eidsberg, 60 in Finland and 8,000 mink in Germany. September in the UK saw another seven fully-laden refrigerated lorries burnt out at the Cherryfield pork processors in Croydon, causing £500,000 damage after devices and petrol-soaked rags were left on and around the wheels. Meanwhile, back in Oxford…

Park Farm: Over The Wall When They Least Expect It

> I have enforced the law against killing certain animals and many others, but the greatest progress of righteousness among men comes from the exhortation in favour of non-injury to life and abstention from killing all living beings.
>
> *King Asoka of India (c. 273-232 BC) from Asoka's Edicts*

Activists and other campaigners have often used local protests to take the opportunity to snoop around places, which weren't on the day's agenda. As paranoid as these places are, there are often opportunities for those who go looking for them to find a way in. At even the most raided locations, it has been known for doors to be left open in the middle of the day, with the inevitable consequence that animals have disappeared and offices been rifled with no one any the wiser. Park Farm had been hit over the years at various times: in the middle of the night, on a Sunday afternoon, and at 6.00am. Nothing big in the world of vivisection, but the lowly Park Farm has provided a wealth of information, spectacular footage and some invaluable experience to a lot of activists over many years. Bit sad it's gone really!

Oxford University Park Farm: the same old story—a complex of windowless buildings imprisoning various species of animals awaiting the vivisectors' carving knife. Or a Home Office approved breeding facility supplying the biomedical research community with the living systems needed to cure all human ills. Whatever you call it, it equals unimaginable animal suffering, a fact which combined with the ease of access at this Oxford site, had some animal liberators from out of town interested.

With a view to lifting as many beagles as could be loaded up before anyone noticed and then getting lost in the early morning rush hour, there were half a dozen activists in the fields out back before it was light and a van waiting nearby. Using ladders to scale the seven-foot wall, the back of the fortified dog unit was silently breached. Some of the pre-dawn raiders then jumped into the corridor and forced access to the kennel block with a sledgehammer. All that was required now was simply to bag as many dogs as possible as quickly as possible and leave. Some came quietly, as beagles so often do, terrified and resigned to whatever will be. Others enjoyed the attention to start with, but then became a little unsure once they were zipped inside the darkness of the holdall and there was no one to play with anymore, but too late by then to do anything about it. One little dog, her eyes wide with fear, was terrified of capture and caused an almighty kafuffle before being finally subdued and bagged, weeing all the way. All was going well and the bags were quickly filling up when disaster struck.

What's the worst thing that could happen? Keys rattling outside the door. The door. There's somebody at the door! An alarm bell sounding is so much more welcoming if there's got to be a problem, devastating, of course, but less so than a real live human turning up. Twenty dogs had been bagged in as many minutes but what of it if they were about to be caught on the job?

The farm manager, James Davys, suddenly appeared at the door, then marched in, closely followed by his colleague, Pete. Instead of starting their day packing beagles to order, they were suddenly looking at Trouble. Difficult to say who was the most shocked, but there was no doubting that everyone in the kennel block was unimaginably unhappy with the situation, though only Davys wanted to fight over it. Sidekick Pete was happy to leave it to the police to sort out and told James so, sensibly grabbing his arm to pull him out. The raiders thought this a happy solution but the main man had outstanding debts to settle and he was not happy. These were his dogs, well, Oxford University vivisectors' dogs, but they were keeping him in work. People would be laughing at the number of times he'd been raided, though he'd never yet suffered the indignity in front of his eyes. This was the fourth raid on his watch and it was no joke.

'No way! Not again,' he growled, as he lunged at the person in a balaclava nearest him. 'You're not taking any more fuckin' dogs.' He landed one good punch in the scuffle that followed, but that was all. While he was grappling with his victim, someone else wearing a head torch head-butted and floored him. He'd been looking to start trouble and he got it, even though everyone else, including his sidekick Pete, had wanted to avoid it. All the beagle burglars had wanted was to get out with their dogs. And would have done so but for Davys who was fuming! His calls for help from Pete fell on deaf ears, as the lad had long since gone to call the police

Time to go. 'Load up.' Davys began to bawl in frustration like a spoilt kid. Their laughter probably echoed in his head for some time to come after they left him to his tears with a parting shot: 'Now you know how it feels. You prick.' They confiscated his keys, which were never recovered and cost Park Farm £5,000 for the replacement of locks.

In the rush to move 18 holdalls up and down the ladders and over to

Above: Shamrock Monkey Farm. For 40 years these sheds held tens of thousands of wild caught monkeys from jungles around the world.
Following a successful 15-month campaign the business was forced to close the site sold and sheds demolished.

Above: The Shamrock site late Summer 2000 cleared of all its cabins following its closure in March.

Above: Regal Rabbits - Hire van at the doors of Shed 1 June 2000.

Above: Dave Blenkinsop & the author filmed loading Regal Rabbits from the sheds into a van in June 2000. A 22-year old business that shipped countless thousand rabbits to vivisection labs across the world was brought to an end in a matter of days by public pressure.

Above: Biosearch Lab Project 6199. Acute Dermal Toxicity Insecticide Test. 5/12/88. (PETA)

Ella Cowley with the first of the Regal Rabbits freed in 2000. Hunt supporters would later decapitate this young animal and leave the remains in the garden. (Keith Mann)

Above: Liberated mink make off from a Swedish fur farm. 2003.

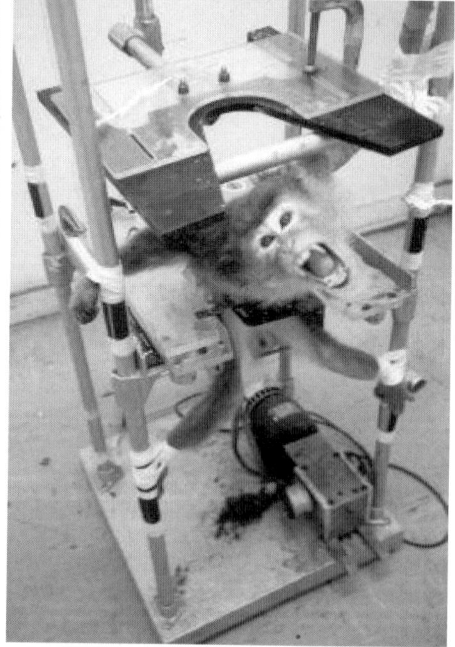

Above left: Activists lock in workers for 10 hours at a vivisection lab.
Above right: Silver Spring monkey undergoing neurological experiment in US laboratory. (PETA)

Above: Thousands march through Oxford against Hill Grove cat farm in 1996.

Above: Hill Grove cats.

Above: Plymouth, Devon UK. Dingles department store burns after ALF incendiary attack in December 1988. The stores sprinkler system failed to douse the flames which caused millions of pounds worth of damage and persuaded the owners to remove fur from their stores.

Right: Lynx anti-fur bus stop advert.
Below: Sussex Police prevent protestors from marching through Brighton town centre against Shamrock Monkey farm. 1999.

Above: Animal Liberation Investigation Unit activists on the roof of the Boots beagle kennels in November 1990.

Above: ALF raiders posing with Boots beagles rescued in November 1990.

Above: SHAC USA. Six campaigners imprisoned in 2006 for up to six years each under sweeping new powers to prevent opposition to vivisection.

Below: SHAC Europe: activists demonstrate their disgust at the daily slaughter of 500 animals inside HLS.

the van, one dog escaped from a bag and took off in a straight line over the field as though he knew where he was going. But he didn't know where he was going; even though he had more chance of a life than he'd had five minutes before, for his liberators it was absolutely heartbreaking. They wished him good luck and sped on themselves. Time was running out. The police were well on the way by the time the van had been loaded, and before there was enough traffic between it and the farm there were blue flashing lights and sirens heading in. Sirens are as undesirable as the sound of door keys. Never as much as meeting head on in a nearby lane, Dan, the driver of the van full of fugitives, slowed down—he had no choice faced with the speeding police car heading for them.

Suspicious but not yet certain that these were the people they were after, the police driver pulled up alongside to the van and instructed: 'Pull over for a quick word.' Dan signalled his compliance, then slammed on the accelerator. He knew he was in trouble now, but there was a still a chance to get some or all of the others out of the way before the police turned round and caught up. The van rounded the next few turns then rapidly decelerated and drew to a halt as the rear doors were thrown open and bodies poured out and into the undergrowth. All but two of the dogs were still in the van, and the police were close. Far too close. It had all happened so fast there had been no time to take out more dogs, which as it turned out was a bad thing. The van sped off but the police were more focused on that than the escapees. What is this obsession with taking these animals back to these places?

Those on foot managed to find wheels and leave the area as initially planned, but Dan Poustie was stopped ten miles from Park Farm by a dozen racing police cars and arrested for aggravated burglary and assault. The 16 dogs on board were returned to Park Farm. The escapee made his way to a house in nearby Northmoor but was taken straight back to the farm by the homeowner. 2649AK and 2781AK made it to safety and are living under assumed names in the South of France. Poustie was later sentenced to 18 months in prison for burglary. Davys was treated for superficial wounds to his face, loin and forehead and went on churning out beagles. But time was running out and before Poustie was through half his sentence, Park Farm shut up shop and became nothing more than a distant memory for the Animal Liberation Movement.

When Park Farm closed during 1999, their entire macaque-breeding colony was sent to Harlan UK for storage, pending the construction of

Oxford University's new vivisection lab where (if built) the primates would eventually be caged and used. Seven years on they're still there. An undercover investigator had been working for ten months in the Leicestershire-based breeding centre which promotes itself as the world's biggest supplier of animals and the by-products of research, selling surgically altered animals and mutants to any one of its customers in 30 countries.

The investigator's responsibilities included hundreds of beagles. She reported, 'In the morning I would open the door to my unit to be greeted by up to three hundred uncontrollable, bored, frustrated dogs clamouring for attention. With so many dogs living in overcrowded conditions and so few staff, it was impossible to give the dogs individual attention. Throughout the day I would hear cries and screeches as dogs bullied and attacked each other. It was awful.'

Her investigation exposed once again the regular mass killing of hundreds of 'excess' guinea pigs, rats and mice—all animals who, if they were actually recorded in Home Office statistics, would double the official statistics for animals killed for vivisection. How little has changed since a similar exposé from Lancashire Poly in 1991 and since the APC announced things were going to get better after the hunger strikes.

Beagle dogs described by Harlan as 'surplus stock' were killed due to excessive breeding, 29 on one day alone. 'Non-conforming products,' or dogs that didn't meet certain 'standards' (with a stumpy tail or one testicle for example) were killed off. Dogs died in fights due to overcrowding and were housed on bare floors without any bedding, any exercise or any stimulation. Breeding females and stud dogs were penned up in this environment all their miserable lives. All of them were considered by their tormentors to be disposable.

This investigator's findings were going to change very little sadly. We might not be about to change the world either but what we had planned would at least have a happy ending.

To Take The Regal Rabbits

A quote from a laboratory animal breeder does tend to suggest that actions may speak louder than words:

> Today because of the activists there is some deterrent to involving oneself in animal industries.

If there was ever any doubt about it, Regal Group UK were going to prove that breeder correct in his assessment. Regal had nestled in the Surrey countryside as a rabbit breeding business for 22 years. William Pitcher and his partner Caroline Smith had built an opulent house in the grounds and owned several posh cars, so they weren't doing badly. Our enquiries suggested that Bill wasn't as vicious towards animals as almost everyone else that works hands-on in the industry seems to be and certainly the condition in the rabbit sheds were the best I've ever seen. That's not to say the rabbits were happy, but the man in charge was somehow proud of what he did and wanted to do it in an orderly fashion.

Unlike Park Farm, Regal advertised their wares, but had for the most part escaped attention from activists. Such was the complacency at the Great Bookham site near Leatherhead, that there wasn't even barbed wire on top of the decorative boundary fence. During 1999, and again the following year, one of the dozen long, windowless wooden sheds was broken into and over 70 rabbits were removed and rehomed. The installation after the first raid of an internal movement sensor alarm at floor level in the sheds (so that the rabbits—held in cages on stilts at waist height—wouldn't trigger them off) did nothing to prevent a second break in. It merely meant that by accessing the unit through an air vent high in the wall, rescuers could use the cages to move around on. It also meant that Bill would have to invest in another security system.

We set up a covert camera nearby to film the comings and goings at Regal. We followed people and asked around and gathered enough information to conclude this was a place of cruelty. With London's able activists only a few miles to the north and the south coast not far in the other direction, it was well placed.

We planned to make a public announcement about our next campaign, but wanted to make sure we were well informed and well prepared (we had spent £7,000 on campaign material) to show we meant business. Within days, the entire local community and many further a field knew all about William Pitcher, The Bunny Butcher of Bookham after seeing his face and phone number posted widely on bus shelters and lamp posts. Worrying enough for anyone, but especially someone keeping secrets in cages.

It was midday Sunday 25 June, 2000 and a bright tranquil day in the Surrey countryside. Bill and Caroline were busy in their house, probably expecting nothing untoward to disturb their peace. Note To Self: Expect the unexpected! Out back, 20 masked trespassers had scaled the fence, and were checking the security system and filming inside the compound to gather information for Close Down Regal Rabbits. Steve, Bill's right hand man, Animal Technician and chief confidante, emerged from the workshop to gaze on in wonder at the scene in front of him. Pitcher arrived on the scene thinking he was being raided; he moaned: 'Oh no! Not again!' He started to push someone and then thought better of it. Too many to push around! It would be over in ten minutes.

Police arrived after the posse had left. Two days later, on Tuesday 27 June, Close Down Regal Rabbits went public at a regional group meeting. We were giving the campaign a year to complete the job. We called Bill and opened dialogue. He was chatty enough and all importantly 'fully regulated by the Home Office,' so he wasn't cruel, and assured us he wouldn't be stopping, because it's what he'd always done and it's legal. The following Sunday, 40 protesters met at the farm gates for the first of many planned vigils. We'd reasoned that as the rabbits get no time out from the monotony of cage life and all that follows, those who send them there should not be allowed to forget this. We told Bill who we were and that we were going to save the rabbits and didn't care for his excuses for being cruel. He seemed not to care, but only very briefly. As for many, Sunday was a day to relax for the Bunny Butchers. Was! An afternoon of Simon and Garfunkel's *Bright Eyes,* through a loud hailer, examples of research projects involving rabbits, and reminders of the movement's past history made uncomfortable listening, and it was made clear that this was just the beginning. He was listening.

On Tuesday 4 July, barbed wire and new fencing went up, but it was not a deterrent type of fence. One of the day's protesters called the campaign number that evening to report on the demo and mentioned the fence, chuckling down the phone that it was 'cute'! A fence like that was more like an invitation. There were London people on site with placards first thing in the morning and again that evening making all kinds of noise. The neighbours didn't like it either, though most of them supported us. Within ten minutes of the start of the evening demo, there was a line of police cars on the drive, all lights flashing. One of the neighbours asked if she'd get such a fantastic response if she had to call them again about something unrelated. 'It took you two days when I reported a burglary,' she told one copper, who didn't want to be doing what he'd been told he might end up doing for the next 12 months. He replied with only slight irony, 'Next time you call, love, say it's animal rights activists that have broken in. That should speed up the response!' He winked at her wryly.

Less sympathetic officers arrested a woman protester for an alleged breach of the peace, then changed their minds on the way to the police station and dropped her off at a busy roundabout two miles away. Back at the farm gate, protesters refused police requests to stop protesting and move on and insisted Pitcher came out to ask personally. Desperate to resolve the situation, he emerged escorted by police to talk face to face. He was seriously balding, had a round face with shifty eyes and he wanted to know what he could expect from the campaign; he wanted clarity on the fate of Shamrock and others, which was interesting. This would be a learning curve for him. He wondered if selling the rabbits for meat would please us! The options were spelled out again.

Not convinced he was grasping the situation, we called Bill early the following morning to clear up any doubt. The rabbit business folds, then we go away. The call was polite but unapologetic. We are not prepared to compromise with the lives of others. We explained we couldn't any longer walk away from these places and allow people to be cruel. He said it wasn't cruel, because they were bred for it. We said we weren't debating it, but if he wanted to see a video or two we'd drop some in. He said he'd already been sent some videos, but he didn't want to be drawn when asked what he thought of what he'd seen. This had him go quiet. 'Hello? Bill? Bill?' He said he had a lot to think about. We suggested he ring Chris Brown at Hill Grove. He said he'd already spoken to him!

On Thursday 6 July, a new five-bar gate went up at the farm entrance complete with a little padlock. It appeared he wasn't thinking quite what we were thinking he was thinking. Locking the animals away further wasn't going to help anyone. The first batch of newsletters were mailed out to thousands the following morning. Some recipients would begin to call and write to Regal to register their disgust, others conspire its demise, fuelled by events that very evening. Things turned nasty when a small Kent contingent of female protesters were pushed around by Pitcher and some hired muscle outside the farm and threatened with rape. The police arrived and, without flinching, arrested one of the women who had been attacked! They released her without charge soon after.

In many respects, the silly arrests and the violence were business as usual, but it was a really stupid thing for Pitcher to be involved in and not what we were expecting from him. We were expecting trouble with the police and a protracted stand off, as was indicated by the creeping security package, but he didn't seem to be the violent type. Anyway, no one had been hospitalised at least, but harm had been done. We rang him the following morning to ask what he was playing at. He said he regretted what had happened and blamed his friends for the trouble. He said he hadn't yet made any decisions about the future, but he was thinking about it. We suggested he might want to speed things up because we had a national demonstration planned for the 23rd that would see a lot more people on his doorstep needing beating up. It was hard to judge whether he was stringing us along or seriously thinking of quitting, but we didn't trust him any more and told him we wouldn't make any further calls. We told him that he might be hearing from other citizens though 'cos the word was out. Some of these people may, it was suggested, make his mind up for him. 'They aren't violent, but they are persistent.'

That evening, 50 masked activists descended on the farm and created a scene, some smashing the new alarm warning system, house windows and attempting to break the door down. It was payback for the night before. By the time the police and helicopter arrived, the culprits had fled, but the chopper harassed the neighbourhood for a few hours as it searched. A small number of protesters gathered at the gate in the middle of it all. The following morning, on Saturday 8 July, just 14 days after the first inspection, Pitcher called the campaign to say he'd had enough. And he wasn't lying! He said he'd decided to close the farm at 4.00pm the previous day, three hours before the attack on his house, but this had confirmed for him he had made the right decision.

This was stunning news. He wasn't just telling us he'd quit, he was begging us to let him be. Seizing the initiative, he was asked whether we were going to get the rabbits. 'Do I have a choice?' was his monumental reply.

'Not really.'

'You want all of them?' he pined.

'Yes, every single one.' A magical moment was upon us. We were gobsmacked! What it meant was we were about to intercept thousands of lab-bound rabbits in one go. Thrown off balance by Shamrock sending on to die the monkeys left there at the end, we called the latest campaign Close Down Regal Rabbits when we should have set out to Save the Regal Rabbits. We'd somehow watered down our demands but were rapidly back where we should be and focusing directly on a rescue mission.

'We need to talk', he was told. And fast, before he thought again about what he was doing or was persuaded to change his mind. Hours later, we had representatives at the farm in talks with Pitcher and a Sussex police officer as mediator, ostensibly so we could seal the deal and call off the campaign. Bill still wanted his rabbits and the wealth they brought, but he didn't want the hassle that came with it. He claimed to love the rabbits but didn't seem able to comprehend the terrible suffering they were subjected to once they were delivered elsewhere. He was dedicated to producing a quality product and wasn't listening to anything we had said about the damage done to that product in laboratories. They weren't just products to him either. He actually seemed to like them for what they were, but switched off his emotions the moment they left his premises. Hating this man for what he was doing, it was hard to really dislike him. He was edgy and didn't like being called cruel. He wasn't stupid or overtly cruel but was involved in vivisection and could only get away from that with our help.

While we were in negotiations with Bill, the mail-out—and visual reminder of vivisection on rabbits—was landing on doorsteps across the country and the campaign phone was ringing off the hook. People wanted extra petitions and transport details for the 23rd and clarification of *Ceefax* news reports claiming that Regal Rabbits was closing. Activists had waited weeks to hear the new target and then the moment it was revealed, before they'd been able to even make a phone call, it was all over! Was this a wind up? Suddenly, rather than getting their leaflets, callers were being asked to take some rabbits home instead. It was hard to believe.

We had overestimated the number of rabbits on site and rather than the 5000 we thought were there we were assured by Bill there were just 1,152. This is still an enormous number of good homes needed. Not something ever readily available for that number of any species. We suddenly had a whole new responsibility. Closing the farm was one thing, though not very much as it turned out, but finding good homes could be a far greater task. By Saturday afternoon, we were effectively The Regal Group, and every last animal was under our care. He agreed to show us inside the sheds for the first time so we could assure a very mistrusting movement that we weren't being misled. He promised us he wouldn't sell a single rabbit.

Bill Pitcher was a defeated man. He shouldn't feel ashamed of this and we didn't want him to, only for his past. This was an intelligent and evolutionary move for him to make. But in reality, he had nothing to bargain with and no longer a business to deal in. We allowed someone we were calling animal abusing scum the day before to look after our rabbits until they were old enough to travel, something unique in my experience. The reality was that the rabbits were all ages, and some simply couldn't be moved until they were old enough. Some were pregnant and it would be weeks before it was safe to move them and their offspring. Throughout Saturday and Sunday the phones rang hot with requests to provide homes, long and short term, and transport to move rabbits.

By early Monday morning, we were on site fully equipped to relocate Regal Rabbits and weren't prepared to wait. Bill was happy to get things moving too. The only proviso was that we didn't film events. Sandy, the police mediator, explained that Bill was humiliated enough without having the clear out made public. We agreed, but it was too good an opportunity to miss, so we put a hidden camera in the back of one of the vans and recorded the operation for posterity but didn't release the footage at the time. There are usually only people in balaclavas taking rabbits from cages in this kind of environment but we were able to wander in and out like we owned the place. The clearout was planned meticulously. Vehicles and drivers were instructed to arrive at set times and provided with delivery details, contact numbers, maps and rabbits. As expected, the movement rallied and offers of help flooded in. The police presence was minimal and passive. Sandy—out of uniform—stood by as an observer. He was polite and helpful, even lending a hand occasionally. It was all very civilised and orderly—an animal activist's utopia.

No one could believe they were being seriously asked to turn up at this rabbit farm and load up with as many laboratory rabbits as they could carry. We were asked time after time: 'Are you sure they aren't lying?' It was only once it started to happen and cages of rabbits started to leave the sheds that the reality dawned on us. One by one throughout the day, vans lined up to wait their turn before leaving loaded with rabbits for delivery around the country. Bill hadn't read our plans and wasn't expecting for us to reverse vans up to his sheds to fill them up, but walking them to the perimeter one at a time and passing them over the new gate as he intended would have taken forever. He complied. Remaining for the most part calm as his business was loaded up before his eyes, he expressed no bitterness or anger at events, just this really peculiar, damned irritating concern for the future of the rabbits!

Bill Pitcher, nice guy or not, was deluded. He didn't know us and didn't know where the rabbits were going. He had sent rabbits to laboratories for years and admitted he didn't know either his customers or the fate of the rabbits, but because he was told the Home Office regulates their demise, he assumed everything would be lovely and his creation respected. Keeping an eye on things and asking the odd question of us, he was regularly in and out of the sheds and back to the house to confer with his wife. His second mistake was to express his comical concern for his animals by suggesting to one of the loading team how to handle the rabbits the rabbit farmer way. As he had no concern for the needs of the rabbits he had been keeping in cages or once he'd sold them on, to tell someone dedicated to their rescue how to look after them was asking for the verbal slating that followed. We had agreed not to have a go at any of his staff on site, but he asked for the response he got and had no idea how to reply so just went back indoors.

There were six of us in the sheds including Sandy and Steve and we'd been working for a couple of hours when Bill returned to see the increasingly barren cages and the emotions spilled out of him. He'd wound himself up so much that the rabbits we were loading into our vans might not be going to good homes that he actually broke down and started crying in front of us! Everyone stopped what they were doing and stared open-mouthed! He had finally found a way to stop us taking his rabbits! After the incredulous looks, he got little sympathy, only more reminders of the fate of the rabbits he'd sent away to be vivisected for 22 years. 'Cry for them,' someone snapped at him. But he still didn't get it and to pacify him we had to assure him that we only had the welfare of the rabbits at heart, and while we had no Home Office stamp of approval that was a good thing for the rabbits as we knew better than them or any of his customers ever will the needs of the animals. Reassuring a blubbering middle-aged man who sold rabbits to vivisectors that we wouldn't hurt his rabbits was a one-off experience.

By the end of the Monday, three sheds had been completely cleared and nearly 600 rabbits were on their way to a better life. This was a special day for everyone concerned. The next three months were taken up entirely with re-homing 1,153 New Zealand White and Half-lop rabbits (he'd miscounted by just one). And it wasn't simply just homing them we had to consider, but homing them well. Very few people have the right idea about how to keep domestic rabbits, even those known as animal rights activists, and with the best of intentions, people can cause them to suffer. Rabbits don't live in hutches and it was very much our intention that every single rabbit would be given the best possible chance of a fulfilling life without breeding.

We did hundreds of home checks but had to rely on the word of third parties on occasion because there were so many to home and some were too far away to follow up. All takers were instructed to return the rabbits to us if they changed their minds. A few rabbits didn't get the best deal and had to be re-homed, a few escaped, some got myxomatosis or coccidiosis and one young girl's rabbit was beheaded by hunt supporters and left on her lawn in response to her family's views on hunting, but all had a chance to thrive and most did. The vast majority lived happy lives and, crucially, not one died in a vivisection laboratory. The Animal Liberation Movement did a remarkable thing for the Regal rabbits.

It took just three months to bring this project to a close and re-home 1,153 rabbits. We took the food stocks and the cages, and all there are now in those sheds are mushrooms. Bill had asked what else he could do in his sheds if he didn't do rabbits. Mushrooms were one suggestion, cannabis another, but he wasn't amused. Then again, he never did smile much, but it is a sad business. This swift victory and happy ending was made possible not just because of those who went there and made noises, but those who made the calls, homed the rabbits and sent the cash, and were prepared to stand up and be counted as friends of the animals.

Huntingdon Life Sciences: A Very Public Disaster

> We don't have an auditor, we don't have a bank and we don't have an insurance company.
>
> *Brian Cass, ITV news Jan 05*

Closing Huntingdon Life Sciences to most people would be a logical thing to do and indeed many people fully expected that to happen after the 1987 exposé. But HLS is a big employer and a key player in the world of harmful product testing, and without them and others like them, product manufacturers wouldn't be able to stamp their chemical goods as safe. Often described by the media as a drug testing company, HLS also test pesticides, herbicides, fungicides, agrochemicals, household products, food additives, GM food and so on. HLS will test anything.

A month after the latest exposé, the HLS laboratory in New Jersey was similarly opened up after secret footage taken by PETA investigator Michelle Rokke over a five-month period, was released; PETA were immediately issued with a gagging order by HLS. Following a court hearing, the order was lifted and the horrific truths were revealed, including workers terrifying and abusing monkeys in their care; threatening to bite their faces off and laughing at screaming, struggling animals in pain. The footage shows one live monkey being cut up on a metal tray and it can be seen twitching and jerking as the scalpel slices into his chest. A technician observes: 'This guy could be out a little more.' Another frightened monkey is tied to a table as a laughing technician squirts lubricant into its mouth. A dog struggles and screams as technicians force a thick tube down its throat. One monkey shown being strapped to a table was one of 48 being used to test a nasal decongestant for Proctor & Gamble. Technicians yell and scream at the terrified animal and each other like they're wild on drugs and leave the animals injured and bruised. These monsters are repeatedly seen acting with total contempt for the suffering of their victims, not to mention a complete absence of any of the rigorous scientific methodology we are always being assured is the tenet of vivisection. One brief exchange between technicians summarises it neatly:

Tech one: 'I'm sure the sponsor will love that'

Tech two: 'Bring up their heart rates just a little bit more.'

Tech three: 'You can wipe your ass with that data.'

Michelle Rokke released 8,000-pages of confidential documents, which revealed all kinds of awful, unimaginable facts. In one long list of gruesome tests, one dog out of a group of 48 being poisoned daily for over a year in a test for Colgate-Palmolive's Ajax kitchen cleanser, had a seizure. Rokke was told not to record it in the observation log, which—considering logging observations is (allegedly) the whole point of carrying out tests—merely substantiated what many have said before: that test results get rigged in order to ensure that sales of products can continue. In another experiment, 37 beagles were to have one of their leg bones sawn then snapped with a stainless steel wire, all without anaesthetic, to test an Osteoporosis drug already tested and on the market for the Japanese company Yamanouchi. This test was cancelled following the storm of publicity that followed, and actress Kim Basinger stepped in and was able to buy the beagles.

The footage taken during the investigation is a genuine horror film and must surely underpin the view that these people are real-life monsters, and that as such, they can surely have little ground to complain when they are exposed to the public and experience the full force of anger felt by those who find them repulsive.

Following investigation by the US Dept of Agriculture, HLS were later charged with five offences under the Welfare of Animals Act, including 'Failure to give animals painkillers and anaesthesia during painful and distressing procedures' and 'Failure to provide primates with psychological enrichment to keep them from self destructive behaviours.' Perversely, they were able to wriggle out of punishment through an agreement with the US DoA and instead agreed to spend $20,000 on new primate caging and promised to invest $20,000 in non-animal testing methods. It was nothing like justice, nor was it likely to prevent further cruelty, and most significantly, it got the lab off the hook. Again.

Established in 1951, the HLS estate of the late 1980s consisted of three sites in the UK: a 28-acre compound in Suffolk, one in Cheshire and the biggest in Cambridgeshire. At any one time they were holding around 35,000 rats, 13,000 mice, 4,000 guinea pigs, 4,000 fish, 3,000 birds, 2,000 rabbits, 1,000 dogs, 450 macaques, 200 marmosets, 10 baboons, and a number of miscellaneous species, all being slowly poisoned to death at a rate of 500 a day by a 1,000-strong work force. These are mind-blowing statistics, made so much worse when each figure is broken down to one complex, creative individual; statistics are designed to obscure the reality, that each figure represents a living being. Each with great capacity to suffer.

Everything is gross about HLS, a fact, which several exposes have clearly demonstrated, but the Labour Government's reaction has to be marvelled at. Their political allegiance to the electorate whom they are meant to represent has been nothing short of a travesty, in particular where they have not merely failed to keep their promises on tackling vivisection, but have encouraged and supported it. HLS does research and testing for others, over half of which involves poisoning healthy animals to death. This government wants to see those numbers increased! These issues have motivated a lot of direct action, and the conspiracy that has evolved to ensure vivisection continues and in secret is serving to radicalise a global movement.

Soon after the exposé, the Huntingdon Death Sciences campaign (HDS) formed and again focused public attention on not just the HLS labs but now also its 1,700 shareholders and clients, suppliers and other associates. Five hundred marched on Huntingdon and smaller weekly demonstrations at the gate once again exposed how tetchy some people are about this kind of public attention. It saw protesters regularly driven at by staff, which was encouraged by security men. One demonstrator was injured by an incensed worker early one evening, then arrested for being run over to be released later without charge! It was a very deliberate act of aggression, and one which numerous workers engaged in before heading home. A natural reaction? Probably not for the majority of us, but for people whose business is the abuse of others, it's to be expected.

Ten thousand leaflets a week were being distributed. Coach companies employed to transport workers out to the Huntingdon site were approached by campaigners and urged to stop assisting the process. Duncan's contacted the campaign to say they were pulling out of the contract following several attacks on their vehicles, including the icing on the cake, which saw several of their coaches very deliberately rammed by one of their own double-decker buses driven by a masked up individual in their compound late one night. A succession of protest camps outside the HLS UK labs attracted widespread support and national publicity and ultimately cost HLS nothing short of £1 million in court eviction costs and land purchase. Their costs were mounting as rapidly as the scramble to do something—anything—to affect HLS.

Following the very public exposé of life inside HLS, confidence in the company collapsed on the Stock Market and in the business world, fuelled in no small part by the endless pressure from animal rights activists. As major clients distanced themselves, the share price plummeted to a few pennies from a peak of £3.50p in 1990. Nine pence! So drastic was the free fall that trading was suspended on the Stock Market to stop total collapse. One hundred and fifty workers were made redundant from the two southern sites, and the recently acquired laboratory in the north, at Wilmslow in Cheshire, was closed, much to the delight of campaigners camped out there and digging in for a long, hard battle. Once reviled under the ownership of Ciba-Geigy, the labs had weathered the storm of the NALL in the 1980s and had secured its small perimeter with high steel fences, alarms and cameras. HLS saw it as a good investment with its purpose-built primate unit in the centre, as they quietly extended their reach. But with it came the daily presence to see the workers in and out again, 24-hour vigils, home visits to workers and directors, blockades of the labs and dozens of ALF raids. It was a brief focused campaign involving a lot of anonymous individuals, but a big victory for a broad-based movement with a purpose.

Desperate to avoid the awkward questions that shareholders were promising to pose at the company AGM, HLS shifted from the usual handy location in Cambridge and ran to Boston in Massachusetts in the USA. This kept away the regular shareholders and most of the 200 campaigners who had invested in one share each, instead limiting the attendance to three uncomfortable directors and a handful of activists, including two pests from the UK. HLS, the Big Bully, was running scared. At the Huntingdon lab, a number of our shareholders attended to inspect company documents in accordance with the rules. But, as is expected, the rules were ignored by HLS, so two shareholders tried to force their way in. They were arrested 'to prevent a breach of the peace' and held for three hours, and never allowed to exercise their right.

The first of the newly established Stop Huntingdon Animal Cruelty (SHAC) national demonstrations in December 1999 attracted 500 marchers. Cambridgeshire Police saw nothing new in this, having weathered many protests before, but they didn't want it all the same, and things were hotting up. They spent £60,000 and set about imposing their will with 500 officers and a Public Order Act, Section 14 Banning Order to keep objectors from reaching the gates of HLS. HLS for their part had shelled out again to erect a seven-foot, solid wooden fence around the perimeter to keep out prying eyes, endless rolls of razor wire and new security cameras. With the Section 14 imposed at the last minute, the site was effectively hidden from the outside world, and word went round that the demo had instead become a 'public meeting', not covered by the order, in Huntingdon Town Centre. By the end of the day, many local shopkeepers were out of pocket and complaining, not specifically about the demonstration, but the massive disruption it had caused.

With all hope of any kind of justice fading with every government comment on vivisection, and the horrors increasing with every revelation, HLS was catapulted headlong into controversy by a powerful build-up of anger at the way animals and people are being treated at the behest of a business interest. Many thousands of people across the world are intent on closing down this one company known as HLS or Huntingdon. They are taking the campaign far beyond disruptive localised demos and cranking up of security costs, to involve every aspect of the business operation.

Shareholders, customers, market makers, financiers, bankers, insurers, cleaning contractors have all been persuaded to dump HLS, causing endless headaches. The counter-reaction of the Labour Government to this has been dramatic, to say the least.

The modern movement is well adept at involving itself in what looks like a mishmash of random passive protest and action far from the target, but it is this that is deliberately and very effectively, turning the screw on Huntingdon on a global level. There are few clients who can claim to not have been affected when targeted in this way once called upon to call in a contract, and fewer still who have survived this relentless pressure.

Early on in the campaign, a lot of effort was put into targeting Huntingdon workers and the lab itself. The pressure clearly took its toll on an already unstable workforce in which—as various undercover investigations have shown—cruelty, absenteeism, stress, drink and drugs, and incompetence are routine. For many of them it was too much and they began dropping like flies. One HLS employee said in 2000:

> It's distressing to say the least. These people arrive at our work place, shout, scream, blow whistles, bang on drums, kick our cars, try to open the doors and bellow down loudhailers all day long. They refer to us as 'scum', 'puppy killers', 'monsters', 'perverts' and 'animal torturers'. As I get close to work on a morning I get a sinking feeling in my stomach. I know they will be there. As the end of the day comes I dread driving out of the complex. I know they will have doubled in numbers throughout the day. The police are always there, but the atmosphere of intimidation still causes me to sometimes wonder if it is worth it.

One evening just before 5.00pm, a team locked onto concrete-filled oil drums outside the gates and blockaded the exit. One worker's brother attending the site thought this a great idea and helped to unload the drums off the truck as it arrived! Unable to manoeuvre a way around this formidable obstruction, workers were forced to leave their cars and walk out to be picked up by taxis. This would be a recurring theme, with protesters happy to present themselves for arrest and possible injury just to hinder the workforce leaving on time.

One ex-worker of three days who didn't know what he was letting himself in for when taking a job at HLS, told me of the final straw for one of his colleagues, Jean, who had been there years. On this particular day, she had been jostled in the morning arriving for work, then while trying to sort her finances over dinner had got locked in the Nat West bank in Huntingdon town centre when protesters arrived; and had been terrified they might recognise her. On arriving back at work, she was reprimanded by bosses for her timekeeping only to then be delayed leaving that evening by a group of activists who had locked themselves with handcuffs under five specially-adapted cars abandoned in the lane outside the lab. As the activists drove these into position at 4.00pm, Security panicked, ran inside and slammed the gates shut. The car drivers then let the tyres down and left the scene. The police poured into the area in their helicopter, riot vans and half a dozen cars but could then only look on in wonder. It was some hours later, before the unhappy workforce was eventually able to clamber their cars up through a hedge decimated by Security, bounce down the kerb and leave. Jean said she couldn't take it any more and never went back. The cruelty hadn't got to her, but the reminders had, and she wasn't alone.

Many of them have no other option for employment, don't know anything else and won't deny it, yet these are the same people who claim they do what they do for the benefit of others. There is no shortage of people like this who will do anything for money, but there's a shortage of people stupid enough to keep pouring money into a flailing business other than the UK taxpayer!

With footage of terrified animals and jovial animal abusers on national TV, HLS plc suffered severe financial loss. Dealing with the allegations of malpractice alone cost them around £3.5 million in legal fees, and lucrative research contracts were cancelled following freefall on the stock market. HLS ended up £4.5 million in the red following the exposé, having made a profit of £11.1 million the year before. A shortfall of over £15 million for a few minutes of footage from inside one of the torture chambers! Makes you wonder what else goes on that the labs and the Government are desperate we don't see, eh? It makes *me* wonder. Makes me cringe. Makes me cry because I actually know.

I always want to know more of the awful facts. I know it isn't healthy; knowledge may well be power but too much of the detail of the inner workings of a vivisection laboratory is the reason why many activists self-destruct. That, and trying too hard to fix it.

According to the British Banking Association, HLS were 'in a nightmare situation.' With the company careering headlong towards bankruptcy in August 1998, they were desperate for investment and called an Emergency General Meeting. There were few options for shareholders other than liquidation, but HLS was given a £15 million lifeline by a consortium of American businessmen led by Andrew Baker, who had taken over as Executive Chairman when Brian Cass took over as Managing Director. That was his role during undercover investigations in 1990 and 1992 at Hazelton Laboratories (now Covance) in Yorkshire when footage revealed awful scenes and stories similar to those at HLS. Covance were once again exposed by an undercover investigator torturing monkeys in their German primate toxicology lab in 2003.

Baker had been alongside Cass at the time. Equipped with the will and the infrastructure for a thriving business, but still unable to secure the sufficient cash injection required, a further £20 million was raised by issuing 177 million new shares. But there was still a desperate shortfall. Enter the National Westminster Bank. The Nat West Bank did itself long-term harm in the eyes of many existing and potential customers in agreeing to lend HLS plc £24.5 million, so saving the company from liquidation. Without this loan, HLS would have sunk and there would have been an awful lot of re-homing to do. As it is, there's a lot of suffering gone on there and a story to tell.

The Nat West, later the Royal Bank of Scotland, was to deeply regret its move. It was a decision which proved far from profitable, something many of those who have done work for the debt-ridden HLS have found. There is nothing more helpful to a campaign wanting to go public than to have 1,700 branches in high streets to target. By the time the bank had decided it wasn't profitable anymore, most branches had been visited several times with lock-ons, sit-ins, rooftop occupations, pickets and sabotage regular occurrences. Eighty cash machines were disabled in one night alone in London. Countless others suffered a similar fate across the country and further afield. Something like this simply cannot be sustained, but it was two years before the bank had had enough, and joined the rush for the door, leaving HLS in dire straits. Again. By then, no other UK banks would go near this public disaster, leaving the once mighty HLS with no banking facilities and unable to even write or cash cheques! Who would be ruthless enough to step in and bail them out? Surely not the same government that had made so many promises to curb vivisection, now granting HLS the use of the Bank of England to conduct its obscene affairs? Oh yes! The UK taxpayer is shoring up HLS!

And not just banking facilities. Following an intense global campaign against HLS insurance broker Marsh, which was costing them £100,000 a week for protecting the properties of UK directors alone, the company did a cost benefit assessment and decided it wasn't cost effective to cough up for insurance. They pulled out, leaving HLS uninsured and knee deep again. Dutifully the Labour Government's Department of Trade and Industry stepped in and bailed them out. Any damage now done to HLS US interests costs the UK taxpayer!

All this still left HLS with a massive debt to pay and a deadline to meet, something the Government weren't quite able to legitimately arrange for this failed commercial concern. That would be a favour too far! Desperately looking elsewhere for friends, HLS had the option of decamping their shares to the US market and merging with Life Science Research (LSR) Inc., a US-registered company. This was far from an attractive proposition, as the MD, Brian Cass, admitted in May 2001: 'If we move off the UK Exchange, they have effectively won. It is a stand that has to be made.'

Within six months, HLS had no leg to stand on and became an American company. This in turn effectively crashed the worth of their investors' stake by turning 50 HLS shares into one LSR share but it was the best deal on the table.

As the final day drew near in January 2001 with the RBS withdrawing its overdraft facility, the movement was on tenterhooks in anticipation of the news that HLS had gone into liquidation, when up popped a mystery backer at the eleventh hour. This was revealed to be Stephens Inc., a US-based company with $33 million to spare, persuaded that HLS was a good investment. It wasn't, and would do no good for Stephens and associates, but their intervention did give HLS the next lifeline it needed. HLS is an international company but the Animal Liberation Movement is a global one. For bailing out HLS, Stephens suffered the wrath of US activists and in just a few months, days after the ALF had hit boss Warren Stephen's home, smashing windows, and racking up $100,000 on his stolen credit card, they were persuaded to sell off their shares and entire HLS debt facility,

Publicly bailing out to the US was the last thing this once successful, secretive UK business wanted to do. Where once they had led the field in this country, in the US they would find themselves the bottom of a pile of like businesses with very little to boast about and still fewer friends. But at least it would be a less hostile environment and would enable them to find their feet again. Crucially, shareholders could be protected by the rules of the Maryland State, where there is no requirement for a public declaration of company shareholder details. The options for HLS were limited to just this one, but still they failed to take account of the fact that many shareholders were the same, and were known to those of us interested. The burgeoning movement in the US was infected by the campaign being waged in the UK and inspired by the undercover exposé of their New Jersey lab. Out of the frying pan into the fire!

At one point in the proceedings, the *Financial Times* newspaper reported that a tiny group of activists were 'succeeding where Karl Marx and the Baader Meinhof gang and the Red Brigades failed.'

The campaign has been well coordinated, tracking the business and all its associates, ensuring that in whatever country there is a link, however tenuous, there have been protests. In the US, the activists focused on destabilising anything to do with HLS. They set straight about Stephens and all their connections, piling on much more pressure than the company could handle. There were marches, phone and Internet blockades, and arson attacks. Office windows were smashed, private homes visited, offices occupied and the business disrupted in many other ways. Within days of HLS' exodus to America, the first of a whole string of market makers had been forced to abandon the company.

The president of the Bank of New York, with 90 million shares in HLS, had his 30' yacht drilled with holes and pushed out to sea as it started taking on water. Paranoia spread far beyond the workforce; it infected banks and the Stock Market to the point where one shareholder phoned the SHAC UK office and offered private information on a fellow big-time conspirator, whom he said he was happy to have harassed in exchange for immunity to continue profiting from his own HLS stock. After teasing the information out of the caller, SHAC did the dirty and passed the story on to the FT, who ran it on the front page and set about releasing the details of the mystery shareholder and the informant. 'We do not do deals with the devil,' was the uncompromising campaign response.

The campaign against HLS galvanised the movement and changed the rules of the game against vivisection. It opened up the fact that the battle against HLS is a war against vivisection between the people and the entire petrochemical/ pharmaceutical/ governmental machine, whose activities are sanctioned, protected, and funded by the State and its various branches, who in turn profits from the power and wealth of those industries. Today there is little incentive for anyone else to give the huge financial input needed to shore up HLS, and side with vivisection, but the government. All that might, yet the prevailing view may very well have been expressed in the City Comment in the *Evening Standard*, which stated that: 'Long term there is a body of opinion that believes that Huntingdon is unlikely to survive.'

HLS was, on the one hand, an obvious choice for targeting, given its precarious public image and the availability of a huge wealth of inside information, which would destroy that in a moment, and, on the other hand, given its status as a key player in the product testing industry, an ambitious choice. So the question still remains: will it be allowed to fall? Some say not, because it is too valuable an asset commercially (or could be again) and significantly keeps a lot of people employed, but more importantly, a victory for the Animal Liberation Movement over the Government/HLS would be a watershed in the battle to end vivisection. The reality is that only for so long can the tide of change be held back and whether or not they maintain the façade of a thriving company HLS has been decimated by public pressure.

Keeping one step ahead activists have inevitably had to adapt new tactics. One of these has been the use of electronic civil disobedience to pressurise HLS and its affiliates (all from the comfort of home). The virtual sit-ins have brought websites to a standstill and crashed email accounts c/o the Animal Liberation Tactical Internet Response Network. Huge numbers of emails have poured into systems causing meltdown. In the US, in response, core SHAC USA activists were arrested, charged and convicted under new legislation intended to stop any campaigns against animal abusers. These laws were introduced to criminalise the use of the Internet to send information and coordinate opposition to animal exploitation, and in the case of the SHAC US, specifically to contain the campaign in the US while HLS tries desperately to find its feet in preparation for critical refinancing.

In the UK, campaign adaptations have been necessary to deal with increasingly unreasonable policing. With the police steadily softening the effect of lawful protest by designating 'protest zones' and dictating what language and images can be used, tactics have had to change. Step over the protest line to get near enough to be heard and risk arrest. Say something that might be deemed offensive to an animal poisoner within the hearing of a police officer and risk arrest. 'Murderer,' for example, is now an illegal use of the English language if you are stood in front of HLS! 'Say it again and you're nicked', became the standard mantra. So protests have moved on from the expected. Some days have seen hundreds of officers wrong footed and left stranded at advertised meeting points while protesters have diverted to different locations. Last minute mobile phone calls finalise arrangements, 'dummy demos' are advertised and flying pickets take in a variety of targets in succession, moving on before the police catch up. At HLS, these mobile demos have complemented the more frustrating conventional static kind of protest.

In today's protest environment, people have been arrested for stepping over the imaginary and sometimes fluid protest line, for waving a picture of a mutilated dog at the people who mutilated him, for placing a placard against a tree, for pointing, and for blowing a horn or whistle in the direction of a moving car. Designed, no doubt, to deter protesters, such tactics are inappropriate in a democracy and serve only to alienate the people from the police and encourage less confrontational tactics to evolve. And crucially, to go elsewhere, even more wound up than if they'd been allowed to vent their anger at the 'murdering scum' leaving the death camp. Unable to keep up with the constantly changing tactics (aided by the availability of many options offered by a PLC with hundreds of customers, over a thousand workers and the need for a lot of essential services) the powers that be have sought to stop people doing anything at all to protest against vivisection.

One Saturday afternoon in 2001 while driving into Slough through the traffic to demonstrate at a Horlicks factory (the mother company being an HLS customer) we noticed there were yellow jackets at the roundabout at the bottom of the dual carriageway. When one of the minibuses ahead of ours left a trail of shredded paper in its wake, we knew there was a problem. The paper trail was the remnant of demo dockets listing intended targets for the day, with directions, times and locations, and critically, not for the police to see. Those plans could have included any one of a number of targets: the lab, utility supplier, bank manager's home, a march through a town—or all of the above.

There had already been an unannounced demo at one chemical company that sends products to HLS to be injected into animals, and someone had broken a couple of windows during a protest at the main entrance. The crowd was moving on when some hothead local drove his car at people marching on the road away from the site and ran one girl over. In the ensuing melee, the thug had his car surrounded and lashed at before he sped off. Next stop for the protest was Slough, but the police had wised up and were on the roundabout stopping anyone heading for the demo. We did a U-turn in the road and drove elsewhere, but another nine minibuses and over 90 innocent people were arrested and detained until all hours of the night because they were going to a demo. All were released without charge and sued the police for illegal everything.

During 2003, 33 suppliers were encouraged by various levels of protest to pull out of HLS, causing endless logistical problems, which have only worsened over time as this tactic of secondary targeting has increased. Workers have remained far from happy either, despite all that has been done to protect them. There were still people outside the lab most days, four years after the campaign kicked in, and no amount of legislation and security is going to keep people away from visiting private homes, something encouraged by increased police oppression on public protests. Curfews and internment are the most likely to succeed in keeping contained those of us concerned enough about animal abuse and fraudulent, dangerous research to act, but history suggests that even those desperate measures won't stem the growing tide of opposition. The Animal Liberation Movement is now, thankfully, beyond control. Over 26 nations attended the AR 2006 Gathering to share tactics and ideas and some of the biggest actions of modern times are occurring in countries like Russia.

The HLS' tally of victims over a period of fifty years is a staggering nine million animals. Animal testing is profitable and cruel. No wonder there is such determination around the world to close them down for good. That this wide-ranging campaign is organised or coordinated by a small number of people is no secret, but what some have been dismayed to find is that it is actually run by hundreds. Taking out the core in the UK, as the police did in 2001, and securing prison sentences on allegations that the defendants had incited a public nuisance did nothing for the HLS cause. The immediate response by activists was to regroup and renew the pledge to close HLS and that's now a global issue.

One campaigner, Niel Hansen, wrote to each of 1,700 HLS shareholders and included details of HLS crimes against creation and science. He invited them to consider the fine detail of their investment and promised random 24-hour home protests outside those who didn't opt to sell up. There were no threats, just implications, but the response, like so many to the gross abuse of small furry creatures in laboratory cages, was truly theatrical. News editors saw an 'extremist attack' and grabbed it hysterically as they have so many times since. This was a signed letter, polite and reasonable, giving shareholders two weeks to sell up or face a 'campaign tour': legitimate protest. HLS didn't help themselves by writing to their investors warning of the threat and advising they call 999 at the first sign of a protester. Thanks to the ensuing coverage by the end of the week, Huntingdon's sorry share price had plummeted again devaluing the company by 40%! Hansen was soon under police surveillance and being harassed but he wasn't the one breaking the law—they were otherwise active and were being encouraged to stay that way by just such police repression.

Over 250 speculators responded in the affirmative, calling in and selling on a million shares. The circulated letter worked a treat. Giving the missive added weight were the unscheduled appearances by protesters outside the homes of some shareholders. One, a retired businessman with 20,000 shares, found his home besieged by not just a dozen pledged protesters, but twice as many journalists and cameramen. He was quoted as saying he was 'More pissed off with all the media than the protesters.' And so say all of us! That said the media has done a remarkably good job of instilling terror in the hardened hearts of animal abusers everywhere who fear irrationally the non-violent advance of this movement.

In reaction to the devastating effect on its shareholder portfolio, HLS called publicly on the ever-compliant Labour Government to create another new specialist police unit to stop people writing letters and daring to demonstrate against animal cruelty. The other stuff, the 'threats', the 'terrorism', and the 'violence' had by the year 2000 long been criminalised and was well recorded and monitored by the forces of law and order. Four weeks after the letter was sent, its author was arrested for blackmail, and his house and office raided; since he had done nothing illegal, no charges were ever brought.

I have not always referred to individuals in this book by their real names: that to a large extent has been dictated by the need to safeguard their anonymity. Some I have focused on. I have met many people who have given their all to the struggle, people with endless shocking, exciting, funny and scary stories of their exploits for the animals but it's not names I seek to share so much as the action and reaction. Lynn Sawyer's name is one that has cropped up before in these pages. Sawyer—who went public when she abandoned her life as a Conservative hunt supporter (and thus overnight turned from Establishment to Extremist)—represented the 'respectable' side of protest but is no different from the others deemed troublesome. She was present at the World Day demo of 2000, one of 1,500 protesters who swamped HLS—coordinated and very visual, many were dressed in black and wearing skull facemasks—this would be a good one that no one could contain or control!

Demonstrators were made to park their vehicles fields away at the back of the lab and walk down the lanes to the front gate. For a lot of protesters, this was the first time they'd seen the lab, its fences, wire and all its electronic surveillance. Like the concentration camps, HLS brings out powerful emotions. The mood was electric; Shamrock had just announced closure and this place would be next! Following inspiring speeches at the gate, protesters made their way around the perimeter. The police in riot gear inside the compound seemed to be relying on the increased security measures to keep people outside the fence, but the mood was for action and there were wire cutters floating around. No one that mattered saw the secure fence being cut in several places, but they soon noticed a hundred people pour through the holes.

The crowd roared as the formidable perimeter was breached. The police panicked and waded in. They weren't just desperate to keep people out and return them from whence they came, but to punish them for getting in. More violence, and no, it still doesn't matter who you are or that you are only stood there, you have taken sides, you are the enemy. A game of cat and mouse ensued and eventually protesters were evicted.

At 2.00pm came the biggest coup so far, when two protesters, including inoffensive Lynn Sawyer, got in again through the mass of razor wire and riot cops and onto the roof of one of the labs in the middle of the sprawling compound. Much of the crowd had opted to be outside the compound by now, as most of the police were inside it, and so leaving the victors to their roof, instead marched over the fields to the busy A1, blocking it southbound with traffic cones, wood and sheer weight of numbers. Confined to one carriageway by police, a second group broke away and stopped traffic heading north. The police tried frantically to restore order but it was too late. Back on the lab roof there was an Inspector trying to coax the squatters down 'with dignity' but they were enjoying watching the people in yellow pursuing people in black around the surrounding area. That, and the long line of stationary traffic on the A1. All that the police helicopter was doing was recording events as they developed. The police, despite all their power, were powerless to stop the protesters who next spilled onto the A14 and marched down the A1, pursued by racing police vehicles bouncing road cones everywhere. Stopping the A1 traffic was a coup, given the disruption it caused, and focused so much attention on HLS—all there is for stranded drivers to see in the immediate area.

It was early evening before things were back to normal on the A1, and a number of spontaneous worker home visits were staged. The intruders were eventually bundled clumsily off the roof and arrested with others for ignoring the Section 14 ban on the day's rally (which allows police to dictate an alternative location for a protest at will and the time it should conclude).

Three months later, a team of activists again hit the A1, first slowing traffic and then stopping it by hastily erecting two 20′ scaffolding tripods, perching one person at the top of each. They were buoyed by the previous stunt and this time intending to stay there for as long as possible, but only lasted five minutes. Local off-duty PC, David Manton, was in the subsequent backup of traffic, and he wasn't feeling at all benevolent towards his force's greatest enemy and their right to protest. It wasn't even as though he'd been personally inconvenienced, since his motorbike could easily have bypassed the obstruction. He should have known better than to drag apart the poles with someone perched precariously 20′ above the road, but he clearly didn't give a damn as the petite 33 year-old woman above him crashed to the ground.

Lynn Sawyer as you know has become so impassioned about animal exploitation that she's now wrapped up, like so many from all kinds of backgrounds, in various tactics and trickery in the defence of animals. Once very much a hunt supporter, she's now very much an activist, particularly at odds with the violence at Huntingdon, which she had been busy making public when PC Manton ejected her from her roost atop the scaffolding. The 5′ tall midwife was left lying on the road in considerable pain with a fractured hip and femur and a gashed and bleeding face, while Manton sped off home and spent the evening partying, utterly remorseless and unfazed by what he'd done, leaving his victim for colleagues to administer first aid on their arrival. Returning home the next day, however, he was to find those same colleagues searching his house and himself under arrest.

Lynn Sawyer spent weeks in hospital, months off work and needed plastic surgery to the wound on her face. As a result of her injuries, she now has one leg an inch shorter than the other, is facially scarred and lives in pain. That'll teach her! Not. Despite the early arrest, itself remarkable, and the testimony of 16 witnesses, it took ten months for Cambridgeshire Police to bring charges of Grievous Bodily Harm against their colleague. Even then, following a less than truthful court hearing and some very sinister intimidation of witnesses, Manton was somehow found not guilty! Not even done for leaving the scene or failing to report what he'd done! 'I didn't expect justice,' Sawyer said later. 'I don't anymore, which is why I do what I do. A hundred years ago the police were treating women in exactly the same way for demanding rights for women. We won then and we'll win now. It's bullies we're fighting against. They won't ever scare me away.'

Four years later, she was awarded thousands of pounds in compensation for her injuries. A year after the police assault, while in the middle of her recovery and to assist it (she said she needed a morale boost and this was it) angry and determined, she had HLS very much in her sights. Driving to the gates one morning to do her own thing in front of the workers she noticed the security guard was new and looked especially dopey so instead of pulling to the left side of the road to park and protest she turned right and drove up to the gates. She kept right on going like she belonged and no one even challenged her! Well! What a peculiar position for someone to be in, especially someone so well known to HLS and the police; someone who had made it her business to access such places by stealth and cause embarrassment. Someone whose picture had appeared in the local papers only the previous week!

Waved in and now inside the compound, she parked up, had a quick look around and limped off to 'M12.' Helpfully, the technician leaving the building held the door open for her! He said later he thought he recognised her! This is Fortress HLS but suddenly they are opening doors and inviting in a regular pain-in-the-arse. Lynn Sawyer again:

> I knew I wouldn't be able to leave without getting caught so I found myself a small office and barricaded myself in and had a

read of the confidential files. After a while the phone rang and I answered it. It was a woman saying she couldn't get into her office and that she needed the key. I explained that it would not be possible to allow her in. Security woke up and finally came to see me about an hour after I set up this HLS branch of SHAC. Animal lib fanatic and road safety expert Sgt Ken Smith next appeared and tried to talk me out. He was acting less smarmy than the thousand times he's stopped my car. I was behind the desk blocking the door and wouldn't move so they decided to break in through the wall. The police and workers rebuked me for reading the files but I just couldn't help myself. After three hours they drilled through the wall, enough for Ken to kick a big hole and come in to arrest me for vagrancy, burglary, theft of electricity and criminal damage. A bit rich when all I did was walk in and sit down! They weren't at all happy that I breached their security so easily.

Indeed not. Not only a centre of excellence where 'Your secret is our secret', but also everyone else's! The immediate aftermath was to see Security stop and check every car as it arrived at the gates. For those of us standing outside having to watch these monsters breeze in every day giving the V sign, this was like a dream come true. There was suddenly no way of them escaping the anger and they were suddenly no longer quite so fuckin' cocky as they sat there, radio up loud, waiting for an age to move along the queue, looking decidedly uncomfortable, desperate not to make eye contact or look at the pictures being rammed in their faces. This made mornings even more uncomfortable for workers, hence police efforts to deter such protests.

In 2000, several workers had their cars firebombed by the ALF on their drives one night in a new wave of attacks. It was only a handful of cars and no one was hurt, but the media-led hype was stunning and spread far more fear throughout the Huntingdon workforce and beyond than a few fires would have done on their own. Children weren't being kidnapped or grandparents blinded with acid, but ask the workforce at HLS if this is a concern and you bet your life! That fear surrounding the Animal Liberation Movement is disproportionate—given that activists don't tend to use violence—but is a positive thing if it makes the exploitation of animals that bit less attractive. On the other hand, it is also unfathomable—given that activists pose less of a threat to the public than the likes of HLS and many of its workers—yet are targeted with much more media venom and government repression than any violent criminals. As always, it comes down to money. Lots of it. It's what's important to politicians and businessmen. And it's the point of vivisection!

Violence is a key word in this struggle and throughout this book. The violence against animals and the violence against protesters is really all there is to discuss. I can't find much 'animal rights violence', just talk of it. However, the violence that some activists have experienced has sorely tested their essentially peaceful dispositions and has driven them to react in kind.

Known in the 1980s for being a committed Liverpool hunt sab, Dave Blenkinsop has been physically assaulted for his objection to animal abuse more times than he can be bothered to remember. Arrested alongside the likes of Dave Callender and others mentioned in these pages and many more who haven't been, he has sought to fight back. For neither man, passionate and hardened as they are, has using violence come easy. Blenkinsop—quiet, undemanding, trustworthy and reliable—was always the one to come to when you needed your engine fixed, often to be seen with his head under a sab Land Rover bonnet, welding one of the vans or fixing things at a rescue centre.

Blenkinsop held Mike Hill as he lay dying in the Cheshire countryside in 1991. He'd got in the way to stop people being hurt before, and knew how dangerous it was to get into a fight in enemy territory. He was the first to call a tactical retreat if trouble was brewing but if trouble came, as it does, he would stand his ground. Dave Blenkinsop was sent to prison for 15 months for participating in the attack on the Cheshire Beagles kennels two days after Mike's death. He was traumatised, he knew he shouldn't have been there because it was inviting trouble, but he didn't know what else to do. None of us did.

If he hadn't been as agile as he was, he might have been the one lying dying under the wheels of the Old Surrey & Burstow supporters Land Rover that nearly killed Steve Christmas in the Surrey countryside nine years later. Blenkinsop shouldn't have been there either, but fox cubs were being hunted down and torn apart—fox cubs like the abandoned and injured cubs he'd tended at an animal sanctuary nearby, where he'd also been building pens for injured ducks and other rescues.

Luckily for Steve Christmas, Dave Blenkinsop was on hand to hold him as he lay there and to call for an air ambulance to take his friend to hospital. It was the final straw. After years of trying to avoid confrontations wherever possible, Dave Blenkinsop changed his mind about the use of premeditated violence.

In February 2001, three men with baseball bats ambushed Brian Cass, an accountant by profession (the much hated, ill-fated HLS MD and cold-hearted public defender of mass animal torture) as he got out of his car on his Cambridge drive one evening. It appears they set out to hurt him, and may very well have hurt him more had things gone differently. It was fortunate for Cass that he stumbled out of the way of a serious blow and that a neighbour rushed to help him. He managed to get indoors, battered, bruised and bleeding before sustaining serious injury. The following day, he was all over the news showing off his injuries, boasting of how he'd survived, and calling for more protection for people like himself.

The chance discovery in Cambridgeshire a few days later of a number of items of clothing, baseball bats and a balaclava sealed the fate of one of the Cass' attackers. A DNA match was made with Blenkinsop from samples in the balaclava, and Cass' DNA was identified on one of the bats along with fibres which linked the two men. Explanations were thin on the ground for this contact! Not that interested in dealing with the violent thug who had driven his Land Rover at Steve Christmas causing him far more serious, life threatening injury, 70 officers turned up at Blenkinsop's door that May to arrest him, and he was charged two days later with causing Grievous Bodily Harm, and remanded in custody.

Justice was very selectively sought and there was one final irony to come. The CPS dropped the case against the thug in the Land Rover because Dave Blenkinsop had been in prison years before, and therefore in their considered opinion he wasn't a reliable witness! He was of course the best witness and indeed there were others who saw exactly what had happened on that day, but this was the tenuous excuse the CPS needed to dump the case and continue the façade that the violence comes from the activists.

Exhaustive forensic tests linked Blenkinsop's DNA and fibres found on clothing with other incidents and gradually a bigger picture began to emerge of his nocturnal activities in the struggle to end animal abuse. Traces of DNA were also discovered on a fragment of a latex glove found at the scene of the Newchurch raid the previous September and on the fuse assembly of a device left at a slaughterhouse in Oxford three days before his arrest for the Cass attack. Given the minute quantities of DNA with which forensics were dealing, there was of course a possibility that they had been transferred by a third party and weren't therefore necessarily proof positive of the defendant's involvement, but it certainly did look suspicious! To make matters worse, further forensic work revealed that devices used in Oxford and others, which had been used to burn the cars of HLS workers in August 2000, were similar. On top of all that, fibres found in a coat pocket recovered from Blenkinsop were also similar to some found on a device that had been recovered from the drive of an HLS worker before it could ignite, and matched those found on clothing abandoned after the Cass attack.

While Blenkinsop awaited trial for one offence, the thorough police investigation revealed the pattern of his recent past, a past that had caught up with him and would be impossible to escape from. There were few plausible explanations. Some plea-bargaining later, he pleaded guilty and was sentenced to 18 months for his part in rescuing 600 guinea pigs, three years for GBH and 5½ years for handling incendiary devices: a total of ten, with no possibility of parole before June 2006. It was good news for Brian Cass and co. but not the answer to their problem, which has only got worse. The OBE he was awarded for his resistance to public pressure in the name of animal testing would be of little long-term comfort.

Premeditated violence is a new phenomenon. It is not widespread. It doesn't seem like it ever would be given the track record thus far and the lack of motivation for bloodshed from animal activists. Every section of society uses physical violence but this section far less than most. It seems to me rather disingenuous to expect it to remain like that given the increasingly diminished alternative outlets for protest.

SHAC offices and volunteers' homes have been repeatedly subjected to police raids, computers have been confiscated and coordinators imprisoned. So driven were the authorities to nail someone for incitement of the regular campaign newsletters which invited readers to 'Go Get' named HLS workers albeit using legal method, that £1.2 million was poured into their investigation and bringing the case to trial. The central focus of the police case was a cartoon in one newsletter featuring Scooby Doo below a list of workers and the headline 'Blood On Their Hands' with Scooby saying: 'HLS workers are animal killers. GO GET 'EM!' Extensive ongoing surveillance proved the involvement of Heather James, Greg Avery and Natasha Dallemagne in the production and distribution of the newsletters and the three were later sent to prison for 12 months. It was little more that a break for them—time out to recharge their batteries, and an unmitigated disaster for the police who confessed later: 'We won't be trying that again.' Does that mean that they will at last be focusing their attention on serious organised crime as most of us would wish? Don't be stupid!

The National Crime Squad were more than pleased that they had been able to persuade the Post Office to close down the SHAC PO Box and deny that service. Certainly it was temporarily disruptive, but did it help HLS? Hardly. They were getting increasingly desperate. By 2003, HLS and its customers—in particular the vital Japanese contingent—had applied to the High Court for legal injunctions to keep protesters away from their premises. The police already had ample powers and the will to arrest people for acting outside the law, but not quite enough to remove the dangerous threat of people waving placards and exposing the truth. There was once upon a time in England of olde the freedom to protest and this was seen as an essential ingredient of our democracy. Mutual heckling both by pro and anti-vivisectionists outside HLS' gates was a part of that democratic tradition. But somehow that's all gone. Democracy has been sold to the highest bidder. The vivisection industry we talk of has been able to buy itself respite from the relentless pressure of public opinion. Even included in the High Court application were references to amongst other things the A1 tripod stunt, which HLS lawyers described as harassment. Now if you go to the gates of HLS, Oxford University or anywhere else, your opinion might affect the flow of business, and if you wave your placard you will probably be arrested and face up to five years in prison. The democratic right to protest we hear so much about is yet another lie among many.

Nor can you publish any details relating to 'protected persons' i.e. HLS, its workers or customers and their staff or suppliers in any way, nor publish articles relating to activities carried out against them. You can protest once a week with no more than twelve people for a few hours if you first contact the police to make sure it's okay.

But overstep the new 'improved' boundaries of protest by setting up a camp, using a megaphone or communicating with anyone protected who is responsible for poisoning animals to death, and the state may try to crush you. Not a word of propaganda nor a lie do I tell.

Taking out injunctions to stop people from mentioning 'protected persons', didn't, oddly enough, stop people from paint stripping cars or targeting the homes of anyone linked to HLS. In fact, it merely exacerbated the situation. According to the stressed out MD of HLS, post injunction: 'We have validated 54 separate attacks on cars alone over the past six months, but what is most concerning is that 28 have occurred since the start of January. It has really picked up.' Indeed, the attacks tripled! As usual, the media responded by reporting that lunatics were killing all hope of medical cures by damaging Executives' cars and forcing support away from HLS. There were yet more calls for increased restrictions on protesters and heavier sentences for those arrested. Given that people can now go to prison for trying to engage in lawful activity, it seems probable there will be a more focus on other tactics, which are already illegal.

In 1992 HLS was valued at $500 million. By 2005 it was worth around $22 million. If you invested £4,500 in HLS in 1992, ten years on it'd be worth £1.50! In 2004 alone over 100 companies associated with HLS withdrew contracts. Citibank dumped 10 million shares, Charles Schwab 5 million, Merrill Lynch 8 million. They have few friends but for those in government, the animal poisoning industry and the town of Huntingdon. HLS are $100 million in debt. Huntingdon Life Science is a company fighting every day for survival against all the odds.

Brian Cass and Andrew Barker, company CEO, flew to the US to join all Huntingdon's executives especially for the moment HLS would be re-listed on the New York Stock exchange in September 2005 after years of nothing but negativity in the financial market. Bustling with excitement of future investment with champagne at the ready, just 45 minutes from trading the walls came tumbling down as the HLS soldiers were informed it wasn't going to happen after all, due to the fear of what animal rights activists might do. This was a spectacular blow for HLS. Brian Cass' reaction on Channel 4 news was: 'Well obviously we were extremely disappointed, distressed, astonished. We were absolutely speechless… We looked at each other not really believing it.' Ho hum!

Since then there have been yet more revelations from within HLS—at least six to date. Two former workers came forward with more of the same to tell and were duly courted by SHAC and their experiences given light of day. They revealed yet more falsifying of data, animal cruelty, drunkenness, and utter, utter incompetence and indifference. In a series of secret meetings the truth poured out.

> On a night out someone from necropsy was boasting about cutting the head open and sawing through the bone to get to the brain and how the smell of blood made them hungry. They admitted that not only one dog was put in a bin bag, odd parts

here and there ended up with another dog. Vans came to collect the dogs at night and took them to be burned. It always made me really sad knowing that these dogs went to be incinerated not even as a whole animal…
A licence holder would grab the dog by its scruff, sometimes lifting the dog up off the chair, have the dog hanging and really shout at it to behave. Sometimes they would hold the scruff, whilst the dog was sitting on the chair, and push its head and neck down whilst shouting at it. The dog was laid on its back and the bone marrow taken from the chest bone. This wasn't pleasant to sit through. The two team leaders I had done this procedure with hadn't given the dog enough anaesthetic and the dog whimpered and moved. This was so upsetting for me. They didn't give more anaesthetic but carried on.

There is somebody who works there now, as a senior technician, and has been reported. He goes down the pub every lunch time, drinks 3 or 4 pints of Stella and then drives back to work. He also has drink in his locker. He goes to drink while he's at work. That's gross misconduct. In the smoking area he sits there in front of us blatantly smoking weed.

The response to this from the authorities was remarkable. No rush to prosecute for anything criminal or cruel going on inside HLS or to prevent any further compromise of the essential medical research taking place there; instead Special Branch detectives honed in and threatened the whistleblowers with prison and perhaps worse if they didn't keep their mouths shut, even 'persuading' them to write retractions of their extensive revelations! Could the HLS story get any worse?

The Primate Lab

> There is strong scientific evidence that animal-based testing is grossly inaccurate in evaluating how a drug or product will affect humans, and is a grave risk to the health and safety of people and animals alike.
>
> *Dr Ray Greek*

With the dawning of draconian injunctions to protect businesses from protest action, extremely aggressive policing and a media campaign working overtime to terrorise the population with the spectre of anti-vivisection extremism, there would appear to be little left to the objectors to this vile practice. And isn't that the case! The injuctions are targeting lawful protesters and so are the police. So what's left then if the industry and Government continue to refuse to debate the issue? It wasn't my idea to encourage illegal behaviour but that seems to be what's happened. To stop protests at the Newchurch breeding site, one application was sought to keep anyone concerned about animal welfare and/or medical progress from entering within a 30sq km exclusion zone around the farm!

The knock-on effect of refusing to legislate better protection for animals, to set up an inquiry into animal testing and to attack those with declared anti-vivisection sympathies hasn't only failed to improve things for HLS and all its associates, but also harmed the cause of others, not least the Newchurch breeders. A similar process has taken shape in Oxford where a significant battle is today underway between truth, honesty and advanced medical research on the one hand—or if you prefer a bunch of violent extremist—and on the other a bunch of violent lying extremists intent on vivisecting more animals come what may. Some, like the arsonists who target the University will claim to have been forced there by the lack of debate and openness that goes with animal research. The researchers claim to want that debate but say they are frightened to speak out, while the opponents of animal research will, it seems, do anything to raise the debate, so why aren't we having one? Only the researchers and those in power know why.

In Cambridge, the University Council had applied for planning permission to open a new primate research laboratory outside the city. The Girton lab was a big issue for everyone with a vested interest in more animal research and for those of us with concerns about the use of extreme violence to generate results and the deceit being used to hoodwink us into accepting such behaviour. The lab was to specialise in inflicting brain damage on monkeys. However, before the Girton project got off the ground, it was scuppered, In spite of some deeply sinister intervention from the top of govt and the ever-present lies that accompany claims of animals aiding medical progress.

The plans to convert the deserted Girton farm into Europe's largest primate brain research centre were originally rejected twice by the local Council and then went to a public enquiry at the end of 2003. Everyone was opposed to it: the police didn't want another site to have to protect from the inevitable protests; the Council didn't want to build on green belt and have to deal with the chaos that protesters would bring; and animal rights groups and scientists gave even better reasons not to give the go-ahead. It wasn't looking good back at the University either, where the fine detail of the proposed plans were revealed to the Regency House's 3000 academics and administrative staff who had voted in favour of the project three years earlier. Their Council had failed to reveal to them that the Girton lab was to be the hub of brain experiments on monkeys in the UK.

As the scandal unfolded, the University's watchdog investigated the affair and concluded the Council had 'failed to reveal the truth' in its application. A Public Inquiry then agreed with the objectors to the lab and concluded that the centre should not go ahead. With a process like this seen to be working the likes of the ALF would lose their thunder. Democracy at work! Enter the self-appointed neuroscientist and Government Minister, John Prescott. The Labour Government decided, without recourse to any kind of public inquiry into the validity of vivisection, but with generous encouragement from the party's biggest financial backer billionaire, pro-vivisection, pro-GM, pro-biotech Science Minister, Lord Sainsbury, that this country's vivisectors need to have as many experimental animals as they can get their hands on. It was the enormous generosity of Mr David Sainsbury that earned him his two titles from the Government. Prescott, without flinching, overruled the Inspector and gave Girton the go ahead, in what he said was 'strongly in the national interest', something the inspector had explicitly disagreed with. The University got their planning permission, albeit through the back door, and Labour once again demonstrated that the democratic process in this country is a sham.

Despite all the wheeling and dealing, Cambridge declined the Government's helpful intervention as security became an increasing issue, aided by the media churning out the usual 'extremists on the rampage' propaganda. The costs had risen by 25% to £32 million before the foundations had even been laid, forcing the University's withdrawal from the project; simply put, they couldn't 'take financial risks of this magnitude.'

This was another hugely significant victory for the Animal Liberation Movement and apparently, a disaster for 'democracy.' Without collusion by the Council to conceal the truth from Cambridge University staff members as to the nature of the project and without government intervention at a high level, the Girton plans would have been laid to rest after the public enquiry, which showed clearly that there were considerable misgivings throughout the community about the project, and that no one wanted a laboratory at Girton. Prescott made a mockery of democracy by overriding the Planning Inspector's decision, so it's ironic really, that the actions of a minority who pledged public disorder achieved what an official public enquiry could not. The combined failure of the democratic process and the lies of self-serving politicians tied to the purse strings of powerful multi-nationals will surely help tip the balance in favour of anti-vivisectionists and against the vivisection industry.

That hurdle overcome, we were about to find out that the Cambridge debacle wasn't quite over. According to information leaked by a sympathetic insider to SPEAK, the grassroots campaign that had sprung up to oppose the Girton project (then called SPEAC—Stop Primate Experiments At Cambridge) building work had begun in March 2004 on the Oxford's South Parks Road for a primate centre to replace the abandoned Cambridge lab. Evidently, there had been discussions for some time for just such a scenario. Oxford University went to some lengths both to hide and deny any such developments or links, and indeed, planning documents were mysteriously unavailable at the Council offices.

There was originally no mention of animals; then, after being challenged, the University claimed that 98% of the work at the new lab would be on rodents, and that the premises would be more like a 'hotel' for the animals than a lab: somewhere they'd stay before going to 'work' elsewhere; a kind of Travel Lodge for mice. The truth, as it turned out, is of course a little different, as Oxford were forced to admit. The new South Parks building (if completed) is to be both a primate breeding facility and a primate research lab where, among others, crude invasive brain experiments will be carried out (i.e. exactly the opposite to what Oxford University had said!) similar to those shown in the shocking exposé covertly filmed by the BUAV in 2002 in a Cambridge lab. This particular investigation revealed that Marmosets had been taught tricks, then, after having parts of their brain cut or sucked out or injected with toxins, were made to perform more tricks to see how the damage affected them. It was 'like taking a lid off' was how one researcher callously described cutting open the clamped head of the little monkeys with an electric saw. 'Moderate' suffering was how the Government classified these experiments which caused pain, distress, bleeding from head wounds, fits, vomiting, tremors, abnormal body movements, head twisting, disability, confusion with blank expressions—described by a researcher as 'watching the birdies'—and lack of self-care.

The re-named SPEAK campaign rose to oppose Oxford's insane obsession with vivisection. Since 2004, hundreds of protesters have been out onto the streets and many have since been banned from Oxford by injunctions. Once the truth about the lab was leaked and with only the skeleton of the building erected, Oxford University was in a vulnerable position, and they knew it. So did SPEAK. Campaigners contacted material supplier Travis Perkins, explained the nature of the building work, which they had been employed to undertake and suggested they carry out their own research into the project and reconsider. Within days, TP gave assurances they would no longer deliver to the construction site. It was the first blow for the University project. Demonstrations sprang up, the police got heavy handed and their Evidence Gatherers' set about taking as many in-yer-face photographs of the same small number of people as is humanly possible.

Rugby police arrested one middle-aged lady for the shocking crime of beating a drum outside the offices of concrete supplier RMC. At the time, she was on the pavement next to a busy dual carriageway and roundabout but was accused of 'Intentionally causing harassment, alarm and distress' to workers inside the building. She was bailed to return to the police station, to give officers time to 'investigate' the crime, but was never charged. Such arrests would become commonplace.

The ALF then stepped in and put Oxford University in an impossible position. Focusing on building contractors Montpellier and aggregate suppliers RMC, both were persuaded to pull out in a matter of months. The machinery, vehicles, and offices of concrete suppliers RMC were sabotaged at several quarries and building sites and Montpellier were threatened. Concluding a series of actions, the ALF burnt out three diggers in a Surrey quarry, sabotaged a dozen earth-moving vehicles and machinery in Dorset, and sent a hoax letter to Montpellier shareholders purportedly by the company chairman which warned of 'prompt activity by the animal rights movement' unless they sold their stock. In the City the signs were ominous. That day Montpelier shares tumbled 19%.

This was the final straw that left Oxford with the shell of a building, no one to finish the job and a crane that would cost them £10,000 to remove. The costs of vivisection, it seems, just keep on rising. There followed another round of media hysterics and reports that the Prime Minister had assured Lord Sainsbury that the Army could be deployed to protect the project if future contractors couldn't complete the job. Lord Sainsbury asserted, 'We will make sure it is built.' A senior scientist said: 'There are a lot of people who wish that this animal unit wasn't going up. Having abuse shouted at you every day by protesters on your way to work isn't pleasant.'

Desperate to attract builders to Oxford, the University went to the High Court for an injunction to ban anyone from protesting near 'Protected Persons'—Members of the University, the Colleges and the Society, University employees, their families, servants or agents of the Members and of the University Employees, the employees and shareholders of the contractors, their families, servants or agents of the Shareholders and of the Contractor and employees or any person seeking to visit the laboratory or any premises or home belonging to or occupied by a Protected Person. Anyone! Additional applications to keep The Banned from entering Oxford, from contacting in any way anyone involved in vivisection at the University or using megaphones or whistles on the weekly protests held on the street outside the vivisection laboratory, were rejected by the judge. But the Order classifies anyone who reads the terms of the injunction a protester and duly bans them from the aforementioned or from entering within 50 yards of the construction site. Objectors to the vile things they seek to do on this site are permitted to enter this area every Thursday, so long as it is between the hours of 1pm and 5pm and any protest is contained within the 'designated area.'

So wide-ranging is the prohibition on protest, that Protected Persons can even be arrested for going to work if the police are minded to take it to its practical conclusion. The potential of these injunctions is awesome. Their immediate impact is to tie up campaigners in legal work and huge volumes of documents, effectively removing their right to protest, and costing the complainants—and thereby the tax payer—dearly. Yet where are the outraged who rail against those who use direct action? Why so little comment about the removal of the right to peacefully protest? With a raft of awful images of animals in distress and these kinds of ludicrous statements from Oxford's vivisectors, coupled with endless evidence of misleading medical research, it seems unlikely we've heard the last from those they call 'extremists.'

> Monkeys are very keen to do things and are very good at and like playing games. In our department, the cages are large and they're happy. They bound into the cages because they are so excited about the tasks they are going to do, they watch and talk to each other and have a television. They have a life of Riley compared to the animals in the wild. Wild rhesus monkeys live to about 12 but some of ours are 25-30. Would you want to spend your days worrying about whether you are going to get your head bitten off by a baboon, or would you prefer watching telly? They love watching television, and I have been told they prefer soaps. I've seen them spellbound by arguments on soaps.
>
> *John Stein, August 2004*

It's not the monkeys that need their brain examining…

Work on Oxford University finally resumed in November 2005 after 17 months of apparent inactivity. But behind closed doors, extensive secret negotiations had taken place to secure all the building supplies and contractors needed and keep their details confidential. But still the facts became public.

A major security operation was put in place and saw labourers working in balaclavas, delivery drivers wearing hoods and hiding their number plates and all being paid well over the odds to work the project and get a bonus when it is complete.

Surveillance revealed that contract workers were billeted at a sprawling fire service college a county away against the wishes of the natural occupants. Further injunction extensions—paid for by the public—have been granted to keep the public from protesting at this location. The police have also taken to arresting protesters for little or nothing, then issuing bail conditions barring entry within the Oxford ring road.

Dozens of security experts including former SAS men have been involved in counter surveillance and in the protection of key workers, but that's nothing. The Government has made available £100 million of UK taxpayer money to underwrite the bill to build this lab! Unbeknown to the public, vivisection is thriving in the UK and is public funded. Its propagation would be impossible otherwise.

There's a concerted campaign going on to crush the Animal Liberation Movement and force the completion of this project at all costs. The battle lines are drawn and the dumb decision to consolidate Oxford vivisection at this one focal point seems likely to haunt the university for a long time to come.

To Close A Guinea Pig Farm

> They may say they love animals, but they scared the hell out of our cat, Winky.
>
> *Lab animal breeder interviewed after raiders break his home window*

When the body of Gladys Hammond was taken at dead of night from its grave (and let's make it clear, since the media machine hasn't, by person or persons unknown) in the otherwise uneventful village of Yoxhall in Staffordshire in October 2004, there was a national media-led outcry. It was a heinous crime: the worst of the worst. Something so depraved it was beyond comprehension though expletives were in free flow. It was a crime symptomatic of the extremism sweeping our land. And so it has continued for the next few years to stir headline writers into teasing the nation to have a greater concern for the long-dead bodily remains of a relative of a man who chose breeding and killing animals for a living, than the animals he killed. And what of the loved ones who have lost family and friends as a direct result of having been administered dangerous animal tested products? Do you, like me, wonder what the hell is going on that has so dramatically turned the truly admirable human concept of compassion and care on its head and made serious physical and emotional suffering equal to an act of criminal damage or a non violent, if distasteful, publicity stunt? It matters not that experts—even those still practising in the field of vivisection—have proven vivisection is a dangerously flawed, cruel practice. Monkey experimenter Stephen Suomi of the US National Institute of Child Health and Human Development was quoted by the *New Scientist* in July 2004 as saying: 'Making cross-species analyses is always a dangerous thing.' Makes you wonder if they think it, why they're still doing it? For some people it's a bad habit, a life choice (mortgage and wife and kids to look after) for others it's a business opportunity, a good way to generate more income (yacht, island, governments to buy).

It had taken 5½ years to close the farm. The grave robbery sealed it. The Save the Newchurch Guinea Pigs campaign kicked in following the ALF rescue raid in September 1999 and decisions on policing it cost local services £2.25 million. The financial cost of the raid was nothing much in itself for the wealthy, business-minded family running this rodent breeding operation. Indeed, without a second thought the greedy Brothers Grim killed off the thousands of animals left behind by the raiders, as their financial worth was reduced by exposure to non-sterile conditions. You know, outdoors where guinea pigs evolved… Still, this was to be a rude awakening for the family, so lost in a world of animal exploitation that they didn't think for one minute that 'the animal rights' need be a consideration of theirs.

The Hall family had their fingers in a lot of pies—all of them money-making animal abuse enterprises; they reared intensively-farmed turkeys, 'dairy' cows and 'beef' cattle and had big financial investments in vivisection, including 50,000 shares in HLS. By definition, this lot cared nothing about the suffering of other animals.

Newchurch was an obvious target for a focused campaign such as we've seen succeed in recent years but did 'they' go too far, as some commentators have suggested and do the cause a disservice? Did they set the movement back ten years and turn the public against the idea of animal liberation or did they do something that no one else was able willing or capable of doing, something ingenious? Is this what happens when you back people into a corner? What we need to remember is this was an isolated act and not the responsibility of a mass movement, many of whom would themselves disapprove. It was a strategic move—more a desperate act than a depraved one: gory perhaps, ghoulish, if you like, immoral, anti social, unreasonable, and hard work. It needs putting into perspective: it wasn't the work of evil monsters.

During the years following the 1999 raid, as a protest movement began to grow around the business, the money making world of the Halls would be reduced to guinea pig supply alone as it became increasingly unprofitable to maintain so many operations. It was a tactical error on their part and could have made the movement look irrational. Had they abandoned the guinea pig business early and continued breeding other animals, they might have been left in peace by a movement focusing on lab breeders. However, stubborn to the core, the Hall family had made it clear from the outset they would not be moved, no matter what, not now, not ever. Guinea Pigs R Us. I had a lengthy conversation with Chris one day. He thought I was a father concerned about my daughter and the animal rights group she was getting into. Hall was an angry man who had a cold heart; he didn't try to convince me of the benefits of vivisection, he seemed unable to suggest any but for claiming it saves lives and instead just spat out about 'that lot' being thugs, bullies and layabouts and so on and to 'keep my daughter away from them.'

Even after years of steady pressure which targeted all aspects of their empire, including family connections and business contacts, and their social life, and even as their business empire crumbled around them, they insisted they would continue to breed and supply guinea pigs *because* people were trying to stop them! And it was profitable. They would claim some concern to further medical research, but after all this time, knew absolutely nothing about medical science or vivisection. Over a dozen workers were forced to quit under pressure of public humiliation and harassment. Others barricaded themselves in their homes behind cameras, shutters and steel bars. With several sites to protect, the costs rose endlessly for the Halls, forcing them to consolidate their empire. Phone poles were cut down, as were power lines, affecting not just the family but also the surrounding neighbourhood. The siege of Newchurch formed the basis of TV documentaries, news exclusives and yet more government legislation to control dissident voices.

The most significant act of retribution against these people was the removal of the skeletal remains of the mother-in-law of one of the brothers. This act spawned what can only be described as a wave of media hysteria second to none. You could be forgiven for thinking that the entire Animal Liberation Movement had been in the graveyard that night and anyone opposing vivisection was at the very least supportive of the act. The police were immediately pointing the finger at animal rights activists and used the event to demand yet more controls on lawful protesters at the farm and elsewhere and more protection for those in vivisection. The media turned a peculiar stunt into a depraved act; made an entire mass movement somehow culpable for the actions of an unknown few, and drummed up calls for further state oppression.

There was initially a consensus of opinion within the movement that this was a put-up job, which the Halls had orchestrated to get them the sympathy vote or that the Government or industry were up to dirty tricks. The reality—and remember no one has yet been charged with the 'robbery'—was that it was a stunt intended to raise an issue and force closure on a long running campaign. It was about individuals thinking laterally, using their initiative to make a difference. If you prefer, it was a sick depraved monstrous act carried out by mindless thugs wanting to abolish medical care, but it worked.

Whatever your views, the media coverage was way over the top. Page after page condemned anything to do with animal rights; there were 'exclusive' character assassinations on known activists unrelated to any grave robbing incident, deeply vicious Editorials and Comments written by journalists who somehow as a consequence of this incident were suddenly all experts and able to speak with authority on vivisection! And anyone whose view differed was probably by definition a grave robbing vulture! One opinion poll for *The Telegraph* even suggested that more people now supported animal testing because of the hype stirred up about the grave-robbing incident. It's a significant measure of just how desperate the defenders of vivisection are that they have to capitalise on these stunts to defend their vile behaviour.

Repeated references to the grave robbing were made during High Court legal proceedings on behalf of the Halls, who were buying extra injunctions to keep protesters away from not just the farm but villages in the surround. The police used the incident to make arrests of so-called suspects at timely intervals to coincide with High Court hearings and issued press releases which the media dutifully repeated. The police and media were busy stirring up the horror factor by suggesting that the grave robbers might next send back the bones to the family one by one or display them somewhere public. Whatever the thinking of the body snatchers, if the intention was to affect the resilience of the farmers, it worked superbly. 'Until now we have been a stubborn family, very British', said one, 'We have refused to give in to what we think is a form of terrorism. But when something like this happens it makes you think. It is a very emotive time for us.' Someone had known the Halls' Achilles heel; knew the name and location of the resting place of this person Gladys Hammond and knew just how this act would hurt them.

This was very much a one off event and not something many would undertake (no pun intended) but media speculation about who might next be targeted and how deserves an honour for upping the fear factor. Will animal abusers instead now opt for cremation? Personally I can't see what all the fuss is about but then I can see far worse crimes committed against the living and worthy of screaming headlines. Don't people dig up dead bodies all the time to make room for building developments, sometimes moving entire cemeteries? Don't archaeologists dig up the mummified remains of Egyptian pharaohs and their possessions and stick them on display in museums, violating the core religious beliefs of that culture? What of 'our boys' on the rampage in Iraq playing football with the skulls of local victims—anyone recall the horror the media felt about that? It was a story for a brief moment. This is hypocritical at best. Digging up a long dead body is not something I would consider or encourage but surely such a critical act invites us to ask why someone finds it necessary to go to such lengths? Demands were sent to the Halls from the Animal Rights Militia offering to return the bones in exchange for the farm closure.

I did media interviews about the incident and repeatedly sought to take the debate away from whether we had gone too far and from condemning animal rights activists; I tried to take it to the crux of the matter and discuss the real violence, the tortured souls in cages, the fourth biggest killer in the West—animal tested drugs, drugs that kill 10,000 people in the UK every year. Forty a day! How often do you hear that fact mentioned?

While all this was going on, the arthritis painkilling drug Vioxx (withdrawn in 2004) had caused up to 320,000 heart attacks and strokes in human patients killing 140,000, and was the fault of animal extremists. No it wasn't, it was Merck, well known drug pushers, but had it been perhaps we would all know a lot more about the victims of this disaster than we do about the grotesque Hall brothers and their troubles. Media commentators and journalists claim some higher moral ground by defending the rights of humans over animals, but dare highlight the damage this does to all parties and they don't want to know, preferring instead to focus on the actions of the so called extremists who have killed no one. It's downright dishonest.

A thirty-strong police team was assigned to recovering the bones and treated it as a murder investigation, but from the outset clues were few and far between and had detectives looking in the most doubtful locations, interviewing the most improbable of suspects and admitting they were unlikely to arrest the perpetrators. Two hundred officers were deployed on one occasion to dig woodland in the area over several days after some suspects were tailed there. No joy, so a four-figure sum was offered for information leading to the discovery of the bones.

It is interesting to note that of the four people initially arrested, three were named on the ongoing Newchurch injunction as farm protesters, adding great weight to the legal application to ban such people from the vast surround of the main breeding farm and its satellites. One was involved very publicly with SNGP, another had a history for something far less involved, but similar some years earlier involving a grave, but was now more into praying away animal abuse and was no longer a fan of this kind of stunt. He even offered publicly to grass on the perpetrators of this act! The third was in her sixties and fighting cancer. There was no evidence linking any of them to the crime; indeed, there was evidence they couldn't have been involved and the case remained unsolved. The Halls said they would consider their position as and when the bones were returned but there was no sign that it was going to happen and given the lies that go with vivisector-speak, it was unlikely to.

So deeply affected by the whole affair and unable to wait forever for a response they knew wouldn't come, the following August the Halls finally issued that long-awaited statement announcing closure of their business and blaming the theft of the remains for the overwhelming emotional pressure they were under. It was the news tens of thousands of people had been waiting for. It was unfortunate it had to be forced the way it was but suddenly there was a conclusion to a vile business practice that caused endless death and suffering. There are few words to describe the feeling these final public statements generate! I was moved not an inch by the news of the grave robbery but hearing this made me emotional. I make no apologies for having deep concern for the well-being of the living and little of the same for cruel heartless monsters who inflict suffering on a daily basis. As for Gladys: she's long dead.

The press weren't so pleased that another centre of exploitation was to close forever and repeated the verbal assault of the previous Autumn, raking over the same ground as if there was second grave digging to report! This flurry of condemnation and attacks on the 'extremists' who oppose vivisection led nicely into Labour plans to introduce their latest terror legislation aimed at train bombers but to include animal rights activists. The industry would be more than satisfied with new powers to hold suspects for three months without charge while their computer is searched for evidence of sympathy for lab raiders or demo plans and to make lab break-ins terrorist offences and the glorifying of them punishable with 7 years in prison. The Halls said they'd take a few months to wind down to ensure the welfare of the guinea pigs. Something similar to what Shamrock had said before sending their animals to be tortured.

The Halls meanwhile asked for the remains to now be returned as they were closing down. But that didn't happen and months later the police re-arrested and remanded into custody three people whom they charged with blackmail, and who they claimed were responsible for the grave robbery on the basis that they were involved in the wider campaign to close the farm. The significance of this can't be overstated as it basically led to the conviction of four people for their bit part involvement in the campaign to close the farm. Blackmail, as they call it.

While there was circumstantial evidence of their role in small scale ALF actions and of their prominent role in the legitimate campaign, they were to be convicted for everyone's efforts over the 5½ years.

Suspicious mobile phone contact, detailed information on the Halls found in computer searches and unconvincing circumstantial evidence surrounding a wave of direct action painted a picture of a 'blackmail plot' involving the defendants. However minor it might be, it occurred within the conspiracy time scale and so made them guilty. That was the legal advice they were given and warned of 14 years if convicted at trial. All four followed that advice and reluctantly pleaded guilty. It would prove to be a bad decision.

John Smith, Jon Ablewhite, Kerry Whitburn were sentenced to a massive 12 years each in May 2006 and Whitburn's partner Josephine Mayo 4 years for a very minor role. The judge said he had read 38 statements taken from victims targeted in the campaign. He told the defendants:

> Your stated aim was to put the Hall family out of business, to that end you targeted them, their employees and their families. You targeted people who did business with them and friends of them. You targeted the pub, the golf club and solicitors, seeking to isolate them [the Hall family] financially and socially. What is clear is that you have, in the vast majority of these cases, ruined their lives over a period of years and perhaps forever.

No consideration was given for guilty pleas or mitigation including the fact all the defendants continue to deny any involvement in the grave robbery, the date of which merely fell within the stated conspiracy timescale.

John Smith was John Hughes but changed his name. He was always going to be a key focus for detectives leading this investigation having been involved in ALF campaigns over many years. He could expect a prison sentence if caught again but 12 years for low-level acts of sabotage demonstrates clearly the low value our justice system places on living beings and the price some people pay for challenging animal research. What the Newchurch team and the wider community of activists achieved here has been overshadowed by the grave-robbing affair but without it an even bigger shadow would have remained. Police recovered the body of Gladys Hammond in May 2006 following a tip off from Smith who was—he says—tipped off about its whereabouts. Appeals against their extreme sentences were rejected in March 2007.

Wickham—The Botox Conspiracy

Why do people laugh at politicians being liars all the time? We should be angry.

Barry Horne on hunger strike 1998

Back to Wickham!

Wickham had become one of those places thought out of bounds for an exposé or break-in because of its notoriety, its status or its security. Wickham Laboratories in the centre of the twee Conservative Hampshire village of the same name was the focus of one of the earliest lab raids of the 1980's and many protests since but it was about to become central to perhaps the biggest scandal of all.

Wickham was brought into the spotlight in 1981, when targeted by the ALF who liberated a pack of beagles from the kennels one evening, and was later to fall foul of opportunistic raiders during which documentary evidence was snaffled. It was highlighted again following the SEALL raid in 1984 in which activists were investigating the use of stolen pets at the lab. The labs were also infiltrated in the early 1990s, and exposed for the sort of atrocities and malpractices found to be so commonplace in this gross environment. The contract testing lab's management have done themselves no favours running a tail docking practice on site and attacking protesters distributing leaflets; nor, indeed, have they won themselves any friends by suggesting that the RSPCA hand over to them for use in product testing any stray dog destined to be put to sleep by the charity rather than they go to waste! To add insult to his profession, Wickham's head, William Cartmell, offers legal opinion in defence of people accused of animal cruelty and neglect, and to top it all were the rumours that in 2003 Wickham were testing cosmetics on animals, something supposedly banned in the UK. To expose that would be a coup!

A trusted colleague and I decided to hover around the village as the lights went down and see what we could see. We soon realised their reputation was a great deal more fearsome than their security. Ironically, their use of the supposedly banned LD50 poisoning test was to prove our biggest problem, and in more ways than one their greatest asset.

From the outset, we had to watch out for workers turning up at all hours to count and kill test 'subjects.' On a couple of occasions, we managed to clamber, crawl and creep across the rooftops of buildings to the Secondary Animal Facility near the rear of the site where staff would pop in intermittently throughout the night to massacre small rodents, then leave again. We got so close, we could hear them talking and laughing and could see them just below us through the frosted glass on the inside of the building. Had we been the type of people they say we are, it would have been the easiest thing in the world to inflict some serious GBH on these people as they were doing to others far less capable of defending themselves right in front of our very eyes.

Focusing instead on recovering evidence and rescuing the animals, we set about formulating a plan to break in through the roof as soon as the site was vacated and leave before anyone returned. Figuring out a suitable time to break in proved the biggest headache of all as the timetable at Wickham was so random. We could get two hours or maybe six with a police patrol in the middle, though that was really nothing to worry about because as close as they came to the SAF, they only tended to drive up, turn round and drive off.

It was mid December 2003; 'Tom', 'Jerry' and Keith were on site, with others waiting in the wings. We'd worked out the best place to park a vehicle for loading, which meant moving a fence to allow us access to a spot behind the old Wickham veterinary practice out back, which wasn't overlooked by neighbouring houses. Between that and the perimeter of the labs was a really helpful area of grassland from where we were able to monitor activity and get over the outer fence without being detected.

We needed a night of 'busy' weather to camouflage the noise we would make in forcing a hole in the gable end of the roof by removing a wooden panel. In such cases, one is often entering an unknown—I was once confronted with a roof so chock-a-block with old cages, it was impossible to move them sufficiently to get in, while on another occasion, I found a brick wall beyond the wooden outer wall! It was going to have to be last minute at Wickham and all concerned were prepared for a call at a moments notice.

The biggest flaw in what was a pretty well thought-out plan was the fact that I am a marked man and was under surveillance at the time and had been seen in the area the day before we decided to break in. That day Tom, Jerry and I had gone there tooled up to break in (spanners, headlights, crowbar, screwdrivers, cutters, saw and so on) with three rucksacks full of large rolled up shopping bags for whatever we might find inside and with backup vehicles to take the animals to a pre-arranged safe house. The weather was good and we were long over our nerves after three hours of squatting in the grass ready for the mindless morons we had under surveillance to follow our whispered willing for them to 'turn the fucking lights out and go home' so we could get on with a long overdue incursion into their sordid world of poisoning small live things to death.

I often claim when speaking publicly that I don't hate these people, just what they do, but that's not strictly true and I soon felt nothing but hatred for these stupid shaven-headed morons as we watched them go about their disgusting business long into the night. The gas chamber is a favourite at Wickham in which survivors of the test substance are piled in heaps and writhe in agony until they are dead or there's the option of cervical dislocation (break the neck in normal speak with the back of the head held to the table and a yank to the base of the tail) or a lethal injection, which offers no sweet passing either. Of course, none of these are actually choices: they all mean the same to the animal that's about to be killed. It's really just a matter of which method the ones with all the power decide they want to use. They really don't care—how could they—just as long as it doesn't take them too long to note down the details.

We knew it was going to be as much about good luck that we weren't disturbed as good planning and I for one expected to be a suspect in the ensuing investigation living only a county away and with a reputation, but there was no question we were at least going to have a go. We had a couple of escape routes worked out and never expected any of the animal killers to take on anyone in a balaclava in a dark eerie walkway. Bullies aren't so brave when confronted by someone they can't push around. Small rodents are one thing, but masked animal liberators with scary reputations and sharp tools are another.

But it wasn't to be. The animal assassins weren't leaving any time soon, so we headed home empty handed again. We decided to stash our equipment and go back in 24 hours. Police documents would later show my car was seen at my partner's home later that night. And there apparently ended the current round of surveillance.

Here for me lies the most interesting aspect of this operation yet to be revealed. The devastating secrets of the vivisection lab were revealed; cosmetics are still tested on animals today. The undercover work of the police was revealed, Operation Gastrula. But how did the raid ever happen at all? To have this big team from the National Crime Squad following me obviously suspecting I was tackling some animal abuse, it must be highly embarrassing that I disappeared from the radar at the most significant moment between Friday and Saturday. I was out of the house early Saturday morning and going about my business as were the rest of us, with no surveillance.

The following night we met up and made our way back to the village. We parked up, waited, and only whispered once in frustration for them to FO home before they did! In a second, we were masked up, over the fence and sneaking our way again along the deserted walkways to the rear of the complex, up the fire escape and onto the roof. Using a ventilation pipe as a platform I unfurled my box of tricks on the roof and set about teasing a hole in it. Oh how wood screeches as it splinters! At that time of night in a tiny rural neighbourhood, splintering wood makes one hell of a racket as I would be reminded. I was trying to keep it quiet but even pulling out nails was cringe worthy. It didn't matter as it turned out because no one was alerted and half an hour later we had access to the roof space.

Seeing no cameras in the attic and hot with the work I dropped my face mask so I could breath and slithered my way along. With all the piping and roof supports running through the attic and the claustrophobic atmosphere, it was no easy feat to move around, but we managed to find our way through the network of rooms below by lifting the roof tiles and peering in. Removing the first roof panel and looking around for security cameras before descending, what was the first thing I saw? A security camera! I looked straight at the thing, looking at me! Forgetting I didn't actually belong here, I hadn't replaced my mask! Oh! I was upside-down admittedly but it would so obviously be me! I spent a moment figuring out how to talk myself out of this one, put my mask back on and got on with the job. Note to self: must get the CCTV film before leaving.

There were mice in ten small rooms, cages in another, a washroom, extermination equipment and documents. We were intending to put the animals into the carry bags and pass them out of the roof but due to the limited space instead had to pass them out cage by cage. This made hard work of moving dozens of mice cages (small plastic storage boxes with a wire lid) up into the roof and through the maze of obstructions. As we had expected, a local police patrol drove by an hour in, but there was nothing for them to see. The police van and its mass of colour glistened in the streetlights and through the windows of the unit where we were busy. It was heart-stopping to hear from the lookout that the police were feet away but no sooner had he told us to be aware of it he was giving the all clear. It was their drive by. With all rooms accessed (in disguise) and cameras now disabled we emptied them of over 700 mice and whatever tools, chambers and documents there were. Hanging on the outside of the lab doors were more precious files, but the security system in the corridor and on the doors meant we weren't able to open them without triggering the alarm. Come back to them shortly.

Bagged up and out in an hour or so, we agreed I would drive the animals away while Tom and Jerry would retrace our steps, this time accessing the corridor, bagging all the documents and the CCTV tapes before beating a hasty retreat. It was midnight, we'd been in there for two hours and it was time for me to leave as we had a load of animals and more to lose if there was a major response to alarm bells ringing, but there were still valuables to recover. However we weren't to get it all our way because as the lads arrived back at the Animal House, they became aware they weren't alone. Entering the rear gate was an animal technician who'd arrived for killing duty. He saw them in their ballies as they saw him and everyone scarpered. He phoned the police on his mobile and they were there in nine minutes. Impressive, but nine minutes too late. Tom & Jerry were free to fight another day. I was in trouble for sure. The burglary-bungling mouse bludgeoner had brought his girlfriend and baby along; they were waiting in the car while he popped in to slaughter some tiny unhappy female rodents. Like you do.

The National Crime Squad and local detectives were called in and the lab was sealed off for three days' forensic examination. The funny thing is, the NCS had been there just 24 hours earlier but hadn't been sure quite why: now it was clear. The worker was questioned and released back into society (where he and his colleagues continue to pose a very serious threat to all life forms).

Back at the safe house we discovered that the mice—700 of them—were at various stages of Botox poisoning tests, their tails marked to indicate the dose levels administered. Some were due injections later that morning, for many others it was already too late. We fed and watered and put them to bed then sat down for a read. It was compelling reading even at 4.00am. The documents were a real treat while at the same time truly awful. It's one thing hearing that it happens, that these people are so callous and the tests so irrational, but to see it all firsthand brings it home. There was page after page of dates; animals recorded by numbers, by species, by sex and by age. Hundreds upon hundreds of individuals, (female in the main) none older than six weeks of age injected into the stomach with Botulinum Toxin, the survivors otherwise disposed of. Anything up to 600 a day, each a number, either poisoned to death or later punished for surviving it with a brutal execution. There were rats, mice, rabbits and guinea pigs in their thousands: tens of thousands every year. We worked on into the early hours and by mid morning, we had sorted and duplicated files, and they were on their way to anyone who might be interested.

Two days later, early on Monday morning, I noticed I was under surveillance again and was arrested later that day while I was cleaning out my car at a garage. I was suddenly surrounded by a dozen detectives who formed like a dark cloud, was handcuffed and led away, the vacuum bag and my car secured as evidence. The early story I was told was that my car had been randomly spotted parked in the Wickham area the night before the raid but it later emerged there was a lot more to it than that. I was released on bail ten hours later, and all my clothes, footwear, electrical equipment and car were retained. It wasn't until eight months later following extensive inquiries, which revealed sufficient circumstantial evidence to put me in the frame, that I was charged.

The night of the raid, I'd dropped the mice in their cages at a farm in the New Forest some 50 miles away in the next county, from where many were later recovered by these over-zealous government agents. This was a big blow for me, but the saddest thing of all was hearing the police had given the mice straight back to Wickham who—it emerged in court—had promptly used their re-found loss in some other cruel, pointless poisoning test.

One national newspaper, *The Daily Mail* exposed the story under the headline 'Outcry Over Mice That Die For Every Batch Of Botox.' The source of the material wasn't credited as coming from an ALF raid on Wickham, rather their exposé, but it did expose the truth about Botox and the number of animals dying in LD50 tests, which have increased dramatically in line with the increased popularity of Botox as a cosmetic treatment (it also has medical application). In the main, baby mice are injected into the stomach, and their suffering is then monitored until half have died. Those that don't die as a consequence of the Botox injections will slowly suffocate as their muscles and lungs paralyse. The remainder are disposed of violently. Wickham of course denied cosmetic testing. A spokesman said: 'It is against the law and we don't do it here. But I refuse to discuss anything further.' Ironically, *The Daily Mail* was the same national newspaper that as part of the ongoing propaganda war on anti-vivisection, was to call me a 'monster' and 'one of the most dangerous men in Britain' following my conviction for this very exposé!

Evidence against me included mobile phone records from a phone I had used once months before and referred to in an email found on my computer, which was investigated and found to be in the Wickham area on the night of the raid and showed text messages had been sent between this phone and my co-defendants, neither of which was actually recovered. Nor was any of the content of the messages. It was, we were told, unusual for a case such as this involving as it did the loss of a few hundred small white mice and some documents from a commercial premises, that phone transmitter records be obtained to pinpoint the location of mobile phones when texts were sent. This I was informed by my lawyer is usually something reserved for murder investigations. There was also a possible fibre match from the roof space and a possible tyre track mark from my car near the lab. Teams of detectives kept me under surveillance following my release and tailed me after my bail appointments at the police station and were eavesdropping on conversations. This was a big thing for the Hampshire police and no expense was spared in their investigation.

The government has repeatedly said all vivisection is absolutely essential and alternatives to animals and the LD50 would be used where available. Well the cosmetic use of Botox is far from essential and there is an alternative. They said the LD50 would only be used in 'exceptional scientific circumstances.' Liars! My defence rested on Section 2/3 of the Theft Act, which I will remind you allows discretion for someone acting in good faith to prevent a crime by committing a crime, if the offence is genuinely honest. It was my argument that the Government isn't acting in the spirit of things and needs to be taken to task over the issuing of licences for the LD50 test for Botox and that the average person would be appalled to hear that Botox is being tested on animals at Wickham this way. None of the paperwork was recovered, despite intense police efforts following my release.

Eighteen months later, Melvyn Glintenkamp, one of the residents of the farm where the mice had been recovered and I were put to trial for conspiracy to commit burglary. He denied involvement and the evidence corroborated our stories. I admitted my role but denied I was guilty on the grounds that the tests we uncovered were illegal and immoral. Not only is the LD50 test crude and irrelevant and there a supposed voluntary ban on cosmetic testing, but there are more accurate methods for testing Botox, one known as the Snap 25.

At Portsmouth Crown Court, it was revealed there were 'undesirable' side effects to the Botox when injected into animals (monkeys and mice were referred to) which were described as 'commercially sensitive' and so edited from the publicly released licence details. The brand product in question, Dysport, contains human albumin, a blood product, which according to internal documents carries the risk of transmitting viral infection, not that anyone really cares because the growth in the use of Botox is far too profitable. One Wickham witness first denied they use the LD50 but was forced to own up under cross-examination after we released the documents we stole and they then had to admit the truth: that it was the poisoning method they preferred.

On one occasion, the judge remanded the two of us into custody after cars in the area near the court were leafleted during the lunch recess re the government lies on vivisection, but we were exonerated and released from the cells after CCTV footage of the court car park gathered by the attendant squad of detectives showed only an unknown female assailant assaulting cars with her propaganda. The judge also became agitated at observers in the public gallery taking notes on proceedings. On one occasion, he confiscated the notes of two people including the Wickham boss Chris Bishop who spent the eight-day trial in the courtroom scribbling away and fidgeting uncomfortably in the presence of others not like him.

The judge was absolutely incredulous at the idea that I claimed to have acted with honest intent in my actions. From the offset it was his stated purpose to publicly exonerate Wickham of any involvement in anything illegal and he did so often. Ignoring the fact that it became clear there is no official monitoring of the use of Botox once it has killed animals in places like Wickham, something that should be of great public concern, and ignoring my legal defence, at the end of the trial the judge summed up the case for the prosecution warning the jury of anarchy should I be acquitted and reminding them that there was nothing wrong with Wickham's work in the eyes of the government, because, it's 'regulated' by them!

His summing up was in the view of all objective observers nothing short of disgraceful and as good if not better than the prosecution case. The jury was easily persuaded to unanimously convict us both. There was nothing but circumstantial evidence against my co defendant, I protested his innocence as did alibi witnesses, but no matter. The judge described the raid, which caused minimal physical damage and generated media coverage leading to calls to address the Botox scandal, as 'a very serious offence' and worse than an ordinary burglary! He reluctantly consented to bail us pending sentencing and warned that prison was highly likely. Weeks later, we returned for sentencing and I was fully expecting to be sent to prison for two or three years, but due to the mitigating circumstance that I was a carer and my imprisonment would adversely affect my partner and because the judge said he didn't want to make me a martyr and attract any further publicity, he agreed to a non custodial community punishment. Amazingly we were free to go! It was to be a remarkably temporary respite for me.

On leaving court I exchanged words with Bishop as had become the norm during our week together in court. I had lived in the same village as him for months and had never even said boo. He mumbled something and looked unhappy I was going home and I told him his troubles had only just started. Well... He promptly jumped up like someone had shoved a hot rod up his arse and squealed 'Mann, you can't say that to me!' and started waving his arms around like a rag doll on acid. I continued outside to celebrate my release. The judge, who hadn't left the courtroom, summoned me back in and convened a mini trial to find out what had gone on! Everyone looked serious and I felt that sinking feeling. He interrogated other witnesses who agreed with my version of the non-event, but concluded I had been in contempt of court! This was helped in no small part by Bishop adding some line about how I said 'something like, 'You will have to look under your bed.'' I said nothing of the sort! This was a lie, which coming from such a man is no surprise. Wickham sustain their business on lies: they denied they used animals at all and then went on to deny they were testing Botox on the animals they denied they use (If you get my meaning). I have the documentary evidence from inside Wickham, which proves them liars.

In a moment of unexplained hysteria, I had all the publicity the judge had said he wanted to avoid and some. I was told I could be re-sentenced, but was instead given six months for contempt of court on top of community service. One minute I had been looking at two years, then I was on my way home and then before my feet had left the courtroom I was on board the prison van on the way to Winchester Prison. That was a memorable day!

Short sentences are known to be as tedious as the long ones as I found out. There is no time to settle in and achieve anything—it's more a case of just killing time until imminent release. To compound this, two weeks before I was due to be released, I took a legal call in prison. It was not good news. I was informed that my actual date of release had shifted slightly from the end of July to the end of the following January. The Appeal Court had agreed with an application by the Attorney General, Lord Goldsmith (the same man who had conspired with Tony Blair to fool people into allowing him to launch an attack on countless defenceless men women and children in Iraq and elsewhere) that community service was an unduly lenient punishment for what I had done. This happened far more quickly than the appeal against conviction, which they later rejected, and got me an additional 12 months to increase the overall sentence for breaking into Wickham to 18 months.

It was another blow, but I got on with it, spent weeks in the Braille class learning to translate, inhaled more second-hand smoke, passed a business studies course, won the 800 meters in the inter wing sports day, shared some propaganda, and helped the three prison kitchens with their vegan menu. I was released on tagging after six months and spent three on curfew. I have behaved myself since and am currently promoting the new blockbuster *Behind The Mask* at cinemas around the UK and Europe.

I made mistakes and paid the price but breaking into Wickham was all anyone could do to expose this scandal. The alternative should be to do what? Write to MP? My MP told me cosmetic testing had been banned in the UK. Liar. My biggest regret is not better preventing them taking the rescued mice back to be reused. There is increasing pressure being applied at Wickham and it is only a matter of time before injunctions start flowing. Workers' vehicles have been sabotaged, the labs have been attacked, and suppliers have been persuaded to pull out. As is the fashion, the website has been hacked, there are phone blockades and so on. Yet Wickham bosses work tirelessly to build a bigger lab in a better location to torture more and more small creatures.

The police kept my car but finally returned my clothing and so on two years later. Meanwhile, the government are so concerned by our little efforts they are seeking laws to make these raids as significant as flying planes into buildings and blowing up passenger trains. Does what we have to say have them worried or not? Compassionate folk—keep talking!

'They ask if I feel remorse. I reply 'Of course, There's so much I could have done if they had let me.'

To Sum Up

> Those who make peaceful revolution impossible will make violent revolution inevitable.
>
> *John F Kennedy, 1962*

Section 2 of the Theft Act worked spectacularly in the defence of an activist from Dorset who was arrested late one night near a battery egg farm in West Sussex in 2003. Donald Currie had entered the waste pits below the cages and was in the process of bagging up a dozen or so fallen hens, when the farmer was alerted by an alarm. Detained near the farm with the help of the force helicopter and dogs, Currie was arrested, his car impounded, and he was later charged with burglary. The birds found in carry bags near the site were returned to the cages and so the food chain, despite having potentially consumed rat poison used to kill rodents in the pits. And a *Sunday Times* editorial (Oct 2005) had the audacity to say that: 'Animal rights activists are a stain on our society'!

At Hove Crown Court a year later, the defendant admitted his role but his defence counsel, Jeremy Chipperfield, invited the jury to find his client acted in good faith and with honest intent, believing as he did that there was no other way to save the neglected birds and that the average person on the street would agree with his actions. The jury agreed and found him not guilty, effectively setting a precedent and in theory legalising the actions of trespassers in these circumstances. The law is open to interpretation of course and this has yet to be tested in a higher court, but this was a huge step in the right direction.

Donald Currie was arrested again near Reading in Berkshire in early 2006 and remanded into custody on arson charges relating to the planting of incendiary devices. Combing the area late in the night looking for the fleeing arsonist, Reading Police had found him holed up in a phone box. They later admitted that had the traffic lights next to it been green when they were passing, they would not have noticed him, and he could have potentially continued his campaign of harassment indefinitely. But the light stayed red too long; a passing glance and enough time to put two and two together was not what Currie needed but it was all that the HLS and the police needed. It was, for him, a monumental moment, and it was to mark the beginning of a long hard slog for a family man with issues and no desire to hurt anyone.

He was later charged with planting a device on the doorstep of a company director linked to HLS and the burning of a warehouse storing cardboard animal shipment boxes. Held as a Category A prisoner, billed in the media as the ALF's top bomber and tormented with the prospect of a life sentence, he faced the conclusion of the case in December. DNA evidence had proved a significant link between Currie and three incidents, and a guilty plea was inevitable. The firebombing of the Williton Box Company was credited to him on the basis of a DNA sample found on a match dropped near the scene of the fire, but the offence was left on file and guilty pleas for the other two incidents were accepted, but since these offences were more serious, it was hardly a good deal. That one fire-starting device left on the doorstep of the worker's home helped ensure a severe punishment. And so it was that Donald Currie was given 12 years with the caveat for an indefinite period of detention under some new law, and potentially on licence for life when he does get out.

Darren Thurston is locked up in America following a series of FBI raids targeting the Environmental/Animal Liberation Movement and dubbed the Green Scare, comparing it the Red Scare of the 1940's and 50's. In January 2006, six people were arrested in dawn raids and charged with acts of domestic terrorism on behalf of the Earth Liberation Front (ELF) and Animal Liberation Front (ALF) over a five-year period. The 65-count indictment alleges the defendants committed acts of domestic sabotage between 1996 and 2001 in Oregon, Wyoming, Washington, California, and Colorado. Specifically, the indictment includes charges related to arson, conspiracy, use of destructive devices, and destruction of an energy facility. The defendants are implicated in seventeen attacks, including the $12 million arson of the Vail Ski Resort in Vail, Colorado, in 1998, an environmentally damaging project and the sabotage of a high-tension power line in Oregon, in 1999. Three suspects named in the indictment are on the run and believed to be outside the U.S and another, Bill Rogers, committed suicide in prison. 'Terrorism is terrorism, no matter what the motive,' FBI Director Robert S. Mueller said during a press conference 'There's a clear difference between constitutionally protected advocacy—which is the right of all Americans—and violent criminal activity.'

Operation Backfire, a year-long investigation by federal, state, and local law enforcement officials, allegedly yielded evidence of an ongoing conspiracy by members of ELF and ALF. The defendants are accused of attacks on federal land and animal management sites, a horse slaughterhouse, a meat packing plant, lumber facilities, and a car dealership with damages reaching $80 million. In 2004, the FBI estimated ELF, ALF and related groups had committed more than 1,100 criminal acts since 1976 with damage estimates over $100 million. This is payback, the USA very much at war with the green movement. Director Mueller called the indictments 'a substantial blow' to domestic terror groups and said they should have a 'dramatic impact on persons who contemplate these crimes. Persons who conduct this kind of activity are going to spend a long time in jail, regardless of their motive.' The sentences these defendants are facing begin at 35 years and evidence is said to come from undercover agents and recorded admissions of complicity.

In the summer of 2006, Rod Coronado was sent down again, this time for 8 months for interfering with a lion hunt and faces further prison time for incitement allegations. Six SHAC USA activists have been convicted under wide-ranging powers of the Animal Enterprise Act, which was created to protect animal testing companies and other abusers. Their offence was to protest against HLS and they were given sentences ranging from 2 to six years.

Sarah Gisbourne was sentenced to 6½ years in February 2005 after admitting her involvement in a series of paint stripper attacks the preceding year on eight cars belonging to people supporting HLS, causing short of £40,000 damage across three counties. Women 100 years ago were similarly punished by men while using similar tactics to defeat male oppression! This was the first serious indication of a concerted state response following two years of media hype and government threats aimed at appeasing a nervous industry. On appeal, a year was taken off her sentence.

A growing number of other individuals (including Gisbourne on her release) have been served with Anti Social Behaviour Orders (ASBO's) to keep them away from vivisection facilities and supply companies and so on. ASBO's were introduced, we were told, to control unruly yobs on housing estates but are being used to contain animal rights protesters and others.

One of the greatest assaults on our civil liberties is in amendments to the Serious Organised Crime Bill made law in the Summer of 2005. These can criminalise even giving out leaflets about vivisection or calling for consumer boycotts of those involved in vivisection. These amendments specifically target campaigners fighting vivisection; breaches will be punishable with up to five years in prison and will be applied against anyone who causes a business to suffer loss or damage of any description, or prevents or hinders the business carrying out any of its activities. This can apply if someone simply writes to a company supplying a lab and asks them to desist.

It has become an offence for 'a person (A) to commit or threaten that he or another will commit, a crime or civil wrong against any person (B) with the intention of harming an animal research organisation; and it is likely or intended to cause B to fail to perform a contractual obligation, or to withdraw from a contract or to not enter into a contract' or 'if he threatens another person with the intention of causing a second person to abstain from doing something which he is entitled to do.' 'Harming' means causing loss or damage of any kind, or preventing or hindering the animal research organisation from carrying on any of its activities.

These proposals are clearly spectacularly wide ranging and have been sold to the public and the media as necessary to stop the kind of activity which Sarah Gisbourne had been involved in, even though such activity has always been illegal. Instead, they have been used to raid the homes and arrest people who have been on demonstrations at labs. Others have been arrested for displaying images of animals in lab tests and face trial.

Quite simply, the UK Government is seeking to criminalise any and all opposition to vivisection in order to appease an industry that causes serious physical harm and death to tens of thousands of people every year. A billion animals dead and still not even a cure for the common cold. Make you wonder? If this law doesn't work, there is also the new perfectly-timed terrorism legislation, supposedly for keeping foreign religious terrorist suspects confined at home following the legal complications that can ensue when shoving them in prison without trial. These Control Orders and others similar will undoubtedly be applied to those of us fighting for animals and to save this planet, who can't be otherwise contained if the industry keeps on demanding, the media keeps on agitating, and the government keeps on delaying the inevitable.

As shameful as the use of injunctions is in a free society, designed as it is to contain protest groups, it may well become redundant. With the latest powers, there will be no need to tell protesters to keep away using costly injunctions when it's possible to lock them in prison for giving out leaflets or lock them in their homes for thinking about giving out leaflets, maybe. Who will stop this happening? The government has also taken to banning people, including outspoken anti-vivisection heart surgeon Jerry Vlasak, from entering the UK if their views are not those of UK Plc. Ironically, it wasn't an animal rights advocate who pleaded publicly: 'If I could only shoot about 30 of them. If I could kill a hundred of them I would be guaranteed to get rid of the problem.' That remark was made by one of the Hall brothers from Newchurch referring to those protesting against their business; a business which was protected by the full weight of the law, the family courted as victims of terror by the media.

None of these tactics in defence of the status quo are new, of course. The Suffragettes were forced to smash up MP's cars and burned their houses, dug up golf courses, set post boxes and hotels on fire, cut down phone lines, stormed Parliament, smashed up the Home Office, ran in front of racehorses, got beaten up, punched policemen to get themselves arrested, starved themselves and were force fed, petrol bombed government buildings and were demonised and brutalised before getting what they fought for. I can't for the life of me see how anyone could say what they did was wrong, given that they did it to put right an injustice. Likewise the ANC and others.

The Animal Liberation Movement has largely focused its efforts in recent times on vivisection and it is likely that activists will continue to do so for the immediate future. The issue has been raised to the level it's at by the use of direct action and such is the impact of this that over 250 MPs' signed an Early Day Motion tabled in 2006 calling for an independent scientific inquiry into vivisection, making it one of the most popular EDM's. This is a clear signal that there is serious discontent in society with the use of animals in this way and proof that the endless propaganda spewed about how extreme vivisection's opponents are is failing to cloud the issue. As significant as this is, it's highlighted by the parallel campaign by pro vivisection campaigners to get MP's to remove signatures from the list. If ever proof were needed that such a test would fail to serve the pro vivisection argument then this is surely it.

There are the many other issues, some involving such vast kill statistics that it is impossible to even imagine the numbers: the meat and dairy industries in particular cause tens of billions to live and die each year in the most appallingly squalid conditions. By comparison, the worldwide figure of animals consumed by vivisection is a minimum of one hundred million or so each year. It may seem as though we are setting aside the importance of greater evils and are only making a piecemeal contribution or at best merely acknowledging the evils of the meat and dairy industries by abstaining. But abstention is perhaps one of the most significant contributions anyone can make towards liberating animals from slavery. Not just anyone, but everyone! The vegan way is the answer to many of our ills. It's not just easy, it's essential!

In some way, the meat industry may be killing itself off: poisoning and killing consumers with CJD via BSE-contaminated animal flesh; foot and mouth; E. Coli; salmonella; campylobacter; Newcastle disease and who knows what other nasties yet to come. With every new epidemic, thousands—millions—of animals are culled piecemeal, costing the industry millions in financial losses, yet brutally wiping them out does not stop the rot. The viruses and diseases keep coming. Asian bird flu apparently threatens us and most recently in June 2006, meat eaters in the UK were warned to avoid mutton and some traditional sausages to reduce the risk from a new animal brain disease.

The Food Standards Agency said it could not rule out a danger from 'atypical scrapie' in sheep, which is similar to BSE in cattle. And let's not forget that BSE is linked to the practise of feeding generations of cattle (as well as most 'farm' animals) diets of meat and bone meal feed made from the slaughterhouse remains of their own kin—a food so far removed from the natural dietary requirements of these placid herbivores, that it must come as no surprise that disease is rampant amongst these wretched creatures. Countless undercover investigations have revealed such horrors as routine and that far worse goes on every day. From the cradle to the grave, the lives of 'farm' animals are a living hell. For the consumer unconcerned by issues of compassion, there are other issues to consider, which should, in theory, be enough to put anyone off the flesh on their dinner plate: the lack of hygiene, the use of drugs to keep disease in animals at bay, growth hormones etc…

When mice did not develop CJD after researchers had injected them with BSE, the government said the results didn't count, because animals are different to people. According to the assistant director of *Nature*, where the results were published, this was 'the best evidence yet' that there's no link between BSE and CJD, though she was careful to add that 'This does not tell us that beef is safe—but at the same time it does not tell us that beef is dangerous.' Duh! Might be an idea to look at humans who ate it? What was the point of killing more mice? All they are likely to learn will only mislead. So on the one hand there is allegedly no link between BSE in animals and CJD in humans because mice experiments prove there it, while on the other hand, the new sheep disease can be transmitted to mice in the laboratory, which suggests there may be a 'theoretical' risk to humans, according to researchers.

What do any of these results prove exactly? Well, for starters, it may tell researchers that mice may or may not be susceptible to this or that, but it proves absolutely nothing that can be usefully extrapolated to other species, including humans. Everything points to the conclusion that it'd be best to leave all the other animals alone and then we'd all be better for it.

Obviously the meat industry isn't going to cave in without external pressure; true, there are fluctuations in consumer trends, which periodically impact directly on the increased consumption of some animal flesh, and a reduction in others, but this has predominantly been dictated by the perceived health benefits or disadvantages of consuming one animal species' dead flesh against that of another, or a potential health risk to humans in circumstances where there is fear of a risk of cross-species infection. Per capita, however, the consumption of animal parts is increasing, and can only increase further as emerging economic powers join the more affluent nations in their free-for-all against the Earth and its inhabitants. What really matters is that humans learn to respect all other animals/life forms before their excesses drive every species to extinction, strip the oceans bare of sea-life and turn what's left of the earth's forests into desert. It starts with recognising the problems with our modern diet.

Viewed from a global perspective, the future may seem bleak, but when we look at the way the animal rights message has spread from one country to the next, we must not doubt there is a future—it just won't be found sitting back in that proverbial armchair. We might ask: surely there won't be live export shipments from the UK to Europe and the Middle East for much longer? The answer to that is: only with pressure. And if this part of the industry goes, others must surely follow, with transport companies being the fragile link in this chain. Live exports must end, but this is only a stopping post: you stop the animals being exported, they will simply suffer the same cruel fate in a UK slaughterhouse—and that's not good for animal welfare. Not eating them and not drinking their milk is…

Meat production is not a single-issue problem, besides the immediate pressing concerns of animal cruelty, the environmental considerations are immense. 'Farm' animals consume vast amounts of water; huge tracts of Amazon forest are razed to the ground in order to graze cattle or grow crops to feed 'farm' animals in Europe, thus contributing to the effects of global warming; the third world poor starve while the food that could be used to help them is fed to the doomed animals destined for the dinner plate of the western consumer. Simply trashing the meat industry isn't going to bring about a change in eating habits and a lot more needs to be done to change them.

If everyone who eats meat and wears animal flesh were brave enough to watch films like the hard-hitting *Earthlings*, narrated by Joaquin Phoenix, I would guarantee many would change overnight. With enough people simply changing diet, we could very well reach a tipping point and destabilise the already heavily subsidised meat industry, thus encouraging the business in healthy plant-based foods to flourish.

Many anti-vivisectionists make a stand against consuming and wearing animal flesh or body parts, and are by definition boycotting such products. By extension, they are also boycotting any businesses with connections to animal abuse industries, third world exploitation and environmental destruction. The ethical consumer's demand for 'clean' foods and clothing has encouraged the growth of the 'alternative' industries, which in turn, attract new custom, making the idea of being vegan increasingly appealing. Satisfaction of the palate is guaranteed for today's vegan with so many delicious choices available, and much of the credit for that must go to the pioneers of early veganism, who introduced the concept and the term vegan into the English language. In the last 20 years or so, with demand for cruelty-free products on the increase and an equal demand for quality, today's vegan need never eat lentils and lettuce!

The battle against the meat and dairy industries, where 'animal machines' and the supply of body parts is endless and life cheap, is one that must be tackled from all fronts; no single method alone can conquer this monster. Widespread education about the facts surrounding 'animal food' production, undercover exposés, lobbying and radical campaigning and a wide availability of alternative foods are all essential aspects of the battle against cruel farming practices. Seeing endless truckloads of sheep, cattle, baby calves or chickens being transported for slaughter; seeing row upon row of packaged animal flesh on supermarket shelves, and chains of fast food outlets belching out endless animal-derived foods, we understand only too well how immense is the trade in animal flesh. Sadly, the simple act of liberating a hundred or a thousand chickens from an intensive unit makes a negligible dent on the farmer's profits. To the liberated chicken, her life is priceless, as life should be; to the farmer that enslaves millions like her, she is almost worthless, reduced to an economic unit. Economic sabotage has been effective against smaller users of animals like fur farmers and vivisection practitioners but the meat industry is so vast.

In the scale of atrocities, which animal abuse system is the greater evil? Whichever you choose to stand against, they are all part of an endemic social problem, which reduces animals to commodities. We can all achieve little victories in every day life—maybe converting a neighbour or a school friend to veganism or just planting the seeds of change at every opportunity. The slow drip feed effect can be seen in the growing number of vegans and the increase in ethical consumer products, which are the direct result of demand. If at times progress seems slow, regrettably that is because it is, but we have achieved a great deal in the short time since we became a movement a few short decades ago. Many of us will remember how little people knew about systems of animal abuse even as recently as the 1970s. Times have changed: in 2007 the vivisection industry is in mortal terror for the future, fighting tooth and claw for its survival because of the unwanted attention it has received as a result of varied methods used by animal rights pressure groups and through direct action. We may as yet be few, but our message is a mighty one.

We have already achieved much, and we can and will continue to do so. What we have to decide is how much we are ready to put into the struggle to ensure that change comes sooner rather than later. If you believe that can be achieved just by signing a petition or writing to your MP, then you haven't followed this story properly. If anyone tells you different, be wary: they are either a law enforcement officer, a politician, or an animal abuser, who care little for the weak and vulnerable.

Since leaving prison in 1999 and again in 2005, I have accepted the possibility that I may go back. As degrading and uncomfortable as it can be, it was never as big a deal for me as the terrible pain some humans inflict on other animals and as a consequence, I have continued (as some might view it) to push my luck by speaking out. It's a minefield out there for activists with so many new law and vast public funds levelled against them. In March of 2007 three perfectly peaceful non-violent protesters were imprisoned for 15 months, 2 years and 4 years under new powers simply for attending a series of demonstrations against HLS customers, their inoffensive banners, megaphone and whistles the key exhibits. For me personally, there has only ever been one choice. I believe passive acquiescence to the system does nothing to further any cause. As British democracy has slowly come to resemble a draconian oligarchy, we have seen our right to free speech stifled, and state laws enforced by increasingly heavy-handed policing. The inevitable result of this erosion is that many who would never otherwise come into conflict with the law will be swept along on the tide of new crimes that are pushing people into a corner and making criminals of dissenting voices. The blame for creating a new generation of law-breakers can then be firmly placed at the feet of the New Labour Government, who did an about-turn on their pre-election promises, who saw instead fit to ally themselves with destructive and dishonest industries, and to deny their citizens the right to object—as befits a democracy—against an oppressive system that murders millions of innocent animals without ever considering it to be one of the most pressing moral issues humanity has to face. The need to ensure that each animal's right to life is upheld is not someone else's responsibility: it's yours and mine—it's all of ours.

There can be few complaints levied at the way the Animal Liberation Movement has conducted itself over the last 40 years, it remains overwhelmingly non-violent and honest. Paradoxically those who defend vivisection have violence are their very heart and seem to increase it daily. Those that argue that society should not be built on the suffering of others and who act to change it are the future of this planet. Time has already run out for the animals that are dying at this very second in abattoirs, in vivisection laboratories, in factory farms and in the fields. But there is great hope for those not yet detained, defiled and destroyed for the profits they generate. We have the power! Every day that we do nothing and those who claim to be civilised turn away is one day too long. It is an issue of such importance that people have died for it, and governments criminalise those who disseminate its message. The world is ours to change and change it must. Although there can be no pretending the work yet to be done isn't anything but immense, fighting as we are the greatest liberation struggle of all time, the time to act is now.

The Final Chapter

> You have just dined, and however scrupulously the slaughterhouse is concealed in the graceful distance of miles, there is complicity.
>
> *Ralph Waldo Emerson*

While keen to keep out of trouble I nevertheless thought it reasonable to take a journalist to see the awful conditions inside a modern British poultry farm in February 2006. That July 2006, teams of detectives from Hampshire and Dorset raided my home and that of Martin Masterman-Lister. They were acting on a warrant issued after an officer who watched the *Dispatches* documentary—*Mad About Animals* by David Modell—and thought she recognised the egg farm shown in one scene where myself and another had apparently rescued half a dozen hens from the waste pits below the cages. The farm in question was Wallops Wood in Hampshire where this book began. Her subordinates were duly dispatched to the scene of the alleged crime to enquire of the owner as the whether he had been the victim of a burglary. Not recently, was his reply. Had any chickens been stolen? No, not so he'd noticed. And that was all the evidence they needed! 'Go, go, go Hampshire Massive, go get them chickens back…' Loads of 'em piled into our homes at 7.00am, they said they were looking for chickens, though they were not sure how many, and they certainly weren't in my partner's underwear drawers! No sign of any battery cage fugitives anywhere so they took all our computers, mobile phones, cameras, wallets, diaries and leaflets to assist their enquiries. We were handcuffed and led away, my partner bullied and left in tears, her computer confiscated.

Unable to further their case, we were later bailed to return. A few weeks later I phoned the police to speak to one Detective who had been in one of the raiding parties requesting my property back. Computer printers and so on were going to be helping with enquiries some time longer but he had said I could get my wallet. I couldn't get hold of the copper who was dealing with the case so had to explain to a colleague of his what it was about. Bearing in mind this is the Serious Organised Crime Squad. The call went something like this:

Him: 'What's it in relation to?'

Me: 'They raided looking for six chickens allegedly rescued from a poultry farm.'

Him: 'Six what?'

Me: 'Chickens. They took our computers, phones, cameras, paperwork, cash…'

Him: Silence.

Him: 'Are you sure you have the right number?'

Me: 'Well if not we've been burgled and I have a serious crime to report.'

Him: Silence.

Him: 'Six chickens?'

Me: 'That's right.'

Him: Silence. Some muffled sniggering.

Him: 'I'll have to make some enquiries and call you back.'

It was to be another week before the wallet was allowed home…

Bailed to return, in September we both made our way to Winchester only to be told to return again in November because of ongoing enquiries i.e. Hampshire Police battling with Channel 4 for their unused footage. Some computer equipment was returned but other property would remain the focus of ongoing enquiries. In the back of the police station the pile of my computer equipment was brought to me in a shopping trolley. 'Not stolen is it?' I enquired of the law enforcer steering my goods back to their rightful owner. He paused for a moment, certain of the enormous contradiction of him handling stolen property while harassing me for allegedly rescuing half a dozen chickens from a certain death, and lied, 'It's borrowed.'

'Of course it is!'

Part of my computer was missing and my co defendant's printer was covered in ink and broken, so civil proceedings began.

Meanwhile the bail date was extended 'til January 2007 as Hampshire Police awaited 'receipt of material from Channel 4 directly related to the investigation. This material needs to be reviewed prior to any disposal decision being made. Therefore, there is no longer a requirement for you to return to bail on 28/11/06. However, it is requested that you attend North Walls Police station on Monday 8 January 2007 at 13.00 hrs instead…If matters can be finalised prior to the 08/01/07, you will be invited to attend North Walls Police station on an earlier date.'

That material was handed over by Channel 4 to the police, but it proved of little value in the investigation to convict the Wallops Wood Two. The Hampshire Massive passed on a message to my solicitor on Jan 5: investigation concluded seven months on — no case to answer!

A further visit to the huge Wallops Wood farm in October 2006 confirmed rumours that it is no more. One officer had claimed a few weeks before that the farm was closing down. Some found it hard to believe, but he was telling the truth. This vile farm has been closed. And it wasn't the RSPCA that did it. The Wallops Wood nightmare is over.

Is that the end of the story? Not by a long shot…

Appendices

Contacts & Websites—Campaigning Groups

For an up-to-date list of contacts and links, please refer to the website for this book, which can be found at: www.fromdusktildawn.org.uk

Animal Aid
The Old Chapel, Bradford Street, Tonbridge, Kent TN9 1AW
Tel: 01732 364546
UK based campaigning group.
www.animalaid.org.uk

Animal Cruelty Investigation Group
PO Box 8, Halesworth, Suffolk IP19 OJL
Carries out undercover exposés.
www.acigawis.freeserve.co.uk

British Anti-Vivisection Association (BAVA)
PO Box 73, Chesterfield SE1 OYZ
Campaigns against vivisection.
www.bava.org.uk

Captive Animals Protection Society
PO Box 573, Preston PR1 9WW
Tel: 0845 330 3911
Campaigns against zoos and circuses.
www.captiveanimals.org

Cetacea Defence Marine Mammal Protection
PO Box 78, Shaftesbury, Dorset SP7 8ST
Campaigns to protect marine animals.
www.cetaceadefence.org

Coalition to Abolish the Fur Trade
PO Box 573, Preston PR1 9WW
Tel: 0845 330 3911
Campaigns against the fur industry.
www.caft.org.uk

Dian Fossey Gorilla Fund
110 Gloucester Avenue, London NW1 8JA
Tel: 020 7483 2681
Working to save remaining mountain gorillas.
www.dianfossey.org

Friends of Animals Under Abuse (FAUNA)
PO Box 156, Cardiff CF5 5YD
Tel: 02920 569914

Gateway To Hell
BCM 8231, London WC1N 3XX
Seeking to stop importation of lab animals.
www.gatewaytohell.net

Hunt Saboteurs Association
BM HSA, London WC1N 3XX
Tel: 0845 450 0727
Works directly in the field to protect wildlife from the huntsmen.
www.huntsabs.org.uk

International Primate Protection League (IPPL)
Gilmore House, 166 Gilmore Rd, London SE13 5AE
Tel: 020 8297 2129
Dedicated to protecting all monkeys and apes, whether wild or captive.
www.ippl-uk.org

League Against Cruel Sports
83-87 Union Street, London SE1 1SG
Tel: 020 7403 6155
Campaigns to end cruelty to animals in the name of 'sport'.
www.league.uk.com

McSpotlight
A focus on McDonalds
www.McSpotlight.org

Naturewatch
14, Hewlett Road, Cheltenham GL52 6AA
Tel: 01242 252871
Campaigns against cruelty to animals in various areas.
www.naturewatch.org

People for the Ethical Treatment of Animals (Europe)
PO Box 36668, London SE1 1AW
Tel: 020 7357 9229
Largest animal rights organisation in the world.
www.petauk.org

Sea Shepherd Conservation Society
The ocean bound sister of the ALF, protecting sea life.
www.seashepherd.org

SPEAK
PO Box 6712, Northampton NN2 6XR
Tel: 0845 330 7985
Campaigning against the Oxford primate lab.
www.speakcampaigns.org

Stop Huntingdon Animal Cruelty (SHAC)
c/o 89 Bush Rd, East Peckham Tonbridge, Kent TN12 5LJ
Tel: 0845 458 0630
Campaigning to close Huntingdon Life Sciences (HLS).
www.shac.net

Southern Animal Rights Coalition (SARC)
PO Box 5668, Poole, Dorset BH15 3ZR
Tel: 0845 4584673
Coordinate campaigns in the South of England, including against Wickham Laboratories.
www.sarconline.co.uk

Uncaged Campaigns
St Mathews House, 45 Carver Street, Sheffield S1 4FT
Tel: 0114 2722220
Anti-vivisection campaigning organisation.
www.uncaged.co.uk

Vegetarians International Voice for Animals (Viva!)
8 York Court, Wilder, Bristol BS2 8QH
Tel: 0117 944 1000
Campaigns to promote cruelty free living.
www.viva.org.uk

Contacts & Websites—Organisations Opposing Animal-Based Research Theories

Americans For Medical Advancement
Advocating for patients and their families.
www.curedisease.com

Europeans for Medical Progress
PO Box 53839, London SE27 OTW
Tel: 020 82652880
Promotes alternative human-specific medical research.
www.curedisease.net

Physicians Committee for Responsible Medicine
Non-profit organization that promotes preventive medicine, conducts clinical research, and encourages higher standards for ethics and effectiveness in research.
www.pcrm.org

Scientific Anti-Vivisectionism
Animal experiments: the vivisectors' claims refuted.
www.freewebs.com/scientific_anti_vivisectionism

Vernon Coleman
International medical expert, best-selling novelist and campaigning author.
www.vernoncoleman.com

Vivisection Information Network (VIN)
A very comprehensive website looking at every aspect of vivisection. An invaluable resource with many links.
www.vivisection-absurd.org.uk

Contacts & Websites—News/Information

Animal Rights Coalition
PO Box 339, Wolverhampton WV10 7BZ
Monthly online animal rights magazine.
www.arcnews.org.uk

ALF Press Office
BM 4000, London WC1N 3XX
Tel: 07752 107515

Animal Liberation Front Supporters Group
BM1160, London WC1N 3XX
Supporters group.
www.alfsg.org.uk

Arkangel For Animal Liberation
BCM 9240, London WC1N 3XX
Online animal rights publication.
www.arkangelweb.org

Bite Back Magazine
222 Lakeview Ave. Ste. 160-231 West Palm Beach, Florida 33401
Quarterly quality US direct action magazine and regularly updated website covering direct action worldwide.
www.directaction.info

Earth First
Environmental direct action.
www.earthfirst.org.uk

Indymedia
Independent news resource.
www.Indymedia.org

NETCU Watch

'Watching them, watching us.' Reports on what the National Extremism Tactical Coordination Unit are up to.
www.vivisection.info/netcu_watch

Undercurrents

Reporting news you don't see elsewhere.
www.undercurrents.org

The Vegan Society

Donald Watson House, 21 Hylton Street, Hockley, Birmingham
Tel: 0121 523 1730
Publish the vegan bible—Animal Free Shopper—300 pages of good news for people who think being vegan means going without. And many other diet related books.
www.vegansociety.com

Vegan Prisoners Support Group

PO Box 194, Enfield, Middlesex EN1 4YL
Tel: 020 8292 8325
Campaigns for the needs of vegan prisoners.
www.vpsg.org

Veggies (Catering campaign)

Vegan catering and comprehensive Animal Contacts' List plus calendar of animal rights events.
www.veggies.org.uk

Violence In Animal Rights

Highlighting the real violence in animal rights campaigning.
www.violenceinanimalrights.org.uk

Recommended Books

The following list is far from comprehensive, merely a personal choice of some of the better ones and those I've referred to in these pages.

Caught In The Act—Melody MacDonald and the ACIG
Covers the investigation of Wilhelm Feldberg at the National Institute of Medical Research in London.
Available for £5.00 from the Animal Cruelty Investigation Group

Free The Animals: Ingrid Newkirk—The Story of the American ALF
Compelling reading.
Available from the PETA website
www.petabookstore.com

Rose Tinted Menagerie—William Johnson (1990)
A very readable history of animals in entertainment from ancient Rome to the 20th century.
Available for £5.00 from CAPS, PO Box 573, Preston PR1 9WW
Tel: 0845 3303911
www.captiveanimals.org

Rage and Reason—Michael Tobias
The ultimate animal liberator's revenge novel.
ISBN 1873176562
Available for £8.00 from www.fromdusktildawn.org.uk

Secret Suffering—BUAV/Sarah Kite
Inside HLS – an 'animal research centre of excellence.'
ISBN 1871416017 (1990)
Available for £4.95 from BUAV, 16a Crane Grove, Islington, London N7 8NN
Tel: 020 7700 4888
www.buav.org

The Silent Ark—Juliet Gellately

A chilling exposé of the meat industry—the global killer.
Available for £6.99 from Viva!, 8 York Court, Wilder, Bristol BS2 8QH, Tel: 0117 944 1000
www.viva.org.uk

Slaughter of the Innocent—Hans Ruesch

Described as the Bible of the Anti-vivisection Movement. Withdrawn from bookshops in the UK and US this is the book the Pharmaceutical industry tried to suppress. Dated but comprehensive and carefully documented, objective yet emotionally compelling, this work kills any argument for vivisection. Once suppressed by fake British anti-vivisection societies it helped spawn the modern anti-vivisection movement in many countries (1983) (2003 by Slingshot Publications)
Available for £4.50 from BAVA, PO Box 73, Chesterfield SE1 OYZ
www.bava.org.uk

Naked Empress—Hans Ruesch

Follow up to *Slaughter of the Innocent*.
Available for £7.50 from BAVA, PO Box 73, Chesterfield SE1 OYZ
www.bava.org.uk

Vivisection Unveiled—Dr Tony Page

An exposé of the medical futility of animal experimentation.
ISBN 1897766319 (1997)
Available for £6.99 from Jon Carpenter, The Spendlove Centre, Charlbury OX7 3PQ or Animal Aid, The Old Chapel, Bradford Street, Tonbridge, Kent TN9 1AW
www.animalaid.org.uk

Vivisection or Science, A Choice to Make—Professor Pietro Croce MD

Written by an ex-vivisector, this book condemns vivisection on scientific and methodological grounds, arguing that there are no such things as 'alternatives' to vivisection because vivisection isn't an option.
Available for £14.95 from Animal Aid, The Old Chapel, Bradford Street, Tonbridge, Kent TN9 1AW
www.animalaid.org.uk

When Elephants Weep—Jeffrey Masson

A powerful challenge to the notion that animals have no feelings therefore the use of violence against them is acceptable.

Available for £6.99 from Animal Aid, The Old Chapel, Bradford Street, Tonbridge, Kent TN9 1AW

www.animalaid.org.uk

Easy Vegan Cooking—Leah Leneman

The perfect introduction to vegan cooking. One of many good books on the subject dispelling the myth that vegans only eat leaves and lentils!

Available for £9.99 from Animal Aid, The Old Chapel, Bradford Street, Tonbridge, Kent TN9 1AW

www.animalaid.org.uk

Outfoxed—Mike Huskisson

(1983) Graphic undercover exposé of hunting with hounds.

Available from the Animal Cruelty Investigation Group

The Price of Meat—Danny Penman

Hard hitting, revealing and deeply unsettling.

ISBN 0575063440 (1997)

Available from Amazon: www.amazon.co.uk

Sacred Cows and Golden Geese: The Human Cost of Experiments on Animals—Ray & Jean Greek

ISBN 0 826412262 (2002)

Invaluable read for anyone doubting the uselessness of animal research.

Available for £14.99 from Animal Aid, The Old Chapel, Bradford Street, Tonbridge, Kent TN9 1AW

www.animalaid.org.uk

What Will We Do If We Don't Experiment On Animals? Medical Research For The Twenty-First Century—Dr's J & R Greek

ISBN 1412020581 (2004)

Available for £14.50 from Animal Aid, The Old Chapel, Bradford Street, Tonbridge, Kent TN9 1AW

www.animalaid.org.uk

Animal Rights-Related Videos and Films

Other related films are available via this book's website: www.fromdusktildawn.org.uk

Safer Medicines

This is a long overdue film released in April 2007, which showcases state-of-the-art approaches to ensuring that drugs in the future will be safer than they have been in the past. World leading scientists from industry and academia present their vision for the future of drug development – with a focus on human biology. There are none of the horrors that usually accompany productions of this nature, just some hard facts and forward thinking from the likes of actor and Thalidomider Mat Fraser who argues powerfully that better means to assess drug safety are needed, Professor Colin Garner of York University and founder of Xceleron who describes how microdosing offers a revolutionary approach to drug testing, Dr Bob Coleman, Senior Scientific Consultant to Asterand, explain how crucial it is to focus on human tissue in drug discovery and development and Tony Benn as ever eloquent and honest argues that the case for a scientific evaluation of animal tests for drug safety is unarguable and should be a priority.
Available for £5 on DVD from: www.curedisease.net/safermedicines

Angels of Mercy

Channel 4 documentary about the ALF & Keith Mann. Can be viewed on Google videos.

Behind The Mask

Another recently released must see documentary focusing on those individuals who take direct action to save animals. See the trailer and show some friends the film. It's life changing!
Available on DVD from: www.thethinkshop.co.uk/mask

Bad Medicine: the human cost of animal experiments

The perfect companion to Hans Ruesch's classic book, *Slaughter of the Innocent*. The film and book that destroy the myth of vivisection!
Available on DVD from: www.bava.org.uk

Earthlings

Narrated by Academy Award Nominee Joaquin Phoenix and featuring music by the critically acclaimed platinum artist Moby, *Earthlings* is a documentary film about humankind's complete economic dependence on animals raised for pets, food, clothing, entertainment and scientific research. Using hidden cameras and never-before-seen footage, *Earthlings* chronicles the day-to-day practices of the largest industries in the world, all of which rely entirely on animals for profit. Powerful, informative, controversial and thought provoking, *Earthlings* is by far the most comprehensive documentary ever produced on the correlation between nature, animals and human economic interest. For those who have no emotions about animal industries this is a must-see film! Available on DVD from: http://isawearthlings.com

Animals Rescued, Recovered and Returned

- On 17 July, 1975, Mike Huskisson was arrested after he left ICI's massive research complex at Alderley Edge in Cheshire, having removed three of their infamous smoking beagles. The dogs were fortunate in this case and remained free, because ICI decided against attracting further adverse publicity, which would have drawn attention to their habit of forcing beagles to smoke cigarettes.
- The next batch weren't so lucky. In February 1977, 125 mice—taken from the Evans Laboratory Animal Breeding Centre in Surrey—were recovered by the police from Ronnie Lee's flat. Despite Lee's pleas, and his offer to buy the mice, and despite the fact that Evans admitted he had a further 10,000 mice at his disposal, every one of the mice was returned to the lab and gassed.
- 1979, 100 hens were returned by police following arrest of raiders on farm in West Midlands.
- July 1985, the Central Animal Liberation League (CALL) raided the Oxford University breeding centre Park Farm and rescued over 30 dogs of all descriptions. A few days later, after several police raids, eight were recovered and returned to Park Farm. A small team later returned to the Farm, and re-liberated several of the dogs confiscated by the police.
- March 1990, a large police operation involving forces from four counties recovered two of the 82 beagles taken from Interfauna laboratory supplier kennels in Cambridgeshire. Interfauna disowned the beagles, saying they were no longer useful for experimentation, having been removed from the 'controlled laboratory environment.' They were temporarily rehoused by police pending the outcome of legal proceedings. At the conclusion of these, they were officially released into the permanent care of their foster homes.
- 1991, activists from the Animal Liberation Investigation Unit removed eight Labradors suspected of being stolen pets during an inspection of Cambridge University's laundry farm. The getaway van carrying seven of them was chased, rammed and stopped by police, who immediately took the animals back to the lab. The eighth dog evaded capture and was last seen

catching up on some missed affection.

- 1997, the police returned five cats to the owner of Hill Grove Farm outside Oxford after taking them from the arms of activists suspected of rescuing them from the farm during an impromptu daytime raid. No attempt was made to establish the true owner's identity, and the police were happy to take the word of a man who supplies animals for experimentation that they were his cats.
- 2003, hundreds of botox test mice were returned to Wickham Laboratories by police following an extensive surveillance operation, all were reused and killed.
- November 2004, fifteen battery hens were returned to cages at West Sussex farm after being recovered with the aid of a police helicopter and their rescuer arrested. He was later found not guilty due to the condition of the birds.
- Bedford, February 2005. Mark Organ and Alan Clarke were arrested after a police patrol stumbled on them loading hens from a battery farm in Bedfordshire. 300 hens were recovered following a pursuit and returned to the cages. The activists were fined £500 with £500 costs.
- June 2005. Dozens of sick and neglected animals rescued from a pet shop breeding operation in Sussex were returned by police against the wishes of the local RSPCA inspector and anyone else with an ounce of decency. They had been traced to the home of activist Sarah Whitehead in Littlehampton. Other animals remained free. The breeder's licence was removed by the council a year later and the filthy operation closed down.

Summary Of Dates

- **1822** First laws passed to protect animals in the UK.
- **1835** Bear and bull baiting, cock fighting and dog fighting are banned in the UK.
- **1898** British Union for the Abolition of Vivisection (BUAV) is founded.
- **1907** The Brown Dog affair sparks disturbances in London, UK.
- **1911** The Protection of Animals Act introduced into UK law.
- **1964** First hunt sabotaged in Devon, UK by Hunt Saboteurs Association.
- **1973** First Band of Mercy arson attack on Hoechst laboratory in Milton Keynes, UK.
- **1976** ALF established in the UK.
- **1976** First recorded fur farm liberation. 1,000 foxes released from Dalchonzie fur farm in Scotland.
- **1977** Condiltox Laboratories, London, UK close after the ALF cause £80,000 damage. It's the first obvious victory for direct action.
- **1977** Dutch ALF rescue hens from an intensive unit at Eindoven.
- **1979** First recorded US ALF lab raid on New York University Medical School, USA—five animals are rescued.
- **1980** First UK 'home visit' to Wellcome vivisector. Garage is painted.
- **1981** French activists rescue dogs from a laboratory. The first of many highly successful French lab raids to follow.
- **1981** First US raid on laboratory at Silver Spring, Maryland, USA exposes shocking conditions.
- **1981** German activists raid a laboratory and rescue 48 beagles.
- **1981** Canadian ALF strike at a butchers shop.
- **1981** Scottish ALF target a vivisector's home.
- **1982** Swiss ALF raid, five mice rescued. Zurich laboratory is the ONLY raid here.
- **1982** First Australian ALF action.
- **1983** Club Row animal market in London, UK closes after a two-and-a-half-year campaign.
- **1983** Actions in Malta, South Africa and New Zealand.

- **1984** Green Mole rescue animals from Eastern Health Board laboratory in Dublin, Eire.
- **1984** First Danish ALF action.
- **1984** First UK contamination hoax, of Sunsilk shampoo.
- **1984** SEALL raid, Royal College of Surgeons.
- **1984** Mars hoax (UK) ends tooth decay experiments and leads to formation of the first dedicated animal squad, the Animal Rights National Index (ARNI).
- **1984** Hunt Retribution Squad emerge promising violence.
- **1985** Swedish activists rescue two beagles from a dental school in Malmö, Sweden.
- **1986** Animals (Scientific Procedures) Act turns the clock back for animals in laboratories in the UK.
- **1987** Sheffield (UK) Trial. Ronnie Lee is sentenced to ten years.
- **1987** First recorded ALF actions in Italy, Austria and Spain.
- **1989** Hudsons Bay Fur Company pulls out of the UK after three hundred years.
- **1991** Veal crates banned in the UK.
- **1991** 18-year-old Mike Hill is killed by Cheshire Beagles Huntsman, UK.
- **1992** First Israel ALF action.
- **1993** Last UK dolphin show closes.
- **1993** 15-year-old Tom Worby is killed by Cambridgeshire Fox Hunt and the Grand National (UK) is sabotaged.
- **1994** First Polish ALF action.
- **1994** Author sentenced to fourteen years in prison.
- **1995** Live Animal Export campaign explodes at Shoreham, UK.
- **1995** First Finnish ALF action sees 600 foxes dyed at various farms.
- **1995** Jill Phipps is killed by a live animal exporter.
- **1996** First Norwegian action.
- **1987** Consort Beagle Kennels, UK has enforced closure.
- **1998** First Belgian ALF action targeting nine meat vehicles.
- **1998** Last UK fur farm liberation.
- **1998** Last Austrian fur farm closes and the practice is banned by law.
- **1999** Hill Grove Farm, UK has enforced closure.
- **1999** Sow stalls and tethers are banned in the UK.

- **1999** (July) Mink farming banned in Holland.
- **2000** Vicky Moore (DOB: 24/12/1955) dies campaigning against Spanish Blood Fiestas.
- **2000** Shamrock Farm, UK has enforced closure.
- **2000** Regal Rabbits, UK has enforced closure.
- **2001** Barry Horne (DOB 17/3/1952) dies in prison following a series of hunger strikes.
    - 1st Jan 6—Feb 10 1997 = 35 days
    - 2nd Aug 11—Sep 26 1997 = 46 days
    - 3rd Oct 6—Dec 13 1998 = 68 days
- **2003** Fur Farming (Prohibition) Act comes into force in UK.
- **2004** Hunting with Hounds is banned in Scotland.
- **2004** First recorded ALF action in Turkey. Three butchers windows are smashed.
- **2005** Hunting with hounds is banned in England & Wales.
- **2006** Sow stalls are banned in Europe.
- **2005** (March) In Israel, the force-feeding of geese is banned.
- **2005/2006** Sweden effectively finishes off fur farming by introducing stringent animal welfare laws.
- **2005/2006** Austria bans wild animal circuses, battery farming (including the use of so called enriched cages) and the shooting of migratory wild birds.
- **2006** Croatia votes to phase out fur farming in 10 years.
- **2007** Veal crates are banned in Europe.
- **2008** (April) Fox and chinchilla farming banned in Holland.

Index

Behind the Mask

The story of the people who risk everything to save animals

Behind the Mask is a 72-minute controversial documentary that focuses on the Animal Liberation Front, direct action, and the current repressive, so-called free governments to which activists are victim. It is produced and directed by Shannon Keith, an animal rights lawyer in America who started her own production company in 2004 with the aim of bringing animal liberation issues to mainstream media.

Using real undercover and underground video, *Behind the Mask* explores the world of those people who choose to break the law for a better cause... for the liberation and freedom of animals. While learning about specific individuals in the movement, the viewer is taken on a journey into the world of animal exploitation as well.

Throughout the film Shannon Keith captures the hearts and souls of people involved in the struggle for Animal Liberation. Judge for yourselves if these men and women really are, as the government would lead you to believe, a terrorist threat to our country today. Well known long-term British activists such as Keith Mann, John Curtin and Ronnie Lee are amongst those who are interviewed and who give excellent accounts of their personal experiences. Other individuals of all ages and backgrounds, from all over the globe, tell their tales of liberation, incarceration, sacrifice and determination, while exclusive underground footage reveals heart-thumping action sure to leave you wondering... who are these people *Behind The Mask*?

Creating Terror

On September 11 2001 the world was treated endlessly to the spectacle of passenger planes slamming into buildings in New York. We were repeatedly warned at the time that the world was going to change as a consequence. We were told 19 terrorists were responsible. It was the fires these people caused in the 110-story towers that caused them to pancake in 10-seconds, so the story goes. But so much about this conspiracy theory is doubtful to say the least, and deserves our scrutiny. It matters to those campaigning in the area explored in this book as much as everyone else, because the first part of the assurance that the world was about to change has proven to be true while little else we were told about this affair has.

As someone who has been in a courtroom many times, some as an observer, others as a witness or defendant I have a fairly good understanding of the process. One aspect—something I seek to draw out throughout my ramblings—is the need to tell the truth, the whole truth and nothing but the truth. If you aren't very bright or careful, or are unlucky and lie deliberately or by accident about something when giving evidence and are caught out, just once, then the rest of your testimony will be discredited endlessly by the prosecutor and your character assassinated mercilessly. Your evidence becomes worthless, tainted by your deception. It strikes me that there are glaring inconsistencies in the official story of the events of 9/11 and it seems obvious we have been told some whopping great lies. Not untruths, lies. Not just omissions, lies.

There is very credible expert testimony, documentary evidence, video footage and a quite dramatic twist to the story to the 9/11 conspiracy theories, which governments and media outlets have sold us. I challenge you not to be at least suspicious of the role of conspirators not yet named on the indictment and not of the Muslim faith after viewing: 'Confronting The Evidence: A Call To Reopen The 9/11 Investigation + Painful Deceptions'—See: http://www.checktheevidence.com/911/orderpage.html
And see: www.911truth.org for a whole heap more!